Jean
Anderson
Cooks

BOOKS BY JEAN ANDERSON:

The Art of American Indian Cooking
(with Yeffe Kimball)

Food Is More Than Cooking

Henry the Navigator, Prince of Portugal

The Haunting of America

The Family Circle Cookbook
(with the Food Editors of Family Circle)

The Doubleday Cookbook (with Elaine Hanna)

Recipes from America's Restored Villages

The Green Thumb Preserving Guide

The Grass Roots Cookbook

Jean Anderson's Processor Cooking

Half a Can of Tomato Paste and Other Culinary Dilemmas
(with Ruth Buchan)

Jean Anderson Cooks

HER KITCHEN REFERENCE
& RECIPE COLLECTION

William Morrow and Company, Inc.

NEW YORK

Library of Congress Cataloging in Publication Data

Anderson, Jean, 1929–
  Jean Anderson cooks.

  Includes index.
  1. Cookery. I. Title.
TX651.A573. 1982   641.5   82-7884
ISBN 0-688-01325-2   AACR2

Printed in the United States of America

First Edition

1 2 3 4 5 6 7 8 9 10

Book Design by Betty Binns Graphics/Martin Lubin

IN MEMORY OF M.M.J.A.,
WHO TAUGHT ME TO COOK

Contents

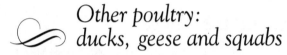

Vegetables: artichokes through zucchini

GRADING / SEASONS / HALLMARKS OF QUALITY / AMOUNTS NEEDED PER SERVING / BEST WAYS TO STORE / BASIC PREPARATION / BEST WAYS TO COOK / RECIPES

Baking: the advantages of metric measures

GETTING SET FOR METRIC (THE EQUIPMENT NEEDED) / THE KEY INGREDIENTS OF BAKING AND THEIR FUNCTIONS (FLOURS, SUGARS, FATS, EGGS, LIQUIDS, LEAVENINGS) / THE METHODS OF MIXING / WHAT WENT WRONG? (THE CLASSIC CAUSES OF FAILURES IN CAKES AND BREADS AND HOW TO PREVENT OR RECTIFY THEM) / BREADS / PUDDINGS, PIES AND PASTRIES / CAKES AND TORTES

Basic & multipurpose recipes

PASTRIES / STOCKS / RISOTTO, WILD RICE AND SPAETZLE / SAUCES AND VARIATIONS / FLAVORED BUTTERS

PART TWO
RECIPE COLLECTION: PARTICULAR FAVORITES

THE BASIC METRIC UNITS USED IN COOKING (THEIR MULTIPLES, PREFIXES
AND ABBREVIATIONS) / CONVERSION AND EQUIVALENTS

American/metric equivalents for:
VOLUMES / WEIGHTS / LINEAR MEASURES / TEMPERATURES /
CONVERSION FORMULAS / WEIGHTS OF COMMONLY USED STAPLES
(FLOURS, SUGARS, CORNSTARCH, COCOA, BUTTER, MARGARINE,
VEGETABLE SHORTENING) / COMMON CAN, JAR AND BOTTLE
SIZES / FROZEN FOOD PACKAGE SIZES / BEER, WINE AND LIQUOR
BOTTLE SIZES / COMMON CASSEROLE AND PAN SIZES

Fahrenheit-Celsius equivalents for:
OVEN TEMPERATURES / MEAT ROASTING / DEEP-FAT FRYING / JELLY
AND CANDY MAKING / CANNING / WINE STORAGE / RECOMMENDED
REFRIGERATOR AND FREEZER TEMPERATURES

Introduction

MY PURPOSE in writing this book is to share my fascination with the alchemy of cooking and also to pass along some favorite recipes that I've gathered in many parts of the world. What I have attempted is to write—to build, if you will—a solid source of information that is at once problem-solving and highly personal, a cook's companion that not only anticipates and answers your basic cooking and marketing questions but also provides you with an unusual and alluring collection of dishes to try.

It is therefore a two-part book. Part One, the **Kitchen Reference**, is concerned with the facts and fundamentals you must have at hand to shop and cook wisely in this day of catapulting food prices. For example, picture yourself at the supermarket, faced with a gorgeous piece of meat at a reasonable price (for a change!)—which, on the spur of the moment, you can't remember how best to cook. **Buy it** and be confident that you will find the answer in these pages when you get home.

Or, conversely, you are in your kitchen planning a menu. You can check out here all your major ingredients and decide how you will cook them **before** you shop. And if money is no object on this occasion, you can be sure you will find in this book precisely the sort of fail-safe information you need to keep anything from going wrong when you cook that extravagant cut of young veal you have set your heart on.

In Part One, I explain how to judge the quality of foods as you shop, then detail ways of storing them back home to preserve every ounce of that quality. I devote considerable space to basic cooking processes and basic recipes as they apply to meats, poultry, seafood, vegetables and baking, then proceed to some easy but creative variations that evolve naturally from these. To make the maximum amount of information quick to look up, I have worked out a series of tables and charts—the cuts of meat, for example, the length of time fresh and frozen foods may be safely stored. You can spot specific topics not only in the many headings and subheadings but also within the text itself because key words are printed in **boldface** type. You will find, too, that having such a handy reference in which to look up the basics will give you the freedom of "cooking without recipes," to say nothing of allowing you to make the best use of the best or freshest or cheapest (preferably all three!) foods available in your local markets and supermarkets.

Part Two, the **Recipe Collection**, is calculated to be fun—an arbitrary but I think original collection of particular favorites, recipes found and tested during my many years of traveling both in America and abroad. Even here, I tend to prefer the more economical folk dishes (so many "ethnic" cuisines being rooted in careful economy), but I do admit that I've slipped in a few delicious exceptions. The Recipe Collection is presented in standard cookbook style, that is, in chapters running from Appetizers to Sweets.

My love affair with food began one sunny autumn afternoon the day I turned five. Of course, I had been lured kitchenward before by the smells of bread baking and been thrilled when my mother would entrust to me the stirring of a cake batter or the decoration of a Christmas cookie. But this October afternoon was my day to solo and it is the birthday gift I shall always cherish.

Because I hadn't yet learned to read, my mother lined up on the counter all the ingredients I would need for making my Grandmother Johnson's Soft Ginger Cake, which I so adored (and still do). Mother sifted the flour for me, measured all the ingredients and turned on the oven. She explained in some detail how the cake should be mixed, then went outdoors with my father.

Being left alone in the kitchen didn't frighten me one bit. Quite the contrary. I was in hog heaven and decided to improvise. Why not add nuts and raisins to the ginger cake? Why not bake it as cupcakes in muffin pans? Why not shove the oven heat up so that they would bake **faster** and I could sample them sooner? I did all these things, and in my burst of creativity forgot to add the baking powder and shortening. I also overfilled the pans (which I had neglected to grease) and—horrors!—slid the cupcakes into a searing-hot oven and trotted outside to play.

So much for my kitchen solo. It's a wonder I didn't burn the house down. I did manage to destroy two perfectly good muffin pans, wreck an oven and smudge an entire kitchen. Mother laid down the law: No more cooking until I learned to follow directions.

I was humiliated that I had let my mother down. Miffed, too, but undaunted and determined to try again. Before long, I had made and frosted a chocolate cake, with Mother looking on this time. The cake was seriously overmixed—about the texture of pumpernickel—but I served it proudly and watched as my mother, father and brother gamely scraped their plates. From that moment on, I was hooked on cooking.

The summer I was nine my neighborhood playmates set up a lemonade stand by the side of the road. I opened a bakery in our front yard—nothing more than a doughnut stand knocked together out of orange crates, but I called it a bakery. Every morning I made fresh doughnuts, not because my supply had run out or because I cared very much about fresh-baked quality. I was simply fascinated by the way the doughnuts puffed up in the hot fat and magically flipped themselves over the instant their undersides browned. My best customers were local deliverymen who, I suspect, would have eaten anything. I lost money on the bakery, of course, but it clinched forever my interest in food and my curiosity about it, compensation enough for a few dollars lost.

It was only natural, I suppose, that after a childhood of conducting kitchen experiments, my college major should have been food chemistry and my very first job that of an assistant home-demonstration agent teaching farm women how to prepare appealing and nutritious meals. I consider myself lucky, for unlike so many young people who haven't the foggiest notion what they want to do, I had always known that I wanted to write and to cook. So I became a food editor, first at *The Raleigh Times,* then after a year off to earn a master's degree in journalism at Columbia University, at *The Ladies' Home Journal* in New York. As an assistant food editor at the *Journal,* I began eating my way around the world, making notes on what I ate and honing my palate as I tried to crack the recipes. I loved the culinary sleuthing and I still do.

Today I spend about half my time traveling, gathering recipes and interviewing unsung country cooks as well as gurus of gastronomy. I then return home to translate the recipes I especially liked from the French or Portuguese or whatever into English, from institutional quantities into family-size portions and, of course, from metric measures into American—which really should not be necessary!

It's astonishing to think that the whole world has now "gone metric"—save the United States, Burma, Brunei and South Yemen. Considering our position in the world market, how can we cling to an archaic system of measures predicated upon such variables as the length of an emperor's foot or the girth of a king's waist?

But cling we do—opposing metrics two-to-one, according to a recent poll—because the Metric Conversion Act of 1975 makes the switchover voluntary rather than mandatory. It's a major change, to be sure. And truth to tell, I resisted metric when first confronted by it in food chemistry labs at Cornell. But I fast became a convert, as did my classmates, when we realized how much easier, quicker and more accurate the metric system is than our own. And we also learned to measure ingredients by weight. What won us over to that, first of all, was the amount of dishwashing that was eliminated, particularly when it came to baking, because flours, sugars and shortenings, instead of being measured in cups and rounded off, were merely scooped onto a piece of wax paper on a scale. But the real clincher was discovering that we were actually cooking better than ever before—not really surprising when you consider the preciseness of the metric system and the chances for error in our own.

In the course of testing and developing recipes for this book, I have once again been cooking the metric way. And these past two years of metric measuring reaffirm my faith in the system and my conviction that it should—must—come to the American kitchen.

If you have any doubts that metric is on the way, you have only to look at the standard cups for measuring liquids now being sold in every five-and-dime. They are calibrated in milliliters as well as in cups. In addition, most thermometers today are marked off in degrees Celsius as well as in degrees Fahrenheit, and some scales register weights dually, in grams and in ounces.

Need further proof? Scrutinize the can and package labels next time you trundle down a supermarket aisle. There, clearly printed, are the metric volumes and weights as well as the American. At last count, 15 percent of America's major industries had switched to metric, the better to compete in the global marketplace. Gas pumps in Hawaii now dispense gasoline by the liter, and as of January 1980, all vintners and distillers bottled their spirits in metric-size bottles. Finally, thirty-four out of America's fifty state boards of education have given metric the nod, meaning that many of our children and grandchildren are already learning the metric system.

My intent here, however, is not to proselytize for the metric system but to point out its merits in the kitchen and to ease the transition for those who are willing to try it. Nowhere is metric more critical to culinary success than it is in baking; therefore, it is in the baking chapter (page 297) that I have included a full discussion of the advantages of the metric system. You will also find in the Appendix complete conversion tables—ounces to grams, cups to milliliters, inches to centimeters, Fahrenheit to Celsius—that can be consulted whenever necessary.

But lest you think that the three-hundred-odd recipes in this book must be made the metric way, let me point out straightaway that I have tested—and written—each of them both ways: in the customary American measures as well as in metric weights and volumes. It's perfectly possible, therefore, to prepare every recipe in this book without ever using the metric measures.

Indeed, the metric system is not the major thrust of this book although I do give it equal time, so to speak, in the recipes. The Kitchen Reference is the core of the book, where I examine the whys of cooking as well as the hows. Why, for example, does a cake hump and crack in the middle? What forms the intricate structure of breads? Why does a sauce separate, and how can it be salvaged? Why do green vegetables turn brown? Why are some pastries leaden and others as light and wispy as onion skin? These and other cooking mysteries I enjoy probing and writing about. My pleasure in this book has been to place between two covers much of what I have learned in my twenty-five years as a food editor, cookbook author and collector of professional tips and techniques. It is not—indeed cannot be in a volume of this size—an all-encompassing basic cookbook. But as a reference, it does cover a vast amount of material that the usual cookbook cannot, and I've larded the text with anecdotes (often born of experiences or disasters from which I've learned) because I want the book to be enjoyable as well as instructive.

My hope is that my own enthusiasm for and love of good food will rub off as you spend time with this volume, that you will discover, as I have, the pleasures of cooking as well as the principles.

JEAN ANDERSON

New York 1982

PART ONE

Kitchen Reference

About meat
in general

Despite rocketing prices, despite flirtations with vegetarianism, we remain a nation of meat-eaters so devout that we consume, on an average, some 120 pounds of meat per person per year. We plan our meals around the meat course, letting it set the tone of what precedes and follows. Not a bad idea, considering the fact that meat is the single most expensive item on the menu today.

For that reason alone, it won't hurt any of us to learn as much as we can about the different kinds, cuts and qualities of meat. And in order to protect our investments, to know how to care for meats in refrigerator and freezer as well as how to cook them to best advantage.

It's also time, I think, that more of us moved beyond the confines of steaks and chops and experimented with the lowlier, less costly cuts. These, to my mind, are far more appealing and challenging than steaks and chops. Every bit as succulent, too, if properly prepared. Such cuts lend themselves to improvisation, to teaming with a vast array of vegetables, grains and pasta that make it possible to stretch one pound of meat over as many as six or eight servings—easily, and often elegantly to boot.

I shall make no attempt here to cover every retail cut of meat (more than 1,000 at last count) because there simply isn't space to do so in a book of this size. Nor shall I include all of the standard recipes for steaks, chops and roasts, which can be found in any good basic cookbook. My purpose is to teach the methods of meat cookery—the broiling and panbroiling, the frying (sautéing), the roasting, braising, poaching and stewing—via my own, sometimes offbeat, favorite dishes. I have concentrated, for the most part, on the less tender, less exorbitant cuts because I truly like them better. What you will find in these pages, then, is a calculated but, I hope, also unexpected collection of recipes for beef, veal, lamb and pork, generously larded with the professional tricks, tips and techniques I have learned over the years.

First, a few points to bear in mind when you next stand before the meat counter, contemplating the bewildering array, plus some of the storage ideas that have served me well.

Inspection and grading: Because meats can be so easily adulterated, because spoiled meats can be disguised to look fresh, because the weight of certain cuts can be pumped up by injecting them with water, because not all meat handlers keep their plants scrupulously clean, the federal government maintains an intricate network of watchdogs to ensure that the meat we eat is both safe and wholesome. *Today, by law, all meats must be federally inspected—and passed— before they can be shipped across state lines.* In addition, many states have adopted stringent standards of inspection for meats produced and sold locally. To tell whether the meat you buy has been federally inspected, look for the round stamp reading "U.S. INSP'D & P'S'D" that appears on the fat of larger cuts, on labels and on containers.

Federal grading, although not compulsory, is welcomed by most major packers. And why not? A piece of meat marked USDA CHOICE (look for the shield-shaped stamp) will move faster than one of unknown quality. Not all meats, by the way, are graded. Pork rarely is. But beef, veal and lamb are. The top grade for them all: USDA PRIME. You're likely to see precious little prime meat, however, because it's reserved for fancy restaurants and butchers. Second and third best—and these are the grades most likely to appear in supermarket counters—are USDA CHOICE and USDA GOOD. What determines grade? Primarily the percentage of meat to bone and of fat to lean. The higher the grade, the meatier the cut will be, the finer-grained its flesh, the greater the marbling (flecking of fat within the lean) and the thicker the outer covering of fat. Prime beef, for example, is almost off-puttingly fat, at least in these days of calorie- and cholesterol-consciousness. As a result, cattlemen are at last beginning to produce slimmer steers and hog growers leaner pork.

Top-quality beef, as it appears in supermarket counters, will be a bright cherry red and lamb a rich carmine because they have been cut some hours earlier (exposure to air is what reddens meat). If you have ever watched a butcher custom-slice steaks or chops, you may have been so dismayed by the color of the just-cut meat—a deep mauve-brown for beef and lamb, a drab gray for pork and veal—that you were tempted to reject it as old or spoiled. On the contrary, it is absolutely fresh. Give the meat an hour or so and it will be as dazzlingly red or pink as supermarket meat.

How to wrap and store fresh meat: Supermarket meats prepackaged in pliofilm can be left in their original wrappers provided you plan to cook them within a day or two. If you intend to hold a piece of meat longer or if it is unpackaged meat you have bought from a butcher, remove the store wrapping, then rewrap *loosely* in wax paper, foil or plastic food wrap. Meats are particularly perishable, and the reason for wrapping them loosely is to allow some air to circulate around them, retarding the growth of anaerobic bacteria (those that thrive in the absence of air and are the culprits of meat spoilage).

TIP: *I like to place large cuts (roasts, for example, or even batches of ground meat) in a shallow bowl and to drape it with a big square of foil, wax paper or plastic food wrap, tucking the four corners underneath. This way all juice oozing out of the meat will be caught instead of dribbling down inside the refrigerator where it will congeal, develop a foul odor and be tedious to clean. Smaller cuts drip even more profusely, so I arrange chops, steaks, shanks, stew meat and so on in one layer on a large platter, draping loosely the same way. It's important that you don't stack pieces of meat because this will accelerate their spoiling.*

However you wrap the meat, put it straightaway into the coldest part of the refrigerator (the temperature should register between 35° and 40°F. or 2° to 4°C.) and leave it there until you are ready to use it. The table below will indicate how long you may safely store the various kinds and cuts of meat.

MAXIMUM RECOMMENDED STORAGE TIMES FOR MEATS

MEAT/CUT	REFRIGERATOR (35°–40°F. OR 2°–4°C.)	FREEZER (0°F. OR −18°C.)
Beef (roasts, steaks, shanks, stew meat)	2 days (prepackaged) 4 days (home-wrapped)	1–2 weeks (prepackaged) 6–12 months (home-wrapped)
Ground Beef	1–2 days (prepackaged) 2 days (home-wrapped)	not recommended (prepackaged) 3–4 months (home-wrapped)
Veal (roasts, chops, scaloppine, steaks, shanks, stew meat)	2 days (prepackaged) 3–4 days (home-wrapped)	1–2 weeks (prepackaged) 6–9 months (home-wrapped)
Ground veal	1 day (prepackaged) 2 days (home-wrapped)	not recommended (prepackaged) 3–4 months (home-wrapped)
Lamb (roasts, chops, steaks, shanks, stew meat, riblets)	2 days (prepackaged) 3–4 days (home-wrapped)	1–2 weeks (prepackaged) 6–9 months (home-wrapped)
Ground lamb	1–2 days (prepackaged) 2 days (home-wrapped)	not recommended (prepackaged) 3–4 months (home-wrapped)
Pork (roasts, chops, ribs, stew meat)	1–2 days (prepackaged) 3–4 days (home-wrapped)	1 week (prepackaged) 3–6 months (home-wrapped)
Ground pork	1 day (prepackaged) 2 days (home-wrapped)	not recommended (prepackaged) 3 months (home-wrapped)
Sausage (fresh)	1 week (prepackaged) 1 week (home-wrapped)	2 months (prepackaged) 2 months (home-wrapped)
Sausage (smoked)	1 week (prepackaged) 3–7 days (home-wrapped)	not recommended (prepackaged) not recommended (home-wrapped)
Sausage (dry, semidry)	2–3 weeks (prepackaged) 2 weeks (home-wrapped)	not recommended (prepackaged) not recommended (home-wrapped)
Luncheon meats	1 week (prepackaged) 1 week (home-wrapped)	not recommended (prepackaged) not recommended (home-wrapped)
Smoked ham (whole or half)	1 week (prepackaged) 1 week (home-wrapped)	2 months (prepackaged) 2 months (home-wrapped)

MEAT/CUT	REFRIGERATOR (35°–40°F. OR 2°–4°C.)	FREEZER (0°F. OR −18°C.)
Smoked ham (slices)	4 days (prepackaged) 3–4 days (home-wrapped)	2 months (prepackaged) 2 months (home-wrapped)
Hotdogs	5 days (prepackaged) 3–4 days (home-wrapped)	1 month (prepackaged) 1 month (home-wrapped)
Bacon	7 days (prepackaged) 5–7 days (home-wrapped)	1 month (prepackaged) 1 month (home-wrapped)
Variety meats (liver, kidneys, sweetbreads, heart, tripe, etc.)	1 day (prepackaged) 2 days (home-wrapped)	1 week (prepackaged) 3–4 months (home-wrapped)

NOTE: *Whenever a range of time is given, e.g. from 3 to 6 months, the smaller the piece of meat, the shorter the storage time.*

How to wrap and freeze fresh meat: First rule: You should freeze top-quality, absolutely fresh meat only. Second, you should concentrate on those cuts that can be plunked solidly frozen into a skillet, kettle or oven because whenever meat must be thawed before it is cooked, it will lose vital juices—and much of the quality for which you paid top dollar.

Neither **ground meat** nor **stew meat** is thus a good candidate for the freezer unless fully or partially prepared first. Ground beef and ground lamb, for example, should be shaped into patties at the very least, then individually wrapped and frozen. Ground veal, on the other hand, is so lean that it will be tasteless as a chip unless fortified with enough ground beef, pork or suet to give it moisture, character and flavor. It's not much work, I find, to mix up a favorite recipe for veal patties or loaves, to shape them, wrap each separately in foil and to freeze them raw (I do the same for all meat loaves, whether beef, ham or lamb). TIP: *I freeze the loaf in the pan in which I'll bake it; as soon as it's brick-hard, I slip it out of the pan and wrap it airtight in foil. Come baking time, all I need do is to unwrap the loaf, ease it back into the pan (it will fit like a glove), then bake according to recipe directions, allowing an extra half hour or so in the oven to compensate for the fact that the loaf went into it solidly frozen.*

As for **stew meat,** it fares best if made into stew and simmered to within about one hour of fork-tenderness. Cool the stew to room temperature, ladle into freezer containers, filling each to within ½ inch (1½ cm) of the top, then snap on the lids. NOTE: *The stew will tenderize somewhat in the freezer, thanks to the cutting action of the ice crystals inside the meat. When you are ready to serve, plop the solidly frozen blocks of stew into a kettle and warm slowly over low or moderately low heat. Keep the kettle covered—in the beginning, at least—and keep an eagle eye out lest the stew threaten to scorch. If it seems dry, add a little additional broth or water. By the time the stew is steaming hot, the meat should be perfectly* *tender. If not, you've only to re-cover the kettle and simmer the stew slightly longer. You can also finish a frozen stew in the oven; simply set the covered kettle or casserole in a cold oven, turn the thermostat to moderately slow (325°F. or 165°C.) and bake about 1 to 1½ hours or until meat is fork-tender.*

If you insist upon freezing raw stew meat, you should make every effort to minimize juice loss by: **(1)** freezing the meat in small quantities (use freezer containers no larger than 1 quart or 1 L and preferably smaller), **(2)** thawing the veal chunks (when you are ready to cook them) *only* until they can be separated, **(3)** dredging them a little more heavily than usual, and **(4)** browning them before they thaw any further, a few at a time, in cooking oil (butter burns too easily) over higher than usual heat. The idea is to sear the surface of the meat cubes as fast as possible, sealing the juices in.

Roasts, steaks, chops, shanks are a snap to package and freeze. They should be individually, snugly wrapped in foil or moisture- and vapor-proof freezer paper and tightly sealed. Once frozen, you can bundle several chops or shanks together so that they won't migrate to the bottom or back of the freezer and get lost.

For scaloppine and minute steaks, I've evolved a special technique: I lay about a two-foot (60 cm) length of plastic food wrap on the counter, then place a piece of *scaloppine* or a minute steak at one end, its length running parallel to the cut edge of the wrap. I then double the plastic wrap smoothly back over the meat, enclosing it in a giant pleat. I top with a second scallop or minute steak, fold the plastic over it, pressing out any wrinkles, then continue in this manner until I have a neat packet of about six to eight pieces of *scaloppine,* or perhaps four minute steaks. This "accordion pleating" keeps the scallops or minute steaks separate—enough for four servings, or if I use only half a packet, enough for two (the balance need only be resealed immediately and returned to the freezer). Before popping the package of raw *scaloppine* or minute steaks into the freezer, I fold the ends of plastic wrap in, then overwrap the packet carefully in foil, seal it, label it and date it.

You should make a point, **always,** of labeling and dating whatever you freeze. And of freezing everything as quickly as possible. To do so, simply set the items to be frozen directly on the "floor" of a freezer registering 0°F. (−18°C.) or lower. Once the packages are frozen solid, you can rearrange them as needed to make the most efficient use of your freezer space. NOTE: *The preceding table will tell you how long the various cuts and kinds of meat may be held in the freezer before they begin to deteriorate. Never, ever, refreeze meat that has thawed; if, however, ice crystals are clearly discernible in a meat that has partially thawed (as during an electrical failure, for example), the meat may be refrozen. Otherwise, cook it and serve it without delay.*

The ways of cooking meat: There are two basic principles of meat cookery into which all methods fall—**dry heat** and **moist heat**—and the method you choose will be determined by the tenderness or toughness of the meat.

The **tough cuts** (or "less tender," as the meat industry prefers to call them) come from well-exercised parts of an animal: **neck, breast, flank, shank (leg).** Three others—**round, rump** and **chuck** (shoulder)—can be **marginally tender** or **downright tough** depending upon how young and pampered the animal is and also whether the meat has been commercially tenderized (as much beef is nowadays, extending "steak row" beyond the pricey confines of porterhouses, sirloins, T-bones and clubs).

Truly **tender cuts,** on the other hand, come from the little-exercised, costly **rib** and **loin,** provided, of course, the animals were not allowed to romp or run (few are in today's world of scientific meat production). In addition, the **legs** of lamb and pork (ham) qualify as **tender cuts,** as does **round** of veal.

Although few of us realize it, no truly tender cut of meat—a filet mignon, for example, or a loin lamb chop—can ever be made any more tender than it is in the raw state. The aim in cooking, then, is to preserve as much of the original succulence as possible, and the way to accomplish this is usually by **broiling, panfrying (sautéing)** or **roasting,** all **dry heat** methods. I say **usually,** because pork and veal both present special problems, veal because it is so lean it will harden and dry unless cooked with additional fat or liquid, pork because it must always be cooked until well done (not to be translated as tasteless and juiceless) if it is to be safe to eat. But more about the special methods for preparing these two meats in the upcoming sections on Veal and Pork.

One of the miracles of cooking is that tough cuts of meat can be made meltingly tender in a skilled cook's hands. There are, in fact, three basic ways of tenderizing meat: **(1) chemically** (by treating with a commercial meat tenderizer, usually a concentrated, crystalline form of the enzyme papain, extracted from papaya, or by marinating in an acid medium such as buttermilk, tomatoes, wine or vinegar—this is the method German cooks use in making *sauerbraten*); **(2) mechanically** (by mincing, grinding, pounding or scoring meat, which breaks up sinew and connective tissue) and finally, **(3)** by **cooking with moist heat,** i.e. **braising** or **stewing.** This, to me, is the most magical method of all because the combination of prolonged but gentle, moist cooking converts collagen (a component of tough connective tissue) into gelatin, making the meat exquisitely succulent. Tougher cuts, by the way, contain more character and flavor than tender cuts—another reason to prefer them.

Next, here are the basic methods of cooking meat, defined and explained, methods that also carry over into the preparation of fish, fowl and game.

DRY HEAT METHODS OF COOKING MEATS
(FOR TENDER CUTS ONLY):

Roasting: Cooking in the oven, uncovered, in a shallow roasting pan without any additional liquid. All meats to be roasted should be placed fat side up (so that they become self-basting), and if they are boned and rolled (or have no protruding bones as does a standing rib roast), they should be placed on a rack in the roasting pan lest they "stew in their own juices." **The most suitable cuts**

to roast: all rib and loin roasts (except milk-fed veal), beef and lamb sirloin, leg and saddle of lamb, fresh ham, and if of top quality, rolled beef rump, beef sirloin tip and rolled lamb shoulder.

There are, it should be said, two schools of thought about roasting: **(1) searers**—those (for the most part chefs) who like to sear a roast at a very high temperature (about 450°F. or 230°C.) for the first half hour or so of cooking, then to finish it off at a lower heat (300°–325°F. or 150°–165°C.) and **(2) nonsearers**—principally home economists, who insist upon keeping the oven heat at a moderate or moderately low level throughout roasting. Searers insist that a roast develops a rich, flavorful crust when seared (it does) and that this crust seals in meat juices (it doesn't; researchers have proved that there is greater shrinkage, i.e. juice loss, when meats are seared than when they are cooked at a uniformly moderate temperature). Still, I must confess that after a lifetime of dutifully cooking roasts at about 325°F. (165°C.) from start to finish, I've defected to the searer's camp. I like a brown "crust" on my roast, and I also like the richer, more plentiful drippings searing produces because they make glorious pan gravies.

Finally, to answer one of the most-often-asked questions about roasting: **Should the meat be salted before or after it's cooked?** It honestly doesn't matter much because the salt will only penetrate the meat about ¼ inch (¾ cm). I do season a roast before it goes into the oven—and "season" is the key word here because I mix salt, freshly ground pepper, crumbled herbs and sometimes crushed garlic together and smear them liberally over the roast. Some favorite combinations: sage and thyme (and sometimes garlic) for pork; rosemary and thyme (and sometimes garlic) for lamb; marjoram, rosemary or tarragon and thyme for beef. TIP: *Always let a roast stand at room temperature both before and after it is roasted. If a roast goes straight from refrigerator to range, it may not cook evenly—an hour on the counter, I find, will take the chill off the meat. The resting period after the roast is done may be even more important because it is during these 20 to 30 minutes that the meat juices have a chance to settle and the flesh to firm up, making carving easier.*

Broiling: Cooking meat on a rack over or under intense heat without any additional fat or oil. The reason for the rack is to keep the meat up out of the fatty drippings. **Most suitable cuts: Beef and lamb steaks, lamb chops, top-quality ground beef or lamb patties.** Some people broil veal and pork chops, but I prefer to braise them for reasons I will discuss in the sections devoted to Veal and Pork. TIP: *A good rule of thumb to remember when broiling meats is that the thinner the meat, the closer it should be placed to the heat.* For example, steaks, chops or patties measuring about an inch (2½ cm) thick should be placed 2 to 3 inches (5 to 8 cm) from the heat; those between 1 and 2 inches thick (2½ to 5 cm) should be broiled 3 to 5 inches (8 to 13 cm) from the heat. TIPS: *Do not salt and pepper meats to be broiled until after they brown; turn the meat with tongs rather than with a fork, which might pierce the meat, releasing precious juices.*

Panbroiling: Cooking in an uncovered heavy skillet over moderately high heat with minimal fat or oil and no additional liquid; excess drippings, moreover, should be spooned off as the meat browns, otherwise it will *fry* rather than panbroil. **Most suitable cuts for panbroiling: Beef and lamb steaks, lamb chops, top-quality beef or lamb patties.** Again, many people panbroil pork or veal chops. I don't (see the sections on Veal and Pork for my explanations). TIPS: *Do not salt meat to be panbroiled before it is cooked because the salt will draw juices from the meat, making it extremely difficult to brown. Use tongs for turning panbroiled meats and turn them once only—about halfway through cooking. A kitchen fork could puncture the meat, causing valuable juices to be lost and the meat to dry out.*

Panfrying (sautéing): Cooking meat uncovered in a large heavy skillet in a small or moderate amount of fat or oil. **Most suitable cuts for panbroiling: Veal chops, steaks, scaloppine and patties; also beef cube steaks.** Pork chops can be panfried, but I prefer to braise them because they're more interesting and less greasy. TIPS: *If meats to be panfried are dredged or breaded, they may, of course, also be salted and peppered because the flour or crumb coating will seal the juices in. Otherwise, they should not be seasoned because the salt will draw the meat juices and make the chops, steaks, scaloppine or patties virtually impossible to brown.*

MOIST HEAT METHODS OF COOKING MEATS (FOR NOT-SO-TENDER CUTS, ALSO CERTAIN CUTS OF VEAL AND PORK):

Braising: Browning a meat well, then cooking, covered, in the oven or on top of the stove with some liquid or moisture-yielding ingredients until fork-tender. Swiss steaks, then, are braised. And so are pot roasts. **Most suitable cuts: Veal chops, steaks and shanks; veal roasts; pork chops; short ribs, spareribs, and riblets; also less tender cuts of all meats, i.e. from the shoulder, breast (brisket), neck, shanks, rump, neck and tail.**

Stewing: Cooking in liquid in a covered container either in the oven or over a burner. Traditionally, the meat is first browned, then cooked in the company of vegetables, herbs, spices, salt and pepper until a fork will pierce it easily. **Most suitable cuts: The tough cuts of all meats, particularly hocks and shanks, tail, and stew meat, such as chuck (shoulder).**

TWO SPECIALTY METHODS OF COOKING MEATS:

Deep-fat frying: Cooking small morsels of tender meat (usually dredged, breaded or batter-dipped) by immersing them in very hot fat (most often at a temperature between 300° and 360°F. or 150° and 182°C.). **Most suitable meats: Sweetbreads, brains, meatballs, croquettes** (and, of course, all manner of fish, shellfish and poultry). TIPS: *Deep-fried foods should always be drained well (I use several thicknesses of paper toweling), then served as soon as possible. The best fats and oils to use for deep-frying are the lightest and least flavorful because they have* *the highest smoking (burning) point. They are also the most economical. My own favorites are vegetable shortening, vegetable oil and peanut oil (I sometimes use a mixture of vegetable and peanut oil).* If you strain the fat or oil each time you use it through a fine sieve or several thicknesses of cheesecloth, then store, tightly covered, in the refrigerator, you can reuse it as many as three or four times for deep-fat frying—provided the foods you fried were not strong-flavored ones (shrimp, for example, or onion rings).

Poaching: Cooking food by immersing it in simmering liquid (usually water, stock or broth). This, to be sure, is a moist method of cooking, but it is the exception to the rule because the foods usually poached are delicate ones. **Most suitable meats: Sweetbreads, brains, meatballs, dumplings** (and, of course, whole fish, shellfish and chicken breasts).

Beef

       In the old days of cowboys and cattle drives, America's beef was so leathery few people could eat it. Pork was our preferred meat then. But once the Golden Spike was driven and railroads connected east coast with west, the beef industry was on its way. Instead of being trotted hundreds of miles to market, losing weight and gaining sinew, steers were crowded into cattle cars where they could scarcely move a muscle. The result: better meat. As beef production became more scientific, cattle growers began to pen their animals instead of giving them free range and to fatten them up on rations of grain. Thus dawned the days of juicily tender T-bones—and our love affair with beef.

       In the past decade, our undying passion for steaks and roasts has driven the cost of these cuts beyond reach for many of us. Indeed, between 1976 and 1980 alone, America's per capita beef consumption dropped sixteen pounds—from 95.6 to 79.6. Most of us simply opted for cheaper meats—principally chicken— instead of giving the lesser cuts of beef a chance.

       I personally find these less tender, less costly cuts more versatile, more appealing than the proverbial prime ribs. Certainly they can be equally delicious if adeptly prepared, certainly they can spur the cook to greater creativity. For this reason, I devote more space to the lowlier cuts of beef in the pages that follow than I do to steaks and roasts. It's time that more of us learned how superb such cuts can be.

       Before plunging into a discussion of the major cuts, however, a few words about "Boxed Beef," a trend gaining momentum across the country that may slash our beef bill as much as 20 percent. "Boxed Beef," quite simply, is the wholesale or subprimal cut, trimmed and accompanied by cutting instructions so that we can slice off our own porterhouse or prime ribs, blade steaks or stew meat.

       Aside from saving us money, "Boxed Beef" will also teach us valuable lessons about the structure, character and quality of meat. People laugh when I say

I studied meat-cutting at Cornell. And truth to tell, I thought the course was a giggle when I signed up for it. But I stopped giggling about five minutes into the first session. It was a tough course, a superbly practical course, one that has stood me in good stead ever since.

Early on I learned that our beef comes from steers between the ages of nine and forty-two months, that steers are males castrated while young so that they develop such feminine characteristics as softer muscles and fatter flesh (these are what make meat juicy and tender). I learned, too, that the breed of animal (i.e. Angus, Hereford, Charolais) affects the quality and flavor of the meat less than what the animal ate and how rambunctious it was (grain + minimal exercise = succulence).

The qualities of beef

As I've already noted in the introduction to this chapter, the top three grades of beef are USDA PRIME, USDA CHOICE and USDA GOOD (these last two are the ones you're most likely to find at your butcher or supermarket). Lower grades are used primarily for processed meats—hotdogs, cold cuts, cubed steaks, etc.

Because the federal grades aren't visible on all cuts, it's important to recognize good-quality beef when you see it: the flesh should be bright cherry red, velvety smooth and liberally flecked with fat; the outer fat covering should be snowy white (yellow fat usually indicates that an animal was old and/or range-fed; in either case, the meat will be tough). Finally, the center of the chine (back) bone will be spongy and red in top-quality beef. NOTE: *What few of us realize is that not every cut of **Prime** or **Choice** beef will be tender. For example, a rib roast of **Good** grade will usually be more tender than a **Prime** rump. Money can be saved, then, by suiting the grade to the cut.*

The cuts of beef and how to cook them

There is space enough here to cover only the major cuts (the tender and the not-so-tender), but I will cover these fully, suggesting how much you should buy per serving and discussing the basic methods for cooking each.

Roasts

Rib roasts are everyone's favorite, but **rump, round** and **sirloin tip** of CHOICE or PRIME grade will usually be tender enough to oven-roast, too. So will "Tendered" (commercially tenderized) blade and arm roasts from the **chuck** (shoulder), which are normally too tough to roast successfully. "Tendered Beef," by the way, will be so labeled.

POPULAR TENDER ROASTS	DESCRIPTION	MARKET WEIGHTS	APPROX. NO. OF SERVINGS PER POUND (½ kg)
Standing rib	The choicest of all, a chunky, curved roast containing ribs, heavily marbled lean, and a thick outer fat covering. Best of the best: First-Rib Roasts from the loin end. EXPENSIVE.	5–8 pounds (2¼–3½ kg)	1⅓–1½
Rolled Rib	Round, elongated, boneless cut heavily blanketed with fat. EXPENSIVE.	4–6 pounds (1⅘–2¾ kg)	2–3
Rib Eye (also called Delmonico)	Long, almost columnar cut composed of lean rib-eye muscle. Boneless. EXPENSIVE.	3–5 pounds (1⅓–2¼ kg)	2–3

NOTE: *The following roasts are "borderline," i.e. tender enough to roast only if of top quality or commercially tenderized. Otherwise, they are pot roasts and best when braised.*

POPULAR NOT-SO-TENDER ROASTS	DESCRIPTION	MARKET WEIGHTS	APPROX. NO. OF SERVINGS PER POUND (½ kg)
Standing Rump	A blocky, bony, lean cut with compact flesh. MODERATE.	4–7 pounds (1⅘–3¼ kg)	1–1½
Rolled Rump	The same cut, boned and rolled. MODERATELY EXPENSIVE.	3–6 pounds (1⅓–2¾ kg)	2–3
Sirloin Tip	A lean, triangular cut. Boneless. MODERATELY EXPENSIVE.	3–5 pounds (1⅓–2¼ kg)	2–3
Top Round	A lean, fairly flat cut with some bone. FAIRLY EXPENSIVE.	3–6 pounds (1⅓–2¾ kg)	2
Eye Round	Unusually lean and compact; boneless. FAIRLY EXPENSIVE.	2–5 pounds (1–2¼ kg)	2–3

NOTE: *The cuts that follow are almost always too tough to roast by conventional methods. Sometimes, however, if cut from prime beef or if commercially tenderized they can be roasted. They are most often used, however, as pot roasts.*

POPULAR POT ROASTS	DESCRIPTION	MARKET WEIGHTS	APPROX. NO. OF SERVINGS PER POUND (½ kg)
Heel of Round	A wedge-shaped, boneless, sinewy pot roast. MODERATE.	3–4 pounds (1⅓–1⅘ kg)	2–3
Blade Roast	Chunky, square shoulder roast with the shoulder blade and some rib ends. MODERATE.	3–5 pounds (1⅓–2¼ kg)	1½
Arm Roast	A meatier but less tender shoulder cut containing the small round arm bone. MODERATE.	3–5 pounds (1⅓–2¼ kg)	2–2½
Boneless Shoulder (or Cross Rib)	Meaty and boneless, chunky and flavorful. If of tip-top quality, may be tender enough to roast. MODERATE.	3–6 pounds (1⅓–2¾ kg)	2–3

About roasting times, temperatures and tables

I have never been one to rely heavily upon roast meat charts because too many variables can affect overall roasting time: the shape of the roast, the size of the roast, whether or not it contains bone, the temperature of the meat when it went into the oven, the temperature of the oven and whether it remains constant throughout, the accuracy of the oven. I disagree, moreover, with many of the "doneness temperatures" charts offer. Most, for example, cite an internal meat temperature of 140°F. (60°C.) as being *"rare"* for roast beef. Not in my book. Roast beef at that temperature will be pink— well on its way to *medium*. For me, *rare* is *really rare*—juicy red, meaning an internal temperature of about 125°F. (52°C.).

Because I like my roast beef **rare,** I think in terms of **15 to 17 minutes per pound** in a moderately slow oven **(325°F. or 165°C.)** for all bone-in roasts **(after the 25- to 30-minute initial searing at 450°F. or 230°C.).** You will be fairly on the mark if you add 2 to 3 minutes per pound for each successive degree of doneness: **17 to 20 minutes per pound for medium-rare, 19 to 23 for medium,** and so on. Boneless cuts, both because of their compactness and because meat conducts heat more slowly than bone, will require 8 to 10 minutes longer per pound to roast than the bone-in cuts—and that's for each degree of doneness. It's important to remember, too, that large roasts will cook proportionately faster than small ones and that flat roasts will cook faster than chunky ones. You should also bear in mind that a roast will continue to cook after it comes from the oven and that its internal temperature may climb several more degrees during the "resting" period.

By all means, use a roast meat thermometer—either the type that you insert at the outset that stays in the meat throughout roasting or the newer spot-check variety. I personally prefer the latter because its probe is as slender as a knitting needle and need only be inserted as the roast approaches doneness, thereby minimizing juice loss.

Doneness (or degrees thereof) is highly subjective, not to mention arguable. And will ever be, I suspect. Here, however, are the ones I recommend.

DEGREE OF DONENESS	INTERNAL MEAT TEMPERATURE	DESCRIPTION OF MEAT
Rare	125°F. (52°C.)	Very red, very juicy but hot throughout.
Medium Rare	135°–140°F. (57°–60°C.)	Rose-pink and juicy.
Medium	150°–155°F. (65°–68°C.)	Gray-pink, moderately juicy.
Medium Well	160°F. (71°C.)	Gray, firm, little juice.
Well Done	165°F. (74°C.) and up	Gray-brown, compact and fairly dry.

Herbed roast beef

SERVES 6 TO 8

This is my favorite way to roast beef, and it's a good basic method that can be used for all tender roasts whether bone-in or boneless. If you prefer your beef "straight," omit the herbs.

5–6 pounds	standing rib roast (have butcher saw through back bone at base of each rib to facilitate carving)	2¼–2¾ kg
1 teaspoon	crumbled leaf marjoram or tarragon	1 teaspoon
½ teaspoon	crumbled leaf thyme	½ teaspoon
1 teaspoon	salt	1 teaspoon
½ teaspoon	freshly ground black pepper	½ teaspoon

Rub the roast well all over with a mixture of the marjoram, thyme, salt and pepper. Stand the roast on its rib ends in a shallow roasting pan so that the curved fat side is on top and let stand at room temperature 1 hour. Place the roast on the middle rack of a very hot oven (450°F. or 230°C.) and sear 30 minutes. Reduce oven heat to moderately slow (325°F. or 165°C.) and roast uncovered for 1¼ to 1¾ hours or until a meat thermometer inserted in the center of the largest muscle (make sure it does not touch bone) registers 125°F. (52°C.). This is for truly rare meat—juicily red. NOTE: *If you prefer your beef more well done, give it another 10 to 15 minutes for medium rare (140°F. or 60°C.) and another 20 to 30 minutes for medium (150° to 155°F. or 65° to 68°C.). Boned and rolled roasts will require about half again as long to cook, i.e. 2 to 2½ hours for* rare. *Trust your meat thermometer; it will be the truest indicator of the roast's degree of doneness.* As soon as the roast is cooked the way you like it, remove it from the oven, transfer to a heated platter and let rest 20 to 30 minutes.

Now is the time to decide what you will do with the roast beef drippings. The easiest option is simply to skim off excess fat, to keep the drippings warm and to serve them as is—*au jus.* But if the drippings seem skimpy, or if you want to jazz them up a bit, here are a number of quick and easy choices:

Red wine gravy: Skim excess fat from the drippings, then set the roasting pan over moderate heat (you may need to use two burners) and pour in ⅓ to ½ cup (80 to 120 ml) of a good Burgundy or Bordeaux. Simmer, stirring up browned bits from the bottom of the pan, for about 10 minutes until gravy reduces slightly. Turn heat to low and keep the gravy warm while the roast rests. Pour into a hot gravy boat to serve.

Cream gravy: Skim excess fat from the drippings and set the roasting pan over moderately high heat. Pour in ½ cup (120 ml) rich beef stock or broth and boil hard, scraping up browned bits on the bottom of the roasting pan. Reduce heat to moderate and boil gently 10 minutes to reduce. Pour in 1 cup (240 ml) of heavy cream, turn heat to low and allow gravy to simmer slowly as long as the roast rests. Taste for salt and pepper and adjust as needed.

Pepper-cream gravy: Prepare exactly as for Cream Gravy above, but grind in enough black pepper just before serving to add plenty of nip and flavor.

Dijon-cream gravy: Prepare exactly like the Cream Gravy above, but smooth in 2 to 3 teaspoons of a good Dijon mustard. Taste for salt and pepper and adjust, if needed.

Tarragon-Dijon-cream gravy (for roasts seasoned with tarragon only): Prepare exactly as for Cream Gravy above, but crumble in about ½ teaspoon of leaf tarragon just after you add the cream. Shortly before serving, smooth in 2 to 3 teaspoons of fine Dijon mustard.

Tarragon-tomato-cream gravy (for roasts seasoned with tarragon only): Prepare exactly like Cream Gravy, but crumble in about ½ teaspoon of leaf tarragon just after you add the cream. Reduce the sauce as directed, then just before serving, smooth in 1 to 2 teaspoons of tomato paste and, if you like, 1 or 2 tablespoons of dry vermouth.

Old German sauerbraten

SERVES 6 TO 8

One of the most effective ways to tenderize a less-than-succulent beef roast is by marinating it in an acid medium or, better yet, by cooking it slowly in acid medium. To prove the point I offer this superlative *Sauerbraten,* which I was served one night at the home of Carol Zaiser, a friend and widely respected travel writer who is, in private life, Mrs. Ewen Gillies.

Carol generously gave me the recipe when I asked for it and said that it's one she learned from her mother during her growing-up years in Philadelphia and one that her mother had learned from *her* mother, Mrs. Bertha Reichelt, who emigrated from Germany to America in the late nineteenth century. I first printed the recipe, together with the accompanying *Kartoffel Kloesse* (German Potato Dumplings), for another cookbook, *Half a Can of Tomato Paste and Other Culinary Dilemmas*, which I coauthored with Ruth Buchan, founding editor of the Cookbook Guild. I reprint both here because they are far and away the best *Sauerbraten* and potato dumplings I've ever eaten.

4–4½ pounds	boned and rolled rump roast with some outer fat covering	1⅘–2 kg
3 cups	dry red wine of the Bordeaux type (or 2 cups—½ L—cider vinegar)	¾ L (700 ml)
2½ cups, in all	cold water	600 ml, in all
2 tablespoons	sugar	2 tablespoons
1 tablespoon	salt	1 tablespoon
12	whole cloves	12
6	bay leaves (do not crumble)	6
6	peppercorns	6
2 medium-size	yellow onions, peeled and sliced thin	2 medium-size
½ medium-size	lemon, sliced thin	½ medium-size
2 tablespoons	butter or bacon drippings	2 tablespoons
6	gingersnaps	6
¾ cup	sifted all-purpose flour	75 g (180 ml)

Place the rump roast in a large, deep bowl (preferably a ceramic one). Mix the wine with 1½ cups (350 ml) of the cold water and pour over the beef. Add the sugar, salt, cloves, bay leaves, peppercorns, onion and lemon slices. Cover with plastic food wrap and marinate in the refrigerator for 3 days. Twice a day, turn the beef in the marinade.

When you are ready to cook the *Sauerbraten*, lift the meat from the marinade and pat it dry on paper toweling; reserve the marinade. Brown the roast well on all sides in the butter or bacon drippings in a large heavy kettle (one with a snug-fitting lid) over moderately high heat. Reduce the heat to low and gradually pour in the marinade (including onions, lemon and all spices); add the gingersnaps, adjust the heat so that the kettle liquid bubbles gently, then cover and simmer slowly for about 3 hours or until the meat is fork tender. Turn the meat in the kettle liquid three to four times as it cooks so that it will be more evenly flavored.

About 30 minutes before the meat is done, spread the flour out on a pie pan, then set, uncovered, in a moderate oven (350°F. or 175°C.) and brown lightly (this will take about 30 minutes). Remove the flour from the oven, then add it gradually to the remaining 1 cup of cold water, whisking briskly to make a smooth paste. Set aside for the moment.

Lift the meat from the kettle to a large plate. Pour the kettle mixture through a fine sieve set over a large heatproof bowl, then return the strained liquid to the kettle; discard the strained-out solids. Set the kettle over moderately low heat, then gradually whisk in the flour paste. Continue whisking until thickened and smooth and no raw starchy taste remains—about 3 minutes. Return the meat to the gravy, cover and heat slowly for 10 minutes.

To serve, lift the meat from the gravy, remove and discard the strings, then slice fairly thin. Arrange the slices of *Sauerbraten* on a large, heated platter, wreathe with *Kartoffel Kloesse* (see following recipe), and spoon some of the gravy on top of both the meat and the dumplings. Pass the remainder in a gravy boat.

Kartoffel Kloesse
(GERMAN POTATO DUMPLINGS)

SERVES 6 TO 8

These dumplings are the traditional accompaniment for Old German Sauerbraten and, like it, come from my good friend Carol Zaiser. NOTE: *Do not make these dumplings more than a few hours ahead of time because they will absorb moisture in the refrigerator and soften so much that they will be difficult to handle. And, when cooking the dumplings, boil for 3 minutes only, after the cooking water returns to a boil; otherwise they may disintegrate.*

5 medium-size	baking potatoes, scrubbed but not peeled	5 medium-size
3 slices	bacon, snipped crosswise into julienne strips	3 slices
2 teaspoons	salt	2 teaspoons
3 large	eggs	3 large
1 cup + 2 tablespoons	sifted all-purpose flour	112 g (270 ml)
½ cup	farina	120 ml
2 slices	stale firm-textured bread cut into ¼ inch (¾ cm) cubes	2 slices
¼ teaspoon	freshly grated nutmeg	¼ teaspoon
⅛ teaspoon	ground cinnamon	⅛ teaspoon
½ teaspoon	sugar	½ teaspoon
2 tablespoons	minced parsley	2 tablespoons
2 gallons	lightly salted water	8 L

Boil the potatoes in their skins in a large, covered saucepan 35 to 40 minutes or just until a fork will pierce them easily. Drain very dry, cool until easy to handle, then peel and rice or mash. Spread the riced potatoes out on a clean, dry dishtowel and allow to stand, uncovered, for 20 minutes (this is so the towel will absorb as much potato moisture as possible and keep the dumplings from being soggy).

Meanwhile, fry the bacon in a small heavy skillet over moderate heat until crisp and brown; drain off all drippings, then crumble the bacon as fine as possible and let stand on a piece of paper toweling until needed.

Empty the drained riced potatoes into a large mixing bowl and make a well in the center. Add the salt and the eggs, breaking them one by one into the well. Sift the flour on top, then add the reserved bacon and all remaining ingredients (except the lightly salted water) and knead together with your hands until uniformly mixed. Shape into balls just slightly larger than golf balls and arrange in one layer on a wax-paper-lined tray or baking sheet. Refrigerate, **uncovered,** until ready to cook (but for no longer than 4 hours).

When ready to cook the dumplings, heat the lightly salted water to the boiling point in a very large kettle—the kind you would cook pasta in. At the same time, preheat the oven to very slow (250°F. or 120°C.). Drop about half of the dumplings into the water, spacing them as evenly as possible so that they won't stick to one another. When the water returns to a boil, adjust the heat so that it ripples gently, then cover the kettle and cook the dumplings for 3 minutes exactly.

Using a slotted spoon, lift the dumplings from the water and arrange in one layer on a large heatproof plate; place a large colander upside down over them, to act like a perforated lid, and set in the preheated oven to keep warm while you cook the remaining dumplings. Cook and drain them just as you did the first batch.

Serve hot with Old German Sauerbraten (recipe precedes), including plenty of its rich, spicy gravy.

Steaks

"Steak," according to Webster's, is a "slice of meat cut from a fleshy part of a beef carcass." And therein lies the problem. Not every "fleshy part of a beef carcass" is tender. Indeed, many are jaw-breakingly tough, so if we're to do justice to steaks (to say nothing of our pocketbooks), we'd best know which is which and be able to identify each as to cut and quality.

Beef varies more in quality than any other meat, and nowhere, perhaps, is this spread more apparent than in steaks, which are usually flung onto a broiler or into a skillet and browned via intense heat. Such dry heat methods of cooking, if abused, can turn the most buttery filet mignon to leather. So you can imagine what they will do to cuts of questionable tenderness.

The quality of steaks, like that of roasts, is determined in large measure by the richness of the marbling and the thickness of the outer fat covering—the greater the percentage of fat to lean, the higher the grade, because fat helps make meat succulent. Exercise—or rather the lack of it—is another major factor; thus the most tender steaks will come from the rib and loin in the meaty but almost immobile midsection. Steaks are cut fore and aft, too, from the shoulder (chuck) and round (hip), but these must be classified as "iffy," tender enough to broil **if** from prime or choice animals or **if** from commercially tenderized—"tendered"—beef.

To categorize, here are the principal steaks, together with descriptions of each, suggested amounts per serving plus recommended methods for cooking them.

TENDER STEAKS	DESCRIPTION	HOW MUCH PER SERVING?	BEST WAYS TO COOK
Rib (from the rib section)	A club-shaped steak containing a rib and consisting chiefly of the lean rib-eye muscle. EXPENSIVE.	A 1-inch (2½ cm) steak; weight: ¾–1½ lbs. (⅓–⅔ kg)	Broil, panbroil, panfry (sauté).
Rib Eye or Delmonico	Oval, boneless steak—a rib steak minus bone, tail, excess fat. EXPENSIVE.	A 1-inch (2½ cm) steak (about ¾ lb. or ⅓ kg)	Broil, panbroil, panfry (sauté).
Club (from the rib end of the loin section)	A smallish, club-shaped steak from the part of the loin adjoining the rib. EXPENSIVE.	A 1–1½-inch steak (2½–4 cm) or ¾–1¼ lbs. (⅓–½ kg)	Broil, panbroil, panfry (sauté).
T-Bone (from the center of the loin)	Exquisitely tender large steak named for its T-shaped bone. Contains some filet mignon. COSTLY.	A 1-inch (2½ cm) steak or 1–1¼ lbs. (about ½ kg)	Broil, panbroil, panfry (sauté).
Porterhouse (from the sirloin end of the loin)	The biggest, choicest loin steak because it has a large nugget of tenderloin. COSTLY.	A 1-inch (2½ cm) porter-house—about 2 lbs. (1 kg)—will serve two.	Broil.
Strip Steak (also called Shell Steak)	A T-Bone or Porterhouse with the filet mignon stripped out. EXPENSIVE.	A 1–1½ inch (2½–4 cm) steak—about ¾–1 lb. (⅓–½ kg)	Broil, panbroil or panfry (sauté).
Tenderloin (filet mignon; it runs the length of the loin).	The single most tender beef muscle; long, boneless, lean, velvety. EXORBITANT.	A 1½-inch (4 cm) thick slice or about ½ lb. (225 g)	Roast (if whole), panbroil, broil, sauté.

TENDER STEAKS	DESCRIPTION	HOW MUCH PER SERVING?	BEST WAYS TO COOK
Sirloin	This granddaddy of steaks comes from the sirloin, adjacent to the porterhouse. It contains tenderloin and COSTS PLENTY.	A single inch-thick (2½ cm) steak weighs 2–2¼ lbs. (½ kg) and will serve two.	Broil.

NOTE: *The following steaks will be tender enough to broil only if they come from prime or choice quality beef or if they have been commercially tenderized. Otherwise, treat them as Swiss steaks and braise them.*

NOT-SO-TENDER STEAKS	DESCRIPTION	HOW MUCH PER SERVING?	BEST WAYS TO COOK
Blade Steak (from the chuck or shoulder)	A "first-cut" blade next door to the rib will be tender enough to broil or panbroil if of top quality. It contains the rib eye and shoulder blade. Other blade steaks are less tender. MODERATE.	These are large moderately bony steaks, so count on about ¾ lb. (⅓ kg) per serving.	Braise unless top-quality "first-cut" (broil, panbroil, or sauté it).
Arm Steak (from the chuck or shoulder)	A fairly tough steak containing only the small round arm bone. MODERATE.	If an inch (2½ cm) or more thick, an arm steak will serve 2–3. Allow ½ pound (225 g) per serving.	Braise.
Flank Steak (from the underbelly or flank)	A long boneless steak about 1 inch (2½ cm) thick recognizable by its coarse longitudinal grain; the steak of London broil. MODERATE.	About ½ lb. (¼ kg)	Broil (if tenderized) or braise.
Round Steak (from the round or hip)	Round is to beef as scallops are to veal. A single round steak is whopping and usually subdivided into Top Round (the tenderest), Bottom and Eye Round (less tender). All round is lean. MODERATELY EXPENSIVE.	About ½ lb. (¼ kg)	If of top quality, Top Round may be broiled. Eye and Bottom should be braised.

How to pamper (cook) a tender steak

To broil: Thick steaks will broil better than thin ones (in no circumstances try to broil a steak less than 1 inch—2½ cm—thick, because it will toughen and dry out), large steaks (porterhouse and sirloin) better than small ones (rib, club, T-bone, etc.), heavily marbled ones better than lean ones, and room-temperature steaks better than refrigerator-cold ones (I usually let the steak stand on the counter about 30 minutes before I broil it). I also preheat the broiler a full 15 minutes so that it will be sizzling hot when the steak goes into it. A FEW ADDITIONAL TIPS: **(1)** Do not salt a steak before you broil it (the salt will draw juices from the meat and make it almost impossible to brown); season it, instead, as it browns—just before you turn it. **(2)** Slash the fat around the edge of the steak every inch (2½ cm) or so so that it will lie flat on the broiler pan throughout cooking. **(3)** Use tongs for turning the steak so that you don't pierce it and lose savory juices. **(4)** Broil thick steaks (1½ to 2 inches or 4 to 5 cm) about 5 inches (13 cm) from the heat and thin ones (1 inch or 2½ cm) about 3 inches (8 cm) from the heat. **(5)** Brown the steak on one side, turn, then brown the flip side, using the following timetable as a guide for **Rare, Medium,** and, if you insist, **Well-done.**

For Rare, allow approximately:

5 to 8 minutes per side for 1-inch (2½ cm) thick steaks
8 to 12 minutes per side for 1½-inch (4 cm) thick steaks
12 to 16 minutes per side for 2-inch (5 cm) thick steaks

For Medium, allow approximately:

6 to 10 minutes per side for 1-inch (2½ cm) thick steaks
10 to 15 minutes per side for 1½-inch (4 cm) thick steaks
16 to 20 minutes per side for 2-inch (5 cm) thick steaks

For Well-Done, allow approximately:

10 to 12 minutes per side for 1-inch (2½ cm) thick steaks
12 to 18 minutes per side for 1½-inch (4 cm) thick steaks
20 to 23 minutes per side for 2-inch (5 cm) thick steaks

NOTE: *Large steaks (sirloin, for example) will take proportionately longer to broil than small ones (rib, club, T-bone, etc.), marginally tender steaks (chuck or round) longer than tender ones, and boneless steaks (filet mignon and eye round) longer than bony ones. The exception is flank steak, which usually takes only 3 to 5 minutes per side for rare to medium-rare despite the fact that it is both boneless and fairly tough; it should not be cooked beyond medium rare because it will be disagreeably chewy. Why then, you may well wonder, is London broil so tender? Because it is carved tissue-thin, across the grain, which effectively breaks up the long, sinewy strands.*

To panbroil: I prefer panbroiling for smallish steaks cut 1 to 1½ inches (2½ to 4 cm) thick—rib, club, filet mignon and so on—because I can control burner heat better than broiler heat and am thus less apt to overcook them. Large steaks are too unwieldy to handle skillfully in a skillet and thick ones too dense to cook evenly. The initial preparation of steak for panbroiling is the same as for broiling.

Let the steak stand at room temperature 30 minutes or so, do not season it, but do slash the fat edge every inch (2½ cm) or so. Technically, no fat should be added to the pan when you panbroil a steak, but I do rub the skillet bottom, once it's good and hot, lightly with a piece of the fat trimmed from the steak—just enough to keep the steak from sticking. When the pan is really sizzling hot (a drop of water will skitter about on it), I add the steak, lower the heat to moderately hot, and brown it about 5 to 7 minutes per side for **rare,** 7 to 10 for **medium** and 10 to 12 for **well-done.** NOTE: *Pan drippings should be poured off as they accumulate in the skillet; I usually do this once only—about halfway through cooking as I turn the steaks—unless, of course, an inordinate amount of drippings collect, in which case I drain the skillet more often.*

To panfry (sauté): The technique is precisely the same as for panbroiling, except that you should cook the steaks in a little fat—2 to 3 tablespoons of margarine, butter, vegetable oil, olive oil, or if you like a half-and-half mixture of vegetable oil and hazelnut, walnut or sesame oil. The pan drippings should not be poured off as the steaks cook, and for this reason the best steaks to panfry are the leaner, smaller ones (rib eye, filet mignon, top round, minute steak, etc.).

NOTE: *It goes without saying that all steaks, no matter how they are cooked, should be served sizzling hot. You may serve them plain or, if you prefer, anoint them with a flavored butter or savory sauce particularly suited to steak such as Béarnaise or Bordelaise (see Index).*

How to handle the less-tender steaks

In a word, **braise** them. The classic recipe, of course, is the Swiss steak. But there are other ways to braise these recalcitrant cuts, too. And they are best demonstrated in the recipe for *Rouladen* that follows the tenderloin recipe below.

Green and black peppercorn steaks with armagnac sauce

SERVES 2

Most trendy food shops and specialty groceries now routinely stock dried green peppercorns. This recipe, by the way, is one of those last-minute dishes that require dexterity and careful timing. So line up all the ingredients and utensils you'll need before you begin. The recipe is easiest, I think, when you're dealing with two portions only. But if you feel up to it, by all means double the recipe. NOTE: *The cooking times suggested below are slightly less than usual because the steaks will continue to cook while you keep them warm and prepare the sauce.*

⅛ teaspoon	green peppercorns, crushed	⅛ teaspoon
¼ teaspoon	black peppercorns, crushed	¼ teaspoon
2 (1¾-inch-thick)	center-cut slices beef tenderloin, trimmed of unnecessary fat	2 (4½ cm thick)
2 tablespoons	unsalted butter	2 tablespoons
	SAUCE	
2 tablespoons	Armagnac or Cognac	2 tablespoons
1 tablespoon	unsalted butter	1 tablespoon
½ teaspoon	Dijon mustard	½ teaspoon
3 tablespoons	Madeira wine (not too sweet)	3 tablespoons
⅛ teaspoon	finely crumbled leaf rosemary	⅛ teaspoon
⅛ teaspoon	salt	⅛ teaspoon
Pinch	freshly ground black pepper	Pinch
4 tablespoons	heavy cream, at room temperature	4 tablespoons

Pound the green and black peppercorns into both sides of the steaks and let stand at room temperature 30 minutes. Heat the butter in a medium-size heavy skillet over moderately high heat until it foams up, then subsides. Add the steaks and brown 3 to 4 minutes on a side for rare, 4 to 5 for medium rare, and 5 to 6 for medium (I don't recommend cooking the steaks **any** longer because you will sacrifice the juiciness and tenderness for which you paid a premium). Transfer the steaks to a small heated platter and keep warm while you prepare the sauce.

Remove the skillet from the heat and pour in the Armagnac, stirring it around to loosen the browned bits. Ignite with a match, and when the flames die (after about a minute), set the skillet over moderate heat. Quickly blend in the butter, mustard, Madeira, rosemary, salt and pepper and heat and stir 2 to 3 minutes or until the mixture cooks down into a rich glaze. Smooth in the cream, heat about 1 minute more, then pour over the steaks and serve.

Hedy Wuerz's Rouladen

SERVES 6

I was never a fan of *Rouladen* until I tasted it one night at the home of Hedy Wuerz, an uncommonly gifted cook and hostess who also happens to be director of public relations, North America, for the German National Tourist Office. Hedy's *Rouladen* is something special, and she graciously consented to share her recipe. It's imperative, she cautions, that you use just the right cut of meat. "In Germany," she says, "we just ask for *Rouladen*. Every butcher knows what it is. But in America, I don't know what the meat is called." I have found out. It's top round. And it should be sliced into thin scallops about 6 inches (18 cm) long, 3 inches (8 cm) wide and ⅜ inch (1 cm) thick, then pounded—gently but thoroughly—so that the meat is about ¾ inch (2 cm) larger all around and about ⅛ inch (½ cm) thick. It is vital that the meat have no ragged edges, thin spots or holes because the filling will ooze out. It's also important that the dill pickles and bacon you use in the filling are not too salty or strong; otherwise they will overpower the flavor of the beef. Serve the *Rouladen* with boiled new potatoes or *spaetzle* (see Index).

3 pounds	top round (preferably a single large muscle), sliced and pounded thin as described in the headnote above (you should have 18 to 20 slices in all)	1½ kg
1 teaspoon	salt	1 teaspoon
¼ teaspoon	freshly ground black pepper	¼ teaspoon
6 tablespoons (about)	Dijon mustard	6 tablespoons (about)
	FILLING:	
4 medium-size	yellow onions, peeled and minced	4 medium-size
½ pound	mildly smoked slab bacon, diced fine	225 g
1 cup	minced parsley	240 ml
3 medium-size	dill pickles (not too sour), minced	3 medium-size
	FOR COOKING THE ROULADEN:	
2 tablespoons	unsalted butter	2 tablespoons
2 tablespoons	peanut oil	2 tablespoons
1 large	carrot, peeled and chopped	1 large
1 large	yellow onion, peeled and sliced	1 large
1 large	celery rib, peeled and sliced	1 large
½ cup	minced parsley	120 ml
2 cans (13¾ oz. each)	beef broth, heated to simmering	2 cans (407 ml each)

GRAVY:

—	the Rouladen cooking liquid and solids	—
4 tablespoons	tomato paste	4 tablespoons
½ cup	heavy cream	120 ml
To taste	salt and freshly ground black pepper	To taste

Cover a counter with wax paper and spread the pieces of beef on top. Trim off and discard any ragged edges, then sprinkle each piece lightly with salt and pepper. Turn and season the flip side the same way. Now thinly spread the top side of each scallop with mustard, using about 1 level teaspoon per scallop. Let stand for the moment.

For the filling: Stir-fry the onions and bacon together in a large heavy skillet over moderate heat 8 to 10 minutes, just until onions are nicely glazed with a little of the bacon fat—no matter if they brown lightly. Mix in the parsley, remove the skillet from the heat and cool. Stir in the pickles.

To shape the Rouladen: Place a mounded tablespoon of filling at one end of a scallop, then spread evenly over the meat, leaving ⅜ inch (1 cm) margins to the right and left and a full inch (2½ cm) at the far end. Now roll the scallop up tightly toward the unspread end and secure the seam with toothpicks or poultry pins. Also pinch each end of the roll together and secure with toothpicks so that the filling will not ooze or fall out as the *Rouladen* cook. Fill, roll, and seal the remaining *Rouladen* the same way.

To cook the Rouladen: Warm the butter and peanut oil in a very large heavy skillet set over fairly high heat until sizzling. Add the *Rouladen* and brown nicely on all sides—this will take about 10 minutes. Reduce the heat to moderate, add the carrot, onion, celery and parsley, and sauté about 5 minutes with the *Rouladen.* Add the broth, bring to a simmer, then adjust the heat so that the liquid just trembles. Cover the skillet and simmer the *Rouladen* 1¼ to 1½ hours or until a fork will pierce them easily. Using a slotted spoon, lift the *Rouladen* to a shallow pan, cover with foil and keep warm while you prepare the gravy.

For the gravy: Strain the *Rouladen* cooking liquid, saving both the solids and the liquid. Return the liquid to the skillet, set over high heat and boil hard for 10 to 15 minutes to reduce by about one-third. Meanwhile, purée the solids with about 1 cup of the liquid in an electric blender or food processor equipped with the metal chopping blade. Smooth the purée into the skillet; lower heat so that mixture simmers gently. Smooth in the tomato paste, and when thoroughly incorporated, blend in the cream. Season to taste as needed with salt and pepper.

Return the *Rouladen* to the skillet and warm slowly in the gravy for about 10 minutes, basting often, then serve. NOTE: *You can prepare the* Rouladen *a full day or two in advance, then bring slowly to serving temperature in a covered skillet— 10 to 15 minutes over low heat should be sufficient.*

Ground beef

Hamburger, as it appears in most supermarkets, consists of beef trimmings and—make a note—about 30 percent fat. It may be priced lower than **ground chuck** or **round,** but it will shrink awesomely during cooking as the fat melts. The leanest ground beef is **ground round,** but at only 11 percent fat it makes a dry and dismal burger unless it is served very rare or fortified with additional fat—a little ground suet, perhaps, or butter. (I have a friend who routinely kneads about a stick of softened butter into every pound of ground round. I personally don't care much for her hamburgers, but her family thinks they're the best.)

My personal choice is **ground chuck** because of its juiciness and flavor. Because I prefer chuck on the lean side (15 to 20 percent fat), I ask my butcher to trim it carefully before he grinds it. And he does.

Not all of us, alas, are blessed with skilled and willing butchers, and the only way for us to control the percentage of fat to lean is to grind our own meat. It's easy if you have a meat grinder—and you'll save yourself money. You can also processor-chop or grind meat, although the texture will not be quite the same. Here's the method I worked out a few years ago when I was writing *Jean Anderson's Processor Cooking.*

To processor-grind meat: The best cuts to use are **top** and **bottom round** because they are relatively free of sinew and connective tissue and thus require the least amount of trimming. I've recently discovered to my delight, however, that **first-blade chuck** (that next to the tender rib section) can also be processor-ground with comparative ease (most parts of the chuck are so shot through with gristle, connective tissue and fat that it's scarcely worth your while to excise them all before grinding.) Whatever the meat you intend to grind, you must scrupulously trim it of sinew and connective tissue lest they become entangled in the blades and stall the motor. Once the meat is trimmed, cut it into ¾ to 1-inch (2 to 2½ cm) cubes. Equip the processor with the metal chopping blade, then place no more than 1 cup of beef cubes in the work bowl at a time. NOTE: *Read your processor's instruction manual carefully; some manufacturers recommend that you drop the cubes of meat down the feed tube while the motor is on and the blade spinning; some even recommend that you partially freeze the meat—just until it offers some resistance to the blade and will shatter into small flakes instead of being ground to a paste).* For a coarse grind, snap the motor on and off 3 to 4 times; for a moderate grind, use 5 to 6 on-offs of the motor; and for a fine grind, let the motor run nonstop for 8 to 10 minutes. Keep an eye on the work bowl at all times and, as soon as the meat reaches the texture you want, shut the motor off. Scrape the ground beef into a bowl, then do another batch the same way—and another and another until you have the amount of meat you need for a particular recipe. NOTE: *One advantage of grinding the meat only as you need it is that there is little danger of your original supply going bad in the refrigerator.*

Ground meat is one of the most perishable of meats and should not be kept beyond one to two days. A solid chunk of meat, on the other hand, can be kept twice as long.

Some tips on shaping burgers: None of these measly little "quarter-pounders" touted by the fast-food chains as something special, please. I like my burgers to contain at least ⅓ pound (160 g) of meat, but better yet, a full half pound (225 g). I sometimes mix seasonings in, but more often simply scoop up the meat and lightly shape it into patties about an inch (2½ cm) thick. It's best, I've found, not to pack or compress the meat too much because the burgers will then be heavy. TIP: *The lighter the touch, the lighter the burger.* You can, of course, crumble in a little leaf marjoram or rosemary and thyme—about ½ teaspoon marjoram or rosemary to a pound (½ kg) of meat and ¼ teaspoon thyme. You might also add a tablespoon or two of dry red wine, if you like; ½ cup (120 ml) of minced yellow onion; a crushed garlic clove; a little Dijon mustard. Indeed, use your imagination, experimenting with the seasonings and making note of those your family especially likes.

About cooking burgers: Thick, top-quality burgers containing a moderate amount of fat (20 percent) can be **broiled** or **panbroiled** if they are served rare or medium-rare (3 to 4 minutes on a side should do it). If you **broil** them, place them on a lightly oiled broiler pan and set 2 to 3 inches (5 to 8 cm) from the heat. If you **panbroil** them, oil the skillet or griddle lightly (or sprinkle it with salt), then cook the burgers over fairly high heat. Any burger can be **panfried** (sautéed), but this method is best for lean ones. The technique is little different from panbroiling; the only real change is that you cook the burgers with a little fat. For general use, I like butter or margarine (2 tablespoons is sufficient for 4 to 6 good-size burgers). If I've seasoned the burgers with marjoram or rosemary, I generally substitute olive oil. It's surprising how much you can vary the flavor of burgers merely by changing the frying medium. Sesame oil will create a new dish altogether as, indeed, will walnut or hazelnut oil. (These, by the way, tend to smoke at fairly low temperatures, so it's best to mix them half-and-half with a standard vegetable, peanut or corn oil—a good idea, also, because these "trendy" oils are too strong in flavor to use solo.)

Mushroom and shallot stuffed hamburgers

SERVES 4

I like a plain hamburger as much as the next person. But I also like gussied-up hamburgers because they're so easy to make and lend themselves to infinite variations. The basic technique is this: Make an even number of thin patties—8, 10, 12, and so on—so that pairs may be sandwiched together enclosing the filling of your choice. Sometimes I do nothing more than stuff the burgers with a little minced onion or Roquefort cheese. Sometimes I tuck in a slice of American cheese and a little chopped pickle. Sometimes I get more elaborate and do these fancy hamburgers.

1½ pounds	lean ground beef chuck	⅔ kg
2 tablespoons	dry red wine	2 tablespoons
1 teaspoon ·	Worcestershire sauce	1 teaspoon
1 teaspoon	salt	1 teaspoon
¼ teaspoon	freshly ground black pepper	¼ teaspoon
3 tablespoons	unsalted butter	3 tablespoons
½ cup	finely minced fresh mushrooms	120 ml
2 large	shallots, peeled and minced	2 large

Mix the meat with the wine, Worcestershire sauce, salt and pepper and shape into 8 thin patties of uniform size. Set aside. Melt 2 tablespoons of the butter in a small heavy skillet over moderate heat, add the mushrooms and shallots and stir-fry about 5 minutes or until most of the juices have cooked away. Spread this mixture on half the patties, dividing the total amount evenly. Top with the remaining patties, then pinch the edges together to enclose the mushrooms and shallots. Heat the remaining 1 tablespoon butter in a large heavy skillet over moderately high heat, then brown the hamburgers 5 minutes on a side for rare, 6 for medium and 7 for well done. Or, if you prefer, broil the burgers 3 inches (8 cm) from the heat, allowing approximately the same cooking time per side for the different degrees of doneness.

Beef loaf Italian style with lemon and anchovies

SERVES 8 TO 10

Not the ordinary meat loaf, but an easy and delicious one that I make often.

1 pound	sweet Italian sausages	½ kg
1½ pounds	ground lean beef chuck	⅔ kg
½ pound	ground lean pork shoulder	¼ kg
2 cups	moderately coarse Italian bread crumbs	½ L
2 large	yellow onions, peeled and minced	2 large
1 small	sweet red pepper, washed, cored, seeded and minced	1 small
1 medium-size	finocchio (Florence fennel) rib, trimmed and finely minced	1 medium-size
2 medium-size	garlic cloves, peeled and minced	2 medium-size
1 cup	drained chopped canned tomatoes	240 ml

¼ cup	tomato liquid (drained from the can)	60 ml
¼ cup	dry white wine	60 ml
2 medium-size	eggs, lightly beaten	2 medium-size
1 teaspoon	crumbled leaf basil	1 teaspoon
½ teaspoon	crumbled leaf oregano	½ teaspoon
¼ teaspoon	crumbled leaf thyme	¼ teaspoon
1 tablespoon	anchovy paste	1 tablespoon
1 teaspoon	finely grated lemon rind	1 teaspoon
½ teaspoon	salt	½ teaspoon
⅛ teaspoon	freshly ground black pepper	⅛ teaspoon

Slit the sausage casings lengthwise, then scoop the sausage meat into a large bowl. Add all remaining ingredients, mix thoroughly and pack into a well-greased 9 × 5 × 3-inch (23 × 13 × 8 cm) loaf pan. Bake in a moderate oven (350°F. or 175°C.) for 1 hour and 45 minutes or until loaf pulls from sides of pan and is nicely browned. Cool the loaf in its pan for 15 minutes, then drain off the drippings. Turn the loaf out onto a platter and serve garnished with lemon twists and fluffs of greenery.

Stew meat

 We tend to think of stew meat as boneless, and yet two of the very best cuts of stew beef have the bones in: **short ribs** and **shanks.** Why we don't take greater advantage of such economical cuts, I cannot say. It's a pity because they are supremely succulent when skillfully cooked.

As for boneless stew meat, it most often comes from the **chuck** and the **rump.** The choicer of the two is chuck because it has a greater marbling of fat, also more gristle and sinew, which can be converted into gelatin via slow moist cooking. And what about those anonymous supermarket packages labeled simply **"stew meat"**? What cuts do they contain? Odds and ends, usually, but these trimmings can make perfectly respectable everyday stews.

You will find here (and in the Recipe Collection in Part II) some superlative recipes for a variety of stew meats.

Jugged beef with cranberries and mushrooms

SERVES 6

Strong-flavored cuts of beef—chuck, fresh brisket, short ribs, shank trimmings—can be "jugged" (made into a spicy oven stew) much in the manner of game. So can the tougher cuts of lamb. This recipe, in fact, works equally well for beef, lamb and venison, even for buffalo, which is now being raised for the table. NOTE: *I prefer to salt and pepper stew meat before I dredge it rather than mix the seasonings with the flour because I like knowing precisely how much salt and pepper I am using. I've also evolved a method for dredging meat that coats each piece evenly and thinly but uses less flour than usual. What I do is cover a counter with wax paper, spread the meat out in one layer, sprinkle it with half the salt and pepper, turn it, season with the remaining salt and pepper, then scatter 4 to 5 tablespoons of flour evenly over all. I then toss the meat vigorously until each piece is uniformly dredged. This technique, I've learned, automatically dislodges excess flour on the meat and minimizes the risk of burning the browning fat because there's no loose flour to settle on the kettle bottom and blacken.*

2½ pounds	lean boneless beef chuck, trimmed of fat and cut into 1½-inch (4 cm) cubes	1¼ kg
1 teaspoon	salt	1 teaspoon
¼ teaspoon	freshly ground black pepper	¼ teaspoon
4–5 tablespoons	all-purpose flour	4–5 tablespoons
½ pound	slab bacon, cut into small dice	225 g
3 large	yellow onions, peeled and chopped	3 large
1 pound	mushrooms, wiped clean and sliced thin	½ kg
8 large (1 pound)	carrots, peeled and cut in 2-inch (5 cm) chunks	8 large (½ kg)
½ teaspoon	crumbled leaf rosemary	½ teaspoon
½ teaspoon	crumbled leaf marjoram	½ teaspoon
¼ teaspoon	crumbled leaf thyme	¼ teaspoon
⅛ teaspoon	freshly grated nutmeg	⅛ teaspoon
1 piece (about 2 inches)	stick cinnamon	1 piece (5 cm)
1 cup	dry red wine	240 ml
¼ cup	dry Port, Madeira or sherry	60 ml
½ cup	whole or jellied cranberry sauce, tart currant or other fruit jelly	120 ml
2 tablespoons	minced fresh parsley	2 tablespoons

Season the beef with the salt and pepper, then dredge as directed above (or use your own favorite dredging method). Set the dredged beef aside. Fry the bacon in a medium-size heavy kettle over moderately high heat until all of the fat cooks out and only crisp brown bits remain—10 to 12 minutes. With a slotted spoon, lift the browned bits to paper toweling to drain; reserve. Pour off all drippings and reserve; return 3 tablespoons of them to the kettle. Brown the beef in the kettle in two to three batches over moderately high heat, transferring each as it browns to a large bowl; add additional drippings to the kettle only if absolutely necessary and then no more than 2 tablespoons in all—the meat will exude considerable fat as it cooks, even though it is lean, so go easy on the bacon drippings.

When all the beef is browned, stir-fry the onions and mushrooms in 2 additional tablespoons of the bacon drippings over moderate heat about 10 minutes until limp and lightly browned. Stir in the carrots, rosemary, marjoram, thyme and nutmeg; drop in the cinnamon stick and stir-fry a minute or two. Return the browned beef to the kettle, add the red wine, Port, and cranberry sauce and bring to a boil over moderate heat.

Cover the kettle snugly, set in a slow oven (300°F. or 150°C.) and cook 2 to 2½ hours or until meat is very tender. Stir in the reserved bacon crumbles and the parsley and serve. NOTE: *This stew is best with potatoes, preferably small new potatoes boiled in their skins, with spaetzle (see Index) or broad buttered noodles.*

Canadian beef and beer pie

SERVES 6

 A cross between a *carbonnade* (Belgian beef and beer stew) and a potpie, this recipe is an old favorite of mine. I sometimes use coffee in place of water and think the coffee enriches the flavor (a trick I picked up from Swedish women, who often baste their roasts with the leftover morning coffee). It's best to cook the stew partially in one kettle, then to transfer it to a cold clean casserole just before you add the crust, because it will be virtually impossible to apply the pastry to a hot pot.

2½ pounds	lean boneless beef chuck, trimmed of fat and cut into 1½-inch (4 cm) cubes	1¼ kg
1 teaspoon	salt	1 teaspoon
¼ teaspoon	freshly ground black pepper	¼ teaspoon
1 teaspoon	rubbed sage	1 teaspoon
4–5 tablespoons	all-purpose flour	4–5 tablespoons
2 tablespoons	peanut or other cooking oil	2 tablespoons
2 tablespoons, in all	unsalted butter	2 tablespoons, in all
3 large	yellow onions, peeled and chopped	3 large
2 large	garlic cloves, peeled and chopped	2 large
6 medium-size	waxy potatoes, peeled and cubed (California long whites are excellent)	6 medium-size
¼ pound	mushrooms, peeled and coarsely chopped	115 g
½ teaspoon	crumbled leaf thyme	½ teaspoon
1 large	bay leaf, crumbled	1 large

2 tablespoons	tomato paste	2 tablespoons
2 tablespoons	freshly minced parsley	2 tablespoons
1 can (12 oz.)	light beer	1 can (355 ml)
½ cup	strong coffee or water	120 ml
1 recipe	Basic Piecrust (see Index)	1 recipe

Cover a counter with paper and spread the beef cubes out in one layer. Sprinkle with half the salt, pepper and sage; turn the cubes and sprinkle with the rest of the salt, pepper and sage. Now scatter 4 tablespoons of the flour evenly on top. Toss vigorously five to six times; if beef seems skimpily dredged, sprinkle with the remaining tablespoon of flour and toss well again. Brown the beef in two to three batches in the 2 tablespoons oil and 1 tablespoon of the butter over moderately high heat; as the beef browns, lift to a bowl with a slotted spoon and reserve. When all of the beef is brown, add the remaining tablespoon of butter to the kettle, then dump in the onions and garlic and stir-fry 5 to 8 minutes until limp and golden over moderate heat; do not brown. Lower heat slightly, add the potatoes and mushrooms and stir-fry about 5 minutes. Add the thyme, bay leaf and reserved beef and allow to mellow a minute or two, then mix in the tomato paste, parsley, beer and coffee. Bring to a simmer, cover and set in a moderately slow oven (325°F. or 165°C.). Bake 1½ hours. Remove the kettle from the oven and let stand while you prepare the pastry.

Make the Basic Piecrust as the recipe directs, then roll out on a lightly floured pastry cloth with a stockinette-covered rolling pin into a circle about 3 inches (8 cm) larger than the diameter of the casserole in which you will finish baking the Beef and Beer Pie (it should have a 2½ quart or 2½ L capacity). Let the pastry rest.

Transfer the stew mixture from the kettle to the casserole. With a pastry brush, moisten the casserole rim all around with water (this will help make the pastry stick). Now lay rolling pin across the center of the pastry circle and lop half of the pastry over it. Very carefully ease the pastry on top of the casserole, letting it settle down over the stew. Trim the overhang so that it measures about 1 inch (2½ cm) all around. Roll the overhang under so that it is even with the casserole rim, then seal by crimping with the tines of a fork, pressing against the rim. Prick the pastry well so that steam can escape while the stew finishes baking, making the pattern as decorative as possible.

Return the pie to the moderately slow oven and bake for 1 hour or until the crust is an even dark tan and the stew bubbly. Serve the stew at table directly from its casserole. Accompany with a crisp green vegetable such as broccoli or Brussels sprouts or by a tart green salad.

Veal

Twenty years ago, it was virtually impossible to buy a decent piece of veal in America except in a few pricey metropolitan markets. Indeed, few Americans had ever eaten good veal, let alone knew what it looked like. Small wonder it wasn't popular.

Then mass America began traveling abroad and tasting such Continental classics as the French *blanquette de veau,* the Austrian *Wiener schnitzel,* the Italian *piccata,* all made with a delicate white meat wholly unlike the chewy, reddish cuts palmed off as veal back home.

Today, fine European-style veal is available across most of America—and not just in fancy French restaurants or gold-plated butcher shops. It has come to the supermarket. This is **true** veal, mind you—"nature," "special-fed," "fancy quality"—meat from bull Hostein calves no more than sixteen weeks old that have been penned since the day they were born, pampered and fattened upon a ration of milk solids, vitamins and minerals.

Wisconsin produces the bulk of America's milk-fed veal, not surprising considering that it is our leading dairy state and that veal is a by-product of the dairy industry (not of the beef industry). Holsteins, from which our best veal comes, are dairy animals, abundant milk producers provided the cows freshen (calve) each year. The female calves usually grow up into the dairy herd. The males become lean, fine-fleshed veal.

The beauty of veal is its versatility, its affinity for an astonishing range of ingredients, its ability to complement everything from tuna (as in *vitello tonnato*) to tomatoes (*ossobuco*) to tarragon. I know of no meat more open to improvisation than veal, or one more dependent upon a cook's talent and technique.

Because the price of fine veal is now climbing through the clouds, it's wise to know precisely how much of it you will need before splurging, also how you intend to prepare it, which, in turn, will determine what specific cut you should buy. Finally, it is imperative that you learn to recognize top-quality veal and that you settle for nothing less.

The kinds and qualities of veal

Bob veal: The meat of new-born calves. It's plentiful but poor because the animals from which it comes were far too young to have developed meat of much character. The best way to recognize bob veal is by the smallness of the cuts (these calves were no more than a week old when slaughtered), the redness and sponginess of the bones, the lack of exterior fat and the soft, translucent, grayish flesh.

Grain-fed veal: As soon as calves go off mother's milk and begin grazing or feeding upon grain, their meat begins to redden. The redder the meat, the more grain or grass the animal has eaten and the older it's likely to be. Most grain-fed veal, in fact, isn't veal at all but "baby beef" (8 to 12 months old). And don't be fooled into thinking that "baby beef" will be better or more tender than mature beef. It won't because it lacks the marbling (flecks of fat in the lean) essential to succulence.

Special-fed (also called **Nature** or **Fancy-quality**): Deluxe, delicate, delicious. The veal to insist upon. Much of it is brand-labeled in the manner of designer clothes. Two names to seek out: **Plume de Veau** and **Provimi Delft Blue.** Both are European-style, milk-fed veals—pale, pale pink of flesh (it turns white almost as soon as you begin to cook it), velvety-firm, fine-grained and moist, with the slimmest exterior covering of creamy-white fat. Most of the butchers and supermarkets that sell either of these superior meats proudly advertise that fact.

As for federal grades, the top two for veal—and the only two with which you should concern yourself—are USDA PRIME (most of which winds up in fine restaurants and butcher shops) and USDA CHOICE (the grade most likely to be found in supermarkets). There are lower grades, true. But because veal is such a difficult meat to cook properly at best, I see no point in compounding the problem by buying inferior quality (this, by the way, will cost plenty, too). Most supermarket packages will have the federal grade clearly marked; it will also be visible on larger cuts (look for the purple shield-shaped stamp on the outer fat covering).

The cuts of veal
and how to cook them

Because veal is so fragile, so lean, so delicate of flavor, it can be ruined if not handled with respect and restraint. Rather than plunge into a detailed analysis of all of the cuts of veal (the primal and subprimal—information which you can get along without and for which there simply isn't space in this book—I will confine myself to those cuts you are most likely to find at your butcher's or supermarket. They include both the bony cuts and the boneless, the tender and the tough, enabling me to cover all the best methods for cooking veal. I will discuss the cuts one by one, tell how much of each is needed for the average-size serving, then move on to the basic method of preparation. NOTE: *You will find details on how best to store and freeze veal at the beginning of the Meat chapter.*

Veal roasts

Because veal comes from cosseted animals too young to have exercised and toughened their muscles, many of its cuts (which in beef would be too sinewy to roast) are tender (i.e. "roastable"). Shoulder (chuck) is one such cut. Breast another. The calf's tender young age, however, also means a meat so lean (no marbling to speak of and only a skimpy outer covering of fat) that it should **not** be "roasted by the book," that is, cooked uncovered in the oven without any basting, without any liquid added to the pan. Indeed, if veal is to retain its initial succulence, it must be lavishly barded (wrapped in sheets of fat) or larded (threaded with strips of fat), buttered, basted or cooked in the company of liquid or moisture-yielding ingredients. Sometimes it should even be covered, or at least tented with foil, to prevent its drying out. Technically, then, roasts of veal are **braised.** But more of this later. First, a few facts and figures to help you save time and money when you shop.

POPULAR ROASTS	DESCRIPTION	MARKET WEIGHTS	APPROX. NO. OF SERVINGS PER POUND (½ kg)
Bone-in Shoulder	Two choices, the triangular Blade Roast (recognizable by the shoulder blade) and oval Arm Roast containing the round arm bone and rib ends. MODERATELY PRICED (for veal).	4–5 pounds (1¾–2¼ kg)	1–1½
Rolled Shoulder	An elongated roll with no bones, no waste. MODERATELY EXPENSIVE.	3½–5 pounds (1½–2¼ kg)	2–3
Standing Loin	A meaty cut containing the T-bone and nuggets of tenderloin. EXPENSIVE.	4–6 pounds (1¾–2¾ kg)	1½
Rolled Loin	A long boneless roast with a large smooth muscle. EXPENSIVE.	3½–5 pounds (1½–2¼ kg)	2–3
Standing Rump	A choice, chunky cut; moderately bony. EXPENSIVE.	4–6 pounds (1¾–2¾ kg)	1–1½

POPULAR ROASTS	DESCRIPTION	MARKET WEIGHTS	APPROX. NO. OF SERVINGS PER POUND (½ kg)
Rolled Rump	Big and blocky enough to roast evenly; no bone. EXPENSIVE.	3–5 pounds (1⅓–2¼ kg)	2–3
Leg (Round)	Center-cut Leg, with one small bone and fine-grained muscles from which *scallopine* comes, is the chef's choice—and EXORBITANT; less tender, somewhat LESS EXPENSIVE, the club-shaped Shank-half Leg.	3–8 pounds (1⅓–3½ kg)	2
Breast	A flat, cumbersome cut full of ribs and cartilage. Best when stuffed. REASONABLE.	3–5 pounds (1⅓–2¼ kg)	1
Rolled Breast	As much connective tissue as meat but no bone. REASONABLE.	3–4 pounds (1⅓–1¾ kg)	2–3

NOTE: *Veal rib roasts seem to be less in demand today than they once were (except for the theatrical, custom-made crown roasts that require two rib sections to make and cost the earth), so butchers usually subdivide this wholesale cut into chops. Similarly, butchers seem to reserve most veal sirloin for steaks and scallops instead of selling it as roasts.*

About veal "roasting" times

The reason I have stuck quote marks around **roasting** is that roasts of veal are to my taste too lean to roast successfully and must be **oven-braised** if they are to remain juicily tender. What this means is that the roast may be covered, it may be blanketed with fat, it may be basted, it may even have liquid added to the pan. True roasting requires nothing more than that the meat be cooked uncovered in the oven with no ingredients added to keep it moist and juicy—chancey for veal. Cooking times would be about the same for roasting as for oven-braising.

I don't put much faith in meat-roasting charts, because so many variables affect the overall cooking time: the size and shape of the cut, whether the roast is boneless (these take almost half again as long to cook as bone-in roasts), the temperature of the meat (was it whisked from the refrigerator to oven or allowed to come to room temperature, first?—the latter a good practice, by the way, because the meat will cook more evenly).

Still, I realize how important it is to have some notion as to overall cooking time so that you can synchronize the preparation of the rest of the meal. Here, then, is a rough timetable:

Allow 25 to 35 minutes per pound for bone-in roasts of veal and 40 to 45 minutes for boneless roasts to reach an internal temperature of 165°F. (74°C.). Then add another 20 minutes for the resting period after the roast comes from the oven. This is important because it gives the meat juices a chance to settle and the meat itself time to firm up, making carving easier.

NOTE: *It's wise to use a meat thermometer when oven-braising veal (I prefer the slender-stemmed, spot-check variety that need only be thrust into the center of the largest muscle toward the end of cooking. Take the roast from the oven the instant the mercury hits 165°F. (74°C.). Resist the impulse to roast the veal to 170°F. (77°C.), as most roasting charts recommend, because the internal temperature of the meat will continue to climb during the resting period and will ultimately reach that level.*

Basic braised loin of veal with shallot-cream sauce

SERVES 6

 Barding, larding or draping a roast of veal with mildly smoky bacon are all tried-and-proved ways of keeping the meat moist as it braises. But I prefer this simpler method, which involves nothing more than rubbing the veal with soft butter. You may leave the butter plain or experiment with seasonings, adding shallot and sage (as below), garlic and rosemary, or freshly minced tarragon. The possibilities are as open as your imagination (try creaming a teaspoon or two of Dijon mustard into the butter, or the juice of a lemon, or a couple of tablespoons of dry vermouth). As the butter melts, it will both moisten and flavor the veal and the pan drippings. As added insurance against dry meat, I tent the veal with foil for about a third of its stay in the oven.

A 4½–5-pound	standing loin of veal (have butcher saw through back bone at base of each rib to facilitate carving)	A 2–2¼ kg
½ teaspoon	salt	½ teaspoon
¼ teaspoon	freshly ground black pepper	¼ teaspoon
2 tablespoons	unsalted butter	2 tablespoons
1 large	shallot, peeled and minced fine	1 large
1 teaspoon	rubbed sage	1 teaspoon
¼ teaspoon	crumbled leaf thyme	¼ teaspoon
1 cup	heavy, light or half-and-half cream	240 ml

Rub the veal loin well all over with salt and pepper and let stand at room temperature 1 hour. Meanwhile, cream the butter with the shallot, sage and thyme. Stand the veal, curved side up, in a large shallow roasting pan and rub well with the flavored butter. Set the roast uncovered in a very hot oven (425°F. or 220°C.) for 30 minutes; reduce the oven heat to moderately slow (325°F. or 165°C.), tent the roast loosely with foil and cook 45 minutes. Remove the tent foil, baste the veal generously with pan drippings, then roast 30 to 45 minutes longer until the roast's internal temperature reaches 165°F. (74°C.). Remove the roast from the oven, transfer to a heated platter and let stand in a warm spot at least 20 minutes.

For the sauce, place the roasting pan over two burners set at moderately low heat, add the cream and cook, stirring constantly, until all brown bits have been scraped up and incorporated into the sauce (these will be nicely flavored with shallot). Transfer the sauce to a small heavy saucepan and keep warm, stirring often, until you are ready to serve.

Garnish the veal, if you like, with wedges or twists of lemon and ruffs of parsley, watercress or chicory. To carve, simply cut the roast down between the ribs, allowing one thick chop per portion. Pass the sauce separately.

Rolled shoulder of veal braised in a crust of black olives and crumbs

SERVES 6 TO 8

 Searching for new ways to keep a roast of veal good and juicy, I hit upon this unlikely-sounding recipe that's really very good. The olives you use should be brined Greek ones, not the withered and dry ones, which will be far too strong. Canned black olives are a poor substitute, so don't attempt this recipe until you have nice, plump, purple-black Greek olives (those from Kalamata are the choicest).

A 3½-pound	boned and rolled veal shoulder, wrapped and tied in a thin layer of barding fat	A 1½ kg
2 tablespoons	heavy cream	2 tablespoons
	BLACK OLIVE–CRUMB CRUST:	
6 slices	stale, firm-textured white bread, buzzed to fine crumbs in a food processor	6 slices
⅓ cup	pitted black olives, minced very fine	80 ml
4 tablespoons	unsalted butter	4 tablespoons
2 tablespoons	finely minced parsley	2 tablespoons
1 medium-size	garlic clove, peeled and crushed	1 medium-size
¼ teaspoon	crumbled leaf rosemary	¼ teaspoon

⅛ teaspoon	freshly ground black pepper	⅛ teaspoon
2 tablespoons	dry vermouth	2 tablespoons
	SAUCE:	
—	pan drippings (from the roast, above)	—
1¼ cups	chicken broth or a good veal stock	300 ml
⅞ cup	heavy cream	210 ml
Pinch	crumbled leaf rosemary	Pinch

Let the roast stand at room temperature 1 hour. Brush generously with the cream. Quickly mix all **crust** ingredients until thick and pasty—four to five quick bursts of speed in a food processor fitted with the metal chopping blade. Place the roast in a shallow roasting pan just large enough to accommodate it, then spread evenly with the olive mixture, using a rubber spatula. Let the roast stand 20 minutes to help make the crust stick. Place the roast, uncovered, in a moderately slow oven (325°F. or 165°C.) and bake about 2½ hours or until a meat thermometer, inserted into the center of the roast, registers 165°F. (74°C.). Remove the roast from the oven and transfer to a heated platter; let rest 20 minutes.

Meanwhile, prepare the sauce: Skim all fat from the pan drippings, then place the roasting pan over moderately low heat (you may have to use two burners), pour in the broth and boil uncovered 5 minutes. Strain this mixture through a fine sieve into a small heavy saucepan and set over moderate heat. Add the cream and rosemary, adjust the heat under the pan so that the mixture bubbles gently and allow to reduce and thicken while the roast rests; stir now and then.

When ready to serve, garnish the roast, if you like, with sprigs of watercress or parsley and clusters of black olives. To serve, carve into slices about ¼ inch (¾ cm) thick, removing the strings used to tie the roast as you go. Pass the sauce separately so that guests may help themselves.

Braised breast of veal stuffed with fresh dill soufflé

SERVES 6

There's not much meat on a breast of veal—you'll need very nearly one pound of it (or half a kilo) per person—but what meat there is, if properly cooked, is choice. To demonstrate, I offer an imaginative Austrian recipe, from a little inn high in the Tyrol, which calls for stuffing the veal with a soufflé-light mixture flecked with fresh dill. If fresh dill is unavailable, wait until it is before attempting the recipe. Neither dill weed nor seed can impart the same exquisite flavor.

BREAST OF VEAL:

5–6 pounds	bone-in breast of veal (have butcher make a pocket for the stuffing)	2–2½ kg
½ teaspoon	salt	½ teaspoon
⅛ teaspoon	freshly ground black pepper	⅛ teaspoon
1–2 tablespoons	unsalted butter, at room temperature	1–2 tablespoons
1 cup	water	240 ml

STUFFING:

2 cups	soft bread crumbs	½ L
4 tablespoons	unsalted butter, at room temperature	4 tablespoons
2 tablespoons	finely chopped fresh dill	2 tablespoons
1 tablespoon	minced parsley	1 tablespoon
¼ teaspoon	freshly grated nutmeg	¼ teaspoon
½ cup	evaporated milk, milk or heavy cream	120 ml
3 very large	eggs, separated	3 very large
¼ teaspoon	salt	¼ teaspoon
Light sprinkling	freshly ground black pepper	Light sprinkling

Rub the breast of veal all over with the salt and pepper; set aside.

For the stuffing, cream together the bread crumbs, butter, dill, parsley and nutmeg until light and fluffy. Beat in the evaporated milk, then the egg yolks. Whip the egg whites with the salt to soft peaks; stir 1 cup of the whites into the yolk mixture along with the pepper. Now fold in the remaining whites gently but thoroughly until no streaks of white or green remain.

Up-end the veal so that you can spoon the stuffing directly into the pocket. Pack it lightly into the bottom of the pocket, then spoon in enough more to come within about an inch (2½ cm) of the top. NOTE: *There will be a little stuffing left over, but no matter. It will be baked separately.* Using 6 to 8 poultry pins, skewer the opening shut, then lace with twine, crisscrossing it from pin to pin as if you were lacing your shoes. NOTE: *Pull the twine as tight as possible because you want to seal in the stuffing so that it will steam, puffing lightly—miraculously—like a soufflé.*

Stand the veal on its rib ends in a large shallow roasting pan and rub the surface well with butter. Spoon the remaining stuffing into a small buttered casserole (a 2-cup or ½ L size should be about right); cover and refrigerate until about 30 minutes before serving.

Set the veal uncovered in a very hot oven (450°F. or 230°C.) and brown for 30 minutes. Remove from the oven and lower heat to moderately slow (325°F. or 165°C.). Pour the water into the roasting pan around the veal, tent loosely with foil, return to the oven and bake 1½ hours. Remove the foil and bake uncovered for another 30 to 45 minutes or until a fork will pierce the meat easily.

Let the veal stand at room temperature 25 to 30 minutes; at the same time, put the casserole of stuffing, now uncovered, into the moderately slow oven. It will be done at about the time that the veal is ready to slice. NOTE: *The point of letting the veal rest after it has cooked is to allow the juices to settle and the meat to firm up slightly.* Remove the poultry pins and twine, then transfer the breast of veal to a large heated platter. To carve, slice down between the ribs. NOTE: *Servings may seem inordinately large. But they aren't really, because each contains a rib bone.* Pass the extra stuffing as "seconds."

Vitello tonnato
(COLD SLICED VEAL WITH TUNA MAYONNAISE)

SERVES 6

 The astronomical cost of veal round has put this Italian classic beyond many budgets, so I began wondering what **less expensive** cut of veal might be substituted. It had to contain a single large muscle that would hold together during cooking, then slice neatly. It had to be fine-grained and gristle-free. My butcher suggested veal shoulder cross rib, which costs about one-third as much as veal round. "It's a nice solid piece of meat," Tony said. "I'll bone it, roll it and tie it for you and it should work just fine." It did.

3½ pounds	boned and rolled veal shoulder cross rib, veal round or rump	1½ kg
3 tablespoons	olive oil	3 tablespoons
3 medium-size	yellow onions, peeled and chopped	3 medium-size
1 large	garlic clove, peeled and crushed	1 large
3 medium-size	celery ribs, washed and sliced	3 medium-size
2 large	carrots, peeled and sliced	2 large
4 large	parsley sprigs	4 large
1 large	bay leaf, crumbled	1 large
¼ teaspoon	crumbled leaf thyme	¼ teaspoon
¼ teaspoon	crumbled leaf rosemary	¼ teaspoon
¼ teaspoon	crumbled leaf marjoram	¼ teaspoon
1 large	strip of lemon rind (yellow part only— simply run a vegetable peeler the length of a lemon)	1 large
1 cup	dry white wine	240 ml
1 can (7 oz.)	white tuna, drained and flaked	1 can (198 g)
2 teaspoons	anchovy paste	2 teaspoons
¼ teaspoon	freshly ground black pepper	¼ teaspoon

	TONNATO SAUCE:	
1½ cups	mayonnaise	350 ml
2 cups	puréed kettle mixture (above)	475 ml
¼ cup	lemon juice	60 ml
2 teaspoons	anchovy paste	2 teaspoons
	GARNISHES:	
2 tablespoons	small drained capers	2 tablespoons
2 tablespoons	finely minced parsley	2 tablespoons

Lightly brown the veal on all sides in the oil in a large heavy kettle set over moderately high heat; remove veal to a large plate and reserve; lower heat to moderate. Add onions, garlic, celery and carrots to kettle and stir-fry 10 to 12 minutes until limp and golden (do not brown). Add parsley, bay leaf, thyme, rosemary, marjoram and lemon rind and let mellow 2 to 3 minutes over moderate heat. Add wine, tuna, anchovy paste and black pepper, adjust heat so that mixture barely simmers, then return the veal to kettle. Spoon some of the vegetables on top of veal, cover the kettle and simmer 2 to 2½ hours or until a fork will pierce the veal with only slight resistance. Remove the veal from the kettle to a large heatproof bowl and set aside. Purée the kettle mixture in two to three batches in a food processor fitted with the metal chopping blade, in an electric blender or a food mill; pour purée over veal, cover and refrigerate at least 24 hours.

Next day, remove veal from bowl and scrape any purée clinging to it back into the bowl. Rinse the veal lightly in cool water and pat dry; remove all strings, then set it aside while you prepare the sauce.

For the tonnato sauce: Combine the mayonnaise with the 2 cups puréed kettle mixture, the lemon juice and anchovy paste (a snap to do in a processor fitted with the metal chopping blade or in an electric blender). NOTE: *There will be some puréed kettle mixture left over. I freeze it and use it as a base for soups and stews. Or I make up a double batch of* tonnato *sauce to have plenty to use to dress chicken, turkey or tuna salads. It's also very good on hot pasta.*

To assemble the vitello tonnato: Carefully carve the veal into thin slices, then arrange them, slightly overlapping, on a platter, spooning a little of the *tonnato* sauce over each slice. Cover and marinate 2 to 3 hours in the refrigerator. Also cover and refrigerate the remaining *tonnato* sauce. Just before serving, ladle a little more *tonnato* sauce artfully over the veal, then scatter capers and parsley on top. If there is any *tonnato* remaining, pass separately.

Veal steaks

I am frankly not terribly fond of veal steaks. I find them insipid and overpriced, so when I want steak, I buy beef because of its greater character, texture and flavor (not to mention its lower cost). Veal steaks, moreover, are too lean to broil or panbroil successfully (they merely toughen and dry by the time they are cooked through—and *cooked through* is what they should be, not because rare veal is unwholesome; it simply isn't very appealing).

Like veal roasts, veal steaks are best when *braised*—browned on both sides, then cooked with a little liquid—if they are to be moist, tender and flavorful. A further disadvantage: Veal steaks are too large to manipulate easily in a skillet, and like veal chops, they do require a fair amount of turning and whisking in and out of the skillet. NOTE: *Any of the veal chop recipes included here can be used successfully for veal steaks, although you may need to increase the overall cooking time slightly to compensate for the steaks' greater heft.*

Still, there are people who like veal steaks, and for them I offer these shopping tips:

The choicest veal steaks are, in this order: sirloin, round, blade and **arm.** The last two will never be as soft and yielding to the touch of a fork as the sirloin and round, but then they are significantly less expensive—only moderately costly compared with outrageous.

The best thickness for veal steaks? Because veal steaks should be cooked medium-well, that is, until their juices run clear, they should not be cut more than 1 inch thick (2½ cm), otherwise there's too much danger of their drying and toughening under prolonged heat. I prefer veal steaks even thinner—from ½ to ¾ inch (1½ to 2 cm)—because they will cook through in the time that it takes to brown them on both sides, then you can warm them briefly in a pan sauce. COOKING TIP: *What I generally do is brown the steaks quickly over fairly high heat in a half-and-half mixture of butter and cooking oil (just enough to coat the bottom of a large skillet), then transfer them to a warmed plate while I deglaze the skillet with about 1 cup (240 ml) of dry white wine, beef or chicken broth (or a half-and-half mixture of wine and broth). I then return the steaks to the pan and let them come just to serving temperature over moderately low heat—a matter of 2 to 3 minutes.* For extra flavor, I sometimes crumble about ¼ teaspoon of leaf tarragon, thyme, rosemary, sage or marjoram into the skillet just before I deglaze it. The pan sauce, it goes without saying, should be spooned over the steaks before serving.

How much veal steak per serving? For average appetites, you should allow about ½ pound (225 g) of bone-in steak per serving and about ⅓ pound (160 g) of boneless steak. Some veal steaks are large enough to serve four persons, but most will serve no more than two.

Veal chops

The choicest chops, I think, are those cut from the **loin** because they contain, in addition to the large smooth rib eye, morsels of tenderloin. **Rib chops** contain the rib eye only, so pound for pound, kilo for kilo, the meatier loin chops are a better buy. But neither one, be forewarned, is cheap.

Best thickness? Because veal chops are smaller than veal steaks, they can—and should—be cut somewhat thicker. For most purposes, chops 1 inch (2½ cm) thick are perfect. It's unwise, I think, to buy chops thinner than ¾ inch (2 cm), because they may dry out during cooking. And I find little reason for their being more than 1½ inches (4 cm) thick. Like veal steaks, veal chops should not be flung into a broiler or upon a barbecue. Nor should they be panbroiled. They have no fat within the lean to keep them moist, so too intense a heat—particularly an intense dry heat— will make them leathery. Considering the profligate cost of veal these days, I can only recommend that chops be handled with reverence (and that means **braising** them), also that every precious drop of drippings be utilized in a pan sauce. NOTE: *See the recipes for veal chops that follow, also those among the Recipe Collection in Part II. You may also be interested to know that the quick pan sauces recommended for* scaloppine *(which see) are also superlative for veal chops.*

How many veal chops per person? It depends upon the size of the chops and the appetites of the persons being served. As a rule of thumb, allow ½ pound (225 g) of bone-in veal chops per portion. Usually two rib chops—or one loin chop—will feed one person amply.

Wheaten veal chops with lemon and capers

SERVES 4

There is no reason not to use whole wheat—or even rye—flour when dredging veal chops. Both add an appealing nutty flavor. To inject even nuttier flavor, substitute a tablespoon of walnut or hazelnut oil for one of the tablespoons of peanut oil used to brown the chops.

4 (1-inch-thick)	veal loin or rib chops, each about ⅓–½ pound (160–225 g)	4 (2½-cm-thick)
½ teaspoon	salt	½ teaspoon
⅛ teaspoon	freshly ground black pepper	⅛ teaspoon
⅓ cup	evaporated milk	80 ml
½ cup	unsifted whole wheat flour	120 ml
3 tablespoons	unsalted butter	3 tablespoons
2 tablespoons	peanut or other cooking oil	2 tablespoons
½ large	lemon, juiced	½ large
2 tablespoons	well-drained small capers	2 tablespoons

Trim excess fat from the chops, then sprinkle each well on both sides with salt and pepper. Dip both sides of chops into the milk, then dip into the flour until well coated all over. Let dredged chops stand at room temperature for 10 minutes on a piece of wax paper; turn carefully and let stand another 10 minutes at room temperature on a wire rack—this will help make the flour coating stick.

Heat 1 tablespoon of the butter and the 2 tablespoons oil in a large heavy skillet over moderately high heat until faint ripples appear in the oil on the bottom of the skillet. Add chops and brown well—3 to 4 minutes on the first side. Turn the chops carefully with tongs, reduce heat to low and cook very slowly 15 minutes longer. Lift chops to a hot platter and keep warm. Pour off skillet drippings. To the skillet add the remaining 2 tablespoons of butter, raise heat to moderate and when butter bubbles and browns (a minute or two), add lemon juice and capers and bring just to a boil. Pour over the chops and serve at once.

Breaded veal chops with parmesan and parsley

SERVES 4

 Here is one of those recipes that is so delicious it seems impossible that it's so easy to make.

4 (1-inch-thick)	veal loin chops, each about ½ pound (225 g)	4 (2½ cm thick)
½ teaspoon	salt	½ teaspoon
Light sprinkling	freshly ground black pepper	Light sprinkling
1 jumbo	egg, lightly beaten	1 jumbo
½ small	garlic clove, peeled and crushed	½ small
1 tablespoon	dry vermouth	1 tablespoon
1 tablespoon	milk or cream	1 tablespoon
1½ cups	fine dry bread crumbs	350 ml
2 tablespoons	freshly, very finely grated Parmesan	2 tablespoons
1 tablespoon	very finely minced parsley	1 tablespoon
⅛ teaspoon	crumbled leaf rosemary	⅛ teaspoon
2 tablespoons	unsalted butter	2 tablespoons
2–3 tablespoons	peanut or other cooking oil	2–3 tablespoons

Trim the chops of excess fat, then sprinkle on both sides with salt and pepper. Combine egg with garlic, vermouth and milk in a pie plate. In a second pie plate, combine crumbs, Parmesan, parsley and rosemary. Dip the chops first into the egg mixture, coating all sides well, then into crumbs to bread evenly but lightly on all sides. Let breaded chops stand at room temperature 10 minutes on a piece of wax paper, turn carefully and let stand another 10 minutes on a wire rack (this drying period helps the breading stick to the chops).

Heat 2 tablespoons each of butter and oil in a large heavy skillet over moderately high heat until faint ripples appear in the oil on the bottom of the skillet. Add chops and brown well—3 to 4 minutes; turn with tongs (a fork will pierce the chops, releasing precious juices); add remaining tablespoon of oil if drippings seem skimpy, turn heat to low and let chops cook 15 to 20 minutes longer or until well browned on the flip side and juices run clear (test by making a tiny slit near the bone of one chop—meat should be creamy-white clear through). Serve at once.

Scaloppine
(VEAL SCALLOPS, CUTLETS, ESCALOPES, SCHNITZEL)

Scaloppine, the Italian word for these exquisitely thin and tender slivers of boneless veal round, has not only slipped into the American vocabulary but also become so firmly entrenched that it is now the preferred term. **Cutlets** and **scallops** are what we used to call them (and the English are using an old term when they refer to them as **collops)**, *escalope* is the French word and *schnitzel,* the German. In any language, these are the choicest cuts of veal, the most popular and **the most costly.** The finest *scaloppine* come from the top round, the next best from eye and bottom round. *Scaloppine* may, however, be cut from any large muscle—rib eye, for example, sirloin, even tenderloin.

Shopping tips: Because you will pay a premium for anything labeled *scaloppine,* you'd better know whether or not you are getting what you are paying for. Sloppily cut *scaloppine* will not do—butchers sometimes "butterfly" smaller, inferior cuts of veal and try to pass them off as the real thing. Luckily such counterfeits are usually recognizable: by the faint crease down the center of each scallop and, if the butcher was hurried or inept, by the "sawtooth" surface of the meat.

Perfectly cut *scaloppine* should be sliced uniformly thin—**across the grain**—about ⅜ inch (1 cm) thick, then evenly pounded until slightly less than ¼ inch (¾ cm) thick. The *scaloppine,* moreover, should be cut from a single large muscle so that they are free of membranes, filaments or connective tissue that will shrink and pucker them during cooking. Finally, there should be no ragged edges: they not only look ugly but because they're thinner than the scallops themselves, they will also shrivel and harden during cooking. As for overall dimensions, I like *scaloppine* measuring 5 to 6 inches (13 to 15 cm) long and 2 to 3 inches (5 to 8 cm) wide. Larger scallops are unwieldy; smaller ones will emerge—after sautéing—little more than bite-size. NOTE: *If you have never cooked scaloppine, you may be startled to see how much they shrink in the skillet even though you coddle them and keep the burner heat at a moderate level. The reason is that veal—particularly that cut across the grain—exudes considerable juice as it* cooks; *all the more reason to salvage the drippings via a savory pan sauce (more about this in the recipes that follow).*

How much scalloppine per serving? Ideally, about ⅓ pound (160 g), but because of today's stratospheric prices, I try to stretch one pound (½ kg) of *scalloppine* over four servings. There are several easy ways to do it: **(1)** by breading the scallops generously (the egg and crumb coating is filling), **(2)** by finishing the *scalloppine* with a rich cream sauce (by "cream" I don't mean a flour-based sauce but one made with real cream—heavy, half-and-half or sour— that has been thickened by reduction), **(3)** by adding other, less costly ingredients such as mushrooms and/or onions, and **(4)** by accompanying the *scalloppine* with plenty of homemade *spaetzle, risotto* or *rösti,* those exquisitely crusty Swiss potato pancakes. (NOTE: *You will find each of these recipes and more* scalloppine *recipes elsewhere in this book; see Index.)*

About pounding veal scallops: If the *scalloppine* you buy are not sufficiently or uniformly thin, you should flatten them before cooking; otherwise they will not cook evenly. But use a gentle—not a hostile—touch. If you attack the fragile scallops too aggressively, you will mangle them. The implement I prefer for the job is a large meat cleaver because its broadside is as large as the scallop and will therefore flatten it evenly without creasing or ripping it. You can, of course, use a cutlet bat, a rolling pin, even the bottom of a sturdy glass jar. Whatever you use, however, pound the meat firmly but **gently**—three to four whacks should do the trick. TIP: *I've discovered that I can pound a scallop more easily and efficiently if I slip it inside a fold of plastic food wrap instead of wax paper, which tears so easily and whitens under impact, making it difficult to see what progress I'm making. Using plastic wrap may seem extravagant. Not really, because it's sturdier than wax paper, it remains nice and clear despite considerable battering and it can be reused for several scallops (wax paper cannot).*

Sautéed veal scalloppine
(BASIC RECIPE PLUS SIX 5-MINUTE VARIATIONS)

SERVES 4

Once *scalloppine* are sautéed, how you deglaze the pan determines the nature of the finished dish. For *piccata,* lemon juice is used to dissolve the buttery brown bits on the bottom of the skillet and form the pan sauce. Other recipes may call for wine or broth or cream. Indeed, the possibilities for easy pan sauces are almost endless. Just make sure you know at the outset how you will finish the dish and that you have everything you need at hand because few *scalloppine* require much more than 5 minutes from pan to platter. NOTE: *Although the basic recipe specifies butter for browning the scallops, you may substitute vegetable oil for up to half the butter (it will keep the butter from browning too fast but will mean a slightly less rich flavor).*

BASIC RECIPE:

1 pound	veal scaloppine, *pounded very thin*	½ kg
½ teaspoon (about)	salt (*for tart or lemony pan sauces, use less; for bland sauces, more*)	½ teaspoon (about)
¼ teaspoon	freshly ground black pepper	¼ teaspoon
5 tablespoons	unsalted butter	5 tablespoons
¼ cup	unsifted all-purpose flour	60 ml

Cut any large *scaloppine* into manageable pieces—I find scallops measuring 3 × 6 inches (8 × 15 cm) an ideal size. Salt and pepper both sides of each scallop; let stand at room temperature 15 to 20 minutes. Heat 4 tablespoons butter in a heavy 12-inch (30 cm) skillet over moderately high heat until it foams, then subsides. Quickly dredge half the *scaloppine* in flour, shaking off excess, and sauté quickly—no more than 1 to 2 minutes per side (the point is not to brown the meat but to cook it through). Whisk to a heated plate and cover loosely with foil. Add 1 tablespoon butter to skillet; dredge and sauté remaining *scaloppine* the same way; transfer to plate and re-cover. Cool skillet a minute or two, then deglaze the pan according to the particular variation below that you have chosen to prepare.

VARIATIONS:

Piccata: Add juice of 1 large lemon to skillet, set over moderate heat and deglaze by scraping browned bits up from bottom. Add 1 tablespoon butter and 2 tablespoons minced parsley and let bubble 1 to 2 minutes over high heat. Reduce heat to low; return *scaloppine* to skillet for about 1 minute, turning pieces in sauce. Arrange *scaloppine*, slightly overlapping, on a heated platter, top with pan sauce, garnish with lemon twists and parsley sprigs and serve at once.

Scaloppine with vermouth and capers: Add ½ cup (120 ml) dry vermouth to skillet and boil 1 to 2 minutes, scraping up browned bits. Raise heat and quickly reduce sauce by nearly half; lower heat. Add 1 tablespoon each butter and drained small capers and 2 tablespoons minced parsley. Replace *scaloppine* in skillet and warm about 1 minute. Arrange, overlapping, on a heated platter, top with sauce and serve straightaway.

Scaloppine al marsala: Smooth 3 tablespoons Brown Meat Glaze (see Index) into skillet along with ½ cup (120 ml) dry Marsala wine. Heat and stir over moderately high heat 1 to 2 minutes, then raise heat and boil 1 to 2 minutes to reduce by one-third. Swirl in 1 tablespoon butter, turn heat to low, replace *scaloppine* in skillet and warm about 1 minute. Arrange on heated platter, pour pan sauce evenly over all and serve.

Scaloppine with wine and mushrooms: Prepare exactly like *Scaloppine al Marsala* above, but omit the final tablespoon butter; instead, mix in ¾ pound (340 g) thinly sliced mushrooms that you have previously sautéed 5 minutes in 3 tablespoons unsalted butter. Return *scaloppine* to skillet and proceed as directed.

Rahmschnitzel (veal scallops in cream): Mix 2 tablespoons Brown Meat Glaze (see Index) into skillet along with 1 cup (240 ml) half-and-half and simmer 1 to 2 minutes, scraping up browned bits. Raise heat and boil about 3 minutes to reduce by about one-half. Return scallops to skillet and warm about 1 minute, then serve smothered with the cream sauce.

Paprikaschnitzel: Add 2 tablespoons unsalted butter to skillet and in it stir-fry 3 finely minced shallots over moderate heat until lightly browned—3 to 5 minutes. Blend in a pinch of ground nutmeg and 1 tablespoon sweet paprika. Add 1 cup (240 ml) half-and-half and boil gently 3 minutes until reduced by about one-half. Warm scallops in paprika sauce briefly, then serve topped by the sauce.

Scaloppine alla Milanese
(VEAL SCALLOPS BREADED WITH CRUMBS AND PARMESAN)

SERVES 4

I like the variation below this recipe (made with soft fresh crumbs and Romano cheese) almost as much as the more authentic main recipe, which calls for finer, drier crumbs and grated Parmesan. Whichever version you choose, do use freshly grated cheese, not the commercially bottled that always seems stale. This recipe is a snap to make for two (just halve all proportions, using one small egg instead of one large).

1 pound	veal scaloppine, *pounded very thin*	½ kg
¾ teaspoon	salt	¾ teaspoon
¼ teaspoon	freshly ground black pepper	¼ teaspoon
¼ cup	unsifted all-purpose flour	60 ml
1 large	egg, beaten with 2 tablespoons milk	1 large
1 cup	fine dried bread crumbs	240 ml
¼ cup	freshly grated Parmesan cheese	60 ml
4–6 tablespoons	unsalted butter	4–6 tablespoons

To make *scaloppine* less unwieldy, halve large pieces; salt and pepper both sides of each. Now line up on the counter—in this order and near the stove—a piece of wax paper containing the flour, a pie plate with the egg-milk mixture and a second pie plate in which you've combined crumbs and Parmesan. Dredge scallops lightly in flour, coat well with egg mixture, then "jacket" evenly in crumbs. Air-dry 15 to 20 minutes on wire racks (this helps breading stick). Heat 4 tablespoons butter in a heavy 12-inch (30 cm) skillet over moderately high heat until a bread cube will sizzle in it. Brown half the scallops quickly—

about 3 minutes per side; they should be a rich nut brown. Watch skillet closely and lower heat if butter threatens to burn. Transfer browned *scaloppine* to a shallow pan lined with paper towels and set, uncovered, in a very slow oven (275°F. or 135°C.) while you brown the balance. Serve at once with wedges of lemon.

VARIATION:

Breaded veal scallops with sage and romano: Prepare exactly like *Scaloppine alla Milanese* above, but use 2 large eggs and 2 tablespoons milk for the egg mixture and for the crumb coating, 1 cup (240 ml) fine soft bread crumbs mixed with ¼ cup (60 ml) freshly grated Romano and ½ teaspoon rubbed sage.

Wiener schnitzel
(VIENNESE BREADED VEAL SCALLOPS)

SERVES 4

The hallmark of perfectly cooked *Wiener Schnitzel* is that the crumb coating is crisp and brown and distinctly separate from the meat (you should be able to slide a knife between it and the veal scallop). The trick is to bread the scallops and cook them straightaway—before the coating has a chance to dry and cling to the meat. The temperature of the fat used for browning is critical, too—it should be hot enough to brown the scallops in about 3 minutes, not so hot that it blackens the breading, and yet not so low that it seeps into it. For best results, use a combination of unsalted butter and peanut or other vegetable oil.

1 pound	veal scalloppine, *pounded very thin*	½ kg
½ teaspoon	salt	½ teaspoon
⅛ teaspoon	freshly ground black pepper	⅛ teaspoon
⅓ cup	unsifted all-purpose flour	80 ml
3	eggs, lightly beaten	3
1 cup	fine dry bread crumbs	240 ml
4 tablespoons	unsalted butter	4 tablespoons
2 tablespoons	peanut or other vegetable oil	2 tablespoons

Halve any *scaloppine* that are large, sprinkle both sides of each piece with salt and pepper and let stand at room temperature 10 to 15 minutes. Meanwhile, line up on a counter near the stove the flour (I simply put it on a piece of wax paper), the eggs (in a pie plate) and the crumbs (in a second pie plate) so that you can whisk the scallops through the breading sequence and into the skillet. Heat the butter and oil in a heavy 12-inch (30 cm) skillet over moderately high heat until a bread cube will sizzle in it. Brown half the breaded scallops quickly—about 3 minutes to a side. Remove to a shallow pan lined with paper towels and set, uncovered, in a very slow oven (275°F. or 135°C.). Brown remaining scallops the same way. Serve at once with thin slices of lemon.

Veal paprikash

SERVES 2 TO 4

I don't pretend that this is an authentic Hungarian *paprikás*. It's a version I like very much, which I've evolved over the years. I prefer using a combination of heavy cream and sour cream for the sauce because it makes for a mellower flavor and helps keep the paprika sauce from curdling. If you accompany the scallops with plenty of buttered noodles, you can serve as many as four persons with just one pound of veal.

1 pound	veal scaloppine, sliced ⅜ inch (1 cm) thick and cut into strips 2 inches long by ⅜ inch wide (5 × 1 cm)	½ kg
3 tablespoons	unsalted butter	3 tablespoons
1 medium-size	yellow onion, peeled and minced	1 medium-size
1 large	shallot, peeled and minced	1 large
1 tablespoon	sweet rose paprika	1 tablespoon
½ cup	chicken broth	120 ml
1 tablespoon	tomato paste	1 tablespoon
½ cup	sour cream, at room temperature	120 ml
½ cup	heavy cream, at room temperature	120 ml
½ teaspoon	salt	½ teaspoon
Light sprinkling	freshly ground black pepper	Light sprinkling

Stir-fry half the veal in 2 tablespoons of the butter in a large heavy skillet over high heat 1 to 2 minutes until milky-white; lift with a slotted spoon to a large bowl. Stir-fry the remaining veal in the drippings until white; transfer to bowl. Add the remaining tablespoon of butter to the skillet and stir-fry the onion and shallot over moderate heat 2 to 3 minutes until limp and golden. Smooth in the paprika, let mellow a minute or two, then mix in the chicken broth and tomato paste. Boil, uncovered, about 5 minutes until juices reduce to a nice thick glaze. Return the veal to the skillet, tossing well with the paprika mixture, turn the heat down low, cover the skillet and simmer slowly 10 minutes. Uncover and simmer slowly another 5 minutes or so, until juices cook down somewhat. Combine the sour cream and heavy cream, mix into skillet and simmer slowly about 5 minutes—do not allow to boil. Season with salt and pepper and serve.

Ground veal

The best cuts of veal to grind are the **tougher, cheaper** ones—**shank, flank, breast, neck, shoulder**—because they contain enough sinew, soft cartilage and/or connective tissue to provide good texture and flavor. Of them all, I prefer shoulder, although it is more expensive, because the proportion of flesh to sinew seem perfect and because the flavor is strong enough to assert itself.

No ground veal, alas, contains fat enough to make for juicy loaves or patties. It must be mixed about half and half with ground beef chuck, pork or lamb shoulder, or about two to one with fatter meats such as sausage or a hamburger less lean than chuck.

For patties, I like to use veal mixed with beef or lamb, not with pork or sausage, which must be thoroughly cooked before they are safe to eat (I frankly find it a bother to keep poking inside the patties to see whether a smidgeon of pink remains.) MONEY-SAVING TIP: *You can also "juice up" ground veal by mixing it about two to one with minced butter-sautéed mushrooms and onions (see the recipe for Veal and Mushroom Patties with Rosemary and Sage, which follows).*

For loaves, on the other hand, I favor a combination of ground veal and pork. Both are light, delicate meats and for that reason particularly compatible. I find ground beef or lamb too strongly flavored for most veal loaves. And they are red meats, which will darken the loaf until it no longer resembles veal.

How much ground veal per serving? From ¼ to ⅓ pound (115 to 160 g), depending upon the richness of the recipe.

Lightly curried veal and vegetable loaf with sour cream gravy

SERVES 14 TO 16

Don't be put off by the number of servings indicated. This recipe makes two standard-size meat loaves, one of which can be frozen to be baked several months later. Veal, by itself, is too lean for patties or loaves but, when combined about two to one with pork, becomes surprisingly juicy. This meat loaf is spicy, too, without being "hot."

	VEAL LOAF:	
2½ pounds	ground veal shoulder	1¼ kg
1½ pounds	ground pork shoulder	675 g (⅔ kg)
2 medium-size	yellow onions, peeled and chopped	2 medium-size
2 medium-size	garlic cloves, peeled and minced	2 medium-size

¼ cup	minced parsley	60 ml
1 medium-size	carrot, peeled and chopped fine	1 medium-size
1 medium-size	tart apple, cored and chopped but not peeled	1 medium-size
2 cups	soft bread crumbs	½ L
1 large	egg, lightly beaten	1 large
1 can (13 oz.)	evaporated milk	1 can (384 ml)
1 can (1 lb.)	tomatoes (do not drain)	1 can (454 g)
¼ cup	sweet pickle relish	60 ml
2 teaspoons	curry powder	2 teaspoons
1½ teaspoons	salt	1½ teaspoons
1 teaspoon	crumbled leaf basil	1 teaspoon
1 teaspoon	crumbled leaf marjoram	1 teaspoon
½ teaspoon	crumbled leaf thyme	½ teaspoon
¼ teaspoon	freshly ground black pepper	¼ teaspoon
	GRAVY:	
½–⅔ cup	pan drippings	120–160 ml
½–⅔ cup	sour cream, at room temperature	120–160 ml

Combine all veal loaf ingredients in a large mixing bowl, using your hands **(by no means taste the mixture at this point, because it contains raw pork)**. Divide between two well-greased 9 × 5 × 3-inch (23 × 13 × 8 cm) loaf pans, packing the mixture in firmly. NOTE: *If you intend to freeze one of the loaves, overwrap in aluminum foil and freeze until firm. Unwrap, remove loaf from the pan and rewrap in heavy-duty foil, smoothing out all creases. The loaf will keep well for about 4 months at 0°F. (−18°C.).*

Bake the veal loaf in a moderate oven (350°F. or 175°C.) for about 1½ hours or until meat pulls from sides of pan and is springy to the touch. NOTE: *No need to thaw the frozen loaf before cooking it; simply unwrap and bake as directed but increase overall baking time by 20 to 30 minutes.* Remove loaf from oven and let stand at room temperature 15 minutes.

For the gravy: Drain off all pan drippings and measure. Combine drippings in a small heavy saucepan with an equal quantity of sour cream and heat, whisking, 3 to 4 minutes. Leave loaf upright in its pan while you bring gravy to serving temperature.

To serve, remove the loaf from the pan, slice about ⅜-inch (1 cm) thick and overlap as attractively as possible on a small heated platter. Ladle some of the gravy down the center of the sliced veal loaf and pass the remainder in a separate bowl so that guests can help themselves to more.

Veal and mushroom patties
with rosemary and sage

SERVES 4 TO 6

Veal is too lean to make successful meat patties unless it is mixed with a little fat or with a fatter meat such as pork. But since I wanted to cook these patties quickly (faster than the raw pork would cook through), I enriched the veal by combining it with onion, garlic and mushrooms sautéed in butter. Result? Marvelously juicy patties. These may be shaped several hours ahead and kept in the refrigerator until you're ready to cook them. Appropriate accompaniment? Lemon-dressed asparagus or broccoli.

1 pound	ground veal shoulder	½ kg
2 tablespoons	freshly grated Parmesan cheese	2 tablespoons
1 teaspoon	salt	1 teaspoon
⅛ teaspoon	freshly ground black pepper	⅛ teaspoon
1 medium-size	yellow onion, peeled and minced fine	1 medium-size
1 medium-size	garlic clove, peeled and minced fine	1 medium-size
5 tablespoons, in all	unsalted butter	5 tablespoons, in all
½ teaspoon	rubbed sage	½ teaspoon
¼ teaspoon	crumbled leaf rosemary	¼ teaspoon
6 medium-size	mushrooms, wiped clean and minced fine	6 medium-size

Place veal, Parmesan, salt and pepper in a large mixing bowl and set aside. Stir-fry onion and garlic in 3 tablespoons of the butter in a medium-size heavy skillet over moderate to moderately low heat 3 to 5 minutes until limp and golden; do not brown. Add the sage, rosemary and mushrooms and sauté, stirring often, 3 to 5 minutes, just until mushrooms give up their juices; remove from heat and cool to room temperature. Add to veal and mix all together well, using your hands. Shape into burger-size patties, then brown lightly in the remaining 2 tablespoons of butter in a large heavy skillet set over moderate heat, allowing about 3 minutes per side. Serve at once.

Veal-stuffed potato croquettes

SERVES 4 TO 6

This ingenious recipe—adapted from a meat-stuffed potato dumpling I once tasted in Bergen, Norway—is one of the best ways I know to stretch a little bit of meat a long way. Not every potato will work for the croquettes, however; you need a "boiling" potato waxy enough to hold together after it's mashed. I find Maine or Eastern potatoes the best choice. Serve these crusty-golden croquettes sizzling hot with a tartly dressed green salad or, if you prefer, with green beans vinaigrette.

VEAL STUFFING:

1 large	shallot, peeled and minced, or 1 large scallion, trimmed and minced	1 large
1 tablespoon	unsalted butter	1 tablespoon
¼ teaspoon	rubbed sage	¼ teaspoon
¼ teaspoon	crumbled leaf marjoram	¼ teaspoon
Pinch	crumbled leaf thyme	Pinch
2 medium-size	mushrooms, wiped clean and minced fine	2 medium-size
⅓ pound (5 ounces)	ground veal shoulder	160 g
¼ teaspoon	salt	¼ teaspoon
Light sprinkling	freshly ground black pepper	Light sprinkling

POTATO CROQUETTES:

2 pounds	Maine or Eastern potatoes, washed	1 kg
2 tablespoons	unsalted butter, at room temperature	2 tablespoons
⅓ cup	freshly grated Parmesan cheese	80 ml
½ teaspoon	salt	½ teaspoon
½ teaspoon	rubbed sage	½ teaspoon
⅛ teaspoon	ground mace	⅛ teaspoon
⅛ teaspoon	white pepper	⅛ teaspoon

FOR DEEP-FAT FRYING:

2 quarts	peanut or other cooking oil	2 L

For the stuffing: Sauté the shallot in the butter in a small heavy skillet over moderately low heat about 3 minutes until limp and golden. Mix in sage, marjoram, thyme and mushrooms and sauté, stirring frequently, 3 to 5 minutes until mushrooms release their juices. Remove from the heat and cool to room temperature. Mix well with remaining stuffing ingredients, using your hands. Cover and chill until ready to use.

For the croquettes: Boil the potatoes in their skins in enough water to cover 30 to 40 minutes until tender; drain and cool until easy to handle. Peel the potatoes and mash through a colander or potato ricer until thick and fluffy. (By no means try to mash the potatoes in a food processor or with an electric beater—they will turn to glue.) Mix in butter, Parmesan, salt, sage, mace and white pepper.

To shape the croquettes, scoop up a rounded tablespoon of the potato mixture, then flatten into a patty about 3 inches across and ½ inch thick (8 × 1½ cm). Now scoop up a rounded teaspoonful of the veal mixture and roll into a small ball. Center the veal ball on potato patty, fold margins of potato patty up over the veal ball and roll gently between your hands until it is completely sealed inside the potato croquette. Repeat until you have used up all the veal and potato mixtures—you should have about 15 croquettes.

To deep-fry: Heat the oil in a deep-fat fryer until it registers 375°F. (190°C.) on a deep-fat thermometer. Fry the croquettes, about a third or a half of the total amount at a time, about 5 minutes or until richly golden. Drain on several thicknesses of paper toweling and serve at once. NOTE: *If croquettes are to cook through without overbrowning or absorbing fat, it's important that you keep the temperature of the deep fat as nearly at 375°F. (190°C.) as possible, so raise or lower burner heat as needed.*

Veal stew meat

One of the fascinating bits of kitchen alchemy is what happens to meat—veal, in particular—during stewing. The tender cuts turn surprisingly stringy and dry. But the tough ones, those filled with cartilage and connective tissue, become so juicy and succulent they drop from the bones.

How can this be? The tender cuts, first of all, can never be made any more tender than they are in the raw state. Heat (cooking) merely shrinks (hardens) their muscles. So the object with such cuts—the steaks, chops, *scaloppine*—is just to cook them through gently, preserving as much original tenderness as possible. In the not-so-tender cuts, on the other hand, the sinew, cartilage and connective tissue magically turn into gelatin under slow, moist cooking. This is what makes a stew succulent.

So the cuts of veal you choose for stew should be those with plenty of these potentially tender elements. My own favorites, in this order, are: **shoulder, neck** and **riblets** (these last, a great favorite of the French, contain bones, also considerable cartilage that cooks down to a marvelous crunchiness). With the exception of veal shoulder, which is moderately priced, these cuts are downright inexpensive. Yet when imaginatively, adeptly prepared, they are as delicious as any of the 24-karat cuts of veal. Even more so, to my mind.

How much veal stew meat per person? Allow approximately ⅓ to ½ pound (160 to 225 g) of boneless stew meat per serving, from ½ to ¾ pound (225 to 340 g) of bone-in meat, and about 1 full pound (½ kg) of riblets because they are mostly bone. NOTE: *These amounts, of course, are flexible and will vary according to the quantity, kind and character of the other stew ingredients.*

Dilled chunks of veal with leeks and chestnuts

SERVES 6 TO 8

3 pounds	boned veal shoulder, cut in 1½-inch (4 cm) chunks	1½ kg
2½ quarts, in all	water	2½ L, in all
3 large	leeks, washed, trimmed and sliced thin	3 large
1 medium-size	yellow onion, peeled and chopped	1 medium-size
2 large	shallots, peeled and chopped	2 large
4 tablespoons	unsalted butter	4 tablespoons
1 teaspoon	dill weed	1 teaspoon
½ teaspoon	crumbled leaf thyme	½ teaspoon
⅛ teaspoon	grated nutmeg	⅛ teaspoon
¾ cup	beef broth	180 ml
½ cup	dry vermouth	120 ml
½ pound	frozen peeled Italian chestnuts (available at specialty food shops)	225 g
½ cup	heavy cream	120 ml
1 teaspoon	salt	1 teaspoon
⅛ teaspoon	freshly ground black pepper	⅛ teaspoon

If "stew veal" is not sautéed *before* it is put to simmer, it will throw off considerable gray scum, which should be removed before you begin a *blanquette de veau* or other stew in which the color and clarity of the sauce is important. To precipitate the scum, which can be quickly skimmed off, simmer veal in 2 quarts (2 L) water 10 minutes; skim cooking liquid of froth and scum, then drain veal and rinse well in cool water.

In a large heavy kettle (about a 4-quart or 4 L size), sauté leeks, onion and shallots in butter over moderately low heat 8 to 10 minutes until golden; do not brown. Mix in dill weed, thyme and nutmeg and stir-fry 1 to 2 minutes. Add veal to kettle along with 2 cups (½ L) water, the beef broth and vermouth; cover and simmer slowly 1½ hours.

Add chestnuts, re-cover and simmer about 45 minutes or until chestnuts are firm-tender. With a slotted spoon, lift veal and chestnuts to a large bowl; halve any chestnuts that are extra large. Boil kettle liquid, uncovered, 15 minutes or until reduced by about one-fourth; add cream and boil uncovered another 10 minutes. You can, if you like, purée the kettle mixture at this point, and pour it back into the kettle, although doing so isn't necessary. Return veal and chestnuts to kettle and season with salt and pepper, adjusting to taste. Lower heat and warm the stew about 5 minutes. Serve with new potatoes boiled in their skins and with an assertive green vegetable such as broccoli or Brussels sprouts.

Macedonian casserole of veal with white beans and cabbage

SERVES 6 TO 8

It was in a little country *taverna* in the north of Greece that I first tasted this unusual stew—chunks of veal shoulder simmered to uncommon succulence with dried white beans, tomatoes, cabbage and a whole bouquet of wild herbs. It came to the table bubbling in an earthen casserole and, I was told, had simmered the better part of the day in a wood-stoked stove. It's a relatively economical party dish, I find, exotic, too, and altogether accommodating because it bakes unattended. It can even be partially prepared a day ahead.

1½ cups	dried navy or pea beans	350 ml
1 quart	cold water	1 L
3 pounds	boned veal shoulder, cut in 1½-inch (4 cm) chunks	1½ kg
1 teaspoon	salt	1 teaspoon
¼ teaspoon	freshly ground black pepper	¼ teaspoon
½ cup	unsifted flour	120 ml
6–8 tablespoons	olive oil	6–8 tablespoons
4 medium-size	yellow onions, peeled and chopped	4 medium-size
2 medium-size	garlic cloves, peeled and minced	2 medium-size
1 teaspoon	crumbled leaf marjoram	1 teaspoon
½ teaspoon	crumbled leaf rosemary	½ teaspoon
¼ teaspoon	crumbled leaf basil	¼ teaspoon
¼ teaspoon	crumbled leaf thyme	¼ teaspoon
1 large	bay leaf, crumbled	1 large
1 can (1 lb.)	tomatoes (do not drain)	1 can (454 g)
1 cup	beef broth	240 ml
½ cup	dry white wine	120 ml
1 strip (½ × 2 inches)	lemon rind (yellow part only)	1 strip (1½ × 5 cm)
1 quart	thinly sliced, cored green cabbage	1 L
2 tablespoons	minced fresh parsley	2 tablespoons

Sort and wash beans; place in a large kettle, add water, cover and soak 8 hours or overnight. Set beans and their soaking water over moderate heat (add water, if needed, so that beans are well submerged) and bring to a boil. Cover and cook ½ hour. Drain beans and reserve.

Spread veal out on wax paper and sprinkle with half the salt and pepper; sift half the flour over veal. Turn veal, sprinkle with remaining salt, pepper and flour and toss well. In a large heavy kettle (about a 4-quart or 4 L size) heat 4 tablespoons of the oil over moderately high heat until ripples appear on bottom of kettle. Brown veal chunks well on all sides, working with about one-third of the total amount at a time (you may need to add an extra tablespoon or two of oil toward the end). As veal browns, remove to a large bowl. Now stir-fry onions and garlic in kettle drippings (add 1 to 2 tablespoons additional oil if drippings seem scanty) 5 to 8 minutes until golden; do not brown. Add marjoram, rosemary, basil, thyme and bay leaf and stir-fry 1 to 2 minutes. Return veal to kettle; add all remaining ingredients except cabbage and parsley. NOTE: *You may prepare recipe up to this point as much as a day ahead of time. Cover and refrigerate until about 3 hours before serving.*

Bring kettle mixture to a gentle simmer over moderate heat, cover, and set in a moderate oven (350°F. or 175°C.) and bake 1¾ hours. Add cabbage, stir gently, re-cover and bake 1 hour longer. Stir in parsley and serve with chunks of garlic bread and a crisp green salad dressed with olive oil and lemon.

Veal shanks

Americans have too long ignored these exquisite, economical cross-sections of the leg. There is nothing intimidating or mysterious about them—in fact, they're one of the easiest cuts of veal to prepare. I serve them often as *ossobuco* in winter and find that guests are invariably surprised and pleased.

Admittedly, shanks are one of the toughest cuts of veal (the leg being one of the most exercised parts of the animal and exercise being what toughens meat). But slow **braising** or **stewing** reduces them to succulence, particularly if, as in *ossobuco*, an acid ingredient (in this case, tomatoes) is added to the pot; acid acts like an enzyme, speeding the conversion of sinew to gelatin.

The choicest veal shanks are those cut from the hind legs because they are meatier, also because the leg bones are bigger, meaning more marrow inside them (the Italian word, *ossobuco*, incidentally, translates to mean "bone with a hole in it"). I'm especially fond of marrow; it cooks down to pâté-richness and can be scooped out at table with a long slender marrow spoon or with the point of a knife (I always save it until last).

How many veal shanks per person? Because these contain as much bone as meat, you should allow from ¾ to 1 pound per serving (340 g to ½ kg), which is about what one thick, meaty shank will weigh. Veal shanks can vary enormously in size, depending upon how high on the leg they were cut (the higher, the bigger). If they are to cook evenly (and if the portions are to be equitable), it's important that the shanks be of as nearly the same size as possible.

I prefer **center-cut shanks** (from the hind leg), measuring 4 to 4½ inches (10 to 11 cm) in diameter and 1½ to 2 inches (4 to 5 cm) thick. TIPS: *Slit the outer skin of each shank vertically, but do not sever it completely, leaving margins of ½ inch (1½ cm) top and bottom (this is to allow the meat to expand as it cooks without pushing up off the bone. The skin, if not slit, will contract like a rubber band, forcing the meat up). You should also tie the shanks around with string (or have the butcher do it), so that they will remain neat and compact throughout cooking. Finally, I've learned that if I arrange the veal shanks in the kettle so that the smaller bone openings are on the bottom, the marrow will remain intact—inside the bone.*

Ossobuco
(BRAISED VEAL SHANKS)

SERVES 6

This particular recipe is one I've evolved over the years. I find it perfect for small dinners because the *ossobuco* can be made ahead (indeed, it profits from a day or two in the refrigerator) and needs only to be reheated shortly before serving. The best accompaniments are the simplest: boiled rice, a tartly dressed green salad and a sturdy loaf of Italian bread.

6 center-cut slices, 2 inches thick	veal shank (outer skin left on and tied with string to hold them together as they cook)	6 center-cut slices, 5 cm thick
1½ teaspoons	salt	1½ teaspoons
½ teaspoon	freshly ground black pepper	½ teaspoon
¼ cup	unsifted all-purpose flour	60 ml
3–4 tablespoons	olive oil	3–4 tablespoons
2–3 tablespoons	peanut or other cooking oil	2–3 tablespoons
4 large	yellow onions, peeled and chopped	4 large
3 large	garlic cloves, peeled and minced	3 large
1 medium-size	carrot, peeled and chopped	1 medium-size
2 medium-size	celery ribs, chopped	2 medium-size
1 teaspoon	crumbled leaf basil	1 teaspoon
1 teaspoon	crumbled leaf marjoram	1 teaspoon
½ teaspoon	crumbled leaf thyme	½ teaspoon
1 large	bay leaf, crumbled	1 large
2 tablespoons	minced parsley	2 tablespoons

2 strips (about ½ × 2 inches)	lemon rind (yellow part only)	2 strips (about 1½ × 5 cm)
1 can (1 lb.)	tomatoes (do not drain)	1 can (454 g)
1 can (13¾ oz.)	beef broth	1 can (407 ml)
1½ cups	dry white wine	350 ml

Sprinkle shanks lightly all over with salt and pepper; dredge in flour, shaking off excess. In a heavy kettle large enough to accommodate all shanks in one layer, heat 2 tablespoons each olive and peanut oil over moderately high heat until a bread cube will sizzle; add shanks and brown well—about 5 minutes per side. NOTE: *Or, to pare calories slightly (about 50 per serving), arrange seasoned, dredged shanks in one layer on broiler pan and broil 5 inches (13 cm) from heat about 10 minutes until browned; turn and brown flip side 5 to 7 minutes.* Lift browned shanks from kettle (*or broiler pan*) and reserve.

Add 1 to 2 tablespoons olive oil to kettle (3 tablespoons if you broiler-browned shanks), and stir-fry onions, garlic, carrot and celery over moderate heat 12 to 15 minutes until limp; do not brown. Add herbs and lemon rind and mellow 5 minutes. Add tomatoes and their juice, broth and wine; return shanks to kettle, pushing them underneath liquid and breaking up any large tomato clumps. Bring mixture barely to a simmer, cover and cook very slowly 5 to 6 hours, stirring now and then, until you can pierce meat easily with a fork. Cool, cover and refrigerate.

About an hour before serving, set kettle on counter and let stand 30 minutes. To reheat, set covered kettle over lowest heat or in a moderate oven (350°F. or 175°C.) and bring slowly to serving temperature (20 to 30 minutes). Taste for salt and pepper and adjust as needed; discard lemon rind. If gravy seems thick, thin with a little beef broth; if it seems thin, boil rapidly, uncovered, to reduce slightly.

Arrange shanks on a heated platter, top with some of the gravy and pass the rest separately. Trim platter with lemon wedges and ruffs of cress. NOTE: *Don't forget to put out small spoons (marrow spoons, if you have them) or pointed knives for getting at the creamy marrow inside the hollow of each bone. It is a special delicacy.*

Belgian casserole of veal shanks with beer and cabbage

SERVES 6

This is one of those accommodating dishes that bake almost unattended. If you are lucky enough to have a food processor to do the slicing and puréeing for you, you'll find the recipe virtually effortless to prepare. Yet it's impressive enough for a party. Accompany with tiny new potatoes boiled in their skins or, perhaps, with dried navy or pea beans that have been cooked in rich beef or veal stock instead of water, then drained very dry.

6 medium-size	veal shanks, cut 1½ inches (4 cm) thick	6 medium-size
1 teaspoon	salt	1 teaspoon
⅛ teaspoon	freshly ground black pepper	⅛ teaspoon
2 medium-size	yellow onions, peeled and sliced thin	2 medium-size
2 medium-size	carrots, peeled and sliced thin	2 medium-size
3 medium-size	parsley sprigs	3 medium-size
1 large	bay leaf, crumbled	1 large
¼ teaspoon	crumbled leaf thyme	¼ teaspoon
⅛ teaspoon	ground nutmeg	⅛ teaspoon
1 cup	beef broth	240 ml
1 cup	flat beer	240 ml
6 medium-size	juniper berries	6 medium-size
1 small (about 1 lb.)	cabbage, quartered	1 small (½ kg)
½ cup	half-and-half cream	120 ml

Sprinkle the veal shanks on both sides liberally with salt and pepper, using about half the total amount of each. Place shanks in a heavy kettle or flameproof casserole large enough to accommodate them all in a single layer. Arrange onions, carrots and parsley sprigs in and around shanks. Sprinkle with the crumbled bay leaf, thyme and nutmeg. Pour in beef broth and beer, then drop in the juniper berries, distributing them as evenly as possible. Sprinkle remaining salt and pepper over all. Bring to a simmer over moderate heat, then cover kettle, set in a moderately hot oven (375°F. or 190°C.) and bake about 1½ hours or until veal is almost tender.

Meanwhile, trim off and discard the cabbage cores (at the point of each quarter), then cut the cabbage in large chunks; spear each chunk with a toothpick, smack through the center, to keep cabbage from separating into layers as it cooks, but *do* leave toothpick ends exposed so that you can remove them quickly before serving.

When veal has cooked almost to the point of tenderness, lay cabbage chunks lightly on top, re-cover kettle and bake another 25 to 30 minutes or until veal is fork-tender and cabbage crisp-tender. Carefully transfer cabbage chunks to a heated plate, cover and keep warm. With a slotted spoon, transfer veal shanks to a second heated plate, cover and keep warm. Quickly purée kettle liquids and solids in a food processor fitted with the metal chopping blade, or in an electric blender (in which case, buzz about half of the total amount at a time), or force all through a food mill. Return puréed mixture to kettle, set over moderate heat and boil uncovered about 10 minutes to reduce slightly. Turn heat to low, smooth in the cream, then return veal to kettle, stirring lightly. Lay cabbage chunks on top, cover and warm about 5 minutes.

To serve, wreathe cabbage chunks around the rim of a heated platter, removing toothpicks as you go. Mound the veal shanks in the center and spoon some of the cream sauce over both the veal and the cabbage. Pass the remaining sauce separately so that guests may help themselves to more.

Lamb

Although the preferred meat in much of the world, lamb has never made it in America. Indeed, we're eating only one-fifth as much of it as we did during the early years of World War II.

Some lamb growers blame World War II for the decline of lamb, pointing fingers at the tough Australian mutton fed to American troops in the South Pacific. Others indict today's inflated prices (lamb costs more than beef), and still others cite long-term prejudices. Strangely, lamb seems to be the least popular in the West and Middle West where it is grown. A holdover of the old range wars? Perhaps. But then lamb has never been popular Down South either, and it's only fairly recently that it has begun to be raised there.

The major reason for lamb's unpopularity, I suspect, is that those who turn up their noses at it have never eaten genuine lamb perfectly prepared. And if they have eaten "lamb," it is more likely to have been over-the-hill young mutton—cooked to death.

A little story to illustrate the point: As a child of the small-town South, my family was considered odd because we ate things like broccoli, artichokes and—heaven forbid—lamb! One day, when I was in maybe the eighth or ninth grade, I brought a girlfriend home after school to play. She stayed for dinner and, after second helpings, turned to my mother and said, "Miz Anderson, that was just the best steak I ever put in my mouth. I've never had it rare before."

My mother smiled, then replied gently, "Why thank you, Naline. But that wasn't steak. Those were lamb chops." Naline blanched, nearly gagged, then stammered, "B-b-but I n-n-never eat *lamb*. I don't *like* it!"

As it turned out, that was the first time lamb had ever passed Naline's lips. She had simply been told all of her young life that she hated lamb. My mother won a convert that night. And who knows? Naline may now be serving lamb to her family.

Difficult as it may be to believe, I had a similar experience just last year in—of all places—New York City. I'd invited some friends to dinner, among them a well-traveled television executive, never dreaming that he—or anyone else—would be turned off by roast saddle of lamb. But he, who daily battled network "lions," was stopped cold by the lamb. He was deeply embarrassed, of course. And he apologized profusely, laying the blame on his "Nebraska upbringing." To his credit, he did manage a couple of bites of lamb that night. And he has since come around to eating lamb occasionally, although I fear that its flavor will forever be tainted by the memory of the strong mutton he was forced to eat as a child.

The qualities of lamb

True lamb is never more than a year old, and I like it a good deal younger—between four and eight months. Like beef, lamb is federally graded as to quality, but the only grades likely to reach your supermarket will be the top two: USDA PRIME and USDA CHOICE. If the grade is not clearly visible on the package or outer fat covering, you can be assured of top quality if the meat is velvety-moist, evenly dark red and faintly marbled with creamy-white fat. The truest indicator of youth will be the look of the large bones—shanks, back bone, etc. If animals are young, bone centers will be spongy and red; if not, they will be harder and whiter (calcified). Why, you may well ask, is lamb so much darker red than beef? And why is its fat yellower? For a single reason. Lambs are grass fed—usually on hardscrabble heights of the Rockies—and a diet of grass will darken both the lean and the fat of any animal.

A sight I shall forever remember is that—a few years ago—of thousands of sheep flowing down the grassy high slopes of the Sangre de Cristo Mountains near Taos, New Mexico, toward the Rio Grande to drink. They were accompanied by Basque shepherds, bereted and mustachioed, and by plucky little sheepdogs who, ever alert to the straying lamb, kept the river of fleece on course.

The cuts of lamb
and how to cook them

These break down into the **tender** and **not-so-tender,** and the determining factors, as with beef and veal, are the animal's age and activity. The most heavily exercised portions of the animal will be the **toughest: neck, shoulder, breast** and **shank.** And the more immobile portions will be the **tenderest: rack (rib), loin** and **leg (sirloin and round). The same cooking methods apply: dry heat (roasting, broiling, panbroiling, panfrying) for the tender cuts and moist heat (braising and stewing) for the less tender.**

Roasts

Leg of lamb is the most popular, but **saddle of baby lamb (a double loin)** and **rack (the rib section)** are equally good. Here, then, to chart them, are the roasts of lamb, both tender and marginally tender:

POPULAR TENDER ROASTS	DESCRIPTION	MARKET WEIGHTS	SERVINGS PER POUND (½ kg)
Leg	The meaty hind leg; available whole (full leg) or as halves: sirloin half (the choicest) and shank half. EXPENSIVE.	6–10 lbs. (2¾–4½ kg) for full leg; 3–5 lbs. (1⅓–2¼ kg) for half legs.	1½–2
Rolled Leg	The hind leg, boned and rolled. EXPENSIVE.	3–5 lbs. (1⅓–2¼ kg)	2–3
Hindquarter	The hind leg plus the sirloin and several loin chops. A hindquarter from anything other than baby lamb will be too big to fit into a home oven. EXORBITANT.	8–10 lbs. (3½–4½ kg)	1½–2
Saddle	A double loin (left and right sides); supremely tender. Single loins, I think, are too small to roast well. EXORBITANT.	4–5 lbs. (1⅘–2¼ kg)	1½–2
Rack (rib)	A small, elongated, bony roast containing as many as 8 rib chops. EXPENSIVE.	3–3½ lbs. (1⅓–1½ kg)	1
Crown	Two racks, bent into a circle with the rib ends sticking up like the points of a crown. The center is usually filled with ground trimmings. COSTLY.	6–7 lbs. (2¾–3¼ kg)	1

NOTE: *The following cuts, even if of young, top-quality lamb, are better when braised.*

POPULAR LESS-TENDER ROASTS	DESCRIPTION	MARKET WEIGHTS	SERVINGS PER POUND (½ kg)
Breast	Very bony, cartilaginous cut beloved by the French. It's flat, with a natural pocket for stuffing. REASONABLE.	2–2½ lbs. (about 1 kg)	1

Boned Breast	The same cut stripped of bones. It's sinewy, best when stuffed and rolled. REASONABLE.	1½ lbs. (⅔ kg)	2
Square Shoulder	A blocky cut containing a fair amount of bone and 4–5 rib chops. MODERATE.	4–6 lbs. (1⅘–2¾ kg)	1½
Cushion Shoulder	This one looks like a square pillow and has a pocket for stuffing. Boneless. MODERATE.	3–5 lbs. (1⅓–2¼ kg)	2–3
Rolled Shoulder	Boned shoulder rolled into a compact, chunky roast. MODERATE.	3–5 lbs. (1⅓–2¼ kg)	2–3

About roasting times, temperatures and tables

 The different lamb roasts vary so much in shape, size and boniness that I find roasting charts virtually useless. I rely, instead, upon my own methods (see recipes that follow). But first a few words about the internal meat temperature most charts recommend for perfectly roasted lamb: 175° to 180°F. (79° to 82°C.) or well-done! To me that is criminal, for at that temperature the lamb will have lost all traces of pink, not to mention considerable juice. It will be dreary, gray-brown and dry. No wonder more people aren't partial to lamb!

There is no reason whatever to serve tender roasts of lamb well done. As far as I'm concerned, there is every reason **not** to. The French like their lamb **very rare**—rose-red and fairly dripping with juice at an internal temperature of about 125° to 130°F. (52° to 54°C.). I prefer mine cooked a shade more, **medium rare** (135° to 140°F. or 57° to 60°C.). At this internal temperature, the meat will be very pink and juicy. I suggest that you try lamb this way before you roast it beyond the point of no return. Then, if you simply insist upon lamb's being **medium** (160°F. or 71°C.) or—horrors!—**well done** (175° to 180°F. or 79° to 82°C.), put it back in the oven. In any event, cook until a meat thermometer inserted in the center of the largest muscle, not touching bone, registers the desired temperature.

Roast leg of lamb cloaked with fresh ginger and garlic

SERVES 6 TO 8

 This is my favorite roast lamb recipe: a whole leg rubbed with a creamy butter-and-flour paste aromatic of fresh ginger, garlic and rosemary. The method is basic and can be used whether or not you choose to cloak the leg of lamb with the paste or roast it in the altogether. TIP: *For crushing the ginger root, use a garlic press.*

A 6-pound	leg of lamb, trimmed of unnecessary fat	A 2¾ kg
1 teaspoon	salt	1 teaspoon
¼ teaspoon	freshly ground black pepper	¼ teaspoon

	PASTE:	
4 tablespoons	unsalted butter, slightly chilled	4 tablespoons
2 medium-size	garlic cloves, peeled and crushed	2 medium-size
A 1-inch cube	fresh ginger root, peeled and crushed	A 2½ cm cube
1 teaspoon	crumbled leaf rosemary	1 teaspoon
½ teaspoon	crumbled leaf thyme	½ teaspoon
2 tablespoons	flour	2 tablespoons

Rub the leg of lamb generously all over with salt and pepper. Cream the butter well with the garlic, ginger, rosemary and thyme; mix in the flour. Using a rubber spatula, spread this paste as evenly as possible all over the leg of lamb. Place the leg on a rack in a large shallow roasting pan and let stand at room temperature 1 hour.

Set the roast uncovered in a very hot oven (450°F. or 230°C.) and sear for 30 minutes. Reduce the oven temperature to moderately slow (325°F. or 165°C.) and roast ¾ to 1 hour longer or until the internal temperature of the lamb (use a spot-check thermometer, making certain its tip rests in meat) registers 135° to 140°F. (57° to 60°C.). This temperature, I should emphasize, is for **juicily pink** lamb. If you insist that yours be **medium** continue roasting for another 15 to 20 minutes or until the meat thermometer registers 160°F. (71°C.). For **well-done** lamb, roast to an internal temperature of 175° to 180°F. (79° to 82°C.)—another 15 to 20 minutes.

Remove the leg of lamb from the oven and let stand at room temperature 25 minutes before you carve it so that the juices will settle and the meat firms up slightly.

Braised cushion shoulder of lamb with eggplant and tahini stuffing

SERVES 6 TO 8

You can, if you like, use this method of cooking a cushion shoulder of lamb but substitute any of your own favorite stuffings for the one suggested here. I particularly like this mellow Middle Eastern mixture, however, and think its mingled flavors of lemon, garlic, sesame and eggplant are a perfect complement for lamb.

A 4–5 pound	cushion shoulder of lamb	A 2–2¼ kg
1 large	garlic clove, peeled and crushed	1 large
1 teaspoon	salt	1 teaspoon
¼ teaspoon	freshly ground black pepper	¼ teaspoon
1 recipe	Eggplant and Tahini Stuffing (see Index)	1 recipe
2 tablespoons	olive oil	2 tablespoons
½ cup	chicken broth or water	120 ml

Rub the cushion shoulder inside and out with a mixture of the garlic, salt and pepper. Using poultry pins, close all but one side. Set aside for the moment. Prepare the Eggplant and Tahini Stuffing as directed, then spoon it lightly into the pocket in the cushion shoulder. Skewer the remaining side shut. Heat the oil in a large heavy skillet over high heat and brown the meat on both sides. Transfer the lamb to a large shallow roasting pan, pour in the broth and tent loosely with foil. Roast the shoulder 1½ hours in a moderately slow oven (325°F. or 165°C.), then remove the foil cover and bake ½ to ¾ hour longer or until a fork will pierce the meat easily. NOTE: *It is not practical to determine the degree of doneness with a meat thermometer, because there is no way of telling whether it is resting in the meat or in the stuffing, which would have a lower temperature. So the fork test is the best.* Remove the lamb from the oven and let it rest at room temperature 20 minutes. Transfer the lamb to a heated platter, remove all poultry pins and serve. NOTE: *To carve the cushion shoulder, simply slice straight down through it as if you were carving a giant sandwich so that everyone gets two slices of meat with a layer of stuffing in between.*

Lamb chops

Far and away the favorites (and the most expensive) are the **rib** and **loin chops.** My own preference is for loin chops because they are meatier and contain small nuggets of tenderloin (a rib chop from a young lamb will scarcely provide two good bites of meat). Another superlative, tender chop is the **sirloin** (sometimes called lamb sirloin steak), which is simply to lamb what a sirloin steak is to beef (much smaller, of course).

There are not-so-tender lamb chops, too, cut from the shoulder: **arm chops** (containing only the small round arm bone), **blade chops,** containing the shoulder blade and sometimes a few rib ends as well, and **boneless shoulder chops** (sometimes called **Saratoga chops).** The boneless chops may be tender enough to broil, panbroil or panfry (as indeed are all rib, loin and sirloin chops), but arm and blade chops may or may not be. It depends upon how old the animal was and how high its federal grade.

Because the tender rib and loin chops are so small, they should be cut thick—no less than 1 inch (2½ cm) but preferably 1½ inches (4 cm). The larger chops—sirloin, blade and arm—are best, I think, when cut about 1 inch (2½ cm) thick.

How to cook lamb chops

To panfry (sauté): This is the method I like best because I think lean and tender young lamb chops profit by being cooked in a bit of butter or oil. Let them stand at room temperature 30 minutes—just long enough to take the chill off (rub first, if you like, with a little garlic or crumbled rosemary). Do not salt the chops before you cook them because the juices will ooze out and make them difficult to brown. For 4 to 6 chops, melt about 2 tablespoons of butter (or oil or a half-and-half mixture of the two) in a large heavy skillet set over moderately high heat. When a drop of water will sputter in the hot fat, add the chops and brown about 3 to 5 minutes on a side, depending upon the size and the thickness of the chops (and how well done you like them). I give them minimal time in the skillet because I like my lamb chops juicily pink. Season with salt and pepper.

Panfrying, of course, produces exquisite pan drippings and you are faced with the option of **(1)** dispensing with them altogether (the best idea if you are cutting down on calories or cholesterol, **(2)** pouring them over the chops as is, or **(3)** gussying them up a bit. *Here are a few fast pan sauces to try:*

Squeeze the juice of a lemon into the pan drippings and warm briefly; add a couple of teaspoons of finely minced fresh mint, tarragon or parsley. Pour over the chops and serve.

Squeeze the juice of a lemon into the pan drippings and warm briefly; smooth in ½ teaspoon anchovy paste, then add 1 to 2 tablespoons small, well-drained capers and about 2 teaspoons minced parsley or chives. Pour over the chops and serve.

If you've rubbed the chops with garlic and/or rosemary before you panfried them, crumble an additional pinch of rosemary into the drippings, then deglaze the pan with ½ cup (120 ml) dry white wine. Boil down slightly and pour over the chops, or first blend in about 1 teaspoon of Dijon mustard or tomato paste.

Deglaze the pan with ½ cup (120 ml) dry white wine and boil down hard until reduced by at least half. Add 1 tablespoon freshly minced tarragon (or ½ teaspoon crumbled leaf tarragon) and ½ cup (120 ml) heavy cream and reduce for about 2 minutes. Pour over the chops and serve.

To improvise a jiffy Châteaubriand Sauce, sauté 1 tablespoon minced shallots in the drippings about 1 minute, pour in ¾ cup (180 ml) dry white wine, add a pinch each of pulverized bay leaf, crumbled leaf tarragon and thyme and boil hard about 2 minutes to reduce slightly. To finish, turn the heat down low, smooth in a tablespoon of unsalted butter, add 1 teaspoon finely minced pars-ley, then season to taste with salt and freshly ground black pepper.

To broil: Let the chops stand at room temperature for 30 minutes. Do not season with salt or pepper. Lightly oil the broiler pan and preheat the broiler a full 15 minutes. Arrange the chops on the broiler pan and set 2 to 3 inches (5 to 8 cm) from the heat; broil 1-inch (2½ cm) chops 4 minutes per side for **rare** and 6 minutes per side for **medium.** NOTE: *1½ inch (4 cm) chops will take 5 to 6 minutes per side for* **rare** *and about 7 for* **medium. Well-done** *chops will require about 2 minutes longer per side, but I urge you not to cook the chops that long because they will suffer. The time to salt and pepper the chops is as each side browns.*

To panbroil: Let the chops stand at room temperature 30 minutes; do not salt or pepper them. Set a large heavy skillet or griddle over fairly high heat, then rub lightly with oil. When good and hot (a drop of water will skitter about over the surface), add the chops and brown 3 to 5 minutes per side, depending upon how thick the chops are and how well done you like them. Salt and pepper the browned side of the chops as you turn them, the flip side just before serving. Six minutes in a skillet over moderately high heat will produce a suc-culent, pink **rare** lamb chop, 10 minutes one that is about **medium.** It's a waste of money to cook fine lamb chops beyond medium (and I frankly think it's profligate to cook them beyond rare).

Ground lamb

While "lamburgers" will never match "Big Macs" in popu-larity, still, lean ground lamb, properly seasoned and cooked, is very good indeed. **Regular ground lamb** usually consists of trimmings, which may be too fatty (lamb fat or tallow is what gives lamb its distinctive—some say, strong—flavor). So I request **ground lamb shoulder** whenever I want to make lamb patties or loaves because I find that it contains the perfect proportion of fat to lean to make it juicy and flavorful.

Although ground lamb may come from a tough cut originally, it is wholly tender (the grinding takes care of all the gristle and sinew) and may thus be cooked by any of the dry heat methods: **roasting** or **baking** (for loaves); **broil-ing, panbroiling** and **panfrying** (for patties).

Lamb and bulgur loaf with apple and mint

SERVES 8 TO 10

I like this loaf best cold, topped with a nippy mustard or curry sauce. It's good hot, too (with the same sauce), but because the loaf is so tender and juicy, it should be cooled a full half hour before it is turned out onto a platter. NOTE: *The juices may bubble over a bit during baking, so place a baking sheet underneath the loaf while it bakes.*

1 cup	bulgur wheat	240 ml
1 cup	apple juice	240 ml
2 pounds	ground lamb shoulder	1 kg
1 pound	ground pork shoulder	½ kg
2 medium-size	yellow onions, peeled and chopped	2 medium-size
1 medium-size	tart green apple, peeled, cored and chopped	1 medium-size
2 medium-size	carrots, peeled and chopped	2 medium-size
½ cup	rolled oats	120 ml
1 can (8 oz.)	tomato sauce	1 can (226 g)
¼ cup	finely chopped chutney	60 ml
¼ cup	minced parsley	60 ml
3 tablespoons	minced fresh mint (or 1 tablespoon mint flakes)	3 tablespoons
2 very large	eggs	2 very large
½ teaspoon	crumbled leaf marjoram	½ teaspoon
¼ teaspoon	crumbled leaf rosemary	¼ teaspoon
⅛ teaspoon	crumbled leaf thyme	⅛ teaspoon
1½ teaspoons	salt	1½ teaspoons
⅛ teaspoon	freshly ground black pepper	⅛ teaspoon

Soak the bulgur in the apple juice in a large mixing bowl for 1 hour. Add all remaining ingredients and mix thoroughly, using your hands. Pack into a well-greased 9 × 5 × 3-inch (23 × 13 × 8 cm) loaf pan, mounding the mixture up in the center, and bake in a moderate oven (350°F. or 175°C.) for 1 hour and 45 minutes or until the loaf has pulled from the sides of the pan and is nicely browned. Remove from the oven, set the loaf on a wire rack and cool in the pan at least 30 minutes. Drain off excess drippings, then invert the loaf onto a large plate. Invert once again onto a platter so that the loaf is right side up. NOTE: *For a party presentation, you might surround with hollowed-out lemon halves filled with chutney and ruffs of watercress.*

Pastichio
(GREEK LAMB AND PASTA)

SERVES 6

This frugal dish is served almost everywhere in Greece and is a great *taverna* staple. I have had it made with thinly sliced potatoes as well as with macaroni, with artichoke hearts, even with green peas. Greek cooks traditionally—and quite sensibly—use *pastichio* as a repository for vegetable leftovers, layering them between the meat and pasta.

2 medium-size	yellow onions, peeled and chopped	2 medium-size
2 medium-size	garlic cloves, peeled and minced	2 medium-size
3 tablespoons	olive oil	3 tablespoons
1 pound	ground lamb shoulder	½ kg
3 tablespoons	tomato paste	3 tablespoons
1 tablespoon	finely minced fresh mint	1 tablespoon
½ teaspoon	crumbled leaf oregano	½ teaspoon
¼ teaspoon	crumbled leaf rosemary	¼ teaspoon
¼ teaspoon	crumbled leaf basil	¼ teaspoon
¼ teaspoon	ground cinnamon	¼ teaspoon
Pinch	crumbled leaf thyme	Pinch
1½ teaspoons, in all	salt	1½ teaspoons, in all
⅛ teaspoon	freshly ground black pepper	⅛ teaspoon
5 tablespoons	unsalted butter	5 tablespoons
8 tablespoons	flour	8 tablespoons
1¼ cups	milk	300 ml
1 cup	half-and-half cream	240 ml
½ pound	elbow macaroni, cooked by package directions and drained well	225 g
1 large	egg, lightly beaten	1 large
⅛ teaspoon	ground nutmeg	⅛ teaspoon
8 tablespoons	freshly grated Parmesan cheese	8 tablespoons

Stir-fry the onions and garlic in the olive oil in a large heavy skillet over moderate heat 8 to 10 minutes until limp and lightly browned. Add the lamb, breaking up large clumps, and stir-fry about 5 minutes or until no longer pink (do not allow the lamb to brown). Mix in the tomato paste, mint, oregano, rosemary, basil, cinnamon, thyme, ¾ teaspoon of the salt, and the pepper. Reduce heat to low and simmer uncovered for 25 to 30 minutes, stirring occasionally, until about the consistency of pasta sauce.

Meanwhile, melt the butter in a large heavy saucepan and blend in the flour to make a thick paste. Whisk in the milk and cream and cook, stirring constantly, over moderate heat 3 to 5 minutes until thickened and no raw starch taste remains. Stir in ½ teaspoon of the remaining salt. Combine 1 cup (240 ml) of the sauce with the macaroni and set aside for the moment. Whisk a little of the remaining sauce into the egg and stir back into pan; season with the nutmeg and the remaining ¼ teaspoon of salt. Set aside off the heat.

To assemble the *pastichio*, layer the different components into a well-oiled 9 × 9 × 2-inch (23 × 23 × 5 cm) baking dish as follows: half the macaroni mixture, 2 tablespoons of the Parmesan, all of the lamb mixture, 2 more tablespoons of Parmesan, the remaining macaroni, and another 2 tablespoons of Parmesan. Pour the reserved sauce evenly on top, then scatter the final 2 tablespoons of Parmesan over the sauce.

Bake uncovered in a moderate oven (350°F. or 175°C.) for 40 to 45 minutes or until bubbling and flecked with brown. Remove the *pastichio* from the oven and allow to stand at room temperature 15 to 20 minutes before serving (this is to allow the juices a chance to settle and the mixture to firm up somewhat so that it can be cut more neatly). To serve, cut into large squares.

Bobotie
(CAPE MALAY BAKED CURRIED MINCED LAMB)

SERVES 6 TO 8

3 slices	stale firm-textured whole wheat bread	3 slices
1 cup	milk	240 ml
3 large	yellow onions, chopped fine	3 large
2 large	garlic cloves, minced	2 large
A 1-inch square	fresh ginger root, peeled and minced	A 2½ cm square
3 tablespoons	unsalted butter	3 tablespoons
2 tablespoons	curry powder	2 tablespoons
¼ teaspoon	ground turmeric	¼ teaspoon
¼ teaspoon	ground allspice	¼ teaspoon
⅛ teaspoon	ground nutmeg	⅛ teaspoon
2 pounds	ground lean lamb shoulder	1 kg
2 small	eggs	2 small
½ cup	golden seedless raisins (sultanas), chopped fine	120 ml
¼ cup	beef broth or water	60 ml
¼ cup	lemon juice	60 ml
1 teaspoon	salt	1 teaspoon
⅛ teaspoon	freshly ground black pepper	⅛ teaspoon
4 large	bay leaves	4 large
	TOPPING:	
2 small	eggs	2 small
¾ cup	milk (use milk squeezed from bread above + enough to total ¾ cup)	180 ml
¼ teaspoon	salt	¼ teaspoon

Soak bread in milk. Meanwhile, sauté onions, garlic and ginger in butter until tender over moderately low heat, about 10 minutes. Smooth in curry, turmeric, allspice and nutmeg and mellow 5 minutes. Dump into large mixing bowl. Squeeze bread as dry as possible and add to bowl along with meat and all remaining ingredients except bay leaves (reserve milk squeezed from bread; you'll use it in the topping). Mix meat well with all other ingredients, using your hands; pat firmly into a buttered 9 × 9 × 2-inch baking dish (23 × 23 × 5 cm). Insert bay leaves into meat, spacing equidistantly and pushing into mixture as far as possible. Bake uncovered in a moderately slow oven (325°F. or 165°C.) for 1 to 1¼ hours until firm and lightly browned. Remove from oven and let stand 10 minutes.

Meanwhile, beat all topping ingredients together. Pour evenly over *bobotie* and broil 5 to 6 inches (13 to 15 cm) from heat 3 to 4 minutes until dappled with brown and set like custard. Cut into large squares and serve with rice or pilaf.

Lamb shanks

It was Joan Fontaine who introduced me to lamb shanks, one of the lowliest but loveliest cuts of all. I'd gone to Los Angeles to interview her for a celebrity cooks series I was writing for *The Ladies' Home Journal,* and Joan grilled the lamb shanks, as I recall, over the living room hearth. She had first marinated them with herbs and wine and, if memory serves, partially cooked them, too. I forget the details—but *not* how superb those lamb shanks were.

I have since come to rely upon lamb shanks for superlative eating. And the more I travel, the more ways I learn to prepare them. I have had lamb shanks curried with fiery spices in southern India . . . braised with white beans, tomatoes and mint in Greece . . . bubbled with grapes in South Africa . . . and simmered with bay leaves and red wine in Italy.

If you have never tried lamb shanks, I urge you to try one of the recipes offered here. I think you'll be surprised at how good they are, and I know you'll be pleased by how cheap they are.

Crusty crumbed and deviled lamb shanks

SERVES 4

A whole lamb shank has an almost Henry VIII proportion, but it does contain considerable bone. So one shank is about right for each hungry person. To make the preparation—and eating—easier, ask your butcher to crack each shank at the knuckle. A rice pilaf and crisp green salad make splendid accompaniments.

4 (each about 1 pound)	lamb shanks, cracked	4 (each about ½ kg)
1 cup	water	240 ml
1 cup	dry white wine	240 ml
1 large	bay leaf	1 large

	CRUMB COATING:	
3 cups	soft, fairly fine bread crumbs	¾ L
1 medium-size	garlic clove, peeled and crushed	1 medium-size
4 tablespoons	melted unsalted butter	4 tablespoons
2 tablespoons	Dijon mustard	2 tablespoons
¼ teaspoon	finely crumbled leaf rosemary	¼ teaspoon
¼ teaspoon	salt	¼ teaspoon
⅛ teaspoon	freshly ground black pepper	⅛ teaspoon
1 very large	egg, whisked with 2 tablespoons milk	1 very large

Arrange the shanks in one layer in a large shallow roasting pan; pour in the water and wine, drop in the bay leaf. Cover snugly with foil and bake in a moderate oven (350°F. or 175°C.) for 1½ to 2 hours or until the meat is very tender. Remove from the oven and cool the shanks until easy to handle; discard the bay leaf and cooking liquid.

For the crumb coating: Place the bread crumbs and garlic in a large bowl. Combine the melted butter, mustard, rosemary, salt and pepper, pour into the crumb mixture and toss well to mix. Transfer mixture to a pie pan. Place the egg mixture in a second pie pan. Dip the shanks first in the egg mixture. NOTE: *The shanks are so irregularly shaped that you may fare better by brushing them lavishly with the egg mixture. Your purpose is to coat them generously so that the crumbs will stick fast.* Next dip the shanks into the crumbs. Again, the shape of the shanks makes dipping difficult, so you may find it easier to pat on the crumb mixture firmly, piling most of it on the top and sides where gravity will work for you and help make the crumb coating stick. Let the coated shanks stand at room temperature about 20 minutes—this air-drying also helps the crumbs to adhere. Arrange the shanks in one layer in a large shallow roasting pan and roast them, uncovered, in a very hot oven (450°F. or 230°C.) for 25 minutes or until sizzling hot and richly browned. Serve at once.

Cappadocian lamb shanks with pea beans and mint

SERVES 4

Cappadocia, if you don't know it, is that south central Turkish province where Göreme, an uncanny "Valley of the Moon," is located. Here, scarps and pinnacles of volcanic tuff are honeycombed with the homes and churches of early Christians who—quite literally—dug in to escape religious persecution. Elaborately domed and frescoed, the cave churches are marvels of Byzantine art and architecture. Here, too, is a robust country cooking that teams lamb with an imaginative variety of vegetables and herbs. This particular recipe is my adaptation of a dish I enjoyed one night in the little market town of Nevsihir.

1 pound	dried navy or pea beans	½ kg
1 quart	cold water	1 L
4 (each about ¾ pound)	lamb shanks	4 (each about ⅓ kg)
1 teaspoon (about)	salt	1 teaspoon (about)
¼ teaspoon (about)	freshly ground black pepper	¼ teaspoon (about)
4 tablespoons	flour	4 tablespoons
3 tablespoons	olive oil	3 tablespoons
4 large	yellow onions, peeled and chopped	4 large
2 large	garlic cloves, peeled and minced	2 large
1 large	bay leaf, crumbled	1 large
½ teaspoon	crumbled leaf rosemary	½ teaspoon
½ teaspoon	crumbled leaf marjoram	½ teaspoon
¼ teaspoon	crumbled leaf thyme	¼ teaspoon
¼ teaspoon	ground cinnamon	¼ teaspoon
2 tablespoons	minced parsley	2 tablespoons
2 tablespoons	minced fresh mint	2 tablespoons

Place the beans and water in a medium-size heavy saucepan, set uncovered over moderately high heat and bring to a boil. Reduce heat so that water bubbles gently, then simmer beans 2 minutes exactly. Turn off the heat, cover the pan snugly and cool to room temperature. NOTE: *This is a way to shortcut the traditional but tedious overnight soaking.*

Salt and pepper each lamb shank generously on all sides, using about half the salt and pepper, then dredge well with flour. Heat the oil in a large heavy skillet over high heat until faint ripples appear, add the shanks and brown well on all sides. With tongs, lift the shanks to a large plate and reserve. Lower burner heat to moderate, dump in the onions and garlic and stir-fry about 5 minutes until limp and golden. Add the bay leaf, rosemary, marjoram, thyme and cinnamon and stir-fry about a minute longer, just to release and mellow the flavor of the herbs.

Pour the cooled beans and their soaking water into a 3-quart (3 L) casserole, add the skillet mixture and the remaining salt and pepper and mix well. Lay the lamb shanks on top, pushing down slightly into the beans. Cover tight. NOTE: *I used a domed-lid flameproof glass baking dish and found it a perfect choice because the lamb shanks do protrude above the level of the casserole.* Bake in a moderately slow oven (325°F. or 165°C.) for 2½ to 3 hours or until the meat literally falls from the shank bones. Take the casserole from the oven, remove the shanks and separate the meat from the bones. Cut the meat into largish chunks, discard the bones and return the meat to the casserole. Add the parsley and mint, stir lightly to mix, re-cover and bake 10 to 15 minutes longer. Serve with a tartly dressed green salad or a sturdy, boiled and buttered green vegetable such as Swiss chard, beet or turnip greens, collards, kale or spinach.

Lamb stew meat

The toughest parts of the **neck** and **shoulder** make especially succulent stew meat because they contain an abundance of connective tissue which, under long, moist cooking, reduces to gelatin. I prefer such cuts boned, then divided into 1- to 1½-inch (2½ to 4 cm) cubes. If I want stew meat with the bones in (and I sometimes do), I resort to **riblets** (the equivalent of beef short ribs or pork spareribs). These, too, can be unbelievably tender. Best of all, they are cheap, as is neck meat. Both are cuts we would all do well to use more often, following the lead, perhaps, of our Mediterranean sisters, who cook them to perfection in an awesome number of ways. I have never eaten lamb more exquisitely or imaginatively stewed, I think, than in Lebanon, Turkey and Egypt, where sinewy chunks were simmered into submission with everything from pomegranates to pine nuts to field peas and spinach.

Lamb kurma

SERVES 6

This mild curry comes from the north of India. It's a relatively "dry" curry, hence the small amount of cooking liquid. The temptation will be to add more water. **Don't.** Considerable liquid will seep out of the onions and lamb as the curry simmers. So, if you keep the heat low enough—and the pot covered—there's little danger of the curry's boiling dry. NOTE: *The reason for using ghee (clarified butter) is that it will not blacken or burn. It also has a purer butter flavor.*

2 pounds	well-trimmed lean boned lamb shoulder, cut into 1-inch (2½ cm) cubes	1 kg
4 tablespoons	ghee (melted butter from which the white milk solids have been skimmed)	4 tablespoons
4 large	yellow onions, peeled and coarsely chopped	4 large
4 large	garlic cloves, peeled and minced	4 large
A 1½-inch cube	fresh ginger root, peeled and minced	A 4 cm cube

5 large	cardamom pods	5 large
5 large	whole cloves	5 large
½ teaspoon	coriander seeds	½ teaspoon
¼ teaspoon	cumin seeds	¼ teaspoon
½ teaspoon	peppercorns	½ teaspoon
¼–½ teaspoon	crushed dried red chili peppers (depending upon how "hot" you like things)	¼–½ teaspoon
½ teaspoon	ground cinnamon	½ teaspoon
½ teaspoon	ground turmeric	½ teaspoon
¼ cup	lemon juice	60 ml
¼ cup	cream of coconut (available in Oriental or Latin groceries)	60 ml
¾ cup	cold water	180 ml
½ teaspoon (about)	salt	½ teaspoon (about)
½ cup	heavy cream, at room temperature	120 ml

Brown about one-fourth of the lamb cubes in 2 tablespoons of the *ghee* in a medium-size heavy kettle over high heat; transfer to a large bowl with a slotted spoon. Proceed, browning the lamb in three more batches the same way, adding an additional tablespoon of *ghee* about halfway through. Transfer each batch to the bowl as it browns. Add the remaining tablespoon of *ghee* to the kettle, reduce the heat to moderate, dump in the onions, garlic and ginger and stir-fry 8 to 10 minutes until limp and lightly browned.

Meanwhile, break open the cardamom pods and remove the dark inner seeds. Place these in a mortar and pestle (discard the pithy outer pods); add the cloves, coriander, cumin, peppercorns and crushed dried red chili peppers and pulverize. NOTE: *You can save considerable time and effort by using one of those small electric coffee grinders or even an electric blender—simply buzz the spices until they are reduced to fairly coarse powder.* Combine the pulverized spices with the cinnamon and turmeric, add to the onions in the kettle and stir-fry a minute or two to mellow the flavors. Return the lamb to the kettle; add the lemon juice, cream of coconut, water and salt. Bring to a slow simmer, then reduce the burner heat to low so that the kettle liquid barely ripples, cover and simmer 2 hours.

Test the lamb for doneness. If it still seems fairly resistant to the probings of a fork, you will need to simmer the curry a little longer. Whether you cover it or not at this point depends upon the quantity of liquid in the kettle. If the curry seems fairly soupy, leave the kettle uncovered. If not, re-cover the kettle. Cook for another 30 to 60 minutes or until the lamb is fork-tender. Smooth in the cream, taste for salt and add more if needed, then simmer about 5 minutes longer.

Serve the *kurma* with fluffy boiled rice and a nice tart chutney.

Highland lamb stew

SERVES 6 TO 8

I come from a long line of good Scottish cooks, and this recipe is one I remember my mother making when I was a child. I don't believe the recipe was hers originally (she was more English than Scottish) but rather one she'd gotten from my Grandmother Anderson, who in turn, had gotten it from my Great-Grandmother Anderson—or so I was told. Whatever its source, this lamb stew is both good and frugal. The only accompaniment needed is a green vegetable. My mother usually served buttered broccoli or Brussels sprouts.

3 pounds	boned lamb shoulder, cut in 1-inch (2½ cm) cubes	1½ kg
1½ teaspoons (about)	salt	1½ teaspoons (about)
¼ teaspoon (about)	freshly ground black pepper	¼ teaspoon (about)
½ cup	unsifted all-purpose flour	120 ml
4 tablespoons	vegetable oil, butter or margarine	4 tablespoons
3 large	yellow onions, peeled and chopped	3 large
1 teaspoon	crumbled leaf marjoram	1 teaspoon
½ teaspoon	crumbled leaf thyme	½ teaspoon
½ teaspoon	crumbled leaf rosemary	½ teaspoon
6 cups	beef, veal or chicken stock or water	1½ L
12 uniformly small	new potatoes, scrubbed but not peeled	12 uniformly small
8 large	carrots, peeled and thickly sliced	8 large
18 uniformly small	silverskin onions, peeled	18 uniformly small

Sprinkle the lamb cubes evenly all over with 1 teaspoon of the salt and the pepper, then dredge in the flour. (Reserve any remaining flour; you will use some of it later to thicken the stew.) Brown the lamb, about one-third of the total amount at a time, in 3 tablespoons of the oil in a large heavy kettle set over moderate heat; as the lamb browns, transfer it to a large bowl with a slotted spoon. Add the remaining tablespoon of oil to the kettle, dump in the onions and stir-fry about 10 minutes over moderate heat until nicely browned. Add the marjoram, thyme and rosemary and stir-fry a minute or two to release their flavors.

Return the lamb to the kettle, add 5⅔ cups (1 L + 160 ml) of the beef stock and the remaining ½ teaspoon of salt and bring to a simmer. Adjust the heat so that the stock ripples gently, cover and simmer 1 to 1½ hours or until the lamb is almost fork-tender. Add the potatoes, carrots and silverskins to the kettle, re-cover and simmer 30 to 45 minutes longer or until both the lamb and vegetables can be easily pierced with a fork. Mix 3 tablespoons of the reserved dredging flour with the ⅓ cup (80 ml) of reserved beef stock to make a smooth paste in a small bowl. Whisk a little of the hot stew liquid into the paste, then stir back into the stew. Keep stirring for about 3 minutes or until the gravy is lightly thickened and no raw starch taste remains. Taste for salt and pepper and add more if needed. Ladle the stew into a large tureen and serve at the table.

Braised lamb riblets with vegetable gravy

SERVES 4 TO 6

There's a lot of good eating on lamb riblets, as this recipe proves. Serve with boiled new potatoes.

4 pounds	lamb riblets, cut in 3-inch (8 cm) lengths	2 kg
1½ teaspoons (about)	salt	1½ teaspoons (about)
¼ teaspoon (about)	freshly ground black pepper	¼ teaspoon (about)
½ cup	unsifted all-purpose flour	120 ml
4 tablespoons	olive oil	4 tablespoons
3 large	yellow onions, peeled and chopped	3 large
2 large	garlic cloves, peeled and minced	2 large
2 large	carrots, peeled and sliced	2 large
2 large	celery ribs, peeled and sliced	2 large
1 large	bay leaf, crumbled	1 large
1 tablespoon	minced fresh sage (or 1 teaspoon rubbed sage)	1 tablespoon
½ teaspoon	crumbled leaf marjoram	½ teaspoon
¼ teaspoon	crumbled leaf rosemary	¼ teaspoon
Pinch	crumbled leaf thyme	Pinch
1 cup	dry white wine	240 ml
1 can (13¾ oz.)	beef broth	1 can (407 ml)
2 tablespoons	minced parsley	2 tablespoons

Sprinkle the lamb riblets well all over with 1 teaspoon of the salt and the pepper. Dredge well in the flour. Heat 3 tablespoons of the olive oil in a large heavy kettle over moderately high heat and brown the ribs well on all sides, tackling only about one-third of the total amount at a time. As the ribs brown, lift them to a bowl with a slotted spoon. Add the remaining tablespoon of oil to the kettle, dump in the onions and garlic and stir-fry over moderate heat about

10 minutes until nicely browned. Add the carrots, celery, bay leaf, sage, marjoram, rosemary and thyme and stir-fry a minute or two. Return the riblets to the kettle, pour in the wine and broth, add the remaining ½ teaspoon of salt and bring to a simmer. Adjust the heat so that the liquid bubbles gently, cover and simmer about 1½ hours or until the riblets are tender.

Remove the riblets to a large deep platter and keep them warm. Buzz the kettle mixture to a smooth purée in an electric blender or a food processor fitted with the metal chopping blade or, if you have neither, put all through a food mill. Taste for salt and pepper and add more, if needed. If the gravy seems thin, pour it into a heavy shallow saucepan and boil hard, stirring often, 3 to 5 minutes until about the consistency of a pasta sauce. Spoon a little of the vegetable gravy over the riblets, sprinkle liberally with parsley and serve. Pass the remaining gravy separately.

Pork
& ham

The news in pork these days is "the new pork," which contains 36 percent fewer calories than "the old pork," 57 percent less fat and 22 percent more protein, thanks to geneticists, who have managed to breed leaner hogs, and packers, who have learned to trim carcasses more closely.

Unlikely as it may seem, today's pork loin actually weighs in at about 600 fewer calories per pound than today's boneless beef rib (1200 calories vs. 1800). And yet pork is one of the most nutritious meats available, providing an outstanding source of thiamin (vitamin B_1), iron and phosphorus and a good source of vitamins B_2 (riboflavin), B_6 and B_{12}.

"Everything but the squeal," people used to say of the edible parts of a hog. And that's very nearly true. I don't know that anyone has ever come up with a smashing recipe for pigs' tails, but virtually every other part of the animal **is** eaten. Even its fat is rendered into lard, which, of course, makes the best pie crust in the world.

The difference between pork and ham? We tend to think of ham as "cured pork." Actually, it is the hind leg of the hog and may be fresh or cured. Many cuts of pork are cured (brined). And they may or may not be smoked: ham, butt (upper shoulder), picnic (lower shoulder), jowl and bacon.

The qualities of pork

Although all pork entered into interstate commerce is federally inspected for wholesomeness, little fresh and cured pork is government graded because their quality is more uniform than that of other meats, also because packers tend to use their own trademarks of quality such as "Premium" or "Star." Your best insurance of top quality, then, is to buy from a butcher you trust, also to learn the visual hallmarks of quality. This is easy for fresh pork: look for meat that is a delicate rosy-beige, with white fat and spongy, red bone centers. The quality of cured pork is less easy to ascertain because the kind of cure and degree of smoking affect the color and texture of the meat. The best policy is simply to buy brands you like.

The cuts of pork
and how to cook them

As with beef, veal and lamb, the cuts of pork can be divided into two categories: the **tender** and the **less-tender.** The logical assumption, then, would be that the tender cuts should be prepared by dry heat (broiling, panbroiling, sautéing, roasting, etc.) and the tougher ones via moist heat (braising and stewing). But there is an added complication with pork. Some hogs (usually those that have been slopped) harbor microscopic parasites, *trichinae,* in their flesh that are wholly undetectable to the naked eye. These, if ingested live, can cause a serious, sometimes fatal disease in human beings known as *trichinosis.* For this reason, pork must always be cooked until well done—not to be translated, however, to mean "tasteless and dry."

Microbiologists have recently determined that *trichinae* are killed at a temperature of 140°F. (60°C.), but pork at that temperature is not palatable. I prefer to cook pork until its internal temperature reaches 170°F. (77°C.), by which time the meat will be the color of ivory and the juices clear. Ten years ago, it was recommended that pork be cooked even longer—to an internal temperature of 180°F. (82°C.)—but few people today subscribe to this cook-it-to-death school because the pork is about as succulent as cardboard.

Cooking pork **roasts** until well done does not present problems because the cuts are large. But cooking **chops** and **steaks** may because they're apt to dry out in the skillet or broiler unless additional fat or liquid is added. To minimize the risk of toughening or drying out these smaller cuts, **braise** them.

Fully cooked hams and **ham steaks,** of course, need only be cooked until they're appetizing—to an internal temperature of 140°F. (60°C.). Other cured cuts of pork **(those not fully cooked)** will be at their best if cooked to an internal temperature of 160°F. (71°C.). The safest and easiest way to determine internal temperature is by using a meat thermometer. (Just make certain that its tip rests in the center of the largest **lean** muscle and does not touch bone, which will give you a falsely elevated reading.)

Pork **chops** and **steaks** are too thin for accurate thermometer readings, so to test for doneness, make a small slit near the bone: if the meat shows no signs of pink, it is done.

Roasts

Hogs are lazy, and for that reason more parts of them are tender enough to roast than of any other meat animal.

POPULAR TENDER ROASTS	DESCRIPTION	MARKET WEIGHTS	SERVINGS PER POUND (½ kg)
Ham	The hind leg; available fresh or cured; bone in, semiboneless or boneless, also as a full ham, butt half (the meaty round) or shank half (bony). MODERATE.	Full hams 8–20 + lbs. (3½–9 + kg); half hams 4–12 lbs. (1⅘–5½ kg); semiboneless and boneless, 4–6 + lbs. (1⅘–2¾ kg)	1½–2 for bone-in hams; 2–3 for boneless hams.
Loin	Available bone-in or boned and rolled. The choicest is center loin because it contains the tenderloin. EXPENSIVE.	3–7 lbs. (1⅓–3¼ kg)	1½–2 for bone-in roasts; 3 for boneless.
Tenderloin	The long, lean, buttery-smooth muscle that is the equivalent of beef fillet. EXPENSIVE. NOTE: *Because of its extreme leanness, tenderloin should be braised.*	¾–1½ lbs. (⅓–⅔ kg)	3
Crown	Custom-made, theatrical roast made by bending two loin sections into a crown. EXORBITANT.	10 lbs. (4½ kg) and up	1½–2
Boston Butt	A chunky, square cut from the top of the shoulder. REASONABLE.	4–6 lbs. (1⅘–2¾ kg)	1½–2
Picnic	Available as cushion-style (boned but not rolled and perfect for stuffing), bone-in and boned and rolled. MODERATE.	3–5 lbs. (1⅓–2¼ kg)	1½–3, depending upon whether bone-in or boneless.

NOTE: *For details on the standard method of roasting pork, see The Ways of Cooking Meat included among the introductory notes to this chapter.*

Specialty hams

Many fine European hams are now available across America: **Prosciutto** (a fine-grained, mahogany-hued, salty Italian ham), **Westphalian, Bayonne** and **Chaves** (the German, French and Portuguese equivalents, respectively). These air-cured hams, by the way, are **raw.** But not to worry. *Trichinosis* is not a problem in Europe. Most often used as accents or ingredients, these butter-smooth hams are too rich to serve as we normally serve ham. They need the counterpoint of a tart fruit, for example, or the crunch of vegetables to be truly enjoyable.

America, too, boasts a variety of specialty hams, the most famous of them being the salty, deep red **Smithfield hams.** By law, these hams may come from peanut-fed hogs in the peanut belt of either Virginia or North Carolina, but they must be smoked, cured and processed in the town of Smithfield, Virginia. Smithfield hams are very expensive (as are similar country-cured hams), and they all require special cooking—usually a long slow simmering in several changes of water. The best plan is to follow to the letter the directions on the ham wrapper. NOTE: *These hams are often heavily molded, but you need only scrub the mold off (together with any accretions of ash and salt) before you cook them.*

Anatolian roast loin of pork with cinnamon

SERVES 8 TO 10

 I like the Middle Eastern way of seasoning meats—that is, of using such spices as cinnamon, allspice or cloves in concert with the more conventional herbs. This particular recipe is adapted from one I enjoyed in Izmir, Turkey, about five years ago and I make it often because I like the faint sweetness of cinnamon with pork. (The Turkish recipe called for lamb because Moslems do not eat pork.) Except for the seasonings, this is the conventional method of roasting pork, one that may be used for any tender pork roast, whether boneless or bone-in.

A 4–5 pound	boned and rolled loin of pork	A 1⅘–2¼ kg
2 tablespoons	unsalted butter, at room temperature	2 tablespoons
2 large	garlic cloves, peeled and crushed	2 large
½ teaspoon	ground cinnamon	½ teaspoon
½ teaspoon	crumbled leaf rosemary	½ teaspoon
¼ teaspoon	crumbled leaf thyme	¼ teaspoon
½ teaspoon	salt	½ teaspoon
¼ teaspoon	freshly ground black pepper	¼ teaspoon

Rub the pork well all over with a mixture of the butter, garlic, cinnamon, rosemary, thyme, salt and pepper. Place on a rack in a shallow roasting pan and let stand at room temperature 1 hour. Roast in a moderate oven (350°F. or 175°C.), allowing 35 to 40 minutes per pound or until a meat thermometer registers 170°F. (77°C.). NOTE: *If you prefer a bone-in roast, allow 30 to 35 minutes per pound.* Do not cover the roast at any time and do not add liquid to the pan. As soon as the meat thermometer reaches the desired temperature, remove the roast from the oven and let it stand 30 minutes before serving. Remove as many strings as possible, then place the pork on a heated platter, and serve. NOTE: *Boneless roasts, of course, are a cinch to carve. But if you have chosen a bone-in roast, ask the butcher to crack the backbone at the base of each rib so that all the carver needs to do is slice down between the ribs, allotting one to two chops per person.*

VARIATION:

Rôti de porc à la boulangère: Omit the cinnamon from the seasoning called for above; otherwise proceed as directed. When the pork has roasted about 1½ hours, take it from the oven; raise the oven temperature to hot (400°F. or 205°C.). Lift the pork from the pan and set aside; remove the rack. To the roasting pan add 8 large peeled and thinly sliced baking potatoes, 2 large peeled and coarsely chopped yellow onions, ¼ cup (60 ml) minced parsley, ½ teaspoon crumbled leaf marjoram, ¼ teaspoon crumbled leaf rosemary, 1½ teaspoons of salt and ⅛ teaspoon freshly ground black pepper. Toss all together in the pan drippings, then dot generously with unsalted butter (you'll need about 3 tablespoons in all). Place the pork on top of the potato mixture, return to the oven and roast, stirring the potato mixture occasionally, about 1½ hours longer or until a meat thermometer registers 170°F. (77°C.) and the potatoes are crusty-brown on top but tender underneath. NOTE: *I think this particular recipe is better if made with a bone-in loin of pork—and a big one—because there seem to be more drippings to combine with and flavor the potatoes.*

Carne de vinho e alhos
(PORK WITH WINE, GARLIC AND HERBS)

SERVES 6

This robust country dish, popular everywhere on the Portuguese island of Madeira, is marinated in wine and herbs for 2 to 3 days before it's cooked.

3 pounds	boned pork loin, trimmed of excess fat and sliced ½ inch (1½ cm) thick	*1½ kg*
1 bottle (⅘ quart)	dry white wine (preferably a Portuguese vinho verde)	*1 bottle (750 ml)*

1 cup	cider vinegar	240 ml
4 large	bay leaves	4 large
½ teaspoon	crumbled leaf savory	½ teaspoon
½ teaspoon	crumbled leaf marjoram	½ teaspoon
6	whole cloves	6
¼ teaspoon	salt	¼ teaspoon
¼ teaspoon	freshly ground black pepper	¼ teaspoon
3 large	garlic cloves, peeled and crushed	3 large
1 long slim loaf	French or Italian bread, sliced about 1 inch (2½ cm) thick	1 long slim loaf
4 tablespoons (about)	olive oil	4 tablespoons (about)
4 tablespoons (about)	unsalted butter	4 tablespoons (about)
1 medium-size	navel orange, sliced thin	1 medium-size
4–5	sprigs watercress	4–5

Layer pork in a large ceramic bowl; add wine, vinegar, bay leaves, savory, marjoram, cloves, salt, pepper and garlic. Cover and marinate in the refrigerator 2 to 3 days, turning pork often in marinade.

When ready to cook pork, transfer it to a large heavy skillet (not iron), add marinade, cover and simmer over low heat ½ hour; drain pork on paper toweling. Quickly moisten bread slices by touching each side to surface of marinade; spread on paper toweling and let dry. Raise heat underneath marinade so that it bubbles gently, and boil uncovered to reduce while you proceed with the recipe.

In a second large heavy skillet, brown each pork slice lightly on both sides in 2 tablespoons each olive oil and butter over moderately high heat. NOTE: *You may think that these cooked pork slices will not brown, but they will—nicely.* Remove to a heated plate and keep warm.

Quickly brown bread on both sides in skillet drippings, adding more oil and butter as needed. Drain on paper toweling.

To serve, arrange slices of bread on a platter, top with overlapping slices of pork, then spoon some of the reduced marinade on top. Garnish with orange slices and watercress. Pour remaining marinade into a sauceboat and pass separately.

Pork chops and steaks

Rib and **loin chops** are the most popular and expensive, but there are other choices: the bigger, cheaper **blade chop** from the shoulder and the still bigger (but not cheaper) **sirloin chop.** As for steaks, there are fresh **blade** and **arm steaks,** both from the shoulder and both relatively inexpensive (the arm steak is the meatier). **Ham steaks** are simply slices from the butt end of a ham and are most often prepackaged and fully cooked so that they only need to be heated.

The best thickness for pork chops and steaks? I like mine cut at least 1 inch (2½ cm) thick and preferably 1½ inches (4 cm). I sometimes have the chops cut two ribs thick, make pockets between the two and stuff the chops.

How to cook
pork chops and steaks

As I've already pointed out, pork chops and steaks are best when braised. Because they must be cooked until well done, they may toughen and dry if broiled, panbroiled or sautéed.

My method of braising: Let the chops or steaks stand at room temperature 30 minutes. Sometimes I rub them first with a little crushed garlic and/or fresh ginger root; often I rub them with a little crumbled sage and thyme. But I do not salt and pepper them—yet. For 4 chops or 2 steaks, I heat 2 tablespoons of peanut, vegetable or olive oil in a large heavy skillet over high heat about a minute, then brown the chops or steaks nicely—about 2 minutes on a side, salting and peppering them as they brown. I then reduce the heat to low, pour in about ½ cup (120 ml) of dry white wine or vermouth, apple or tomato juice (it all depends upon what I'm in the mood for), cover the skillet and let the chops or steaks cook slowly for 20 to 30 minutes, depending upon their thickness. Usually I can tell by the texture of the meat whether or not it's done (if it's firm, it usually is). But if I'm in doubt, I make a tiny slit near the bone and take a look. When the chops or steaks are done to my satisfaction, I transfer them quickly to a hot plate and keep them warm.

If I've used wine, vermouth or apple juice as the cooking liquid, I boil it down by about two-thirds, then either pour straightaway over the chops and serve them or smooth in about ½ cup (120 ml) of room temperature heavy cream and boil this down by about half. This, too, gets poured over the chops or steaks before serving.

SOME EXCELLENT ADDITIONS: About ½ pound (225 g) of thinly sliced mushrooms sautéed in a little butter with 1 to 2 minced shallots, then seasoned with a little crumbled leaf rosemary and thyme. I simply stir this mixture into the reduced skillet liquid before I pour it over the chops or steaks.

As for ham steaks, I brown them quickly in a little oil or butter—2 to 3 minutes on a side, turn the heat down low, pour in about 1 cup of Madeira wine (not too sweet), cover and cook 15 to 20 minutes. I lift the steaks to a hot platter to keep warm, then reduce the pan liquid by about three-fourths—it should be glistening and brown, about as thick as a thin glaze. This is poured over the ham steaks straightaway. That's all there is to it.

Braised pork chops
with orange and mustard

SERVES 4 TO 6

You will not need to add any salt to this recipe because of the saltiness of the soy sauce and mustard.

6 (1-inch-thick)	pork loin or rib chops, each about $\frac{1}{3}$–$\frac{1}{2}$ pound (160–225 g)	6 (2½ cm thick)
2 tablespoons	peanut or vegetable oil	2 tablespoons
1 large	orange, juiced	1 large
3 tablespoons	dark soy sauce	3 tablespoons
2 tablespoons	Dijon mustard	2 tablespoons
1 tablespoon	honey	1 tablespoon
1 tablespoon	finely minced fresh ginger root	1 tablespoon
1 large	garlic clove, peeled and crushed	1 large
Pinch	freshly ground black pepper	Pinch

Brown the chops on both sides in the oil in a large heavy skillet set over moderately high heat; transfer to a large shallow baking dish large enough to accommodate all of the chops in a single layer—a flameproof 13 × 9 × 2-inch (33 × 23 × 5 cm) baking dish should be perfect. Combine all remaining ingredients and pour evenly over the chops. Cover with foil and bake in a moderate oven (350°F. or 175°C.) for 45 minutes. Uncover the chops, baste generously with the pan drippings and bake 15 to 20 minutes longer until nicely glazed and cooked through. (To test, make a small slit near the bone; if the meat is white, the chops are done.)

Ground pork

Ground pork and ham are too lean and characterless to use by themselves. But mixed with beef, lamb or veal—and with one another—they make dandy loaves and meatballs.

Pork and caper loaf
with fresh sage and marjoram

SERVES 8 TO 10

This light and lemony loaf can be made with dried rather than fresh sage and marjoram, but it will not have the same country-fresh flavor. It's equally good hot or cold.

2 pounds	ground pork shoulder	1 kg
½ pound	ground veal shoulder	225 g
½ pound	ground smoked ham	225 g
2 cups	soft bread crumbs	½ L
1 cup	evaporated milk	240 ml
2 medium-size	yellow onions, chopped fine	2 medium-size
2 medium-size	eggs	2 medium-size
¼ cup	well-drained capers	60 ml
2 tablespoons	minced parsley	2 tablespoons
1 tablespoon	minced fresh sage (or 1 teaspoon rubbed sage)	1 tablespoon
1 tablespoon	minced fresh marjoram (or ½ teaspoon crumbled leaf marjoram)	1 tablespoon
1 teaspoon	finely grated lemon rind	1 teaspoon
½ teaspoon	salt	½ teaspoon
⅛ teaspoon	freshly ground black pepper	⅛ teaspoon

Mix all ingredients together well and pack into a well-greased 9 × 5 × 3-inch (23 × 13 × 8 cm) loaf pan. Bake in a moderate oven (350°F. or 175°C.) for 1 hour and 45 minutes or until the loaf is nicely browned and pulls from the sides of the pan. Cool the loaf upright in its pan on a wire rack for 15 minutes; drain off drippings. NOTE: *The drippings, mixed with an equal quantity of plain yogurt or sour cream and seasoned to taste with a little Dijon mustard, make an excellent accompanying sauce for the loaf.* Turn the loaf out on a platter and garnish, if you like, with lemon twists and fresh sprigs of sage, marjoram or watercress.

Frikadeller
(DANISH MEATBALLS)

SERVES 6

 The reason these meatballs are so moist and light is that the liquid ingredient is carbonated water, which bubbles through the meat mixture much like a leavening agent. Serve with Hedy's Braised Red Cabbage with Apples and Onion in Red Wine Sauce. (see Index).

¾ pound	ground pork shoulder	340 g
¾ pound	ground veal shoulder	340 g
4 slices	firm-textured white bread, buzzed to moderately fine crumbs	4 slices
1 medium-size	yellow onion, peeled and finely minced	1 medium-size

1 teaspoon	salt	1 teaspoon
¼ teaspoon	dill weed	¼ teaspoon
⅛ teaspoon	freshly grated nutmeg	⅛ teaspoon
Pinch	ground caraway	Pinch
1 teaspoon	salt	1 teaspoon
⅛ teaspoon	freshly ground black pepper	⅛ teaspoon
½ cup	club soda	120 ml
4 tablespoons	unsalted butter	4 tablespoons

Mix all ingredients except the butter well, then chill 2 hours or until firm enough to shape. Pinch off chunks of the meat mixture and roll into fat little "logs" measuring about 3 inches long and 1½ inches in diameter (8 cm × 4 cm). Arrange these on a large tray, in one layer, cover loosely with wax paper and chill several hours or until quite firm. NOTE: *This chilling is important because if the meat mixture is too soft, the frikadeller will fall apart in the skillet.*

Melt the butter in a large heavy skillet over moderate heat and brown the *frikadeller* well on all sides in two to three batches; as each batch is browned, lift to a large plate with a slotted spoon. When all of the *frikadeller* are browned, return all to the skillet, turn burner heat down low, cover and cook slowly 25 to 30 minutes until well done. For a particularly pretty presentation, mound the *frikadeller* on a bed of red cabbage and sprinkle lightly with freshly minced dill or parsley.

Spareribs

There's a surprising lot of meat on pork ribs, and these, properly cooked by moist heat, make superlative eating. I adore them barbecued the Deep South way (see recipe that follows), also as the Chinese prepare them, darkly glistening with soy and ginger. Spareribs are very good, too, deviled or curried. They may also be broiled or grilled, provided they have first been braised or simmered until tender. **How many spareribs should you allow per person?** One full pound (½ kg).

Old-fashioned Carolina barbecued spareribs

SERVES 6

Too many Southerners today barbecue spareribs with a gloppy ketchup mixture. But not Mrs. Oscar McCollum of Rockingham County, North Carolina, whom I interviewed a few years ago for a series of articles I was writing for *Family Circle* magazine entitled "America's Great Grass Roots Cooks." Mrs. McCollum's barbecued ribs are very much like those I remember eating as a child in Raleigh. The perfect accompaniment: coleslaw and fresh-baked cornbread.

6 pounds	spareribs, cut in 3-rib widths	2¾ kg
3 quarts	cold water	3 L
	BARBECUE SAUCE:	
1 cup	cider vinegar	240 ml
½ cup (1 stick)	unsalted butter	115 g
¼ cup	firmly packed light brown sugar	60 ml
1 teaspoon	freshly ground black pepper	1 teaspoon
⅛ teaspoon	cayenne pepper	⅛ teaspoon
¼ teaspoon	salt	¼ teaspoon

Simmer the spareribs in the water in a heavy, deep, covered kettle over low heat 1 hour and 15 minutes. Meanwhile, bring all sauce ingredients to a simmer in a small saucepan; turn off the heat, but keep the sauce warm at the back of the stove or by setting near the kettle of ribs. Lift the ribs from the kettle when they have cooked the proper length of time and arrange in one layer in a very large shallow roasting pan. Brush lavishly with the sauce, set in the broiler about 5 inches (13 cm) from the heat and broil 10 to 12 minutes, basting the ribs after they have broiled 5 minutes. Turn the ribs, brush generously with the sauce and broil 10 to 12 minutes longer, again basting with sauce after 5 minutes. Pour any remaining sauce into a bowl (also add any sauce and juices in the bottom of the roasting pan), and pass so that guests may spoon additional barbecue sauce over their portions.

Pork stew meat

The cut I like best for stewing is the shoulder because it contains sinew and fat enough to make succulent eating. The meaty neck bones can also be stewed, but I usually don't like to have to fish around for bones as I eat, so boned pork shoulder is my choice, cut into 1- to 1½-inch (2½ to 4 cm) cubes. Because of its delicate flavor, pork is versatile and can be substituted for lamb or veal—even beef—in almost any stew. But through some magical alchemy that seems to heighten its flavor, it's best, I think, when teamed with such strong-flavored vegetables as cabbage, cauliflower, Brussels sprouts, leeks, turnips, parsnips or rutabaga.

Pork stew with apple, cauliflower and tarragon

SERVES 6 TO 8

This may sound an unlikely combination of ingredients, but the results are outstanding. Serve with an assertive salad of crisp greens, tartly dressed with oil and lemon.

3 pounds	boned pork shoulder, cut in 1–1½-inch (2½ to 4 cm) chunks	1½ kg
3 quarts, in all	water	3 L, in all
2 medium-size	yellow onions, peeled and sliced thin	2 medium-size
2 medium-size	carrots, peeled and sliced thin	2 medium-size
1 large	tart green apple, peeled, cored and diced	1 large
2 large	parsley sprigs	2 large
½ teaspoon	crumbled leaf tarragon	½ teaspoon
¼ teaspoon	crumbled leaf thyme	¼ teaspoon
¼ teaspoon	crumbled leaf rosemary	¼ teaspoon
1 can (13¾ oz.)	beef broth	1 can (407 ml)
1 cup	apple juice	240 ml
½ cup	dry white wine	120 ml
2 teaspoons	Dijon mustard	2 teaspoons
½ cup	heavy cream	120 ml
1 teaspoon (about)	salt	1 teaspoon (about)
1 large (2½ lbs.)	cauliflower, washed, trimmed and divided into flowerets	1 large (1¼ kg)

Place pork and 2½ quarts (2½ L) of the water in a large heavy kettle, bring to a boil, reduce heat so that water barely ripples and simmer 10 minutes. NOTE: *This is to force the pork chunks to throw a scum, which can be discarded before you begin the stew proper.* Drain pork in a large colander; then rinse well under cool running water, washing off all clinging bits of scum; also wash the kettle well and return it to the stove. When pork chunks are scum-free, drain thoroughly and add to the kettle along with the onions, carrots, apple, parsley sprigs, tarragon, thyme, rosemary, beef broth, apple juice and wine. Bring all to a simmer, cover and cook over very low heat for 3½ to 4 hours or until a fork will pierce the pork with only the slightest resistance. NOTE: *This may seem rather a long time to cook a pork stew, but you are using gentler than usual heat so that you can control the texture of the pork more precisely. If you were to boil the pork, it might cook in half the time, but it might also disintegrate into shreds quite suddenly—less than 10 minutes after it had seemed tough.*

With a slotted spoon, transfer pork chunks to a large heatproof bowl. Boil the mixture left in the kettle, uncovered, about 20 minutes or until reduced by about one-fourth. Then purée kettle mixture in a food processor fitted with the metal chopping blade, or in an electric blender (do only one-third to one-half of the total amount at a time), or put through a food mill. Return puréed mixture and pork chunks to kettle. NOTE: *You may prepare the recipe up to this point a day or two ahead of time. Simply let the covered, refrigerator-cold kettle stand at room temperature ½ hour to take some of the chill off the stew before proceeding with the recipe.*

Set the kettle over low heat and bring slowly to a simmer. Reduce heat to lowest point so that stew merely "mellows"; you do not want the sauce to boil—or even to simmer—so place a flame-tamer under the kettle, if need be. Smooth in the mustard, then the heavy cream and let stew stand, uncovered, for a few minutes.

Bring the remaining 2 cups (½ L) of water to a boil in a large saucepan, sprinkle in the salt, then add the cauliflowerets, cover and simmer 5 to 7 minutes until crisp-tender. Drain the cauliflowerets well, then return to pan. Shake the pan vigorously for a minute or two over low heat to drive off excess steam (important, so that you don't water down the stew's marvelous sauce). Add cauliflowerets to the stew, spooning some of the gravy over them, and warm 2 to 3 minutes to allow flavors to mingle. Dish up and serve.

Bacon

True bacon comes from the pork belly and is leaner of late than it once was. (**Canadian bacon** is the lean eye of loin of pork, cured and smoked, and is much more like ham than bacon.) Most supermarkets today do sell bacon by the slab as well as sliced thin (35 slices to the pound or ½ kg), medium (16 to 20 slices per pound or ½ kg) or thick (12 to 15 slices per pound or ½ kg). Many of the better butchers also now carry bacon that has been cured **without sodium nitrite,** the preservative that has been shown to cause cancer in laboratory animals. Look for it.

In addition, specialty food shops sell Danish bacon (a mild, sweet cure), Irish bacon (deeply smoky) and home-cured bacon (heavily salted and smoked). These specialty bacons, particularly when bought by the slab, may show a thick encrustation of salt and ash. Sometimes there may even be mold. No harm done. Simply rinse (or scrub) away the salt, mold and ash before using the bacon. NOTE: *Heavily cured bacons are often so salty that if you are using them in a recipe, you may have to reduce the amount of salt called for to compensate. The bacon may also be blanched in boiling water to remove excess salt.*

Salt pork and fat back

These two are in fact what their names imply. **Salt pork** is brined (salt-preserved) pork fat often streaked with a little lean, and **fat back** is fresh creamy-white fat cut from the layer that covers the shoulder and back of a hog. The two may be used interchangeably in many recipes, even though salt pork may contain some lean, which fat back usually does not. And, of course, salt pork is so salty that you may need to reduce the quantity of salt called for in a recipe—and/or blanch the salt pork—if you substitute it for fat back.

How are they used? To add richness and flavor to stews and casseroles, primarily. Both are often diced and rendered (melted) and their drippings used for browning meat. (The crisp browned bits or cracklings left after the fat back or salt pork has been rendered are saved and tossed into a casserole or stew shortly before serving so that they do not lose their crunch.)

Fresh fat back is the soul of soul food, and a big chunk is routinely plunked into every pot of green beans, turnip greens, kale, collards or black-eyed peas and put to simmer with them for the better part of the day. It seems difficult to believe that I grew up on such vegetables (they were integral to every school lunch). I don't remember complaining, particularly, but now I certainly do intensely dislike greasy, overcooked vegetables swimming in water.

Smoked ham baked in rye bread crust à la Parkhotel Adler

SERVES 8

If you want to wow dinner guests, this recipe from the Black Forest's Parkhotel Adler is the recipe to try. It's theatrical yet, backstage, easy to make. The crust does more than bestow magical succulence upon the ham baked inside it; it's also served alongside the ham, underneath ladlings of pan drippings, in the manner of Yorkshire pudding. NOTE: *The metric equivalents given here are precise as they often need to be in baking where exact proportions are critical to a recipe's success.*

	RYE DOUGH:	
2¼ cups, in all	**unsifted** rye flour	210 g, in all
4¼ cups (about)	sifted all-purpose flour	425 g (about)
3 cups, in all	warm water, about 105–115°F. (41–46°C.)	710 ml, in all
2 packages	active dry yeast	2 packages
1 teaspoon	salt	1 teaspoon

	HAM:	
6–6½ pounds	fully cooked smoked half ham (shank end), trimmed of rind and all but ⅛ inch (½ cm) outer layer of fat	3 kg
	EGG GLAZE:	
1 large	egg	1 large
2 tablespoons	cold water	2 tablespoons

For the dough: Make a "sponge" by mixing ¾ cup (180 ml) each of the rye and all-purpose flour with 1 cup (240 ml) of the warm water. Place in an oiled bowl, lightly brush the surface with oil, cover with a clean dry cloth and let stand in a warm, draft-free spot overnight.

Next day, dissolve the yeast in 2 cups (480 ml) warm water, mix in the sponge and the salt and beat hard until smooth. Mix in the remaining rye flour, then enough of the remaining all-purpose flour to make a soft but manageable dough; beat hard until elastic. Place the dough in a large well-oiled bowl, brush the top with oil, cover with a cloth and let rise in a warm spot about 45 minutes until doubled in bulk. Punch the dough down, re-cover with the cloth and let rise again 45 minutes. Punch the dough down once more and knead hard for 5 minutes on a well-floured pastry cloth.

To wrap the ham in dough: Roll about one-third of the dough into an oval ⅜ inch (1 cm) thick and as wide and long as the ham (including the shank bone); place in the bottom of a large shallow roasting pan and center the ham on top. Roll the remaining dough into a slightly larger oval about ¾ inch (2 cm) thick and drape it on top of the ham (the weight of the dough will pull it down over the ham). Fit the dough around the ham by molding gently as you would modeling clay; trim off excess overhang. Moisten the edges of the top and bottom crusts with warm water, pinch together to seal and tuck underneath the ham. Also patch any thin spots, using dough scraps, and seal by moistening with warm water. If there are scraps enough, make leaf and stem cutouts and "glue" them in a decorative pattern on the crust with the egg glaze. (To make it, simply whisk the egg and water together until smooth.)

Refrigerate the dough-wrapped ham, uncovered, for 2 to 3 hours; then brush the entire surface of the dough lightly with the egg glaze. Bake the ham, uncovered, in a slow oven (300°F. or 150°C.) for 3 hours or until the crust is nicely browned and sounds hollow when thumped.

Carefully transfer the ham to a large heated platter and keep warm. Remove and discard bits of dough clinging to the pan. Pour pan drippings into a small saucepan and set aside. Pour about an inch (2½ cm) of water into the roasting pan, set over moderate heat and reduce by half, scraping up browned bits; combine with the reserved drippings in the saucepan and boil 1 to 2 minutes. Pour into a sauceboat. (Strain first, if you like.)

To carve the ham: Cut straight through the dough crust down the center "back" and pull the two halves apart. Also cut down the center "back" of the ham to the bone, then along the bone from the large end of the ham to the shank bone; finally, carve into thin slices by cutting at right angles to the original cut. Break the crust into smallish chunks and include some with each portion. Pass the pan drippings so that everyone may ladle some over both ham and rye crust.

Chicken

In the last twenty years, America's per capita consumption of chicken has more than doubled. And why not? Chicken is choice, chicken is cheap, and now that our gastronomical gurus have discovered what a dandy substitute it makes for veal, chicken is even chic.

What few of us realize, however, is that chicken is a nutritional heavyweight. Its high-quality protein is a match for that of red meat, and yet its calories (particularly of white meat) weigh in at less than half those of beef, lamb or pork. For example, three ounces of skinned chicken breast add up to 115 calories while an equivalent portion of hamburger totals 245 calories, roast pork, 310, and lamb rib chops, 340.

More important, the quality of chickens shipped to market today is reliably high, thanks to streamlined poultry production that approaches sci-fi proficiency. Some food snobs insist that we've traded character and flavor for tenderness. I wonder. I don't recall that the chickens of my childhood were so all-fired tasty. But I do remember they were tough as all get-out. Most, it seemed to me, were rangy cocks or broody hens past their prime. I remember going with my mother down to the old central market in Raleigh, North Carolina, and seeing wooden crates filled with poultry in from the farm—scrappy Leghorns, their white feathers rouged with the red clay soil in which they'd been allowed to scratch, plump Rhode Island Reds and scruffy Barred Rocks.

During World War II we raised our own chickens in the backyard—both for eggs and for eating. But the chickens destined for our dinner table were inevitably tough old birds. It was my job to pluck, singe and draw them. How I loathed it! But I learned a lot about chickens that has proved valuable ever since. Our chickens, if memory serves, were fed cracked corn and some sort of meal. And, of course, they scratched around in the dirt.

Not so today's pampered birds. Most never touch ground but are raised in elevated cages, feasting all day long upon nutritionally enriched rations. I remember when I was interviewing a poultryman's wife a few years ago on the Delmarva Peninsula (the eastern shore of Delaware, Maryland and Virginia and one of America's major poultry-producing areas), she told me that it took only six to seven weeks to raise a hatchling into a three-pound broiler-fryer.

The broiler-fryer is today's "wonder bird." It's plump and fleshy, tender enough to broil, fry or roast. Some 90 percent of the chickens marketed today are broiler-fryers, but there are other types available with which we should have more than a passing acquaintance.

The kinds and qualities of chickens

Like red meat, chicken is federally inspected for wholesomeness if it is shipped across state lines to be sold (look for the round inspector's seal on the package or wing tag). It may also be federally graded as to quality—if the poultryman or processor opts for it.

The top grade for chicken is USDA GRADE A, and the shield-shaped grade emblem usually appears on the wing tag or label alongside the inspection seal. Grade A chickens are the ones you're mostly likely to see in your supermarket or butcher shop. These birds are amply fleshed, smooth and unbroken of skin, generally attractive. The skin color can range from deep yellow to white and says less about the grade of a chicken than about its diet and breed. The only other grades for chicken are USDA GRADE B and USDA GRADE C and, truth to tell, in my twenty-five years as a food editor, I have yet to see either of them in a store. Few Grade B or C birds, I'm told, ever reach the supermarket because they're used for processed foods (canned soups and stews, chicken franks, luncheon meats and the like).

In red meat, the federal grade is an indicator of tenderness. In poultry, it is not. What matters more is the **class (age)** of the bird:

Broiler-fryers: Tender young birds between seven and nine weeks of age weighing 2 to 3½ pounds (1 to 1⅓ kg). Reliably succulent and astonishingly versatile, broiler-fryers are sometimes marketed as "broiling chickens," "fryers" and even "roasting chickens."

Roasters: A little older than broiler-fryers (about 16 weeks) and a good bit bigger—3½ to 6 pounds (1⅓ to 2¾ kg), roasters are tender and, as their name implies, particularly suited to roasting. Their body cavities are big enough to hold from 2 to 3 cups (½ to ¾ L) of stuffing.

Capons: Males castrated while young so that they will flesh out tenderly, developing some of the female's plumpness. Capons weigh between 4 and 7 pounds (1⅘ to 3¼ kg) and are usually about 16 weeks old. They are meatier than roasters and contain significantly more fat. TIP: *Be sure to pull all fat deposits from the body and neck cavities before you stuff a capon.*

Heavy hens: These are what used to be called "stewing hens." They're mature (a euphemism for "old") and usually "tough as old Nick." The best way to cook hens is to stew them because the combination of heat and moisture miraculously converts the sinew to gelatin just as it does with the tougher cuts of red meat. Hens average between 4½ and 6 pounds (2 to 2¾ kg) and are the birds to cook when you need chicken meat for a casserole, soup, stew or salad. TIP: *About 50 percent of a hen will be meat, so you can count on 2¼ pounds (1 kg) of meat from a 4½-pound (2 kg) hen and 3 pounds (1⅓ kg) of meat from a 6-pounder (2¾ kg).*

Rock Cornish: These lightweights are specially bred and fed chickens averaging 1½ pounds (⅔ kg) or less. They're tender enough to roast, but their meat is largely white and dry, so frequent basting is necessary to keep Rock Cornish hens moist. Allow ½ to 1 bird per person.

Knowing the different classes of chickens available today is a help when you approach the poultry counter of your supermarket, but it's also wise to know the forms in which chicken is sold:

Whole chickens: Broiler-fryers, roasters, capons, heavy hens and Rock Cornish are all sold whole with packets of giblets (heart, liver and gizzard plus the neck) tucked inside their body cavities. Be sure you fish the giblets out before you begin to prepare the bird.

Halves: Small broiler-fryers are sold halved—split right down the center—to accommodate aficionados of the broiler and backyard barbecue. Halved birds may also be baked.

Quarters: Broiler-fryers split down the center and from left to right along the midsection. Like chicken halves, these are most suitable for broiling or barbecuing.

Pieces: Whole broiler-fryers disjointed so that there are drumsticks, thighs, breast halves and wings. The back may be separated or attached to the breasts and thighs. Also usually included, a sack of giblets (liver, heart and gizzard) and the neck. Chicken pieces are also sometimes marketed as "frying chickens" and, as that label implies, are good for frying or deep-frying.

Chicken parts: These, not to be confused with chicken pieces, are simply packets containing many like parts. The variety available simply staggers. On a recent run down the poultry counter of my neighborhood supermarket, I noted the following: **whole breasts** weighing 12 to 16 ounces (⅓ to ½ kg) each; **boned breasts** (sometimes called "cutlets"); **thighs** (dark, meaty cuts weighing about ¼ pound or 115 g each); **drumsticks** (dark, less meaty cuts also weighing about ¼ pound or 115 g each); **wings** (light meat but precious little of it); **giblets** (gizzard, liver, heart) and **chicken livers.**

How much chicken should you allow per person?

Chicken is available in so many different forms that it's best, perhaps, to offer this little table:

WHOLE CHICKEN	POUNDS PER PERSON		KILOS PER PERSON
Broiler-Fryer	1–1½		½–⅔ kg
Roaster, Capon, Hen	1		½ kg
Rock Cornish	¾–1½		⅓–⅔ kg

CHICKEN PARTS	POUNDS PER PERSON	PIECES PER PERSON	GRAMS PER PERSON
Breasts	½	½ breast	225 g (¼ kg)
Thighs	½	2 thighs	225 g (¼ kg)
Drumsticks	½	2 drumsticks	225 g (¼ kg)
Wings	½	3–4 wings	225 g (¼ kg)
Giblets, Livers	¼	—	115 g

The care and keeping of chicken

In the refrigerator: Tray-packed or supermarket-sealed whole chickens, chicken parts, even giblets may be kept safely in the refrigerator for two days in their original wrappers **provided** you waste no time getting them home and into the coldest part of the refrigerator. Chicken from a butcher should be unwrapped, placed in one layer on a large plate or tray, covered loosely with plastic food wrap, foil or wax paper and placed in the coldest part of the refrigerator. Handled thus, it will keep safely for about three days, but the giblets only two days. NOTE: *Occasionally, tray-packed chicken will smell "strong" or "off" when the plastic covering is first removed. Don't panic. Let the chicken stand about five minutes on the counter, then sniff again. The odor (caused by oxidation within the supermarket package) will most likely have vanished. If not, by all means return the chicken to the supermarket for a refund or replacement.*

In the freezer: Whole chicken and chicken parts, properly wrapped and frozen, will keep well at 0°F. (−18°C.) for 4 to 6 months. The best wrapping materials: aluminum foil, freezer paper and plastic food wrap. Wrap each whole chicken, or **each piece,** individually, pressing out all wrinkles and sealing tight. The reason for wrapping pieces individually is that you can take them out as you need them—one, two, three or four pieces at a time. Pieces frozen *en masse* will stick together and be difficult to separate without thawing. Once small pieces—wings, thighs, drumsticks, etc.—are frozen, bundle them into a plastic bag so that they don't get lost in the back or bottom of the freezer. It goes without saying that you should date and label each packet so that you have some notion as to what it contains and some idea, too, as to its age.

How to thaw frozen chicken: The safest way is in the refrigerator. Simply set the still-wrapped chicken or chicken parts in the refrigerator. Whole frozen chickens weighing 4 pounds (2 kg) or less will take 12 to 16 hours to thaw in the refrigerator; chicken parts, 4 to 9 hours. You can determine the progress of the thawing, of course, simply by feeling the package. To thaw chicken more quickly, immerse it, still tightly wrapped, in cold water. NOTE: *Never refreeze chicken once it has thawed—you will be flirting with food poisoning and you will also have destroyed most of the chicken's original quality.*

The ways of cooking chicken

Like red meats, chickens can be divided into two categories—the tender and the tough—and which they are will, in turn, determine how you should cook them. NOTE: *It isn't necessary to thaw frozen chicken or chicken parts before you cook them. In fact, it's better not to because it is during the thawing period that chicken loses considerable juice and quality. To compensate for the fact that the bird went into the pot or oven solidly frozen, you need only add 15 to 30 minutes to the overall cooking time.*

FIRST, THE TENDER CHICKENS:

To fry: Choose a young broiler-fryer weighing about 2½ pounds (1¼ kg) and have it disjointed. Sprinkle each piece lightly on both sides with salt and freshly ground black pepper (for variety, try seasoned salt and/or lemon pepper). Dredge the chicken lightly in flour (or cornstarch or rice flour, which make exceptionally crispy-crusted chicken). Pour corn, peanut or vegetable oil into a very large heavy skillet to a depth of ¼ inch (¾ cm) or, if you like, use about two-thirds oil and one-third unsalted butter—but not 100 percent butter because it will blacken under the intense heat needed to brown the chicken. Set the skillet over high heat, then heat until there seem to be currents in the oil—these will show as ripples on the bottom of the skillet and indicate that the oil is sizzling hot. Place the largest pieces of chicken—breasts, thighs, back—in the skillet first, skin sides down, then fit the smaller pieces in and around. Brown the chicken pieces about 15 minutes over moderately high heat, turning once or twice with tongs; reduce heat to moderately low, cover the skillet and cook 20 to 25 minutes or until the breasts and thighs are cooked through—when you pierce them with a fork, the juices should run clear, not pink or red. Turn the chicken once, about midway through this slow-cooking period, so that it will cook evenly. Uncover the chicken and cook about 5 minutes more or until it crisps a bit. NOTE: *Remove the liver and heart after 5 to 10 minutes in the skillet and keep warm—they do not need the whole 35 to 45 minutes, indeed will be as hard as India rubber if cooked that long.* Drain the chicken well on several thicknesses of paper toweling before serving.

To sauté: Sauté is just the French word for frying. But when it comes to cooking chicken, there is a significant difference between the French method and the American. For starters, the French use **very little** fat—usually 2 to 3 tablespoons per large skillet. All that's needed is enough to coat the skillet bottom lightly so that the chicken won't stick. Second, the French rarely dredge pieces of chicken. They simply brown them lightly on both sides—*au naturel*—season them, then turn the heat way down low and let the chicken cook until tender, usually about 45 minutes altogether. They may slosh in a little wine or stock or cream—but doing so shifts the method of cooking from sautéing to braising, described a little later on.

To stir-fry: This Oriental technique of tossing chunks of food as they sear over intense heat in a small amount of oil in a wok or skillet is suitable only for small pieces of chicken—preferably boneless ones. Speed and dexterity are of the essence when it comes to stir-frying because the aim is merely to brown the pieces lightly on the outside and to heat them through. A few minutes are all it takes.

To deep-fat fry: See the recipe that follows.

To oven-fry: This is a superlative way to fry chickens for a crowd, because you can spread two to three disjointed chickens out in a big, shallow baking pan. Season and dredge the chicken pieces as directed for fried chicken above. Pour about ½ cup (120 ml) of melted butter or margarine into a very large shallow pan. Roll the chicken pieces in the butter, then arrange, skin side up, **in one layer.** NOTE: *You should have enough chicken pieces to fill the pan without crowding it.* Bake the chicken uncovered in a moderate oven (350°F. or 175°C.) for about 1 to 1¼ hours or until nicely browned and fork-tender. Drain well on paper toweling before serving.

To broil: Small chickens (2½ to 3 pounds or 1 to 1½ kg) are better choices for broiling because they will cook through by the time their skins are crackly brown. (Larger chickens may actually char by the time they are done.) The broiler-fryers should be halved or quartered, lightly sprinkled with salt and pepper (seasoned or celery salt make a nice change of pace, as does lemon pepper). Brush lightly with melted butter or margarine, or olive oil, sesame, hazelnut or walnut oil. (I sometimes even brush the chickens with a good vinaigrette or Italian dressing—the low-calorie variety when I am trying to shed a few pounds.) Place the pieces of chicken, skin side **down,** on a lightly oiled broiler pan (line it first with foil to simplify cleanup), then place in the broiler about 8 inches (20 cm) from the heat and broil 15 minutes. Turn the chicken, brush well again with melted butter, oil or whatever you used the first time and broil about 10 minutes longer or until fork-tender, richly browned and crisp.

An easy diet variation: Sprinkle the pieces of chicken with pepper and seasoned salt, place them, skin side **up,** on an oiled broiler pan, then top each piece with 3 to 4 ribs of celery. Place in the broiler as directed above and broil 15 minutes. Turn the chicken pieces, place fresh celery on the flip side, and broil 10 to 15 minutes longer. I don't know what it is about celery juice, but it has a marvelous buttery flavor and makes you think that the chicken was actually basted with butter. **Total calories:** About 180 per quarter-chicken (the breast part).

To roast: Broiler-fryers, of course, **can** be roasted. But I prefer a big roaster or capon, about 6 pounds (2¾ kg) minimum, because it can accommodate a decent amount of stuffing. As a rule of thumb, you can figure about ½ cup (120 ml) of stuffing per pound (½ kg) of bird—not counting, of course, any extra stuffing that you may want to make *en casserole.*

Pull all clumps of fat from the body and neck cavities of the chicken and discard. (Or, you may melt it and use it to brush the bird later.) Rub the bird inside and out with salt and freshly ground pepper and, if you like, a little garlic and a mixture of crumbled herbs—sage and thyme, for example, marjoram and/ or rosemary and thyme. Use any of your favorite stuffings or, if you like, simply shove a couple of whole peeled onions into the body cavity, or onions and carrots, or onions, carrots and celery. Or you might do as the French do and thrust a bouquet of fresh herbs into the cavity—a fresh handful of parsley, thyme and marjoram, tarragon, or a few sprigs of rosemary. You can tuck almost anything inside the bird as long as its flavor is compatible with that of chicken.

If you are using a proper stuffing, spoon it first into the neck cavity— **lightly**—then fold the neck skin back against the back of the bird and skewer shut with a poultry pin. Also fold the wings against the back of the bird. Now upend the bird so that you can spoon the stuffing directly into the body cavity. Again, spoon it in **lightly**—do not pack, because the stuffing will swell as it cooks, and if you tamp it down, it will become gummy and possibly even rupture the bird. Now, using soft twine, tie the drumsticks together, then the tail to them—this is an easy way of "trussing" the bird and enclosing the stuffing. NOTE: *Once you have stuffed the chicken, roast it without delay because uncooked stuffing spoils rapidly.*

Place the bird, breast side up, on a rack in a shallow open roasting pan and brush liberally with melted butter or chicken fat, or olive or other oil. Set uncovered in a moderately hot oven (375°F. or 190°C.) and roast approximately 30 minutes per pound or until the chicken is a glistening amber brown and you can move the drumstick easily (this is the classic test of doneness for a chicken and, I think, as good as any). You should not need to baste the chicken during roasting, but if it seems to be drying out, brush again generously with melted butter or oil. Remove the chicken from the oven and let stand 15 to 20 minutes before serving so that its juices will settle. Remove and discard the strings and the poultry pin used to secure the neck skin.

This resting period is the time to decide what you will do about the pan drippings. The easiest solution is simply to skim them of excess fat, pour into a gravy boat and serve as is.

For a brown gravy: Skim off all fat drippings and measure them. If there are less than 4 tablespoons, round out the measure with melted butter or margarine. Place in a small heavy saucepan, smooth in 4 tablespoons of flour and brown lightly over moderate heat. Measure the remaining drippings, meanwhile, and add enough good strong chicken broth, if needed, to equal 2 to 2½ cups (½ L). Whisk this mixture into the saucepan and cook, stirring constantly, until thickened and smooth—about 3 minutes. Turn heat to low and let gravy mellow 2 to 3 minutes. Season to taste with salt and pepper.

For a cream gravy: Prepare exactly as directed for the Brown Gravy, but use 2 to 2½ cups (½ L) milk or half-and-half cream in place of the broth.

For a giblet gravy: Prepare either the Brown or Cream Gravy, then mix in the finely minced giblets, which have first been simmered about 30 minutes in 2 cups (½ L) water with a chunked carrot and celery rib, a peeled and quartered small onion, a big bay leaf and 6 peppercorns. NOTE: *This stock should be saved, strained and used in making the gravy. Use in place of chicken broth in the Brown Gravy. For the Cream Gravy, use 1 cup (240 ml) each of giblet broth and milk + ½ cup (120 ml) heavy cream.*

AND NOW, FOR THE TOUGH CHICKENS:

To stew: The purpose of stewing is usually to obtain chicken meat for another recipe (casserole, loaf, salad, sandwich spread, etc.). Remove and discard excess body fat; also remove the packet of giblets from the body cavity (if any) and unwrap. Plop the chicken or hen into a large heavy kettle, add a peeled and quartered onion or two, a couple of chunked carrots and ribs of celery (include some green tops), a couple of bay leaves, 6 to 8 peppercorns and the giblets. Pour in enough water to almost cover the chicken and, if you like, a cup (240 ml) or so of dry white wine. Bring to a simmer over moderate heat, adjust the burner so that the kettle liquid bubbles very gently, cover the kettle and simmer the bird 2 to 3 hours or until a fork will pierce it easily. NOTE: *Broiler-fryers, roasters and capons can all be simmered, but because they are tender birds, they will be done in a fraction of the time; plump broiler-fryers or roasters in about 45 minutes, a capon in about 1 hour. The best policy is to watch the pot and test the chicken after the first 30 minutes, then again after another 15 minutes of simmering.*

When the bird is tender, lift it from the pot and cool until easy to handle. Remove the meat from the bones and cut into chunks, cubes, strips or dice as individual recipes direct. Strain the chicken broth, cool, then skim off all fat.

Pour into 1-pint (½ L) freezer containers or jars, leaving ½ inch (1½ cm) of head room at the top, snap or screw on the lids, label and date, then refrigerate or freeze. The stock will keep well in the refrigerator for about 1 week, in a 0°F. (−18°C.) freezer for about 6 months.

To braise (fricassee): Tender birds as well as the tough are frequently braised. It is a method found in a very wide variety of recipes that call for the bird (or parts thereof) to be browned in a little fat, then simmered until succulent with a bit of liquid, or with vegetables or fruits that will produce liquid. You will find here—and in Part II—a number of recipes in which the chicken is technically braised. The French call these recipes *sautés* because they begin with the initial browning of the chicken.

Crispy yogurt-dipped fried chicken

SERVES 2 TO 4

 This is scarcely the conventional fried chicken, but it's marvelously juicy inside and crusty-brown outside. The secret is in the coating: tart yogurt and lemon, mellowed ever so slightly with honey, then dipped in self-rising flour, which on contact with the acid "dip" magically forms a leavened batter. Do not attempt this recipe in rainy or humid weather, however, because the batter will become soggy. It's important, too, that the chicken you choose to fry be a young and tender one, no more than 3 pounds (1½ kg), or the pieces may not cook through by the time they are very brown outside. Finally, it's critical that the temperature of the fat be just right—between 325° and 335°F. (165° and 168°C.). If it gets much hotter, the chicken will over-brown by the time it's done; if it drops too low, the chicken will be greasy.

A 3-pound	broiler-fryer, disjointed	A 1½ kg
¼ teaspoon	salt	¼ teaspoon
¼ teaspoon	freshly ground black pepper	¼ teaspoon
1 cup	plain yogurt	240 ml
½ cup	milk	120 ml
2 teaspoons	light honey	2 teaspoons
1 teaspoon	finely grated lemon rind	1 teaspoon
1½ cups	unsifted self-rising flour	350 ml
1½ teaspoons	paprika	1½ teaspoons
3 quarts	peanut or vegetable oil (for deep-fat frying)	3 L

Sprinkle each piece of chicken lightly on both sides with salt and pepper. In a shallow bowl, combine the yogurt, milk, honey and lemon rind. In a pie pan, mix the flour and paprika. Dip each piece of chicken into the yogurt mixture until evenly coated (let excess drip back into the bowl), then roll in the flour until evenly coated. NOTE: *This is messy work. To save cleanup, cover a counter with wax paper, then line up the ingredients in this order: chicken, yogurt mixture, flour and finally, a large extra sheet of wax paper to contain the dipped and floured pieces of chicken.* Let the coated chicken stand at room temperature 20 to 25 minutes.

Meanwhile, place the oil in a large deep-fat fryer and insert a deep-fat thermometer. Heat over moderately high heat until the temperature registers 350°F. (175°C.). This is higher than the temperature recommended for frying chicken in the headnote above, but the minute you add the chicken to the hot fat, the temperature will plummet. The pieces to fry first are the larger, meatier ones—breasts and thighs. Being larger, these take a bit longer to cook than the smaller, bonier pieces, but they will also retain their heat better, so they are not likely to cool down too much while you cook the balance of the chicken.

Fry the breasts and thighs for about 10 minutes, keeping the temperature of the fat as nearly between 325° and 335°F. (165° and 168°C.) as possible by raising and lowering the burner heat. As soon as these pieces are done—they will be deeply brown—lift them with tongs to a metal tray lined with several thicknesses of paper toweling to drain. Cover loosely with several additional layers of paper toweling (these not only help sop up any excess oil but also help to insulate the chicken and keep it warm).

Raise the burner heat under the oil so that the temperature quickly returns to 350°F. (175°C.). Add all remaining pieces of chicken and fry about 8 minutes, again keeping the temperature as nearly constant as possible by raising and lowering the heat. NOTE: *Take the liver out after 2 to 3 minutes in the deep fat and add to the tray with the other pieces of chicken.* When the last batch is done, drain quickly on more paper toweling. Serve the chicken hot—it suffers on standing because the crust goes limp.

Pecan-crumbed chicken breasts with parsley and parmesan

SERVES 6

Exceedingly rich but exceedingly good.

3 large (about 1 pound each)	whole chicken breasts, halved	3 large (about ½ kg each)
½ teaspoon	salt	½ teaspoon
¼ teaspoon	freshly ground black pepper	¼ teaspoon
½ cup (1 stick)	unsalted butter, melted	120 ml (1 stick)
1 small	garlic clove, peeled and crushed	1 small
2 cups	soft fine bread crumbs	½ L

1 cup	finely chopped pecans	240 ml
1/4 cup	freshly grated Parmesan cheese	60 ml
2 tablespoons	finely minced parsley	2 tablespoons
2 teaspoons	rubbed sage (measure loosely packed)	2 teaspoons
1/4 teaspoon	crumbled leaf thyme	1/4 teaspoon

Sprinkle each chicken breast lightly on both sides with the salt and pepper; set aside. Combine the butter and garlic in a pie pan. In a second pie pan, mix the crumbs, pecans, Parmesan, parsley, sage and thyme well. Dip each breast first in butter until evenly coated all over, then in crumbs. You want a thick coating of crumbs, so pat the mixture onto each breast to help it stick. Arrange the crumbed breasts, skin sides up, in one layer, in a large shallow roasting pan. (The pan should be just large enough to accommodate the pieces of chicken without crowding them but not so large that the bottom of the pan is exposed at any point.) Drizzle any remaining garlic butter (there won't be much) over the chicken. Set uncovered in a moderate oven (350°F. or 175°C.) and bake 1¼ hours or until the chicken is sizzling and richly browned. Two to three times during baking, baste the pieces of chicken evenly with the pan drippings. Serve hot or at room temperature.

Chicken scallops in mustard cream

SERVES 4

This is such an easy, elegant recipe, my version of the one served at Jacqueline's, a lovely little wine bar in New York's East 60s. But it's one of those last-minute affairs that requires a bit of dexterity. Have ready all ingredients and implements you will need before you begin.

2 large (1 pound each)	chicken breasts, boned, skinned and split	2 large (½ kg each)
1/2 teaspoon	salt	1/2 teaspoon
1/4 teaspoon	crumbled leaf thyme	1/4 teaspoon
1/8 teaspoon	freshly ground black pepper	1/8 teaspoon
1/3 cup	unsifted all-purpose flour	80 ml
4 tablespoons	unsalted butter	4 tablespoons
1/4 cup	dry white wine	60 ml
1 tablespoon	mild French mustard	1 tablespoon
1/2 cup	heavy cream	120 ml

Pound each chicken breast lightly with a cutlet bat or rolling pin or heavy bottle to flatten somewhat. Sprinkle on both sides with salt, thyme and pepper, then dredge lightly in flour. Heat the butter in a large heavy skillet over moderate heat until it bubbles up, then subsides. Add the chicken breasts and brown nicely—about 3 to 4 minutes on each side. Remove the chicken to a heated platter and keep warm. Pour the wine into the skillet and heat and stir, 1 to 2 minutes, scraping up browned bits on the bottom of the skillet; smooth in the mustard, add the cream and boil hard 2 to 3 minutes until reduced by about half—the sauce should be about the consistency of sour cream. Pour over the chicken breasts and serve.

Roast chicken stuffed with chopped chicken livers

SERVES 4

What's unusual about this recipe is that the chopped chicken liver mixture is stuffed not into the body cavity but spread underneath the skin into a smooth layer on top of the breast. Into the body cavity go an onion, carrot and celery rib so that their mingled flavors permeate the bird.

A 4-pound	ready-to-cook roaster (reserve the liver to use in the stuffing; freeze remaining giblets to use another time)	A 2 kg
1 small	carrot, peeled and halved	1 small
1 medium-size	celery rib, trimmed and halved	1 medium-size
1 small	yellow onion, peeled and quartered	1 small
1 tablespoon	unsalted butter, at room temperature	1 tablespoon
¼ teaspoon	salt	¼ teaspoon
	STUFFING:	
3 large	shallots, peeled and minced	3 large
1 teaspoon	finely minced fresh ginger	1 teaspoon
2 tablespoons	unsalted butter	2 tablespoons
½ teaspoon	crumbled leaf marjoram	½ teaspoon
¼ teaspoon	crumbled leaf rosemary	¼ teaspoon
Pinch	crumbled leaf thyme	Pinch
Pinch	freshly grated nutmeg	Pinch
¼ cup	dry vermouth	60 ml
½ pound	chicken livers + the liver from the roaster above	225 g
1 cup	fine soft bread crumbs	240 ml
2 tablespoons	finely minced parsley	2 tablespoons
¼ teaspoon	salt	¼ teaspoon
Light sprinkling	freshly ground black pepper	Light sprinkling

Separating the skin of a chicken from the meat is surprisingly easy, but it's important to work slowly (also to remove any rings from your fingers) so that you don't rip or puncture the skin. Place the bird on its back on a counter, then starting at the neck opening, run your fingers down underneath the skin, pulling it free of the breast. It comes loose quickly, but should there be any recalcitrant strands of connective tissue, snip them with kitchen shears. Continue freeing the breast skin until you have worked your way clear down to the legs. Do not loosen the skin all the way to the vent (body cavity); what you want is a large pocket over the breast meat into which you can scoop the stuffing. Set the bird aside while you prepare the stuffing.

For the stuffing: Stir-fry the shallots and ginger in the butter in a medium-size heavy skillet over moderate heat 2 to 3 minutes until limp and golden. Add the marjoram, rosemary, thyme and nutmeg and stir-fry a minute or so to heighten their flavors. Pour in the vermouth, raise the burner heat and reduce until only a thin glaze remains on the bottom of the skillet—4 to 5 minutes. Reduce the burner heat to moderate, dump in the chicken livers and stir-fry 3 to 4 minutes—just until no longer pink. Purée the skillet mixture in a food processor fitted with the metal chopping blade or in an electric blender at high speed. NOTE: *If you have neither processor nor blender, put the skillet mixture through a meat grinder fitted with the fine blade.* Combine the liver purée with the bread crumbs, parsley, salt and pepper. (I simply dump these last four ingredients into the processor work bowl on top of the puréed livers and buzz briefly three to four times until creamy-smooth.)

To stuff the chicken: Using a rubber scraper, scoop up a gob of the liver stuffing; hold the neck skin up with one hand, then shove the scraperful of stuffing gently down underneath the skin toward the legs; turn the rubber scraper as needed so that you can "wipe" the liver stuffing off on the breast. Continue in this fashion, working your way from the bottom of the "pocket" to the top, until you have used up all of the stuffing. TIP: *Massage the skin of the bird from time to time as you add the stuffing so that it is evenly distributed.* When you have finished stuffing the pocket, fold the neck skin back against the back of the bird and fasten with a poultry pin. Also fold the wings against the back of the bird. Tuck the pieces of carrot, celery and onion into the body cavity. Tie the legs of the bird together, then tie the tail to the legs so that the body cavity is more or less closed.

Now rub the bird lightly all over with the softened butter and sprinkle with the salt. Place the bird, breast side up, on a rack in a shallow roasting pan. Set, uncovered, in a very hot oven (450°F. or 230°C.) and sear for 15 minutes. Reduce the oven temperature at once to moderately slow (325°F. or 165°C.) and roast the chicken about 1 hour and 15 minutes longer or until the leg moves easily in the hip socket.

Take the bird from the oven and let stand at room temperature 15 minutes. Remove the strings and poultry pin; also remove the vegetables from the body cavity and discard. (If your Scottish soul rebels against throwing the vegetables out, save them to use in a soup, stew or casserole.)

A word about carving the chicken: It's not as difficult as you may think. In fact, the method is the standard one. Slice off each leg at the hip joint, then each wing at the shoulder. Next, starting in the middle of the breast and following the line of the rib cage, remove each breast intact. Divide up the light and dark meat, honoring family's or guests' preferences, and make certain that each person receives an ample spoonful of the stuffing.

Gravy? I don't make it for this particular recipe because the bird is so moist, the skin so crisp and the stuffing so rich. But certainly you may make a gravy from the pan drippings, if you like. Follow any of the methods described earlier in this chapter under **To roast,** in The Ways of Cooking Chicken.

Cornish game hens indienne with raisin, rice and pine nut stuffing

SERVES 4

The stuffing is lightly curried as is the buttery wine mixture used to baste the birds as they roast. There is more stuffing here than you can spoon into the game hens (each holds precious little); foil-wrap it and bake it alongside the birds so that everyone can have more. NOTE: *If you prefer to use this stuffing in chicken, by all means do. There is enough here for a 4- to 5-pound (2 to 2¼ kg) roaster.*

4 small (about 1 pound each)	Cornish game hens, preferably fresh, although thawed frozen birds may be substituted	4 small (about ½ kg each)
	RAISIN, RICE AND PINE NUT STUFFING:	
1 medium-size	yellow onion, peeled and minced	1 medium-size
2 tablespoons	unsalted butter	2 tablespoons
½ teaspoon	curry powder	½ teaspoon
¼ teaspoon	crumbled leaf rosemary	¼ teaspoon
¼ teaspoon	crumbled leaf thyme	¼ teaspoon
—	the game hen hearts and livers	—
1⅓ cups, in all	converted rice	315 ml, in all
2 cups	chicken broth	½ L
¼ teaspoon	salt	¼ teaspoon
⅛ teaspoon	freshly ground black pepper	⅛ teaspoon
⅓ cup	finely minced golden seedless raisins (sultanas)	80 ml
⅓ cup	coarsely chopped pine nuts	80 ml

¼ cup (½ stick)	*melted unsalted butter*	60 ml (½ stick)
2 tablespoons	*dry Port, sherry or Madeira*	2 tablespoons
1 teaspoon	*curry powder*	1 teaspoon

Take the giblets from the body cavity of each game hen. Mince and reserve the hearts and livers; you'll use these in the stuffing. Wrap and freeze the remaining giblets to use another day in making chicken stock or broth. Now wipe the birds inside and out with well-dampened paper toweling; set the birds aside while you prepare the stuffing.

For the raisin, rice and pine nut stuffing: Stir-fry the onion in the butter in a medium-size heavy saucepan over moderate heat about 5 minutes until limp and golden; blend in the curry powder, rosemary and thyme and allow to mellow 2 to 3 minutes to take the raw edge off the curry. Now add the reserved minced hearts and livers and sauté, stirring now and then, 2 to 3 minutes until they are no longer pink. Stir in 1 cup (240 ml) of the rice and stir-fry until translucent and golden—2 to 3 minutes. Pour in the broth, sprinkle in the salt and pepper, raise the burner heat slightly and bring all to a rapid boil. Adjust the burner heat so that the broth bubbles gently, then boil uncovered for 3 minutes. Stir in the remaining rice, cover and cook about 15 minutes or until almost all water is absorbed. Uncover the pan, turn burner heat down low, fork the rice up, then cook another 2 to 3 minutes, just until the rice seems dry. NOTE: *The rice will still be quite firm, but that's as it should be because it will cook further in the oven.* Take the rice from the heat and fold in the sultanas and pine nuts.

Now stuff each of the hens, filling the neck cavity first (you will be able to get only a teaspoon or so of the stuffing into each). Spoon in the stuffing lightly—never pack it down—because it will expand as it bakes. Fold the neck skin against the back, sealing the stuffing in, then fasten with a toothpick. Now stuff the body cavities of each bird (I simply upend the birds and spoon the stuffing in, letting it drop in lightly). As you stuff each bird, fold the wings against the back, then close the body cavity by tying the tail and drumsticks together. Wrap the remaining stuffing in foil and refrigerate for the time being.

Place the birds, breast side up, in a shallow roasting pan just large enough to accommodate them without crowding. Whisk together all basting ingredients and brush liberally over each bird. Roast the birds, uncovered, in a moderately hot oven (375°F. or 190°C.) for 1 to 1¼ hours, brushing with the basting mixture every 15 to 20 minutes.

After the birds have roasted ½ hour, set the foil-wrapped packet of stuffing on the oven shelf beside the birds. Continue roasting the birds until they are richly browned and a drumstick moves easily at the hip joint when you nudge it (one of the most reliable tests of doneness for all poultry). Remove the hens from the oven and remove all toothpicks and string. Allow the birds to rest 10 minutes, then serve. Pour the pan drippings into a heated gravy boat and pass the extra dressing separately in a small bowl.

Old-fashioned fricassee of dark meat of chicken

SERVES 4

You can, if you prefer, prepare chicken breasts this way instead of thighs and drumsticks, or use a combination of dark and light meat, or a disjointed chicken. Just make sure that the total amount of meat comes to about 4 pounds (2 kilos). Serve with mashed potatoes, rice or fresh-baked biscuits (for catching every last drop of gravy) and a crisp green vegetable such as Brussels sprouts or broccoli.

4 large	chicken thighs	4 large
4 large	drumsticks	4 large
4 tablespoons	unsalted butter	4 tablespoons
1 large	yellow onion, peeled and minced	1 large
¾ pound	mushrooms, wiped clean and sliced thin	⅓ kg
1 teaspoon	crumbled leaf marjoram	1 teaspoon
¼ teaspoon	crumbled leaf rosemary	¼ teaspoon
Pinch	crumbled leaf thyme	Pinch
Pinch	ground mace	Pinch
1 teaspoon	finely grated lemon or orange rind	1 teaspoon
2 cups	chicken broth	½ L
⅓ cup	dry vermouth	80 ml
2 tablespoons	lemon juice	2 tablespoons
5 large	egg yolks, lightly beaten	5 large
¼ cup	heavy cream	60 ml
To taste	salt and white pepper	To taste
2 tablespoons	minced parsley	2 tablespoons

Brown the thighs and drumsticks well on all sides in 3 tablespoons of the butter in a medium-size heavy kettle over moderate heat; lift to a large bowl and reserve. Add the remaining tablespoon of butter to the kettle, then stir-fry the onion and mushrooms 8 to 10 minutes until limp and all juices have evaporated. Add the marjoram, rosemary, thyme, mace and lemon rind and stir-fry a minute or two to release their flavors. Add the chicken broth and vermouth and bring to a simmer. Return the thighs and drumsticks to the kettle, distributing them evenly, cover and simmer 45 to 50 minutes or until a fork will pierce a thigh easily. Lift chicken to a warmed plate, cover loosely with foil and keep warm.

Strain the kettle liquid, reserving both the solids and the liquid. Purée the solids with about 1 cup (240 ml) of the liquid in a processor fitted with the metal chopping blade or in an electric blender at high speed or by forcing through a food mill. Return purée to the kettle and add the reserved liquid and the lemon juice. Turn the burner heat up high and boil this mixture hard for about 15 minutes or until reduced in volume by about one-third. Turn burner heat to low. Briskly stir a little of the hot kettle liquid into the egg yolks, then stir back into the kettle. Add the cream and heat, stirring constantly, for about 3 minutes, or until thickened and smooth. In no circumstances allow the mixture to boil or it will curdle. Season to taste with salt and white pepper, then return the thighs and drumsticks to the kettle. Warm them slowly for about 2 minutes, then transfer all to a deep platter, scatter the parsley on top and serve.

Turkey

Of all the meats available today, turkey is the only one that costs *less* than it did fifteen years ago. But that's only part of the good news.

Today's turkey is 50 percent meatier than the birds of Thanksgivings past, and yet it is quicker to cook because of its greater tenderness. It is low in calories and cholesterol but loaded with top-quality protein. Best of all, turkey is now available the year round—both fresh and frozen. Finally, turkey has come of age gastronomically, thanks to innovative chefs who have capitalized upon its versatility.

The kinds and qualities of turkeys

As with red meats and chicken, all turkey shipped interstate must be inspected for wholesomeness, and their wrappers or labels will bear the round USDA (U.S. Department of Agriculture) inspection seal. Turkeys may also be graded for quality (it's the packers' or producers' option). The top grade for turkey—and the only one you're likely to see—is USDA GRADE A. These are plump-breasted birds, well shaped, with smooth, unbroken skin. The two lesser grades for turkey—USDA GRADE B and USDA GRADE C—are used primarily for processed foods.

In the old days (25 to 30 years ago), it seemed, you just went out and bought a turkey big enough to feed a given number of people. In other words, a turkey was a turkey. Not so today, as these categories quickly prove:

Fryer-roasters: These are either young turkeys or especially bred Beltsvilles, small meaty birds weighing from 4 to 9 pounds (1⅘ to 4 kg). They are small enough and tender enough to panfry but are equally delicious when roasted, braised or barbecued. And there are additional bonuses: two small turkeys, for example, instead of one whopping bird will mean double the number of drumsticks, breasts and thighs—even accommodate two kinds of dressing, if you like.

Hens: Plump and tender females weighing from 12 to 16 pounds (5½ to 7¼ kg). Best when roasted.

Tom turkeys: These are the big boys—males tipping the scales at 20 pounds (9 kg) or more. They're smooth-grained, meaty and tender, however, and the perfect choice for large parties. Like turkey hens, toms should be roasted.

Fryer-roasters, hens and toms are all available either frozen through supermarkets or fresh-chilled—trade lingo for fresh, iced birds—sold primarily through custom butchers. Occasionally, a supermarket will offer fresh-chilled turkeys, too.

There are, in addition to whole birds, literally dozens of other forms of turkey available today:

Half turkey: Just what it says, half a bird; available either fresh or frozen.

Turkey breast: You can buy these with the bone in or boneless, fresh or frozen. They are ready to roast and, of course, all white meat.

Turkey steaks and cutlets: These are a godsend because they look—**and cook**—like veal steaks and *scaloppine,* but they cost "mere pennies" by comparison. Turkey steaks are generally cut from ½ to ¾ inch (1½ to 2 cm) thick and cutlets ¼ to ⅜ inch (¾ to 1 cm) thick. Both are boneless, both are solid white meat and both can be substituted in any recipes for veal steaks or *scaloppine* (see the section on Veal in the Meat chapter).

Thighs: Juicy pieces of dark meat from the second (upper) joint of the turkey leg. One of the more economical parts of the bird, thighs are best when oven-fried or barbecued.

Drumsticks: Inexpensive and easy to prepare, turkey drumsticks contain considerable dark, succulent meat. Like thighs, these are best, I think, when oven-fried, braised or barbecued.

Wings: One of the most economical of all turkey parts. I prefer wings for "meat," that is, I poach or stew them, separate the meat from the bones and skin, then use it for soups, stews, salads and casseroles.

Hindquarter roasts: Drumstick, thigh, tail and back—all dark meat and a particularly good buy.

Ground turkey: This is to turkey as hamburger is to beef—raw ground meat and the perfect choice for patties, loaves and croquettes. Unlike hamburger, however, turkey meat is too lean to use solo and will be juicier combined about half-and-half with ground pork or sausage.

Turkey giblets, necks and tails: You can buy giblets (the heart, gizzard and liver), by the packet in many supermarkets, also the necks and tails. They're ideal for soups and stews.

Turkey rolls: Fully cooked and ready to slice or dice into soups, salads, and casseroles. No bones. Good hot or cold.

Rolled turkey roasts: Unlike turkey rolls, these are **raw** turkey breasts or hindquarters that have been boned and rolled, then frozen. They are ready to thaw and roast. You can buy a rolled turkey roast of white meat only, dark meat only or a mixture of the two.

Turkey pan roast: Like rolled turkey roasts, these are available with all white meat, all dark meat or a combination of white and dark. But unlike them, they are packed in a foil roasting pan and can be shoved into the oven solidly frozen. Many even come packing their own gravy.

The modern turkey is getting to be like the "shmoo," that lovable, accommodating critter dreamed up by the late cartoonist Al Capp, if you look at the list of **processed** turkey products available today. "Shmoos," remember, could—and would—turn themselves into almost anything edible; their sole purpose was to please. The turkey's, it would seem, is the same, given its many guises: turkey ham, smoked turkey, turkey franks and weiners, turkey bologna, salami, pastrami and sausage, even baconlike turkey strips. All can be bought in almost every supermarket.

How much turkey should you allow per person?

Large turkeys contain proportionately more meat to bone than small turkeys, so they will serve more persons per pound or half kilo than small birds. I like to allow from ½ to ¾ pound (¼ to ⅓ kg) of turkey per person if the bird weighs more than 12 pounds (5½ kg) and ¾ to 1 pound (⅓ to ½ kg) per person if it weighs less than 12 pounds (5½ kg). As for turkey parts, I allow 1 full pound (½ kg) per person for bony cuts (wings, backs, etc.) and ½ to ¾ pound (¼ to ⅓ kg) for the meaty ones (breasts, thighs, drumsticks). For boneless turkey roasts (or turkey meat), I figure on about ½ pound (¼ kg) per person.

The care and keeping of turkey

Frozen turkeys—and the majority of them sold today **are** frozen—should simply be placed in a 0°F. (−18°C.) freezer in their original wrappers without delay and kept there until you are ready to cook them.

Fresh-chilled turkeys should be unwrapped, placed on a large plate and draped loosely with wax paper, plastic food wrap or foil. I take the packet of giblets from the body cavity, unwrap them, place in a small bowl, cover with plastic wrap and refrigerate separately. Fresh-chilled turkeys should be cooked within two days after purchase.

SHOULD FROZEN TURKEYS BE THAWED BEFORE THEY'RE COOKED?

Whole turkeys, **yes**—except for those that are commercially stuffed. Roast these as package labels direct. The three methods of thawing recommended by the National Turkey Federation (and the ones I use) are as follows:

In the refrigerator: Slow but safe. Place the turkey (still in its original wrapper) on a tray and set in the refrigerator. Do not open or puncture the wrapper. **Thawing time:** 3 to 4 days, depending upon the size of the bird. Check the bird often after the second day; as soon as it feels soft and you can move a leg or wing, it is thawed.

On the kitchen counter: A much quicker way to thaw a turkey. Pop the bird (still in its own wrapper) inside a heavy brown paper bag, then set on a metal tray on an out-of-the-way counter. The reason for the paper bag is to provide some insulation from the room temperature so that the skin of the turkey doesn't become too warm and spoil. **Thawing time:** about 1 hour per pound (½ kg) of bird.

In cold water: This is the fastest way of all. Submerge the wrapped turkey in a kettle of cold water and let stand, changing the water every hour or so. **Thawing time:** about ½ hour per pound (½ kg) of turkey.

As soon as the turkey is thawed, remove the bag of giblets from the body cavity and the neck from the neck cavity. Roast the turkey at once or refrigerate it—but for no more than 24 hours. NOTE: *Never, ever refreeze a turkey once it has thawed, because you will be flirting with food poisoning.*

To stuff or not to stuff a turkey

Turkey with all the trimmings is our Thanksgiving tradition. But researchers at Cornell University now question the wisdom of stuffing a turkey because of the possibility of food poisoning. Poultry stuffing, alas, is a perfect medium for bacterial growth—warm, dark and moist. Heat penetrates a roasting turkey so slowly there is time enough for the microbes to grow and produce toxins.

The Cornell researchers' conclusions are:

Roast turkeys weighing 18 pounds (8 kg) or more **unstuffed.**

When stuffing smaller birds, avoid adding ingredients to the stuffings that increase the likelihood of spoilage: broth, giblets, raw egg, cornbread, oysters. NOTE: *Broth, giblets and oysters should all be heated to the boiling point before they are added to a stuffing.*

To minimize the risk of spoilage, substitute orange or cranberry juice for half of the liquid called for in a stuffing recipe (the acid of these juices inhibits bacterial growth). Also effective: chopped fresh cranberries or raisins.

Make certain that all implements or utensils you use when making a stuffing are spotlessly clean—and this means **chopping boards** (not to mention your own hands).

Stuff the bird **just before you roast it,** not earlier. You can, of course, partially prepare the stuffing ahead of time. But keep the dry and liquid ingredients separate, each tightly covered in the refrigerator, and combine them just before you stuff the bird.

To bake the stuffing separately: Since a very little turkey flavor permeates the stuffing, there's little reason to stuff a turkey. And as I've just pointed out, there are a good many reasons **not** to. My favorite way to cook the stuffing is to bake it in a large, shallow buttered casserole that's pretty enough to come to the dinner table. I simply make up a big batch of my favorite stuffing, allowing 1 cup (240 ml) per serving, cover it snugly with foil, then set it in the oven an hour before the turkey is done and let it cook along with the turkey. To give the stuffing a bit of turkey flavor, I mix in 4 to 5 tablespoons of the pan drippings, then re-cover the turkey and return it to the turned-off oven to keep warm while I let the turkey rest and make the gravy. This method is so much simpler—and safer—than our traditional way of stuffing the big bird.

How to roast a turkey

If the turkey is a frozen one, thaw by one of the three methods described earlier. Remove the wrapping from the thawed turkey; also remove the giblets and neck from the body and neck cavities. Release the legs from the band of skin near the vent (body cavity) or from the wire hock lock, rinse the turkey inside and out with cool water, then pat dry with paper toweling.

If you intend to stuff the turkey, allow about ¾ to 1 cup (180 to 240 ml) of stuffing per pound of bird. Spoon the stuffing first into the neck cavity—but don't pack it in, just let it drop from the spoon into the cavity. When the neck cavity is full, fasten the neck skin back against the back of the turkey with a poultry pin. Now upend the turkey so that you can spoon the stuffing directly into the body cavity. When the body cavity is full, reinsert the legs in the band of skin or return them to the hock lock. Tuck the wing tips akimbo against the back of the turkey. NOTE: *Trussing is almost a thing of the past (thank goodness) with these new "tucked turkeys"—turkeys with skin bands or hock locks to hold the legs snugly to the body. The whole purpose of trussing was merely to make the bird as compact as possible so that it would roast more evenly.*

Place the turkey, breast side up, on a rack in a shallow open roasting pan. If you want to use a meat thermometer, insert it into the center of the inside thigh, next to the body, but make certain that its tip rests in meat, not against bone, which will give you a false reading. Tent the turkey lightly with foil, shiny side down (this is to prevent overbrowning), then roast the turkey in a constant, moderately slow oven (325°F. or 165°C.), using the following timetable as a guide. Baste the bird, if you like, every half hour or so with melted butter or with a half-and-half mixture of melted butter and chicken broth, wine or—my favorite—beer. Remove the foil during the last half hour of cooking so that the skin browns richly.

APPROXIMATE ROASTING TIME FOR TURKEY IN A 325°F. (165°C.) OVEN

WEIGHT	UNSTUFFED	STUFFED
8–12 lbs. (3½–5½ kg)	3–4 hours	4–5 hours
12–16 lbs. (5½–7¼ kg)	3½–5 hours	4½–6 hours
16–20 lbs. (5½–9 kg)	4½–6 hours	5½–6½ hours (not recommended for birds more than 18 lbs. or 8 kg)
20–24 lbs. (9–10¾ kg)	5½–6½ hours	not recommended

Tests for doneness: A meat thermometer will register between 180° and 185°F. (82° and 85°C.); the thickest part of the drumstick will feel soft, and the drumstick itself will move easily in the hip socket.

As soon as the turkey is done, remove from the oven and let stand on the counter 15 to 20 minutes to allow the juices to settle so that carving will be easier.

To make gravy: Use the pan drippings, of course. But first pour them into a measuring cup and let the fat rise to the top. For each 1 cup of gravy that you want, spoon 2 tablespoons of the fat drippings back into the roasting pan and blend in 2 tablespoons of flour. Set over moderately low heat and cook, stirring browned bits up from the bottom of the pan, for 3 to 5 minutes or until the fat-flour mixture is a pale topaz brown. Now for each 2 tablespoons of fat and flour used, pour in 1 cup (240 ml) of liquid—use pan drippings skimmed of fat **plus** chicken broth and/or milk, depending upon whether you want a brown gravy or a "cream" one. Cook the gravy, stirring constantly, 3 to 5 minutes until thickened and no raw starch taste remains. **For Giblet Gravy:** Simply mix in the minced turkey giblets, which have first been simmered until tender in a little water—the gizzard, heart and neck can simmer 2 to 3 hours, but the liver only 10 to 20 minutes, so add it at the very end. For extra flavor, add a little salt to the cooking water, also 4 to 5 peppercorns, 3 whole cloves, a small bay leaf and a chunked small onion, carrot and celery rib. Strain this broth and use for part of the gravy liquid.

Caring for roast turkey leftovers: If you have stuffed the turkey, you should "unstuff it" before you refrigerate the bird. I simply spoon the stuffing into a plastic container, snap on the lid and set it in the coldest part of the refrigerator. I also cut all meat from the turkey carcass, place it in a large bowl, then cover the bowl with plastic food wrap. Any leftover gravy should be poured into a small jar, covered tightly and refrigerated. If I think that I'll be unable to eat up the balance of a turkey within three days, I separate the dark meat from the white, then foil-wrap each snugly in quantities I'm apt to use for a recipe—2 cups (½ L), for example—label and store in the freezer. Frozen cooked turkey will retain most of its original quality for about one month in a 0°F. (−18°C.) freezer.

Other ways of cooking turkey

Turkey production has become so controlled, so scientific that you can count on a tender bird nearly every time. So the ways of cooking turkey are determined less by degree of tenderness than by personal choice and by size of bird. Anything heavier than 8 pounds (3½ kg) I automatically roast because I frankly find big birds too cumbersome to prepare any other way. The small fryer-roasters, however, can be panfried or oven-fried, braised and barbecued.

To panfry: Choose a fairly small turkey—about 4 to 6 pounds (1⅘ to 2¾ kg)—and have it disjointed just as you would chicken so that there are 2 drumsticks, 2 thighs, 4 breast pieces (each half breast should be halved horizontally), 2 wings and 4 back pieces. Sprinkle the pieces lightly with salt and pepper, then dredge in about 1 cup (240 ml) flour (for added flavor, mix about 1 teaspoon of paprika and/or rubbed sage into the dredging flour).

Pour vegetable oil into a large heavy skillet to a depth of ½ inch (1½ cm), set over moderately high heat until a cube of bread will sizzle in it, then starting with the large meaty pieces—breasts and thighs—begin browning the turkey. When all pieces are nicely browned on all sides—about 20 minutes altogether—turn the heat down to low, add 2 to 3 tablespoons of water, wine or broth, cover tightly and simmer ¾ to 1 hour or until you can pierce the largest pieces easily with a fork. Remove the cover and cook about 10 minutes longer—just until the skin crisps a bit.

To oven-fry: Disjoint and dredge a 4- to 6-pound (1⅘ to 2¾ kg) turkey as directed above for panfrying. Pour 1 cup (240 ml) of melted butter or margarine into a large shallow baking pan, then add the pieces of turkey, rolling them in the butter as you place them in the pan and ending with all of them skin side down. NOTE: *The turkey pieces should be in a single layer, so choose a pan big enough to accommodate them all.* Bake, uncovered, in a moderate oven (350°F. or 175°C.) for 45 minutes. Using tongs, turn the pieces of turkey skin side up and bake 45 minutes longer or until the breasts and thighs are fork-tender.

To braise (fricassee): This really is an extension of panfrying, with dozens of variations on a single technique. Braising, quite simply, means browning a meat, then cooking it in the company of liquid or moisture-yielding ingredients until tender. So begin as directed for panfrying: Season, dredge and brown the pieces of turkey. Remove the browned pieces to a large bowl and reserve. Drain all but about 2 tablespoons of the oil from the skillet. Your options now are many: You might brown a large yellow onion or two in the drippings along with a couple of crushed cloves of garlic, then slosh in a little white wine and/or tomato juice, return the turkey to the skillet, cover and simmer about 1½ hours until tender. Or you might sauté a few minced leeks and ½ pound (¼ kg) of sliced mushrooms in the drippings, add a little chicken broth and sherry, return the turkey to the skillet, cover and simmer until tender. The possibilities are as broad, really, as your imagination.

To barbecue: See the recipe that follows; it's an old North Carolina specialty.

Roast turkey with lemon and ham stuffing balls

SERVES 8 TO 10

 For America's Bicentennial, I wrote a cookbook-cum-travel guide that featured more than three dozen of America's beloved restored villages. One of the most imaginative of all the recipes I discovered during my research is this one from Old Sturbridge Village in Massachusetts, where the women have been uncommonly inventive about using up the extra stuffing. Instead of baking it *en casserole*, they shape it into small balls, brown them in butter, then use them to garnish the platter.

A 10–12-pound	ready-to-cook turkey	A 4½–5½ kg
¾ teaspoon	salt	¾ teaspoon
¼ teaspoon	freshly ground black pepper	¼ teaspoon
¼ cup	unsifted all-purpose flour	60 ml
1 cup (2 sticks)	melted unsalted butter (for basting)	240 ml (2 sticks)
	LEMON AND HAM STUFFING:	
6 cups	soft fine bread crumbs	1½ L
1 cup (firmly packed)	ground suet	240 ml (firmly packed)
1¼ cups	minced Smithfield or Virginia ham	300 ml
2½ teaspoons	crumbled leaf marjoram	2½ teaspoons
1 teaspoon	finely grated lemon rind	1 teaspoon
1 large	lemon, juiced	1 large
1½ teaspoons	salt	1½ teaspoons
⅛ teaspoon	freshly ground black pepper	⅛ teaspoon
⅛ teaspoon	freshly grated nutmeg	⅛ teaspoon
2 large	egg yolks	2 large
¼ cup (½ stick)	melted unsalted butter (for browning stuffing balls)	60 ml (½ stick)

	GIBLET GRAVY:	
—	the turkey neck and giblets	—
6 cups	water	1½ L
7 tablespoons	fat, skimmed from the pan drippings	7 tablespoons
6 tablespoons	all-purpose flour	6 tablespoons
½ teaspoon	salt	½ teaspoon
⅛ teaspoon	freshly ground black pepper	⅛ teaspoon

Rub the turkey inside and out with the salt and pepper, then rub the skin of the bird well all over with the flour to coat evenly but lightly.

For the stuffing: Mix together with your hands the bread crumbs, suet, ham, marjoram, lemon rind and juice, salt, pepper, nutmeg and egg yolks. Fork the mixture up until it is fluffy, then drop lightly into first the neck cavity, then the body cavity of the turkey. Cover the remaining stuffing and refrigerate until about an hour before serving. Skewer the neck skin of the turkey flat to the back, enclosing the stuffing in the neck cavity, then reinsert the legs in the band of skin or return them to the hock lock. Tuck the wing tips akimbo against the back of the bird. Place the bird, breast side up, on a rack in a large shallow roasting pan and roast, uncovered, in a moderately slow oven (325°F. or 165°C.) for 1 hour. Baste lavishly with melted butter and roast 2½ to 3 hours longer, basting often with the remaining butter and pan drippings, until the turkey is richly browned and the leg joint moves easily.

While the turkey roasts, start the giblet gravy: Place the turkey neck and giblets in a large heavy saucepan, add the water and simmer uncovered for 20 minutes; remove the liver and heart and refrigerate. Continue simmering the neck and gizzard as long as the turkey roasts; discard the neck and mince the gizzard, liver and heart. Strain the giblet stock, measure out 2½ cups (600 ml) and add the minced giblets (save any remaining stock to use in making a soup or sauce another time).

About 1 hour before the turkey has finished roasting, shape the remaining stuffing into balls about the size of crab apples (about 2 inches or 5 cm in diameter). Brown lightly in a skillet in the ¼ cup melted butter over moderate heat. Transfer the stuffing balls to a small baking pan, arranging them in one layer. Pour any skillet drippings over the balls, cover snugly with foil and set in the oven with the turkey to bake for 1 hour. When the turkey is done (it will take about 4 hours for a 10-pound or 4½ kg bird), remove from the oven and let rest 20 minutes on the kitchen counter so that the juices will settle, facilitating carving. Turn the oven off but leave the stuffing balls in the oven to keep warm.

To finish the giblet gravy: Quickly skim 7 tablespoons of fat from the turkey drippings and place them in a medium-size saucepan; blend in the flour. Heat and stir the mixture (roux) until it turns a pale brown. Add the reserved 2½ cups (600 ml) giblet stock and the minced giblets and heat and stir until the mixture thickens, 2 to 3 minutes. Turn the heat to the lowest point, add the salt and pepper and let the gravy mellow until you are ready to serve the turkey.

Arrange the turkey on a heated large platter. Surround with stuffing balls, ruffs of watercress and, for added color, clusters of whole raw cranberries. Pour the gravy into a gravy boat and pass separately.

Old-time barbecued turkey the Tar Heel way

SERVES 4

The Tar Heel state is North Carolina, and this way of barbecuing turkey or chicken (for chicken is equally good prepared this way) is the one I remember from my early days as an assistant home demonstration agent in Iredell County. This barbecue sauce, you'll note, is **without** ketchup— which is as it should be, I think. The ideal accompaniment: a cool, crisp coleslaw.

A 4-pound	fryer-roaster turkey, disjointed	A 2 kg
2 large	garlic cloves, peeled and halved	2 large
1½ cups	water	350 ml
	BARBECUE SAUCE:	
1 tablespoon	honey or light corn syrup	1 tablespoon
¼ teaspoon	dry mustard	¼ teaspoon
1 teaspoon	salt	1 teaspoon
⅛ teaspoon	freshly ground black pepper	⅛ teaspoon
1 cup	tomato juice	240 ml
¼ cup	cider vinegar	60 ml
¼ cup (½ stick)	melted unsalted butter	60 ml (½ stick)
1 tablespoon	Worcestershire sauce	1 tablespoon

Place the pieces of turkey, skin side down, in a large shallow roasting pan; drop in the garlic cloves and pour in the water. Set, uncovered, in a moderately hot oven (375°F. or 190°C.) and bake 45 minutes, turning occasionally.

Meanwhile, prepare the barbecue sauce: In a small heavy saucepan, blend together the honey, mustard, salt and pepper; mix in the tomato juice, vinegar, melted butter and Worcestershire sauce. Set over low heat and bring slowly to a boil, stirring frequently. Turn heat to its lowest point and keep the sauce warm.

When the turkey has cooked 45 minutes, pour the barbecue sauce evenly over all and cook the turkey about 1 hour longer, basting frequently with the sauce in the pan. NOTE: *If the sauce should thicken too much before the turkey is tender, blend about 1 cup (240 ml) of boiling water with the sauce in the pan.*

To serve, lift the turkey to a hot platter, strain the barbecue sauce remaining in the baking pan into a small sauceboat and pass separately.

Other poultry

Once sold almost exclusively by fancy butchers, ducks, geese, even squabs, are showing up with surprising frequency in supermarkets today. Usually they are frozen, but if you live near the source, you may be able to buy chilled fresh-killed birds between May and January, which is considered "the season."

All of these birds, if sold interstate, must be federally inspected for wholesomeness—look for the U.S. Department of Agriculture's (USDA's) round inspection stamp on the wing tag or package. Most ducks and geese, moreover, are also graded as to quality, although grading is entirely voluntary (a grower or producer must request it). The top grade for ducks and geese is the same as for chickens and turkeys: USDA GRADE A (the shield-shape grade stamp will appear alongside the inspection seal on the wrapper or wing tag). As for the lower grades—USDA B and C—you will rarely see them.

Ducks

All ducks and ducklings raised for the table today are descended from a single small flock of White Pekins introduced into Long Island, New York, about a hundred years ago. Although now grown in seven other states, these are still marketed primarily as "Long Island ducklings." **Ducklings,** by the way, is precisely what they are: young birds of from 7 to 8 weeks, weighing 4 to 5 pounds (1⅘ to 2¼ kg). **Ducks** are older (10 weeks or more), bigger (over 5 lbs. or 2¼ kg) and tougher.

How much duck or duckling per person? All ducks contain a lot of fat and a lot of bone, so allow 1¼ pounds (about ½ kg) per person.

Best ways to store: As I've already pointed out, most ducks and ducklings sold today are frozen, usually inside tightly fitting plastic wrappers, so they need only be rushed home from the store and put straightaway into a 0°F. (−18°C.) freezer. **Storage time:** about 3 months.

As for fresh ducks, remove their store wrappers, also the bag of giblets inside the body cavity. Place the bird on a large plate, cover loosely with plastic food wrap, wax paper or foil and set in the coldest part of the refrigerator. The giblets may be placed on the plate beside the bird if there is room for them. Otherwise, unwrap them, empty into a small bowl, cover and refrigerate. **Storage Time:** 2 to 3 days.

Best ways to cook: I personally like to **roast** or **braise** ducklings. Because of their high fat content, I find them too hazardous to broil—with fat sputtering all over the inside of the broiler, there's a good chance of fire. As for stewing, I again find the duck's fattiness objectionable because its musky flavor permeates absolutely everything (duck fat, by the way, is extremely difficult to digest). By roasting or braising the birds, you can easily drain the fat off as it collects.

Geese

Almost all geese that come to market today will be solidly frozen and encased in plastic wrappers. They will be young birds (usually between 4 and 6 months of age) and weigh from 6 to 14 pounds (2¾ to 6½ kg).

How much goose per person? Geese are slightly meatier than ducks (but only slightly), so you should allow 1 full pound (½ kg) of bird per person.

Best ways to store: Frozen birds should be thrust into a 0°F. (−18°C.) freezer in their original wrapper the minute you get them home from the store (and waste no time getting them home lest they begin to thaw). **Storage time:** 6 months.

Fresh birds, if you should be so lucky as to find them, should be unwrapped. Remove the bag of giblets and the neck from the body and neck cavities. Place these in a small bowl (I usually empty the giblets out of the bag), then cover and refrigerate. The bird itself should be placed on a tray or in a shallow pan, then loosely covered with plastic food wrap, wax paper or foil and stored in the coldest part of the refrigerator. **Storage time:** 2 to 3 days.

Best ways to cook: Most of the geese marketed today are young and tender enough to roast, and for me, that is the ideal way to cook a goose. The French, of course, have raised the preparation of goose to high culinary art: they braise them, stew them, poach them, cook them *en daube* (braised with herbs in a big pot in red wine stock) and *en casserole*. But I stick with **roasting** because I like roast goose best (see the recipe that follows).

Squabs

These are nothing more than domesticated pigeons, far fairer and sweeter of flesh than their wild, gamy cousins. Squabs are pint-size, rarely more than a pound (½ kg) apiece.

How much squab per person? 1 whole bird.

Best ways to store: Squabs will invariably be frozen (unless you live next door to a squab farm), so hurry the birds home from the market and place them in a 0°F. (− 18°C.) freezer in their original wrappers. **Storage time:** 6 to 8 months.

Best ways to cook: I prefer squabs **roasted** or **braised.** Some people split them and broil them, but I think the intense heat of the broiler merely dries and toughens these vulnerable young birds.

SHOULD FROZEN DUCKLINGS, GEESE AND SQUABS BE THAWED BEFORE THEY ARE COOKED?

Yes! And here's how:

REFRIGERATOR METHOD: This is the safest method, also the one that is kindest to the bird because there will be less juice and flavor loss. Simply place the solidly frozen bird, still in its original wrapper, on a plate or tray and set in the refrigerator. **Thawing time:** 3 to 4 hours per pound (½ kg) of bird.

ROOM TEMPERATURE METHOD: Place the still-wrapped, frozen bird inside a heavy brown paper bag and set on the kitchen counter. **Thawing time:** about 1 hour per pound (½ kg) of bird.

COLD WATER METHOD: Immerse the still-wrapped frozen bird in cold water; change the water every 30 minutes or so until the bird is thawed. **Thawing time:** about ½ hour per pound (½ kg) of bird.

Care of the thawed bird: Remove the bag of giblets from the body cavity and the neck from the neck cavity as soon as they are no longer frozen fast; unwrap the giblets and empty into a small bowl, add the neck, cover and set in the coldest part of the refrigerator. Usually the bag of giblets and neck can both be removed when a bird is about half thawed.

If you do not intend to cook the thawed bird right away, place it on a large plate or tray, cover loosely with plastic food wrap, wax paper or foil and set in the coldest part of the refrigerator. NOTE: *Do not try to hold a thawed bird in the refrigerator for longer than 24 hours, and never refreeze it.*

How to roast a duck or goose

1. If the bird is frozen, thaw as directed above.

2. Rinse the bird inside and out with cool water, then pat very dry with paper toweling. Rub the body cavity lightly with salt and pepper. Save the giblets to use another time for soup or stock or set them to simmer in enough water to cover (the liver will be done in about 20 minutes, the remaining giblets in about 1½ hours). Use the giblet broth for making pan gravy; mince the giblets and add to the gravy shortly before serving.

3. Prepare your favorite stuffing, allowing about ¾ cup (180 ml) per pound of (½ kg) bird. NOTE: *Some people like to stuff ducks. I don't, because the stuffing—particularly if it's a bread stuffing—becomes a repository for much of the heavy fat that will melt and drain off as the bird roasts. There is the same problem—to a lesser degree—with geese. But you can nicely counteract the greasiness of the drippings by using a tart fruit stuffing instead of a bread stuffing.*

To stuff a goose, spoon the stuffing lightly into the neck cavity, then fold the neck skin back against the back of the bird and fasten with a poultry pin. Now upend the bird and spoon the stuffing lightly into the body cavity. Never pack the stuffing in, because it will expand as the bird roasts. Now close the vent, either by sewing it shut with heavy thread or by using poultry pins and twine. Simply stick the poultry pins through the skin flap on one side of the vent, then push through to the opposite side. Now loop a piece of twine around the bottom skewer and lace the vent shut, crisscrossing the twine from skewer to skewer just as if you were lacing shoes.

4. Fold the wings against the back of the bird and, if you have not already done so, skewer the neck skin against the back. I've found that this is all that's really needed in the way of trussing ducks and geese. Both of these birds are broader, flatter and more compact than either chickens or turkeys. Their legs, scarcely more than "pipestems," lie fairly close to the body—but too far apart to tie together as is usually done for trussing without wrinkling or deforming the bird. I usually don't bother unless the bird seems "spread-eagled," in which case I simply lap a length of string around the legs several times, pulling it just tight enough to draw the legs against the body—no tighter.

5. Place the bird, breast side up, on a rack in a large shallow roasting pan. With a large needle, prick the skin all over at frequent intervals to allow the fat underneath the skin to run out as the bird roasts. Do not salt and pepper the bird, do not rub it with fat and do not add liquid to the pan.

6. Set the pan, uncovered, in a very hot oven (425°F. or 220°C.) for 25 minutes, then lower the heat to moderate (350°F. or 175°C.) and roast ducks and geese up to 10 pounds (4½ kg) for 1 to 2 hours (larger geese may require 2½ to 3 hours) or until the skin is richly browned and a leg moves easily in its hip socket. NOTE: *Continue pricking the skin throughout cooking so that as much fat drains off as possible.* Both ducks and geese should be basted often—every 15 to 20 minutes—with their own pan drippings if you wish. But for a really crisp skin, and moist meat, baste the birds instead with ice water; **each time,** drain off all drippings first because the ice water will cause them to sputter wildly. NOTE: *If the birds seem to be browning too fast, tent them loosely with foil.* Pour off excess pan drippings as they accumulate, because if you merely let them collect in the bottom of the pan, there is some danger of a fat fire. NOTE: *If you want to use a meat thermometer to determine the exact degree of doneness, insert it in the meaty inner thigh, not touching bone. When the bird is done, the temperature will register 180°F. (82°C.).*

7. As soon as the bird is done, remove it from the oven and let stand at room temperature about 20 minutes to allow the juices a chance to settle and the meat to firm up. Remove all twine and poultry pins.

8. Goose drippings make a splendid gravy, but duck drippings do not—at least in my view. Duck, in fact, is so rich that I don't think it needs a pan gravy. If you insist, use melted butter for the fat instead of drippings. **The standard proportions for pan gravy:** 2 tablespoons fat and 2 tablespoons flour to each 1 cup (240 ml) of liquid. For goose, I like a half-and-half mixture of beef and chicken broths with maybe a tablespoon or two of skimmed pan drippings to each 1 cup (240 ml) of liquid. Simply blend the fat with the flour and brown lightly, over moderate heat; pour in the liquid and heat, stirring constantly, until thickened and smooth and no raw starch taste remains—usually 3 to 5 minutes.

FLAVORFUL ADDITIONS: a little grated onion browned with the fat-flour mixture, crumbled leaf thyme or rosemary. I also sometimes mix in a little dry Madeira or Port, or finely grated orange or lemon rind—just a teaspoon or so. The idea is to experiment, tasting as you go, and making a note of successful combinations so that you can duplicate them next time around.

9. Place the bird on a heated platter and garnish with ruffs of watercress or curly chicory. Appropriate garnishes: clusters of whole cranberries; pickled peaches or crab apples; or hollowed-out lemon or orange halves filled with whole cranberry sauce. Pass any gravy separately in a heated sauceboat.

Ben Etheridge's boneless duckling à l'orange

SERVES 2 TO 4

Ben Etheridge, a transplanted Tar Heel (North Carolinian) working in New York as an editor at Reader's Digest Books, is a true and inventive cook. This unorthodox but delicious way of making Duckling à l'Orange is his, a method evolved over the years because no single recipe seemed to suit him. "Most duck sauces are too bland," explains Ben. "I think a duck sauce should have a lot of pizzazz." This one has. "This is an excellent dish for a dinner party," Ben continues, "because the sauce and the duck, except for the brief final broiling, can be made in advance"—well in advance if you freeze the duck and the sauce. What Ben usually does is prepare the sauce a day ahead. "But do not add the orange liqueur, lemon juice, salt or butter," he cautions, "until shortly before serving." As for his unconventional method of "roasting" the duckling, Ben says, "This is better than the conventional method in many ways. The duck is steamed, almost completely boned, then broiled. The skin is crisper and there is no fat." All true, I discovered, when Ben came down one night to demonstrate his way of making Duckling à l'Orange. NOTE: *A frozen, thawed duckling may be used, but it will not be as tender and moist as a fresh one because there is juice loss during the thawing period.* Ben usually serves half a duckling per person, but adds that if several courses are served at dinner, a quarter duckling per person will be ample.

A 5-pound	oven-ready duckling	A 2¼ kg
1 large	navel orange (zest only, cut into julienne)	1 large
1 quart (about)	cold water	1 L (about)
¼ teaspoon (about)	salt	¼ teaspoon (about)
	SAUCE:	
—	the duckling neck, gizzard, heart and liver (giblets)	—
3 tablespoons	peanut or vegetable oil	3 tablespoons
2 medium-size	yellow onions, peeled and sliced thin	2 medium-size
2 medium-size	carrots, peeled and sliced thin	2 medium-size
3½ cups (about)	beef broth	830 ml (about)
4 large	parsley sprigs	4 large
1 medium-size	bay leaf	1 medium-size
Pinch	crumbled leaf thyme	Pinch
2 large	navel oranges (zest only, cut into julienne)	2 large
1 quart	boiling water	1 L
3 tablespoons	sugar	3 tablespoons
¼ cup	red wine vinegar	60 ml
2½ tablespoons	cornstarch blended with 3 tablespoons dry Madeira (Sercial)	2½ tablespoons
2 teaspoons	Brown Meat Glaze (see Index) or use a bottled meat glaze	2 teaspoons
⅔ cup	dry Madeira (Sercial)	160 ml
3 tablespoons	Grand Marnier or other orange liqueur	3 tablespoons
2 teaspoons	lemon juice	2 teaspoons
To taste	salt	To taste
2 tablespoons	unsalted butter, at room temperature	2 tablespoons

Pull away as much fat as possible from inside the duckling, then cut off the tail and remove any residue around the oil glands that were at the base of the tail (a good butcher will take care in removing these lest they rupture and affect the flavor of the duckling). Quickly rinse the duckling inside and out under cold running water. There is no need to dry it. Place the julienned orange zest in the body cavity. Now place the duckling on a footed rack in a kettle large enough to accommodate it without cramping it. Pour in the water (make sure that it does not touch the bird), bring to a simmer over moderate heat, cover tightly and steam the duckling for 1½ hours exactly. Check the pot from time to time, and if it threatens to boil dry, add a bit more water.

While the duckling steams, begin the sauce: Cut the giblets into 1½-inch (4 cm) pieces or smaller and pat very dry on paper toweling. Divide the oil between two medium-size heavy skillets and set each over moderate heat. Dump the giblets into one and the sliced onions and carrots into the other; brown both well, stirring now and then—this will take 8 to 10 minutes for the vegetables, slightly less for the giblets. Transfer the browned giblets and vegetables to a medium-size heavy saucepan. Add the beef broth, parsley, bay leaf and thyme. If the broth does not cover the giblets and vegetables, pour in a little water until it does. Set over moderately low heat, bring to a simmer, put the lid on the pan askew and simmer 1½ hours. Strain the broth, discarding all solids; also skim off any grease. Measure the stock. It should total 2 cups (½ L). If there is too much stock, boil, uncovered, over moderate heat until it has reduced to 2 cups (½ L). If there is insufficient stock, you can do one of two things: You can add enough strained and degreased broth (from steaming the duck) to round out the measure or you can do so with additional beef broth.

The duck should now be done. Lift it **very gently** from the pot so as not to break the skin. Place the duck on a rack and let it cool to room temperature. (Save any broth to use another time.)

While the duck cools, proceed with the sauce: Blanch the julienned orange zest in the boiling water for 15 minutes, drain well and reserve. Combine the sugar and vinegar in a medium-size heavy saucepan, set over moderate heat and allow to cook down until a brown amber glaze remains on the bottom of the pan. Off heat, stir in a little of the stock, stirring until all hardened bits of glaze dissolve. Add the remaining stock, whisk in the cornstarch mixture and reserved orange zest, set over moderate heat and cook, stirring constantly, until the sauce bubbles up, thickens and clears—about 3 minutes. Blend in the brown meat glaze; set off the heat for the time being. Pour the ⅔ cup of Madeira into a small heavy saucepan set over moderately high heat and boil, uncovered, until almost all of the wine cooks away, leaving only 2 to 3 tablespoons in the bottom of the pan. Add this wine reduction to the sauce. NOTE: *You may prepare the sauce up to this point well ahead of time. Pour into a small bowl, cover and refrigerate until ready to use.*

It is now time to get on with the duckling. First remove the orange zest from the body cavity and discard. Then, using poultry shears, cut through the breast lengthwise. Turn the bird over and cut along both sides of the back bone and remove. Twist off the first two wing joints. Carefully remove the breast bone and all other bones, including the wing bone attached to the shoulder, but leave the drumsticks intact. Remove the wing bone as follows: From the underside, cut the tendons from the ball joint. Then, from the outside, hold the meat tightly around the bone and push, **do not pull,** the bone through to the underside and remove it. Trim away any ragged pieces of skin around the bird to make the halves as handsome and shapely as possible. Save these pieces of skin and broil them when broiling the duck. (They make a delicious—and well-deserved—reward for the cook.)

Now, depending upon whether you are serving two persons or four, leave the duckling halves intact or halve each horizontally, making four portions of as nearly equal size as possible. Place each piece, skin side up, on the counter and flatten gently with the palms of your hands so that the surface of each piece is as uniform as possible and will thus brown more evenly under the broiler. NOTE: *You may prepare the duckling up to this point as much as two days ahead of time. Wrap in aluminum foil and refrigerate. Or, if you prefer, the duckling may be foil-wrapped, frozen and kept as long as two months. Thaw the duckling thoroughly before proceeding.*

About 15 minutes before you are ready to serve, pour the reserved sauce into a small heavy saucepan and set over low heat. Arrange the pieces of duckling, skin side up, on a broiler pan, sprinkle evenly with the ¼ teaspoon of salt, then set about 3 inches (8 cm) from the heat. While the duckling broils (and this will take 5 to 8 minutes only), finish the sauce: Stir in the Grand Marnier, lemon juice and salt. Finally, swirl in the butter. Do not let the sauce boil at any point because it will not only thin out (cornstarch, once thickened, will thin if overheated) but also lose its potent Grand Marnier flavor.

As the duckling broils, check it from time to time to see that it is not overbrowning in spots. If it is, simply cover any dark spots with bits of heavy-duty aluminum foil. Don't worry about the duckling's overcooking or drying. It won't when broiled this quickly.

As soon as the duckling is crisply browned, arrange it, skin side up, on a small heated platter and spoon some of the orange sauce on top. Garnish with twists or segments of orange, if you wish, and frills of curly chicory. Pour the remaining sauce into a heated sauceboat and pass separately so that guests may help themselves to more.

FINAL NOTES: *This is one of the pleasantest of all Ducklings à l'Orange to eat because you can cut straight through it without encountering bones every inch of the way. The only bones at all are those in the drumsticks and it won't be amiss if you— or your guests—pick them up to gnaw at table. You will be grateful to Ben Etheridge, too, for degreasing the duck so completely that it leaves the broiler almost pristine— even the broiler pan is a breeze to clean.*

How to roast squabs

1. If the birds are frozen, thaw them according to one of the three methods described earlier in this chapter.

2. Rinse the squabs inside and out with cool water, then pat very dry with paper toweling. Rub the body cavities lightly with salt and pepper. Place the giblets and neck, if any, in a small saucepan, cover with cold water and bring to a simmer; remove the liver after 10 minutes and refrigerate. Cook the remaining giblets as long as the squabs roast. You will use them (and the giblet broth) for making pan gravy.

3. Stuff the body cavities of the birds, if you like, allowing about ½ cup (120 ml) of your favorite stuffing per bird. Spoon the stuffing in lightly, then using poultry pins and twine, lace the vent shut. **To truss:** Fold the wings back "akimbo" against the back of each bird, then tie the legs together.

4. Place the birds, breast side up, on a rack in a shallow roasting pan; rub each lightly all over with softened butter or bacon drippings.

5. Roast the birds, uncovered, in a moderately hot oven (375°F. or 190°C.) for 35 to 40 minutes or until nicely browned and the juices run clear (to test, prick a thigh with a sharp-pronged fork). Brush the birds about halfway through cooking with a little additional softened butter or bacon drippings.

6. As soon as the birds are done, remove them from the oven and let stand at room temperature for 15 minutes.

7. For a pan gravy, skim the pan drippings of fat. Combine the skimmed drippings with the giblet broth and measure. For each 1 cup (240 ml) of liquid, you will need 2 tablespoons of fat drippings (if these are skimpy, round out the amount with butter or bacon drippings) and 2 tablespoons flour. Warm the fat in a small saucepan over moderate heat, blend in the flour, pour in the liquid, then heat, stirring constantly, until thickened and smooth—3 to 5 minutes. Add the minced giblets and serve.

NICE ADDITIONS: a large shallot, minced, browned in the fat drippings; a little apple cider (substitute about ½ cup or 120 ml of it for an equal measure of giblet broth or other liquid); a pinch of crumbled leaf rosemary and/or thyme; ½ teaspoon of finely grated orange or lemon rind; ¼ cup (60 ml) tart apple or currant jelly; a splash of dry sherry, Port or Madeira.

8. Arrange the birds on a heated platter and garnish with ruffs of parsley, rose geranium, lemon verbena, watercress or chicory. For color, add lemon or orange twists, preserved kumquats or crab apples, clusters of green and/or red grapes. Pass the gravy separately in a heated gravy boat.

Seafood

It's easy to sort out the sea's bounty when you realize that all of the major categories are divisible by two. **Seafood** breaks down into **fin fish** and **shellfish. Fin fish** may be subdivided into two basic types: **fat or oily fish** (such as salmon, trout, tuna, halibut, herring, anchovies, sardines, mackerel, pompano, swordfish and bluefish, in which the natural oils are evenly distributed throughout the flesh) and **lean fish** (red snapper, sea bass, haddock, flounder, sole, perch, pickerel, pike and cod, to name a few of the most popular species, in which the oils are concentrated in the liver—remember the cod liver oil we all had to swallow as children "to build up our strength"?).

Shellfish are divisible by two, also: the **crustaceans** (the legged creatures such as **lobsters, crabs** and **shrimp** with exterior, armorlike shells) and **mollusks** (soft, spineless animals—**clams, mussels, oysters** and **scallops**—that live inside hard shells). There are, of course, further subdivisions. (All of the mollusks just named, for example are **bivalves**—meaning that they have double, hinged shells.) The basic broad categories are the ones that will concern us most here.

Fish

You no longer need to live within the sound of the surf to enjoy fresh fish—and an astonishing variety of it—thanks to refrigeration and air freight. Fresh fish is available to you in the following forms:

WHOLE: Fish as they're pulled from the water. Before such fish are cooked, they must be scaled and drawn (eviscerated). The fins must be removed, but whether the head and tail are left on or lopped off is entirely up to you.

DRESSED OR PAN DRESSED: Whenever a large fish—salmon, for example—is completely cleaned (eviscerated, definned, trimmed of head and tail and, if necessary, scaled), it is said to be "dressed." But small fish given the same treatment are "pan-dressed," presumably because they are small enough to fit into a frying pan.

FILLETS: These are boneless, skinless, ready-to-cook strips taken from the sides of a fish. When the two sides are left connected by the belly skin, they are called a **butterfly fillet.**

STEAKS: Nothing more than cross-sections cut from large dressed fish—salmon, swordfish or tuna, for example. They can vary from ½ to 1½ inches (1½ to 4 cm) in thickness. They contain a cross-section of the backbone, but that's all, and they are ready to cook.

CHUNKS: These, too, are cross-sections of large dressed fish; like steaks, they contain the backbone. Unlike them, they tend to come from less meaty fish and are thus cut thicker than steaks.

Inspection and grading: The U.S. Department of Commerce's National Marine and Fisheries Service sets the grade standards for fish and shellfish and provides grading services. These are entirely voluntary, however, and grades are rarely seen except on processed frozen fish sticks, breaded shrimp, fish portions and fillets. The top grade and the one that is most likely to show up in your grocery is U.S. GRADE A (the lower two grades are B and C). Any fish product may be inspected for wholesomeness, but here, too, the "seal of approval" is rarely seen.

Hallmarks of quality: The best advice I can offer is to find a good fish store and make a friend of its owner, or failing that, the manager of a good fish department in a supermarket. A knowledgeable fishmonger is a font of information. My "man" is Mike DeMartino of DeMartino's on New York's unfashionable Eighth Avenue. I hang about DeMartino's on unhectic days just to see the fish laid out on beds of shaved ice with the expertise and artistry you'd expect of a jeweler. Mike has taught me much about the different kinds of fish, about their best seasons, not to mention the best methods for cooking each of them.

Most important, Mike has taught me **how to buy fish.** Know first, he stresses, what kinds of fish you like and how you intend to cook them. Know, too, the times of the year when these fish are at their best. Then, learn how to recognize a fresh fish when you look it straight in the eye:

EYES: They should be bright, clear and bulging. As a fish becomes stale, its eyes begin to cloud and sink into the head.

FLESH: It should be springy-firm and translucent and cling to the bones.

GILLS: If the fish is fresh and has been handled carefully, the gills will be red and free from slime. As a fish ages, the color of its gills fades to pink, then gray, then brown or green.

SKIN: When fish are first pulled from the water, they iridesce brightly. But soon their colors begin to pale. So the fresher the fish, the more gleaming and colorful the skin.

ODOR: If a fish is old or bad, you will know it by its smell. Truly fresh fish have a sea-sweet aroma. Although the fishy odor gathers strength with the passage of time, it should never be disagreeably strong. A friend of mine once remarked that anyone who thought a fish could smell "sea-sweet" had never visited a fish market. "Have you ever been in a fish market that smelled sea-sweet?" she asked. Not really, I had to confess. But what my friend failed to take into account is that "out back," behind the store proper, men are scaling and gutting fish and shucking shellfish. The fall-out isn't emptied out more than a couple of times a day and *that's* what begins to smell "high"—even in the most prestigious fish markets.

As for top-quality frozen fish, look for fish that is snugly wrapped in moisture- and vaporproof material and, it goes without saying, in packages devoid of rips or tears. If the fish has been cut into steaks or fillets, scrutinize the flesh: it should be translucent, of good fresh color, and it should show no browning or "burning" or cottony patches, all indications of freezer burn and improper wrapping.

How much fish per serving? Much depends, of course, on the fish, the degree of bone it contains, the richness of the flesh, and, of course, how you intend to cook it. You can eat more poached fish, for example, than you can batter-fried fish simply because the batter itself is filling. Still, general guidelines can be a help. Here are the ones that I've used over the years:

Whole Fish	1 pound (½ kg) per serving
Dressed Fish	½ to ¾ pound (¼ to ⅓ kg) per serving
Fillets, Steaks or Chunks	½ pound (¼ kg) per serving (less if the fish is to be richly sauced)

Best way to store:

FRESH FISH: Rinse the fish well in cool water, pat dry on paper toweling, then arrange in one layer on a plate or platter. I prefer a ceramic surface to a metal one because I think fish can take on a metallic taste; perhaps it's my imagination, but I don't think so. Cover the fish with plastic food wrap, making sure that it is sealed in, and place in the coldest part of the refrigerator. **Maximum storage time:** 2 days and, if you caught the fish yourself, gutted it straightaway, wasted no time getting it into the refrigerator and are lucky, 3 days.

FROZEN FISH: Commercially frozen fish should be rushed home from the store (it should also be the last item you buy so that it doesn't thaw in your grocery cart) and stuck at once on the freezing surface of your freezer. If you are freezing fish that you have caught, scale it, eviscerate it and remove the fins. Leave the head and tail on if you wish. Rinse the fish inside and out with cool water, pat dry on paper toweling, then wrap snugly in foil or freezer paper, pressing out all wrinkles and sealing with freezer tape. Label and date and place directly on the freezing surface of the freezer. **Maximum storage times: Fat or oily fish** (salmon, trout, tuna, swordfish, bluefish, mackerel, pompano and the like) do not keep as well as lean fish because their flesh is apt to go rancid; 3 months at 0°F. (− 18°C.) is the maximum recommended storage time. **For lean** fish (sole, flounder, cod, red snapper, haddock, etc.) it is about twice as long—6 months at 0°F. (−18°C.).

The best ways to cook fish: Again, much depends upon the fish. A whopping salmon is obviously a poor candidate for the frying pan, and a small sole or flounder a bad choice for the oven because the dry heat of baking will toughen and dry it beyond edibility. Here then are the ways I like best for cooking the commonly available kinds of fish.

To SAUTÉ OR PANFRY: Fillets are best, particularly those of lean white fish such as flounder or sole, although small trout or perch may also be sautéed with great success. I personally like to dredge the fish in flour or cornmeal because I like a browned coating. My favorite frying medium is butter, although for trout or stronger-flavored fish I will occasionally use olive oil or bacon drippings, either solo or in tandem with butter. If there is any advice I can pass along about sautéing fish successfully, it would be: "Easy does it!" Keep the heat at a moderate level. And brown the fish lightly—about 2 minutes per side for thin fillets, 3 to 4 for thicker ones, for steaks or whole fish. Fish are naturally tender. The idea is merely to heat them through, to "set" or coagulate the flesh. If you do more than that, you will surely toughen the fish.

To STEAM: Weigh the fish and note the weight, then wrap in cheesecloth (to keep the fish intact and facilitate lifting it in and out of the pan). Lay it on a rack, then ease into a fish poacher or large kettle containing 2 inches (5 cm) of boiling water. (The fish should not touch the water; if it does, tip out a little of the water). Cover the kettle and steam as follows: **1 minute per ounce** (30 g) of fish **less than 2 inches** (5 cm) thick at the thickest point. Thicker fish are not particularly good candidates for steaming because the outside will overcook by the time the inside is heated through.

To POACH: The perfect method for salmon and other large fish. The fish can be poached in a court bouillon (see the recipe for Poached Salmon in this section), in plain water, or in a half-and-half mixture of water and dry white wine (and by all means add an onion to the kettle, a celery rib, some parsley or dill sprigs). The ideal cooking time is **10 minutes for each inch** (2½ cm) **of thickness** (measure the fish at its thickest point). Because fish is fragile and tends to break apart easily, it's wise for poaching as well as steaming to wrap it in several thicknesses of cheesecloth before you cook it. If you leave some overhang at each end and twist and tie these, you will have built-in handles with which to lift the fish in and out of the kettle). **Some points to remember: (1)** Make sure that the fish is immersed in the poaching medium; **(2)** begin timing the cooking of the fish from the moment the poaching medium **returns** to a simmer; **(3)** adjust the burner heat so that the poaching medium stays at a slow simmer and never boils; **(4)** cook the fish with the kettle **covered.** As soon as the fish has cooked the allotted period of time, lift it from the kettle, unwrap it and peel off any skin.

Serve hot, or chill well and serve cold. Serve with Watercress Sauce (see the recipe in this section), with tartar sauce or with any favorite fish sauce.

To bake: I find this a lovely way to cook salmon, haddock and bluefish, but not nude or unadorned, because I consider oven heat too harsh for fish that is simply plunked down into a baking pan *au naturel.* My favorite ways to bake a variety of fish (tuna, haddock, pompano, etc.) are included in both this section and among the Recipe Collection in Part II (see Index).

To braise: Because braising involves an initial browning, then cooking in the company of liquid or moisture-yielding ingredients, it is more a recipe-oriented method than a basic method. To prove the point, see the recipe in this section for Braised Salmon Steaks the Austrian Way with Bacon, Chives and Dill Pickle.

To broil: I'm not as quick to broil fish as most people are, and I'm fussy about the fish I choose to broil because, with few exceptions, the intense heat of the broiler merely dries and toughens it. For that reason, I usually broil only oily fish—swordfish, salmon, pompano, etc.—although occasionally an enticing recipe comes along to make me break my rule. My favorite cuts for broiling are steaks—again of swordfish or salmon—because steaks can be cut fairly thick. I find 1 to 1½ inches (2½ to 4 cm) the ideal thickness—thin enough for the fish to cook through, thick enough for it not to go rubbery. For best results, I brush the fish with melted butter or olive oil before I broil it, place it about 6 inches (15 cm) from the heat and allow 4 to 5 minutes per side. When I turn the steaks, I lavish the flip side with additional melted butter or olive oil.

About cooking frozen fish: Should it be defrosted before it is cooked? **Yes**— but as gently as possible in the refrigerator. Thawing is the thief of flavor because there is so much juice loss. You can minimize this by keeping the still-wrapped frozen fish in the refrigerator. Tip: *Place the fish on a tray so that it does not drip down inside the refrigerator, causing one foul-smelling mess.* Most fillets and steaks will require 8 to 10 hours to thaw; whole fish, overnight. Caution: *Never refreeze fish once it has been thawed, and cook it as soon after thawing as possible.*

The best ways to cook thawed, frozen fish? I do not favor baking or broiling because the thawed fish has already lost much of its original juiciness. No point in drying it out altogether—a lesson too many restaurant chefs have yet to learn, alas. For fillets, steaks and small whole fish, **sautéing** is best; for large fish, **poaching, steaming** or **braising.**

Bridie's butter-browned breaded fillets of lemon sole

SERVES 4

When I first started out some twenty years ago as a recipe tester at *The Ladies' Home Journal,* there was a wonderful woman there named Bridie Dolan, who cooked the best fillets of sole I had ever eaten (or have eaten since, I might add). We recipe-testers used to look forward to the days when we tested desserts or cakes, cookies or pies and so that we could ask Bridie to cook fillets of lemon sole for our main course at lunch in the test kitchen. NOTE: *Lemon sole, of course, is not true sole, but a type of flounder. No matter, it is superlative prepared Bridie's way.*

2 large	eggs, lightly beaten	2 large
¼ cup	light cream or milk	60 ml
1½ cups	fine dry bread crumbs or cracker meal	350 ml
1½ pounds	fillets of lemon sole	⅔ kg
¼ pound (1 stick), in all	unsalted butter	115 g (1 stick), in all
Light sprinklings	salt and freshly ground black pepper	Light sprinklings
1 large	lemon, cut into slim wedges	1 large

Combine the eggs and the cream and pour into a pie pan. Place the crumbs in a second pie pan or on a large piece of wax paper. Dip each fillet first into the egg mixture until evenly coated, then into crumbs, patting firmly to make them stick. Heat half (4 tablespoons) of the butter in a large heavy skillet over moderate heat until it foams up, then subsides, and begin browning the sole nicely on both sides—no more than 3 to 4 minutes altogether. NOTE: *You'll only be able to brown about 4 fillets at a time, so keep the first batches warm by setting uncovered in a very slow oven (250°F. or 120°C.) while you fry the subsequent batches.* Continue browning the sole the same way, adding more butter as needed. Sprinkle the browned fillets lightly with salt and pepper, drizzle with any of the browned butter remaining in the skillet, arrange on a heated platter and garnish with lemon wedges.

Sautéed swordfish steaks in mustard sauce with capers and fresh dill

SERVES 4

This is a last-minute recipe, so have everything measured and at hand before you begin. Also have at the ready all implements you will need: pancake turner, wooden spoon, heated platter, etc.

2 pounds	fresh swordfish divided into 4 steaks of equal size, about 1 inch (2½ cm) thick	1 kg
¼ teaspoon	salt	¼ teaspoon
Light sprinkling	freshly ground black pepper	Light sprinkling
¼ cup	unsifted all-purpose flour	60 ml
3 tablespoons	unsalted butter	3 tablespoons
¼ cup	dry vermouth	60 ml

1 tablespoon	lemon juice	1 tablespoon
1 tablespoon	Dijon mustard	1 tablespoon
½ cup	heavy cream	120 ml
3 tablespoons	freshly snipped dill	3 tablespoons
2 tablespoons	well-drained small capers	2 tablespoons

Sprinkle each swordfish steak lightly on both sides with salt and pepper, then dredge well in flour, shaking off the excess. Heat the butter in a large heavy skillet over moderately high heat just until it froths up and subsides. Add the swordfish steaks and brown 4 to 5 minutes on each side—no longer or the fish will toughen. Using a pancake turner, lift the browned swordfish steaks to a heated platter and keep warm. Quickly deglaze the skillet by pouring in the vermouth and lemon juice and stirring with a wooden spoon to dislodge the browned bits on the bottom of the skillet. Smooth in the mustard, then boil, uncovered, for a minute or two until the mixture has cooked down to a rich amber glaze. Stir in the heavy cream and again boil hard until reduced by about half. Stir in the dill and capers, pour evenly over the swordfish steaks and serve.

Fresh poached salmon the Nordic way with watercress sauce

 SERVES 6 TO 8

The trick in poaching salmon is to keep the water at a tremble, *not* at a boil or even a simmer, both of which will toughen the fish. It will take 30 to 35 minutes to poach the salmon to perfection—to the point at which it will fall into moist chunks at the touch of a fork. NOTE: *This Watercress Sauce is delicious with any cold cooked fish or shellfish.*

4 quarts (about)	water	4 L (about)
2 cups	dry white wine	½ L
10 large fronds	fresh dill	10 large fronds
4 large	parsley sprigs	4 large
1 medium-size	yellow onion, peeled and quartered	1 medium-size
1 large	bay leaf	1 large
½ large	lemon, sliced thin	½ large
12 large	peppercorns	12 large
6 large	juniper berries	6 large
2 teaspoons	salt	2 teaspoons
A 3- to 4-pound	piece of center-cut salmon, cleaned and dressed	A 1½ to 2 kg

WATERCRESS SAUCE:

3 medium-size	scallions, trimmed and sliced thin (include some green tops)	3 medium-size
1 large	shallot, peeled and minced	1 large
3 tablespoons	unsalted butter	3 tablespoons
1 cup	firmly packed tender young spinach leaves (or use ⅓ of a package—10 oz. or 283 g—frozen chopped spinach)	240 ml
1 cup	firmly packed young watercress leaves	240 ml
1½ cups	mayonnaise	350 ml
1 teaspoon	lemon juice	1 teaspoon
1 teaspoon	prepared horseradish	1 teaspoon
½ teaspoon	Dijon mustard	½ teaspoon
3 to 4 drops	liquid hot red pepper seasoning	3 to 4 drops
To taste	salt	To taste

Place a rack in a large heavy kettle or fish poacher and add the water, wine, dill, parsley, onion, bay leaf, lemon slices, peppercorns, juniper berries and salt. Bring to a simmer and cook, covered, for 15 minutes. Meanwhile, rinse the salmon in cool water and wrap in several thicknesses of cheesecloth. NOTE: *The cheesecloth serves three purposes: It keeps the seasonings from coming into direct contact with the salmon as it poaches, it facilitates lifting the salmon in and out of the kettle and it helps to keep it intact—once cooked, salmon is very fragile.* Ease the salmon onto the rack in the kettle; the liquid should just cover it and if it does not, add a bit more water. Now let the liquid return to a tremble; as soon as it does, cover the kettle and begin timing the poaching. NOTE: *I set a timer for 30 minutes, then check the fish at that point—if it offers only slight resistance when pressed with a finger, it is done; if it is underdone, it will feel soft, almost mushy, and I then cook it 5 to 10 minutes longer.*

While the salmon poaches, prepare the watercress sauce: Stir-fry the scallions and the shallot in the butter in a large heavy skillet over moderate heat about 5 minutes until limp and golden. Dump in the spinach and watercress and stir-fry 2 to 3 minutes, just until wilted. Cover the skillet and cook 5 minutes. Now uncover the skillet and cook until the mixture is very dry. Purée the skillet mixture in a food processor fitted with the metal chopping blade (or in an electric blender at high speed). Add the mayonnaise, lemon juice, horseradish, Dijon mustard and liquid hot red pepper seasoning. Buzz a few seconds until creamy-smooth, taste and add salt as needed. NOTE: *This recipe makes about 2 cups of sauce; if stored tightly covered in the refrigerator, it will keep well for about a week.*

As soon as the salmon is done, lift it from the kettle and remove the cheesecloth. Starting at the bottom (belly side), carefully peel off and discard all skin. TIP: *I work with the salmon on a large plate. After I've removed all of the skin on the top side, I place a second large plate on top of the salmon and invert it just as I would a cake. I then peel the skin from the second side.* Cover the salmon with foil or plastic food wrap and chill several hours. Also cover and chill the sauce. TIP: *As a desperation measure—when time has gotten away from me and guests are about to arrive—I quick-chill both the sauce and the salmon by setting them in the freezer. After about 40 minutes, they will be as cold as they would be after 3 hours in the refrigerator.*

To serve, ease the salmon onto a chilled platter (my favorite is a bright red platter against which the salmon pink fairly glows) and garnish with twists of lemon and ruffs of watercress. Pass the sauce in its own bowl.

NOTE: *If you are as Scottishly frugal as I am, you will strain the court bouillon in which you poached the salmon and freeze it to use later for poaching other fish or shellfish.*

Kolja
(SWEDISH-STYLE HADDOCK BAKED WITH DILL, WINE AND CREAM)

SERVES 4

With six ingredients only, *Kolja* (pronounced COAL-ya) is one of the easiest recipes imaginable. And one of the best. It will take you less than five minutes to get the fish into the oven and about forty minutes to bake. No, the fish will not overcook, because the coverlet of dill helps to insulate it from the heat. If you follow the directions below to the letter and if your **oven is accurate,** I promise you that the fish will be exquisitely moist and tender and aromatic of fresh dill.

1 pound	skinned and filleted haddock, in one piece	½ kg
Light sprinklings	salt and freshly ground black pepper	Light sprinklings
½ cup	dry white wine or dry vermouth	120 ml
⅔ cup	heavy cream	160 ml
18 large fronds	fresh dill	18 large fronds

Sprinkle the haddock lightly on both sides with salt and pepper, then place flat in a shallow baking pan just large enough to accommodate it. Pour in the wine and cream, then blanket the fish with fresh dill. Bake, uncovered, in a hot oven (400°F. or 205°C.) for 35 to 40 minutes until the fish flakes at the touch of a fork, basting every 10 minutes with the cream mixture. Discard the dill, ease the fish onto a heated deep platter, then spoon the pan liquids on top. Serve with boiled new potatoes (and spoon some of the pan drippings over them, too).

Baked fresh tuna steaks
with capers and olives

SERVES 6

Tuna is Sicily's most important catch, and few people know better than the Sicilians how to prepare it. This particular recipe, a favorite in the western port of Trapani and the offshore island of Favignana, is one of those effortless recipes that seem exotic. If fresh tuna is unavailable, substitute fresh swordfish. To round out the meal, precede with steamed artichokes and accompany with a lemon-and-oil-dressed salad of arugula.

9–10 slices	lean sliced bacon	9–10 slices
6 (1-inch-thick)	fresh tuna steaks (each steak should weigh about ½ pound or 225 g)	6 (2½ cm thick) steaks
3–4 tablespoons	olive oil (top quality)	3–4 tablespoons
2 tablespoons	dry vermouth	2 tablespoons
Light sprinkling	freshly ground black pepper	Light sprinkling
⅓ cup	chopped pitted green olives	80 ml
2 tablespoons	small capers, well drained	2 tablespoons
3 tablespoons	minced parsley	3 tablespoons
2 cups	soft, moderately fine bread crumbs	½ L

Line bottom of a 13 × 9 × 2-inch pan (33 × 23 × 5 cm) with bacon and lay tuna on top; brush with 1 to 2 tablespoons olive oil, drizzle with vermouth and sprinkle with pepper. Mix olives with capers and parsley, then spoon over tuna. Toss bread crumbs with 2 tablespoons oil and scatter on top of tuna. Marinate uncovered in the refrigerator for 3 to 4 hours. Let tuna stand at room temperature 30 minutes, then bake, uncovered, in a moderately hot oven (375°F. or 190°C.) 35 to 40 minutes until crumbs are browned and fish flakes at the touch of a fork.

Braised salmon steaks the Austrian way
with bacon, chives and dill pickle

SERVES 4

Although I don't remember precisely where in the Tyrol I was introduced to this unusual salmon dish (it was that long ago), I do recall with peculiar clarity the dish itself. And how delicious it was. This recipe is my approximation of the original.

4 slices	bacon, snipped crosswise into julienne strips	4 slices
4 (about ½ pound each)	center-cut salmon steaks, sliced 1-inch (2½ cm) thick	4 (about 225 g each)
Light sprinklings	salt and freshly ground black pepper	Light sprinklings
⅓ cup	unsifted all-purpose flour	80 ml
2 tablespoons	unsalted butter	2 tablespoons
⅓ cup	dry white wine or dry vermouth	80 ml
⅓ cup	half-and-half or heavy cream	80 ml
2 tablespoons	freshly snipped chives	2 tablespoons
1 tablespoon	finely minced dill pickle	1 tablespoon

Fry the bacon in a large heavy skillet over moderate heat 8 to 10 minutes until all of the fat has cooked out and only crisp brown crumbles remain. With a slotted spoon, lift the browned bacon to paper toweling to drain. Pour all drippings from the skillet, then spoon 1 tablespoon of them back into the skillet. Sprinkle the salmon steaks lightly on both sides with salt and pepper, then dredge in the flour. Add the butter to the skillet, let it foam up and subside, add the salmon steaks and brown about 2 minutes on a side. Transfer them to a shallow baking pan just large enough to accommodate them in a single layer and set aside.

Deglaze the skillet with the wine, scraping the browned bits up from the bottom of the skillet as the wine bubbles, then boil hard until reduced to a thick amber glaze—3 to 5 minutes. Pour in the cream and reduce by about one-third, stirring often. Stir in the reserved bacon crumbles, the chives and dill pickle, let simmer a minute or two to mellow the flavors, then pour over the salmon steaks. Bake, uncovered, for 10 to 12 minutes in a moderate oven (350°F. or 175°C.) until the salmon will flake at the touch of a fork. Serve straightaway accompanied by boiled new potatoes and a green vegetable such as asparagus or broccoli.

Shellfish

When I was a child, we used to spend part of each summer at a cottage on Chesapeake Bay near Whitestone, Virginia, and among my fondest memories are those of the days we went crabbing. Sometimes we'd bait a safety pin with a piece of bacon, tie it to a length of string, drop it into a bed of seaweed and wait for a crab to grab hold—it usually didn't take long. Sometimes the crabs were so thick we'd simply scoop them up with a net.

We'd take the crabs back to the cottage, Mother would put a big pot of water on the wood stove and we'd hang around waiting for it to boil. As soon as it did, Mother would drop the live-and-kicking crabs into the kettle and we'd scurry about setting the table. Within twenty minutes, we'd be cracking crabs and digging out the sweet, snowy meat, all of us so absorbed in the task at hand that we scarcely spoke.

We had oysters aplenty at the cottage, but we bought these from the local fish market—about a twenty-minute boat ride up the Rappahannock River— and all the fin fish we could eat, too. But it is the crabs that I remember with particular fondness, those glorious East Coast blue crabs that grow fatter and sweeter in Chesapeake Bay than anywhere else on earth.

I also remember eating plenty of shrimp and scallops during my childhood. My hometown of Raleigh, North Carolina, is about 150 miles inland and even in those days—the 1940s—fresh shrimp and scallops would be trucked up from the coast despite World War II and gasoline rationing. It wasn't until I went off to college in New York State, however, that I first tasted lobster, clams and mussels. And it was later still before I learned to cook them properly. Those who've taught me the most were women at the source—a lobsterman's wife in Maine, a waterman's wife on Maryland's Eastern shore, a shrimper's wife on the Gulf Coast—women I've had the privilege of interviewing during my years as a food writer. Much of what I pass along now is the wisdom they shared with me. **Crustaceans** come first; **mollusks** follow.

Crabs

For me, crabs will forever be blue crabs because I grew up on them. But I like the West Coast Dungeness very much, too, and even the frozen Alaska king crab legs (these sometimes measure six feet across!).

Season: Hard-shell blue crabs are available the year round, but supplies are often short in winter simply because it's too cold for the watermen to go out and also because the crabs themselves make things difficult by "going to ground" and nestling among the rocks and seaweed on the ocean or bay floor. **Soft-shell blue crabs** are hard-shell crabs that have molted. (This, incidentally, is the only way crabs can grow, shedding one shell and growing a new one the next size larger.) They are in season from May through October. The **Pacific Dungeness** are in best supply in California between mid-November and August. Farther north in Oregon and Washington, they're available year round.

Hallmarks of quality: Both blue crabs and Dungeness should be alive and kicking when you buy them. They should also be intact—missing no claws or legs. Have the fish market pack them in seaweed for you so that they will stay alive longer—also so that they can't flail about. NOTE: *Cooked blue crab meat, both the choice snowy lump or backfin meat and the darker, stringier "picked" or "regular crab meat," are available iced or frozen from top fish stores and supermarkets. The best advice I can offer here is to buy brands you know and trust. I've settled upon a Georgia brand that is meticulously picked and devoid of shell and cartilage.*

How much per serving? Crabs vary tremendously in size. **Blue crabs,** for example, can be mere babies—about ¼ pound (115 g) each—or they can be whoppers—1 to 1¼ pounds apiece (about ½ kg). As a general rule, however, you won't go wrong allowing about 1 pound (½ kg) of unshelled crab per person—and that goes for **Dungeness** as well as for blue crabs. **Soft-shell** crabs are another matter. They are usually quite small—2 to 3 inches (5 to 8 cm) across, including legs. A decent portion, I think, is 4 soft-shell crabs. But I have crab-loving friends who can wolf down a dozen or more at a sitting. For **crab meat,** I allow ¼ to ⅓ pound (115 to 160 g) per serving.

Best way to store: Live crabs do not keep for long. If packed in seaweed in a heavy paper bag, I've managed to keep them live and kicking for about 24 hours in the coldest part of the refrigerator. But that's the maximum. TIP: *The cold anesthetizes the crabs, so that when you first remove them from the refrigerator, they will be uncharacteristically calm. But a few minutes at room temperature will activate them.* Chilled **cooked crab meat** should be stored in its original container in the coldest part of the refrigerator. **Maximum storage time:** About 3 days under optimum conditions. **Frozen crab,** of course, should be kept in the freezer in its original carton. **Maximum storage time:** About 2 months.

Basic preparation: Hard-shell crabs need only to be washed in cool water if they are to be cooked whole. But **soft-shell** crabs, which are eaten shell and all, must first be cleaned. Lift the pointed ends on each side of the soft top shell (they are to the right and the left as you face the crab), then pull out and discard all spongy portions. Also peel off the tail or "apron," which tucks underneath the back of the crab and snip off the "face." The crabs are now ready to cook.

Best ways to cook crabs:

Hard-shell crabs: As far as I'm concerned, there are only two proper ways to cook live hard-shelled crabs—by steaming or by boiling.

TO STEAM: Pour about 2 inches (5 cm) of water into a very large kettle (the sort you would use for cooking pasta), add a rack, pile some seaweed on top (use the seaweed in which the crabs were packed)—a couple of inches of seaweed is about right. NOTE: *If you have no seaweed, don't worry. The crabs will steam very well without it; I use it because I think it adds the tang of the sea.* Bring the water to a slow boil, adjust the burner heat so that it bubbles gently, then wearing gloves (I use the garden variety to protect myself from the crabs' flailing claws and if you've ever been nipped by an angry crab, you'll understand why), grasp the crabs by the top shell and pile them onto the seaweed. Cover the kettle and steam the crabs for 20 minutes exactly. As an old Maryland "salt" explained to me, "Crabs don't take to too much cooking."

Lift the crabs from the kettle and serve with plenty of melted butter. Put out nutcrackers and picks so that guests can get at their crabs easily. **If you've never tackled a whole hard-shell crab, here's how to go about it:** Break the claws off close to the body, then pull off each of the legs. Yank the top shell off and scrape away and discard the yellowish stomach and digestive tract, also all of the spongy portions or "dead man's fingers," as they're called. These are rumored to be poisonous, but as a waterman's wife once said to me, "I don't think they can be. If you've ever been to a crab fest and seen people go at the crabs, you'd know that they eat absolutely everything—**including** the dead man's fingers." I personally discard them, however, because they just aren't very appetizing. What you're after, of course, is the snowy lump or backfin meat tucked inside the top shell. Also the claw meat, which you can dig out easily once you've crunched the claws open with a nutcracker.

To BOIL: About half-fill a big kettle with water, add about 2 cups (½ L) of dry white wine or cider vinegar, drop in a couple of bay leaves or, if you prefer, a tablespoon of pickling spice or, if available, crab boil. Bring to a rolling boil, drop in the live crabs, and, as soon as the water returns to a boil, clap the lid on the kettle and boil 15 minutes. Lift the crabs from the kettle and serve with melted butter, picks and nutcrackers just as you would steamed crabs.

Soft-shell crabs: These require fat—butter or oil.

To SAUTÉ: Wash and clean the crabs as directed above under Basic Preparation, sprinkle lightly with salt and freshly ground black pepper, then dredge in flour and shake off the excess. In a large heavy skillet set over moderately high heat melt about 1 stick (¼ pound or 115 g) of unsalted butter, let it foam up and subside, then sauté the crabs, about 4 at a time, until crisply golden brown—about 3 minutes per side. Drain on paper toweling and keep warm while you sauté the re᷄ .aining crabs.

To DEEP-FRY: It's my southern background, I guess, that makes me like deep-fried soft-shell crabs despite the more sophisticated ways that I've tried them. Here's the way I usually prepare them: Clean the crabs as directed, sprinkle lightly with salt and freshly ground black pepper or lemon pepper, dip in buttermilk, letting the excess drip off; then dredge in **self-rising** flour. Deep-fry, 2 to 3 crabs at a time, in cooking oil at 375°F. (190°C.) for 2 to 3 minutes until nut-brown and crisp. Drain on paper toweling and keep warm while you fry the balance of the crabs. NOTE: *A simpler way of dredging the crabs is to sprinkle them with salt and freshly ground pepper, then to dredge them in all-purpose flour, shaking off the excess. But I do prefer the rich, batterlike crust the buttermilk dip and self-rising flour produce.*

Eastern Shore deviled crab

SERVES 6

The Eastern Shore of Maryland, a peninsula washed by the Atlantic on one side and Chesapeake Bay on the other, is blue-crab country. Cooks here prepare crab in more ways than would seem possible, but few of them can top this exquisitely light deviled crab.

1 medium-size	yellow onion, peeled and chopped	1 medium-size
½ medium-size	sweet green pepper, cored, seeded and chopped	½ medium-size
5 tablespoons, in all	melted unsalted butter	5 tablespoons, in all
1 pound	lump crab meat, picked over for bits of shell and cartilage	½ kg
1 cup	moderately fine soft bread crumbs	240 ml
1 large	hard-cooked egg, peeled and finely chopped	1 large
2 tablespoons	minced parsley	2 tablespoons
2 tablespoons	Dijon mustard	2 tablespoons
¼ teaspoon	dry mustard	¼ teaspoon
¼ teaspoon	cayenne pepper	¼ teaspoon
¼ teaspoon	salt	¼ teaspoon
Light sprinkling	freshly ground black pepper	Light sprinkling
	TOPPING:	
4 tablespoons	fine dry bread crumbs tossed with ½ teaspoon melted unsalted butter	4 tablespoons

Stir-fry the onion and green pepper in 2 tablespoons of the butter in a medium-size heavy skillet over moderately low heat about 10 minutes until limp and golden. Scrape into a mixing bowl, add all remaining ingredients (except those for the topping) drizzle with the remaining melted butter and toss lightly to mix. Spoon the mixture into large buttered scallop shells or individual ramekins, mounding the mixture up. Then sprinkle lightly with the topping and bake, uncovered, in a moderately hot oven (375°F. or 190°C.) for 20 minutes. Serve as a main course accompanied by a crisp, cool green salad.

Sherried crab and mushrooms

SERVES 6

If you double or triple this recipe and bake it in two batches, you have an elegant buffet entrée. Accompany by boiled rice, a crisp salad sharply dressed, dinner rolls and, because of the richness of the crab, follow with a light fruit dessert.

2 large	shallots, peeled and chopped	2 large
5 tablespoons, in all	unsalted butter	5 tablespoons, in all
½ pound	mushrooms, wiped clean and chopped	225 g
¼ cup	moderately dry sherry or Madeira	60 ml
1 tablespoon	lemon juice	1 tablespoon

2 tablespoons	flour	2 tablespoons
¼ teaspoon	freshly grated nutmeg	¼ teaspoon
¼ teaspoon	cayenne pepper	¼ teaspoon
½ teaspoon	salt	½ teaspoon
Pinch	freshly ground black pepper	Pinch
1 cup	half-and-half cream	240 ml
¼ cup	freshly snipped dill	60 ml
¼ cup	minced parsley	60 ml
1 pound	lump crab meat, picked over for bits of shell and cartilage	½ kg

TOPPING:

1 cup	moderately fine dry bread crumbs tossed with 1 tablespoon melted unsalted butter	240 ml

Stir-fry the shallots in 3 tablespoons of the butter in a large heavy skillet over moderate heat 3 to 5 minutes until limp; dump in the mushrooms and sauté, stirring frequently, 8 to 10 minutes until they have released their juices and these have evaporated. Pour in the sherry and lemon juice, then adjust heat to its lowest point and allow the mixture to mellow while you proceed with the recipe.

In a small heavy saucepan, melt the remaining 2 tablespoons of butter over moderate heat. Blend in the flour, nutmeg, cayenne, salt and pepper and mellow about a minute. Mix in the cream and heat, stirring constantly, until thickened and smooth—about 3 minutes. Reduce the heat to its lowest point, mix in the dill and parsley and allow to mellow 5 minutes.

Dump the crab into a mixing bowl, add the mushroom mixture, then the parsley-and-dill sauce. Toss well to mix, spoon into a buttered 6-cup (1½ L) shallow casserole or *au gratin* pan, and scatter the topping evenly over all. Bake, uncovered, in a moderately hot oven (375°F. or 190°C.) for 30 minutes until bubbling and browned, and serve.

Lobster

If you've priced lobsters lately, you know that they are very nearly worth their weight in silver, if not in gold. And inflation is less responsible for their sky-high cost than are pollution and greed. So threatened, in fact, is our lobster supply that there is presently a federally funded program for the development of lobster farming.

The lobsters in question are the lordly American lobsters (*Homaris americanus*), those giant-clawed beauties whose lives are such a series of crises and threats that only two out of ten thousand freshly hatched eggs ever make it to maturity. That's right—just two eggs. There are natural predators—sea birds and fish that pluck the larvae from the sea—but a greater peril are the unscrupulous fishermen who do not throw back undersize or "berried" lobsters (females carrying eggs on their swimmerets). The result, of course, is that our supplies dwindle (more than half of the fifty million pounds of lobsters that we Americans consume each year are now imported from Canada). And as supplies are depleted, prices rocket. All the more reason to treat the lobster with utmost respect and to give it kid-glove care in the kitchen.

Season: Year round, although supplies may be short in winter.

Hallmarks of quality: Like live crabs, live lobsters should be very active, thrashing about when you pick them up. (Be sure that your fish store pegs the claws or secures them with bands so that you don't get nipped.) Big is not better when it comes to lobsters. The sweetest and most tender will weigh 3 pounds (1½ kg) or less apiece. All Maine lobsters (and many of those available in this country are from Maine) are carefully graded according to weight before they are shipped. Here are the classifications:

Chickens or Chicken Lobsters	1 pound (455 g)
Heavy Chickens	1–1⅛ pounds (455–515 g)
Quarters	1¼ pounds (570 g)
Selects	1½–1¾ pounds (675–800 g)
Deuces or Two-Pounders	2 pounds (907 g)
Heavy Selects	2–2¼ pounds (907 g–1 kg)
Small Jumbos	2¼–2½ pounds (1–1¼ kg)
Jumbos	2½–4 pounds (1¼–1⅘ kg)

It's also possible now to buy cooked, chilled lobster meat by the pound (½ kg) in many fine fish markets. And, of course, frozen rock lobster tails are available everywhere. I frankly think very little of these because they are stringy and tough. I'd just as soon do without lobster at all as to settle for a frozen rock lobster tail.

How much lobster per serving? I like to allow about 2 pounds (1 kg) live lobster per person and about ¼ to ⅓ pound (115 to 160 g) of lobster meat.

Best way to store: Live lobsters will keep best when packed in seaweed in a large heavy paper bag and stuck in the coldest part of the refrigerator. **Maximum storage time:** 48 hours, but cook sooner, if possible.

Chilled, **cooked lobster meat** should be stored in the refrigerator in its original carton and **frozen lobster tails** in a 0°F. (−18°C.) freezer in their original wrappers. **Maximum storage times:** About 3 days for the chilled lobster meat, 2 months for the frozen tails.

Basic preparation: If the lobsters are to be cooked whole, they require no preparation at all. But if you are going to split them live, read the next paragraph carefully.

Some special techniques: Some recipes—primarily French classics—call for splitting or cutting up **live** lobsters, not jobs for the squeamish. The first task is to kill the lobster instantly. This can best be done by driving the point of a knife (or better yet, an ice pick) through the center-back of the lobster just where the carapace (body shell) joins the tail. Next turn the lobster over and split the tail lengthwise, using a knife sharp enough to sever the shell. NOTE: *The lobster will quiver as you work with it, but this is merely a muscular spasm.* Now split the body of the lobster in two and discard the stomach (paper sac near the eyes) and intestinal vein that runs the length of the tail.

How you proceed from here will depend upon the individual recipe. Usually the **tomalley** (buttery green liver) and **coral** (ovary with undeveloped eggs) are removed and blended into stuffings or sauces. NOTE: *Every now and then you may come upon a lobster filled with a gelatinous green-black mass. I was horrified the first time I split open a lobster to find such a sight, and called Mike DeMartino, my fish man, straightaway. He hooted! "That's the roe," he said. "You've got a female lobster just ready to lay eggs. The roe is considered one of the greatest delicacies of all." Mike was right. But since that first encounter almost ten years ago, I haven't lucked onto another roe-rich female. (Lobstermen are required by law to throw them all back into the sea.)*

Best ways to cook: I think it's a sacrilege to broil or bake lobster because the delicate flesh merely shrivels and toughens under intense dry heat. If you insist upon learning how to broil or bake a lobster, you will have to look elsewhere for directions. My feeling is that lobster must be coddled and that there are only two ways to do it:

TO STEAM: The first rule is not to steam too many lobsters in a single kettle. Two lobsters per 4-gallon (16 L) kettle is about right. Place a rack in the bottom of each kettle, pour in about 2 quarts (2 L) of boiling water and add **no** salt. Grasping the lobsters around the back, lower them, head first, onto the racks in the kettles. As soon as the water returns to a boil, cover the kettle and steam the lobsters 20 minutes exactly. Have ready plenty of paper toweling and a sharp knife. Using tongs, lift the lobsters from the kettle and bed on the paper toweling on a countertop. Now split each tail lengthwise, letting all of the water ooze out onto the towels. When the lobsters have drained thoroughly, pile on a big platter. Put out plenty of melted butter, nutcrackers and picks so that guests may help themselves. Also put out a big bowl to catch the fall-out of shells (there's always plenty).

TO BOIL: Again, don't try to cook more than two lobsters in a single kettle. Half fill with lightly salted water (about 1 tablespoon of salt per kettle) or better yet, with sea water. Bring to a slow boil over moderate heat, then adjust the heat so that the water just trembles. If it boils hard, you will toughen the lobsters. Holding the lobsters by the back, ease them, head first, into the kettle and as soon as the water returns to a tremble (**not** a full rolling boil), cover the pot and begin timing the cooking. Chicken lobsters will be done in about 12 minutes; for anything larger (up to 3 pounds or 1½ kg), add 2 to 3 minutes cooking time for each additional ½ pound (225 g). Larger lobsters—4 to 5 pounders (1¾ to 2¼ kg)—should be perfectly cooked in 25 minutes. Again, have lots of paper toweling ready to catch the juice that trickles out of the lobsters as you split them. Serve as directed above for steamed lobsters.

Shrimp

Of all the species of shellfish, shrimp are the best known, best loved, most available and most versatile. They abound in coastal waters surrounding much of the United States, but the bulk—not to mention the best—of them come from the warm waters of the Gulf of Mexico. These are plump, sweet-meated shrimp, sometimes such jumbos that you get only fifteen of them to the pound. Cold-water shrimp, on the other hand (notably those from the Pacific Northwest and Baltic), are truly "shrimps," so tiny that it may take two hundred of them to make a pound. Far more popular, more common and more reasonably priced are the average-size, all-purpose shrimp that number between twenty and forty to the pound. And what about prawns? Another species altogether, a European relative, not often seen in this country outside of posh restaurants or fancy fish markets. What are usually pawned off here as prawns are nothing more than jumbo shrimp.

Season: Year round.

Hallmarks of quality: Look for clean, sweet-smelling shrimp that have not been so roughly handled that they are battered or broken. If the shrimp have been shelled, their flesh should be moist, not slimy, firm yet resilient, translucent and pale mauve-gray. Cooked shrimp are also sold by many fish markets, but I rarely buy them because they are invariably overcooked. I don't think much of frozen shrimp, either, because their texture is alternately rubbery and mushy.

How much shrimp per serving? There is considerable waste when you buy shrimp in the shell, something to bear in mind each time you plan to serve shrimp. I figure upon **1½ to 2 servings per pound** (½ kg) of **unshelled** shrimp. From **shelled** raw shrimp, I expect to get **2 to 3 servings per pound** (½ kg).

Best way to store: Shrimp, like other shellfish, spoil quickly, especially when **raw.** As soon as I get shrimp home from the store, I rinse them under cool water whether or not they have been shelled. I then pat them dry and arrange in one layer on a large plate, cover snugly with plastic food wrap and store in the coldest part of the refrigerator. **Maximum storage time:** About 2 days. **Cooked shrimp** will keep slightly longer if properly stored. I pile them into a bowl, drop in an ice cube or two to provide both chill and moisture, cover snugly with plastic food wrap and refrigerate. **Maximum storage time:** About 3 days.

Frozen shrimp, it goes without saying, should be kept in the freezer—one that can maintain a temperature as low as 0°F. (−18°C.). **Maximum storage time:** 6 months, although I frankly think that frozen shrimp begin to lose quality after 3 months.

Basic preparation: Fresh raw shrimp should first be rinsed in cool water. How you prepare them from here on out depends pretty much upon the recipe you're following, also upon your personal taste. They may be shucked raw, in which case, simply peel the shell off in segments, starting with the feelers on the curved underside of the shrimp. Once the shell is off, devein each shrimp by making a shallow slit the length of the outer curved edge and pulling the black vein out, starting at the large end and working toward the tail. NOTE: *The vein is harmless, merely unsightly. A lot of good cooks I know never bother to devein shrimp, but that somehow strikes me as being aesthetically insensitive, not to mention lazy.* Once you've deveined all of the shrimp, rinse them well under cool running water and pat dry in paper toweling. NOTE: *If you choose to shell and devein the shrimp after they're cooked, use the same technique. The only difference is that the shells are harder, so work carefully lest you cut yourself.*

A special technique: Many recipes call for **butterflied shrimp,** which means simply that the shrimp have been cut almost—but not quite—through, then spread flat like a butterfly or an open book. Butterflying is one of the easiest techniques to learn: All you need to do is deepen the slit you made when deveining the shrimp, cutting to within about ⅛ inch (½ cm) of the opposite side. The next step is to place the shrimp on the counter, cut side down, and to press lightly to spread the halves.

Best ways to cook shrimp: Here, too, I part company with many of the cooks I respect, to say nothing of good friends. They like to broil and bake shrimp. I don't, certainly not unless there is plenty of moisture to bathe the shrimp and keep them succulent. Never, ever, do I bake or broil shrimp unprotected from the harsh oven heat because they quickly turn to rubber. My theory about cooking shrimp is that it must be coddled, and the best ways to do that, I think, are by boiling, sautéing, stir-frying or deep-frying (my southern upbringing surfaces again).

To BOIL: Actually, shrimp shouldn't be boiled, but merely simmered, because boiling makes them leathery. They may be simmered in the shell or out—the procedures are identical. Some people add more salt to the water for unshelled shrimp. I don't. I don't care for the briny taste it imparts or the hardness it gives to the shrimp. My technique is simply to half-fill a big pot with water, court bouillon, or a two-to-one mixture of water and dry white wine, and bring it to a gentle simmer, to add the shelled or unshelled raw shrimp, to let the water return to a simmer, then to cover the kettle and cook the shrimp just until they have turned a dazzling flamingo pink—2 to 3 minutes, usually, but never more than 5. I drain the shrimp at once and, if I intend to serve them cold, plunge them into a large bowl of ice water to quick-chill. NOTE: *You can, of course, cook shrimp in beer. It's a waste of good beer, I think, although friends of mine wouldn't cook shrimp any other way.*

To STIR-FRY OR DEEP-FRY: See the recipes that follow.

Stir-fried shrimp with cucumber, water chestnuts and ginger

SERVES 4

Have at hand everything you will need to prepare this dish, for once you begin, things must move quickly and smoothly without your having to hunt for this or that.

3 medium-size	scallions, trimmed and sliced thin (include some green tops)	3 medium-size
1 medium-size	garlic clove, peeled and minced	1 medium-size
1 tablespoon	finely minced fresh ginger root	1 tablespoon
3 tablespoons	peanut oil	3 tablespoons
1 tablespoon	toasted sesame seed oil	1 tablespoon
1 pound	shelled and deveined small raw shrimp	½ kg
1 small	cucumber, peeled, halved lengthwise, seeded and sliced	1 small
¼ cup	dry vermouth	60 ml
2 tablespoons	mirin (Japanese sweet rice wine)	2 tablespoons
3 tablespoons	soy sauce	3 tablespoons
½ cup	sliced water chestnuts (preferably fresh)	120 ml

Stir-fry the scallions, garlic and ginger in the peanut and sesame oils in a large heavy skillet over moderately high heat 1 to 2 minutes until limp; add the shrimp and stir-fry 2 to 3 minutes, just until pink. With a slotted spoon, lift the shrimp to a large plate and reserve. Add the cucumber to the skillet and stir-fry 1 to 2 minutes; using the slotted spoon, transfer to the plate of shrimp. Pour the vermouth, *mirin* and soy sauce into the skillet and boil hard 2 to 3 minutes until reduced by about half. Dump in the water chestnuts and turn them in the soy mixture a minute or so. Return the shrimps and cucumbers to the skillet and turn in the soy mixture 1 to 2 minutes until nicely glazed and flavors are mingled. Serve with fluffy boiled rice.

Crispy buttermilk-dipped fried butterfly shrimp

SERVES 4

First of all, if you are to have success with this recipe, the shrimp must be small—about 30 to 35 per pound—otherwise they will not cook through by the time the batter is brown. Second, you must use very hot fat— about 375°F. or 190°C.—so that the shrimp cook quickly without toughening.

1 pound	shelled and deveined small raw shrimp	½ kg
1 teaspoon	lemon pepper	1 teaspoon
1 cup	buttermilk	240 ml
1½ cups	unsifted self-rising flour	350 ml
2 quarts	peanut, corn or vegetable oil (for deep-fat frying)	2 L

Butterfly the shrimp by deepening the cut made for deveining and spreading each flat like an opened book. Sprinkle with lemon pepper; dip into buttermilk, then dredge in the self-rising flour. Fry the shrimp in three to four batches, in 375°F. (190°C.) deep fat until crisply golden—1 to 1½ minutes, **no longer,** or the shrimp will toughen. Drain on several thicknesses of paper toweling and serve hot.

Clams

"Those little treasures hid in the sand." That's what the Pilgrims called clams, with good reason, for clams helped to sustain them during lean times in the New World. Clams are not as plentiful today as they were in the day of our founding fathers, but their supply is not threatened in the way that the lobster supply is, and there are clams enough to go around.

Although there are perfectly delicious Pacific clams (razors, pismos, butter clams and those long-necked giants known as Geoducks—pronounced *gooey-ducks*), East Coast clams are better known and more widely available. These are of two types:

Hard-shell clams or quahaugs (the best of these come from New England and Long Island):

LITTLENECKS—So called because of their small necks. These are delicate, diminutive clams, usually between 1½ to 2 inches (4 to 5 cm) across at the widest point. The best way to serve them? On the half-shell.

CHERRYSTONES—The same clam as the littleneck, only bigger. Cherrystones average 2 to 2½ inches (5 to 6½ cm) across. Also best on the half-shell because their meat is so succulent.

CHOWDER CLAMS—The same clams grown up. Chowders measure 3 inches (8 cm) across or more and, because their meat is apt to be tough, are best when minced and used in chowders or other recipes.

Soft-shell clams: These are usually known as "steamers" because they are the preferred clams for steaming. New Englanders also insist that they make the best chowder and fritters. Steamers, most likely, were the Pilgrim's "treasures in the sand," because they are dug along sandy beaches at low tide. They are sold in their shells.

Season: Year round, although steamers are at their most plentiful and succulent in summer.

Hallmarks of quality: It's difficult to determine the quality of **unshucked clams.** The best advice I can offer is to buy from a reputable dealer and to specify the type of clam you want. A good fishmonger will handle the clams gently lest their shells chip or crack; he also will not load your order with dead clams—those that do not "clam up" when tapped. **Shucked hard-shell clams** should be sweet-smelling, opalescently pink and covered—although not swimming—in their own liquor.

How much per serving? Allow 10 to 12 clams per person if they are to be served on the **half-shell.** For **shucked clams,** I count on 3 to 4 servings per pint (½ L); this amount will go further if I'm using the clams in a rich recipe.

Best way to store: **Unshucked clams** should be stored in a bucket of ice in a cool corner of the cellar or, if there is room, in the refrigerator. **Maximum storage time:** 2 days. **Shucked clams** should be stored in the coldest part of the refrigerator in their original carton. **Maximum storage time:** 24 hours.

Basic preparation: All unshucked clams—and most especially steamers—must be purged of sand and grit. But first, scrub the shells well under cool running water. If the clams are hard-shell, reject any that do not close tightly as you handle them—they are probably dead or full of mud. NOTE: *Soft-shell clams do not clamp as tightly shut as the hard-shells, but you can tell, nonetheless, as you handle them whether there's movement. If not, the clams are probably dead or duds.*

The second step is to submerge the clams in a bucket of cold water, to toss in a handful of cornmeal or sprinkle in 3 tablespoons of vinegar, then to let the clams stand for at least 10 hours, or better still, 24. Cornmeal and vinegar both act as irritants, forcing the clams to cleanse themselves. NOTE: *If the weather is hot, I also drop several ice cubes into the bucket and keep adding them as needed to maintain the water temperature at ocean coolness.* Drain the clams after the purge, then rinse well in cool water. They are now ready to cook or shuck. NOTE: *Shucked clams need no special treatment, but their liquor should be strained through a fine sieve to remove bits of grit.*

To shuck clams: Equip yourself first of all with a clam knife—a sturdy, stubby blade strong enough to withstand considerable shell-prying. Holding the clam securely in one hand, slip the side of the knife between the top and bottom shells at the front (the nonhinged side). Now twist the blade in the crack, forcing the halves apart. Run the knife around the shell to the hinge at the back. Twist off the top shell, then use the knife to cut the clam from the shell. Pour any juice (clam liquor) through a fine sieve into a cup and reserve. (It's marvelous for soups and sauces if the recipe you're preparing does not call for it.)

Best ways to cook clams:

TO STEAM: Soft-shell steamers are the best choice for steaming, although littlenecks and cherrystones can also be steamed. Pour 2 inches (5 cm) of water into a deep kettle with a close-fitting lid. Add a rack to the kettle, bring the water to a boil, then pile the cleaned and purged clams on the rack. Cover the kettle and steam the clams 6 to 10 minutes, just until their shells open (discard any that do not). Serve the clams with plenty of melted butter and wedges of lemon.

TO BAKE: See recipe that follows.

NOTE: *Other than steaming clams, baking them or eating them on the half-shell, I like them best in chowder and pie or prepared à la marinière, as in Moules Marinière, substituting an equal quantity of clams for mussels (see Index).*

Baked clams on the half-shell with herb butter

SERVES 4

One advantage of this recipe is that you can make the herb butter well ahead of time, then spoon it over the clams just before they go into the oven. TIP: *To keep the clams upright as they bake, bed them in rock salt in the baking pan. If you have four pie tins attractive enough to go to the table, make beds of rock salt in each, then arrange half a dozen clams in a circle in each tin.*

¼ pound (1 stick)	unsalted butter, at room temperature	115 g (1 stick)
1 medium-size	shallot, peeled and minced fine	1 medium-size
1 small	garlic clove, peeled and minced fine	1 small
2 tablespoons	minced parsley	2 tablespoons
2 tablespoons	freshly snipped chives	2 tablespoons
2 tablespoons	minced fresh tarragon (or 1 teaspoon crumbled leaf tarragon)	2 tablespoons
1 tablespoon	dry vermouth	1 tablespoon
1 teaspoon	Dijon mustard	1 teaspoon
Few drops	liquid hot red pepper seasoning	Few drops
1 cup	moderately fine soft bread crumbs	240 ml
24	littleneck or cherrystone clams on the half-shell	24

Cream the butter with the shallot, garlic, parsley, chives, tarragon, vermouth, mustard and liquid hot red pepper seasoning until creamy-smooth, then mix in the bread crumbs. Arrange the clams in a bed of rock salt in a large shallow baking pan or in four pie tins half filled with rock salt. Spoon the herb butter over each clam, dividing the total amount evenly. Bake uncovered in a very hot oven (425°F. or 220°C.) for 8 to 10 minutes until bubbly and lightly browned. Serve as a first course or main course.

New England clam chowder

SERVES 6

Never allow clam chowder to boil. If you do, the clams will toughen and the milk will curdle. NOTE: *I favor Spanish or Bermuda onions for this recipe because they are milder and sweeter than yellow onions.*

2 ounces	salt pork, cut into small dice	60 g
1 large	Spanish or Bermuda onion, peeled and chopped	1 large
4 large	Maine or Eastern potatoes, peeled and cut into small cubes	4 large
1½ cups	water	350 ml
1 pint	shucked clams (do not drain)	½ L
1 pint	milk, at room temperature	½ L
1 pint	half-and-half cream, at room temperature	½ L
¼ teaspoon	cayenne pepper	¼ teaspoon
To taste	salt and freshly ground black pepper	To taste

In a large heavy kettle set over moderate heat, brown the salt pork until most of the fat has been rendered and the dice are reduced to crisp browned bits. With a slotted spoon, lift these to paper toweling to drain; reserve. Dump the onion and potatoes into the drippings and stir-fry 5 to 10 minutes, until limp and golden. Add the water, cover and simmer 15 to 20 minutes until the potatoes are tender. Drain the liquor from the clams, strain through several thicknesses of cheesecloth (to remove any grit or bits of shell) and add to the kettle along with the clams. Heat gently 3 to 4 minutes—no longer or the clams may toughen.

In a separate heavy saucepan, bring the milk and half-and-half to the simmering point. Very slowly pour into the clam mixture, stirring gently all the while. Add the cayenne, the reserved salt pork, then salt and black pepper to taste. Ladle into large soup plates and serve with pilot biscuits or oyster crackers.

Mussels

Unlike oysters, scallops and clams, mussels have never been very popular in this country despite the fact that abroad they're so fashionable that they must be "farmed" if the demand for them is to be met. I personally prefer mussels to either oysters or clams because I find them sweeter, milder and more interesting. But few people, I dare say, would agree with me.

Because they've never gained much favor here, mussels are plentiful along both Atlantic and Pacific coasts—from Alaska to San Francisco on the West

Coast, from the Arctic to North Carolina's Outer Banks on the East Coast. Best of all, they are cheap. **Really** cheap, often less than a dollar a pound.

Season: Year round. NOTE: *Because of the dangerous warm-weather "red tide" along the Pacific Coast, mussels (and other mollusks, too) are available there principally from November through April. In recent years, alas, "red tides" have begun to affect East Coast supplies of shellfish, too.*

Hallmarks of quality: Look for mussels with relatively clean, tightly closed shells that have not been cracked or broken. NOTE: *Fresh mussels are rarely, if ever, sold out of the shell.*

How many mussels per serving? From 1 pound (½ kg) of unshelled mussels, you can count upon 1 to 2 servings—it all depends upon how the mussels are prepared. And upon appetites.

Best way to store: The less mussels are handled, the better. I simply shove them—without rinsing or scrubbing—into the bottom of the refrigerator in their heavy brown-paper fish-market wrapper. **Maximum storage time:** 24 hours.

Basic preparation: Although often muddy outside, mussels do not suck grit and muck inside their shells the way clams do, so they need not be purged. All they require, really, is a good scrubbing under cool running water, then a meticulous "bearding." The "beards" are the brown, fibrous tufts that protrude from the shells of mussels (they are actually the means by which mussels cling to rocks and pilings). They're unsightly but easy to remove. You can snip the beards off with scissors, cutting as close to the shell as possible. Or—and this is the method I prefer—you can pull them out, tugging from the narrow end of the mussel shell around toward the broader rounded end. If a little of the mussel meat should come away with the beard, no matter. If there are small barnacles or bits of stone clinging to the mussel shells, flick or pry them off with the point of a knife.

You should inspect the mussels carefully as you prepare them and reject at once any that are broken, cracked or chipped. Also reject any that appear to be lifeless. It's easy to tell whether a mussel is alive when you pull the beard away, because it will clamp its shell tightly shut—so tightly that you won't be able to budge it. Thump any questionable mussels with your fingers; if they sound hollow, pitch them out. A live mussel will give off a dull, thudding sound. NOTE: *Cookbooks used to recommend that you submerge mussels in a bucket of water and reject as dead any that float. Misleading advice, I've found, because mussels often suck in enough air to make themselves buoyant. A truer test comes after you've cooked the mussels: If the shells do not open, the mussels should be discarded.*

To open raw mussels: Few people realize that mussels are as delicious on the half-shell as oysters and clams. And I think they're even better. Serving them this way means that you must open the shells. Fortunately, it's easier than opening either clams or oysters because mussel shells are less tough and less tightly hinged. Holding the mussel in one hand, insert the point of a paring knife between the two shells but nearer the narrow end than the center; tilt it upward so that the point rests against the inside of the top shell, then slowly move the knife around the mussel. When it has gone full circle, lift the two halves apart. Discard the top shell.

Best ways to cook: Aside from the basic method of steaming mussels just below, my favorite ways to prepare mussels are included as recipes, both in this section and among the Recipe Collection in Part II.

To STEAM: Pour about 2 inches (5 cm) of water into a very large heavy kettle; place a rack in the bottom of the kettle, then bring the water to a boil. Pile the scrubbed and bearded mussels on the rack, cover the kettle and steam the mussels 5 to 7 minutes, just until their shells open wide. **Discard any mussels that do not open.** Serve with melted butter into which you have squeezed a little lemon juice and/or mixed a little minced garlic.

Moules marinière

SERVES 4

Of all the recipes that I have tried for this French country classic, I like this one best. Scrubbing and bearding the fresh mussels is tedious, it's true, but as you labor away, you can take solace in the fact that the cooking goes quickly. NOTE: *For cooking the mussels, choose a large, heavy, broad-bottomed kettle so that you can reduce the cooking liquid with due speed.* It is this boiling down of the cooking liquid, the concentration of the sea-sweet essence of the mussels, that sets this recipe apart. NOTE: *You will not need to add any salt to this recipe because mussels are naturally salty. Indeed, make sure that the butter you use for finishing the sauce is unsalted.* You'll be pleased to know that littleneck or cherrystone clams can be substituted in this recipe for the mussels with splendid results.

2 large	yellow onions, peeled and chopped	2 large
2 large	shallots, peeled and minced	2 large
2 medium-size	garlic cloves, peeled and minced	2 medium-size
2 tablespoons	olive oil (top quality)	2 tablespoons
4 pounds	fresh unshelled mussels, scrubbed in cool water and bearded, OR littleneck or cherrystone clams, scrubbed and purged of grit	2 kg
1 cup	dry white wine	240 ml
1 cup	water	240 ml
2 tablespoons	unsalted butter	2 tablespoons
½ cup	minced parsley	120 ml
Light sprinkling	freshly ground black pepper	Light sprinkling

Stir-fry the onions, shallots and garlic in the oil in a large heavy kettle over moderate heat 10 minutes until limp and golden. Add the mussels, wine and water, and as soon as the liquid trembles gently, cover and simmer 8 minutes. With a slotted spoon, lift the mussels to a large heatproof bowl, discarding any that did not open. Cover the bowl loosely with foil. Raise the burner heat to its highest point and boil the cooking liquid hard for about 15 minutes until reduced by almost half. Swirl in the butter, and when it melts, return the mussels to the kettle. Reduce the burner heat at once to its lowest point, sprinkle in the parsley and pepper and warm the mussels in the reduced liquid about 2 minutes, turning them often. Spoon into soup plates and top each portion with a generous ladling of the cooking liquid. Accompany with garlic bread and a cool, crisp salad.

Oysters

Connoisseurs will forever quibble about the merits of one oyster over another: the subtle bluepoints of Long Island, for example, versus the briny Wellfleet of Cape Cod, the coppery Chincoteagues of Virginia versus the fragile varieties along the subtropical Gulf Coast. Heredity may affect the size, shape and color of a particular species, but habitat—particularly the salinity of the water—appears to determine flavor.

Once blessed with an abundance of natural oyster beds off the shores of every surf-washed state, America's supply is now so severely depleted that we, like the Romans almost two thousand years before us, must grow our own if our appetites are to be satisfied. Judging from the middens of oyster shells found along our coasts, American Indians were almost as gluttonous in their consumption of oysters as the Romans. But America's first all-out oyster binge began early in the last century with the coming of "The Oyster Express," lightweight wagons that raced from Baltimore to Pittsburgh, carrying fresh cargoes of oysters bedded in wet seaweed. Soon the craze spread farther west—to Cincinnati, where the places to be seen were the city's proliferating "oyster parlors," and then farther still to Springfield, Illinois, where the young Mr. and Mrs. Abraham Lincoln threw oyster parties at which nothing but oysters was served.

Oyster madness abated only when the nation's supplies were imperiled in the late nineteenth century. And it is unlikely to resurface given our conservationist turn of mind, to say nothing of the price of fine oysters.

Season: There **is** something to the "R months" theory. It is not, as many of us have been taught, hazardous to our health to eat oysters in May, June, July or August. It's just that this is the oyster spawning season and that most states forbid the taking of oysters during these months. No matter, oysters are not very plump or palatable while they spawn. You can stretch the oyster season, of course, by resorting to canned or frozen oysters—but they are sorry substitutes.

Hallmarks of quality: Most oysters today are sold shucked, although big-city markets (and oyster pounds at the source) also sell them in the shell and opened on the half-shell. The best oysters will be plump, moist and ivory-hued to pale tan. They will smell sweet but also exude a sharp marine tang. Their liquor should be clear, never cloudy.

How many oysters per serving? If you are going to serve oysters on the half-shell, allow 6 to 12 per person, depending upon the size of the oysters and the richness of the meal to follow. As for shucked oysters, 1 pint (½ L) will serve 2 to 3 persons, depending upon the way in which they're prepared.

Best way to store: In the refrigerator, tightly covered in their original carton. **Maximum storage time:** 24 hours.

Basic preparation: Shucked oysters require little other than that they be drained (reserve and strain the liquid through a fine sieve to remove any bits of shell or grit), then rinsed in cool water. As you rinse the oysters, probe them gently for small stones, bits of grit, even pearls. (I once found a tiny pearl when I was helping my mother prepare oysters, and I was ecstatic for weeks. The pearl was worthless, of course, but not to my young mind.) Needless to say, anything hard found among the oysters should be discarded lest someone break a tooth. NOTE: *If you intend to serve oysters on the half-shell, most fish markets or oyster pounds, praised be, will bill and open the oysters for you. Let them! It's a nasty job because oyster shells are rough, hard and razor-sharp about the edges.*

Best ways to cook: I'm afraid I belong to the school of purists who think oysters are best raw, although I do occasionally batter-fry, scallop or stew them, and include recipes for each of these here.

Batter-fried Chesapeake oysters

SERVES 4

This no-nonsense recipe was given to me by the late Mrs. Charles Seymour, a Chesapeake Bay waterman's wife, whom I interviewed some six years ago for a series I was writing for *Family Circle* magazine called "America's Great Grass Roots Cooks." I include it here because it is quite simply the best recipe for batter-fried oysters I have ever eaten.

24 large	shucked oysters, patted dry on paper toweling	24 large
Light sprinklings	salt and freshly ground black pepper	Light sprinklings
½ cup	oyster liquor	120 ml
⅓ cup	milk	80 ml
⅔ cup (about)	sifted all-purpose flour	160 ml (about)
1 cup	vegetable shortening or oil	185 g (240 ml)

Sprinkle the oysters lightly all over with salt and pepper. Combine the oyster liquor and milk in a small bowl, then add just enough of the flour to make a batter about the consistency of pancake batter. Heat the shortening in a heavy, medium-size skillet over moderate heat until a bread cube will sizzle vigorously when dropped into the skillet. Dip the oysters into the batter, then drop into the hot fat and brown 3 to 4 minutes on a side—just until a rich topaz brown. NOTE: *Do not attempt to fry more than 6 oysters at a time, because they will crowd the skillet and cool the fat. To keep each batch warm as successive ones cook, spread the oysters out on a shallow baking pan lined with paper towels and set, uncovered, in a keep-warm oven (250°F. or 120°C.).* Serve sizzling hot.

Scalloped oysters

SERVES 6

1 small	yellow onion, peeled and minced	1 small
3 tablespoons	unsalted butter	3 tablespoons
2 tablespoons	flour	2 tablespoons
Pinch	crumbled leaf thyme	Pinch
Pinch	freshly grated nutmeg	Pinch
1 quart	shucked oysters, drained	1 L
¾ cup	oyster liquor, strained	180 ml
¼ cup	heavy cream	60 ml
½ large	lemon, juiced	½ large
½ teaspoon	salt	½ teaspoon
⅛ teaspoon	freshly ground black pepper	⅛ teaspoon
1 cup	crushed soda crackers	240 ml
	TOPPING:	
½ cup	moderately fine dry bread crumbs mixed with 1 tablespoon melted unsalted butter	120 ml

Stir-fry the onion in the butter in a small heavy skillet over moderate heat 3 to 5 minutes until limp and golden. Blend in the flour, thyme and nutmeg, turn heat to its lowest point and allow to mellow while you cook the oysters. Heat the oysters in the oyster liquor in a medium-size heavy saucepan over moderate heat 3 to 5 minutes, just until their "skirts" ruffle. Stir in the onion mixture, heavy cream, lemon juice, salt and pepper. Mellow a minute or two over low heat, then remove from the heat and stir in the crushed soda crackers. Spoon into a well-buttered 6-cup (1½ L) baking dish, sprinkle evenly with the crumb topping, then bake uncovered in a moderately hot oven (375°F. or 190°C.) for 25 to 30 minutes until bubbly and flecked with brown.

Old-fashioned oyster stew

SERVES 6 TO 8

A Down East cook once told me that the ideal proportions for oyster stew are one part oysters to two parts milk and/or cream. This straightforward, ungussied recipe proves his point. It's rich enough to serve as a main course and is a nourishing way to take the chill off a cold, raw day.

1½ pints	shucked oysters	¾ L
5 tablespoons (⅔ stick)	unsalted butter	5 tablespoons (⅔ stick)
1 quart	milk, at room temperature	1 L
1 pint	half-and-half cream, at room temperature	½ L
½ teaspoon (about)	salt	½ teaspoon (about)
¼ teaspoon	cayenne pepper	¼ teaspoon
Pinch	freshly grated nutmeg	Pinch

Drain the oysters, reserving the liquor. Line a large, fine sieve with several thicknesses of cheesecloth, set over a large bowl, pour in the oyster liquor and let it drip through undisturbed. Meanwhile, warm the oysters in the butter over moderately low heat 2 to 3 minutes—just until their edges begin to ruffle. Pour in the strained oyster liquor and set aside. Bring the milk and half-and-half almost **but not quite** to the simmering point over moderate heat in a second large saucepan, stirring occasionally. Stir about 1 cup of the hot milk mixture into the oysters, then pour all of the oyster mixture into the milk. Add the salt, cayenne and nutmeg, stir gently, then taste for salt and add more, if needed. Ladle into large soup bowls and serve with pilot or oyster crackers.

Scallops

"The caviar of mollusks," scallops have been called. I would agree with that judgment, particularly if the scallops in question are the tiny nut-sweet bay scallops from the waters of eastern Long Island. They are to me as delectable as lobsters or blue crabs, and infinitely more enjoyable than clams, mussels and oysters. I even prefer the large sea scallops to these mollusks.

Now plentiful, sea scallops were once so rare and costly that disreputable fishmongers faked them by punching disks out of cod. But the discovery in the mid-1930s of vast scallops beds off the New England shore assured us at last of a good supply of the real thing and put the shyster merchants out of business.

Season: Year round for sea scallops; from September through April for bay scallops.

Hallmarks of quality: The characteristics are the same for both bay scallops and sea scallops: moistness, plumpness, cleanliness, a fresh sweet aroma with the merest suggestion of the sea, and a minimum of accompanying liquid.

How much per serving? About ⅓ to ½ pound (160 to 225 g), depending upon the heaviness of the recipe.

Best way to store: Almost all scallops sold today are shucked. As soon as I get them home from the fish market, I transfer them to a deep plate (without first rinsing them), cover snugly with plastic food wrap and set in the coldest part of the refrigerator. Avoid storing scallops in a metal container because they will taste metallic. **Maximum storage time:** 48 hours under optimum conditions, but try to cook the scallops within 24 hours, if possible.

Basic preparation: So simple! Rinse the scallops under cool running water, then if they are to be sautéed, pat them dry on paper toweling. Nothing more is needed.

Best ways to cook: Scallops, I think, are more versatile than any other mollusks, thanks to a firmness of texture and delicacy of flavor. Some people insist that there is nothing more eloquent than bay scallops, sliced raw across the grain, graced with the lightest brushing of olive oil and a scattering of freshly ground black pepper. I'm frankly too chicken to eat bay scallops raw—even in *seviche*, where the lime juice is supposed to "cook" them. I studied too much pathogenic bacteriology in college and remember too vividly how fast microbes multiply. It's hepatitis I'm nervous about, and for this reason, I cook bay scallops—*always*. (I'm also pretty persnickety about the clams and oysters I serve raw.) As for sea scallops, they just aren't very good raw.

I also happen to think that scallops, unlike other shellfish, are best when dressed up a bit. You'll find all of my favorite ways of preparing scallops included, either here or among the Recipe Collection in Part II.

Sautéed bay scallops with dill and vermouth

SERVES 4

This is one of those last-minute recipes that require split-second timing, so line up all ingredients before you start. Also have handy a slotted spoon and a medium-size bowl to hold the scallops when you whisk them out of the skillet.

3 tablespoons	unsalted butter	3 tablespoons
1½ pounds	bay scallops, washed and drained	⅔ kg
½ cup	dry vermouth	120 ml
2 tablespoons	lemon juice	2 tablespoons

2 tablespoons	snipped fresh dill	2 tablespoons
1 tablespoon	minced parsley	1 tablespoon
¼ teaspoon	salt	¼ teaspoon
Light sprinkling	freshly ground black pepper	Light sprinkling

Melt the butter in a large heavy skillet over moderately high heat; when it foams up and subsides, dump in the scallops and stir-fry 4 to 5 minutes—just until the scallops have released considerable juice. With a slotted spoon, transfer scallops to a bowl. Pour the vermouth and lemon juice into the skillet and boil down with the scallops' juices until only a thick glaze remains on the bottom of the skillet—2 to 3 minutes should be sufficient. Quickly drain any juices that may have collected in the bowl of scallops into the skillet and boil these down also to a thick glaze. Return the scallops to the skillet, turn the heat down fairly low and toss the scallops in the glaze until nicely coated. Sprinkle in the dill, parsley, salt and pepper and toss the scallops lightly until the seasonings are evenly distributed. Serve immediately.

Baked breaded sea scallops

SERVES 4

I can think of few recipes more accommodating than this one: the scallops can be breaded several hours ahead of time, then kept refrigerated until you are ready to bake them. Once in the oven, they require nothing more than a brief basting or two.

1 pound	sea scallops of as nearly the same size as possible (for this recipe, I like them about 2 inches—5 cm—across)	½ kg
1 cup (2 sticks)	melted unsalted butter mixed with 2 tablespoons lemon juice	240 ml (2 sticks)
1½ cups	moderately fine soft bread crumbs	350 ml
3 tablespoons	freshly grated Parmesan cheese	3 tablespoons
2 tablespoons	minced parsley	2 tablespoons
Light sprinklings	salt and freshly ground black pepper	Light sprinklings

Rinse the scallops well in cool water, then pat dry on paper toweling; set aside for the moment. Pour the melted lemon butter into a small bowl; combine the bread crumbs, Parmesan and parsley and place in a pie tin. Now sprinkle the scallops lightly on both sides with salt and pepper, dip into melted butter, then into the crumb mixture. NOTE: *Pat the crumbs onto the scallops fairly liberally— you want a good thick coating.* Arrange the scallops in one layer in a shallow baking pan just big enough to contain them; drizzle any remaining melted butter evenly on top, taking care not to dislodge the crumb coating.

Bake the scallops uncovered in a moderately hot oven (375°F. or 190°C.) for 15 minutes, basting them once or twice with the buttery pan drippings. Serve hot with a simply prepared green vegetable—asparagus, beans or broccoli, for example—or, if you prefer, with a mixed green salad.

Vegetables

For years little more than an adjunct to a meal (or an afterthought), vegetables have at last come of culinary age. There are many reasons. More of us have access to first-rate fresh vegetables than ever before, thanks to the flowering of boutique greengroceries across the country. More of us have traveled—to Europe, the Middle and Far East, Africa, South America. And if we aren't whizzing off to other continents, we are at least exploring the excellent ethnic restaurants in our own country. We are learning about new vegetables, not to mention new ways of preparing old favorites, and supermarkets, keeping stride with our greater sophistication and curiosity about food, are expanding their inventories beyond such standard staples as cabbage, carrots and potatoes by stocking fresh ginger root, bean sprouts and mushrooms on a more or less daily basis.

Considering the variety of today's provender, it's hard for me to believe that just fifteen years ago in the small-town South where I grew up, mushrooms were a "special order." Whenever I wanted them, I hunted up the manager of the town's "gourmet grocery" and asked him to have mushrooms for me three to four days hence. He always did, although I think he had to order them from Richmond, Virginia, nearly two hundred miles away. Today, of course, that same market has mushrooms in ready supply along with such other former "special orders" as broccoli, cauliflower and artichokes. I even saw shallots and snow peas there on my last trip home.

But buying "fresh vegetables," alas, is no guarantee of freshness, because too many vegetables are picked green and shipped cross country to be prepacked in plastic and loll about supermarket bins for days. If it's a "just-picked" flavor that you crave, patronize local greengrocers or farms, where you can pick your own. Better yet, grow your own vegetables in your backyard. You don't need much ground to grow a bumper crop, and you may be surprised, as I once was, to discover what a green thumb you have.

Most fresh vegetables are graded as to quality by the federal government at the wholesale level, but the grades only occasionally appear on supermarket packages. The top grade is U.S. FANCY, the second best (and the one you're most likely to encounter) is U.S. NO. 1, and the third, U.S. NO. 2. Your best guide to quality, however, will simply be a vegetable's appearance, which is why I go into some detail in discussing the hallmarks of quality, vegetable by vegetable, in the pages that follow.

It may sound as if I am opposed to canned and frozen vegetables. Not completely. I find canned tomatoes preferable to the fresh for most recipes because they are mellower and have truer tomato flavor than the fresh ones I can usually get; certainly they are infinitely superior to those miserable tomatoes sold four-to-a-carton in supermarkets. I also think most canned tomato sauces, purées and pastes are superb. (Have you see the tomato paste available by the tube that can be kept in the refrigerator and squeezed out as needed? What a good idea!)

As for frozen vegetables, I consider most of them pretty poor. I do rely heavily on frozen chopped spinach, however, because fresh spinach is not available year round, because it is so tedious to wash and trim and because once it is chopped and cooked, I can frankly see little difference between it and the frozen. Baby limas are surprisingly good, too. I rate frozen green peas only so-so, but do use them on occasion when fresh green peas are unavailable. And I sometimes use frozen asparagus spears for purées and a favorite asparagus pie of mine. But I've never succeeded in making the spears acceptable if simply dressed with butter. By my standards, at least. They can never approach the exquisite crisp-tenderness of perfectly cooked fresh asparagus. I've tried every way I know to cook frozen asparagus, even reducing the cooking time to a brief blanching in boiling water. But the spears are always limp (scarcely surprising when you consider that the ice crystals formed, as the stalks freeze, rupture their fragile structure). Two other frozen vegetables I find acceptable are artichoke hearts and Brussels sprouts, but I use them only as fill-ins during the off-season.

In the pages that follow, you will find full discussions of the most popular and interesting vegetables available today. You will also find additional vegetable recipes among the Recipe Collection in Part II.

Artichokes (globe)

Until recently, only the plump **Green Globe** artichokes were widely available, but today the small, conical Italian **Violets** and **Green French**—Europe's choice—are being routinely stocked by many big-city greengrocers. Sometimes not much bigger than a rosebud, these tender young artichokes contain no "choke" and thus can be halved, stir-fried and eaten as is.

Season: September through June with April being the peak month.

Hallmarks of quality: Plumpness, compactness, **tightly** closed buds (for artichokes are the buds of an edible thistle). The green of Globe and French artichokes should be a clear spring or apple green. Violet artichokes will be greenish at the base, shading into lavender, midleaf, then deepening to purple at the tip. Globe artichokes vary tremendously in size, ranging anywhere from an ounce (28 g) to a pound (½ kg), depending not so much upon age as upon position on the stalk. The smallest artichokes grow at the bottom of the stalk, the medium-size ones in the middle, and the choice, jumbo artichokes at the apex. NOTE: *Truly fresh artichokes will squeak when you squeeze them.*

How many artichokes per serving? Allow one medium-size or large globe artichoke and 3 to 4 small French or Italian ones per person.

Best way to store: Unwashed, first of all. If you wash artichokes before you refrigerate them, they may blacken. I simply pop the unwashed artichokes into small plastic bags—one globe artichoke (but about four small French or Italian artichokes) per bag—as soon as I get them home from the store, then set them in the bottom of the refrigerator *unsealed* (it's important that some air circulate around them. I try to cook the artichokes within a day or two of purchase, but have managed to hold them successfully, bagged in plastic, for about a week **provided** the artichokes were tightly budded when I bought them.

Basic preparation: All artichokes, regardless of how you will ultimately prepare them, should first be soaked in a sinkful of lightly salted cold water for about 30 minutes. Drain them well, pat dry on paper toweling, then prepare as individual recipes direct or according to the following special techniques (because of their unique anatomy, artichokes call for a greater variety of preparation techniques than any other vegetable):

Some special techniques needed for artichokes:

TO TRIM: Slice the stem off even with the bottom of the artichokes, then snip off the prickly tip of each leaf and, if you like a tidier look, lay the artichoke on its side and slice off the top inch (2½ cm) or so. This is all the preparation an artichoke needs if it is to be simply steamed. NOTE: *It isn't necessary to dechoke an artichoke unless you intend to stuff it. Each person will dechoke his own artichoke at the table after he has plucked the outer leaves off, one by one, and nibbled the nut-sweet nugget of flesh at their base. The way I attack the choke at table is to cut around its base with a sharp knife, then to slide the knife underneath it and lift it off in one simple operation.*

TO DECHOKE RAW ARTICHOKES: Only globe artichokes will need to be dechoked, and these only if they are to be stuffed or sliced. After you have soaked and trimmed the artichokes as directed above, spread their leaves at the top, then using a sturdy teaspoon or a ball scoop, reach down into the heart of the artichoke and scoop out all of the prickly bits of thistle.

TO SLICE: Wash, trim and dechoke globe artichokes as directed. Lay them on their sides on a cutting board, and using a very sharp, heavy knife, cut straight through them crosswise, slicing as thick or as thin as you like. For most purposes (omelets, stir-frying and such), I find ¼ to ½ inch (¾ to 1½ cm) ideal. TIP: *Artichokes will discolor a carbon steel knife, so if that is what you use for slicing, clean the knife at once, using a fine steel-wool pad and a little lemon juice. My knife sharpener, who comes round regularly to sharpen my battery of knives and scissors, says that the best way to remove stains from carbon steel knives is to rub the blades with a lightly oiled cork in a gentle circular motion. I've tried Fred's technique and it works, although it does require patience and persistence. As soon as the knives are bright, wipe them carefully with paper toweling and return them to the knife rack.*

To STUFF: Wash, trim and dechoke the artichokes as directed. Spread the leaves and lightly spoon your favorite stuffing down into the hollow in the center of each artichoke and then, if you like, scatter more of the stuffing down between the leaves. You won't need much stuffing for each artichoke—usually from ½ to 1 cup (120 to 240 ml), depending upon size. Bread-crumb stuffings are unusually compatible with artichokes and can be varied in myriad ways. **A favorite stuffing of mine** (enough for 2 large or 4 small to medium-size artichokes): Lightly toss 2 cups (½ L) fine soft bread crumbs with 3 tablespoons melted unsalted butter in which you have crushed ½ very small garlic clove, then toss in 3 tablespoons freshly grated Parmesan. FLAVORFUL ADDITIONS: 1 to 2 tablespoons finely minced parsley; 1 to 2 finely minced shallots sautéed in the melted butter just until limp; a pinch of crumbled leaf rosemary, marjoram, oregano and/or thyme. **The best way to cook stuffed artichokes:** Steam them or bake them (directions follow).

To MAKE ARTICHOKE HEARTS: These are nothing more than the tender centers of globe artichokes, minus the chokes, and they couldn't be easier to prepare: first strip away all outer leaves of the uncooked artichoke until you reach the pale, yellow-green leaves at the center. Lay the artichoke on its side, slice the stem off even with the bottom, then slice off the prickly leaf tips. Spread the leaves of the heart and scrape out the choke. Artichoke hearts may be stir-fried and served as a vegetable or steamed, chilled and dressed with lemon juice or wine vinegar and oil. They also make a superlative addition to tossed salads and casseroles.

To MAKE ARTICHOKE BOTTOMS: These are even easier. Simply pull all leaves from the artichoke, scrape out the choke, then slice the stem off even with the bottom. You will now have a solid cup-shaped piece of artichoke that can be stir-fried in a little oil or steamed until tender, then stuffed with a variety of hot or cold savory mixtures: vegetable purées, meat or fish salads or such classic sauces as hollandaise or béarnaise. Filled artichoke bottoms make showy edible garnishes for meat, fish and poultry platters, as French chefs have long known.

TIP: *To prevent the cut surfaces of artichokes from darkening, rub them at once with half a lemon or dip them into lemon juice.*

Best ways to cook: I used to boil artichokes, but lately I've become a convert to steaming because steamed artichokes are firmer and more flavorful. You lose something when you boil an artichoke because much of its delicate flavor leaches out into the cooking water.

TO STEAM: Place the prepared artichokes on a rack and lower them into a kettle (stainless steel or enameled cast iron, preferably, because aluminum can discolor artichokes) containing about 1 inch (2½ cm) of boiling water. Cover and steam just until you can pluck a leaf from the base of an artichoke easily. **Cooking times:** 40 to 45 minutes for large whole artichokes; 30 to 35 minutes for dechoked large artichokes or medium-size whole artichokes; 25 to 30 minutes for small artichokes, artichoke hearts or bottoms or dechoked medium-size artichokes. NOTE: *If you intend to use the artichoke hearts or bottoms in casseroles or other recipes, partially cook them only for about 15 minutes.* Using a skimmer or slotted spoon, lift the artichokes from the kettle and stand on several thicknesses of paper toweling to absorb the excess moisture.

TO BAKE: Technically speaking, this is oven-steaming, for the artichokes are cooked in a covered casserole with a little bit of liquid. It's the best way, I think, to cook stuffed artichokes. Choose a small heavy kettle with a tight-fitting cover—it should be just large enough to accommodate the artichokes without crowding them. Pour in about 1 inch (2½ cm) of boiling water or beef or chicken broth. Stand the artichokes in the kettle so that each touches and supports its neighbor, add a couple of peeled garlic cloves, if you like, a bay leaf and parsley sprig or two. Drizzle olive or vegetable oil *very* lightly over each artichoke. Cover and bake in a moderate oven (350°F. or 175°C.) for about 1 hour or until you can remove a leaf from the base of an artichoke easily. Using a skimmer or slotted spoon, lift each artichoke from the kettle and set briefly, base down, on several thicknesses of paper toweling. (This is to draw any excess moisture from the artichokes so that they don't "weep" on the dinner plate or platter.) Serve the artichokes hot, or do as the Italians do and serve them at room temperature.

TO STIR-FRY: Heat a large peeled and halved garlic clove in 2 to 3 tablespoons of olive or vegetable oil in a large heavy skillet over moderate heat 2 to 3 minutes; discard the garlic. Raise the burner heat to moderately high, dump in 1 to 1½ quarts (1 to 1½ L) of sliced globe artichokes (or hearts or bottoms) and stir-fry 4 to 5 minutes—just until crisp-tender (hearts and bottoms may take as long as 10 to 12 minutes). Sprinkle lightly with lemon juice, dry white wine or vermouth and stir-fry about a minute longer. Season to taste with salt and freshly ground black pepper and serve. SOME FLAVORFUL ADDITIONS: 1 to 2 peeled and minced shallots (sauté them in the oil before adding the artichokes), a pinch of crumbled leaf rosemary, thyme, marjoram or tarragon.

NOTE: *If the artichoke hearts or bottoms are to be used in a recipe, do not season them.*

Globe artichokes stuffed with bacon, carrots, shallots and thyme

SERVES 4

Stuffing artichokes may seem an impossible task. Not at all. It goes quite quickly, in fact, if you know a few tricks. First of all, parboil the artichokes briefly—just long enough to limber the leathery leaves. Drain the artichokes well, then stand them upside down on a counter. With the heel of your hand resting on the center-bottom of an artichoke, press down gently but firmly. This will fan the leaves out like a full-blown rose, exposing the choke and leaving spaces between the leaves to cup the stuffing. Serve the stuffed artichokes at the start of an elegant small dinner or serve as the main course of a light luncheon.

4 medium-size (about ¾ pound each)	globe artichokes, soaked 30 minutes in lightly salted water	4 medium-size (about ⅓ kg each)
4 quarts	water	4 L
½ large	lemon, juiced	½ large
1 tablespoon	salt	1 tablespoon
	STUFFING:	
4 slices	lean bacon, snipped crosswise into julienne strips	4 slices
2 tablespoons	olive oil	2 tablespoons
4 large	shallots, peeled and minced	4 large
2 medium-size	carrots, peeled and minced	2 medium-size
2 large	garlic cloves, peeled and minced	2 large
1 teaspoon	finely minced thyme (or ½ teaspoon crumbled leaf thyme)	1 teaspoon
3 cups	fine soft bread crumbs	¾ L
½ teaspoon (about)	salt	½ teaspoon (about)
Light sprinkling	freshly ground black pepper	Light sprinkling
	FOR COOKING THE ARTICHOKES:	
1 cup	water	240 ml
½ cup	dry white wine	120 ml
3 large	garlic cloves, peeled	3 large
3 small	fresh thyme sprigs (optional)	3 small

Slice the stem off of each artichoke so that it will stand squarely without wobbling. Cut about 1 inch (2½ cm) off the top of each artichoke, then with kitchen shears, snip off the prickly leaf tips. Heat the water with the lemon juice and salt in a very large heavy kettle over moderate heat until it reaches a full boil. Drop in the artichokes, cover and parboil for 5 minutes exactly. Drain the artichokes well, then cool until they are easy to handle.

Stand the artichokes upside down on the counter, then one at a time, press down firmly on each artichoke bottom so that the leaves "blossom," exposing the choke. Turn the artichokes right side up. Using a teaspoon, scrape out the choke—all thistly bits at the heart of the artichoke. This takes a bit of doing, but persist, making sure that you have removed all of the choke from each artichoke. Set the artichokes aside while you prepare the stuffing.

For the stuffing: Sauté the bacon slowly in the olive oil in a small heavy skillet over moderately low heat about 10 minutes or until all of the drippings have cooked out of the bacon and only browned bits remain. Using a slotted spoon, lift the browned bits to paper toweling to drain; reserve. Stir-fry the shallots, carrots, garlic and thyme in the drippings over moderate heat 2 to 3 minutes—just until limp; do not brown. Chop the reserved bacon bits so that they are uniformly fine, then combine with the bread crumbs, salt and pepper, tossing lightly to mix. Dump in the skillet mixture and toss well again. Taste for salt and add more, if needed.

To stuff the artichokes: Starting with the bottom leaves, and working your way up and around the artichoke, spoon a little bit of stuffing down at the base of each leaf, so that the artichoke stands open like a flower. Finally, spoon stuffing into the heart where the choke was, mounding it up lightly. Do not pack the stuffing at any time, just spoon it lightly between the artichoke leaves.

To cook the artichokes: In a heavy kettle just large enough to accommodate all of the artichokes without crowding, place the water, wine, garlic cloves and, if available, the thyme. Bring to a boil over moderate heat. Adjust the burner so that the liquid barely trembles, then stand the artichokes, stem down, in the kettle. Cover and cook about 45 minutes or until you can remove a lower leaf from an artichoke easily. Cook the artichokes uncovered for 5 minutes more. Using a slotted spoon, lift them from the kettle, stand briefly on several thicknesses of paper toweling (to absorb excess liquid), then serve hot or at room temperature.

NOTE: *For years we've been cautioned never to serve wine with artichokes because, to quote one old cookbook, "Both will taste terrible!" I've always followed that advice. But when I was testing this recipe, I decided to serve a well-chilled, crisp, dry white Italian wine to see if there really was anything to the old wives' tale. I couldn't see that any curious alchemy had taken place. In fact, my luncheon guests and I all thought that the stuffed artichokes and crisp white wine complemented one another beautifully. Now a dry red wine might have an altogether different effect; I suspect that it might because it is more tannic.*

Artichokes (Jerusalem)

How Jerusalem artichokes came to be named—or rather misnamed—remains a mystery. They are not artichokes but a knobby, fawn-skinned tuber of the sunflower family also known as **"sunchokes."** Certainly Jerusalem artichokes are not from Jerusalem. Probably they are native to North America, because they were a great favorite of the American Indians and to this day still grow wild in open lots and along highway rights-of-way throughout the eastern United States. The most plausible explanation for their unlikely name is that "Jerusalem" is a corruption of *girasole*, the Italian word for sunflower. As for "artichoke," some people liken the flavor of Jerusalem artichokes to that of true artichokes. I think they taste more like potatoes.

Until recently, about the only way to enjoy Jerusalem artichokes was to go out and dig them up yourself. Today, however, they can be bought in the splendid Korean fruit and vegetable markets proliferating in big cities, across the country, also in health food stores (inulin, the starch of Jerusalem artichokes, cannot be assimilated by the body, making them a good choice for diabetics and calorie counters).

Season: Now that they are being grown for the table, Jerusalem artichokes can be had very nearly the year round. **Peak months:** October through February.

Hallmarks of quality: Plumpness, firmness, the absence of nicks and blemishes.

How much per serving? Allow about ¼ pound (115 g) or 3 to 4 artichokes.

Best way to store: Jerusalem artichokes are most often bagged in plastic by the grower, so I simply pop the bag of chokes into the refrigerator as is. Washing them beforehand, alas, merely hastens their demise. Unfortunately, Jerusalem artichokes soften fairly fast once dug, so use them within several days of purchase.

Basic preparation: Jerusalem artichokes are as knobby and misshapen as ginger root and, thus, the very devil to peel. Luckily, they need not be peeled, only scrubbed well in cool water, then patted dry on paper toweling.

Best ways to cook: Because it is so very easy to overcook Jerusalem artichokes (they will be firm one instant, then turn to tasteless mush the next), I frankly prefer them raw. They have a magnificent crunch—not unlike that of water chestnuts—and can enliven fish, poultry and vegetable salads, not to mention such humdrum cooked vegetables as buttered green peas, beans and carrots. I also add Jerusalem artichokes to all manner of meat loaves. And southern ladies have been making them into superlative pickles and pickle relishes for generations. TIP: *Jerusalem artichokes darken rapidly once they are cut, so plunge them at once into acidulated water (1 quart or 1 L cold water mixed with 1 tablespoon of lemon juice or white vinegar) and leave them there to keep them nice and white. Before using, drain the artichokes well and pat them dry on paper toweling.*

Old-time Tar Heel
Jerusalem artichoke pickle relish

MAKES ENOUGH TO FILL 6 HALF-PINT (¼ L) JARS

When I was growing up in North Carolina, this crunchy pickle relish was put up by local canneries and sold through supermarkets. My mother used to buy it and serve it with baked ham or roast turkey. I didn't learn to make the relish, however, until after I'd graduated from college and gone to work as an assistant home demonstration agent in Iredell County. One of the good local country cooks shared this recipe with me.

2½ pounds	Jerusalem artichokes	1¼ kg
2 large	sweet red peppers, washed, cored, seeded and coarsely chopped	2 large
2 large	sweet green peppers, washed, cored, seeded and coarsely chopped	2 large
4 large	yellow onions, peeled and coarsely chopped	4 large
1 gallon	cold water mixed with 4 teaspoons pickling salt (brine)	4 L
1⅓ cups	sugar	315 ml
1½ cups	cider vinegar	350 ml
1 cup	white (distilled) vinegar	240 ml
4 teaspoons	mustard seeds	4 teaspoons
1 tablespoon	ground turmeric	1 tablespoon
1 tablespoon	pickling spice, tied in cheesecloth	1 tablespoon

Scrub the artichokes well with a vegetable brush under cool running water, scrape away any dark or blemished spots and rinse well. Coarsely chop the artichokes and place in a very large enameled or stainless steel kettle. Add the red and green peppers and onions, toss lightly to mix, then cover with the brine. Allow to stand for 3 hours at room temperature. Line a large colander with a clean dish towel, then dump in the artichoke mixture. Allow to drip-dry until most of the brine has drained off, then bundle the artichoke mixture up in the towel and twist and squeeze, extracting as much liquid as possible. Empty the artichoke mixture into a large bowl.

In a large stainless steel or enameled saucepan, bring the sugar, vinegars, mustard seeds and turmeric to a boil, stirring frequently. Drop in the spice bag and boil 2 full minutes. Remove the spice bag, then pour pickling liquid over the artichoke mixture and stir well. Pack into 6 hot sterilized half-pint (¼ L) preserving jars, filling each to within ¼ inch (¾ cm) of the top. Run a thin-blade spatula around the inside of each jar to release trapped air bubbles, wipe the rims and seal. Process the jars for 10 minutes in a boiling water bath

(212°F. or 100°C.). Lift the jars from the water bath, complete the seals, if necessary, then cool to room temperature, label and store on a cool, dark dry shelf. Let the relish season 3 to 4 weeks before serving.

Asparagus

Unlikely as it may seem, asparagus and onions are related—distantly—for both belong to a lily family of the eastern Mediterranean. Ancient Greeks hiked into the hills above Athens each spring to stalk the wild asparagus, and Romans, at the height of their empire, grew asparagus on rooftops and balconies. Louis XIV had extensive beds of asparagus planted at Versailles and, years later, Thomas Jefferson at Monticello.

Americans today, as in Thomas Jefferson's day, favor green asparagus, Europeans, the white, especially the chunky, buttery Argenteuil, grown at the town of the same name near Paris. Although the common supermarket asparagus is the green, fancy produce shops now sell the rarer white asparagus in season.

Season: Early March through June. **Peak months:** April and May.

Hallmarks of quality: Smooth, tightly closed green tips shaded with mauve (white asparagus will have pale yellow tips); crisp, straight stalks devoid of blemishes; moist rather than fibrous or rubbery bases; scales that lie flat on the stalk. NOTE: *Stalk size is not necessarily an indicator of tenderness, because stalks an inch thick (2½ cm) can be every bit as succulent as those one-quarter their size. The age of the stalk is a truer test of tenderness (old asparagus will be woody), also the freshness of the asparagus (stalks that have been lying around will be withered and dry).*

How much asparagus per serving? If the asparagus was not trimmed before it was packaged or bundled, there will be considerable waste. All of the lower white stalks will be too tough to cook with the tender green tops (they *can* be simmered into soup, however, so don't pitch them out). You should probably allow between ½ to 1 full pound (¼ to ½ kg) per person, depending upon how closely the stalks have been trimmed (and how fond you are of asparagus).

Best way to store: Supermarkets usually bind stalks of asparagus together, and you should unbind them as soon as you get them home. Next, cut ½ inch (1½ cm) off the bottom of each stalk; dampen several thicknesses of paper toweling, then, gathering 6 to 8 stalks together, wrap their bases in the moistened toweling. Continue this way until you have wrapped all of the asparagus. Place a sheet of paper toweling in the bottom of a medium-size plastic bag, lay a bundle of asparagus flat on top of it, add a second sheet of paper, a second bundle of asparagus, reversing the direction of its tips, and so on until you have about two-thirds filled the bag. Fold the top over and slip the bag into the refrigerator vegetable crisper. **Storage time:** 4 to 5 days maximum. Asparagus deteriorates rapidly, so cook it within a day or two, if possible.

Basic preparation: Cut or break off the tough stem ends. I prefer the breaking technique because the stalk will snap just where "tough" turns to "tender."

Next, peel the asparagus. Holding a stalk by the tip and beginning at about where the first scale appears, run a vegetable peeler the length of the stalk toward the base, pressing almost not at all. The idea is to pick up the thin outer skin and scales only, not to cut into the white heart of the stalk. Soak the peeled stalks in a sinkful of cold water to which you have added 2 tablespoons each of salt and sugar (these will crisp the stalks like magic). Drain the asparagus well.

Best way to cook: After years of cooking asparagus, I've evolved a pet method that I think beats the traditional tying-the-stalks-into-bundles way of steaming or the standing-the-stalks-in-a-double-boiler method of boiling. It's easier than either and yields perfectly cooked asparagus—tender but with crunch.

First of all, choose stalks of as nearly the same size as possible—I like those measuring about ½ inch (1½ cm). Bring about 6 cups (1½ L) of lightly salted water to a rolling boil. Meanwhile, lay the asparagus stalks flat in one layer in a large heavy skillet (preferably stainless steel or enameled cast-iron or one of the new nonstick alloys) so that their tips all face the same direction. If your skillet is big enough—I use a 12-inch (30 cm) one—you can accommodate enough asparagus for 4 to 6 persons. As soon as the water comes to a boil, pour enough of it into the skillet to submerge the asparagus. Cover the skillet tight, set over moderate heat and cook 4 minutes for stalks less than ½ inch (1½ cm) in diameter, 5 minutes for those between ½ and 1 inch (1½ and 2½ cm) and 6 minutes for larger stalks. Drain the asparagus at once, then return to the skillet and set briefly over moderate heat, shaking the pan gently to drive off excess moisture. Season to taste with salt and freshly ground pepper, then dress with a little melted butter (I like to add about 1 tablespoon of snipped fresh dill or ½ teaspoon of dill weed to the butter as it melts), or with browned butter, oil and lemon or vinaigrette. Or serve with Hollandaise or Beurre Blanc (see Index).

To serve asparagus cold: Plunge the asparagus into ice water as soon as it is cooked and dress shortly before serving. NOTE: *The acidity of vinaigrette and many other dressings will turn the asparagus an appalling khaki color. The technique I use is to marinate the asparagus in the oil and herbs of whatever dressing I've chosen, then to sprinkle the lemon or vinegar on just before serving. This way the asparagus remains vibrantly green. If you intend to marinate the asparagus for only an hour or two, do so at room temperature; otherwise marinate the asparagus in the refrigerator.*

Easy asparagus purée noisette

SERVES 4 TO 6

Frozen asparagus is not something I often cook—**except** for this splendid purée with browned butter flavor. In fact, the frozen asparagus's tendency to become mushy is precisely why it is perfect for puréeing. And, of course by using frozen asparagus, you save yourself all the labor of washing, trimming and peeling. When puréed, frozen asparagus remains vibrantly green and deceptively "fresh-tasting."

3 packages (10 oz. each)	frozen asparagus spears	3 packages (283 g each)
3 cups	boiling water mixed with 2 teaspoons salt	¾ L
2 tablespoons	unsalted butter	2 tablespoons
Pinch	ground mace	Pinch
To taste	salt and freshly ground pepper	To taste

Lay the asparagus spears flat in a large heavy skillet, pour in the boiling salted water, cover, set over moderate heat and boil 10 to 12 minutes until very soft. Meanwhile, brown the butter slowly in a small heavy saucepan over low heat until a rich topaz hue. Drain the asparagus well, return to the skillet and shake briefly over moderate heat to drive off all excess moisture. Now purée the asparagus in a food processor fitted with the metal chopping blade, drizzling the browned butter down the feed tube. NOTE: *Several churnings—about 20 seconds each—are preferable to a single 60-second one. Uncover the work bowl after each churning and scrape the sides down before proceeding.* Churn in the mace and salt and pepper to season, then serve. NOTE: *If you do not have a processor, you can purée the asparagus, about one-third of the total amount at a time with about one-third of the browned butter, in an electric blender at high speed. Or you can force the asparagus through a food mill, then mix it with the browned butter, mace, salt and pepper.*

Asparagus and Gruyère pie

SERVES 6

Here's one of the few recipes in which frozen asparagus spears work well. Serve as the main course of a light luncheon or supper accompanied by tartly dressed salad or sliced tomatoes.

1 package (10 oz.)	frozen asparagus spears, cooked by directions and drained well	1 package (283 g)
A 9-inch	unbaked pie shell	A 23 cm
3 ounces	Gruyère cheese, coarsely grated	90 g
1 cup	milk	240 ml
½ cup	heavy cream	120 ml
2 medium-size	eggs, lightly beaten	2 medium-size
¼ cup	freshly grated Parmesan cheese	60 ml
1 teaspoon	salt	1 teaspoon
½ teaspoon	dill weed	½ teaspoon
Pinch	ground mace	Pinch
Pinch	freshly ground black pepper	Pinch

Trim the asparagus spears so that they are 3½ inches (9 cm) long, then arrange them in a sunburst pattern in the bottom of the pie shell with their tips pointing toward the center. Sprinkle the Gruyère evenly on top. Combine the milk, cream, eggs, Parmesan, salt, dill weed, mace and pepper and pour evenly over all. Bake uncovered in a moderate oven (350°F. or 175°C.) for 35 minutes. Cool 20 minutes, then cut into wedges and serve.

Beans (fresh)

"With corn they put in each hill three or four beans which are of different colors." Thus wrote Champlain of the Kennebec Indians in 1605. But he was not the first New World explorer to comment upon beans. Columbus remarked in 1492 that he had found "a sort of bean" in Cuba "very different from those of Spain."

The New World beans the explorers found are one of America's gifts to good eating: green beans, wax beans and limas. Those available today bear little resemblance to their early ancestors, however, for geneticists have developed modern varieties that are consistently tender and flavorful—and this goes for green and yellow wax beans, baby limas (often called butterbeans) and the big starchy Fordhooks. They have also bred plenty of snap into green beans and most of the woodiness out, meaning that you will find few strings attached.

Season: Year round for all beans. **Peak months:** June for green and wax beans, August and September for limas.

Hallmarks of quality: Straight, moist, slim, unblemished, pods (only over-the-hill beans bulge) and uniform green or yellow color.

How many beans per serving? ⅓ pound (160 g) green or wax beans; 1 pound (½ kg) unshelled lima beans. NOTE: *Always shell limas yourself.*

Best way to store: I simply bundle untrimmed, unwashed beans into a medium-size plastic bag, slip in several pieces of paper toweling, top and bottom (to absorb excess moisture), fold the top of the bag over loosely, and set in the vegetable crisper. If refrigerator space is tight, you can shell the limas into a plastic container, snap the lid on and refrigerate. But they will fast lose their just-shelled flavor, so cook within a day or two. **Storage time:** 4 to 5 days for green and wax beans and unshelled limas.

Basic preparation: Green and wax beans need only to be washed (I soak them in a sinkful of lightly salted cool water for about 20 minutes), then tipped (have their tapered ends snipped or snapped off). Limas must be shelled. NOTE: *To open the pods zip-quick, run a swivel-bladed vegetable peeler down the outside edge, then press the cut edge gently and the beans will tumble out.*

Best ways to cook: Boiling (the French way, which is really parboiling), **steaming** and **stir-frying** are my favorite ways to cook green and wax beans. Limas I prefer to simmer in a small amount of water.

To boil green or wax beans: Prepare the beans as directed, then boil uncovered in a very large kettle (the sort you would use for spaghetti) in about 1 gallon (4 L) of lightly salted water (1 teaspoon salt per quart or liter of water is a good ratio) about 10 to 15 minutes, depending upon the size of the beans. As soon as they are crisp-tender, drain and plunge into ice water. (This "refreshing," as the French call it, helps to set a vegetable's color, crunch and flavor.) Chill 10 to 15 minutes, then drain and pat dry on paper toweling. The chilled beans may be stored, tightly covered, in a plastic container and held in the refrigerator for as long as 24 hours. **To finish the beans:** Warm the beans 3 to 5 minutes, stirring often, in a large heavy skillet or sauté pan in a little fat or oil, allowing about 2 tablespoons per pound (½ kg) of beans. What you choose as the warming medium can completely alter the character of the beans. For example: Olive oil and garlic and, perhaps, a bit of freshly minced basil or marjoram will inject an Italian accent; peanut and/or sesame seed oil plus freshly minced ginger, garlic and a splash of soy sauce will give the beans a Japanese flavor; melted butter and freshly minced tarragon or chervil will make them French, and melted butter plus freshly snipped dill, Scandinavian. Of course, you may simply warm the beans 3 to 4 minutes in boiling water, drain them and serve with a classic sauce such as Hollandaise or Beurre Blanc (see Index). The point is to improvise, tasting as you go.

To boil lima beans: These are starchy beans, so it's best, I think, not to salt the cooking water because the salt has a toughening effect. For 1 to 1½ pounds (½ to ⅔ kg) of shelled beans, I use 1½ cups (⅓ L) of boiling water and for 1½ to 3 pounds (½ to 1½ kg) of beans, 2 cups (½ L) of boiling water. Simply drop the shelled beans into the rapidly boiling water, cover and simmer about 20 minutes until tender and no raw starch flavor remains. Drain well, and return to the pan. Shake briskly over the heat to drive off excess moisture. Add about 2 tablespoons of butter (or bacon fat) and/or ⅓ cup (80 ml) of heavy cream per pound (½ kg) of beans and warm 2 to 3 minutes over low heat—just until flavors mellow. Season to taste with salt and freshly ground black pepper and serve.

To steam green or wax beans: Prepare as directed, then lay the beans flat in a steamer basket; lower into a large saucepan containing about 1½ inches (4 cm) of boiling water (the basket should not touch the water). Cover the pan tight and steam the beans 20 to 25 minutes if they are whole, 15 if cut into chunks, and 10 to 12 if Frenched—taste a bean toward the end of cooking and as soon as it is tender but crunchy, remove from the heat. Top with melted butter (warmed, if you like, with a little chopped fresh tarragon, chervil, marjoram, summer savory, thyme or dill). Or top instead with hollandaise or a zippy mustard sauce. NOTE: *Any of the seasonings suggested for boiled beans can be used for steamed beans.* Add salt and freshly ground black pepper to taste.

To stir-fry: The Chinese method of dry-sautéing is my favorite for green beans because it heightens their color, mellows their flavor but at the same time preserves most of their original crunch and nutritive value. Prepare the beans as directed, and pat dry. For each pound (½ kg) of beans, use about 3 tablespoons of peanut oil (or 2 parts peanut oil to 1 part toasted sesame seed oil). Heat the oil a minute or two over high heat, dump in the beans along with 1 to 2 minced cloves of garlic and 1 tablespoon of finely minced fresh ginger root. Reduce the heat slightly, and stir-fry 4 to 5 minutes, just until the beans are an intense green. NOTE: *You must toss the beans constantly as they cook, otherwise they may scorch.* Splash in a little soy sauce instead of salt, if you like, then season to taste with freshly ground black pepper and serve.

To serve green or wax beans cold: Boiled or steamed beans are as good cold as hot, either alone or in tandem with other vegetables. Quick-chill them as soon as they are crisp-tender by plunging into ice water, then drain well. Dress with any favorite salad dressing: oil and vinegar, oil and lemon, herb, garlic—anything you fancy. NOTE: *If you intend to marinate green beans in a tart dressing, mix together only the oil and the seasonings and pour this mixture over the beans, cover and let stand 1 to 2 hours at room temperature or a day or more in the refrigerator. Only at the last minute should you add the vinegar or lemon juice, for both quickly turn green beans a dreary brown.*

Green beans and walnuts in tarragon-mustard sauce

SERVES 6

These beans will be more fragrant if seasoned with fresh tarragon—especially the heady French tarragon. The mustard you choose for this recipe should be mellow rather than salty or biting. Beans prepared this way are especially good with broiled chicken, salmon or swordfish.

1½ pounds	tender young green beans, tipped and snapped in half	⅔ kg
2 quarts	boiling water mixed with 1 teaspoon salt	2 L
¾ cup	coarsely chopped walnuts	180 ml
2 large	shallots, peeled and minced	2 large
3 tablespoons	unsalted butter	3 tablespoons
¼ teaspoon	crumbled leaf thyme	¼ teaspoon
3 tablespoons	flour	3 tablespoons
2 tablespoons	mild French mustard	2 tablespoons
1 cup	reserved bean cooking water	240 ml
¾ cup	heavy cream	180 ml
2 tablespoons	freshly minced tarragon (or 1½ teaspoons crumbled leaf tarragon)	2 tablespoons
To taste	salt and freshly ground black pepper	To taste

Cook the beans in the salted boiling water in a covered saucepan over moderate heat about 15 minutes until tender. Drain, reserving 1 cup (240 ml) of the cooking water. Return the beans to the pan in which you cooked them, add the walnuts, and set aside for the moment. In a small heavy saucepan set over moderate heat, stir-fry the shallots in the butter about 3 minutes until limp and golden. Add the thyme and flour and stir to make a smooth paste. Now blend in the mustard. Add the reserved cooking water and cream and cook and stir about 3 minutes until thickened and smooth. Stir in the tarragon, salt and pepper to taste, then pour the sauce over the beans and walnuts. Let mellow over very low heat about 5 minutes, stirring occasionally. Taste for salt and pepper, add more, if needed, then serve.

Marinated green beans with zucchini, red onion and tarragon

SERVES 6

For large parties, I double or triple this recipe. It's perfect for buffets because it's colorful and easy to spoon out of the bowl with one hand. TIP: *To keep the beans nice and green, add the vinegar shortly before serving, not earlier, because it will turn the beans brown. Also do any fine tuning of seasonings just before serving.* These beans are superlative with chicken in almost any form.

1½ pounds	tender young green beans, tipped and snapped in half	⅔ kg
4 quarts	boiling water mixed with 1 tablespoon salt	4 L
1 pound	tender young zucchini, cut into matchstick strips about 2 × ¼ inch (5 × ¾ cm)	½ kg
1 large	red onion, peeled and quartered	1 large
2 tablespoons	finely minced scallions	2 tablespoons
1 large	garlic clove, peeled and finely minced	1 large
⅓ cup	freshly minced tarragon (or 2 teaspoons crumbled leaf tarragon)	80 ml
1 teaspoon	crumbled leaf marjoram	1 teaspoon
1 teaspoon (about)	salt	1 teaspoon (about)
⅛ teaspoon	freshly ground black pepper	⅛ teaspoon
4 to 6 tablespoons (about)	olive oil (a good assertive oil)	4 to 6 tablespoons (about)
4 to 5 tablespoons (about)	tarragon vinegar	4 to 5 tablespoons (about)

Boil the beans in the salted water in a covered kettle over moderate heat 10 to 15 minutes until crisp-tender. Meanwhile, place the zucchini in a large heatproof bowl. Slice each onion quarter thin and add to the zucchini along with the minced scallions and garlic. When the beans are done, drain them well, then return them to the kettle and shake vigorously over moderate heat to drive off excess moisture. Dump the hot beans on top of the zucchini, onion, scallions and garlic and let stand until cooled to room temperature. Now add the tarragon, marjoram, salt and pepper and toss well to mix. Add 4 tablespoons of the oil and toss well. Taste and add more oil, if needed. Let the bean mixture marinate at room temperature 3 to 4 hours. Or cover and marinate overnight in the refrigerator (bring to room temperature before proceeding). Toss the bean mixture well again, add 4 tablespoons of the vinegar and toss well. Taste and if not tart enough, add an extra tablespoon or so of vinegar. Also add more oil or salt, if needed. Toss well again and serve.

Limas with bacon, basil and mint

SERVES 4

The limas I use for this recipe are the big, starchy Fordhook type. Their pods are so tough that to speed shelling, I snip them open along the curved outer edge with kitchen shears. Try to use fresh mint and basil—both should be in season when the limas are at their peak.

2 pounds	large lima beans (in the shell)	1 kg
3 cups	boiling water mixed with 2 teaspoons salt	¾ L
2 ounces	smoked slab bacon, cut into small dice	60 g
3 large	shallots, peeled and minced	3 large
1 tablespoon	freshly minced basil (or ½ teaspoon crumbled leaf basil)	1 tablespoon
1 tablespoon	freshly minced mint (or 1 teaspoon mint flakes)	1 tablespoon
⅓ cup	light or heavy cream	80 ml
To taste	salt and freshly ground black pepper	To taste

Boil the limas in the salted water in a covered saucepan 18 to 20 minutes until firm-tender. Meanwhile, fry the bacon in a small heavy skillet over moderately low heat 10 to 15 minutes until all of the drippings have cooked out and only browned bits remain. With a slotted spoon, lift the browned bits to paper toweling to drain; reserve. Pour off all drippings, then spoon 3 tablespoons of them back into the skillet and stir-fry the shallots over moderate heat 3 to 5 minutes until limp and golden; reserve. When the limas are done, drain them well, return them to the pan and shake briefly over moderate heat to drive off excess moisture. Dump in the shallot mixture, add the basil, mint and reserved bacon and toss lightly to mix. Add the cream, salt and pepper to taste, stir gently, then allow to mellow a minute or two over moderate heat before serving.

Beans (dried)

What bounty! What beauty! There are beans, it seems, of every size, shape and color: black (turtle beans), white (navy or pea, Great Northern and limas), pink, red (kidney), ivory (garbanzos or chick peas), speckled (cranberry and pinto), even "eyed" beans (cowpeas and black-eyed peas). Most of them come from Michigan, most can be bought in almost every big supermarket, all are remarkably versatile and all make economical meat substitutes because of their top-quality protein. Less widely available (but no less versatile or nutritious) are the giant, mealy favas, beloved by Mediterranean peoples (your best bets for finding them will be Greek, Italian or Middle Eastern groceries).

Hallmarks of quality: Unbroken beans of good color with a minimum of grit or gravel.

How much per person? A pound (½ kg) of dried beans will serve 4 to 6.

Best way to store: Tightly covered in a glass jar (to keep weevils and roaches at bay) on a cool, dark shelf. Stored thus, dried beans will keep indefinitely.

Basic preparation: All beans should be sorted (for bits of stone, misshapen, broken or shriveled beans), then placed in a colander and rinsed well in cool water. They must also then be soaked so that most of the water lost in the drying process is replaced, softening the beans. There are two methods: fast and slow.

STANDARD METHOD OF SOAKING BEANS: Place the beans in a large bowl and for each 1 pound (½ kg) of them, add 6 cups (1½ L) of water and 2 teaspoons of salt. Let stand overnight at room temperature. Next day, drain the beans well. NOTE: *Beans soaked by this slower method will retain their shape better than those soaked by the quick method; they will also have more uniform texture.*

QUICK METHOD OF SOAKING BEANS: For each 1 pound (½ kg) of beans, use 6 cups (1½ L) of water. Bring the water to a boil, dump in the beans, cover and boil 2 minutes. Turn the heat off and let the beans stand, covered and undisturbed, until they have cooled to room temperature. Drain well.

Best way to cook: No matter how they will ultimately be used, dried beans must first be boiled until tender, and the method is the same for all varieties. Only the cooking time varies because some beans are tougher than others.

TO BOIL: Sort and soak the beans as directed, add 6 cups (1½ L) of hot water. Bring to a gentle simmer over moderate heat, cover and cook until firm-tender: approximately 35 minutes for cowpeas and black-eyed peas; 50 to 60 minutes for limas and favas; 1 to 1½ hours for kidney beans, pink beans and garbanzos; and 1½ to 2 hours for black beans, pintos, navy (or pea) and Great Northern beans. Test the beans about 15 minutes before their cooking time is up, and if they are *al dente* (tender but still a bit firm between the teeth), drain them at once. They are now ready to season and serve or to use as individual recipes direct.

COOKING TIPS: *To minimize the risk of the kettle of beans boiling over, add a pat of butter or a tablespoon of cooking oil to the cooking water. . . . To prevent the skins from bursting, cook the beans at a gentle simmer instead of a hard boil. . . . To keep the beans from sticking to the pot, stir them from time to time. . . . Finally, if a recipe calls for an acid ingredient (vinegar, for example, or tomato paste or lemon juice), add it at the end of cooking, not at the beginning, because acid reacts with the starch of the beans and keeps them from softening properly.*

Purée of red beans, bacon and onions with dry red wine

SERVES 6 TO 8

 This rich, porridge-thick purée is magnificent with roast venison, turkey, chicken or game birds, served in place of potatoes or puréed chestnuts. Or serve it as the centerpiece of a light luncheon or supper, accompanying with crisp chunks of garlic bread and a tartly dressed green salad. NOTE: *The processor makes short shrift of this once awkward recipe because it chops the vegetables and purées the beans in seconds.*

1 pound	dried kidney beans, washed and sorted	½ kg
6 cups	cold water	1½ L
4 slices	lean bacon, snipped crosswise into julienne strips	4 slices
2 medium-size	yellow onions, peeled and chopped	2 medium-size
1 large	garlic clove, peeled and minced	1 large
1 large	carrot, peeled and chopped	1 large
½ teaspoon	crumbled leaf thyme	½ teaspoon
½ teaspoon	crumbled leaf marjoram	½ teaspoon
¼ teaspoon	crumbled leaf rosemary	¼ teaspoon
1 large	bay leaf	1 large
1½ cups	dry red wine	350 ml
2 to 4 tablespoons (about)	bean cooking water	2 to 4 tablespoons (about)
2 tablespoons	unsalted butter	2 tablespoons
½ teaspoon (about)	salt	½ teaspoon (about)
⅛ teaspoon	freshly ground black pepper	⅛ teaspoon

Place the beans in a large heavy kettle, add 5 cups (1¼ L) of the water and bring to a boil over moderate heat; boil uncovered for 2 minutes, then remove from the heat, cover the beans and allow to cool to room temperature. Add the remaining cup (240 ml) of cold water to the beans, bring to a simmer, adjust burner heat so that the beans bubble gently, cover and cook 2 to 2½ hours or until the beans are very tender.

Meanwhile, brown the bacon slowly in a medium-size skillet over moderately low heat until all of the drippings have cooked out and only crisp brown bits remain. With a slotted spoon, lift the browned bacon to paper toweling to drain. Pour off all drippings, then spoon 3 tablespoons of them back into the skillet. Set over moderate heat, dump in the onions, garlic and carrot and stir-fry about 10 minutes until limp and lightly browned. Mix in the thyme, marjoram and rosemary and stir-fry 1 to 2 minutes to release and intensify their flavors. Drop in the bay leaf, add the wine and turn burner heat down low. Let the mixture simmer slowly until the wine has cooked down by about three-fourths, leaving only a thin layer in the bottom of the skillet. If you keep the heat properly low, this will take almost as long as it will take for the beans to cook. Remove the skillet from the heat when the wine has cooked down sufficiently; remove and discard the bay leaf.

When the beans are tender, drain them, reserving about ½ cup of the cooking liquid. Place the beans in a food processor fitted with the metal chopping blade (if you have one of the smaller work bowls, you will probably have to purée the beans in two batches), add all of the wine mixture and the reserved bacon crumbles and buzz for about 30 seconds nonstop. Add 2 tablespoons of the reserved bean cooking water and buzz about 30 seconds longer. If mixture still seems very stiff, add a third and, if necessary, a fourth or fifth tablespoon of cooking water. The bean purée should be the consistency of whipped potatoes. NOTE: *If you do not have a food processor, force the beans through a food mill, together with the skillet mixture and reserved bacon, then beat in just enough bean cooking water to give the purée a fluffy consistency.* Add the butter, salt and pepper and beat hard to combine. Taste for salt and add more, if needed, and serve.

Navy bean salad with lemon and dill

SERVES 6

One of the cold marinated vegetable dishes at which Turkish women excel.

1 cup	dried navy or pea beans, washed and sorted	240 ml
1 quart	water	1 L
2 small	carrots, peeled and cut in fine dice	2 small
1 large	Spanish or Bermuda onion, peeled and chopped	1 large
1 small	garlic clove, peeled and minced	1 small

4–5 tablespoons	olive oil	4–5 tablespoons
3 tablespoons	minced fresh dill (or ½ teaspoon dried dill weed)	3 tablespoons
3 tablespoons	minced parsley	3 tablespoons
3 tablespoons	lemon juice	3 tablespoons
1–1¼ teaspoons salt	salt	1–1¼ teaspoons
Light sprinkling	freshly ground black pepper	Light sprinkling

Bring beans and water to a boil in a large heavy saucepan over moderate heat; boil a minute, turn heat off, cover pan and let stand 1½ hours. Bring to the boil once again, adjust burner heat so that water ripples gently, re-cover and cook beans 45 minutes. Add carrots, re-cover and cook about 45 minues or until beans and carrots are tender.

Meanwhile, lightly sauté onion and garlic in 3 tablespoons of the olive oil in a large heavy skillet over moderately low heat about 3 to 5 minutes—just until golden but still a bit crisp; set aside. When beans are tender, drain well and empty into a large heatproof bowl. Add sautéed onion mixture, dill, parsley, lemon juice, salt and pepper and enough of the remaining olive oil to coat beans lightly. Cover and marinate several hours in the refrigerator. Toss well again and if salad seems dry, add a little additional olive oil. Let stand at room temperature 30 minutes before serving.

Beets

The beet would never win first prize as America's favorite vegetable, but ancient Greeks made offerings of it to the god Apollo. It was the Romans, however, who first wrote down recipes for cooking beets, and those of Apicius have come down to us today in facsimile editions of his famous cookbook.

Season: Year round. **Peak months:** June through September.

Hallmarks of quality: Smooth, dark red skin unbroken about the crown, a round rather than an oblong shape, slender tap roots and crinkly dark green leaves. NOTE: *For greater tenderness and flavor, select beets from 2 to 2½ inches (5 to 6½ cm) in diameter.*

How many beets per serving? ⅓ to ½ pound (160 to 225 g) or 2 to 3 smallish beets.

Best way to store: If the beets still have the tops on, cut them off about 1 inch (2½ cm) above the crown. (Beet greens, by the way, are delicious cooked like spinach.) Do not wash the beets before you store them, and do not trim off the tap roots. Simply bundle them loosely into a plastic bag and set in the refrigerator. **Storage time:** 7 to 10 days, but use the beets sooner, if possible, because they will lose flavor in cold storage.

Basic preparation: Beets need only to be scrubbed lightly in cool water, but use a gentle touch so that you don't break the skin. Do not peel the beets, do not cut off the inch (2½ cm) or so of tops remaining and do not remove the tap roots. NOTE: *The reason for leaving some of the tops and all of the roots on, and for cooking beets unpeeled, is so their exquisite color doesn't wash out into the cooking water.*

Best way to cook: Boiling is about the only method that works well for beets. Simply prepare them as directed above, place in a large heavy saucepan, cover with boiling unsalted water, clap the lid on the pan and boil 40 to 45 minutes or until you can pierce a beet easily with a fork. Drain the beets, quick-chill by plunging into ice water, then drain. Peel and slice, dice, cube or shred. Warm in a little melted butter (with a little dill weed or crushed caraway seeds added) for extra flavor, then sprinkle lightly with lemon juice, vinegar or a little tart red wine. Season to taste with salt and freshly ground black pepper and serve. NOTE: *Anthocyanin, the red pigment of beets, is an indicator rather like litmus, meaning that acids and bases (those compounds—baking soda, for one— at the high end of the pH scale) can change its color. Acids—of which lemon juice and vinegar are prime examples—turn the maroon of beets to a dazzling ruby red (which is why they are both so often used to flavor beets). And bases? I shall never forget stirring a little baking soda into shredded beets in a lab at Cornell and seeing them turn navy blue!*

Beets the Swedish way
with fresh dill and sour cream

SERVES 4 TO 6

 I've been serving beets this way ever since I tasted them at a Stockholm *smörgåsbord* some fifteen years ago. It was the most opulent *smörgåsbord* I've ever seen, but the beets held their own with the more theatrical offerings. For this recipe, Swedish cooks would use only the freshest beets and dill. I urge that you do the same because the recipe's success depends upon the mingled subtle flavors of just-pulled beets and just-picked dill. Choose beets that are uniformly small, preferably no bigger than crab apples.

1½ pounds	uniformly small beets	⅔ kg
6 cups	boiling water	1½ L
1 tablespoon	finely minced yellow onion	1 tablespoon
1 large	lemon, juiced	1 large
1 teaspoon	sugar	1 teaspoon
½ teaspoon (about)	salt	½ teaspoon (about)
Light sprinkling	freshly ground black pepper	Light sprinkling
½ cup	sour cream, at room temperature	120 ml
3 tablespoons	freshly snipped dill	3 tablespoons

Cut off all but about 1 inch (2½ cm) of the beet tops, but do not remove the root or peel the beets. Scrub them well in cool water, then place in a large heavy saucepan, add the boiling water, set over moderate heat, cover and boil about 45 minutes or until you can pierce a beet easily with a fork. Drain the beets well, and let cool until easy to handle. Peel the beets, removing both the tops and the root; slice about ⅜ inch (1 cm) thick directly into a mixing bowl. Add the onion, lemon juice, sugar, salt and pepper and toss lightly to mix. Add the sour cream and dill and toss more thoroughly—until the dill is evenly distributed. Taste for salt and add more, if needed. Reheat the beets briefly, but do not allow to boil or the cream may curdle. Serve hot or—and I like this way better—do not reheat the beets; let them stand instead at room temperature 1 hour before serving. NOTE: *You can prepare the beets as much as a day ahead of time; in fact they're more flavorful after a stay in the refrigerator. Simply cover and keep refrigerated until about 30 minutes before serving; the chilled beets should stand at room temperature at least 30 minutes so that the flavors heighten.*

Broccoli

Thomas Jefferson, who introduced spaghetti to America by serving it at the White House, grew another Italian favorite—broccoli—in his gardens at Monticello from seeds he had picked up abroad. One of the first American recipes for cooking broccoli appears in a Virginia cookbook of Jefferson's day. "Cook the vegetable as asparagus," it advises, "and dress it as cauliflower." Good advice, for broccoli is first cousin to cauliflower, a fragile cousin, hence the recommendation to cook it tenderly—like asparagus.

Season: Year round. **Peak months:** October and November; also January through April.

Hallmarks of quality: Dark green or mauve-tinged, tightly budded heads; moist, succulent stalks free of nicks and blemishes, crisp leaves. If the broccoli's curd (budding head) is beginning to yellow or flower, reject it.

How much broccoli per person? About ½ pound (¼ kg). NOTE: *The average bunch of broccoli weighs between 1½ and 2 pounds (⅔ and 1 kg), but there will be a fair amount of waste in the woody stem ends.*

Best way to store: Remove, first of all, the twist-band around the broccoli. Next remove any wilting leaves and slice off the coarse stem ends. Wrap the base of each stem in damp—**not wet**—paper toweling, pop the broccoli into a medium-size plastic bag (do not seal) and refrigerate. **Storage time:** 3 to 4 days, but for top quality, cook the broccoli sooner.

Basic preparation: Divide the broccoli into stalks of as nearly the same size as possible. (For *flowerets*, separate the stalks from the budded head, then divide into flowerets of about the same size, taking advantage of the plant's natural branching.) Trim all leaves from the stalks, and if these still seem fibrous, cut them off and discard. Make deep crisscross cuts in the base of each broccoli stalk (this is to make them cook as quickly as the tender flowerets). Now soak the broccoli 20 to 30 minutes in a sinkful of cool water to which you have added 1 tablespoon *each* of salt and sugar (these crisp the broccoli). Drain well.

Best ways to cook:

To BOIL: Taking a leaf from the old Virginia cookbook that recommended cooking broccoli like asparagus, I do precisely that. I lay the prepared broccoli stalks or flowerets flat in a very large heavy skillet (preferably not aluminum, which might affect both the color and the flavor of the broccoli), pour in enough lightly salted boiling water to submerge them, then clap the lid on and boil gently as follows: 4 to 5 minutes for flowerets and about 10 minutes for stalks— just until they are brilliant green and tender but crisp. NOTE: *Do not, as poor restaurants sometimes do, add a pinch of baking soda to the cooking water. It will turn the broccoli a poisonous green and give it a disagreeably soapy texture and flavor. It will also destroy most of the vitamin C (of which broccoli is a prime source).*

As soon as the broccoli is cooked the way you like it, drain it, return it to the skillet and shake gently over moderate heat to drive off excess steam. Sprinkle with salt and freshly ground black pepper, then dress with melted butter (a little lemon, anchovy paste, crushed garlic or snipped fresh dill make nice additions to the butter), or, if you prefer, dress with oil and lemon, vinaigrette, or top with a nice tart hollandaise, or a mustard or cheese sauce. NOTE: *For 4 portions, ¼ to ⅓ cup (60 to 80 ml) of melted butter or tart dressing should be sufficient, and 1 to 1½ cups (240 to 350 ml) of sauce.*

To STEAM: Prepare the broccoli as directed above, then lay the stalks flat in a steamer basket. Lower the basket into a large saucepan containing about 1½ inches (4 cm) of boiling water (*it should not touch the bottom of the basket*), cover and steam 15 to 20 minutes or until the broccoli is crisp-tender. Lift the broccoli from the basket, sprinkle lightly with salt and freshly ground black pepper and serve with any of the flavored butters, dressings or sauces suggested for boiled broccoli.

To serve broccoli cold: Boil or steam as directed but do not season. Plunge the broccoli into ice water, and when thoroughly chilled, drain well and pat dry on paper toweling. Like asparagus, broccoli will turn brown if marinated in an acid mixture, so follow the directions for serving asparagus cold (see page 197).

To STIR-FRY: Follow the recipe below.

Dry-sautéed broccoli

SERVES 4

The Chinese way of cooking vegetables has become a favorite of mine not only because it is so fast but also because it preserves a vegetable's nutritive value and original crunch and, at the same time, heightens its beauty. Broccoli, for example, emerges from the skillet a dazzling emerald green. What's best about this method, however, is that you can change the character of a vegetable completely merely by using different oils for sautéing and by adding or subtracting a few last-minute seasonings. Olive oil (and the addition of a little garlic and lemon), for example, injects an Italian accent, toasted sesame oil (and perhaps a splash of soy sauce) an Oriental one. Most flavored oils are too strong and heavy to be used by themselves. They will also smoke and burn at the intense heat needed for stir-frying, and they will overpower the flavor of all but the most assertive vegetables. The perfect ratio, I've found, is about one part sesame, hazelnut or walnut oil to two parts peanut or vegetable oil. NOTE: *The basic recipe and variations given below work equally well for asparagus tips and tender young green beans.*

A 2-pound head	broccoli, trimmed of leaves and coarse stem ends	A 1 kg head
3½ teaspoons, in all	salt	3½ teaspoons, in all
1 tablespoon	sugar	1 tablespoon
3 tablespoons	peanut or vegetable oil	3 tablespoons
Light sprinkling	freshly ground black pepper	Light sprinkling

Cut the broccoli flowerets from the stems, then divide them into smaller flowerets roughly 1 to 1½ inches (2½ to 4 cm) long and 1 inch (2½ cm) wide at the widest point. Slice the stems, slightly on the diagonal, about ¼ inch (¾ cm) thick. NOTE: *Halve any unusually chunky stems vertically so that they will cook in approximately the same time as the more fragile flowerets.* Wash the broccoli carefully, then soak 1 hour in a sinkful of ice water to which you have added 1 tablespoon of the salt and the sugar. NOTE: *These both help to crisp the broccoli because it will absorb the salted and sugared water quickly, gaining snap and crunch.* Drain the broccoli well and pat dry on several thicknesses of paper toweling.

Heat the oil in a very large heavy skillet over high heat until small ripples appear on the skillet bottom. Dump in the broccoli, lower heat to moderately high and stir-fry 4 to 5 minutes until crisp-tender. Sprinkle with the remaining ½ teaspoon salt and the pepper and serve.

VARIATIONS:

Chinese gingered broccoli with sesame oil: Prepare, soak and dry the broccoli as directed. In a very large skillet set over high heat, heat 2 tablespoons peanut oil and 1 tablespoon toasted sesame seed oil with 2 slivered large cloves of garlic about 1 minute; discard the garlic. Add 1 tablespoon finely minced fresh ginger root and the broccoli and stir-fry as directed. Omit the final ½ teaspoon of salt and sprinkle the broccoli instead with 2 to 3 tablespoons dark soy sauce. Season with pepper and serve.

Italian broccoli with oil and lemon: Prepare, soak and dry the broccoli as directed. In a very large skillet set over high heat, heat 3 tablespoons top-quality olive oil with 4 large slivered cloves of garlic about 1 minute; remove and discard the garlic. Add the broccoli and stir-fry as directed. Just before serving, squeeze in the juice of 1 small lemon, season with salt and pepper, toss lightly and serve. NOTE: *You might also toss in, if you like, about ⅓ cup (80 ml) coarsely chopped, toasted* pignoli *(pine nuts) about 2 minutes before the broccoli is done.*

Sautéed broccoli with hazelnuts or walnuts: Prepare, soak and dry the broccoli as directed. In a very large skillet set over high heat, heat 1 tablespoon of hazelnut or walnut oil and 2 tablespoons of peanut or vegetable oil until small ripples appear on the skillet bottom. Dump in the broccoli and stir-fry as directed. About 1 minute before the broccoli is done, sprinkle in about ¼ cup (60 ml) of coarsely chopped walnuts or blanched hazelnuts. Season to taste with salt and pepper and serve.

Butter-sautéed broccoli with lemon: Prepare, soak and dry the broccoli as directed. In a very large skillet over high heat, heat 2 tablespoons peanut oil and 1 tablespoon unsalted butter about 1 minute. Dump in the broccoli and stir-fry as directed. Just before serving, squeeze in the juice of 1 lemon. Season to taste with salt and pepper and serve.

NOTE: *If you want to sauté the flowerets only, you can do so by any of the above methods. You will reduce the number of servings, however, by about half. Save the stems to use in a soup or casserole.*

Brussels sprouts

These delicate little vegetables are the babies of the cabbage family. French kings and queens used to turn up their noses at any of them that were larger than a pea, and Belgians (yes, the first sprouts really did come from around Brussels) still like them about the size of a grape. Whether Brussels sprouts were originally a distinct species isn't known, for almost any cabbage plant will put out dozens of miniature heads once the big head has been picked.

Season: September through February. **Peak months:** October and November.

Hallmarks of quality: Uniformly small, tightly closed heads that are crisp of leaf and bright green of color. Yellowing sprouts are old (i.e. tough and strong-flavored); puffy or loose-leafed ones have stood too long in the supermarket. The choicest sprouts are those between 1 and 1½ inches (2½ and 4 cm) in diameter.

How many Brussels sprouts per serving? About a third of a 1-pint (½ L) carton.

Best way to store: In the refrigerator in their original carton, covered with plastic food wrap. **Storage time:** 5 to 6 days, maximum, if the sprouts were really fresh to begin with. Otherwise, 2 to 3 days.

Basic preparation: Pull off and discard the outer layer of leaves, then cut off the stems, but not so close that the sprouts fall apart. NOTE: *Sprouts need not be washed, because most of the grit and grime come off with the outer leaves.* To speed the cooking of sprouts, make a tiny X-shaped cut in the base of each.

Best ways to cook:

To BOIL: Place the prepared sprouts in a large heavy saucepan (preferably one made of a nonreactive material such as stainless steel, flameproof glass or enameled cast iron). For every pint (½ L) of sprouts, pour in 1 cup (240 ml) of lightly salted boiling water. Cover, set over moderate heat and boil 15 to 20 minutes or until you can pierce a sprout easily with a fork. Drain the sprouts well, then dress with melted butter or browned butter, heavy cream and with grated Parmesan or finely minced walnuts, pecans or hazelnuts. **Additional ways to season:** Dress with olive oil and garlic or with one of the mellow nut oils such as walnut or hazelnut. For each pint (½ L) of cooked sprouts, you will need about 4 tablespoons of melted butter, 3 tablespoons of oil or ⅓ to ½ cup (80 to 120 ml) of cream. Just before serving, season the sprouts to taste with salt and freshly ground pepper. NOTE: *Tart salad dressings, lemon, wine and vinegar will all toughen and brown Brussels sprouts if used in any but the most minute quantities.*

To STEAM: Place the sprouts in a steamer basket, lower into a kettle containing about 1½ inches (4 cm) of boiling water (the basket should not actually touch the water), cover and steam for 15 to 20 minutes or until crisp-tender. Use any of the seasonings suggested for boiled sprouts above.

NOTE: *Boiled or steamed Brussels sprouts team magnificently with seedless green grapes or boiled chestnuts in a cream sauce. Use about 4 parts sprouts to 1 part grapes or chestnuts and about 1½ cups (350 ml) Medium White Sauce or Béchamel (see Index) for each quart or liter of sprouts. They are also delicious tossed in bacon drippings with crisp crumbled bacon or topped with a sharp cheese sauce. Finally, because they are so closely kin to cabbage, Brussels sprouts are compatible with any of the herbs and spices commonly used for cabbage: nutmeg, mace, caraway, dill, chives, shallots and so on.*

Scalloped Brussels sprouts and walnuts with rye crumb topping

SERVES 6

Because caraway and the cabbage family of vegetables to which Brussels sprouts belong are so compatible, I decided to make the crumb topping partly with caraway rye bread. A light rye bread is best, and even that should be mixed about half-and-half with white bread so that the caraway flavor does not overpower that of the Brussels sprouts. NOTE: *For each cup of crumbs, you'll need about two slices of bread.* This, strictly speaking, is not just a crumb topping, because it is layered into the casserole along with the sprouts. What I like about this recipe is that it can conveniently be made several hours ahead of time, then whisked from refrigerator to oven about 30 minutes before serving. It is a splendid accompaniment to baked ham or boiled tongue (either hot or cold) and is rich enough to serve as the main dish of a light lunch or supper.

2 cartons (10 oz. each)	fresh small Brussels sprouts, trimmed of coarse leaves and stems	2 cartons (283 g each)
1 quart	boiling water mixed with 1 teaspoon salt	1 L
4 tablespoons	unsalted butter	4 tablespoons
4 tablespoons	flour	4 tablespoons
¼ teaspoon	dill weed	¼ teaspoon
Pinch	pulverized caraway seeds	Pinch
Pinch	ground mace or nutmeg	Pinch
Light sprinkling	freshly ground black pepper	Light sprinkling
1 cup	rich chicken broth	240 ml
½ cup	heavy cream	120 ml
2–3 tablespoons	Brussels sprouts cooking water	2–3 tablespoons
To taste	salt	To taste
	TOPPING:	
1 cup	moderately fine soft white bread crumbs	240 ml
1 cup	moderately fine soft rye bread crumbs	240 ml
½ cup	finely ground walnuts	120 ml
3 tablespoons	freshly grated Parmesan or Romano cheese	3 tablespoons
2 tablespoons	melted butter	2 tablespoons

Parboil the Brussels sprouts in the salted water in a covered saucepan over moderate heat 10 to 12 minutes until crisp-tender; drain the sprouts, reserving 3 tablespoons of the cooking water. While sprouts cook, melt the butter in a small heavy saucepan over moderate heat and blend in the flour to make a smooth paste; mix in the dill weed, caraway, mace and pepper and mellow 1 to 2 minutes over moderate heat. Combine the broth, cream and 2 tablespoons of the Brussels sprouts cooking liquid and whisk quickly into the flour-and-butter paste. Cook, stirring constantly, until thickened and smooth and no raw floury taste remains— 3 to 5 minutes. If sauce seems thick, smooth in the remaining tablespoon of reserved cooking water. Taste the sauce and add salt, if needed, pour over the sprouts and toss well to mix.

Quickly prepare the topping by tossing all ingredients together; layer one-third of this mixture into the bottom of a lightly buttered 6-cup (1½ L) casserole; top with half of the sprouts mixture, another one-third of the crumbs, the remaining sprouts, and finally, the remaining crumbs. Bake, uncovered, in a moderate oven (350°F. or 175°C.) for about 30 minutes or until bubbling and lightly browned.

Brussels sprouts soup creamed with chèvre

SERVES 4 TO 6

If you cannot find a creamily soft *chèvre* (French goat cheese) for thickening and flavoring this soup, substitute cream cheese. The soup won't be quite the same but it will be good. NOTE: *Because of the saltiness of the cheese, you will probably not need to salt the soup. But taste it before serving and add a smidgeon of salt if it seems bland.*

1 carton (10 oz.)	fresh Brussels sprouts, trimmed and sliced very thin	1 carton (283 g)
1 large	shallot, peeled and minced (or substitute a large scallion)	1 large
2 tablespoons	unsalted butter, at room temperature	2 tablespoons
2½ cups	rich chicken broth	600 ml
1 pint	half-and-half cream	½ L
⅛ teaspoon	crumbled leaf rosemary	⅛ teaspoon
⅛ teaspoon	crumbled leaf savory	⅛ teaspoon
⅛ teaspoon	freshly grated nutmeg	⅛ teaspoon
Light sprinkling	freshly ground black pepper	Light sprinkling
2 ounces	soft chèvre, at room temperature (or use cream cheese)	60 g
1 tablespoon	dry vermouth	1 tablespoon

Stir-fry the Brussels sprouts and shallot in the butter in a large heavy skillet over moderately low heat about 15 minutes or until soft and lightly browned. At the same time, combine chicken broth and cream in a large heavy saucepan, set uncovered over moderately low heat and simmer until slightly reduced—15 to 20 minutes (do not allow mixture to boil, however, or it may curdle). When Brussels sprouts are soft, mix in rosemary, savory, nutmeg and pepper and mellow 1 to 2 minutes over moderately low heat. Cut the cheese into small cubes and drop, 4 to 5 at a time, into the broth mixture; whisk until smooth. Continue adding the remaining cheese the same way. When all of the cheese has been smoothed into the broth, stir in the Brussels sprouts mixture, then the vermouth. Warm 3 to 5 minutes (do not boil). Purée the mixture, about half of the total amount at a time, in a food processor fitted with the metal chopping blade or in an electric blender, or put through a food mill. Return soup to pan and bring just to serving temperature. Ladle into soup bowls and serve. NOTE: *Garnish, if you like, with a scattering of finely sliced Brussels sprouts that have been lightly sautéed in butter or, if you prefer, with a sprinkling of freshly grated Parmesan or Romano cheese.*

Cabbage

Few vegetables are as ancient as cabbage, and few figure more prominently in history or legend. Aristotle, it's said, thought that gorging upon cabbage would keep him from getting drunk (as did the Romans later on). Young Scottish girls believed that they could determine the physiques of their future husbands by going blindfolded into the garden on Halloween night and picking a cabbage at random (the bigger the cabbage, the bigger the husband). And old German legend had it that the man in the moon was put there for stealing cabbages on Christmas Eve. (The Germans, I think, remain the masters at cooking cabbage.)

Today, four types of cabbage are widely available: the common **green, red, Savoy** (crinkly, dark green outer leaves, but a pale chartreuse heart), and **bok choy** (the delicate cylindrical yellow Chinese celery cabbage, in truth not cabbage at all but a member of the mustard family).

Season: Year round for all cabbages. **Peak months:** Winter.

Hallmarks of quality: For all varieties, smooth, unblemished, crisp, compact heads of vibrant color that feel heavy for their size. NOTE: *Savoy is more sprawling than the other cabbages, but still its inner leaves should be tightly headed.*

How much cabbage per person? About ⅓ to ½ pound (160 to 225 g) per person. NOTE: *1 pound (½ kg) of cabbage will yield 4 cups (1 L) of shredded cabbage and 3 cups (¾ L) of cooked cabbage.*

Best way to store: Loosely bagged in plastic in the refrigerator. NOTE: *Remove outer leaves only if they are wilting or blemished, then trim stem flush with the bottom of the cabbage.* **Storage time:** About 2 weeks, maximum.

Basic preparation: All that's needed is to remove any limp or discolored outer leaves. **A quick way to core cabbage:** Quarter a head of cabbage, then slice off the hard white core at the point of each quarter. (The heart of *bok choy* is tender and mild enough to eat and need not be removed.)

Some special techniques:

TO PROCESSOR-SLICE: Cut cored cabbage into columns about the width and height of the processor feed tube. Equip the machine with the medium or coarse slicing disk. Stand a column of cabbage in the feed tube, then snap the motor on and push gently down the tube. NOTE: *The texture of processor-sliced cabbage is about the same as that put through the coarsest (slicing) side of a four-sided hand grater.*

TO PROCESSOR-SHRED: Cut cored cabbage into 1-inch (2½ cm) chunks. Equip the processor with the metal chopping blade, place 2 cups (½ L) of cabbage chunks in the work bowl, distributing them evenly, then shred, using about 5 on-offs of the motor. NOTE: *The texture will be very much like that of cabbage put through the second-coarsest side of a four-sided hand grater. For finer texture, use 7 to 8 fast bursts of the processor motor.*

Best ways to cook:

TO BOIL (except *bok choy*): Quarter, core and, if you like, chunk or slice the cabbage. Place in a large heavy saucepan (preferably not aluminum, which may affect the flavor of cabbage), pour in just enough lightly salted boiling water to cover the cabbage, and place the lid on the pan. Boil gently as follows: about 10 minutes for chunks and slices, 15 to 20 for cabbage quarters—just until crisp-tender. Drain the cabbage well, return to the pan and shake gently over moderate heat for a minute or two to drive off excess moisture. Add a good lump of butter and/or a little heavy or light cream, season to taste with salt and pepper and serve. **Other compatible seasonings:** Minced fresh dill, fennel or chives; freshly grated nutmeg or ground mace, caraway or fennel seeds; freshly grated Parmesan; finely chopped walnuts, pecans or toasted almonds. NOTE: *Red cabbage also profits from the addition of a little vinegar, lemon, orange or cranberry juice or red wine (all of which will intensify its color), also from a tablespoon or two of a tart red jelly.*

TO STEAM: Quarter and core green, red or Savoy cabbage; leave as is or cut into about 2-inch (5 cm) chunks. Slice *bok choy* about 1½ inches (4 cm) thick. Place cabbage in a steamer basket, lower into a large saucepan containing about 1½ inches (4 cm) of boiling water (make certain that the steamer basket does not touch the water), cover tight and steam as follows: about 15 minutes for *bok choy* and cabbage chunks and 25 to 30 minutes for cabbage quarters. Use any of the seasonings recommended for boiled cabbage above or one of your own favorites.

TO STIR-FRY: See recipe that follows.

TO BRAISE: See recipe that follows.

Stir-fried green cabbage the East Indian way

SERVES 4

Stir-frying is one of the most successful ways to cook cabbage because it remains crisply succulent and develops a faintly sweet, nutlike flavor. I like to serve this particular recipe with broiled chicken, roast pork or baked ham.

2 teaspoons	mustard seeds	2 teaspoons
2 tablespoons	ghee (melted unsalted butter from which the milk solids have been skimmed)	2 tablespoons
1 tablespoon	peanut or vegetable oil	1 tablespoon
½ cup	chopped yellow onion	120 ml
2 tablespoons	finely minced sweet green pepper	2 tablespoons
2 teaspoons	finely minced fresh ginger	2 teaspoons
2 teaspoons	curry powder	2 teaspoons
Pinch	ground cinnamon	Pinch
Pinch	ground nutmeg	Pinch
A 2-pound	green cabbage, trimmed, quartered, cored and sliced thin or 2 quarts (2 L) sliced bok choy	A 1 kg
To taste	salt and freshly ground black pepper	To taste

In a large heavy skillet set over moderately high heat, stir-fry the mustard seeds in the *ghee* and oil about 2 minutes or until they begin to sputter and skitter about the skillet. Reduce the heat to moderate, add the onion, green pepper and ginger and stir-fry 3 to 5 minutes until limp and golden. Smooth in the curry powder, cinnamon and nutmeg and mellow over moderate heat about a minute. Dump in the cabbage and stir-fry about 5 minutes or until nicely glazed. Turn the heat down low and cook the cabbage, uncovered, stirring frequently, 5 to 10 minutes longer or until as crisp or tender as you like it. Season to taste with salt and pepper and serve.

Hedy's braised red cabbage with apples and onion in red wine sauce

SERVES 6

I do believe this is the best red cabbage I've ever eaten. The recipe comes from my friend Hedy Wuerz, a Bavarian now living and working in New York City, who is a sensational cook. I first tasted it at Hedy's one evening and liked it so much I asked for the recipe. Hedy graciously obliged. She serves the red cabbage with her remarkable Rouladen (see Index), but it's equally delicious with Frikadeller (see Index), baked ham, roast pork, turkey or venison.

A large (about 2-lb.)	red cabbage	A large (about 1 kg)
3 tablespoons	unsalted butter	3 tablespoons

1 tablespoon	sugar	1 tablespoon
1 large	yellow onion, peeled and minced	1 large
2 large	tart green apples, peeled, cored and coarsely chopped	2 large
¼ cup	red wine vinegar	60 ml
1 cup, in all	beef broth	240 ml, in all
½ teaspoon	salt	½ teaspoon
2 large	bay leaves	2 large
2 tablespoons	all-purpose flour	2 tablespoons
1 cup	dry red wine	240 ml
2 tablespoons	red currant jelly	2 tablespoons

Trim the coarse outer leaves from the cabbage and discard; quarter the cabbage, slice off the hard white core at the point of each quarter and discard, then slice each quarter very thin. Set the cabbage aside for the moment. In a very large heavy skillet, melt the butter over moderately high heat; sprinkle in the sugar and heat 2 to 3 minutes—just until dissolved. Dump in the onion and apples and stir-fry about 5 minutes until limp and golden. Add the cabbage and stir-fry about 5 minutes until nicely glazed. Pour in the red wine vinegar, and ½ cup (120 ml) of the beef broth and allow to come to a slow simmer; adjust burner heat so that the liquid bubbles very gently. Sprinkle in the salt, add the bay leaves, pushing them down into the cabbage, then cover the skillet and simmer 20 to 25 minutes or until the cabbage is crisp-tender. Sprinkle the flour over the cabbage and toss well to mix; add the wine and the remaining ½ cup (120 ml) beef broth. Heat, stirring gently, 3 to 5 minutes until liquids are thickened and no raw starch taste remains. Remove and discard the bay leaves, add the jelly and toss lightly to mix. Warm another 5 minutes and serve.

Warm German slaw with bacon and caraway

SERVES 6

If it seems that I am using an inordinate number of German recipes in this section, it is because Germans cook cabbage better than anyone else I know. This particular recipe also comes from my Bavarian friend, Hedy Wuerz, who has kindly allowed me to print it here. NOTE: *It's imperative that you don't overcook the cabbage—5 minutes in heavily salted boiling water should be sufficient—also that you drain the cabbage very dry so that it does not water down the dressing.* This slaw is delicious with pork chops or roast pork and also with any of the wide variety of wursts.

½ pound	smoked lean bacon, cut into ¼-inch (¾ cm) cubes	225 g
1 medium-size (3 pounds)	cabbage, quartered, cored and sliced about ½ inch (1½ cm) thick	1 medium-size (1½ kg)
4 quarts	water	4 L
5 tablespoons	salt	5 tablespoons
¼ cup (about)	bacon drippings (from cooking the bacon above)	60 ml (about)
⅓ cup	strong beef broth	80 ml
3 tablespoons	red wine vinegar	3 tablespoons
1 tablespoon	sugar	1 tablespoon
4 teaspoons	caraway seeds	4 teaspoons
Light sprinkling	freshly ground black pepper	Light sprinkling

Sauté the bacon in a medium-size heavy skillet over moderately low heat about 15 to 20 minutes, stirring often, until most of the drippings have cooked out and the bacon is golden and translucent but not brown. While the bacon cooks, halve or quarter any cabbage slices that are exceptionally large. Bring the water and salt to a rolling boil in a very large kettle (the type you would use for cooking pasta) over high heat, dump in the cabbage and cook 5 minutes until barely tender; drain at once, return the cabbage to the kettle and shake well over moderate heat 1 to 2 minutes to drive off all excess moisture. Dump the cabbage into a large mixing bowl.

Drain the bacon drippings into a measuring cup; you will need ¼ cup (60 ml) minimum, so if there are insufficient drippings, round the measure out with corn oil. Sprinkle the bacon cubes over the cabbage. Place drippings in a small saucepan, add the broth, red wine vinegar, sugar and caraway seeds and bring quickly to the boil. Pour over the cabbage and toss lightly to mix. If the slaw seems skimpily dressed, add another tablespoon or two of bacon drippings (if you have them) or of corn oil—every leaf should glisten with dressing. Sprinkle the slaw with pepper and toss lightly again. Let stand about 15 minutes before serving.

Carrots

Although known to Arabs as early as the twelfth century, carrots weren't grown for the table until three hundred years later when the Dutch developed an appetite for them. These were sweet, chunky, red-orange carrots, not the slimmer, paler variety that we enjoy today (and which became such a rage in seventeenth-century London that fashionable women wore the frilly tops in their hair).

Season: Year round.

Hallmarks of quality: Crispness and moistness; uniformity of size, shape and color; absence of knicks, blemishes, bumps, splits or cracks. NOTE: *If possible, buy carrots with the tops on; if these are nice and frilly, you may be sure the carrots are fresh.*

How many carrots per serving? ¼ to ⅓ pound (115 to 160 g). NOTE: *There are 12 to 14 slim carrots per pound (½ kg) and 6 to 8 medium-size ones.*

Best way to store: Loosely bagged in plastic in the refrigerator's vegetable crisper. NOTE: *If you have bought carrots with the tops on, cut them off about an inch (2½ cm) above the crown before storing them.* **Storage time:** 2 to 3 weeks.

Basic preparation: Peel the carrots, using a swivel-bladed vegetable peeler, then slice about ¼ inch (¾ cm) off the top and bottom. Leave the carrots whole or chunk, slice, dice, shred or cut into strips.

Best ways to cook:

To BOIL: Prepare the carrots as directed, then simmer in about ½ inch (1½ cm) of lightly salted boiling water or beef or chicken broth in a covered saucepan as follows: about 10 minutes for diced or sliced carrots; 10 to 15 for carrot strips or chunks; 20 to 25 minutes for slim whole carrots; and 30 for the medium-size. NOTE: *Perfectly cooked carrots will be firm-tender, not mushy.* Drain well, return the carrots to the pan, shake a minute or two over moderate heat, then add 2 to 3 tablespoons of butter and salt and pepper to taste. **Compatible seasonings:** Dill, tarragon, rosemary, thyme, chervil, marjoram, mint, parsley, savory; also nutmeg, ginger, mace and cinnamon; grated lemon and orange rind.

To STEAM: Prepare the carrots as directed, place in a steamer basket and lower into a large saucepan containing about 1½ inches (4 cm) of boiling water (the water should not touch the basket). Cover the pan and steam as follows: 15 to 20 minutes for sliced or diced carrots; 20 to 30 for carrot chunks, strips or small whole carrots; and 30 to 40 for medium-size whole carrots. Season as you would boiled carrots (see the suggestions above, or improvise).

To BRAISE: See recipe that follows.

Carottes râpées

SERVES 4 TO 6

In the Midi, French women make a sunny dish of shredded carrots by dressing them with olive oil and lemon, then lacing liberally with garlic, marjoram and thyme. *Carottes râpées,* they call the recipe after the French verb *râper,* meaning "to grate." The beauty of this particular dish is that it is equally good hot or cold. I could honestly make a meal of it, although I usually serve *carottes râpées* with broiled chicken, salmon or swordfish, even with roast pork. NOTE: *The carrots you use for this recipe must be absolutely fresh—just pulled, if possible. Otherwise, they will have the flavor and succulence of cardboard.*

1½ pounds	medium-size carrots, peeled	⅔ kg
1 large	Italian (red) onion, peeled and chopped	1 large
1 medium-size	garlic clove, peeled and minced	1 medium-size
¼ cup	olive oil (top quality)	60 ml
½ teaspoon	crumbled leaf marjoram	½ teaspoon
¼ teaspoon	crumbled leaf thyme	¼ teaspoon
¼ cup	lemon juice	60 ml
To taste	salt and freshly ground black pepper	To taste

Coarsely shred the carrots, using the second-coarsest side of a four-sided grater or a food processor fitted with the shredding disk. Stir-fry the carrots, onion and garlic together in the olive oil in a large heavy skillet over moderately high heat 5 minutes—just until crisp-tender. Sprinkle in the marjoram and thyme and stir-fry a minute or two longer. Add the lemon juice and toss lightly, then season to taste with salt and pepper. Toss well again and serve hot or cold.

Braised curried carrots and onions

SERVES 6

It was in the temple town of Mahabalipuram south of Madras that I first enjoyed this unusual dish. I've tempered the fire of the original to accommodate those without asbestos palates and substituted the supermarket variety of carrots for the yam-sweet red Indian ones.

2 medium-size	yellow onions, peeled and sliced thin	2 medium-size
1 tablespoon	finely minced sweet red pepper	1 tablespoon
1 teaspoon	finely minced fresh ginger	1 teaspoon
¼ cup	ghee (melted unsalted butter from which the milk solids have been skimmed)	60 ml
½ teaspoon	curry powder (Indians would use more)	½ teaspoon
1 pound	slim young carrots, peeled and sliced thin	½ kg
3 tablespoons (about)	water	3 tablespoons (about)
1 tablespoon	lemon juice (Indians would use tamarind juice)	1 tablespoon
To taste	salt and freshly ground black pepper	To taste

In a large heavy skillet over moderate heat, stir-fry the onions, red pepper and ginger in the *ghee* 3 to 5 minutes until limp and golden; blend in the curry powder and allow to mellow a minute or two. Add the carrots and stir-fry 3 to 4 minutes, just long enough to glaze. Turn the heat to low, add the water, cover tight and simmer 15 to 20 minutes or until the carrots are crisp-tender; check the skillet now and then and if the carrots seem to be cooking dry, add an additional tablespoon or so of water. Sprinkle with lemon juice, season to taste with salt and pepper and serve.

Cauliflower

Chou-fleur (cabbage flower), the French call cauliflower, with good reason, for botanically speaking cauliflower is both flower (a mass of fragrant white "blossoms" nestling in a ruff of frosty green leaves) and cabbage. A classy cabbage, to be sure, or as Mark Twain dubbed it, "The cabbage with the college education."

Season: Year round. **Peak months:** September through December.

Hallmarks of quality: Ivory or snowy, tightly curded, unbruised, unblemished, firm heads with crinkly green leaves at the base.

How much cauliflower per person? About ¾ pound (⅓ kg).

Best way to store: Loosely bagged in plastic in the refrigerator. **Storage time:** About 5 days, but the cauliflower will begin to lose crispness and develop a strong "cabbagey" flavor after a couple of days.

Basic preparation: Strip away all green leaves and cut the stem off so that it is even with the base of the head. If you intend to cook the cauliflower whole, make a deep X-shaped cut in the base of the stem. (This is to speed the cooking of the stem so that it will be done at the same time as the more delicate head.) Scrape away any darkened spots on the curd, then soak the head about 30 minutes in a sinkful of cool water to which you have added 1 tablespoon each of salt and sugar (this is to crisp the cauliflower). Drain well.

To make flowerets: Trim the cauliflower as directed, then, starting at the base, cut off the individual branches of curd, halving or quartering any that are overlarge so that all flowerets will be approximately the same size and cook in the same amount of time. Soak the flowerets as directed for whole cauliflower.

Best ways to cook:

TO BOIL: Place the cauliflower, stem down, in a large heavy saucepan (preferably stainless steel, enameled aluminum or cast-iron, flameproof glass or other nonreacting material that will not affect the delicate flavor of the cauliflower), then pour in 2 cups (½ L) of boiling water to which you have added 1 teaspoon salt. Set over moderate heat, cover and boil gently 20 to 30 minutes or until you can pierce the head easily with a fork. NOTE: *Flowerets will take only about 10 minutes.* Drain the cauliflower well, then return to moderate heat and shake gently 1 to 2 minutes to drive off all excess moisture. Top with browned butter or hollandaise and serve. NOTE: *To help keep cauliflower white as it cooks, add a pinch of cream of tartar to the cooking water, or a tablespoon of lemon juice or a slice of lemon.*

TO STEAM: Place the cauliflower or flowerets in a steamer basket and lower into a large saucepan containing about 1½ inches (4 cm) of boiling water, and do make certain that the basket does not touch the water. Cover and steam flowerets 12 to 15 minutes and whole heads 30 to 40 minutes until crisp-tender.

To serve cauliflower cold: Boil or steam as directed, then drain and quick-chill by plunging into ice water. Let the cauliflower stand in the ice water 15 to 20 minutes or until well chilled, then drain and pat very dry on several thicknesses of paper toweling. Dress with a good, tart vinaigrette, oil and lemon, or mayonnaise (either plain or flavored with garlic, lemon, mustard or anchovy).

Cauliflower au Gruyère

SERVES 6

A marvelous accompaniment to roast pork, chicken or turkey, this is a casserole of cauliflower creamed with a satin-smooth Gruyère sauce.

A 3-pound	cauliflower, trimmed and divided into bite-size flowerets	A 1½ kg
2 cups	boiling water mixed with 1 teaspoon salt	½ L
	GRUYÈRE SAUCE:	
2 tablespoons	unsalted butter	2 tablespoons
2 tablespoons	flour	2 tablespoons
¼ teaspoon	crumbled leaf summer savory	¼ teaspoon
Pinch	crumbled leaf rosemary	Pinch
Pinch	ground mace	Pinch
½ teaspoon	salt	½ teaspoon
⅛ teaspoon	white pepper	⅛ teaspoon
1½ cups	milk	350 ml
½ cup	reserved cauliflower cooking water	120 ml
5 ounces	Gruyère cheese, coarsely grated	140 g
¼ cup	dry vermouth	60 ml
	TOPPING:	
1 cup	moderately fine dry bread crumbs	240 ml
1 tablespoon	melted unsalted butter	1 tablespoon

Parboil the cauliflower in the salted water in a covered saucepan over moderate heat 5 to 8 minutes until barely tender. Drain the cauliflower, reserving ½ cup (120 ml) of the cooking water; return the cauliflower to the heat and shake briefly to drive off excess moisture. Remove the cauliflower from the heat and set aside.

For the sauce: Melt the butter in a medium-size heavy saucepan over moderate heat; blend in the flour, savory, rosemary, mace, salt and pepper to make a smooth paste. Combine the milk and reserved cauliflower cooking water, pour into the saucepan and cook, stirring constantly, until thickened and smooth—3 to 5 minutes. Off heat, add the cheese and stir until melted, then mix in the vermouth.

Arrange the cauliflowerets in a lightly buttered 2-quart (2 L) *au gratin* pan or shallow casserole; pour the Gruyère sauce evenly over all. Combine the topping ingredients and scatter evenly over the cauliflower. Bake, uncovered, in a moderately hot oven (375°F. or 190°C.) for 30 minutes or until bubbly and touched with brown.

Celeriac
(KNOB CELERY OR CELERY ROOT)

This is the "celery" of celery rémoulade, the celery preferred by European cooks because of its more pronounced flavor, firmer texture and lower water content. Celeriac is crisp and white, not unlike a turnip, and, praised be, it is becoming more and more available in supermarkets as well as in "boutique" greengroceries.

Season: August through May. **Peak month:** October.

Hallmarks of quality: Hard, unblemished knobs with a minimum of root ends. Choose celeriac between 2 and 4 inches (5 and 10 cm) in diameter that has few knicks or "warts" and that is not softening around the crown.

How much celeriac per person? About ¼ pound (115 g).

Best way to store: Loosely bagged in plastic in the refrigerator. Do not trim or wash celeriac before you store it. **Storage time:** 7 to 10 days.

Basic preparation: Cut off any stalks and root ends, then peel and slice, dice, cube or cut into julienne strips as individual recipes instruct. NOTE: *When dealing with raw celeriac, use your sharpest knife and work very carefully, very slowly. Celeriac is very hard and if you force the knife, it may slip.*

Best way to cook: Initially, celeriac must be boiled or parboiled before it can be creamed, mashed, baked or batter-dipped and deep-fried.

TO BOIL: Trim and peel the celeriac as directed above, then slice, dice or cut into julienne strips (whatever individual recipes require). Place in a heavy saucepan, pour in just enough lightly salted boiling water to cover, then boil, covered, 15 to 20 minutes until crisp-tender. If you intend to mash or purée the celeriac, cook 25 to 30 minutes or until very soft.

To PARBOIL: Boil as directed but for 10 to 15 minutes only, just until the celeriac is **barely** tender. Use for salads or recipes such as fritters, scalloped or *au gratin* dishes in which the celeriac will be quickly heated through.

To serve cold: Boil **or** parboil the celeriac as directed, then quick-chill in ice water. Drain well and pat dry on paper toweling. Dress with a tart vinaigrette, with rémoulade sauce, with oil and lemon, or do as the Germans do and mix with homemade mayonnaise (just enough to bind the cubes or julienne of celeriac together) and stir in some finely chopped walnuts—about 1 cup (240 ml) of walnuts for 1½ pounds (⅔ kg) of celeriac (or enough for about 6 servings).

Céleri rémoulade

SERVES 4 TO 6

Celeriac, or celery root, is mahogany-hard to the core—or so it seems to me whenever I tackle it. The only way to cleave through the fibrous brown skin to the pale ivory heart is with a razor-sharp chef's knife. There's a lot of waste with celeriac because of the thickness of the skin and the convolutions of the root, but all the trimming and cutting for this superlative recipe are in the end worthwhile. Céleri Rémoulade can be served as an appetizer, cold vegetable or salad. And it keeps well for several days in the refrigerator. NOTE: *Rather than blanch the matchstick strips of celeriac, which could soften them too much, I dress them well ahead of time and let the Rémoulade Dressing "temper" the celeriac as it seasons. I also give the celeriac a preliminary marinating in vinegar, lemon juice and salt. Any leftover Rémoulade Dressing can be used to dress cold cooked asparagus, broccoli or green beans. It will keep well in a tightly covered jar for about one week in the refrigerator.*

1½ pounds	celery root, trimmed, peeled and cut into matchstick strips	675 g
1 tablespoon	lemon juice	1 tablespoon
1 tablespoon	white wine vinegar	1 tablespoon
½ teaspoon	salt	½ teaspoon
	RÉMOULADE DRESSING:	
⅓ cup	Dijon mustard	80 ml
2 large	egg yolks	2 large
¼ cup	boiling water	60 ml

2 tablespoons	hot red wine vinegar	2 tablespoons
⅔ cup (about)	olive oil (top quality)	160 ml (about)
2 tablespoons	minced parsley	2 tablespoons
1 tablespoon	minced fresh tarragon (or 1 teaspoon crumbled leaf tarragon)	1 tablespoon
⅛ teaspoon	freshly ground black pepper	⅛ teaspoon

In a large nonmetal mixing bowl, toss the celery root with the lemon juice, vinegar and salt; cover and marinate several hours in the refrigerator.

For the Rémoulade Dressing: In the work bowl of a food processor equipped with the metal chopping blade or in the container of an electric blender, place the mustard and egg yolks. Snap the motor on and off a couple of times to combine. Now with the motor running, drizzle in first the boiling water, then the hot vinegar, down the feed tube. With the motor still running, add the olive oil drop by drop—at least the first one-third of it; once the mixture begins to emulsify, you may add the olive oil in a fine stream. NOTE: *If you have neither blender nor processor, you must beat the dressing by hand. A wire whisk is the best implement to use, but you must apply plenty of vigor to the job.* Once all of the oil has been added, beat the dressing hard another 30 seconds or so until the consistency of thin mayonnaise. Transfer to a bowl, fold in the parsley, tarragon and black pepper, cover and refrigerate until ready to use.

Remove the celeriac from the refrigerator, toss well, then drain off any liquid that may have accumulated in the bottom of the bowl (there won't be much). Add several heaping tablespoonfuls of the Rémoulade and toss well. Add more Rémoulade as needed—the celeriac should be generously coated. Cover and marinate in the refrigerator 6 to 8 hours before serving, or better yet, make it the night before you intend to serve it.

Just before serving, toss the celeriac well and add a bit more Rémoulade, if needed, to make it nice and moist.

Celery

The first mention of celery in this country appears in the *American Gardener's Calendar*, published in Philadelphia in 1806, although it had been known to ancient Greeks (they considered it a purifier of the blood). The French prized celery, too, but the seeds, not the stalks that are so integral to our cooking today. There are two basic varieties of celery now widely available: the white and the green (Pascal).

Season: Year round.

Hallmarks of quality: Ultracrisp ribs (individual stalks), free of cracks or blemishes; crinkly yellow-green leaves. If possible, buy unbagged celery because you can determine its condition at a glance (not true of commercially packaged celery because the bags are often heavily lettered and the leaves are chopped off).

How much celery per person? About ⅓ pound (160 g) to serve as a vegetable.

Best way to store: Loosely bagged in plastic in the refrigerator crisper. Before bagging the celery, remove any coarse outer ribs that may be bruised. I package these separately after I've cut away any discolored, cracked or soft portions. **Storage time:** 7 to 10 days, but use the celery sooner if possible, because it will soon lose crispness and flavor.

Basic preparation: Simply pull off the number of ribs you need, wash in cool water, cut off the rough stem ends and, if you like, the green tops (I save these to use in stocks, soups and salads). If the outer ribs are unusually coarse, it's a good idea to pull off the coarser strings: simply slip a paring knife under the strings at the base of the celery ribs, lift up until you can catch the strings in your fingers, then peel them off much as you would the strings on a banana. TIP: *To rehabilitate limp celery ribs, cut the stems off diagonally at the base, rather as though you were cutting the stems off roses, then soak the ribs in a sinkful of cool water to which you have added 2 tablespoons each of salt and sugar (these miraculously crisp the celery).*

To make celery hearts: These are nothing more than the innermost ribs— usually 5 to 6 of them. So you need only strip away all outer ribs (bag these in plastic, refrigerate and use as soon as possible). To finish the celery hearts, trim off the knobby base, then the leaves, so that each celery heart is about 5 inches (13 cm) long.

Best ways to cook: You can boil celery. Or steam it. But unless the celery is to be used in other recipes (in which case it may be parboiled), I can't imagine why anyone would want to cook it because it is so exquisitely good raw. I do, however, like braised celery provided it is still plenty crisp (too often it is mushy), and I like celery stir-fried the Chinese way with other crunchy vegetables.

TO PARBOIL: Prepare celery hearts as directed, lay flat in a large skillet (preferably not aluminum), pour in just enough lightly salted boiling water to cover, set over moderate heat, cover the skillet and boil gently for 8 to 10 minutes or just until a fork will pierce a celery heart with only slight resistance. Drain well, and use as individual recipes direct. NOTE: *If the celery hearts are to be served cold—*à la Grecque, *for example—or vinaigrette—quick-chill them by submerging for about 15 minutes in ice water. Drain well before using and pat dry on paper toweling.*

To braise: Prepare celery hearts as directed, then sauté in 3 to 4 tablespoons of butter, olive oil or bacon drippings in a large heavy skillet over moderate heat, turning gently, about 5 minutes until uniformly golden. Pour in about 1 cup (240 ml) of boiling beef or chicken broth or water, cover, reduce the heat slightly and simmer about 15 minutes until crisp-tender. Season to taste with salt and freshly ground black pepper (add a little freshly grated nutmeg, if you like) and serve topped with a little of the cooking liquid. **Seasoning suggestions:** Sprinkle about 2 tablespoons of freshly snipped dill or chives or minced tarragon or fennel over the celery 2 to 3 minutes before serving.

Celery hearts à la Grecque

SERVES 4

Almost any vegetable that is good cold—artichoke hearts, Belgian endive, finocchio, leeks, carrots, cucumbers, zucchini, for example—is good prepared this way. Simply parboil the vegetable until crisp-tender, then proceed as directed for the celery hearts, but reduce or increase the cooking time in the marinade according to the size and tenderness of the vegetable. (See the sections on the individual vegetables in this chapter for an indication of overall cooking times.)

4 medium-size	celery hearts, parboiled 10 minutes in enough lightly salted water to cover, then drained well	4 medium-size
1/3 cup	olive oil (top quality)	80 ml
1½ cups	cold water	350 ml
3 tablespoons	lemon juice	3 tablespoons
2 tablespoons	white wine vinegar	2 tablespoons
1/4 teaspoon	fennel seeds	1/4 teaspoon
1/8 teaspoon	coriander seeds	1/8 teaspoon
1/8 teaspoon	crumbled leaf thyme (or 1 medium-size sprig of fresh thyme)	1/8 teaspoon
1/8 teaspoon	peppercorns	1/8 teaspoon
1 large	bay leaf, crumbled	1 large
1/4 teaspoon	salt	1/4 teaspoon

Lay the celery hearts flat in a large skillet (not aluminum). Add the oil, water, lemon juice and vinegar. Tie the fennel and coriander seeds, the thyme, peppercorns and bay leaf in cheesecloth and drop into the skillet, then add the salt. Set over moderate heat and bring to a simmer; adjust the burner so that the liquid trembles gently, cover and simmer the celery hearts 15 to 20 minutes or until tender—but not mushy. Remove from the heat, cool the celery hearts in the liquid, then cover and refrigerate until shortly before serving. Let the celery hearts stand at room temperature, still in the marinade, for 20 minutes so that the flavors intensify, then lift out to serve, topped by a little of the marinade.

Celery soufflé

SERVES 6 TO 8

This is a lovely, light accompaniment for roast pork, turkey or chicken that can be partially made a day ahead of time. All that remains to be done is to beat the egg whites, fold them in and bake the soufflé.

3 pounds	celery (about 2 bunches), trimmed of root and leaves and coarsely cut up	1½ kg
1 large	yellow onion, peeled and minced	1 large
2 large	parsley sprigs	2 large
1 large	thyme sprig (or ½ teaspoon crumbled leaf thyme)	1 large
1 large	bay leaf, crumbled	1 large
1 small	rosemary sprig (or ¼ teaspoon crumbled leaf rosemary)	1 small
1 cup	milk	240 ml
1 cup	beef or chicken broth	240 ml
3 tablespoons	unsalted butter	3 tablespoons
4 tablespoons	all-purpose flour	4 tablespoons
4 large	egg yolks	4 large
⅛ teaspoon	white pepper	⅛ teaspoon
½ cup	soft fine white bread crumbs	120 ml
5 large	egg whites	5 large
1 teaspoon	salt	1 teaspoon
Pinch	cream of tartar	Pinch

Place the celery and onion in a large heavy saucepan (not aluminum). Tie the parsley, thyme, bay leaf and rosemary in cheesecloth and drop into the pan; add the milk and broth, set over moderate heat and bring to a simmer. Adjust the heat so that the liquid barely trembles, cover and simmer 1 hour or until the celery and onion are both mushy. Drain, reserving the cooking liquid; discard the cheesecloth bag. Purée the celery and onion with all but ½ cup (120 ml) of the cooking liquid in a food processor equipped with the metal chopping blade, or in an electric blender at high speed, or by putting through a food mill.

Melt the butter in a medium-size saucepan over moderate heat and blend in the flour; slowly add the ½ cup (120 ml) of reserved cooking liquid and half of the purée. Heat, stirring constantly, 3 to 5 minutes until thickened, smooth and no raw starchy taste remains. Lightly beat the egg yolks, blend a little of the hot mixture into them, then stir back into the pan and cook, stirring all the while, 1 to 2 minutes; do not allow to boil or the mixture may curdle. Combine the saucepan mixture with the remaining celery purée, the pepper and bread crumbs, cover loosely and let cool to room temperature. NOTE: *You can, if you like, prepare the recipe up to this point several hours—or even a day—ahead of time. Cover tight and refrigerate until about 2 hours before serving. Let the mixture stand at room temperature 45 minutes before proceeding.*

Beat the egg whites with the salt and cream of tartar to soft peaks, then fold about one-fourth of the beaten whites into the celery mixture. Now dump the remaining whites on top of the celery mixture and fold in gently but thoroughly, using a rubber spatula. Pour into an ungreased 2-quart (2 L) soufflé dish and bake, uncovered, in a moderately hot oven (375°F. or 190°C.) for ¾ to 1 hour or until dramatically puffed and golden. Rush the soufflé to the table and serve.

Corn

Botanists believe that corn first grew in Peru because motifs of it appear on pre-Incan pottery that has been unearthed around Cuzco. They also believe that corn spread gradually northward, one tribe teaching another how to grow it, and that by the coming of Columbus, it was growing abundantly throughout North and South America.

This corn, however, was a far cry from the juicy, sweet hybrids available to us today. **Sweet** is the key word here, for in my view the only corn fit to eat is sweet (or sugar) corn. The kernels may be white, yellow or both—all on one cob, as in the delectable "butter-and-sugar" corn of the Northeast.

Season: May to October. **Peak months:** July and August.

Hallmarks of quality: Because corn sugar turns to starch almost as soon as ears are pulled from the stalk, I never waste money on prepackaged supermarket corn. I'd rather do without than eat anything so tough and tasteless. I frequent roadside farmer's stands whenever I get the chance, choosing ears that are still moist, tightly sheathed in crisp green husks and tasseled with silvery-gold. (Withered, brown or dry tassels indicate that the corn has been off the stalk for a while.) If in doubt, I pull the husks apart for a look at the kernels. (Many greengroceries discourage this, reasonably enough, because the ear will never again be tightly sheathed.) In fresh young corn, a kernel, when pressed, will spurt sugary milk. The rows of kernels will be even, plump and moist with no signs of "denting" (dimpling), which indicates age. TIP: *Do not buy sweet corn until you are ready to cook it.* My mother always had the kettle boiling when my father went out to pick corn, and my brother and I hung around waiting to husk it. I don't suppose more than 30 minutes elapsed between pot and plate, and for that reason, I consider any but the freshest sweet corn a waste of money.

How much corn per person? 2 to 3 ears; or 1 cup (240 ml) of cream-style or whole-kernel corn. NOTE: *If your family is as addicted to fresh-boiled sweet corn as mine is, allow 4 to 5 young ears per person.* When I was a child and fresh corn was in season, we'd eat nothing but corn on the cob about one night a week and I remember putting away 6 big ears at a sitting.

Best way to store: I don't recommend storing sweet corn, but if it cannot be helped, bag the tightly sheathed ears loosely in plastic and set in the refrigerator. Cook as soon as possible, because corn loses its just-picked flavor faster than any other vegetable.

Basic preparation: When you are ready to cook the corn—**no sooner**—strip off the green husks and remove all strings. Cut the stalk off even with the base of the cob and slice off the undeveloped tip. If there are any blemished or discolored kernels, dig them out with the point of a paring knife.

Special techniques:

FOR WHOLE-KERNEL CORN: Stand a husked cob on end in a flat-bottomed bowl, then, using a very sharp paring knife, cut straight down the cob from top to bottom, freeing two to three rows of kernels at a time. NOTE: *One medium-size cob will yield ½ to ¾ cup (120 to 180 ml) of kernels.*

TO MAKE CREAM-STYLE CORN: Husk the corn, remove strings, then with a sharp knife, score each row of kernels right down the center. Stand the cob on end in a flat-bottomed bowl, and holding the blunt side of a paring knife against the top of the cob at about a 45° angle, scrape down along the cob, pushing the pulpy corn into the bowl. If you have a food processor, there's a quick, neat way to make fresh cream-style corn. Simply cut the whole kernels from the cob by running a sharp knife the length of the cob, freeing three to four rows at a time, then dump the kernels into a food processor fitted with the metal chopping blades. Four to five fast zaps of the motor and you have cream-style corn. Do not overprocess. NOTE: *One medium-size cob will yield about ½ cup (120 ml) of cream-style corn.*

Best way to cook:

TO BOIL: Drop just-husked ears into a big kettle of boiling water (the sort of kettle you would use for cooking lobsters or pasta) that has been sweetened with 2 tablespoons of sugar. Let the water return to a rolling boil, then cover and boil the corn 3 to 5 minutes, depending upon the size of the ears. With tongs, lift the ears of corn out onto several thicknesses of paper toweling and roll them gently to blot up all excess moisture. Serve straightaway with plenty of butter, salt and pepper. NOTE: *Never salt the cooking water; salt will toughen the corn.*

Fresh corn and scallion chowder with salt pork

SERVES 2 TO 4

As a main dish, this will serve two amply if accompanied by a green vegetable or crisp salad and crusty chunks of bread. As a first course, it will serve four.

¼ pound	salt pork, cut into small dice	115 g
4 large	scallions, trimmed, washed and sliced thin (include some tops)	4 large
2 medium-size	ears of sweet corn, husked and cut from the cob cream-style	2 medium-size
½ teaspoon	paprika	½ teaspoon
¼ teaspoon	crumbled leaf thyme	¼ teaspoon
¼ teaspoon	crumbled leaf marjoram	¼ teaspoon
1 cup	half-and-half cream	240 ml
1 cup	milk	240 ml
½ teaspoon (about)	salt	½ teaspoon (about)
⅛ teaspoon	freshly ground black pepper	⅛ teaspoon

Render the salt pork slowly in a large heavy skillet over moderately low heat until all of the fat has cooked out, leaving crisp browned bits; with a slotted spoon, lift the browned bits onto several thicknesses of paper toweling to drain; reserve. Pour all drippings from the skillet, then spoon 2 tablespoons of them back into the skillet. (Save the remainder to use another time.) Stir-fry the scallions in the drippings over moderately low heat 8 to 10 minutes until limp; add the corn, paprika, thyme and marjoram and sauté, stirring frequently, about 15 minutes or until the corn has begun to caramelize and no longer tastes raw. Pour in the half-and-half and milk and warm over moderately low heat, stirring often, about 20 minutes until flavors are well blended. Add the salt, pepper and reserved browned bits of salt pork, taste (making sure that you include at least one piece of salt pork in the tasting spoon because it will affect the overall impression of saltiness), then add a little more salt, if needed. Ladle into soup bowls and serve.

Corn, bacon and green chili pie

SERVES 6 TO 8

For best results, use fresh cream-style sweet corn for this recipe and a good smoked bacon. I like the bite of the green chili (I use canned jalapeño peppers), but the pie is very good without them.

3 slices	bacon, snipped crosswise into julienne strips	3 slices
2 medium-size	yellow onions, peeled and chopped	2 medium-size
2 cups	fresh cream-style sweet corn (about 4 medium-size ears)	½ L
½ teaspoon	crumbled leaf marjoram	½ teaspoon
¼ teaspoon	crumbled leaf thyme	¼ teaspoon
Pinch	crumbled leaf rosemary	Pinch
1 teaspoon	sugar (optional)	1 teaspoon
¾ teaspoon	salt	¾ teaspoon
⅛ teaspoon	freshly ground black pepper	⅛ teaspoon
1 to 2 tablespoons	minced canned green chilies	1 to 2 tablespoons
1 cup	light or heavy cream	240 ml
¼ cup	freshly grated Parmesan cheese	60 ml
2 large	eggs, lightly beaten	2 large
A 9-inch	unbaked pie shell	A 23 cm

Brown the bacon slowly in a medium-size skillet over moderately low heat about 10 minutes until all of the drippings have cooked out and only crisp brown bits remain. Using a slotted spoon, lift the browned bacon to paper toweling to drain; reserve. In the drippings, stir-fry the onions over moderate heat 10 to 12 minutes until limp and lightly browned. NOTE: *This browning of the onions is important for flavor.* Add the corn, marjoram, thyme, rosemary and sugar (but add sugar only if the corn does not seem naturally sweet) and stir-fry about 5 minutes until the herb flavors have intensified and the corn no longer tastes raw. Remove from the heat, stir in the salt, black pepper and green chilies and let cool about 10 minutes. Combine the cream and the cheese. Brush a little of the beaten egg over the pie shell, then stir the remaining egg into the cream mixture. Let the pie shell air-dry for 15 minutes—this is to seal the surface so that the crust will not become soggy during baking.

Combine the cream-egg mixture and the cooled skillet mixture, then pour into the pie shell. Scatter the reserved bacon crumbles evenly on top, and bake, uncovered, in a moderate oven (350°F. or 175°C.) for 30 minutes until set like custard. Cool 15 minutes before cutting into wedges and serving.

Cucumbers

Ever since the first cucumbers were carried out of the valleys of the Himalayas thousands of years ago, they have reigned as one of the world's favorite foods. It was Columbus who introduced cucumbers to the New World by planting them in Haiti in 1494. A mere forty years later, Jacques Cartier made note of "the very great cucumbers" grown by Indian tribes near Montreal. DeSoto saw cucumbers almost everywhere he traveled, Captain John Smith found them in Virginia and the Pilgrims in Massachusetts.

It's odd, then, that we know so few ways to prepare cucumbers. We pickle them, yes, and munch them raw. But few of us do much more despite the fact that three different varieties are widely available today: small, firm, yellow-green **pickling cucumbers;** medium-size, dark green **slicing cucumbers** (these are the ubiquitous supermarket cucumbers), and foot-long, slim European **seedless cucumbers.**

Season: Year round.

Hallmarks of quality: Straight, uniformly firm cucumbers devoid of nicks and blemishes.

How many cucumbers per person? ½ to 1 medium-size cucumber.

Best way to store: Tightly bagged in plastic in the refrigerator crisper. Any partly used cucumbers should be sealed **airtight** in plastic food wrap so that they neither absorb refrigerator odors nor inject their own unique flavor into everything else. **Storage time:** About 1 week, but use the cucumbers sooner if possible because they will begin to lose crunch. TIP: *If you stick a couple of pieces of paper toweling in the bag of cucumbers, they will absorb excess moisture and help slow the softening process.*

Basic preparation: In the old days before cucumbers were **waxed** to increase their longevity, we ate them skins and all. Not a good idea today, because the wax coating is both heavy and sticky. Peel it all off, using a swivel-blade vegetable peeler. **To seed cucumbers:** Halve them lengthwise, then with a teaspoon, scoop out and discard all central seedy portions.

Best ways to cook: Cucumbers usually suffer from cooking unless they are treated with respect and cooked as quickly as possible. They are best, I think, when chunked, sliced or diced and stir-fried the Chinese way: 2 to 3 minutes in a little peanut, sesame or olive oil over intense heat should be sufficient. Cucumbers may be cooked solo or in tandem with other compatible, crunchy vegetables such as bean sprouts, snow peas, scallions or water chestnuts. **Seasoning ideas:** Stir-fry a crushed garlic clove and about 1 tablespoon of finely minced ginger along with the cucumbers; slosh with a couple of tablespoons of good dark soy sauce and, if you like, a tablespoon or two of dry sherry. Or do as the Scandinavians do: Stir-fry the cucumbers 1 to 2 minutes in butter, pour in about ½ cup (120 ml) of heavy cream and sprinkle lavishly with freshly snipped dill. Season to taste with salt and freshly ground black pepper and serve.

Minted cucumber crescents with yogurt

 A superbly refreshing appetizer or salad that averages out at a mere 45 calories per serving.

4 small to medium	cucumbers, peeled and halved lengthwise	4 small to medium
1¼ teaspoons	salt	1¼ teaspoons
¼ cup	finely chopped fresh mint	60 ml
1 carton (8 oz).	plain yogurt	1 carton (226 g)
¼ teaspoon	dill weed	¼ teaspoon
Light sprinkling	freshly ground black pepper	Light sprinkling

Using a teaspoon, scoop seeds from cucumbers and discard. Slice cucumbers thin, letting crescents drop into a large mixing bowl and sprinkling with salt as the bowl fills up. Let stand at room temperature 1 hour, then drain cucumbers of all liquid and pat dry on several thicknesses of paper toweling. Return cucumbers to bowl, add remaining ingredients, toss well, cover and chill several hours before serving.

Cucumbers à la dijonnaise

The perfect accompaniment to cold broiled chicken, cold poached salmon or shrimp during the sultry days of summer. NOTE: *For this recipe, choose small, firm cucumbers, because these will best retain texture during cooking.*

8 small	cucumbers, peeled, quartered and seeded	8 small
⅓ cup	olive oil (top quality)	80 ml
1½ cups	cold water	350 ml
1 large	lemon, juiced	1 large
2 tablespoons	white wine vinegar	2 tablespoons
¼ teaspoon	fennel seeds	¼ teaspoon
⅛ teaspoon	coriander seeds	⅛ teaspoon
¼ teaspoon	crumbled leaf thyme	¼ teaspoon
8 large	peppercorns	8 large
1 large	bay leaf, crumbled	1 large
¼ teaspoon	salt	¼ teaspoon
1 tablespoon	Dijon mustard	1 tablespoon

Lay the prepared cucumbers flat in a large heavy skillet (not aluminum); add the oil, water, lemon juice and vinegar. Tie the fennel and coriander seeds, the thyme, peppercorns and bay leaf in cheesecloth and drop into the skillet. Sprinkle in the salt, set over moderate heat and bring to a simmer. Adjust the burner so that the liquid trembles gently, cover and simmer 8 to 10 minutes until cucumbers are crisp-tender. Let the cucumbers cool in the marinade, then cover and marinate in the refrigerator several hours, turning them occasionally. Remove from the refrigerator and drain off the marinade, reserving 1 cup (240 ml) of it. Blend the mustard into the reserved marinade, pour over the cucumbers, turn over to mix well, then cover and chill ½ to 1 hour. Serve the cucumbers, topped with a little of the Dijonnaise marinade as a cold vegetable, a salad or an appetizer.

Eggplant

"Doubtless these apples have a mischievous qualitie the use whereof is utterly to bee forsaken." The "apples" in question were eggplants, and the skeptic was the famous sixteenth-century English herbalist John Gerard. Like Europeans of his day, he believed eggplants to be dangerous, "mad apples" of the deadly nightshade family (hadn't the Romans named them *mala insana?*) with strange and terrifying powers over man.

So for centuries Europeans avoided eggplants, leaving them to Arabs and Orientals, who prepared them in strange and wondrous dishes (many of the best eggplant recipes available today come from the Middle East or the Mediterranean).

Until recently, the only eggplants to be had in America were the big dark purple ones. Big-city greengrocers, however, now routinely stock baby Italian eggplants and, occasionally, an exotic white hybrid as well.

Season: Year round. **Peak months:** July, August and September.

Hallmarks of quality: Firm, unscarred eggplants that feel heavy for their size. **Small** is better when it comes to eggplant because the flesh will be less pithy and the seeds smaller (well-developed eggplant seeds are unpleasantly bitter).

How much eggplant per person? About ¼ to ⅓ pound (115 to 160 g). A medium-size purple eggplant will weigh about 1 pound (½ kg).

Best way to store: Unwrapped, in the refrigerator crisper. **Storage time:** 3 to 4 days.

Basic preparation: Eggplants really require nothing more than a good washing in tepid water. Peel them or not as individual recipes instruct, then slice or dice.

Special techniques: Many Middle Eastern recipes call for a preliminary **roasting** of eggplant, a far less complicated process than it sounds. I simply place the whole eggplant on a baking sheet, then bake in a moderate oven (350°F. or 175°C.) for about ¾ hour or until quite soft. The next step is to cool the eggplant until it is easy to handle, then to halve it and scoop out the "roasted" flesh. NOTE: *If the seeds are large and dark, remove as many of them as possible because they will taste quite acrid.*

TO "DRY" EGGPLANT SLICES OR CHUNKS: Eggplants are largely water and for that reason do not fry well unless they have first had some of their moisture removed. It's a routine technique often integral to the basic preparation, regardless of how the eggplants will eventually be cooked. Simply slice or dice the eggplant to whatever thickness or size a specific recipe suggests, then sprinkle liberally with salt. Place the eggplant, in one layer, between several thicknesses of paper toweling and weight down with heavy plates for an hour or so. The salt will draw excess moisture from the eggplant and the paper toweling will absorb it.

Best ways to cook eggplant: With the exception of frying, the simple methods of cooking do little for eggplant in my opinion. Eggplant must be given full creative treatment. (See recipes that follow and those in the Recipe Collection in Part II.)

TO PARBOIL (often necessary before eggplant can be used in recipes): Prepare the eggplant as directed, peel or not, then slice or dice as individual recipes direct. Place the eggplant in a large saucepan (not aluminum, which will darken the eggplant), cover with lightly salted boiling water, cover and boil 5 to 10 minutes until crisp-tender. Drain well, then pat the eggplant dry on paper toweling. TIP: *If firmness of texture is important, steam the eggplant instead: place the slices or cubes in a steamer rack, set over boiling water in a large saucepan, cover and steam about 10 minutes until crisp-tender. The eggplant is now "parboiled" and ready to use in recipes.*

TO FRY: Prepare the eggplant as directed, then slice about ½ inch (1½ cm) thick. Sprinkle liberally with salt and weight down between several thicknesses of paper toweling as directed above in "To Dry Eggplant Slices." Dredge the slices first in flour, then dip in lightly beaten egg (for 1 medium-size eggplant, use 2 medium-size eggs, lightly beaten with 2 tablespoons milk or cream). Then coat with fine dry bread crumbs (about 2 cups or ½ L of crumbs for a medium-size eggplant). Let the breaded eggplant slices air-dry on a wire rack at room temperature for 20 to 30 minutes—this encourages the breading to stick. Brown the eggplant slices in about ¼ inch (¾ cm) of olive, peanut, corn or vegetable oil in a large heavy skillet over moderately high heat, allowing 2 to 3 minutes per side. As the eggplant slices brown, transfer them to paper toweling to drain. Add more oil to the skillet as needed for subsequent batches of eggplant. Serve hot. NOTE: *To keep the first batches from cooling as the final ones brown, lay them in one layer on a baking sheet lined with several thicknesses of paper toweling, then set uncovered in a very slow oven (250°F. or 120°C.).*

Hunanese braised eggplant
with sesame, garlic and ginger

SERVES 4

    This fifteen-minute recipe is an exception to the rule that eggplant must always first be sprinkled with salt and weighted down between several thicknesses of paper toweling before it can be fried. The heat used here for stir-frying is intense—just enough to sear the surface of the eggplant. Then liquids are added, the heat lowered, the skillet covered and the eggplant braised. I like to leave the eggplant peel on for color and texture, but if you object to it, by all means peel the eggplant before you cube it. Eggplant prepared this way is delicious with broiled chicken, steak or lamb chops.

1 medium-size (1 pound)	firm young eggplant, washed and cut into 1-inch (2½ cm) cubes	1 medium-size (½ kg)
2 tablespoons	peanut oil	2 tablespoons
1 tablespoon	roasted sesame seed oil	1 tablespoon
1 large	garlic clove, peeled and minced	1 large
2 tablespoons	finely minced fresh ginger	2 tablespoons
3 tablespoons, in all	soy sauce	3 tablespoons, in all
1 tablespoon	mirin (Japanese sweet rice wine) or cream sherry	1 tablespoon

Stir-fry the eggplant in the peanut and sesame oils along with the garlic and ginger in a large heavy skillet, wok or sauté pan over very high heat 1½ to 2 minutes until golden. NOTE: *The eggplant will soak up the oil like a sponge, but resist the temptation to add more oil because the finished dish will be greasy if you do. Just keep tossing the eggplant, garlic and ginger vigorously as they sear so that they do not char.* Reduce the heat to moderately low, add 2 tablespoons of the soy sauce, toss well, then cover and braise 8 to 10 minutes, stirring now and then, just until the eggplant looks translucent but still has a bit of crunch. Sprinkle the remaining tablespoon of soy sauce and the *mirin* evenly over the eggplant, stir-fry about 1 minute over high heat, then serve.

Roasted whole eggplant
studded with bacon and garlic

SERVES 4

    If you're wary of garlic, better skip this recipe. But if not, try eggplant this way. It's such an easy recipe, equally good warm or cold, and delicious with roast lamb, chicken or turkey.

1 medium-size (1 pound)	firm, glossy eggplant, washed	1 medium-size (1 pound)
2 slices	bacon, cut crosswise into julienne strips	2 slices
4 large	garlic cloves, peeled and quartered lengthwise	4 large
1 teaspoon	salt	1 teaspoon
½ teaspoon	crumbled leaf thyme	½ teaspoon
½ teaspoon	crumbled leaf marjoram	½ teaspoon
¼ teaspoon	freshly ground black pepper	¼ teaspoon
2 tablespoons	olive oil (top quality)	2 tablespoons

With a sharp paring knife, mark the eggplant into quarters from top to bottom by making four "dotted lines" of deep slits spaced 1 inch (2½ cm) apart.

Dip the bacon pieces and garlic slivers into a mixture of the salt, thyme, marjoram and pepper to coat them evenly. Now stuff each of the eggplant slits, alternating the garlic and bacon. (You may have a little bacon and garlic left over, but no matter; they can be added to the baking pan.)

Spoon the olive oil into a pie pan, add the whole scored eggplant and turn it in the oil so that it is evenly coated all over. Now drop in any remaining bacon, garlic and herb mixture. Bake, uncovered, in a slow oven (300°F. or 150°C.) for 1½ hours. Remove the eggplant from the oven and cool 30 minutes. Quarter lengthwise by cutting midway between each row of slits and serve. Top each portion with a little of the pan drippings, extra bacon and garlic.

Belgian endive

Ever since the ancient Egyptians discovered how cool and crisp endive was, it has been a popular salad green. In his *Paradisi* of 1629, John Parkinson, herbalist to Charles I, writes that endive was "much used in winter as a sallet herbe with great delight."

While the English were busily tossing salads of endive, the French and Belgians were elevating the cooking of it to high art and amassing an impressive recipe repertoire for the succulent ivory stalks.

Season: September through May.

Hallmarks of quality: Firmness, plumpness and compactness of stalks. Individual leaves should be crisp, uniformly ivory except at the tips, where they may be tinged with yellow-green. Reject any endives that are loose-leafed, limp or streaked with rust or brown.

How many endives per person? Usually 2 medium-size stalks—6 to 7 inches (15 to 18 cm) in length—will be ample to serve as a cooked vegetable; 1 to serve raw dressed as a salad.

Best way to store: Both water and light turn endive bitter, so do not wash the stalks before you put them away. Also to help keep light out and moisture in, bundle 2 to 3 stalks together in several thicknesses of paper toweling, then bag loosely in plastic and store in the refrigerator crisper. **Storage time:** 3 to 4 days.

Basic preparation: Do not wash endives; merely pull off any wilted or discolored outer leaves, then slice, dice or leave whole as individual recipes direct.

Best way to cook: By braising; see recipe which follows.

Braised Belgian endives with bacon, lemon and shallots

SERVES 6

The trick in braising endives is not to overcook them, which means watching the pot and taking the endives from the heat the instant they are crisp-tender. Overcooking will make them both bitter and mushy.

¼ pound	lean smoked slab bacon, cut into ¼-inch (¾ cm) cubes	115 g
1 tablespoon	unsalted butter	1 tablespoon
1 tablespoon	sugar	1 tablespoon
6 medium-size	Belgian endives, trimmed	6 medium-size
4 large	shallots, peeled and minced	4 large
¼ cup	rich beef broth	60 ml
1 medium-size	lemon, juiced	1 medium-size
⅛ teaspoon	freshly grated nutmeg	⅛ teaspoon
To taste	salt and freshly ground black pepper	To taste
1 tablespoon	minced parsley	1 tablespoon

Sauté the bacon in the butter in a large heavy skillet over moderately low heat 12 to 15 minutes until most of the fat has cooked out of the bacon, leaving crisp brown bits. With a slotted spoon, lift the browned bits to paper toweling to drain; reserve. Pour all of the drippings from the skillet, then spoon 3 tablespoons of them back into the skillet. (Reserve the remaining drippings; you may need some to finish this recipe and the balance can be used for other recipes later.) Add the sugar to the skillet, set over moderate heat and stir a minute or two until dissolved. Add the endives and sauté about 5 minutes, turning in the drippings, until lightly but evenly browned and nicely glazed. Lift the endives to a plate with a slotted spoon and reserve. If the skillet drippings seem skimpy, add another tablespoon. Add the shallots and stir-fry 3 to 5 minutes over moderate heat until limp and golden. Pour in the beef broth and lemon juice and boil a minute or two to combine the flavors. Return the endives to the skillet, turn the heat to low, cover and simmer 8 to 10 minutes until crisp-tender. Uncover the skillet, sprinkle the reserved bacon crumbles and nutmeg evenly over all, then turn the endives in the skillet mixture to glaze. Season to taste with salt and pepper. Lift the endives to a heated, small, deep platter and keep warm. Quickly reduce the skillet liquids by boiling hard a minute or two, pour over the endives, sprinkle with parsley and serve.

Finocchio
(FLORENCE FENNEL)

This crisp, anise-flavored, bulbous celerylike stalk figures prominently in ancient alchemy and legend. Roman gladiators, it's said, ate fennel to increase their strength; fennel seeds were strewn across the path of newlyweds to bring good fortune, much as we throw rice today; and early herbalists believed fennel could cure everything from mad-dog bites to drunkenness.

Today fennel or finocchio is more highly prized for its culinary versatility. It is delicious sliced raw into salads, boiled or steamed and buttered, braised and as Sicilian cooks have long known, teamed with fish (try the recipe for Broiled Red Snapper Stuffed with Finocchio; see Index).

Season: June, July, August and early September.

Hallmarks of quality: Compactness, crispness and moistness of the bulb and frilliness of the green tops. Reject any finocchio that is overly coarse, nicked, blemished or limp.

How much finocchio per person? A medium-size bulb will make 1½ to 2 servings.

Best way to store: Loosely bagged in plastic in the refrigerator crisper. **Storage time:** 5 to 7 days, but use sooner if possible.

Basic preparation: Remove any coarse, softening or discoloring outer ribs and cut off the feathery green tops. I wrap these in a small plastic bag, refrigerate them and use to season steamed, poached or broiled lean white fish, broiled chicken, tomato soups and sauces, even yeast breads. The feathery tops should be snipped just as you would fresh dill. As for the finocchio bulbs, they may be cooked whole, quartered, sliced or diced.

Best ways to cook:

To BOIL: Half immerse the prepared finocchio in beef or chicken broth or very lightly salted boiling water, cover and cook as follows: about 30 minutes for whole bulbs, 15 for quartered bulbs, and 8 to 10 for sliced or diced—just until crisp-tender. Drain well, then season to taste with butter, salt and freshly ground black pepper. NOTE: *I also toss in a tablespoon or two of freshly snipped finocchio tops to heighten the fennel flavor.*

TO STEAM: Because finocchio is so hard and compact, whole bulbs will not steam evenly—the outer ribs will be mushy before the inner ones are tender. So the best plan is to quarter the bulbs lengthwise or to slice or dice them. Arrange the finocchio in a steamer basket, then cook **over** boiling water in a large covered saucepan until crisp-tender as follows: about 15 minutes for sliced or diced finocchio, 20 to 25 for the quartered. Season as directed for boiled finocchio above.

TO STIR-FRY: Trim the finocchio bulbs of coarse outer leaves and feathery tops, then quarter each bulb lengthwise and slice crosswise about ¼ inch (¾ cm) thick. Stir-fry in 2 to 3 tablespoons of butter, or bacon drippings, olive or peanut oil, or about two parts peanut oil and one part toasted sesame oil in a large heavy skillet over high heat just until translucent and crisp-tender—about 5 minutes altogether. Season to taste with salt and freshly ground pepper and, if you like, a tablespoon of the snipped finocchio tops (or a half-and-half mixture of these and snipped fresh dill or minced parsley). You might also add a little soy sauce (particularly good if the finocchio was stir-fried in peanut and/or toasted sesame oil), a little dry sherry or vermouth, even a little mellow tomato sauce (preferably homemade).

TO BRAISE: See the recipe for Braised Finocchio with Bacon, Lemon and Shallots (see below).

To serve cold: Steamed or boiled finocchio can be quick-chilled in ice water, then drained well and dressed with oil and lemon or vinaigrette. (Try adding a tablespoon or two of freshly minced tarragon.) Also see the recipe for Celery Hearts à la Grecque in the celery section of this chapter. Trimmed finocchio bulbs, quartered lengthwise, may be substituted for the celery hearts.

VARIATION:

Braised finocchio with bacon, lemon and shallots: Trim the tops from 4 medium-size bulbs of finocchio and reserve. Also remove any coarse or blemished outer stalks and discard. Quarter each finocchio bulb lengthwise, then slice each quarter crosswise about ½ inch (2½ cm) thick. Now braise the finocchio exactly as directed above for Belgian endives, but reduce the cooking time in the covered skillet to 3 to 5 minutes; because the finocchio is sliced, it will cook more quickly than whole stalks of endive. Just before serving the finocchio, sprinkle with 2 tablespoons of the finely snipped finocchio tops instead of parsley. NOTE: *Bag the remaining finocchio tops in plastic, refrigerate and use for seasoning salads, soups, stews, casseroles, breads. Finocchio, by the way, is particularly compatible with lean white fish, so try sprinkling freshly snipped tops over broiled, baked or poached fish instead of dill or parsley.*

Leeks

Leeks, the most elegant member of the onion family, have been the national emblem of Wales ever since the sixth century when the Welsh defeated the Saxons. According to legend, St. David, on whose day the battle was fought, ordered the Welsh lads to tuck leeks into their caps for easy identification. The Welsh handily won, attributed their victory to the leek and made it their national emblem.

In that day leeks were peasant food. But not so today, considering that leeks sometimes cost as much as a dollar apiece.

Season: Year round. **Peak seasons:** There are two of them—April, May, June and July and September through December.

Hallmarks of quality: Clean, compact unblemished stalks with moist root ends and tops. Always try to buy leeks of as nearly the same size as possible.

How many leeks per person? Much depends upon how the leeks are to be served, to say nothing of your pocketbook. Leeks are usually used more as a seasoning than an appetizer, vegetable or salad to be served solo, but should you want to serve them thus, allow 2 medium-size leeks per person.

Best way to store: Loosely bagged in plastic in the refrigerator crisper. NOTE: *Do not trim or wash leeks before you store them because doing so will merely hasten their deterioration.*

Basic preparation: The most difficult part about preparing leeks is cleaning them. They are grown in sandy soil, and grit tends to work its way down inside the many layers of the stalk. But first of all, cut off the root ends and all but the most tender green top (most of it will be tough). The next step is to flush out as much grit as possible. My technique is to hold the leek, root end down, directly under the cold water faucet and let the water push the grit out the bottom of the stalk. Usually this works. If not, I make two long slits on opposite sides of the stalk, cutting deep into the center but leaving ½-inch (1½ cm) margins top and bottom. I again hold the stalk under the faucet, this time horizontally so that the water can work its way through the various layers, washing out the grit. When the leeks are clean, pat them dry on paper toweling, then leave whole, chunk or slice as individual recipes direct.

Best ways to cook:

To BOIL: Lay trimmed and cleaned whole leeks flat in an enameled, stainless steel or flameproof glass saucepan; pour in about 2 inches (5 cm) of boiling beef or chicken broth or lightly salted water. Cover and boil about 10 minutes, just until firm-tender. Drain (reserve broth to use in soups, stews or sauces), season to taste with butter, salt and pepper, and, if you like, a little snipped fresh dill or finocchio tops. **Other compatible seasonings:** Thyme, marjoram, chervil, summer savory, rosemary, nutmeg and mace.

To STEAM: Lay trimmed and cleaned whole leeks in a steamer basket and cook **over** boiling water in a large covered saucepan 10 to 15 minutes until firm-tender. Serve hot, using any of the seasonings suggested for boiled leeks above.

To braise: Sauté the leeks in a little butter or olive oil in a large heavy skillet (not aluminum) over moderately high heat about 5 minutes, turning them often, until evenly glazed and golden. Add a sprig of thyme (or about ¼ teaspoon crumbled leaf thyme), a grating of nutmeg, about 1 cup (240 ml) good beef broth and, if you like, a tablespoon or two of dry white wine. Cover and simmer 5 to 10 minutes, just until the leeks are tender. Season to taste with salt and pepper and serve, topped with some of the braising liquid.

To serve cold: Boiled or steamed leeks can be quick-chilled in ice water, then drained and marinated an hour or two in a good tart vinaigrette or herb or oil and lemon dressing. Serve as a first course or salad. Also see the recipe for Celery Hearts à la Grecque in the celery section of this chapter. Trimmed whole leeks may be substituted for the celery hearts in this recipe. Note: *You may need to reduce the overall cooking time slightly. The leeks should be firm-tender, not mushy.*

Leeks au gratin

SERVES 4 TO 6

A glamorous accompaniment to roast chicken or turkey.

2 tablespoons	unsalted butter	2 tablespoons
2 tablespoons	flour	2 tablespoons
¼ teaspoon	crumbled leaf thyme	¼ teaspoon
Pinch	crumbled leaf rosemary	Pinch
Pinch	freshly grated nutmeg	Pinch
½ teaspoon	salt	½ teaspoon
Light sprinkling	freshly ground black pepper	Light sprinkling
½ cup	beef broth	120 ml
1 cup	milk or half-and-half cream	240 ml
2 tablespoons	freshly grated Parmesan or Romano cheese	2 tablespoons
2 pounds	leeks, trimmed, cleaned, boiled 10 minutes in lightly salted water and drained well	1 kg
	TOPPING:	
1 cup	fine soft bread crumbs	240 ml
1 tablespoon	melted unsalted butter	1 tablespoon
2 tablespoons	freshly grated Parmesan cheese	2 tablespoons

Melt the butter in a small heavy saucepan over moderate heat, blend in the flour, thyme, rosemary, nutmeg, salt and pepper and allow to mellow about 1 minute.

Combine the broth and milk, pour into the saucepan and heat, stirring constantly, 3 to 5 minutes until thickened and smooth and no raw starch taste remains. Off heat, stir in the grated Parmesan. Set aside. Arrange the leeks in an unbuttered 6-cup (1½ L) *au gratin* pan or shallow casserole. Pour the cheese sauce evenly on top. Combine the topping ingredients and scatter uniformly over all. Bake, uncovered, in a moderate oven (350°F. or 175°C.) for 30 minutes, then brown quickly under the broiler and serve.

∽ Lentils

I live a fast walk from New York City's "Little India" on the lower reaches of Lexington Avenue and love to go in just to sniff the air, heavy with the scent of curry spices. Here you will also find burlap bags overflowing with lentils—red lentils, brown lentils (the common supermarket variety), green lentils and lentils the color of ripe corn. The red, green and yellow lentils, I've found, are slightly softer and waxier than the brown, somewhat mellower, too. But all can be prepared the same way.

Season: Lentils are dried and thus available year round.

Hallmarks of quality: A high percentage of unbroken lentils and a low percentage of extraneous grit. Also look for lentils that are of uniform color.

How many lentils per person? About ¼ pound (115 g).

Best way to store: In a tightly covered glass jar on a cool, dark shelf. **Storage time:** Properly stored, lentils will keep indefinitely.

Basic preparation: Wash and sort the lentils well, discarding all bits of stone and any lentils that are discolored. NOTE: *Unlike dried peas and beans, lentils do not need a preliminary soaking.*

Best way to cook: Only one, and that is **boiling.** How much liquid you use for cooking the lentils will determine whether you end up with a soup or a vegetable of porridge consistency. And what liquid you use—i.e., lightly salted water, beef, chicken or vegetable broth—will completely alter the final flavor. NOTE: *Do not cook lentils in tomato juice because its acid will make them disagreeably firm, which no amount of cooking will correct. If you want to season lentils with tomatoes, do so after they are tender.*

To BOIL: Place 1 pound (½ kg) of washed and sorted lentils in a large heavy saucepan, pour in 3 cups (¾ L) of lightly salted boiling water, or beef, chicken or vegetable broth, set over moderate heat and as soon as the liquid returns to a gentle boil, adjust the burner as needed so that the liquid barely trembles. Add any or all of the following to the pot: a large peeled and chopped yellow onion, a large crushed garlic clove, a large whole bay leaf, a ham bone, a sprig of thyme (or ¼ teaspoon crumbled leaf thyme). Cover and simmer the lentils 40 to 45 minutes until firm-tender. Toward the end of cooking, watch the pot closely lest the lentils stick. If the pot is in danger of boiling dry, add a bit more water or broth. Season the lentils to taste with salt and freshly ground pepper and serve. **For soup:** Use 5 to 6 cups (1¼ to 1½ L) of liquid to 1 pound (½ kg) of lentils, then add any of the seasonings suggested for boiled lentils. Cover and simmer 1 to 1½ hours until the lentils are mushy-tender. NOTE: *If you have used a ham bone, remove the bone at the end of cooking, cut off the meat, dice it and return it to the lentils.*

Austrian sour lentils

SERVES 6 TO 8

These lentils will forever do for me what madeleines did for Proust. One spoonful and I am whirled back two dozen years to one snowy January day in Vienna. I'd been out all day, photographing the city under its cloak of new-fallen snow, and was chilled to the bone. After a long soak in a hot tub, I headed for the dining room of the little hotel where I was staying, and ordered a big bowl of sour lentils. They were as good as anything I ever remember eating—steaming-hot, tart of lemon and vinegar, an entire meal in themselves. I'm sure they had nothing to do with my not catching cold—but I like to think that they did, attributing to them the sort of magical powers that other people do to chicken soup.

2 cups	brown lentils, washed and sorted	½ L
4½ cups	beef broth	1 L + 120 ml
¼ teaspoon	crumbled leaf thyme	¼ teaspoon
1 large	bay leaf	1 large
2 medium-size	yellow onions, peeled and chopped	2 medium-size
3 tablespoons	unsalted butter	3 tablespoons
2 tablespoons	flour	2 tablespoons
2 tablespoons	finely chopped drained capers	2 tablespoons
1 teaspoon	finely grated lemon rind	1 teaspoon
2 tablespoons (about)	red wine vinegar	2 tablespoons (about)
2 tablespoons	lemon juice	2 tablespoons
To taste	salt and freshly ground black pepper	To taste

Simmer the lentils in 3½ cups (830 ml) of the broth along with the thyme and bay leaf in a covered saucepan over moderately low heat 1 to 1¼ hours until firm-tender and all broth is absorbed. Meanwhile, stir-fry the onions in the butter in a medium-size heavy saucepan 10 to 15 minutes over moderate heat until limp and nicely browned. Blend in the flour and mellow 2 to 3 minutes, then stir in the capers and lemon rind. Combine the remaining cup (240 ml) of broth with the wine vinegar and lemon juice, pour into the flour mixture and heat, stirring constantly, until thickened and smooth. Turn the heat down low and mellow the sauce about 5 minutes longer; set aside.

As soon as the lentils are firm-tender, remove and discard the bay leaf. Pour in the reserved sauce and stir well to mix. Season to taste with salt (you probably will not need much of it) and pepper and serve as the main course of a cold-weather lunch or supper.

Mushrooms

Until recently, the only mushrooms widely available were the snowy supermarket variety. And even these, I discovered not so many years ago when I'd gone home to visit my family, had to be especially ordered in the small-town South. Today, of course, these mushrooms are routinely stocked by supermarkets everywhere. And specialty shops are beginning to offer fresh yellow, funnel-shaped French *chanterelles*, webbed brown morels, plump Italian *boletus* (also called *cèpes* or *porcini*), pungent brown Black Forest mushrooms and two new Japanese exotics: fleshy, black *shitake* and delicate white *enok* mushrooms that are no bigger than thumbtacks. You will pay a premium for such mushrooms, but then mushrooms have for centuries been the prerogative of the privileged. The Pharaohs of ancient Egypt, it's said, prized mushrooms so highly that they forbade common men to eat them.

Season: Year round for the common mushrooms, also the exotic *enoks*, now being grown in California. Morels are the mushrooms of May; *chanterelles* and *porcini* come to market in the summer and fall; the other varieties appear erratically. NOTE: *Morels,* chanterelles, *and* porcini *are all available dried and need nothing more than rejuvenation in cool water.*

Hallmarks of quality: Regardless of variety, mushrooms should feel spongy-firm and look clean, fresh and succulent, not withered or wet. When buying the common mushrooms choose those of medium size with firm stems and snowy, unspotted caps that are still attached about the edge to the stem, hiding the brown gills on the caps' undersides.

How many mushrooms per person? About ⅓ to ½ pound (160 to 225 g).

Best way to store: The object is to keep the mushrooms damp but at the same time to prevent them from becoming wet, which will hasten their deterioration and which will most certainly happen if they are bagged in plastic or left sealed in their supermarket cartons. The method that mushroom growers recommend for storing mushrooms is to spread them out on a tray, in one layer, and to cover them loosely with several thicknesses of paper toweling that have been dipped in cool water, then wrung out fairly dry. Moisten the paper toweling each day by sprinkling lightly with water. **Storage time:** About 5 days.

Basic preparation: Trim off woody or discolored stem ends, then wipe the mushroom caps with a damp cloth. Never soak or wash mushrooms—except for morels—because most of their flavor will be lost. Morels have intricately webbed crowns, which trap grit, and for that reason must be more carefully washed than other mushrooms. I usually rinse them quickly under cool running water, then pat them dry at once on several thicknesses of paper toweling. *Enok* mushrooms, sold in perforated plastic bags, are ready to use as purchased (they can be tossed raw into salads or added to almost any stir-fried dish). NOTE: *If you are to use mushroom caps only, save the stems to use later in soups, stews and casseroles. I usually just bundle the stems in dampened paper toweling and store in the refrigerator (they will keep well 2 to 3 days).*

Best ways to cook: Stir-fried or sautéed mushrooms are best, I think, although the caps can be stuffed and baked. If you intend to cook mushrooms whole, choose small ones. Otherwise, quarter or slice them.

TO SAUTÉ OR STIR-FRY: Prepare the mushrooms as directed. Use a large heavy skillet and for 1 pound (½ kg) of mushrooms, 3 to 4 tablespoons of butter, olive oil or bacon drippings. For **sautéing,** use moderate heat, and stir occasionally; for **stir-frying,** use high heat and stir constantly. Cook 5 to 10 minutes, just until the mushrooms are lightly browned, have released their juices and these have evaporated. Once the mushrooms are done, you have a number of options as to how you will finish them. I like to blend in 1 cup (240 ml) of room-temperature sour cream or ½ cup (120 ml) of heavy cream and 2 tablespoons of freshly snipped dill or minced parsley. Another choice would be to add ¼ cup (60 ml) of dry sherry or white wine to the sautéed mushrooms and to cook it down by about half. If you have sautéed the mushrooms in olive oil, you might dress them with a little lemon juice or white wine vinegar and freshly minced tarragon; these are delicious hot or cold.

Mushrooms à la provençale

SERVES 4

This is a marvelous—and marvelously easy—way to prepare almost any edible mushrooms: the supermarket champignons, the fleshy boletus (or *porcini,* as the Italians call them) and the golden, vase-shaped *chanterelles.* Whatever the variety, the mushrooms should be of as nearly the same size as possible. If small, they may be used whole; otherwise they should be halved or quartered or cut into slim wedges. Serve as a first course, salad or vegetable side dish.

1 pound	small whole mushrooms or quartered medium-size mushrooms, wiped clean	½ kg
4 tablespoons, in all	olive oil (a top-quality, richly flavored oil is best)	4 tablespoons, in all
1 medium-size	garlic clove, peeled and minced	1 medium-size
¼ teaspoon	crumbled leaf thyme (or, if available, a small sprig of fresh thyme)	¼ teaspoon
1 tablespoon	dry vermouth	1 tablespoon
2 tablespoons	freshly minced parsley	2 tablespoons
¼ teaspoon (about)	salt	¼ teaspoon (about)
Pinch	freshly ground black pepper	Pinch

Stir-fry the mushrooms in 3 tablespoons of the oil in a large heavy skillet over moderate heat 5 minutes. NOTE: *The mushrooms will soak up the oil within less than a minute, but do not add more oil—yet.* After the mushrooms have cooked 5 minutes, add the garlic, thyme and the remaining tablespoon of oil, drizzling it as evenly as possible over the mushrooms. Stir-fry 2 minutes, add the vermouth and stir-fry another 2 to 3 minutes until all liquid has evaporated. Add the parsley, salt and pepper and stir-fry 1 to 2 minutes longer until the mushrooms are firm-tender and flavors well blended. Taste for salt and add more, if needed. Serve hot or at room temperature.

Baked mushroom and potato strata

SERVES 8

This recipe, like a good many, was born of a failure. I was attempting to make a complicated Lithuanian potato dough that is rolled out, spread with mushroom filling, then twirled up jelly-roll style. But the potatoes never formed a smooth and elastic dough. They tasted perfectly splendid, and so did the mushroom mixture, so I decided to layer them into a baking dish. Friends who sampled the recipe were none the wiser and thought the recipe superb. It's a good choice, by the way, for a buffet and is wonderful with roast beef, pork, turkey or chicken.

	POTATO MIXTURE:	
2½ pounds (about 8 medium-size to large)	Maine or Eastern potatoes, boiled in their skins until tender, peeled and mashed until smooth	1¼ kg (about 8 medium-size to large)
¼ cup	unsifted potato starch or all-purpose flour	60 ml
2½ teaspoons	salt	2½ teaspoons
⅛ teaspoon	freshly ground black pepper	⅛ teaspoon
⅛ teaspoon	freshly grated nutmeg	⅛ teaspoon

1 very large	egg, lightly beaten	1 very large
3 to 4	tablespoons light or heavy cream	3 to 4
	MUSHROOM MIXTURE:	
1 pound	mushrooms, wiped clean and finely chopped	½ kg
1 small	yellow onion, peeled and finely chopped	1 small
1 large	shallot, peeled and minced	1 large
3 tablespoons	unsalted butter	3 tablespoons
¼ teaspoon	crumbled leaf thyme	¼ teaspoon
⅛ teaspoon	freshly grated nutmeg	⅛ teaspoon
3 tablespoons	all-purpose flour	3 tablespoons
3 tablespoons	sour cream	3 tablespoons
½ teaspoon	salt	½ teaspoon
⅛ teaspoon	freshly ground black pepper	⅛ teaspoon

Mix the potatoes with the potato starch, salt, pepper, nutmeg and egg, and beat until smooth. Now add just enough cream to lighten the potatoes slightly—they should be creamy-thick but not stiff. Set aside while you prepare the mushroom mixture.

For the mushroom mixture: Stir-fry the chopped mushrooms, onion and shallot in the butter in a large heavy skillet over moderate heat about 10 minutes or until thick and pastelike. Blend in the thyme and nutmeg and let mellow a minute or two over moderate heat to intensify their flavors. Blend in the flour, then the sour cream, salt and pepper.

To assemble the strata: Spread half of the potato mixture in the bottom of a well-buttered 9 × 9 × 2-inch (23 × 23 × 5-cm) baking dish. Top with all of the mushroom mixture, then spread the remaining potato mixture on top, roughing it up a bit as you would meringue for a prettier appearance.

Bake uncovered in a moderate oven (350°F. or 175°C.) for about 45 minutes or until tipped with brown. Serve at table directly from the baking dish.

Fresh mushroom soufflé spiked with dry white wine

SERVES 6

I like this delicate soufflé with broiled fish or chicken and a crisp green salad, but if topped with a nippy cheese sauce, it can become the main dish of a light luncheon or supper. NOTE: *If you want to give the soufflé a "top hat" (raised center), draw a circle in the soufflé mixture about 1½ inches (4 cm) in from the edge of the dish.*

2 large	shallots, peeled and minced	2 large
6 tablespoons, in all	unsalted butter	6 tablespoons, in all
1 pound	mushrooms, wiped clean and minced fine	½ kg
¼ teaspoon	crumbled leaf thyme	¼ teaspoon
¼ teaspoon	crumbled leaf rosemary	¼ teaspoon
⅛ teaspoon	freshly grated nutmeg or mace	⅛ teaspoon
¼ cup	dry white wine or vermouth	60 ml
4 tablespoons	flour	4 tablespoons
2 cups	milk	½ L
1 teaspoon, in all	salt	1 teaspoon, in all
⅛ teaspoon	freshly ground black pepper	⅛ teaspoon
6 large	eggs, separated	6 large

Stir-fry the shallots in 2 tablespoons of the butter in a large heavy skillet over moderate heat 3 to 5 minutes until limp and golden. Add the mushrooms, thyme, rosemary and nutmeg and stir-fry about 10 minutes until the mushrooms have released their juices and these have evaporated. Pour in the wine and simmer slowly until the mixture is thick, dry and pastelike—5 to 10 minutes.

Meanwhile, melt the remaining 4 tablespoons of butter in a medium-size heavy saucepan over moderate heat and blend in the flour to make a smooth paste. Add the milk, ½ teaspoon of the salt and the pepper, and cook, stirring constantly, until thickened and smooth—3 to 5 minutes. Whisk the egg yolks lightly, mix a little of the hot sauce into the yolks, then stir back into pan, reduce heat to low, and heat, whisking vigorously, about 2 minutes—do not allow to boil or the sauce may curdle. Empty the sauce into a large bowl and mix in the mushroom mixture; cool to room temperature, stirring frequently to prevent a skin from forming on the surface of the sauce.

Sprinkle the remaining ½ teaspoon of salt evenly over the egg whites and beat them to soft peaks. Blend about one-fourth of the beaten whites into the mushroom mixture to lighten it, then spoon the remaining whites on top and fold in lightly but thoroughly until no streaks of white or brown remain. Spoon into an ungreased 2½-quart (2½ L) soufflé dish and bake uncovered in a moderate oven (350°F. or 175°C.) for 1 to 1¼ hours or until lightly browned, puffed and the soufflé quivers gently when you nudge the dish. Rush the soufflé to the table and serve.

Okra

 Not much is known of the okra of old. Probably it originated in Ethiopia above the Blue Nile, was carried into southern Europe by the Moors and to the New World by either the Spaniards or black slaves. Certainly it

is in the Deep South that okra is most popular in this country. And certainly it is southern women who know best how to cook it, whether they are slipping whole or minced young pods into gumbo (it serves as both flavoring and thickener) or dusting slices with stone-ground corn meal and frying them to a rich amber. What makes okra objectionable to many people (and I count myself among that number) is not its delicate eggplantlike flavor but its slimy texture. Properly prepared, however—and in my book, that means *frying*—okra will be crisply tender.

Season: Spring, summer and fall. **Peak months:** July and August.

Hallmarks of quality: Small, firm-tender pods between 2 and 4 inches (5 and 10 cm) long with pliable tips. The okra should be an "alive" green and devoid of yellow or brown spots, nicks or rips. Reject all large okra—it will be woody.

How much okra per person? ¼ to ½ pound (115 to 225 g), depending upon how it is prepared.

Best way to store: Unwashed and untrimmed, loosely bagged in plastic in the refrigerator. **Storage time:** 3 to 4 days.

Basic preparation: Wash the pods well in cool water, pat dry, then carefully cut off the stems so that you do not open the stem end of the pod. (This is important if you intend to cook the pods whole and don't want the insides to ooze out.) Leave the pods whole or slice thin (about ½ inch or 1½ cm is a good thickness for frying). NOTE: *For gumbos, Cajun women chop the okra fairly fine, then fry it a half hour or so in bacon or ham drippings until it reduces to a thick paste. One Cajun I interviewed a few years ago makes huge batches of fried, chopped okra— "gumbo base," she calls it—and freezes it in half-pint (240 ml) portions—"just enough to thicken a big batch of gumbo."*

Best ways to cook: If okra is to be served by itself as a vegetable, the only way it's fit to eat—in my view, at least—is fried.

TO FRY: Wash and slice the okra, then dredge well in flour or stone-ground corn meal. NOTE: *It's important that you use stone-ground cornmeal, not the gritty variety, because its floury texture makes it stick to the okra better.* Now stir-fry in bacon drippings, butter or vegetable oil (about 3 tablespoons for 1 pound or ½ kg of okra) in a large heavy skillet over moderately high heat just until nicely browned on both sides—4 to 5 minutes altogether. TIP: *Never cook okra in an iron skillet or kettle because the okra will turn black. The best material for cooking okra is enameled cast iron because this hard, nonporous, inert surface will not react in any way with the okra.*

Onions

What a big, beautiful family the onion family is. There are the slim, peppery spring onions and scallions; the fawn-colored Spanish giants; the sweet, flat, white Bermudas; the pungent purple-red Italian onions; the versatile all-purpose yellow onions; and the succulent little silverskins that are plunked whole into stews. There are also leeks (see the discussion of them that appears earlier), mellow-sweet shallots, nippy chives and garlic.

Season: Year-round for garlic, shallots, chives, scallions, spring onions, red, white and yellow onions. Bermudas are primarily available from March through June and Spanish onions from August through May.

Hallmarks of quality: They vary from type to type. **Chives** should be springy and intensely green; **scallions** and **spring onions,** moist, succulent, unscarred and clean. When buying **garlic, shallots** or any of the other varieties of onions, choose firm specimens that show no signs of sprouting (sprouted onions, garlic and shallots will quickly soften and spoil; moreover, they have an unpleasant, pervasive bitter taste). Buds (heads) of garlic should be compact, hard and completely encased in papery skin.

How many onions per person? Except for silverskins, which are often creamed or braised alongside roasts, and yellow onions, which are sometimes stuffed, the question is irrelevant because onions are used primarily as seasoners. Allow 4 to 5 silverskins per person and one medium-size yellow onion.

Best ways to store: Again, it varies from onion to onion. I roll **chives,** untrimmed and unwashed **scallions** and **spring onions** in a little lightly moistened paper toweling, pop them into a small plastic bag and refrigerate (they will keep well for about 1 week). All **garlic, shallots** and **dry onions** should be kept well ventilated (I store them in baskets) in a cool, dark, dry place that will discourage sprouting. **Storage time:** All conditions being right, 3 to 4 weeks.

Basic preparation: Scallions and **spring onions** should be trimmed of root ends and withered or discolored tops, then washed well in cool water. **Chives** need only to be rinsed in cool water, patted dry, then snipped or minced. **Garlic** and **shallots** are usually simply peeled and minced or crushed in a garlic crusher. **All other onions** need only to be peeled and sliced, chopped or minced as individual recipes direct. **Silverskins** and **yellow onions,** however, are often also peeled and cooked whole, and there's a tearless way to do the job: Blanch the onions in boiling water for 30 to 60 seconds, cool under running water and their skins will slip right off.

Best ways to cook: The most popular techniques to know are how to boil, parboil and braise onions.

TO BOIL: This method is used primarily for silverskins. Peel the onions, submerge in lightly salted boiling water or, if you prefer, beef or chicken broth, cover and boil gently about 20 to 30 minutes until a fork will pierce an onion easily. Don't overcook or the onions will collapse.

TO PARBOIL (necessary for yellow onions that are to be stuffed, also for silverskins that are added whole to stews or other recipes in which they will receive further cooking): Boil whole peeled onions as directed, but reduce cooking time to 10 to 15 minutes for silverskins and 15 to 20 for medium-size yellow onions. NOTE: *Parboiled silverskins or small yellow onions may be added to a roast pan during the last 45 to 60 minutes of cooking and braised in the pan drippings; baste or turn the onions often so that they brown evenly.*

To BRAISE: The best onions to braise are silverskins or small yellow onions. Peel them, then brown lightly in several tablespoons of butter, olive oil or bacon drippings in a large heavy skillet over moderate heat for about 5 minutes; turn the onions often in the fat as they cook. Pour in about 1 cup (240 ml) of water, beef or chicken broth, tuck in a bay leaf, a sprig of thyme and/or rosemary, cover and cook the onions over moderate heat 15 to 20 minutes until crisp-tender and nicely glazed. Season to taste with salt, freshly grated nutmeg and freshly ground black pepper and, if you like, a tablespoon of minced parsley, tarragon or dill. When serving, spoon some of the pan juices over the onions. Another good addition: a couple of tablespoons of dry vermouth, sherry, red or white wine, added just minutes before serving.

Sopa de cebola à Madeirense
(MADEIRA ONION SOUP)

SERVES 6

 This onion soup from the Portuguese island of Madeira is quite unlike the French classic. It's spicy (thanks to whole cloves), sweet (dried currants or golden raisins simmer along with the onions) and, depending upon how many egg yolks the cook has on hand, lightly thickened. Needless to say, the soup is spiked with Madeira wine just before serving.

2½ pounds	yellow onions, peeled and sliced thin (10–12 medium-size onions)	1¼ kg
3 tablespoons	unsalted butter	3 tablespoons
2 tablespoons	olive oil	2 tablespoons
6	whole cloves	6
1 teaspoon	paprika	1 teaspoon
2 tablespoons	dried currants or golden seedless raisins (sultanas)	2 tablespoons
5 cups	rich beef broth	1¼ L
¼ teaspoon (about)	salt	¼ teaspoon (about)
⅛ teaspoon (about)	freshly ground black pepper	⅛ teaspoon (about)
4 large	egg yolks, lightly beaten	4 large
¼ cup	dry Madeira wine (Sercial)	60 ml

Sauté onions in butter and oil in a large heavy kettle over moderate heat about 30 minutes, stirring occasionally, until limp and golden and lightly touched with brown. Don't rush this process or the soup will not have proper onion flavor. Add cloves, paprika, currants and broth, cover and simmer 1 hour. Then uncover and simmer ½ hour. Season to taste with salt and pepper.

NOTE: *The soup will be far superior if at this point you cool it, cover it and refrigerate for 24 hours.* Bring slowly to serving temperature. Mix a little hot broth into beaten egg yolks, stir back into kettle, then cook and stir 3 to 4 minutes until slightly thickened. Mix in Madeira. Serve with sprinklings of freshly grated Parmesan cheese and crisp chunks of garlic bread.

Braised onions agrodolce

SERVES 6

*A*grodolce is an Italian word meaning "bittersweet" or "sweet-sour," and these brown, glistening onions are precisely that underneath a glaze of caramelized sugar and vinegar. I find them a marvelous accompaniment to roast beef, venison, lamb or pork. TIP: *The fastest way to peel the onions is also wholly tearless: blanch them in boiling water for about a minute, plunge at once into cold water, then slip the skins right off.* The best onions to use for this recipe are the firm white or silverskin onions measuring about 1¾ inches (4½ cm) in diameter.

2 tablespoons	olive oil (top quality)	2 tablespoons
2 tablespoons	unsalted butter	2 tablespoons
1 tablespoon (slightly rounded)	sugar	1 tablespoon (slightly rounded)
2 pounds (about 20 medium-size)	silverskin onions, peeled	1 kg (about 20 medium-size)
¼ cup	beef broth	60 ml
¼ cup	medium-sweet Madeira or Port	60 ml
⅓ cup	red wine vinegar	80 ml
¼ cup (optional)	golden seedless raisins (sultanas)	60 ml (optional)
To taste	salt and freshly ground black pepper	To taste

Heat the oil, butter and sugar in a large heavy skillet over moderately high heat until the sugar has dissolved and mixture is beginning to brown. Add the onions and brown them lightly, turning them often so that they are uniformly glazed—8 to 10 minutes. With a slotted spoon, lift the onions to a large plate and reserve. To the skillet add the broth and Madeira and boil hard until reduced to a rich brown glaze—3 to 5 minutes. Pour in the vinegar and stir until well blended.

Return the onions to the skillet, reduce burner heat so that the skillet liquid barely bubbles, then cover and simmer 20 minutes. Turn the onions in the skillet liquid, re-cover and cook 20 minutes longer. Uncover, again turn the onions in the skillet liquid, add the raisins, if you like, salt and pepper to taste, re-cover and simmer 5 to 10 minutes longer until you can pierce an onion easily with a fork. Serve the onions topped with some of the skillet liquid, now a rich, amber sweet-sour glaze.

Parsnips

Parsnips, pale beige-skinned cousins of the carrot, are one of those old-fashioned, hard-to-find vegetables that few of the younger generation have ever heard of, let alone tasted. As a matter of fact, they were out of favor during my childhood (or perhaps they were simply out of favor in the South). But I do remember my mother preparing them, and my school chums thinking we were odd for eating such peculiar vegetables. The Roman Emperor Tiberius didn't think parsnips peculiar. He ordered that they be grown for him in the Rhineland and that his cooks sauce them with mead.

Season: Year round. **Peak months:** October through March. New Englanders plant parsnips in summer, but pull them only after first frost, believing that a cold snap finishes them to sugary perfection.

Hallmarks of quality: Uniformity of size, succulence, absence of nicks and blemishes, featheriness of the green tops (if any). Choose parsnips of as nearly the same size as possible so that they will cook evenly.

How many parsnips per person? About 2 medium-size.

Best ways to store: Cut off any tops (they will sap the parsnips), then bag loosely in plastic in the refrigerator. **Storage time:** About a week.

Basic preparation: Parsnips are prepared in very much the same way as carrots. If you intend to boil or steam them whole, you can peel them or not— whatever you wish. Because parsnips are more irregularly shaped than carrots, however (they're quite bulbous at the top, then abruptly taper off to a slender root), I think it's preferable to slice or dice them so that they will cook more evenly. First cut off the crown and root end, and peel, using a swivel-blade vegetable peeler. Then cut into about ½-inch (1½ cm) slices or cubes.

Best ways to cook:

To boil: Prepare and cut up the parsnips as directed, place in a heavy saucepan and add just enough lightly salted boiling water, beef or chicken broth (or even beer) to about two-thirds cover—2 cups (½ L) water should be sufficient for 1 pound (½ kg) of parsnips. Cover the pan and boil gently 8 to 10 minutes until firm-tender. Drain (if you used broth for cooking the parsnips, save it to use in soups, sauces or stews), then season to taste with butter, salt and pepper. **Some compatible seasonings:** Lemon, orange, allspice. NOTE: *Any of the seasonings or sauces that complement carrots will do as much for parsnips.*

To STEAM: Prepare and cut up as directed. Place the parsnips in a steamer basket, then cook **over** boiling water in a covered saucepan for 10 to 15 minutes or until they can be pierced easily with a fork. Season as you would boiled parsnips.

To ROAST: Trim, scrub and halve the parsnips lengthwise. Pour about ¼ cup (60 ml) melted butter, bacon or ham drippings into a shallow baking pan. Arrange the parsnips in one layer in the pan, turn in the butter until evenly coated, sprinkle lightly with freshly grated nutmeg, then roast uncovered in a moderate oven (350°F. or 175°C.) until fork-tender—about 45 minutes. Turn the parsnips once or twice in the drippings as they roast. Season to taste with salt and freshly ground black pepper and serve.

Hannah Perry's creamed parsnips

SERVES 4 TO 6

"**B**oy! This takes me right back to my childhood and Thanksgiving dinner at my grandmother's house," said Margaret Perry, a friend and fellow writer who reached back in her memory to share this Connecticut Yankee specialty with me. It's delicious with roast turkey, chicken, pork or lamb.

1 pound	medium-size parsnips, peeled and sliced ½ inch (1½ cm) thick	½ kg
2 cups	water mixed with ½ teaspoon salt	½ L
2 tablespoons	unsalted butter	2 tablespoons
2 tablespoons	flour	2 tablespoons
⅛ teaspoon	freshly grated nutmeg	⅛ teaspoon
Pinch	ground cinnamon	Pinch
1 cup	half-and-half cream	240 ml
¼ teaspoon	salt	¼ teaspoon
Pinch	freshly ground black pepper	Pinch
	TOPPING:	
1 cup	moderately fine soft bread crumbs	240 ml
1 tablespoon	melted butter	1 tablespoon

Boil the parsnips in the salted water in a covered, medium-size heavy saucepan over moderate heat 8 to 10 minutes until firm-tender; drain well, return to pan and reserve. In a small heavy saucepan set over moderate heat, melt the butter, blend in the flour, nutmeg and cinnamon and mellow 1 to 2 minutes. Pour in cream and cook, stirring constantly, 3 to 5 minutes until thickened and smooth and no raw floury taste remains. Mix in salt and pepper, pour over reserved parsnips and toss lightly. Spoon into a buttered 1-quart (1 L) shallow casserole or *au gratin* pan. Lightly toss topping ingredients together, then scatter evenly over parsnips. Bake uncovered in a moderate oven (350°F. or 175°C.) 20 to 25 minutes or until bubbling and browned.

Purée of parsnips, apple and Irish potatoes

SERVES 6

Parsnips had fallen so far from favor that they were virtually impossible to find until the splendid Korean greengroceries, popping up in America's biggest cities, began stocking them along with a number of Oriental exotics. A different way to prepare parsnips? I like this spicy purée. It's particularly good with baked ham, roast pork, turkey and chicken.

1 pound	parsnips, peeled and sliced thin	½ kg
1 large	tart apple, peeled, cored and sliced thin	1 large
2 small	all-purpose potatoes, peeled and diced	2 small
1 cup	chicken or beef broth	240 ml
⅛ teaspoon	crumbled leaf thyme	⅛ teaspoon
Pinch	ground mace	Pinch
Pinch	ground cinnamon	Pinch
6–8 tablespoons	heavy cream	6–8 tablespoons
To taste	salt and freshly ground black pepper	To taste

Place the parsnips, apple, potatoes, broth, thyme, mace and cinnamon in a medium-size heavy saucepan and bring to a boil over moderate heat; adjust heat so that liquid bubbles gently, cover tight and cook 10 to 12 minutes until all vegetables are very tender. Turn burner heat down low and cook uncovered about 15 minutes until almost all liquid has evaporated—but do keep an eagle eye on the pot and stir the vegetables from time to time to keep them from sticking or scorching. Mash the vegetables into a silky purée, using a potato masher, or purée them in a food processor fitted with the metal chopping blade. NOTE: *If you use the processor, add 6 tablespoons heavy cream along with the vegetables, then switch the motor on and purée, using 8 to 10 short bursts of speed.* Beat in enough heavy cream to make a soft and fluffy purée, then season to taste with salt and pepper. Serve at once.

Peas

Archaeologists have found peas at ancient Troy and in Swiss lake mud, which seems to trace their trek from Central Asia, where they are believed to have originated, into Europe. A twelfth-century inventory shows that among the provisions of the Barking Nunnery near London were "green peas for Lent." **English peas,** they came to be known, as well as **green peas,** and are still today. But there are other varieties of peas: **field peas,** which are dried both whole and split, **snow peas** (those exquisitely sweet and crisp Chinese pea pods that take about only minutes to cook), and **sugar snaps,** the newest entry, which resemble the French *mange-tout* and like them are eaten pod and all as their name implies. They are sweet and crunchy—and almost as much a fad today as green peas were at the court of Louis XIV. ("It is both a fashion and a madness," wrote Madame de Maintenon of the green pea craze at the French court.)

Season: March through July for green peas and sugar snaps, year round for snow peas. Field peas, of course, are dried and available the year round.

Hallmarks of quality: All fresh peas, regardless of variety, should be intensely green and succulent. The pods should feel moist and velvety. Sugar snap and snow pea pods should be slim with no individual peas discernible; green pea pods should be plump, but not lumpy or bursting at the seams, both of which indicate peas too mature to be sweet and tender. NOTE: *Never buy shelled green peas, because much of their original sweetness will have vanished.*

How much per serving? Allow about ½ pound (225 g) of unshelled green peas per person (which will yield approximately ½ to ⅔ cup or 120 to 160 ml of shelled peas), and ¼ pound (115 g) of snow peas or sugar snaps. As for split and dried whole peas, 1 pound (½ kg) will serve 4 to 6 persons.

Best way to store: All fresh peas should be stored unwashed and untrimmed in plastic bags in the refrigerator. **Storage time:** About 1 week for all varieties.

Basic preparation: Green peas need only to be shelled, but do so just when you are ready to cook them, no sooner. TIP: *If you shell the peas inside a large bag, you will waste no time scrambling around looking for the occasional peas that normally pop across the room or down upon the floor. Discard each pod as you shell it, then when you are ready to cook the peas, simply empty the bag into the pan.* Snow peas should be trimmed at each end, then "stringed" much as green beans used to be stringed. TIP: *The quickest way to string snow peas, I discovered as I watched a Chinese cook level a mountain of them recently, is with the swivel-blade vegetable peeler. Simply run it down the seam on each side of the snow pea pod and the strings will zip right off.* Sugar snaps need only be trimmed at both ends, and both snow peas and sugar snaps should be washed well in cool water. As for dried peas, they should be carefully sorted; reject any discolored or withered peas, also any bits of grit.

Best ways to cook:

To BOIL: Green peas, sugar snaps, snow peas and dried peas may all be boiled, but the techniques vary because the peas themselves are so different. **Snow peas** and **sugar snaps** should be plunged into a huge kettle of boiling water (add a little sugar to the water, if you like, but no salt, which may toughen the pods). Boil about 1 minute—just until a dazzling green. No longer. Drain at once, season to taste with butter, salt and pepper and serve. **Green peas,** on the other hand, should be cooked in a minimum of water—only enough to keep them from scorching. For 2 to 3 pounds (1 to 1½ kg in-the-pod weight) of peas, shelled, ½ cup (120 ml) of boiling water will be sufficient. Add a hefty pinch of sugar, then the peas, cover tight and simmer 2 to 3 minutes for *petits pois* (tiny spring peas), 5 to 8 minutes for peas of average size. Drain at once and season with a little butter or cream, salt and pepper. **Other compatible seasonings:** mint, thyme, shallots, onion, chives, rosemary, soy sauce. As for **dried peas, split peas** disintegrate so when they are cooked they are best made into soup. **Whole dried peas,** like dried beans, must first be soaked. For each 1 pound (½ kg) of peas, allow 5 cups (1¼ L) of water. You can soak the peas overnight or, if you're in a hurry, boil them for 2 minutes, then remove from the heat, cover and let stand for 1 hour. The peas are now ready to be drained and used as individual recipes direct.

To STEAM: All fresh peas steam magnificently. Shelled green peas, snow peas and sugar snap pods should be laid in a steamer basket, then cooked **over** boiling water in a covered pan as follows: about 5 to 7 minutes for sugar snaps, snow peas and very small green peas, about 15 minutes for average-size green peas. TIP: *Green peas are done when they are vividly green, firm-tender and no longer taste raw.* Season as you would boiled peas.

To STIR-FRY (snow peas): See the recipe below. NOTE: *Raw snow peas and sugar snaps are splendid tossed raw into seafood or poultry salads or mixed green salads. A generous handful of them is usually about right for a salad that will serve four persons. If the peas are small, toss into the salad whole; otherwise cut crosswise, slightly on the diagonal, into thirds or fourths.*

Creamed green peas with shallots and shredded romaine

SERVES 4 TO 6

Shallots have a naturally sweet flavor that partners perfectly with green peas, and romaine adds a tempering taste of salt. This is one recipe in which I think frozen green peas are almost as good as the fresh. Certainly they simplify things because they are already shelled and need not be parboiled. So take your pick.

2½ pounds (in the pod)	fresh green peas, shelled, or 2 packages (10 oz. or 283 g each) frozen peas, partially thawed	1¼ kg (in the pod)
1 quart	boiling water	1 L
2 large	shallots, peeled and minced	2 large
2 tablespoons	unsalted butter	2 tablespoons
¼ teaspoon	crumbled leaf marjoram	¼ teaspoon
⅛ teaspoon	crumbled leaf chervil	⅛ teaspoon
½ cup	beef broth	120 ml
⅓ cup	heavy cream	80 ml
4 large	romaine leaves, washed, patted dry and sliced crosswise very thin	4 large
To taste	salt and freshly ground black pepper	To taste

If you are using fresh peas, parboil them 3 minutes in the boiling water; drain well and set aside. Stir-fry the shallots in the butter in a large medium-size saucepan over moderate heat 8 to 10 minutes until limp and lightly browned. Blend in the marjoram and chervil and mellow a minute or two to intensify their flavors. Pour in the beef broth and cream, bring to a simmer, then dump in the parboiled fresh peas or the partially thawed frozen peas. Adjust burner heat so that the cream mixture just trembles, cover and cook 8 to 10 minutes until the peas are tender and no longer taste raw. Uncover, stir in the romaine and simmer uncovered about 3 to 5 minutes longer. Season to taste with salt and pepper and serve.

Snow peas stir-fried with sesame, ginger and garlic

SERVES 4

Before you begin this recipe, have all ingredients measured and lined up in order of use on the counter beside the skillet, because once you begin, the sequence must move with split-second timing. The object is to temper the crispness of the snow peas, not destroy it (which will surely happen if you overcook them).

2 tablespoons	peanut oil	2 tablespoons
1 tablespoon	roasted sesame oil	1 tablespoon
¼ teaspoon	salt	¼ teaspoon

2 medium-size	garlic cloves, peeled and minced	2 medium-size
2 tablespoons	minced fresh ginger	2 tablespoons
1 pound	snow peas, trimmed, stringed, washed in cool water and patted very dry on paper toweling	½ kg
1 tablespoon	water	1 tablespoon
¼ cup	soy sauce	60 ml

Heat the peanut and sesame oils in a large heavy skillet over moderately high heat a minute or two until ripples appear on the bottom of the skillet. Add the salt, garlic and ginger, reduce heat slightly and stir-fry about 1 minute—just until the garlic and ginger are golden; do not brown them or they will taste bitter. Dump in the snow peas and stir-fry 2 minutes. Add the water and soy sauce, toss the snow peas lightly, cover and steam 2 minutes. Uncover, toss again lightly and serve.

Peppers

Imagine Columbus's surprise when, en route to India, he not only found land sooner than expected but also peppery red and green pods. They were not the priceless black pepper of the East that he sought, but he called them peppers anyway. The New World peppers belong to the broad family of *capsicums*, which can be divided into two categories: the hot and the sweet. The **sweet** ones are green (bell) peppers, red and yellow peppers (nothing more than ripened green peppers), pimientos, paprika and slim, sweet yellow-green Italian peppers. Not all **hot peppers** are equally hot, so to give you some notion as to their degree of fire, I list here some of the more popular ones in ascending order from mild to incendiary: *ancho* (plump, dark red peppers that are usually dried, *poblano* (the green, unripe *ancho*), New Mexican chilies (Pueblo Indian women fashion these scarlet peppers into Christmas wreaths and *ristras* or swags), *jalapeño* (small, round and green), *serrano* (skinny green chilies), *pequin* (very small, red and red-hot) and finally, the tiny, torrid *tabasco*. It's interesting to note that the bigger the chili, the milder it's apt to be.

Season: Sweet peppers are available the year round but will be at their best during the summer. Hot peppers are in season from August through December; dried, they are available the year round.

Hallmarks of quality: Whether sweet or hot, peppers should be dazzlingly green, red or yellow, firm, plump and succulent with no breaks in the skin, no signs of softening or discoloring. If you intend to stuff peppers, choose those that are plump enough to hold a respectable amount of stuffing and straight enough to stand.

How many peppers per serving? About 1 medium-size sweet green or red pepper per person and 2 Italian peppers. Hot peppers, of course, are used primarily for seasoning except for the *poblanos*, which are often stuffed for *chiles rellenos*; allow 1 to 2 *poblanos* per person, depending upon their size.

Best way to store: Because fresh peppers so easily soften and spoil, I store them in well-perforated plastic bags in the refrigerator with sheets of paper toweling between the peppers to absorb moisture. **Storage time:** 5 to 7 days. Dried peppers, stored airtight in glass jars on a cool, dark, dry shelf, will keep almost indefinitely.

Basic preparation: Peppers should first be washed in cool water. What happens next depends upon how the peppers are to be used. If they are to be cut up, they should be cored and seeded. NOTE: *If you are working with hot peppers, remove all seeds and veins (these are hotter than the flesh of the pepper), then wash your hands well. Avoid touching your face or body while you are working with hot peppers—a lesson I learned the hard way when I inadvertently rubbed my eyes while mincing chilies (excruciating!).* If sweet peppers are to be marinated or mixed into salads, they will be mellower if roasted. If they are to be stuffed, they should be parboiled so that they will cook more evenly.

Special techniques:

TO ROAST SWEET PEPPERS: Lay whole, uncored peppers on their sides in a pie pan or shallow baking pan and set in the broiler 2 inches (5 cm) from the flame. Broil about 20 minutes altogether, giving the peppers a quarter-turn every 5 minutes until their skins are uniformly charred. Rinse the peppers under cool running water, then slake off the black skins. Core and seed the peppers, then drain well on paper toweling.

TO PARBOIL SWEET PEPPERS: Lay whole uncored peppers on their sides in a heavy kettle and pour in just enough boiling water to submerge them. Cover the kettle and boil the peppers 5 to 6 minutes until a vibrant green. Remove the peppers from the kettle, cool under running water, then slice off the tops and scrape out all seeds and pith. Stand the peppers upside down on several thicknesses of paper toweling to drain for 10 to 15 minutes. They are now ready to stuff. NOTE: *You can sauté the whole peppers 10 to 15 minutes in a couple of tablespoons of olive, peanut or corn oil instead of parboiling them; in fact, the peppers will have richer flavor if you do (see the recipe for Eggplant-Stuffed Peppers à la Gritti Palace that follows).*

Best ways to cook: Unless they are stuffed and baked or roasted (see above), peppers are more often stir-fried in the company of meats and/or other vegetables than cooked and served solo. One exception, of course, are the sweet and succulent Italian "frying peppers," as the following adapted recipe for Peperonata proves.

Peperonata
(SAUTÉED SWEET PEPPERS AND ONIONS WITH
OLIVES AND CAPERS)

SERVES 4 TO 6

I've improvised here on the traditional Sicilian *peperonata* (a mix of green bell and sweet red peppers) by teaming the even sweeter Italian "frying" peppers with red Italian onions. I've also taken the liberty of adding capers for bite and a mellowing tablespoon of dry vermouth. Serve *peperonata* as one of the components of antipasto, as a salad or vegetable. It is good hot or at room temperature as an accompaniment to grilled or sautéed chicken, swordfish, salmon or tuna steaks.

1 pound	sweet Italian (yellow-green) peppers	½ kg
1 large	Italian (red) onion, peeled and cut into very slim wedges	1 large
1 small	garlic clove, peeled and minced	1 small
3 tablespoons	olive oil (top quality)	3 tablespoons
1 teaspoon	crumbled leaf oregano	1 teaspoon
1 cup	very coarsely chopped pitted green olives	240 ml
2 tablespoons	capers, drained	2 tablespoons
2 tablespoons	minced parsley	2 tablespoons
1 tablespoon	dry vermouth	1 tablespoon
To taste	salt and freshly ground black pepper	To taste

Halve the peppers lengthwise, remove cores, seeds and pithy inner portions, then cut crosswise into 1-inch (2½ cm) slices. Stir-fry the peppers, onion and garlic in the oil in a large heavy skillet over moderate heat 8 to 10 minutes until nicely glazed. Sprinkle in the oregano, cover, turn heat down low and simmer 15 minutes. Uncover the peppers, add the olives, capers, parsley and vermouth and stir-fry 1 to 2 minutes over moderate heat. Season to taste with salt (you may not need any salt because of the saltiness of the olives and capers) and the pepper. Serve hot, or marinate at room temperature for 1 to 2 hours and serve.

Eggplant-stuffed peppers à la Gritti Palace

SERVES 6

When I was attending Julie Dannenbaum's splendid cooking school at the Gritti Palace Hotel in Venice a few years ago, I watched with fascination one day as Chef Giovanni Caione deftly stuffed scarlet peppers with an eggplant risotto. I learned that day a couple of professional tricks that I have used ever since: (1) If you sauté whole peppers prior to stuffing instead of parboiling them, they will have richer, mellower flavor, and (2) if you bake the peppers upside down, both they and the stuffing will be moister. No, the stuffing won't fall out if you save the caps and set each firmly in place before you invert the peppers. This recipe is Chef Caione's and I think as delicious a way to prepare stuffed peppers as you're likely to find. The peppers are rich enough to serve as a main course and need nothing more than a tartly dressed green salad and a well-chilled dry white wine to accompany them.

3 tablespoons, in all	olive oil (top quality)	3 tablespoons, in all
6 large	sweet red or green peppers, washed but not cored	6 large
1 cup	finely chopped sweet red or green pepper	240 ml
2 cups	peanut or corn oil	½ L
1 medium-size	unpeeled eggplant, cut into ½-inch (1½ cm) cubes	1 medium-size
1 medium-size	yellow onion, peeled and chopped	1 medium-size
1 cup	converted rice	240 ml
2½ cups	boiling chicken broth	600 ml
⅓ cup	freshly minced basil (or ⅓ cup minced parsley mixed with ½ teaspoon crumbled leaf basil)	80 ml
2 tablespoons	freshly grated Parmesan cheese	2 tablespoons
1 tablespoon	unsalted butter, at room temperature	1 tablespoon
To taste	salt and freshly ground black pepper	To taste
½ teaspoon	crumbled leaf oregano	½ teaspoon

Heat 2 tablespoons of the olive oil in a large heavy kettle over moderate heat about 1 minute, add the whole peppers and sauté, turning often in the oil, 5 minutes. Turn the heat to low, cover the kettle and braise the peppers 10 minutes. Remove the peppers from the kettle and set aside to cool. Stir-fry the minced pepper in the kettle drippings about 5 minutes until limp; remove and reserve.

Heat the peanut oil in a deep-fat fryer or deep skillet to 400°F. (205°C.). Add about one-third of the cubed eggplant and fry 1 minute until golden. Remove with a slotted spoon and drain on paper toweling. Deep-fry the remaining eggplant the same way in two batches and drain.

In a medium-size heavy saucepan, heat the remaining tablespoon of olive oil over moderate heat for about a minute. Add the onion and stir-fry 8 to 10 minutes until limp and lightly browned. Add the rice and stir-fry 1 to 2 minutes until translucent. Raise the burner heat to moderately high, then begin adding the boiling chicken broth, ½ cup (120 ml) at a time, cooking and stirring each time until the broth is absorbed before adding more (this is the classic method for making a *risotto*). When the last of the broth has been added and absorbed by the rice, mix in the basil, Parmesan, butter, reserved minced pepper and eggplant. Season to taste with salt and pepper.

To stuff the peppers: Slice ½ inch (1½ cm) off the top of each pepper and reserve. Scrape out and discard all seeds and pithy portions from the inside of each pepper. Now fill each pepper with the eggplant and rice mixture, packing it in fairly firmly. Replace the top of each pepper, and stand the peppers upside down in a baking dish just large enough to accommodate them without crowding (the peppers should just touch and support one another). Sprinkle the peppers evenly with oregano, then bake, uncovered, in a moderate oven (350°F. or 175°C.) for 1 hour. Serve hot or at room temperature.

Potatoes

When fifteenth-century European explorers went looking for the riches of the East, they found the West and an unsuspected treasure: the potato, which would one day become "poor man's meat." Today there are dozens of varieties of potatoes, all of which may be divided into two basic categories: the starchy (or baking potatoes) and the waxy (or boiling potatoes). The four varieties stocked by almost every supermarket and grocery are: **Maine** or **Eastern potatoes** (sometimes billed as "all-purpose potatoes"), **new potatoes,** and **California Long Whites;** these three are all of the waxy type. Fourth are the superbly starchy **russets** or **baking potatoes,** often called simply **Idaho potatoes** because that state grows the bulk of our supply.

Season: Russets and Eastern potatoes are available the year round; new potatoes and California Long Whites are in best supply in the spring and summer.

Hallmarks of quality: Look for potatoes that are firm, clean, smooth-skinned, devoid of nicks, soft spots, sprouts or green patches. These green patches, by the way, are not only bitter but also indicate high concentrations of solanine, which the body converts into a poison called solanidine. Could this be why for centuries potatoes were considered poisonous? Possibly.

How many potatoes per serving? 1 medium to large russet or Eastern potato, 3 to 4 small new potatoes and about 2 average-size California Long Whites.

Best way to store: Unwashed in a cool, dark, dry place. If you store potatoes in strong light, green patches and sprouts will develop. If you store them in the refrigerator or too cold a spot, the potato starch will turn into sugar, making the potatoes unpleasantly sweet and watery. NOTE: *This, happily, is a reversible process. Any potatoes that have wintered over in cold storage should be allowed to stand at room temperature about 2 weeks before they are cooked so that the sugar reverts to starch.* **Storage time:** Several weeks.

Basic preparation: Potatoes should first be scrubbed in cool water, trimmed of any green spots, eyes or blemishes, then peeled or not, as you prefer. Leave the potatoes whole or slice, dice, cube, shred or cut up as recipes direct. TIP: *Never cut potatoes ahead of time because they will turn pink, then beige-brown. If circumstances force you to prepare them ahead of time, keep the cut potatoes submerged in cold water to which you have added a healthy pinch of cream of tartar or some lemon juice. The acidulated water will keep the potatoes white and crisp.*

Best ways to cook:

To BOIL: Eastern potatoes, California Long Whites and new potatoes all boil superbly. I prefer to cook them whole in their skins, then to peel and cut them after they are cooked, because I think the flavor is richer and the texture less watery. Prepare the potatoes as directed, place in a large heavy saucepan, cover with lightly salted boiling water and boil gently with the lid on the pan until you can pierce a potato easily with a fork. So many factors affect overall cooking time—the size and shape of the potato, its age, how it was stored—that it's difficult to set precise cooking times. I have had new potatoes cook tender in 20 minutes one time, then take as long as 45 the next. My best advice is to begin testing the potatoes after they've cooked about 20 minutes, then to test every 10 minutes thereafter. Medium-size Eastern potatoes usually will be fork-tender in 30 to 40 minutes. As soon as the potatoes are done, plunge into cold water until they are cool enough to handle, then peel and cut up as recipes direct.

To PARBOIL: Whole potatoes that are to be baked in casseroles or cooked in oven stews or those that are to be roasted alongside a joint of beef, lamb or pork should be partially cooked first. Boil them as directed above, but for 15 to 20 minutes only.

To BAKE: I'll never understand why so many restaurants persist in baking potatoes in foil—it makes them so limp and dreary (and the skin positively soggy). For me, the perfect baked potato is simply scrubbed, then stuck *au naturel* on the middle rack of a hot oven (400 to 425°F. or 205 to 220°C.) and baked about 1 hour or until the aroma is irresistible, the skin crisp and the flesh tender enough to yield to a gentle pinch. I like nothing more on my baked potatoes than a fat lump of sweet butter, a light sprinkling of salt and a heavier one of freshly ground black pepper. To open the baked potatoes, I make an X-shaped cut in the top, then holding potholders to protect my fingers, push the sides of the potatoes in so that the steaming, ivory fluffs of potato burst forth. **Other compatible seasonings:** Sour cream and chives, of course, California's favorite; finely crumbled, crisply cooked bacon teamed with finely minced dill pickle and a little melted butter; sour cream and snipped dill or caraway seeds; any soft, quickly melting cheese (I favor Gorgonzola or Fontina); heavy cream and paprika; finely minced onion or shallots and sour cream—so many possibilities!

To FRY: Cold, sliced cooked potatoes are what are usually fried—or rather, "hashed." But a wonderful old Pennsylvania Dutch woman taught me to fry raw potatoes. Allow 1½ medium-size all-purpose potatoes per person—that is, 6 potatoes for 4 people. Peel them, quarter them lengthwise, then slice each quarter very thin. In a large heavy skillet set over moderate heat, melt 3 tablespoons of lard (hot lard, **not** vegetable shortening) or, if you prefer, 2 tablespoons of lard and 1 tablespoon of unsalted butter. When good and hot, dump in the potatoes and fry, scraping the skillet often with a pancake turner so that you bring the browned potatoes on the bottom up on top. Keep scraping and frying the potatoes until they are cooked through, nicely browned and no raw starch taste remains—about 25 minutes in all. Season to taste with salt and freshly ground black pepper and serve. Ambrosia! Hashed browns are cooked precisely the same way—they just don't take as long because the potatoes are already cooked.

To FRENCH-FRY: Figure on 1½ to 2 medium-size baking potatoes per person; peel them, cut lengthwise into slim finger-shaped strips and soak 10 to 15 minutes in ice water. (This is to firm up the potatoes and keep them from darkening.) Pat the potato strips very dry on several thicknesses of paper toweling, then fry in 375°F. (190°C.) deep fat until crisply golden brown—8 to 10 minutes. Drain well on paper toweling, sprinkle with salt and pepper and serve. NOTE: *It's best to use a fryer basket for French fries so that you can whisk them out of the fat en masse the instant they're done, also to fry them in relatively small batches so that they will cook evenly. You can keep the "first fried" crisp and hot by spreading them out on a baking sheet lined with several thicknesses of paper toweling and setting, uncovered, in a very slow (250°F. or 120°C.) oven.*

Kilkenny
(SCOTTISH CREAMED POTATOES AND CABBAGE)

SERVES 4 TO 6

 Scottish women would use leftover boiled potatoes and cabbage for making this recipe, but I like it so well that I make it from scratch. Kilkenny partners superbly with roast beef, lamb, pork, turkey or chicken.

1 pound	Maine or Eastern potatoes, scrubbed	½ kg
⅔ cup	chicken broth	160 ml
1 cup	water	240 ml
1 pound	cabbage, trimmed, cored and cut into 1½-inch (4 cm) chunks	½ kg
1 tablespoon	unsalted butter	1 tablespoon
⅛ teaspoon	freshly grated nutmeg or mace	⅛ teaspoon
¾ teaspoon (about)	salt	¾ teaspoon (about)
Light sprinkling	freshly ground black pepper	Light sprinkling
¾ cup	light or heavy cream	180 ml

Peel the potatoes and cut into 1-inch (2½ cm) cubes. Bring the broth and water to a boil in a medium-size heavy saucepan, add the potatoes, cover and boil about 15 minutes until fork-tender. Meanwhile, pile the cabbage chunks into a steamer basket, set **over** boiling water, and steam in a covered saucepan 10 minutes until crisp-tender. Drain the potatoes, add the steamed cabbage, butter, nutmeg, salt and pepper and toss lightly. Add the cream and toss lightly once again, then cover and simmer slowly 3 to 5 minutes, just long enough to mingle and mellow the flavors. Taste for salt and add more, if needed, and serve.

Lacy Lithuanian potato pancakes

SERVES 6

Properly cooked, these pancakes are crusty-brown outside and soft inside. They aren't difficult to make (especially if you have a processor to shred the potatoes), but there are several points to bear in mind: use a well-tempered skillet for cooking the pancakes, otherwise they will stick (even with the proper skillet, the first batch may stick a bit); press the pancakes down hard just before you turn them, using a pancake turner; and keep the burner heat between moderate and moderately low. If too hot, the pancakes will burn before they cook inside, if too low, they will be soggy. NOTE: *It's also important to use a waxy type of potato for this recipe—Maine or Eastern potatoes are the best, I find—so that the pancakes stick together.*

2 pounds (about 5 large)	Maine or Eastern potatoes	1 kg (about 5 large)
¼ cup	unsifted potato starch or all-purpose flour	60 ml
1 tablespoon	finely grated yellow onion	1 tablespoon
1¾ teaspoons	salt	1¾ teaspoons
⅛ teaspoon	freshly ground black pepper	⅛ teaspoon
⅛ teaspoon	freshly grated nutmeg	⅛ teaspoon
3 large	eggs, lightly beaten	3 large
2 to 4 tablespoons	unsalted butter	2 to 4 tablespoons
	OPTIONAL TOPPING:	
1 cup	sour cream, at room temperature	240 ml
2 tablespoons	freshly snipped chives or dill	2 tablespoons

Peel the potatoes and submerge at once in cold water to which you have added a pinch of cream of tartar (this acidulated water helps keep the potatoes from darkening). One at a time, lift the potatoes from the water and shred moderately coarsely in a food processor fitted with the shredding disk or by pushing through the second-coarsest side of a four-sided grater. Sprinkle each potato lightly with a little of the potato starch as you shred it. When all potatoes are shredded, add the remaining potato starch, if any, the grated onion, salt, pepper, nutmeg and beaten eggs. Stir well to mix. NOTE: *It will seem that there is very little batter—and in fact there is. But it will be sufficient if you follow these directions.*

Place 2 tablespoons of the butter in a very large heavy skillet and melt over moderate heat. Stir the potato mixture well again, then, using medium-size kitchen tongs, take up some of the shredded potatoes (about a rounded table-spoonful) and place in the skillet. Flatten at once with a pancake turner, evening up any unusually ragged edges, then spoon a little (about ½ tablespoon) of the eggy pancake batter on top of the potatoes; press down well again. Repeat this procedure for each pancake. With a 12-inch (30 cm) skillet, you should be able to cook five small pancakes at a time. Brown the pancakes about 4 minutes on one side, once again press down firmly with the pancake turner, then turn and brown the flip sides about 4 minutes also. If the pancakes seem to brown too fast, lower the heat slightly. When the pancakes are done, lift to a metal tray and set, uncovered, in a very slow oven (250°F. or 120°C.) to keep warm while you fry subsequent batches, adding a third or fourth tablespoon of butter to the skillet, if needed. As the pancakes brown, continue adding them to the tray, but keep them in a single layer only (use two trays, if necessary). If you stack the pancakes, they will lose their lovely crispness.

Serve on heated plates, allowing 4 to 5 pancakes per person. If you like, top each portion with a hefty dollop of sour cream and a sprinkling of chives or dill.

NOTE: *These pancakes are rich enough to serve as the main course of a light luncheon or supper. Accompany with a green vegetable such as broccoli and, if you like, tartly dressed sliced tomatoes.*

Rutabaga

(See *Turnips*)

Sorrel

(SOUR DOCK)

Sorrel is not a green Americans know well, although Europeans have long prized its lemony bite. They purée sorrel into soups, sauces and stuffings; toss it into salads and steam it with spinach to temper the tartness.

Season: Spring and summer.

Hallmarks of quality: Sorrel, if you don't know, has crisp, tongue-shaped green leaves about 3 inches (8 cm) long and 1 to 1½ inches (2½ to 4 cm) wide. *Crisp* is the key word here, for freshly plucked sorrel will be almost frostily succulent. The best sorrel will also be young and tender, clean and blemish-free.

How much sorrel per person? No matter how you prepare it, a little sorrel goes a long way because of its intense sour flavor. I allow about ¼ pound (115 g) per person, maximum.

Best way to store: Unwashed and untrimmed, loosely bagged in plastic in the refrigerator crisper. **Storage time:** 2 to 3 days.

Basic preparation: Trim off the stems, then slosh the leaves very gently in a sinkful of cool water so that the grit drifts to the bottom of the sink and stays there. Lift the leaves from the water and drain between several thicknesses of paper toweling.

Best ways to cook: The most glorious way I know to prepare sorrel is to simmer it into soup (see the recipe that follows). You can also steam it with spinach (which see), using about 1 part sorrel to 3 or 4 parts spinach.

Potage Germiny
(FRESH SORREL SOUP)

SERVES 6

I've tried many different sorrel soups, but this one, which I developed for *Jean Anderson's Processor Cooking*, published by William Morrow in 1979, is still my favorite, so I include it here.

1 quart	rich chicken broth	1 L
1 medium-size	yellow onion, peeled and chopped	1 medium-size
3 tablespoons	unsalted butter	3 tablespoons
3 large	egg yolks, lightly beaten	3 large
1 cup	heavy cream	240 ml
¼ teaspoon	cayenne pepper	¼ teaspoon
Pinch	white pepper	Pinch
½ teaspoon (about)	salt	½ teaspoon (about)
1 pound	fresh sorrel, trimmed of stems, washed in cool water and patted dry on paper toweling	½ kg
1 to 2 tablespoons	lemon juice (if needed to increase the tartness of the soup)	1 to 2 tablespoons

Gently boil the chicken broth uncovered in a heavy medium-size saucepan about 30 minutes or until reduced by about one-fourth. Meanwhile, stir-fry the onion in the butter in a very large heavy skillet over moderate heat about 5 minutes until limp and golden; reduce the heat under the skillet to the lowest point and allow the onion to mellow while you proceed with the recipe.

Whisk together the egg yolks and cream, ladle in a little of the reduced hot broth, blend well, then stir back into the saucepan. Add the cayenne, white pepper and salt. Heat and stir over lowest heat about 5 minutes until slightly thickened and smooth (do not allow to boil), then remove from the heat and allow to stand while you prepare the sorrel.

Pile the sorrel into the skillet with the onion, cover and warm about 30 seconds; stir well, re-cover and warm 30 seconds longer or just until the sorrel is wilted. Now purée the skillet mixture in a food processor equipped with the metal chopping blade (two to three fast zaps of the motor will do it) or, a little bit at a time, in an electric blender at high speed. Stir the sorrel mixture into the soup and return the saucepan to low heat just long enough to bring the soup to serving temperature—3 to 5 minutes. Stir occasionally and do not allow the soup to boil because it will curdle. Taste for seasonings and add more salt, if needed—also add 1 to 2 tablespoons of lemon juice if the soup is not tart enough to suit you. Serve hot, or chill well and serve cold.

Spinach

Spinach is believed to have come from Persia and to have been carried long ago into China by Arab caravans, where it quickly became (and remains to this day) a great delicacy. It was the Moors who introduced spinach to Europe—via Spain. The early Dutch always thought of spinach as a Spanish vegetable. And so did John Parkinson, the seventeenth-century English herbalist, who noted that the Dutch "doe stew the herbe in a pot or pipkin without any other moisture than its owne." An early cooking method, perhaps, but one we have yet to improve upon.

Season: Year round. **Peak months:** January through June. NOTE: *Frozen spinach—particularly the chopped—is one of the few frozen vegetables that I use. Its flavor, color and texture remain remarkably unchanged by its stay in the freezer—in fact, I find little difference between frozen and freshly chopped spinach except in the time it takes to prepare them.*

Hallmarks of quality: If I must choose between bagged "fresh" spinach or frozen spinach, I will opt for frozen every time. In my experience, the bagged spinach is miserable stuff, filled with woody stems and decaying leaves—about 50 percent waste. The only fresh spinach I will buy is that that I can hand-pick, choosing crispest, tenderest young leaves devoid of holes, rips, blemishes and soft spots.

How much spinach per serving? About ½ pound (¼ kg).

Best way to store: Unwashed and untrimmed in a brown paper bag in the refrigerator crisper. **Storage time:** About 2 days.

Basic preparation: Trim off all coarse stems and remove any blemished or softening leaves. Fill a sink with tepid water, mix in about 2 tablespoons of salt, then very gently move the spinach leaves about in the water, loosening any grit and sand and sending them to the bottom of the sink. Carefully lift the spinach from the water, empty and rinse the sink, then fill it with cool water and rinse the spinach. NOTE: *If there is still considerable grit on the bottom of the sink, rinse the spinach a second—and if need be, a third—time.* Drain the spinach between several thicknesses of paper toweling.

Best ways to cook:

TO STEAM: Pile the rinsed spinach in a large heavy kettle (not aluminum, because the spinach will blacken the kettle). For extra flavor, add a generous handful of fresh sorrel or watercress. But do not add any water. The rinse water clinging to the leaves will be more than sufficient for steaming the spinach; in fact, there should not be too much. Cover the kettle, set over moderate heat and steam the spinach 3 to 5 minutes until slightly wilted (it will be an eye-popping emerald green). Drain the spinach very dry and, if you like, chop, or purée in an electric blender at high speed or in a food processor fitted with the metal chopping blade. Season the spinach with melted butter and/or cream and salt and freshly ground pepper to taste. **Other compatible seasonings for leaf or chopped spinach:** Butter-browned chopped onion and freshly grated nutmeg and, if you like, a dollop of sour cream as well; butter-browned minced onion, yogurt and curry powder; olive oil, garlic and lemon, perhaps also toasted chopped *pignoli* (North Africans also add a few chopped raisins); bacon drippings and crumbles; a tart vinaigrette; a sharp Cheddar sauce; hollandaise.

TO STIR-FRY: This is the Italian way and my own favorite. Heat 2 to 3 tablespoons of top-quality olive oil (or butter or bacon drippings) in a large heavy kettle (not aluminum) over moderate heat, add a minced garlic clove, if you like, and a medium-size chopped yellow onion; stir-fry 2 to 3 minutes, dump in the spinach and stir-fry 2 to 3 minutes, just until every leaf glistens. Clap the lid on the kettle and steam the spinach 1 to 2 minutes. Season to taste with salt and pepper, toss well and serve.

Troucha
(PROVENÇAL BASIL-SPINACH OMELET)

SERVES 6

When I was last in Provence, I stopped by a little inn in the foothills of the Alpes-Maritimes for lunch and feasted on this spinach omelet, heady with the scent of fresh basil. Cut into wedges like quiche and served at room temperature, it was plain country fare and so filled with herbs and spinach, so crusty on top and bottom, that it was really more a thick egg pancake than an omelet. With a crisp dry wine to accompany it, great chunks of bread and a breath-catching view of the Mediterranean, it made a memorable meal. NOTE: *It is essential to use a well-seasoned skillet or omelet pan when making troucha; otherwise it may stick and break apart as you attempt to turn it. The easiest*

way to turn the troucha *is to invert it upon a plate, then to slide it back into the skillet,*
flip side down.

2 ounces	smoked bacon or salt pork, cut into very small dice	60 g
3 tablespoons, in all	olive oil	3 tablespoons, in all
1 medium-size	Italian (red) or yellow onion, peeled and minced	1 medium-size
1 large	garlic clove, peeled and crushed	1 large
2 packages (10 oz. each)	frozen chopped spinach, partially thawed	2 packages (283 g each)
5 large	eggs, lightly beaten	5 large
½ cup	minced fresh basil	120 ml
½ cup	minced fresh parsley	120 ml
½ cup	freshly grated parmesan cheese	120 ml
⅛ teaspoon	freshly grated nutmeg	⅛ teaspoon
¾ teaspoon	salt	¾ teaspoon
⅛ teaspoon	freshly ground black pepper	⅛ teaspoon

Stir-fry the bacon in 1 tablespoon of the oil in a large heavy skillet over moderate heat about 10 minutes or until most of the fat has cooked out and only crisp browned bits remain. Add the onion and garlic and stir-fry 3 to 5 minutes until limp and golden. Add the spinach and stir-fry 2 to 3 minutes, breaking up large clumps. Turn the heat to low, cover and cook 10 minutes; uncover and cook 3 to 5 minutes longer until very dry. Cool 10 minutes.

Meanwhile, spoon 1 of the remaining tablespoons of oil into a 10- to 12-inch (25 to 30 cm) omelet pan or round-bottomed skillet, set over moderate heat and swirl the oil around for a minute. Turn the heat off and let the pan "season" until you are ready for the omelet.

Combine the eggs with the basil, parsley, Parmesan, nutmeg, salt and pepper. Stir in the cooled spinach mixture. Set the "seasoned" skillet over moderate heat. After 1 minute, pour in the spinach mixture and cook about 5 minutes, just until nice and crusty on the bottom (the top will still be quite moist). Lightly oil a heatproof plate that is larger in diameter than the skillet (or use a round metal tray). Using a small spatula, loosen the *troucha* all around the edge, then invert onto the plate. If some of it should stick to the bottom of the skillet (as will sometimes happen if a skillet is not used exclusively for omelets), lift the recalcitrant pieces with a pancake turner and replace them on the top of the *troucha*, pressing in lightly. Also get up any bits clinging to the skillet, because they will cause the flip side to stick, too. Now add the remaining tablespoon of oil to the skillet, heat about 1 minute, then slide the *troucha* back into the skillet, uncooked side down. Reduce heat to moderately low and let the *troucha* cook slowly about 10 minutes—just until cooked through. Again loosen around the edges with a spatula, ease onto a plate and serve hot or at room temperature. The ideal accompaniments: sun-ripened tomatoes, sliced thin and brushed with olive oil, chewy chunks of country bread, and a crackling white wine such as the Portuguese *vinho verde*.

Wilted spinach salad with hot bacon and scallion dressing

SERVES 4 TO 6

Because the spinach is merely wilted for this salad, not cooked, you can get more servings per pound of spinach than usual. Hand-pick the spinach, rejecting any but the tenderest young leaves. The most tedious part of this recipe is washing the spinach. Be meticulous about it, gently sloshing the spinach up and down in several changes of cool water to make sure that you remove all bits of grit and sand. Then pat the spinach very dry between several thicknesses of paper toweling so that you don't water down the dressing.

1½ pounds	tender young spinach leaves, trimmed of coarse stems and ribs, washed well and patted dry on paper toweling	⅔ kg
	DRESSING:	
8 slices	bacon, cut crosswise into julienne strips	8 slices
6 large	scallions, trimmed, washed and sliced thin (include some tops)	6 large
1 large	garlic clove, peeled and minced	1 large
½ teaspoon	crumbled leaf tarragon	½ teaspoon
¼ teaspoon	crumbled leaf marjoram	¼ teaspoon
2 tablespoons	ketchup	2 tablespoons
½ cup (about)	tarragon vinegar	120 ml (about)
To taste	salt and freshly ground black pepper	To taste

Place the spinach in a very large heatproof bowl and set aside while you prepare the dressing. Brown the bacon slowly in a medium-size heavy skillet over moderately low heat about 10 minutes until all of the drippings have cooked out, leaving crisp brown bits. With a slotted spoon, lift the browned bits to paper toweling to drain; reserve. Now stir-fry the scallions and garlic in the drippings over moderately low heat about 5 minutes until limp and golden. Mix in the tarragon and marjoram and mellow for a minute or two to intensify their flavors, then smooth in the ketchup. Pour in the vinegar (stand back, it may sputter at first), and simmer 2 to 3 minutes to reduce slightly. Pour the dressing over the salad all at once, distributing it as evenly as possible, and toss well. Keep turning and tossing the spinach in the hot dressing until it wilts—a minute or two. Taste for salt and pepper and add as needed; also add a little more tarragon vinegar if the salad is not tart enough. Sprinkle in the reserved bacon crumbles, toss well again and serve.

Squash

"A kind of melon or rather gourd," is the way one early writer described New World squash. "Some of these are green, some yellow, some longish like a gourd, others round like an apple, all of them pleasant food boyled and buttered and seasoned with spice. But the yellow . . . about the size of a pome . . . is the best kind." The varieties of squash available today are even greater, but they can be divided into two categories: **summer squash** (the most common being **yellow squash, zucchini** and **pattypan** or **cymbling**) and **winter squash (acorn, butternut, spaghetti squash, turban, hubbard)** and, of course, **pumpkin,** a not too distant relative.

Season: The designations "summer" and "winter" are misnomers, because those two popular summer squashes—zucchini and yellow squash—are available the year round. Pattypans are more seasonal and at their best in the months of July and August. As for "winter" squashes, acorn and spaghetti squash can be bought the year round in most areas; butternut, hubbard and turban squash are in good supply from late September through about March. The season for pumpkins is shorter—usually from September through December.

Hallmarks of quality:

SUMMER SQUASH: Look for firm, tender young squash with clear, smooth, unblemished skins. The French, when buying *courgettes* (zucchini), insist that the blossom still be attached, proof positive that the squash is a mere baby (American Indians do the same with yellow squash). Avoid buying oversize zucchini; it will be pithy, watery and bitter-skinned.

WINTER SQUASH: Choose hard-skinned squash or pumpkins that feel heavy for their size. Reject any that are nicked or softening.

How much per serving? About ½ pound (¼ kg) of either summer or winter squash.

Best way to store: Summer squash will fare best if loosely bagged in plastic and stored in the bottom of the refrigerator. **Storage time:** 3 to 4 days. **Winter squash** need not be refrigerated, but it *should* be kept in a cool dry area of the house. **Storage time:** 1 week to 10 days, even longer if stored in an unusually cool, dark, dry cellar.

Basic preparation:

SUMMER SQUASH: If truly young, scrub the squash well under cool water but do not peel; leave whole or cut up as recipes direct.

WINTER SQUASH: These are much more difficult to cope with than summer squash because they are so tough and hard. I don't relish the idea of attacking a raw squash with a sharp knife because it's too easy for the knife to slip. So I play it safe. I first wash the squash in cool water, place it in a shallow pan, and "parbake" it, whole and uncovered, for 20 to 30 minutes in a moderate oven (350°F. or 175°C.) until it can be cut up easily. I then halve the squash lengthwise and scoop out all seeds and stringy portions. If I intend to cook the squash as halves, I do not peel it. Otherwise, I do, then slice or chunk it.

Best ways to cook:

SUMMER SQUASH: Many people boil summer squash. I don't because it becomes so tasteless and watery. It's far better, I think, to steam, stir-fry or sauté summer squash. NOTE: *Summer squash that is to be stuffed or baked en casserole should first be parboiled, however, so that it cooks more evenly and quickly. Halve the squash lengthwise, then simmer gently in just enough lightly salted water to cover for 5 to 10 minutes, depending on size, until the squash is slightly softened. Drain well.*

To STEAM: Prepare the squash and halve, slice or cube, as you wish. Place in a steamer basket and cook **over** boiling water in a covered saucepan as follows: 10 to 15 minutes for cut-up squash; 15 to 20 minutes for halves; and 20 to 25 minutes for small whole squash. TIP: *I've found that it's preferable to "parsteam" squash that is to be stuffed or used in baked dishes rather than to parboil it because the squash has a firmer texture. Steam as directed here, but reduce cooking time by half.*

To STIR-FRY OR SAUTÉ: If you are to cook summer squash successfully by either of these methods, you must first draw the excess moisture out of it, otherwise the squash will exude so much liquid in the skillet that it will stew in its own juices and refuse to brown. Scrub the squash as directed, then slice, dice or shred. Spread the cut squash out on several thicknesses of paper toweling, sprinkle fairly liberally with salt, top with more paper toweling and weight down with heavy plates or—and this, I find, works better—with a tray on which you stand some half a dozen large bottles or cans of food. Let the squash stand 30 to 40 minutes, then quickly pat the slices dry between fresh sheets of paper toweling. Now heat 2 to 3 tablespoons of melted butter or olive oil (this amount will be sufficient for about 2 pounds or 1 kg of squash) in a large heavy skillet over moderate heat a minute or two, dump in the squash and either sauté, allowing 2 to 3 minutes per side for sliced or diced squash, or stir-fry 4 to 6 minutes, total, until the squash is lightly browned and crisp-tender. NOTE: *A favorite recipe of mine that's a snap to make is to stir-fry 4 to 6 young shredded zucchini 5 to 8 minutes over moderately high heat with a chopped large yellow onion and a healthy pinch each of rosemary and thyme. Sometimes I add a minced clove of garlic.*

Winter Squash: Wash, then "parbake" the squash as directed above under Basic Preparation. Cool the squash until easy to handle, then halve and remove all seeds and strings.

To BOIL **(for Acorn and Butternut Squash):** Peel the partially cooked squash and cut into 1-inch (2½ cm) chunks, place in a large saucepan, cover with lightly salted boiling water, put the lid on the pan and boil gently over moderate heat about 5 minutes or until you can pierce the squash easily with a fork. Drain well, then season with melted butter, bacon drippings and salt and pepper to taste. **Other compatible seasonings:** Honey; freshly grated nutmeg; finely minced fresh ginger; ground cinnamon, allspice, mace or cloves; crumbled leaf thyme, marjoram or rosemary; freshly snipped dill, chives or finocchio tops; minced parsley; orange or lemon juice and/or rind, or Parsley Sauce (see Index). TIP: *For richer flavor, try boiling the squash in apple cider, beef or chicken broth instead of water.*

To STEAM: Peel the partially cooked squash and slice about ¼ inch (¾ cm) thick or cut into 1-inch (2½ cm) chunks. Lay the squash in a steamer basket and cook **over** boiling water in a tightly covered saucepan about 10 to 15 minutes or until fork-tender. Season as you would boiled squash, above.

To BAKE: This, I think, is the **best possible way to cook winter squash** because the oven's dry heat gives it a rich nutty flavor and because there is no chance of the squash becoming watery.

For Acorn and Butternut Squash: Wash the squash, then partially bake in a moderate oven (350°F. or 175°C.) about 20 minutes or until it is tender enough to cut easily. Halve the squash and scoop out all seeds and stringy inner portions. Arrange the halves, hollow sides up, on a baking sheet. Place a generous pat of butter in each hollow and, if you like, add a tablespoon of honey, brown sugar, orange juice or marmalade. Sprinkle lightly with salt and freshly ground black pepper. Return the squash to the oven and bake, uncovered, 20 to 30 minutes longer or until very tender.

For Spaghetti Squash: Wash the squash, place on a baking sheet and bake, uncovered, in a moderate oven (350°F. or 175°C.) for 45 minutes to 1 hour or until you can pierce the squash easily with a sharp fork. Remove the squash from the oven, halve lengthwise and scoop out all seeds and strings attached to them. Now fluff the meat of the squash up with a fork—it will fall into strands just like spaghetti. Toss with butter, salt and pepper and top, if you like, with your favorite pasta sauce.

For Pumpkin and Hubbard Squash: To my mind, these two giants are best baked **whole.** And what could be easier? Simply stand the pumpkin or hubbard squash on a baking sheet and bake, uncovered, in a moderate oven (350°F. or 175°C.) until you can pierce it easily with a fork. How long this will take will vary with the size of the squash or pumpkin, but as a rule of thumb, you can count on a smallish pumpkin or squash (about 6 inches or 15 cm in diameter) being done in 1¼ to 1½ hours. Remove from the oven, halve and scoop out all seeds and strings. Cut the squash or pumpkin into small chunks (peel or not, as you like) and season to taste with melted butter or bacon drippings, salt or pepper. Or, if you prefer, peel the chunks and mash or purée them in a food processor with a little butter and cream, salt and pepper and crumbled leaf thyme or rosemary. If you prefer a sweeter purée, add a little honey instead of cream, then lightly spice with ground cinnamon and nutmeg or ginger.

Courgettes paysanne
(COUNTRY-STYLE ZUCCHINI)

SERVES 4

This pretty Provençal dish is simple to make. For more variety (and flavor), I slice the zucchini diagonally—at about a 45° angle—so that the "rounds" are "ovals," creating more cut surface to brown and caramelize. The object is to sear the zucchini so quickly that it remains crisp.

4 medium-size	tender, young zucchini, trimmed, washed and sliced on the diagonal about ¼ inch (¾ cm) thick	4 medium-size
½ teaspoon	salt	½ teaspoon
3 tablespoons	olive oil (top quality)	3 tablespoons
½ teaspoon	minced fresh thyme (or ¼ teaspoon crumbled leaf thyme)	½ teaspoon
2 tablespoons	minced parsley	2 tablespoons
⅛ teaspoon	freshly ground black pepper	⅛ teaspoon
2 tablespoons	lemon juice	2 tablespoons

Spread the zucchini slices out in one layer on several thicknesses of paper toweling and sprinkle generously with salt; top with several more thicknesses of paper toweling, then weight the zucchini down by placing a heavy cutting board or tray on top and standing several heavy jars or cans on the board or tray. Let stand for 1 hour (this is to draw moisture from the zucchini so that it will brown more quickly). Heat the olive oil in a very large heavy skillet over high heat for about a minute; dump in the zucchini and stir-fry 3 to 5 minutes, just until all slices are lightly browned but still crisp. Add the thyme, parsley and pepper and toss lightly. Sprinkle with lemon juice, toss lightly again and serve.

Baked yellow squash pudding with buttered crumb topping

SERVES 6

When I was growing up in Raleigh, North Carolina, there was an old-fashioned tea room on Hillsborough Street called the Rineland House that served the best yellow-squash pudding in the world. Or so I thought at the time. Even as a girl, I tried to duplicate that recipe—without much success—because I never dared ask the two old ladies who ran the tea room for their recipe. I feel sure now that they would have obliged me. I have since tried countless times to "crack" their recipe, relying largely on nostalgic memories. This version, I think, comes pretty close to what I remember.

8 small	young yellow squash, scrubbed and cut into ¼-inch (¾ cm) dice	8 small
2 medium-size	yellow onions, peeled and coarsely chopped	2 medium-size
5 tablespoons	unsalted butter	5 tablespoons
⅓ cup	beef or chicken broth or water	80 ml
½ teaspoon	crumbled leaf marjoram	½ teaspoon
¼ teaspoon	crumbled leaf thyme	¼ teaspoon
⅛ teaspoon	freshly grated nutmeg or mace	⅛ teaspoon
1 teaspoon	salt	1 teaspoon
Light sprinkling	freshly ground black pepper	Light sprinkling
2 large	eggs, beaten until frothy	2 large
⅔ cup	coarsely crumbled soda crackers	160 ml
2 teaspoons	light brown sugar or sugar	2 teaspoons
	TOPPING:	
1 cup	fine dry bread crumbs	240 ml
1 tablespoon	melted unsalted butter	1 tablespoon

In a large heavy skillet over moderately high heat, stir-fry the squash and onions in the butter about 5 minutes until touched with brown. Turn heat to moderately low and add the broth, marjoram, thyme, nutmeg, salt and pepper. Cover and simmer about 15 minutes or until squash is very soft. Remove from the heat and mash the squash and onions well with a potato masher. Mix in the eggs, cracker crumbs and sugar, then spoon into a buttered 1½-quart (1½ L) baking dish. Toss the topping ingredients together and scatter evenly over the squash. Bake, uncovered, in a moderately hot oven (375°F. or 190°C.) for 40 to 45 minutes or until richly browned.

Purée of winter squash and sweet potato with apricots and apple

SERVES 4 TO 6

Too often, I think, we treat winter squash and sweet potatoes like "desserts" by sugaring them or sloshing them with syrup. If you like these vegetables pudding-sweet, you will probably not care for this rather tart purée, which has nothing more in the way of sweeteners than the natural sugars of the fruits and vegetables. I like this purée with roast pork, turkey and chicken, also with roast goose, duck and baked ham. NOTE: *I think that both winter squash and sweet potato have superior flavor when baked rather than boiled. Besides, it's easier simply to plunk the whole acorn or butternut squash and sweet potato or yam into a shallow baking pan and to bake them than it is to cut them up raw, peel them and boil them.*

1 large (about 2 pounds)	acorn or butternut squash	1 large (about 1 kg)
1 large (about 1 pound)	sweet potato or yam	1 large (about ½ kg)
1 large	tart green apple, peeled, cored and cut into slim wedges	1 large
4 large	dried apricot halves	4 large
½ cup	apple cider	120 ml
3 tablespoons, in all	unsalted butter	3 tablespoons, in all
Pinch	crumbled leaf rosemary	Pinch
Pinch	ground nutmeg	Pinch
Pinch	ground cinnamon	Pinch
To taste	salt and freshly ground black pepper	To taste

Place the uncut squash and sweet potato in a shallow roasting pan and bake, uncovered, in a moderately hot oven (375°F. or 190°C.) for 1 to 1¼ hours or until both are soft to the touch. Remove from the oven and cool until easy to handle. Meanwhile, place the apple, apricots, cider, 2 tablespoons of the butter, the rosemary, nutmeg and cinnamon in a small heavy saucepan; bring to a simmer over moderately low heat, cover and simmer 20 minutes until apricots and apple are soft. Uncover and simmer about 5 minutes longer until the liquid has almost all cooked away.

Halve the squash; scoop out and discard all seeds and stringy portions. Scoop the flesh into a food processor equipped with the metal chopping blade, dump in the apple mixture, then purée by buzzing about 60 seconds nonstop. Scrape the work bowl sides down, and buzz another 60 seconds until uniformly smooth. (If you do not have a processor, purée the squash and apple mixtures together, about half of the total amounts at a time, in an electric blender at high speed until creamy. Or force all through a food mill.) Now quickly halve the potato, scoop out the flesh and mash well with the remaining tablespoon of butter. Combine the squash and potato purées in a medium-size heavy saucepan and bring slowly to serving temperature, stirring constantly, lest the mixture scorch. Season to taste with salt and pepper and serve.

Baked acorn squash with sausage and onion stuffing

SERVES 4

Here's an easy, inexpensive main dish that's wonderfully warm and fortifying on a raw winter's day. NOTE: *Because of the saltiness of the sausage, you will probably not need to add salt to the stuffing.*

2 medium-size (about ½ pound each)	acorn squash	2 medium-size (about 225 g each)
2 tablespoons	melted unsalted butter	2 tablespoons
	STUFFING:	
½ pound	bulk sausage meat	225 g
1 large	yellow onion, peeled and chopped	1 large
½ teaspoon	crumbled leaf marjoram	½ teaspoon
¼ teaspoon	crumbled leaf thyme	¼ teaspoon
2 cups	moderately coarse soft bread crumbs	½ L
1 tablespoon	freshly grated Parmesan cheese	1 tablespoon

Place the uncut acorn squash in a shallow baking pan and bake, uncovered, in a moderately hot oven (375°F. or 190°C.) for 1 to 1¼ hours or until soft to the touch. Remove from the oven and cool until easy to handle; leave the oven on because you will again bake the stuffed squash in it.

Meanwhile, prepare the stuffing: Cook the sausage slowly in a large heavy skillet over moderately low heat, breaking up large clumps with a wooden spoon, until uniformly brown and crumbly—about 15 to 20 minutes. With a slotted spoon, lift the sausage to paper toweling to drain. Pour all drippings from the skillet, then spoon 3 tablespoons of them back into the skillet; reserve the balance of the drippings. Stir-fry the onion, marjoram and thyme in the drippings over moderate heat about 10 minutes until the onion is limp and lightly browned. If the sausage meat still seems fairly lumpy, chop it until uniformly fine. Return it to the skillet along with 1 additional tablespoon of the reserved drippings and the bread crumbs; toss all lightly to mix.

Now halve the squash; scoop out and discard all seeds and stringy portions. Brush the hollows of each squash half liberally with melted butter; also brush the rims so that they don't dry out during baking. Mound the stuffing into each hollow and sprinkle lightly with the grated Parmesan. Stand the squash in a shallow baking pan just large enough to accommodate them, and bake, uncovered, in the moderately hot oven about 30 minutes until flecked with brown. Serve hot with a green vegetable such as broccoli or Brussels sprouts, or, if you prefer, accompany with a sharply dressed green salad.

Sweet potatoes and yams

Sweet potatoes are another of the wondrous New World foods Columbus found. Presumably they were carried back to Europe at the same time as the "Irish" potato, for mention is made early on of their sweetness and rainbow range of colors (from "purple to red to palest yellow"). But little else is said about them. What we in the United States call yams, by the way, are not yams. (True yams are fleshy, less-sweet tubers of a climbing plant native to the Caribbean.) Our "yams" are merely a plumper, rounder, redder and sweeter variety of the everyday sweet potato. It is elongated, rather like an Idaho potato, but pointed at both ends.

Season: Year round.

Hallmarks of quality: The best yams and sweet potatoes are plump and firm with clean skins, few nicks and blemishes.

How many sweet potatoes or yams per person? 1 medium-size.

Best way to store: In a basket in a cool, dark, dry place. **Storage time:** Only 7 to 10 days if the conditions are less than optimum. Otherwise, about a month.

Basic preparation: Scrub the potatoes well under cool water.

Best ways to cook:

TO BOIL: Scrub the potatoes, but do not peel (sweet potatoes and yams darken quickly when peeled raw). Place the potatoes in a large saucepan, cover with boiling water, clap the lid on the pan and boil gently for 40 to 60 minutes or until you can pierce a potato easily with a fork. Drain well, then peel. NOTE: *You now have several options as to how you will finish the potaotes:* You can mash them with a little butter or heavy cream and season to taste with salt and freshly ground pepper. (A pinch each of nutmeg and rosemary are nice additions.) You can candy the potatoes—a perfectly wretched way to prepare them, I think—by mashing them with pineapple or orange juice, a tablespoon or two of brown sugar and a fat chunk of butter, mounding in a casserole, topping with marshmallows, and browning quickly under the broiler. Or you can slice the potatoes and butter them or glaze them with a little honey, or maple or dark corn syrup. In my opinion, the less added sweetness the better.

TO BAKE: Place the scrubbed sweet potatoes directly on the middle rack of a hot oven (400°F. or 205°C.) and bake 45 minutes to 1 hour or until you can pierce a potato easily with a fork. Remove from the oven, make an X-shaped slit in the top of each potato, then, using potholders to protect your fingers, press the sides of the potatoes, forcing the sweet orange flesh up. Push a generous pat of butter down into each potato, sprinkle lightly with salt and pepper and serve.

Breaded sweet potatoes

SERVES 4 TO 6

I learned to prepare sweet potatoes this way on the West Indian Island of Grenada. Instead of using commercially packaged dry bread crumbs, I make my own by toasting about eight slices of firm-textured white bread in a slow oven (300°F. or 150°C.) until uniformly amber-colored and crisp.

I then break the toast into chunks and whir them to crumbs in a processor equipped with the metal chopping blade. These crumbs have an exquisite, faintly caramel flavor and can be used for breading all manner of food.

2 pounds (about 4 large)	sweet potatoes of as regular shape as possible, scrubbed	1 kg (about 4 large)
2 quarts	boiling water	2 L
2 large	eggs	2 large
2 tablespoons	honey	2 tablespoons
Pinch	freshly grated nutmeg	Pinch
1½ cups	fine dry bread crumbs	350 ml
6 to 8 tablespoons, in all	butter	6 to 8 tablespoons, in all

Place the sweet potatoes in a large heavy saucepan, pour in the boiling water, set over moderate heat, cover and boil about 1 hour or until you can pierce the potatoes easily with a fork. Drain the potatoes, cool until easy to handle, then peel. Now chill the potatoes about 1 hour or until they are very firm. Beat the eggs lightly with the honey and nutmeg and place in a pie pan. Place the bread crumbs in a second pie pan or on a large piece of wax paper. Slice the potatoes lengthwise about ⅜ inch (1 cm) thick. Dip first into the egg mixture until evenly coated, then into the bread crumbs, patting the crumbs firmly and uniformly onto the potato slices just as you would when breading veal scallops.

Heat 4 tablespoons of the butter in a large heavy skillet over moderate to moderately high heat until it froths up, then subsides. Add about one-third of the potato slices and brown nicely, allowing 1 to 2 minutes per side. Drain on paper toweling and keep warm by setting, uncovered, in a very slow oven (250°F. or 120°C.). Brown the remaining slices the same way, adding more butter to the skillet as needed. Serve hot with roast pork or turkey, baked ham or chicken cooked almost any way at all.

NOTE: *See also the recipe for Purée of Winter Squash and Sweet Potato with Apricots and Apple in the section on Squash.*

Swiss Chard

Although nearly a staple in Europe, this silver-stalked, crinkly, green-leafed vegetable isn't much in favor in America. And yet it is a delicacy, a highly nutritious and versatile vegetable with an elusive flavor that seems to me about two parts spinach and one part asparagus. If you should happen to come upon Swiss chard in your local market, by all means buy it and learn to use it.

Season: June through October.

Hallmarks of quality: Youth, first of all—tender leaves and slim succulent stalks. The leaves and stalks should also be clean and blemish-free.

How much chard per person? ½ pound (¼ kg).

Best way to store: Untrimmed and unwashed, loosely bagged in plastic in the refrigerator crisper. **Storage time:** 3 days.

Basic preparation: Cut off all root ends, then separate the leaves from the stalks. To wash the leaves, fill a sink with tepid water, add 2 tablespoons of salt, then move the leaves very gently in the water to dislodge bits of grit which will sink to the bottom of the sink; your aim is to keep them there by agitating the water as little as possible. Lift the leaves to several thicknesses of paper toweling and cut out and discard any heavy ribs—they will be woody. Now wash the stalks in cool running water and, if they are heavily ribbed, peel off the coarse strings as you would with celery; pat dry on paper toweling and coarsely chop or slice thin.

Best ways to cook: Even though the stalks are chopped, they will take far longer to cook than the leaves and should thus go into the saucepan first and be boiled several minutes before the leaves are added.

To BOIL: Place the chopped stalks of 1½ to 2 pounds (⅔ to 1 kg) of Swiss chard in a large heavy saucepan (not aluminum, which will react with the chard), pour in ¾ cup boiling water, add a healthy pinch of salt, cover and boil gently over moderate heat for 5 to 8 minutes, just until beginning to soften. Meanwhile, lightly chop the leaves. Add them to the pan, re-cover and simmer 5 to 10 minutes. Drain well, return the pan of chard to moderate heat and shake vigorously for a minute or two to drive off excess moisture. Season to taste with butter or bacon drippings, salt and freshly ground pepper to taste.

To STEAM: Place the coarsely chopped chard stalks in a steamer basket, then steam **over** boiling water in a covered saucepan for 10 to 12 minutes. Add the coarsely chopped leaves, re-cover and steam 10 to 12 minutes longer. Season as directed for boiled chard above.

To STIR-FRY: Tender young Swiss chard leaves, coarsely chopped, may be stir-fried successfully in bacon drippings, butter or olive oil (about 3 tablespoons for 2 pounds or 1 kg of chard) in a large heavy skillet over moderate heat. I favor the olive oil and like to add 3 to 4 peeled whole garlic cloves to the skillet. The chard will only take 4 to 5 minutes to cook. Discard the garlic cloves as soon as the chard is tender, then drizzle with white wine vinegar or lemon juice, toss lightly and serve.

Swiss chard quiche with bacon and leeks

SERVES 6 TO 8

This is one of the best ways I know to prepare Swiss chard. Serve as a main course accompanied by tartly marinated vine-ripened tomatoes.

1 pound	Swiss chard	½ kg
¾ cup	hot beef broth	180 ml
3 slices	bacon, snipped crosswise into julienne strips	3 slices
2 large	leeks, trimmed, washed and sliced thin	2 large
⅛ teaspoon	freshly grated nutmeg	⅛ teaspoon
½ teaspoon	salt	½ teaspoon
Light sprinkling	freshly ground black pepper	Light sprinkling
A 9-inch	unbaked pie shell	A 23 cm
2 ounces	Gruyère cheese, coarsely grated	60 g
1¼ cups	half-and-half cream	300 ml
2 medium-size	eggs, lightly beaten	2 medium-size
3 tablespoons	freshly grated Parmesan cheese	3 tablespoons

Trim the chard of all coarse stem ends and blemished leaves, then separate the stalks from the leaves. Also cut out all heavy central ribs in the leaves and add these to the stalks. Wash the leaves in several changes of cold water to which you have added salt (about 2 tablespoons for each sinkful of water). Pat the leaves dry between several thicknesses of paper toweling, then chop them coarsely and set aside. Scrub the stalks well with a vegetable brush and if they are heavily ribbed like celery, pull off and discard as many of the coarse strings as possible. Now slice the stalks about ¼ inch (¾ cm) thick and place in a small heavy saucepan (not aluminum, which will react with the oxalic acid of the chard, leaving a dark residue on the pan and a metallic taste in the chard). Pour in the hot broth, set over moderate to moderately low heat (it should be just hot enough to keep the broth at a gentle simmer), cover and cook 15 to 20 minutes or until the chard stems are very tender. Uncover and continue to cook until the broth cooks down to an amber glaze.

Meanwhile, fry the bacon in a large heavy skillet (again not aluminum) over moderate heat until all of the fat cooks out, leaving crisp browned bits. With a slotted spoon, lift the browned bits to paper toweling to drain. To the drippings add the leeks and stir-fry about 3 minutes until limp and golden. Sprinkle in the nutmeg, salt and pepper, then dump in the chard leaves and stir-fry 3 to 5 minutes until glistening. Turn burner heat to low, cover the skillet and steam the chard leaves 10 minutes. Uncover the skillet, add the cooked stems and any remaining broth and cook, uncovered, over low heat about 5 minutes until the mixture is quite dry. Remove from the heat and cool 15 minutes. Spread the chard mixture evenly over the bottom of the pie shell and top with the grated Gruyère. Combine the half-and-half with the eggs and Parmesan and pour evenly over all. Sprinkle the reserved bacon bits on top.

Bake, uncovered, in a moderate oven (350°F. or 175°C.) for 35 minutes. Remove from the oven, cool 20 minutes, then cut into wedges and serve.

Tomatoes

America's tomatoes are in a sorry state. At least those that come to supermarkets. They were picked green and will **never** be fit to eat. Cherry tomatoes have better flavor, as do the Italian plum tomatoes. But even the beefsteaks and basic all-round garden variety of tomato are completely taste-less unless they are locally or home-grown. I'd sooner use canned tomatoes for recipes—and usually do.

Season: Summer, for the properly grown and ripened. Yes, I know that tomatoes—if you can call them that—can be found year round in almost every supermarket, but I won't give them house room.

Hallmarks of quality: My number one criterion for buying tomatoes is aroma. If a tomato doesn't smell warmly, ripely, *deliciously* of tomato—the way the tomatoes my dad used to grow in our back yard smelled—I pass them by no matter how big and round and red they are. I'll settle faster for an honest-to-God tomato with a minor blemish or two than for a perfect "plastic" one.

How many tomatoes per person? 4 to 5 cherry tomatoes, a medium-size Italian plum or ordinary home-grown tomato, or 2 to 3 slices of a beefsteak tomato—but the manner of serving or cooking can altogether change these estimates.

Best way to store: Spread out on a cool, dark dry shelf. Stacked tomatoes (as in a basket or bowl) will quickly soften wherever they touch their neighbors. And the tomatoes at the bottom of the bowl will go bad in short order. NOTE: *If you want to ripen tomatoes that you have picked too green, place them in a perforated brown-paper bag with an apple and set on an out-of-the-way counter. Check every day or so. They will ripen with surprising speed.*

Basic preparation: If you are to serve tomatoes raw, you need only wash and core them and cut into slices or wedges. I like raw tomatoes with the peel on, despite the fact that my mother **always** served them peeled. I think she left them too long in the blanching water to peel them; they always tasted half cooked. However . . .

Some special techniques for tomatoes:

To PEEL: Spear the stem end of a tomato with a long-handled fork, thrust into a saucepan of rapidly boiling water and leave 15 to 30 seconds, turning the tomato all the while. Plunge at once into ice water to stop the cooking action, then core the tomato and peel (the skin will slip right off). NOTE: *The skins of dead-ripe, home-grown tomatoes will loosen in 15 to 20 seconds, so get them out of the hot water fast lest you end up with an unattractive layer of mush on the outside of your tomatoes.*

To SEED AND JUICE: Peel the tomato as directed, then halve it horizontally. Now, holding the tomato in one hand so that the cut side is down, squeeze gently—the seeds and juices will spurt out. (For obvious reasons, it's best to do this over a sink.) Continue to squeeze the tomato until it is quite dry. Soups, stews and sauces often call for seeded and juiced tomatoes because the seeds detract from both the appearance and the texture of the final dish and the juice waters down the tomato flavor as well as the sauce or soup or stew.

Best ways to cook: For me, tomatoes are better in recipes than as a solitary cooked vegetable. It embarrasses me to admit that I cannot—to this day— swallow stewed tomatoes without gagging. They have affected me this way ever since I was a small child (did I once get sick after eating stewed tomatoes?) and they still do. But I do like broiled tomatoes:

To BROIL: Select firm-ripe tomatoes, wash them and core them, but do not peel. Halve the tomatoes crosswise, then brush liberally with olive oil (olive oil in which a clove or two of peeled, slivered garlic have marinated for a couple of hours, if you like.) Arrange the tomatoes, cut sides up, on a shallow pan and set in the broiler about 5 inches (13 cm) from the heat. Broil 8 to 10 minutes or until dappled with brown. Season to taste with salt and pepper and serve. NOTE: *I sometimes pull the tomatoes from the broiler when they are about half done and sprinkle with dry bread crumbs that I have mixed with a little freshly grated Parmesan cheese and melted butter. I then return them to the broiler to finish cooking. If you want to add a fresh or dried herb, sprinkle it on the cut face of the tomato first, then add oil (or butter).*

Sopa de tomate e cebola
(PORTUGUESE TOMATO AND ONION SOUP)

SERVES 6

The success of this hearty soup depends upon vine-ripe tomatoes bursting with true tomato flavor. If they are unavailable, substitute canned whole tomatoes; your soup won't be as good as the original, but it will surpass anything made with pithy, flavorless mass-produced tomatoes. Like most soups, this one will taste mellower if made a day ahead, then finished off just before serving.

4 large	yellow onions, peeled and coarsely chopped	4 large
⅓ cup	olive oil	80 ml
8 large	juicily ripe tomatoes, peeled, cored, seeded and finely chopped OR 2 cans whole tomatoes (1 lb. or 454 g each)	8 large
4 large	garlic cloves, peeled and minced	4 large
5 cups (1 quart + 1 cup)	rich beef broth	1¼ L
¼ pound (1 stick), in all	unsalted butter	115 g (1 stick), in all
¼ teaspoon (about)	salt	¼ teaspoon (about)
⅛ teaspoon (about)	freshly ground black pepper	⅛ teaspoon (about)
1–2 teaspoons	sugar (if needed to mellow the soup)	1–2 teaspoons
8 small	eggs	8 small
12 thick slices	French or Italian bread (use slim baguettes)	12 thick slices
¼ cup	minced parsley	60 ml

Stir-fry onions in oil in a heavy broad-bottomed kettle about 15 minutes over moderate heat until limp and lightly browned. Add tomatoes and garlic, cover and simmer 1 hour; uncover, and simmer 30 minutes, stirring occasionally, until thick and pastelike. Add broth, 3 tablespoons of the butter, salt and pepper to taste and, if needed, sugar. Simmer, uncovered, 1½ to 2 hours or until flavors are richly blended. Cool to room temperature, cover and refrigerate until about 1 hour before serving. Bring soup slowly to serving temperature. Carefully break eggs into soup, spacing them evenly, cover and simmer slowly 15 minutes. What you are doing is poaching the eggs.

Meanwhile, brown bread slices on both sides in remaining 5 tablespoons butter in a large heavy skillet over moderately high heat; drain on paper toweling. Ladle soup into large shallow soup bowls, including an egg with each portion. Garnish each bowl with 2 bread slices and a sprinkling of parsley.

Baked plum-tomato mousse with fresh basil

SERVES 6

I use Italian plum tomatoes for this moist and quivery mousse because I think that they, of all the fresh tomatoes available to us, have the best flavor. Buy them, if possible, at the source, because only then will they truly taste like tomatoes. And seed them before you use them in this recipe. It's easy: Slice off the core end of each tomato, then holding them cut side down over the sink, squeeze gently. The seeds will spurt out. NOTE: *You can, if you like, prepare the tomato base for this mousse a day ahead of time; in fact the flavor will be richer for it.*

2 medium-size	yellow onions, peeled and chopped	2 medium-size
1 large	garlic clove, peeled and minced	1 large
3 tablespoons	olive oil	3 tablespoons
½ teaspoon	crumbled leaf marjoram	½ teaspoon
¼ teaspoon	crumbled leaf thyme	¼ teaspoon
1½ pounds	vine-ripe Italian plum tomatoes, peeled, cored, seeded and finely chopped	⅔ kg
½ cup	firmly packed fresh basil leaves, washed and finely chopped	120 ml
⅓ cup	dry white wine	80 ml
½ cup	beef broth blended with 4 tablespoons flour	120 ml
2 tablespoons	tomato paste	2 tablespoons
2 tablespoons	unsalted butter	2 tablespoons
¼ cup	freshly grated Parmesan cheese	60 ml
5 large	eggs, separated	5 large
1 teaspoon, in all	salt	1 teaspoon, in all
⅛ teaspoon	freshly ground black pepper	⅛ teaspoon
	TO PREPARE THE BAKING DISH:	
1 teaspoon	unsalted butter	1 teaspoon
2 tablespoons	freshly grated Parmesan cheese	2 tablespoons

Stir-fry the onions and garlic in the oil in a large heavy skillet over moderate heat 8 to 10 minutes until limp and lightly browned. Add the marjoram and thyme and mellow a minute or two to intensify their flavors. Add the tomatoes, basil and wine, turn burner heat down low and simmer, uncovered, stirring occasionally, 1 to 1½ hours or until about as thick as you would use for a pasta sauce. Quickly blend in the broth-flour mixture and heat and stir 3 to 5 minutes until thickened and no raw floury flavor remains. Smooth in the tomato paste, butter and grated Parmesan. NOTE: *You may prepare the tomato base up to this point a day ahead of time. Transfer to a medium-size bowl, cover and refrigerate. Bring the tomato base to room temperature before proceeding.*

Now prepare the baking dish: Butter the bottom and sides of a 6-cup (1½ L), straight-sided baking dish or soufflé dish. Add the Parmesan and coat the bottom and sides liberally by tilting the dish to one side and the other. Tap out excess cheese and set the dish aside.

Lightly beat the egg yolks and blend into the tomato base along with ½ teaspoon of the salt and the ⅛ teaspoon pepper. Sprinkle the remaining ½ teaspoon of salt over the egg whites and beat to soft peaks. Stir about one-fourth of the beaten whites into the tomato base, then dump the remaining whites on top and fold in gently but thoroughly until no streaks of red or white remain. NOTE: *This is the same method that you would use in making a soufflé, but this mousse will not puff as dramatically because of the moistness and quantity of the tomato base and also because you smoothed butter into it toward the end, which, in effect, "greases" the egg whites and prevents them from rising to stratospheric soufflé heights.*

Pour the mousse mixture into the prepared baking dish and bake, uncovered, in a moderately hot oven (375°F. or 190°C.) for 45 to 50 minutes until lightly browned. Waste no time in serving—the mousse, like a soufflé, will fall within minutes.

Turnips and rutabaga (yellow turnip)

It's written that Henry VIII liked turnips roasted in ashes and the tender young tops served raw as salad, but there's no record that the court shared his enthusiasm. For the most part, this most ancient of vegetables (about 4,000 years old) has come down through the ages as a lowly root, eaten in lean times by the poor and in fat times by the cattle of the poor.

In the strictest botanical sense, **rutabagas,** often called **yellow turnips,** are not turnips but turnip-cabbage hybrids. But their flavor and texture, if not their whopping size, so closely resemble **true turnips** that they can be prepared and cooked the same way.

Season: Year round. **Peak months:** October and November.

Hallmarks of quality: Generally speaking, the smaller the turnips and rutabagas, the sweeter and the more tender they will be. Select those that feel firm and succulent, are clean and free of nicks, scratches and blemishes. If turnips have the tops attached (few do in these days of supermarket prepackaging), the leaves should be crinkly green. NOTE: *Rutabagas are often heavily waxed today to prolong their storage life, so it is more difficult to ascertain their quality. The best practice is to buy fairly small rutabagas (those about the size of a large grapefruit) that seem heavy for their size.*

How much per person? ¼ to ⅓ pound (115 to 160 g) of either turnips or rutabaga.

Best way to store: If turnips have the tops on, cut them off and bag loosely in plastic and store in the refrigerator crisper. (The greens are a great favorite down South.) Now bag the turnips also loosely in plastic and refrigerate. Rutabagas need not be refrigerated—just stored in a cool spot. **Storage time:**

About 2 days for turnip greens, a week for turnips and 1½ to 2 weeks for rutabagas.

Basic preparations: Small young turnips can—and **should**—be cooked whole in their skins because they will be sweeter and firmer. Large turnips and rutabagas should be peeled and cubed. Don't cut the pieces too small because the turnips or rutabagas will become watery. CAUTION: *Work carefully and slowly when cutting rutabagas. And use a very sharp knife that will cleave cleanly and quickly to the heart without being forced. It's the dull knife, the one that has to be forced, that tends to slip.* **To prepare turnip greens:** They should be washed gently in a sinkful of tepid water like spinach (which see).

Best ways to cook:

TO BOIL: If turnips are small, whole and unpeeled, submerge them in boiling water in a large heavy saucepan, cover and cook gently over moderate heat 20 to 30 minutes, depending upon size. When done, you will be able to pierce the turnips easily with a fork. Drain the turnips well, then peel and slice, dice or mash. Dress with butter, heavy cream or bacon drippings and salt and pepper to taste. For large cubed turnips or rutabagas, I prefer to use beef or chicken broth as the cooking medium. Place the turnips or rutabagas in a heavy nonaluminum pan, pour in enough boiling broth to about two-thirds cover them, set over moderate heat, put the lid on the pan and cook about 15 to 20 minutes until fork-tender. Drain the turnips. (I freeze the cooking broth to use in soups.) Return the turnips to the pan and shake briefly over moderate heat to drive off excess moisture. Season as directed above for turnips cooked whole.

NOTE: *Young and tender turnip greens may be cooked exactly like spinach (see Index), although the traditional southern way is to cook the "turnip salad," as they call it, or "mess o' greens," in a big pot with plenty of water and a chunk of fat back or a ham bone. Southerners let turnip greens laze over a slow burner the better part of the morning, then cool them in the cooking liquid. "Soul food," they call it. I call it "school lunch," because I was subjected, it seems to me, to huge cauldrons of turnip "salad" every day in the school cafeteria. For twelve years! I tried them once and once was definitely enough.*

TO STEAM: Peel and cube the turnips or rutabagas. Place in a steamer basket, then cook **over** boiling water in a large covered saucepan for 15 to 20 minutes until fork-tender. Season as recommended for boiled turnips above.

NOTE: *To enliven mashed turnips or rutabagas, mix about half-and-half with mashed "Irish" or sweet potatoes, or mashed carrots, pumpkin, winter squash or parsnips. Or combine, measure for measure, with any two or three of these vegetables. Season with a little butter, heavy cream and freshly grated nutmeg.*

TO ROAST: Peel whole small turnips, then place in a pie pan or shallow casserole and pour in about ⅔ cup (160 ml) of ham or bacon drippings. Turn the turnips in the drippings until they are evenly glazed, then sprinkle lightly with freshly grated nutmeg, salt and freshly ground black pepper. Place in a hot oven

(400°F. or 205°C.) and roast, uncovered, basting often with the drippings, for about 45 minutes until fork-tender and nicely browned. Remove the turnips from the drippings and serve.

Cream of turnip soup

SERVES 4 TO 6

Turnips are not to everyone's taste, but I suspect that this delicately spicy soup will win converts. It's delicious hot or cold and can precede—or be—the main course. Accompany by plenty of sturdy bread (homemade whole wheat would be splendid) and a salad of assorted greens, tartly dressed.

¼ pound (6 slices)	lean sliced bacon, cut crosswise into julienne strips	115 g (6 slices)
1 pound (about 3 large)	white turnips, peeled and chopped	½ kg (3 large)
2 medium-size	yellow onions, peeled and chopped	2 medium-size
2 medium-size	parsnips, peeled and chopped (optional)	2 medium-size
2 medium-size	carrots, peeled and chopped	2 medium-size
1 medium-size	all-purpose potato, peeled and chopped	1 medium-size
1 large	tart apple, peeled, cored and chopped	1 large
1 teaspoon	dill weed	1 teaspoon
¼ teaspoon	ground allspice	¼ teaspoon
1 tablespoon	minced parsley	1 tablespoon
2 quarts	rich veal stock, beef and/or chicken broth	2 L
1 cup	half-and-half cream	240 ml
To taste	salt and freshly ground black pepper	To taste

Stir-fry bacon in a large heavy kettle over moderate heat until crisply brown—10 to 12 minutes; with a slotted spoon, lift bacon crumbles to paper toweling to drain and reserve. In the drippings, stir-fry turnips, onions, parsnips (if you like), carrots, potato and apple 10 to 15 minutes until limp and lightly browned. Stir in dill weed, allspice and parsley, add veal stock, bring to a gentle simmer, set lid on kettle askew and cook slowly for 3 to 4 hours—until vegetables are mushy. Strain, reserving liquid and solids. Purée the solids in a food processor or by putting through a food mill or fine sieve, and return to kettle along with reserved liquid. Simmer, uncovered, about 1 hour to reduce somewhat. Blend in the half-and-half and simmer very slowly ¾ to 1 hour (put a flame-tamer underneath kettle, if need be, to keep soup from bubbling). Season to taste with salt and pepper, ladle into soup plates and serve hot, topped by the reserved bacon crumbles. Or, if you prefer, cool to room temperature, then chill well before serving. NOTE: *The soup will thicken somewhat as it chills, so thin as needed with a little cold milk before serving. Garnish with finely minced bacon crumbles and, if you like, minced parsley or dill.*

Sliced turnips au gratin with fresh ginger

SERVES 4 TO 6

I like fresh ginger with turnips because it heightens their sweetness and bite. I also find the combination the perfect accompaniment to roast pork, turkey or chicken. NOTE: *This recipe is equally good made with rutabaga (yellow turnip).*

1 pound	firm young turnips or rutabagas, trimmed, peeled and sliced thin	½ kg
1¼ cups	hot beef broth	300 ml
3 tablespoons	unsalted butter	3 tablespoons
1 tablespoon	finely minced fresh ginger	1 tablespoon
¼ teaspoon	crumbled leaf thyme	¼ teaspoon
⅛ teaspoon	freshly grated nutmeg or mace	⅛ teaspoon
3 tablespoons	flour	3 tablespoons
1 cup (about)	light or heavy cream	240 ml (about)
¼ cup	freshly grated Parmesan cheese	60 ml
¼ teaspoon	salt	¼ teaspoon
Light sprinkling	freshly ground black pepper	Light sprinkling
	TOPPING:	
1 cup	moderately fine soft bread crumbs	240 ml
1 tablespoon	melted unsalted butter	1 tablespoon
2 tablespoons	freshly grated Parmesan cheese	2 tablespoons

Cook the turnips in the broth in a medium-size covered saucepan over moderate heat 10 to 15 minutes until crisp-tender. Drain the broth into a large measuring cup and set aside. Arrange the turnips in a shallow 1-quart (1 L) baking dish or *au gratin* pan; set aside. Melt the butter in a small heavy saucepan over moderate heat, add the ginger, thyme and nutmeg and stir-fry 2 to 3 minutes until the ginger is limp and golden. Blend in the flour to make a smooth paste, then lower heat and allow the butter-flour mixture (roux) to turn a pale topaz brown. NOTE: *This delicate browning is essential for flavor.* To the measuring cup containing the broth, add enough cream so that the combined liquids total 1½ cups (350 ml).

Pour into the saucepan and cook, stirring constantly, until thickened and smooth and the sauce no longer tastes of raw flour—3 to 5 minutes. Mix in the grated Parmesan, salt and pepper and allow the sauce to mellow another minute or two over moderate heat, then pour evenly over the turnips.

For the topping: Toss the bread crumbs lightly with the melted butter, add the grated Parmesan and toss well again. Scatter the topping evenly over the turnips.

Bake, uncovered, in a moderately hot oven (375°F. or 190°C.) for 35 minutes until bubbling and browned.

Baking

When I sailed into my first experimental cooking lab at Cornell University, I panicked. There, in each of the work units, stood gram scales and liter beakers. We would be cooking (perish the thought) in metric. No more familiar cups, half cups and quarter cups. From here on it would be grams, milliliters, centimeters and Celsius.

How archaic, we students thought. What we didn't realize in our smugness was that we were the ones who were out of date. But it took maybe thirty minutes for the professor to show us the light: Grams, liters and meters are computed in simple multiples of ten—ever so much more orderly than our lunatic system in which twelve inches equal a foot, thirty-six inches a yard, thirty-two ounces a quart and sixteen ounces a pound.

How ever did we devise such a system? Much of it came down to us from the Romans, who dreamed up the mile (the distance covered by a thousand five-foot paces) and determined that the inch (originally "the length of three barleycorns, round and dry") equaled one-twelfth of a foot. And the yard? It is Anglo-Saxon—the length, it's said, of the sash that girdled an early king. The history of ounces, quarts and pounds is involved and inconsistent—the British Imperial quart containing, for instance, forty ounces rather than thirty-two, while the British pound remained at sixteen ounces like the American.

Historically, metric measures are comparatively new. They were formulated in the late eighteenth century by the French National Academy of Sciences as "an invariable standard for all the measures and weights." Today the metric system is used by all industrialized nations of the world save one: the United States. We've got our backs up about metric. The Metric Conversion Act of 1975 makes the switch-over voluntary, so we've dug in our heels, refusing to jettison our haphazard, albeit colorful, way of measuring for an eminently more logical system. What few of us consider is that we've been using certain metric measures all along without complaint or confusion. The watt, for example. Whenever we buy a 100-watt lightbulb, we are buying metric, so to speak. The same holds true for foreign cars with speedometers worked out in kilometers per hour, not to mention camera lenses, both domestic and foreign, whose focal lengths are measured in millimeters—20 mm, for example, or 50 mm or 200 mm. Doctors write—and pharmacists fill—our prescriptions in milligrams. And, of course, the "quart" of Scotch we buy at our neighborhood liquor store is now a liter.

One instant miracle of the Cornell experimental cooking course was that it taught us just how easy the arithmetic of the metric system is to master, at the same time ensuring much more accuracy in calculating amounts and their subdivisions. Simultaneously, we had another change thrust upon our way of doing things—dry ingredients and solids were to be weighed! Measuring them by cups, pints or quarts was not only out, we would be allowed to use the liter (or subdivisions thereof) only for liquids. What a shock. But the metric system and the use of scales, both for the purpose of accuracy, became so indelibly associated in our minds that we came to think of the weighing of ingredients as a given of the metric system. This is not strictly correct, but there is no better time to go back to the "old-fashioned" method of weighing ingredients for recipes than when you also shift to metric measures. Within a week, we were weighing flours, sugars and fats like old pros. And as recent converts are wont to do, alas, we were proselytizing our classmates by raving about how much more efficient and reliable metric measures were than our antiquated cup system—not to speak of how much neater it was to use scales.

Nowhere are the advantages of the weighing of ingredients more apparent than in baking, because baking is as much science as art. Consider, for example, the margin for error in our conventional way of measuring flour: (1) Sift the flour onto a piece of wax paper; (2) using a spoon, scoop the flour lightly into a dry-cup measure; then (3) using the edge of a straight-blade spatula or knife, level off the surface of the flour until it is flush with the rim of the cup. Our very first class exercise, as I remember, demonstrated just how risky this method is and how dramatically the quantity contained in a cup can vary according to the technique (or clumsiness) of the cook. Use a heavy hand and you will knock the air out of the flour, compacting it—sometimes so much that 1 cup of flour may actually equal 1½ cups. Such imprecision can be critical to a cake or quick bread, often spelling the difference between disaster and success.

But where we students were finally and irrevocably won over to weighing was in the measuring of butter, lard and shortening. How messy and time-consuming it is to let a fat soften until plastic, then pack it into a dry-cup measure, only to scrape it right out again. (And of course, it's impossible to get every smidgeon of fat out of the cup, so here, too, is an unnecessary variable.) With a gram scale, we needed only to lay a piece of wax paper on the scale, then spoon the fat directly onto the paper until we had exactly the number of grams called for in a particular recipe. Five times as fast—and a hundred times as neat (no dishwashing needed).

It's only natural that we should resist changing anything so habitual as our way of cooking. And truth to tell, most of us may never be called upon to weigh flour in grams or measure milk in milliliters, although it's fairly certain that the children now in school will grow up knowing how. Let's hope so. I honestly think it behooves all of us who travel abroad, who enjoy collecting foreign cookbooks and trying out at home the specialties we've enjoyed overseas, to give metrics our best shot. Many foreign cookbooks are translated into English, but often not into American measures. Because metrics are far less mystifying and a lot more accurate than our present cup system, I urge you at least to try **to bake** the metric way. You may discover, as I did, that your pastries are flakier and your cakes more feathery than you dreamed possible.

About the recipes in this baking chapter

For those of you who wish to continue using cup measures, the American measures in the left-hand columns of the lists of ingredients are expressed in the accustomed way. In the metric right-hand columns, however, with only a few exceptions (for small quantities), the amounts for dry ingredients and shortening are given by weight in grams only because I do believe this is the best way to take advantage of the metric system for baking. You will notice in other parts of the book that I am more lenient and less "European" and use quite a few metric volumes for solid and dry ingredients. But when you get to more baking recipes in Part II in the chapter on Sweets, you'll see that I have stuck to my principles—in the metric columns, it's grams all the way. NOTE: *The gram (and milliliter) amounts are all carefully calculated and in some instances highly specific wherever necessary to ensure the recipe's success. Be sure to follow them.*

About metric equivalents

Thanks to the easy subdivision of metric amounts, the approximate rounded-out conversions from American to metric are sensible numbers that are nevertheless accurate. If you decide to "cook metric," each recipe in this book tells you all you need to know for that recipe. However, in the **Appendix** you will find a full set of **tables of equivalents,** which show you the difference between approximate and precise conversion and provide a fast reference to many details that you will find useful in marketing, using other cookbooks and foreign cookbooks and handling the measuring of ingredients in either the metric or American system.

Getting set for metric—
the equipment needed

A gram scale: A good scale is a major investment, so be choosy. Insist, first of all, upon a scale that has a large flat pan for holding the food to be weighed (the pan should be removable so that it can be washed easily). Second, select a gram scale calibrated in increments as fine as five or ten grams. I recently happened upon a trim import marked off in two-gram increments with a digital read-out and overall capacity of one kilogram (1000 grams or 2.2 pounds) that meets my needs perfectly. One kilogram may seem a limited capacity. For weighing a turkey or joint of beef, perhaps (but is there any reason to reweigh these, since the butcher or supermarket marks the weights on the packages or sales slips?). When baking, you will rarely deal in quantities larger than one kilogram. (This, after all, amounts to a lot—10 cups of sifted all-purpose flour.) As for dual scales (those calibrated in both grams and ounces), I see no real necessity for them.

Liquid measuring cups: If you've recently bought one of the new spouted plastic cups or the standard flameproof glass cups, you know that they are already being calibrated in both cups and milliliters. I presently have two 1-cup (240 ml), two 1-pint (500 ml) and two 1-quart (1 L) measures and keep them all busy.

Dual thermometers: You will need them for your oven, for roasting meats, for making candies and jellies and for deep-fat frying. Here, I **do** find it helpful to have the Fahrenheit and Celsius scales side by side. Besides, it's easier to find dual thermometers today than those calibrated only in Celsius. A trip to your local hardware store should be all that's necessary to equip yourself.

Straightedge: For measuring pots and pans, pastry thicknesses and diameters, etc., you will need a ruler marked off in centimeters. Any good art supply store will stock them.

Measuring spoons: These will remain the same. When European cooks use standardized measuring spoons, the capacities of the spoons are virtually the same as our own and I call for them throughout this book. I think it's absurd to specify such infinitesimal volumes as 1.5 ml (about ¼ teaspoon) or even 5 ml (1 teaspoon) or 15 ml (1 tablespoon).

NOTE: *I've broken one of the rules set up by the Metric Committee of the American Home Economics Committee by calling here and there for half kilos and liters. I do so because I have lived and cooked abroad and am simply following the system used there, which has passed the test of nearly two centuries. A person going into a market in, say, Lisbon, would never ask for 500 grams of grapes or 500 milliliters of wine. He or she would quite simply and sensibly request half a kilo or half a liter.*

The key ingredients of baking and their functions

Flours: These provide the framework for breads, cakes and pastries, thanks to an elastic protein contained in flours called **gluten.** The flour you choose (i.e., cake, pastry, all-purpose or bread flour) and the percentage of gluten it contains will determine the tenderness or toughness, fineness or coarseness of the final product. Rough, chewy country breads, for example, are made with bread flours, which contain a high proportion of gluten; tender-crumbed cakes and pastries are made, respectively, with silken, low-gluten cake or pastry flours—at least by chefs. (Home cooks tend to use all-purpose flour for everything, and a good choice it is. It contains moderate amounts of gluten that can be developed through kneading or left alone). NOTE: *Unbleached flours, the choice of many cooks today because they contain no chemical bleaches, produce cakes of slightly lower volume and coarser texture than do the bleached flours.*

Whole wheat (or graham) flour is simply the whole kernel, milled, with none of the husk or oily germ removed. (Because of the oil in the germ, whole wheat flour has poor keeping qualities and quickly turns rancid; I store mine in a tightly sealed screw-top jar in the refrigerator and find that it stays fresh for about a year.) Whole wheat flour is usually too glutenous to make good bread unless tempered by the addition of all-purpose flour or tenderized by the addition of sugar and butter. (Both interfere with the development of gluten strands during kneading and soften the end product.) Rye flour, on the other hand, is virtually glutenless, and thus rye breads must rely upon bread or all-purpose flour to provide the necessary framework.

Sugars: Flavor is not their sole function. As I've just pointed out, sugar has the power to tenderize gluten. It also supplies food for the yeast used to leaven bread and accelerates browning. (Browning, after all, is nothing more than caramelization of sugar or starch.) Brown sugars, because of their ability to absorb atmospheric moisture (hydrolize), make unusually moist breads and cakes.

Fats: Lard (the rendered fat of hogs), vegetable shortenings, butter and margarine are the principal fats used in baking. Their function is to tenderize the crumb of cakes and breads, to separate the "flakes" or "leaves" of pastry by melting between the starchy layers as they crisp during baking. They also impart flavor and sometimes color. NOTE: *Butter and margarine have less shortening power than lard or vegetable shortenings because they are only 80 percent fat. And in my experience, butter has even less shortening power than margarine (because of the milk solids), as you know only too well if you have ever substituted margarine for butter in a favorite cookie recipe and watched the individual cookies run together as they bake, forming a solid sheet. The moral of this? Do not substitute one shortening for another unless a recipe spells out the alternatives for you. And never, ever, substitute a cooking* *oil for a fat. Its physical and chemical properties are different and willy-nilly substitutions can ruin perfectly good recipes.*

Eggs: Largely protein, eggs coagulate when heated, firming up the framework of breads and cakes. Egg whites, when beaten, can hold an impressive amount of air, which expands when heated (together with the moisture of the whites), pushing soufflés, sponge and angel cakes to stratospheric heights. Eggs also add color, flavor and considerable food value to baked goods. NOTE: *Fresh eggs will whip to greater volume than old ones, and room-temperature eggs will beat up more rapidly than refrigerator-cold ones. If eggs are truly over the hill, the whites will be so thin and watery that they will collapse almost as fast as you can beat them. And even the freshest egg whites, if overbeaten, will deflate because you've stretched them beyond their limits. To minimize this risk, chefs routinely stabilize the foam of beaten whites by adding a pinch of salt and/or cream of tartar when the whites are at the frothy stage, then as added insurance, gradually beat in a little of the sugar called for in a recipe. We all know, of course, that the tiniest speck of fat in a bowl of whites will keep them from mounting to stiff peaks, which not only means that there should be no yolk among the whites but also that the bowl, beater and cook's hands be pristine.*

Liquids: Their roles are multiple. First, they dissolve sugars, salt and yeast, enabling their uniform distribution throughout a batter or dough. They also hydrate (moisten) both the starch and the gluten of flours, helping to build the foundation of breads, cakes and pastries. Finally, they activate baking powders, initiating the leavening process.

Leavenings: Air and steam, as we've already seen, are the powerful leaveners of soufflés, sponge cakes and angel cakes. But there is a third and more important leavener used to make baked goods light and porous: carbon dioxide gas, which can be produced either chemically or biologically.

CHEMICAL LEAVENING AGENTS: These are **baking powders** or **baking soda** used in conjunction with an acid ingredient such as sour milk, molasses, honey, fruit juice or vinegar. Two basic types of commercial baking powders are widely available today: **the single-acting** (either slow phosphate powders or fast tartrates, which cake specialists favor because they produce cakes of uncommonly fine texture) and **the double-acting** (combination powders that react first when moistened and then again in the oven). Double-acting powders are the best all-round leaveners because they are efficient and relatively fail-safe. NOTE: *If you should be caught short, mid-recipe, with insufficient baking powder, you can easily improvise one as follows: Blend ¾ teaspoon cream of tartar with ¼ teaspoon of baking soda. It will have the leavening power of 1 teaspoon of baking powder.*

BIOLOGICAL LEAVENINGS: The best known is yeast, now available as dry granules in handy dated foil packets or compressed into cakes. The cakes are much more perishable than active dry yeast and less readily available. All yeast should be stored in the refrigerator to prolong its life. Yeasts are microscopic organisms that feed upon sugar, breaking it down into carbon dioxide, which does the leavening, and alcohol, which volatilizes during baking. But certain bacteria also have the power to leaven breads as our great-great-great-grandmothers knew when they made their way west in covered wagons, coddling their sourdough starters. (These starters, actually, contained both bacteria and wild airborne yeasts.) The salt-rising bread of the Old South is a less well known but no less lovely bacteria-leavened bread, and I include a recipe for it in this section.

The methods of mixing

How you mix a batter or dough determines the degree of gluten development and thus the ultimate texture of a bread, cake or pastry: spongy vs. flaky, coarse vs. fine, tender vs. tough. Here are the classic methods:

The muffin method (*used for muffins, quick breads, pancakes, waffles, popovers and Yorkshire puddings*): The dry ingredients are sifted together into the mixing bowl and a well is made in the center of them. The eggs are beaten, then combined with the liquid and melted fat and dumped into the well of the dry ingredients. For muffins and most quick bread loaves, the object is to stir only enough to moisten the dry ingredients (no matter if the batter is lumpy; it will smooth out during baking and the muffins will be meltingly tender on the tongue). Pancakes and waffles should be beaten slightly longer—but only until the batter is smooth or they will be tough. Popovers and Yorkshire puddings, on the other hand, should be beaten hard. Your aim is to develop the gluten as much as possible so that they will puff dramatically without collapsing.

The pastry method (*used for pastries and biscuits*): The dry ingredients are sifted together into the mixing bowl, then the fat is cut in with a pastry blender or two knives until crumbly (I cut the fat in until about the texture of uncooked oatmeal). The liquid is then scattered over the fat-flour mixture while you toss all lightly with a fork. The point is to mix just until the pastry holds together, no longer, or you will develop the gluten and toughen the pastry.

The standard cake method (*used for most butter cakes and many quick breads*): The fat and sugar are creamed until silvery-light, the eggs are beaten in together with the flavoring, then the sifted dry ingredients (flour, leavening and salt, if any) are added alternately with the liquid. NOTE: *You should always begin and end with the dry ingredients and stir after each addition only enough to combine the last ingredient. For the average cake, you should use about five additions for the dry ingredients and three for the liquid.* A variation on this method is to separate the eggs, beat the yolks in as above, then fold the beaten whites in at the end.

The dump method (*used for butter cakes and quick breads*): The combined and sifted dry ingredients go into the mixing bowl first (usually the largest electric mixer bowl), then the combined liquids (including the beaten eggs) are dumped in and the two are beaten a minute or two at moderate mixer speed until combined.

The angel food cake method: The flour and sugar are both sifted, and often some of the sugar is combined with the flour. The egg whites are beaten until frothy, then cream of tartar, salt and flavorings are beaten in; next, some of the sugar is beaten in gradually until the whites are stiff and glossy. Finally, the flour or flour-sugar mixture is sifted, a little bit at a time, over the beaten whites, and folded in very gently so as not to deflate them.

The sponge cake method: The egg yolks are beaten hard and long with the sugar and flavorings until the color and consistency of mayonnaise (the mixture should be thick enough to form flat ribbons that fall back upon themselves when the beater is withdrawn). The sifted dry ingredients are added next, a little bit at the time, and finally, the egg whites, beaten to soft peaks, are folded in. There are also shortcut sponge cake methods, and you'll find an excellent one among the recipes in this chapter.

What went wrong?
(THE CLASSIC CAUSES OF FAILURES IN CAKES AND BREADS)

	FAULT	CAUSE
CAKES AND QUICK BREAD LOAVES	Batter overflows pan	Too much sugar, or pan too full
	Sticky or gritty crust	Too much sugar
	Fallen center	Too much sugar
	Coarse texture	Too much sugar, or undermixing, or too slow an oven
	Rubbery texture	Too much egg, or undermixing
	Uneven texture; lumps	Undermixing
	Fallen loaves; heavy or greasy bottom layer	Too much shortening, or too little flour
	Compact, leaden texture	Too little baking powder
	Collapsed loaves and bitter flavor	Too much baking powder, or too little flour
	Compact, dry texture	Too much flour
	Humped or cracked surface	Too much flour
	Tunnels, tough crumb	Too much flour and/or overmixing
	Lopsided loaves	Unlevel oven
	Uneven browning	Pans touching oven walls or one another

MUFFINS	Humped or peaked centers	Overmixing
	Tunnels, coarse texture	Overmixing
	Tough crumb	Too much egg and/or overmixing
BISCUITS	Heavy, flat biscuits	Too little baking powder and/or overmanipulation of dough
	Sour, mottled biscuits	Too much baking powder and/or undermixing
YEAST BREADS	Off or sour odor, gray color	Too much yeast
	Coarse texture, misshapen loaves	Overrisen dough
	Collapsed or compact, heavy loaves	Overrisen dough
	Mushroom-shaped loaves with "overhanging eaves"	Overrisen dough, or too slow an oven
	Loaves with sunken centers	Overrisen dough, or underkneading
	Small, poorly browned loaves	Overrisen dough, or too little liquid or yeast, or too much salt (salt inhibits yeast growth)
	Loaves with cracked sides	Underrisen dough
	Heavy, doughy loaves	Too much flour and/or underbaking
	Loaves streaked with gluey strands	Not removing crust that forms on dough as it rises. TO PREVENT: *Keep dough surface buttered.*
	Foul-smelling, ropy or slimy loaves	Dough contaminated by bacteria. NOTE: *Do not eat such bread!*

Pão
(PORTUGUESE COUNTRY BREAD)

MAKES TWO 7-INCH (18 CM) ROUND LOAVES

The Portuguese may be the world's best bakers of bread, as those lucky enough to live near such Portuguese-American communities as Provincetown or New Bedford, Massachusetts, know well. The most famous Portuguese bread, perhaps, is the egg-and-butter-rich "sweet bread." Less well known, but no less delicious, is the rough country bread of Portugal. It's served everywhere, fresh from the oven and richly aromatic of yeast.

3 packages	active dry yeast	3 packages
4 cups (about)	sifted all-purpose flour (enough to make a stiff but workable dough)	400 g (about)
¼ cup	sugar	50 g
1¼ cups	warm water (105–115°F. or 41–46°C.)	300 ml
2 teaspoons	salt	2 teaspoons
	OPTIONAL SALT GLAZE:	
2 tablespoons	water	2 tablespoons
1 teaspoon	salt	1 teaspoon

Combine yeast, 1 cup (100 g) flour, the sugar and ¾ cup (180 ml) warm water in a large bowl; cover with a clean dry dishtowel, set in a warm, dry spot and let rise until light and spongy—about 1 hour. Stir down; add salt and remaining warm water. Beat in remaining flour, about 1 cup (100 g) at a time, to make a stiff dough. Knead hard on a lightly floured board for 5 minutes.

Shape dough into a ball, place in a large buttered bowl, turn dough in bowl so buttered side is up, cover with cloth, set in a warm, dry spot and let rise until doubled in bulk—1 to 1½ hours. Punch dough down, knead, shape and let rise as before.

Punch dough down once again, knead quickly until satiny and elastic, divide in half and shape into two high round loaves. Place each in a lightly greased pie tin, cover and let rise ¾ to 1 hour until doubled in bulk. If you want to give the bread a "hard" finish, mix the salt glaze ingredients and brush loaves lightly. Bake in a hot oven (400°F. or 205°C.) for 10 minutes, reduce temperature to moderately hot (375°F. or 190°C.) and bake 10 to 15 minutes longer or until loaves are richly browned and sound hollow when thumped. Cool on wire racks, then break or cut into chunks and serve with plenty of soft sweet butter.

Yogurt batter bread

MAKES TWO 9 × 5 × 3-INCH (23 × 13 × 8 CM) LOAVES

Batter bread dough, as compared to conventional bread dough, is too thin and sticky to knead. To develop the gluten (the wheat protein that provides the framework of bread), you must beat the batter until you think your arm will drop off. If you have a large-bowl, heavy-duty processor or an electric mixer, you're in luck because either will do the beating for you without complaint. This particular bread has an irresistible yeast bouquet and an uncommonly tender crumb. Cool the bread thoroughly before you cut it, and slice with a serrated knife so that you don't damage or deflate the loaves.

| 2 packages | active dry yeast | 2 packages |
| ⅓ cup | warm water (105° to 115°F. or 41° to 46°C.) | 80 ml |

⅓ cup	sugar	65 g
2 cartons (8 oz. each)	plain yogurt, at room temperature	2 cartons (226 g each)
¾ cup (1½ sticks)	melted unsalted butter	180 ml (1½ sticks)
6 cups (about)	sifted all-purpose flour	600 g (about)
1½ teaspoons	baking powder	1½ teaspoons
1 teaspoon	baking soda	1 teaspoon
½ teaspoon	salt	½ teaspoon

Combine the yeast, water and sugar in a small bowl and set aside for the moment. In the work bowl of a large-bowl, heavy-duty food processor equipped with the metal chopping blade or in the largest bowl of a heavy-duty mixer, combine the yogurt and butter; beat in the yeast mixture. NOTE: *If you have neither processor nor mixer, hand-mix the ingredients in a large bowl.* Sift half the flour with the baking powder, soda and salt and mix, 1 cup (100 g) at a time, into the yeast mixture. With a food processor, this will mean three to four on-offs of the motor, no more. Now add the remaining flour the same way, 1 cup (100 g) at a time, to make a very soft and sticky dough. The dough should not seem runny, and if it does, mix in a bit of additional flour. Now beat the dough hard—about four to five 10-second churnings of the processor or about 3 minutes at moderately high mixer speed. If you hand-beat the dough, you must keep at it until the dough is extremely elastic and begins to blister. Turn the dough into a warm, buttered bowl (to warm the bowl, rinse it with hot water and dry it), then brush the surface well with melted butter. Cover with a clean dry cloth and let the dough rise in a warm, dry, draft-free spot about 1 hour or until doubled in bulk.

Stir the dough down with a wooden spoon, then beat hard with the spoon for a minute or two—just until all large bubbles in the dough have been broken. Divide the dough in half and place in two well-buttered 9 × 5 × 3-inch (23 × 13 × 8 cm) loaf pans, smoothing the surface of each loaf as much as possible. Cover the loaves with a cloth and let rise about 30 minutes or until doubled in bulk.

Bake the loaves, uncovered, in a moderate oven (350°F. or 175°C.) for 40 to 45 minutes or until they are nicely browned and sound hollow when you thump them with your fingers. Remove the loaves to wire racks, turn the pans on their sides and allow the loaves to cool in the pans for 15 minutes. Loosen the loaves around the edges with a thin-blade spatula, turn out, then cool, right side up, for 1 hour before cutting.

NOTE: *This bread freezes superbly. Wrap snugly in aluminum foil or several thicknesses of plastic food wrap, date and label, then quick-freeze by setting directly on the freezing surface (usually the "floor") of a 0°F. (−18°C.) freezer. Use the frozen loaves within 3 months.*

Colonial salt-rising bread

MAKES A 9 × 5 × 3-INCH (23 × 13 × 8 CM) LOAF

In the days before commercial yeasts, women leavened their breads with starters—bubbly mixtures of flour, milk and sugar that provided the mediums in which airborne yeasts or bacteria could thrive, producing carbon dioxide (the gas that does the leavening in breads). Sourdoughs, of course, are well known. Less familiar, and I think superior, is the old southern salt-rising bread that has a distinctly sour taste and an uncommonly tender crumb. Be forewarned, however. It takes **time** to get the "starter" started—several days, at best. But once the starter is bubbly, you can keep it from one batch of bread to the next, provided you bake bread as often as once a week. I usually take out about half a cup (120 ml) of the sponge, add a teaspoon or so of sugar, then place it in a small crock, cover it with cheesecloth and keep it in a warm, dry spot. Is salt-rising bread worth all the time and trouble it takes to make it? I think so. The bread is wonderful as is, even better when toasted and buttered. But you must judge for yourself.

1 cup	scalded milk, cooled to room temperature	240 ml
¼ cup	unsifted stone-ground cornmeal	60 ml
3 tablespoons, in all	sugar	3 tablespoons, in all
1 tablespoon	salt	1 tablespoon
7 large	dried white beans (navy, pea or Great Northern beans)	7 large
1 cup	warm water (105° to 115°F. or 41° to 46°C.)	240 ml
4½ cups	sifted all-purpose flour	450 g
2 tablespoons	melted unsalted butter	2 tablespoons

Place the milk in a half-gallon (2 L) preserving jar; add the cornmeal, 2 tablespoons of the sugar, the salt and the dried beans (these help get the starter going). Cover tight, shake well to blend, then uncover. Place a piece of cheesecloth over the jar and secure with a rubber band. Place a rack or trivet in the bottom of a kettle deep enough to contain the jar. Set a flame-tamer on a burner, set the kettle on the flame-tamer, then pour in enough water to two-thirds fill the kettle. Heat until the water reaches 120°F. (49°C.). Set the bottle of starter on the rack in the kettle and let stand about 24 hours. NOTE: *It isn't worthwhile staying up all night to keep the water at the proper temperature! What I do is begin the starter first thing in the morning, maintaining the proper temperature by turning the burner heat to its lowest point for 15 to 20 minutes, then snapping it off for another 15 to 20—all day long. When I'm ready for bed, I simply shut the burner off and let the starter stand in the water overnight. Next day, I have a look at it. It should by now be becoming bubbly. If not, I start the on-off cycle of the burner all over again, keeping the water as nearly as possible at 120°F. (49°C). until the starter is bubbly. If you can find a warm spot somewhere in your house where the starter can be maintained at about this temperature, you're in luck. Simply set the starter there and let it ferment unattended. That, of course, is what colonial women did.*

Once the starter is good and bubbly, you are ready for the next step, which is to make the sponge. Using a slotted spoon, fish out and discard all 7 white beans. Now add the remaining tablespoon of sugar, the warm water, 2 cups (200 g) of the flour and the melted butter to the starter in the jar; stir well to mix, then replace the cheesecloth. Now keep the sponge in the water bath at a slightly lower temperature (115°F. or 46°C.), again raising and lowering the burner heat as necessary to keep the temperature constant. Also add more water to the kettle as needed to keep the jar half submerged. It will take 24 to 48 hours for the sponge to become spongy (partially leavened). I try to keep the sponge warm during the day, then shut the burner off at night just as I did with the starter. If you have a warm spot somewhere, keep the jar of sponge there and check it more often; the fermentation will probably take place more rapidly if you keep the sponge warm day and night.

As soon as the sponge has large bubbles about the surface and looks light and foamy (it should also smell distinctly yeasty or sour), empty it into a large, **warm** mixing bowl. NOTE: *If you intend to save a starter for your next batch of salt-rising bread, now is the time to spoon ½ cup (120 ml) of it into a small crock. Mix in 1 teaspoon of sugar, cover with cheesecloth and set in a warm, dry spot. The starter should keep for about 1 week under optimum conditions; if it seems to go flat, stir in another teaspoon of sugar (food).* Mix the remaining flour into the dough, then beat hard until shiny and elastic; at high mixer speed in the heavy-duty electric mixer fitted with the flat beater, 3 to 4 minutes should be sufficient.

Shape the dough into a ball, place in a **warm,** buttered bowl and butter the top of the dough generously. Cover with clean dry cloth and set in a warm, dry, draft-free spot until doubled in bulk. NOTE: *Salt-rising bread rises much more slowly than yeast bread and will probably require 12 hours to double in bulk. You must keep the surface of the dough well buttered, otherwise it will form a crust that will have to be scraped off and discarded. For this reason, it's best to let the dough rise during the day when you can keep an eye on it and brush the surface of the dough with melted butter whenever it looks dry.*

Once the dough has risen fully, punch it down, then beat hard once again until smooth and elastic. Shape into a loaf, place in a well-buttered 9 × 5 × 3-inch (23 × 13 × 8 cm) loaf pan, again cover with cloth and set in a warm, dry, draft-free spot to rise until double in bulk—this will take 1½ to 2 hours.

Bake the risen loaf for 10 minutes in a moderately hot oven (375°F. or 190°C.), then reduce the heat to moderate (350°F. or 175°C.) and bake 25 to 30 minutes longer until the loaf is nicely browned and sounds hollow when you thump it. Take the loaf from the oven and lay it on its side (still in its pan) on a wire rack. Cool for 15 minutes; loosen the loaf around the edge with a thin-blade spatula, then turn out. Cool upright on a wire rack to room temperature before serving. To slice the loaf, use a sharp serrated knife and a gentle sawing motion. This bread is uncommonly light and may break apart or compact into a doughy mass if cut with a dull knife.

Stone-ground whole wheat bread

MAKES TWO 9 × 5 × 3-INCH (23 × 13 × 8 CM) LOAVES

Stone-ground whole wheat (available at most health food stores) makes a denser, richer loaf than mass-produced whole wheat or graham flour. But what really makes this bread unique is the addition of ginger and nutmeg—just enough to give the bread tang, but not so much as to make it spicy. This bread freezes superbly, by the way, so foil-wrap and freeze one of the loaves to enjoy later.

1½ cups	warm water (105° to 115°F. or 41° to 46°C.)	350 ml
2 packages	active dry yeast	2 packages
1 tablespoon	granulated sugar	1 tablespoon
½ cup	milk	120 ml
¼ pound (1 stick)	unsalted butter	115 g (1 stick)
¼ cup	firmly packed light brown sugar	55 g
1 tablespoon	salt	1 tablespoon
¼ cup	molasses	60 ml
3½ cups	unsifted whole wheat flour	450 g
2½ cups	sifted all-purpose flour	250 g
½ teaspoon	ground ginger	½ teaspoon
¼ teaspoon	freshly grated nutmeg	¼ teaspoon

In a small mixing bowl, combine the water, yeast and granulated sugar; set aside in a warm spot. Place the milk, butter, brown sugar and salt in a small heavy saucepan and bring just to the simmering point over moderate heat. Remove from the heat and mix in the molasses. Cool until slightly more than lukewarm (105° to 115°F. or 41° to 46°C.), then stir into the yeast mixture.

Place the whole wheat flour, all-purpose flour, ginger and nutmeg in a large mixing bowl. (If you have a heavy-duty electric mixer, use the large mixer bowl.) Stir well to combine. Make a well in the center of the dry ingredients, pour in the yeast mixture all at once and mix slowly, pushing the "walls" of flour down into the well and stirring until they are moistened and incorporated into the dough. Now beat the dough hard—at high mixer speed with the flat beater (**not** the dough hook) for 2 to 3 minutes. If you are beating the dough by hand, you must keep at it for about 5 minutes until it is shiny and elastic. The dough is too soft at this point to knead, hence the necessity of beating it hard enough to develop the gluten (protein) in the flour, which will provide the framework of the bread.

Shape the dough into a ball, place in a **warm** buttered bowl, turn it in the bowl so that it is buttered all over, cover with a clean dishtowel, set in a warm, draft-free spot and allow the dough to rise until doubled in bulk—about 1½ hours. Punch the dough down, turn onto a lightly floured pastry cloth and knead vigorously for 3 to 5 minutes, just until smooth and satiny.

Divide the dough in half, shape into two loaves and place in well-buttered 9 × 5 × 3-inch (23 × 13 × 8 cm) loaf pans. Cover with a cloth and set in a warm draft-free spot to rise. It will take only ¾ to 1 hour for the loaves to double in bulk. Bake, uncovered, in a moderately hot oven (375°F. or 190°C.) for 40 to 45 minutes or until the loaves are richly browned and sound hollow when you thump them with your fingers.

Remove the loaves from the oven and lay the pans on their sides on a large wire rack to cool for 15 minutes. (Putting the pans on their sides rather than right side up allows the bread to firm up without deflating.) Loosen the loaves with a thin-blade spatula, turn out on wire racks and cool, right side up, before cutting.

Ljugarn almond-cardamom coffee ring

MAKES 2 LARGE ROUND COFFEE RINGS

Cardamom is the spice Swedish cooks prefer for sweet breads, cakes and cookies. You can use commercially ground cardamom, but you'll find the flavor fuller and fresher if you grind the spice yourself (the inner dark seeds only, not the pale, puffy outer pods), using a mortar and pestle or one of the compact electric coffee grinders. On a recent trip to the Baltic island of Gotland, I sampled several versions of this butter-and-almond-rich coffee ring and think that this one—my version of the one baked by a tiny Konditori in the resort village of Ljugarn—far and away the best. This recipe makes two large coffee rings, so freeze one of them to enjoy later. Simply wrap snugly in foil and store in the freezer. When ready to serve, pop the foil-wrapped, solidly frozen ring into a moderately slow oven (325°F. or 165°C.) and warm 20 to 30 minutes.

	DOUGH:	
2 packages	active dry yeast	2 packages
¼ cup	warm water (about 105–115°F. or 41–46°C.)	60 ml
¼ pound (1 stick)	unsalted butter, at room temperature	115 g (1 stick)
½ cup	sugar	100 g
1 teaspoon	cardamom seeds, pulverized (use inner dark seeds only) or ½ teaspoon ground cardamom	1 teaspoon

¼ teaspoon	salt	¼ teaspoon
⅔ cup	scalded milk	160 ml
1 large	egg	1 large
3½ cups (about)	sifted all-purpose flour	350 g (about)

FILLING:

1 package (7 oz.)	sweetened almond paste	1 package (198 g)
2 tablespoons	sugar	2 tablespoons
6 tablespoons	heavy cream	6 tablespoons
¼ teaspoon	almond extract	¼ teaspoon
¼ teaspoon	vanilla extract	¼ teaspoon
¼ pound (1 stick)	unsalted butter, at room temperature	115 g (1 stick)
1 cup	finely chopped blanched almonds	240 ml

GLAZE:

| 1 large | egg white, whisked with 2 tablespoons cold water | 1 large |

For the dough: Mix the yeast with the water in a measuring cup and let stand until foamy, 5 to 10 minutes. Meanwhile, combine the butter, sugar, cardamom, salt and scalded milk in a large mixing bowl and cool to lukewarm, stirring occasionally. Mix in the yeast, the egg, then 2 cups (200 g) of the flour, beating until smooth and elastic. Work in the remaining 1½ cups (150 g) flour or enough to make a moderately soft, manageable dough. Turn the dough onto a lightly floured board and knead 5 minutes. Shape the dough into a ball, place in a large buttered bowl, turn it buttered side up, cover with a dry cloth and let rise in a warm, dry spot until doubled in bulk—about 1½ hours.

Meanwhile, begin the filling: Blend together the almond paste, sugar, cream, almond extract and vanilla until smooth. Set aside.

Punch the risen dough down and knead 5 minutes; divide in half. Roll half the dough very thin on a lightly floured pastry cloth with a lightly floured, stockinette-covered rolling pin into a rectangle about 22 × 14 inches (55 × 35 cm). Spread with half the butter, then with half the almond filling, leaving ¼-inch (¾ cm) margins all round. Sprinkle with half the nuts, then roll up jelly-roll style from the short side so that you have a roll about 22 inches (55 cm) long.

Ease the roll, seam side down, onto an ungreased baking sheet and bend into a ring, tucking one end into the other and moistening the edges to secure them. Using a very sharp knife, slice almost—but not quite—through to the inner edge of the ring at 1-inch (2½ cm) intervals. Twist the "slices" on their sides so that the filling shows, overlapping them as you move around the ring. Roll, fill and shape the remaining dough the same way; place on a separate baking sheet.

Cover the rings with dry cloths and let rise until doubled in bulk—about 1½ hours.

Brush the rings lightly with the glaze, then bake in a moderately hot oven 375°F. or 190°C.) for 25 to 30 minutes or until richly browned. Serve piping hot or at room temperature—no extra butter needed!

Julkaka (Norwegian Christmas cake)

MAKES A 9 × 5 × 3-INCH (23 × 13 × 8 CM) LOAF

Cake is perhaps the wrong word, for this fruit-strewn, yeast-raised loaf is more bread than cake. The recipe comes from Margaret Perry, a Connecticut-Yankee friend and fellow writer whose roots are Norwegian. Peg says that her mother used to make *Julkaka* every Christmas and because the Connecticut winters of her childhood were so cold, she remembers her mother letting the bread rise overnight in a bowl wrapped in her fur coat. "First came a dishtowel," explained Peg, "then a metal tray that just fit inside the top of the dough bowl, then my mother's sealskin coat with the fox collar." It's a marvelous image. Of course, we needn't take such measures in these days of superheated houses and superactive yeasts. I found that the first rising took just one hour, the second rising even less. NOTE: *For this recipe you must grind the cardamom seeds yourself—not the puffy, white outer pods but the dark inner seeds. For a teaspoon of ground cardamom, you'll need the seeds of about twenty large pods. And how does one grind cardamom seeds? You can pulverize them easily with a mortar and pestle; I use one of the compact little electric coffee grinders, which whirs them to powder in seconds. I keep one of these sturdy little machines on hand specifically for grinding spices and making curry powders.*

3 tablespoons	sugar	3 tablespoons
1 teaspoon	freshly ground cardamom	1 teaspoon
1 teaspoon	salt	1 teaspoon
1½ cups	milk, scalded and cooled to 105°–115°F. or 41°–46°C.	350 ml
1 package	active dry yeast	1 package
4 cups	sifted all-purpose flour	400 g
1 cup	seedless raisins, coarsely chopped	240 ml
¼ pound	candied citron, cut into small dice	115 g
1 large	egg, lightly beaten	1 large
¼ cup (½ stick)	melted unsalted butter	60 ml (½ stick)

In a teacup, combine the sugar, cardamom and salt and set aside. Pour the milk into a large mixing bowl, sprinkle in the yeast and stir until dissolved. Now sprinkle 1 cup of the flour (100 g) over the raisins and citron; toss well to mix and reserve. Blend 1 cup (100 g) of the remaining flour into the yeast mixture; blend in the reserved cardamom mixture, then stir in another 1 cup (100 g) of the flour. Beat in the egg, then the melted butter. Now work in the remaining flour, then the dredged fruits and all dredging flour. Beat hard for several minutes—the dough is too soft and sticky to knead—then turn onto a lightly floured board and allow the dough to stand unattended at room temperature for 15 minutes.

Place the dough in a well-buttered bowl, shaping it into a ball with well-buttered hands so that the top is nicely buttered, too. Cover with a clean cloth and set in a warm, dry, draft-free spot until doubled in bulk—this will take about an hour. Punch the dough down and beat hard for a minute or so. NOTE: *You will find this extremely difficult because the dough at this point will be very rubbery with a life of its own. But persist! It's important to knock the big bubbles of gas out of the dough if the* Julkaka *is to have the proper fine and feathery crumb.*

Now place the dough in a well-buttered and floured 9 × 5 × 3-inch (23 × 13 × 8 cm) loaf pan, patting into a loaf shape with well-buttered hands. Cover with cloth and let rise in a warm, dry, draft-free spot until doubled in bulk—45 to 50 minutes.

Bake the *Julkaka* in a moderately hot oven (375°F. or 190°C.) for 45 to 50 minutes or until the loaf has risen well above the rim of the pan, is richly browned and sounds hollow when thumped with your fingers. Remove the bread from the oven and cool it in the pan, laid on its side, on a wire rack for 10 minutes. With a thin-blade spatula, loosen the bread around the edges, turn out onto a wire rack and cool, right side up, for at least 30 minutes before cutting.

Because of the bread's delicate crumb and abundance of fruits, use your sharpest serrated knife and a gentle sawing motion for slicing it. Serve with softened unsalted butter. NOTE: *I like to toast the bread lightly—just enough to crisp the outside, then spread with a little butter. Snugly wrapped in foil, this bread keeps well in the freezer. You need only slice from the frozen loaf the amount of bread you need, then rewrap the balance and return to the freezer.*

Soft and tender cream biscuits

MAKES 10 BISCUITS

Note that this recipe contains four ingredients only—and no shortening or milk, only heavy cream, which takes the place of both by moistening and shortening the biscuits. You **must** use heavy cream for this recipe and make certain that you shake the container well before you use the cream. Light cream or half-and-half simply will not do because neither has enough butterfat to shorten the biscuits properly. These biscuits are not as flaky as conventional biscuits made with vegetable shortening, but I think they're un-usually good and urge you to try them.

2 cups	sifted all-purpose flour	200 g
½ teaspoon	salt	½ teaspoon
1 tablespoon	baking powder	1 tablespoon
1 cup	heavy cream	240 ml

Sift the flour, salt and baking powder into a large bowl and make a well in the center. Whip the cream to soft peaks, dump into the bowl and mix in briskly with a fork—the dough should just hold together. Turn out onto a lightly floured pastry cloth and knead gently for about half a minute. Roll the dough out ½ inch (1½ cm) thick and cut into rounds, using a floured 2¾-inch (7 cm) biscuit cutter. Arrange the biscuits on ungreased baking sheets, spacing them about 1½ inches (4 cm) apart. Bake in a very hot oven (450°F. or 230°C.) for 10 to 12 minutes until risen and lightly browned. Serve at once with plenty of butter.

VARIATIONS:

Shortcakes: Prepare precisely as directed but stir ¼ cup (50 g) of granulated sugar into the sifted dry ingredients before mixing in the whipped cream. Cut and bake as directed, then use in making strawberry, blueberry, blackberry, peach or any other fruit shortcake.

Sesame sticks: Prepare the dough as directed, then roll ¼ inch (¾ cm) thick on a lightly floured pastry cloth. Cut into sticks about 3 inches (8 cm) long and ⅜ inch (1 cm) wide. Brush lightly with milk, then sprinkle with sesame seeds. Bake on ungreased baking sheets 5 to 7 minutes in a very hot oven (450°F. or 230°C.)—just until pale tan. Serve with cocktails or as a snack.

Poppy seed sticks: Prepare exactly as directed for Sesame Sticks above, but sprinkle with poppy seeds instead of sesame seeds. Serve with cocktails or as a snack.

Salt sticks: Reduce the amount of salt in the recipe to ¼ teaspoon, then prepare exactly as directed for Sesame Sticks above, but sprinkle with coarse or kosher salt instead of sesame seeds. Serve with cocktails or as a snack.

Crofter's scones

SERVES 6 TO 8

Scottish scones are not unlike Irish soda bread, particularly in this farm-style version, which is baked as a single pone (flat loaf) rather than as "cutouts." It's a fast and frugal bread, too. Best of all, it reheats splendidly if foil-wrapped and warmed about 10 minutes in a moderate oven.

1½ cups	sifted all-purpose flour	150 g
⅓ cup	sugar	65 g
½ teaspoon	salt	½ teaspoon
1½ teaspoons	baking powder	1½ teaspoons
¾ teaspoon	baking soda	¾ teaspoon
¼ pound (1 stick)	unsalted butter, cut into pats	115 g (1 stick)
½ cup	dried currants	120 ml
1 large	egg, beaten well with 2 tablespoons milk	1 large
	GLAZE:	
1 large	egg yolk beaten with 1 tablespoon milk	1 large

Sift the flour, sugar, salt, baking powder and soda together into a large mixing bowl. Using a pastry blender, cut in the butter until the mixture has the texture of coarse meal. Add the currants and toss well to dredge. Drizzle the egg-milk mixture evenly on top, tossing briskly with a fork just until you have a soft dough. Turn out on a lightly floured pastry cloth, knead gently once or twice, then roll into a circle about ¾ inch (2 cm) thick. Ease onto a lightly greased baking sheet. Score the surface of the scone in 12 pie-shaped wedges, then brush the glaze evenly on top. Bake in a hot oven (400°F. or 205°C.) for 20 to 25 minutes until touched with brown and the scone sounds hollow when you tap it. Cool briefly, then break into wedges. Split each wedge horizontally, tuck in a lump of sweet butter and serve.

Fresh blueberry scones

MAKES 8 TO 10 SCONES

Normally scones are rolled and cut like biscuits, but these, because of the plumpness and fragility of the blueberries, must be dropped from a spoon. I scoop up the dough in a tablespoon (it should be a well-rounded spoonful), drop it onto ungreased baking sheets, then flatten the surface of each scone with a lightly floured pancake turner. This flattening of the scones is important, indeed essential, if they are to bake evenly and be done inside by the time they are browned outside.

2 cups	sifted all-purpose flour	200 g
1 cup	fresh blueberries, washed, sorted, stemmed and patted very dry on paper toweling	240 ml
⅓ cup	sugar	65 g
1½ teaspoons	baking powder	1½ teaspoons
½ teaspoon	baking soda	½ teaspoon

¼ teaspoon	salt	¼ teaspoon
5 tablespoons + 1 teaspoon (⅔ stick)	unsalted butter, cut into pats	75 g (⅔ stick)
¾ cup	milk	180 ml

Sprinkle ½ cup (50 g) of the sifted flour over the blueberries and toss well to dredge; set aside. Sift the remaining flour with the sugar, baking powder, soda and salt into a large mixing bowl. Using a pastry blender, cut in the butter until the mixture is the texture of coarse meal. Add the berries and all dredging flour and toss well to mix. Drizzle the milk over the surface of the crumbly mixture, tossing briskly with a fork, just until the dough holds together. Drop by rounded tablespoonfuls onto ungreased baking sheets, spacing the scones about 3 inches (8 cm) apart. Dip a pancake turner into flour, then flatten each scone until it is uniformly 1 inch (2½ cm) thick. Bake the scones in a very hot oven (425°F. or 220°C.) 12 to 15 minutes until nicely browned. Remove the scones from the oven and cool about 3 minutes, then split, butter and serve.

Fine and feathery muffins

MAKES 10 TO 12 MUFFINS

There is a great temptation to overbeat muffin batters, and if you do, the muffins will be tough and filled with tunnels. Muffin batter should be stirred just until the dry ingredients are moistened by the combined liquids— no longer. It does not matter if there are lumps in the batter, even a few flecks of flour showing. These will disappear in the baking and you will be assured of crumbly-tender muffins of uniformly fine texture. TIP: *If you grease the bottoms of the muffin pan cups only, you'll get bigger muffins because they can cling to the pan sides as they rise. No, the muffins won't stick to the pans.*

2 cups	sifted all-purpose flour	200 g
1 tablespoon	baking powder	1 tablespoon
¾ teaspoon	salt	¾ teaspoon
3 tablespoons	granulated or light brown sugar	3 tablespoons
3 tablespoons	melted vegetable shortening	3 tablespoons
1 tablespoon	melted unsalted butter	1 tablespoon
1 large	egg, lightly beaten	1 large
1 cup	milk, at room temperature	240 ml

Sift the flour, baking powder and salt into a large bowl; stir in the sugar. Combine the shortening, butter, egg and milk. Make a well in the center of the dry ingredients, pour the combined liquids in all at once and stir briskly with a fork just until the dry ingredients are moistened. Spoon into muffin pan cups (with only the bottoms greased), filling each about two-thirds full. Bake, uncovered, in a hot oven (400°F. or 205°C.) for 20 minutes or until rounded on top and a rich amber brown. Remove the muffins from the oven, loosen each around the edges with a thin-blade spatula, then turn out and serve hot with plenty of butter.

VARIATIONS:

Date muffins: Sift the dry ingredients into the mixing bowl as directed; then stir in 4 tablespoons of light brown sugar and 1 cup of finely snipped pitted dates. Toss the dates in the dry ingredients well to dredge them. Make a well in the center of the dry ingredients, then pour in the combined liquids, mix and bake as directed.

Orange muffins: Sift the dry ingredients into the mixing bowl as directed, then stir in 4 tablespoons of light brown sugar and 1 tablespoon of finely grated orange rind. Make a well in the center of the dry ingredients, then pour in the combined liquids, mix and bake as directed.

Wheat germ muffins: Sift the dry ingredients into the mixing bowl as directed, then stir in 3 tablespoons of light brown sugar and ½ cup of wheat germ. Make a well in the center of the dry ingredients, then pour in the combined liquids, mix and bake as directed.

Golden corn muffins: Sift 1 cup (100 g) of sifted all-purpose flour into a mixing bowl with 4 teaspoons of baking powder and the salt. Stir in 2 cups (300 g) of yellow cornmeal and 4 tablespoons of light brown sugar. Stir well to mix. Combine the egg with the milk and ⅓ cup (80 ml) of melted vegetable shortening. Make a well in the center of the dry ingredients, pour in the combined liquids, then mix and bake as directed.

Fresh mushroom and sage bread

MAKES A 9 × 5 × 3-INCH (23 × 13 × 8 CM) LOAF

One of the characteristics of mushrooms is that they absorb and hold considerable moisture, even after they are cooked. So do not attempt to make this bread in wet or humid weather—as I first did—because the bread will become dismayingly soft and damp, almost like steamed pudding. It's essential, too, in sautéeing the mushrooms and onion, that you keep them over the heat until they have released all their juices and these have evaporated, leaving the skillet mixture thick and pastelike. I find this bread an excellent accompaniment to roast pork, chicken or turkey. And it toasts magnificently. Spread with a little softened butter, sprinkle lightly, if you like, with freshly grated Parmesan and toast in a moderately slow oven (325°F. or 165°C.)—15 to 20 minutes should be sufficient.

1 medium-size	yellow onion, peeled and finely minced	1 medium-size
3 tablespoons	unsalted butter	3 tablespoons
½ pound	mushrooms, wiped clean and finely minced	225 g
2 cups	sifted all-purpose flour	200 g
1 cup	yellow cornmeal	150 g
2 tablespoons	sugar	2 tablespoons
1 tablespoon	baking powder	1 tablespoon
1 teaspoon	rubbed sage	1 teaspoon
½ teaspoon	salt	½ teaspoon
¼ teaspoon	freshly ground black pepper	¼ teaspoon
⅛ teaspoon	crumbled leaf rosemary	⅛ teaspoon
⅛ teaspoon	crumbled leaf marjoram	⅛ teaspoon
4 tablespoons	freshly grated Parmesan cheese	4 tablespoons
⅓ cup (firmly packed)	vegetable shortening	60 g
2 very large	eggs, lightly beaten	2 very large
1¼ cups	milk	300 ml

Sauté the onion in the butter in a medium-size heavy skillet over moderate heat 5 to 8 minutes until limp and lightly touched with brown. (The faint caramel taste that develops in the browning of the onion improves the bread's flavor.) Add the mushrooms and sauté, stirring occasionally, 10 to 12 minutes until they are very dry and thick. Remove from the heat and let cool.

Meanwhile, combine the flour, cornmeal, sugar, baking powder, sage, salt, pepper, rosemary, marjoram and Parmesan in a large mixing bowl. Cut the shortening in, using a pastry blender or two knives, until the texture of coarse meal. Combine the eggs and milk. Make a well in the center of the dry ingredients and pour the milk mixture in all at once. Stir lightly—just enough to mix, no matter if a few small specks of dry ingredients show. If you overstir this delicate batter, the bread will be tough and coarse of grain. Gently, but thoroughly, fold in the mushroom mixture.

Spoon the batter into a generously greased and floured 9 × 5 × 3-inch (23 × 13 × 8 cm) loaf pan and bake, uncovered, in a moderate oven (350°F. or 175°C.) for 45 to 50 minutes, or until the loaf has begun to pull from the sides of the pan and is very springy to the touch. Remove the bread from the oven and cool it upright in its pan on a wire rack for 10 minutes. Carefully loosen the loaf around the edges with a spatula, then invert on a wire rack. Turn right side up and cool before slicing. NOTE: *Do not store this bread in the refrigerator, as it will absorb moisture and soften. The best way to store it is loosely wrapped in wax paper at room temperature. Eat within three days—not difficult to do, by the way.*

Oatmeal and chopped apple bread with walnuts

MAKES A 9 × 5 × 3-INCH (23 × 13 × 8 CM) LOAF

If you happen to have on hand a couple of large tart apples that are in danger of spoiling, you can put them to superlative use in this easy, quick, nutritious bread.

1½ cups	peeled, cored and coarsely chopped tart apples	350 ml
2 tablespoons	lemon juice	2 tablespoons
⅓ cup	firmly packed light brown sugar	70 g
2 cups	sifted all-purpose flour	200 g
1 cup	coarsely chopped walnuts	240 ml
2½ teaspoons	baking powder	2½ teaspoons
1 teaspoon	baking soda	1 teaspoon
½ teaspoon	ground cinnamon	½ teaspoon
¼ teaspoon	ground allspice	¼ teaspoon
¼ teaspoon	freshly grated nutmeg	¼ teaspoon
⅛ teaspoon	salt	⅛ teaspoon
1 cup	granulated sugar	200 g
1 cup	quick-cooking rolled oats	240 ml
1 cup	milk	240 ml
1 large	egg, lightly beaten	1 large
¼ cup (½ stick)	melted unsalted butter	60 ml (½ stick)

Sprinkle the apples with the lemon juice, add the brown sugar, stir well and set aside. Sprinkle ¼ cup (25 g) of the sifted flour over the walnuts, toss well to dredge and set aside also. Now sift the remaining flour with the baking powder, soda, cinnamon, allspice, nutmeg and salt directly into a large mixing bowl. Add the sugar and rolled oats and stir well to mix. Combine the milk with the egg and melted butter. Make a well in the center of the dry ingredients, pour the combined liquids in all at once and stir briskly, just enough to mix. Dump in the apple mixture and dredged walnuts (also all the dredging flour) and fold the two in together. Do not overmix the batter or the bread will be tough. Spoon into a well-greased and floured 9 × 5 × 3-inch (23 × 13 × 8 cm) loaf pan, spreading it well to the corners and smoothing the top as much as possible.

Bake the bread, uncovered, in a moderate oven (350°F. or 175°C.) for 1 hour or until the bread has pulled from the sides of the pan and is springy to the touch. NOTE: *This bread will have a flat top (because of the weight of the batter), not a rounded one, so do not be alarmed if the bread does not rise dramatically above the rim of the pan.*

As soon as the bread pulls from the sides of the pan and is springy to the touch, remove it from the oven and let it cool, right side up, in the pan on a wire rack for 10 minutes. Carefully loosen the bread around the edges with a thin-blade spatula, and turn out on a wire rack. Cool the bread completely before cutting. To serve, slice about ¼ inch (¾ cm) thick. Butter the slices or not as you wish—the bread is rich enough not to need butter.

Pumpkin-pecan bread

MAKES A 9 × 5 × 3-INCH (23 × 13 × 8 CM) LOAF

Because of the difficulty of obtaining fresh pumpkins the year round (to say nothing of the tedium of reducing fresh pumpkin to purée), I rely upon canned, unsweetened pumpkin purée for making this recipe. Note **unsweetened.** What you want for this recipe is pure, unadulterated solid-pack pumpkin that contains no other ingredient. Pumpkin pie mix simply will not do.

¼ pound (1 stick)	unsalted butter	115 g (1 stick)
1 cup	firmly packed light brown sugar	215 g
3 large	eggs	3 large
1 can (1 lb.)	solid-pack unsweetened pumpkin	1 can (454 g)
2½ cups	sifted all-purpose flour	250 g
2½ teaspoons	baking powder	2½ teaspoons
1 teaspoon	ground ginger	1 teaspoon
1 teaspoon	ground cinnamon	1 teaspoon
½ teaspoon	ground allspice	½ teaspoon
¼ teaspoon	freshly grated nutmeg	¼ teaspoon
¼ teaspoon	salt	¼ teaspoon
1 cup	coarsely chopped pecans	240 ml

Cream the butter and sugar until fluffy, then beat the eggs in, one at a time. Stir in the pumpkin. Sift together the flour, baking powder, ginger, cinnamon, allspice, nutmeg and salt and add to the pumpkin mixture about one-fourth of the total amount at a time, stirring after each addition just enough to mix. NOTE: *It's better to have a few lumps of flour showing than to overmix, because you will toughen the bread and coarsen its texture.* Stir in the pecans, then spoon the batter into a well-greased and floured 9 × 5 × 3-inch (23 × 13 × 8 CM) loaf pan, spreading it well to the corners and smoothing the surface as evenly as possible. Bake in a moderate oven (350°F. or 175°C.) for 45 to 50 minutes or until the bread pulls from the sides of the pan and feels springy to the touch. Cool the bread upright on a wire rack 10 minutes, then loosen around the edges with a thin-blade spatula and turn out. Cool the bread 30 minutes before cutting. NOTE: *This waiting period is to allow the bread to firm up and dry out a bit; it's an unusually moist bread, thanks to the quantity of pumpkin, also to the brown sugar, which tends to absorb and hold liquid. If you cut the bread too soon, it will be as dense and damp as steamed pudding.* Cut into thin slices and serve with or without butter. I think this bread makes superlative toast, particularly if buttered lightly, then toasted 10 to 15 minutes in a very slow oven (300°F. or 150°C.)

Highland shortbread

SERVES 6 TO 8

 The secret of good shortbread is to cream the butter and sugar until no sugar grains are discernible on the tongue, and this means having the butter at the proper temperature. It should not be refrigerator cold, nor should it be so warm that it runs. Somewhere between the two extremes is the ideal. I usually take the butter from the refrigerator and let it stand about twenty minutes at room temperature—unless my kitchen is boiling-hot, in which case I let the butter stand on the counter only ten to fifteen minutes. The reason for using rice flour is to help tenderize the shortbread. (Rice flour, unlike wheat flour, is largely starch and will produce an uncommonly tender crumb.)

¼ pound (1 stick)	unsalted butter	115 g (½ stick)
⅓ cup	superfine sugar	65 g
1½ cups	sifted all-purpose flour	150 g
½ cup	unsifted rice flour	50 g

Cream the butter and sugar vigorously until fluffy and almost white; taste and if you can feel any sugar grains on your tongue, cream the mixture longer still until the sugar is completely dissolved in the butter. Combine the flour and rice flour in a large bowl, add the butter mixture and work it in slowly with your fingertips until the mixture is uniformly crumbly but will hold together when you squeeze a handful of it together. Shape the dough into a round flat pone about ¾ inch (2 cm) thick in the center of an ungreased baking sheet. If you have a wooden shortbread mold, press firmly on top of the shortbread until the imprint is distinct, then lift off carefully. Bake the shortbread, uncovered, in a moderately slow oven (325°F. or 165°C.) for 35 to 40 minutes until firm to the touch and evenly pale ivory. Remove from the oven, cool 30 minutes, then break or cut into small pieces and serve.

Blueberry-buttermilk cake
with sugar and spice topping

MAKES A 9-INCH (23 CM) SQUARE LOAF CAKE

Because the batter for this cake is so stiff, the blueberries are distributed throughout the finished cake. (In other batters they usually sink to the bottom.) This is an exceptionally delicate cake with a fine and buttery crumb.

2 cups	sifted all-purpose flour	200 g
1 cup	fresh blueberries, washed, sorted, stemmed and patted very dry on paper toweling	240 ml
1 teaspoon	baking powder	1 teaspoon
1/8 teaspoon	salt	1/8 teaspoon
1/4 pound (1 stick)	unsalted butter	115 g (1 stick)
1 cup	sugar	200 g
1 large	egg	1 large
1/4 cup	molasses	60 ml
1 cup	buttermilk	240 ml
1 teaspoon	baking soda	1 teaspoon
	TOPPING:	
2 tablespoons	sugar	2 tablespoons
1/2 teaspoon	ground cinnamon	1/2 teaspoon
1/4 teaspoon	freshly grated nutmeg	1/4 teaspoon

Sprinkle 1/3 cup (35 g) of the sifted flour over the blueberries; toss well to dredge, then set aside. Sift the remaining flour with the baking powder and salt onto a piece of wax paper and set aside also. Cream the butter and sugar until smooth; beat in the egg, then the molasses. Now combine the buttermilk and baking soda and add to the creamed mixture alternately with the sifted dry ingredients; begin and end with the dry ingredients and stir after each addition only enough to mix. Finally, fold in the blueberries and all the dredging flour, again stirring just enough to combine. Spoon the batter into a well-greased and floured 9 × 9 × 2-inch (23 × 23 × 5 cm) baking pan, spreading it well to the corners and smoothing the top as much as possible. Mix topping ingredients and sprinkle evenly over the surface of the batter.

Bake, uncovered, in a moderate oven (350°F. or 175°C.) for 45 to 50 minutes or until the cake begins to pull from the sides of the pan and feels springy to the touch. Remove the cake from the oven, set on a wire rack and cool 30 minutes. Cut into large squares and serve.

Grenadian spice cake

MAKES A 9 × 5 × 3-INCH (23 × 13 × 8 CM) LOAF CAKE

As buttery and smooth as a pound cake, this recipe comes from the Caribbean island of Grenada, known the world over as "The Spice Island." All of the cake's distinctive seasonings are home-grown: lime, cinnamon, allspice and nutmeg. (The sugar used is likely to be Grenadian, too.) It is essential that you grate the nutmeg for this cake and not resort to commercially ground nutmeg. Freshly grated nutmeg has a lemon-sweet delicacy that does not exist in the commercially ground; indeed, this has an unpleasant, bitter aftertaste. Although Grenadians sometimes spread a vanilla or chocolate buttercream icing over the cake, I think it's best unfrosted.

2 cups	sifted all-purpose flour	200 g
½ teaspoon	baking powder	½ teaspoon
⅛ teaspoon	salt	⅛ teaspoon
½ pound (2 sticks)	cold unsalted butter, cut into pats	230 g (2 sticks)
1½ cups	sugar	300 g
1½ teaspoons	finely grated lime rind (green part only)	1½ teaspoons
1 teaspoon	freshly grated nutmeg	1 teaspoon
½ teaspoon	ground cinnamon	½ teaspoon
¼ teaspoon	ground allspice	¼ teaspoon
3 large	eggs, at room temperature	3 large
½ cup	milk, at room temperature	120 ml

Sift the flour, baking powder and salt together onto a piece of wax paper and set aside. Cream together the butter, sugar, lime rind, nutmeg, cinnamon and allspice until silvery and light—no sugar grains should be discernible on the tongue when the mixture has been properly creamed. (This may take as long as 5 minutes at high mixer speed.) Beat the eggs in, one at a time. Now add the sifted dry ingredients alternately with the milk, beginning and ending with the dry. (I usually mix the flour in in about five separate additions and the milk in in three.)

Spoon the batter into a well-buttered and floured 9 × 5 × 3-inch (23 × 13 × 8 cm) loaf pan, pushing the batter well to the corners and smoothing the surface as much as possible. Bake in a slow oven (300°F. or 150°C.) for 1 to 1¼ hours or until the cake begins to pull from the sides of the pan and leaves an imprint that vanishes slowly when you press the top with your fingers.

Remove the cake from the oven, stand the pan upright on a wire rack and allow the cake to cool in the pan for 10 minutes. Loosen the cake around the edges with a thin-blade spatula, turn out on a wire rack and cool to room temperature. To serve, slice just as you would pound cake. This cake is especially good with fresh sliced peaches, nectarines, plums or sectioned navel oranges. It's even better with any of these fruits spooned on top.

Pepparkaka
(SWEDISH SPICE CAKE)

SERVES 6 TO 8

Dark, dense and delicious, this "peppery" cake owes its bite to ginger, cinnamon, cloves and freshly ground cardamom seeds and its pudding moistness to a honey glaze. It needs no frosting but can be dusted lightly with confectioner's sugar, if you like. Serve as is or drift with softly whipped cream.

	FOR PREPARING THE CAKE MOLD:	
1 tablespoon	unsalted butter, at room temperature	1 tablespoon
2 tablespoons	very fine dry bread crumbs	2 tablespoons
	CAKE:	
1½ cups	sifted all-purpose flour	150 g
1 teaspoon	baking powder	1 teaspoon
½ teaspoon	baking soda	½ teaspoon
1½ teaspoons	ground ginger	1½ teaspoons
1½ teaspoons	ground cinnamon	1½ teaspoons
½ teaspoon	ground cloves	½ teaspoon
½ teaspoon	cardamom seeds, pulverized (use dark inner seeds only)	½ teaspoon
¼ teaspoon	ground mace	¼ teaspoon
Pinch	salt	Pinch
¼ pound (1 stick)	unsalted butter, at room temperature	115 g (1 stick)
¾ cup	sugar	150 g
¼ cup	molasses	60 ml
2 large	eggs	2 large
1 cup	sour cream, at room temperature	240 ml
	GLAZE:	
2 tablespoons	mild light honey	2 tablespoons
⅓ cup	warm water	80 ml
A 1-inch-long piece	stick cinnamon	A 2½ cm long piece

Prepare the cake mold first: Butter an 8-cup (2 L) Bundt or fluted tube mold well, then coat evenly with crumbs, tapping out the excess.

For the cake: Sift the flour with the baking powder, soda, spices and salt and set aside. Cream the butter and sugar until fluffy-light, then beat in the molasses. Add the eggs, one at a time, mixing well after each addition. Add the sifted dry ingredients to the creamed mixture alternately with the sour cream, beginning and ending with the dry ingredients. Spoon the batter into the prepared mold; rap lightly on the counter once or twice to level the batter and burst any trapped air bubbles that would coarsen the cake's texture. Bake the cake in a moderate oven (350°F. or 175°C.) for about 40 minutes or until it pulls from sides of the mold and the top feels springy. Cool the cake upright in its mold for 10 minutes, then loosen around the edges with a spatula and invert onto a wire rack.

For the glaze: Simmer all glaze ingredients slowly in a small saucepan 3 to 5 minutes. Strain, then spoon evenly over the cake.

Allow the *Pepparkaka* to cool completely, then cut into slim wedges and serve.

Madeira cake

MAKES A 10-INCH (25 CM) TUBE CAKE

This dark fruit cake is a Portuguese classic. The baked cake does not contain Madeira wine, but later it is often saturated—or served—with it.

4½ cups	sifted all-purpose flour	450 g
½ cup	finely diced candied citron	120 ml
½ cup	finely diced candied lemon peel	120 ml
½ cup	coarsely chopped candied red cherries	120 ml
1 tablespoon	baking powder	1 tablespoon
1 pound (4 sticks)	unsalted butter, at room temperature	455 g (4 sticks)
1½ cups	sugar	300 g
¼ cup	dark corn syrup	60 ml
¼ cup	molasses	60 ml
8 large	eggs	8 large
2 packages	active dry yeast softened in ¼ cup (60 ml) warm water (about 105–115°F. or 41–46°C.)	2 packages
1 large lemon	juice and finely grated rind	1 large lemon
⅓ cup	sweet Madeira (Boal or Malmsey)	80 ml

Place 1 cup (100 g) of the flour in a small bowl, add the candied fruits and toss well to dredge. Set aside. Sift the remaining flour with the baking powder onto a piece of wax paper and set aside also. Cream the butter and sugar until fluffy-light; beat in the corn syrup and molasses. Add the eggs, one at a time. Mix in the yeast mixture, the lemon juice and rind. Add the flour gradually, beating lightly after each addition. Fold in the fruits and dredging flour. Pour into a well-greased and floured 10-inch (25 cm) tube pan and bake in a moderately hot oven (375°F. or 190°C.) for about 1¼ hours or until the cake begins to pull from the sides of the pan and is springy to the touch. Cool the cake upright in its pan on a wire rack 10 minutes, loosen and invert on the rack. Cool to room temperature, then drizzle evenly with Madeira. Let stand at least 1 hour before cutting.

Bolos de mel
(PORTUGUESE TREACLE CAKES)

MAKES 2 LOAVES, EACH 9 × 5 × 3 INCHES (23 × 13 × 8 CM)

Translated literally, *bolos de mel* means "honey cakes," but the Portuguese word *mel* denotes both true honey (*mel de abelhas* or "honey of the bees") and treacle or molasses (*mel de cana* or "honey of cane"). Sugar cane is one of the important crops on the Portuguese island of Madeira, so it's not surprising that this dense, fruity cake is a beloved sweet there.

⅔ cup	moderately finely chopped mixed candied fruits	160 ml
⅔ cup	moderately finely chopped walnuts	160 ml
⅔ cup	moderately finely chopped blanched almonds	160 ml
4½ cups	sifted all-purpose flour	450 g
2 teaspoons	baking soda	2 teaspoons
½ teaspoon	ground cloves	½ teaspoon
½ teaspoon	ground cinnamon	½ teaspoon
½ teaspoon	ground anise	½ teaspoon
½ pound (2 sticks)	unsalted butter, at room temperature	230 g (2 sticks)
½ cup	vegetable shortening	95 g
1 cup	sugar	200 g
3 large	eggs	3 large
2 packages	active dry yeast softened in ½ cup (120 ml) warm water (about 105–115°F. or 41–46°C.)	2 packages
1¼ cups	light unsulfured molasses	300 ml

Dredge the fruits and nuts in about ½ cup (50 g) of the sifted flour; set aside. Sift the remaining flour with the baking soda, cloves, cinnamon and anise onto a piece of wax paper and set aside also. Cream the butter, shortening and sugar until fluffy-light; beat in the eggs, one at a time. Mix in the softened yeast. Add the sifted dry ingredients alternately with the molasses, beginning and ending with the dry. Fold in the fruits and nuts (include all dredging flour).

Transfer the batter to a large well-greased bowl, cover with clean dry cloth and allow to rise in a warm, draft-free spot for 2 hours. (The batter will rise only slightly, but it **will** become spongy and lighter.) Stir the batter down, divide between two well-greased and floured 9 × 5 × 3-inch (23 × 13 × 8 cm) loaf pans; cover with a cloth and allow to rise 1½ hours.

Bake the cakes in a moderately hot oven (375°F. or 190°C.) for 50 to 60 minutes or until the loaves begin to pull from the sides of the pans and feel springy to the touch. Cool the cakes upright in their pans on wire racks 10 minutes; loosen around the edges with a spatula, turn the cakes out and cool to room temperature before cutting.

Decorate, if you like, with bands of sifted confectioner's sugar. Or serve plain. NOTE: *Snugly wrapped in foil, these cakes will keep well in the freezer for about six months.*

Fauchon's fabulous chocolate-raspberry torte

MAKES AN 8-INCH (20 CM), 3-LAYER CAKE

 Fauchon, Paris's famous *épicerie* (grocery), *confiserie* (confectioner) and *pâtisserie* (pastry shop) on the Place de la Madeleine, is renowned for this devastatingly rich chocolate torte, which uses not one but three different kinds of chocolate. The cake is dense and dark, compounded principally of almond paste, the filling is as fluffy as freshly whipped country butter and the frosting, a glaze of bittersweet chocolate. It's not a difficult cake to make but it does take time.

	TORTE:	
3½ ounces	almond paste, cut into small pieces	100 g
4 tablespoons	**unsifted** confectioner's (10X) sugar	4 tablespoons
4 large	eggs, 3 of them separated	4 large
4 tablespoons	Dutch cocoa powder (not a mix)	4 tablespoons
3 tablespoons	melted unsalted butter	3 tablespoons
½ teaspoon	vanilla extract	½ teaspoon
5 tablespoons	**unsifted** all-purpose flour	5 tablespoons
3 tablespoons	granulated sugar	3 tablespoons

	GANACHE (CHOCOLATE BUTTER CREAM):	
½ cup	half-and-half cream	120 ml
½ cup	heavy cream	120 ml
2 bars (4 oz. each)	German's sweet chocolate	2 bars (113 g each)
2 tablespoons	granulated sugar	2 tablespoons
5 tablespoons	Dutch cocoa powder (not a mix)	5 tablespoons
½ pound (2 sticks)	unsalted butter	230 g (2 sticks)
	FILLINGS:	
¾ cup	bottled raspberry syrup mixed with ¼ cup (60 ml) eau de vie de framboise	180 ml
1 cup	sieved raspberry jam	240 ml
	FROSTING:	
8 squares (1 oz. each)	semisweet chocolate, melted over simmering water	8 squares (28 g each)

For the torte: In an electric mixer set at high speed (or a food processor equipped with the metal chopping blade), beat the almond paste, confectioner's sugar, 1 egg and 3 egg yolks hard until as smooth as sponge cake batter (about 5 minutes in the mixer, three 1-minute churnings in the processor). Lightly beat in, one at a time, the cocoa, butter and vanilla, and finally the flour. Beat the egg whites until frothy; add the granulated sugar, a tablespoon at a time, beating well after each addition. Continue whipping until the meringue stands in stiff peaks. Mix about ½ cup (120 ml) of the meringue into the chocolate mixture to lighten it, then very carefully fold in the remaining meringue until no streaks remain.

Pour the batter into a heavily buttered and floured 8-inch (20 cm) springform pan and bake in a hot oven (400°F. or 205°C.) for 25 to 30 minutes until springy to the touch. Remove the torte from the oven, cool upright in its pan on a wire rack 10 minutes, then loosen and remove the springform sides. Cool the cake completely, remove pan bottom, then slice the cake horizontally into three layers of equal thickness. Set aside.

For the ganache: Place the half-and-half, heavy cream, chocolate, sugar and cocoa in a double boiler top, set over boiling water and heat, stirring now and then, until mixture is creamy-smooth. Cool completely. Cream the butter with the chocolate mixture until light. Chill well, then beat hard until fluffy.

To assemble the torte: Place the bottom layer of the torte, cut side up, on a cut-to-fit cardboard circle and set on a wire rack on a paper-covered counter. Saturate the surface with one-third of the raspberry syrup mixture, spread with half the jam, then half the *ganache*. Set the middle layer in place, drizzle with another third of the syrup, then spread with the remaining jam and *ganache*. Set the top layer in place, cut side down, and saturate with the remaining syrup. Let stand 30 minutes, then frost the top and sides of the torte with the melted

semisweet chocolate. Set in the refrigerator or freezer to quick-harden the chocolate (this will take about 30 minutes), then let the torte stand 1 hour at room
temperature before cutting.

Schwarzwälder Kirschtorte
(BLACK FOREST CHERRY TORTE)

MAKES A 9-INCH (23 CM), 3-LAYER CAKE

It's imperative that you grate the chocolate for this recipe
very fine, otherwise it will not melt as the cake bakes and may sink to the bottom
of the pan. The ground almonds, too, must be fine and feathery.

TORTE:

¾ cup	sifted cake flour	60 g
2 teaspoons	baking powder	2 teaspoons
Pinch	salt	Pinch
¼ pound (1 stick)	unsalted butter, at room temperature	115 g (½ stick)
½ cup	sugar	100 g
6 large	egg yolks	6 large
½ teaspoon	vanilla extract	½ teaspoon
¼ teaspoon	almond extract	¼ teaspoon
4 squares (1 oz. each)	semisweet chocolate, very finely grated	4 squares (28 g each)
6 large	egg whites, beaten to soft peaks with 3 tablespoons sugar	6 large
½ cup	very finely ground **un**blanched almonds	45 g

FILLING:

6 tablespoons	Kirsch	6 tablespoons
1 jar (1 lb.)	whole cherry preserves	1 jar (454 g)
1 cup	heavy cream, stiffly whipped	240 ml

TOPPING:

2 cups	heavy cream	½ L
⅓ cup	**unsifted** confectioner's (10X) sugar	80 ml
2 squares (1 oz. each)	semisweet chocolate, shaved into curls with a vegetable peeler	2 squares (28 g each)
8 large	maraschino cherries, patted dry on paper toweling	8 large

For the torte: Line the bottom of a 9-inch (23 cm) springform pan with wax
paper; butter the paper and pan sides well, then coat with flour, tipping out the

excess. Sift the cake flour with the baking powder and salt and set aside. Cream the butter and sugar until fluffy-light; beat in the egg yolks, vanilla and almond extract, then fold in grated chocolate. Stir in about 1 cup (240 ml) of the beaten egg whites (this is to lighten the mixture), then fold in the balance—gently but thoroughly—until no streaks of white or brown remain. Sift about a fourth of the dry ingredients over the batter and fold in gently; repeat until all of the flour mixture is incorporated. Finally, fold in the ground almonds, using as light a touch as possible. Spoon the batter into the prepared pan, smooth the top and bake in a moderately slow oven (325°F. or 165°C.) about 45 minutes or until torte begins to pull from sides of pan and feels springy to the touch.

Remove the torte from the oven and cool upright in its pan on a wire rack 10 minutes. Loosen torte around the edges with a spatula; release and remove the springform sides. Cool torte completely, remove the pan bottom and peel off the wax paper. NOTE: *Easier to slice into layers if you wrap it snugly in plastic wrap and let stand at room temperature for at least 24 hours before proceeding.*

To assemble the torte: Using a serrated knife, divide the torte horizontally into three equal layers. Place the bottom layer on a cut-to-fit cardboard circle and set on a cake plate or, better yet, a lazy susan. Drizzle the layer evenly with 2 tablespoons of the Kirsch, spread with half the cherry preserves, then with half the whipped cream for the **Filling.** Top with the middle layer, drizzle with 2 more tablespoons of Kirsch, then spread with the remaining cherry preserves and whipped cream. Set the top layer in place, pressing down lightly. Drizzle with the remaining 2 tablespoons of Kirsch.

For the topping: Whip the cream and confectioner's sugar to fairly stiff peaks, then use to frost the top and sides of the torte, swirling it into peaks and valleys. Sprinkle the chocolate shavings on the top and sides of the torte, then decorate the top with the cherries, arranging them in a circle around the edge. Let stand 2 to 3 hours (in the refrigerator if your kitchen is hot) before serving.

Easy sponge cake

MAKES A 10-INCH (25 CM) TUBE CAKE

The method of mixing is more or less the unorthodox "dump-and-beat" variety. But it produces a handsome cake.

1¼ cups	sifted cake flour	100 g
1¼ cups	sugar	250 g
½ teaspoon	baking powder	½ teaspoon
¼ teaspoon	salt	¼ teaspoon
6 large	eggs, at room temperature, separated	6 large
¼ cup	cold water	60 ml
1½ teaspoons	vanilla extract	1½ teaspoons
½ teaspoon	cream of tartar	½ teaspoon

Sift the flour, ¾ cup (150 g) of the sugar, the baking powder and salt into the largest electric mixer bowl. Dump in the egg yolks, water and vanilla and beat at medium speed for 1 minute. In a separate large bowl, beat the egg whites until frothy. Sprinkle the cream of tartar on top and beat just until the whites are beginning to thicken. Now add the remaining ½ cup (100 g) of sugar gradually (about 2 tablespoons at a time) until the whites stand in stiff, glossy peaks when the beater is withdrawn. (It is imperative that the peaks be stiff.) With a rubber spatula, fold about one-fourth of the beaten whites into the yolk mixture, using a quick, light touch. Fold the remaining whites in the same way in three separate additions. Spoon the batter into an **ungreased** 10-inch (25 cm) tube pan and bake in a moderate oven (350°F. or 175°C.) for 40 to 45 minutes until the cake begins to pull from the sides of the pan, is lightly browned and feels springy to the touch. Remove the cake from the oven, invert and cool the cake in the upside-down pan until it has reached room temperature. Loosen the cake around the edges with a thin-blade spatula (also around the pan's central tube) and turn out on a cake plate. Leave the cake plain, dust lightly with confectioner's sugar or frost—whatever you like.

VARIATIONS:

Lemon sponge cake: Prepare as directed, but for the liquid ingredient use 2 tablespoons of lemon juice combined with 2 tablespoons of cold water (instead of the ¼ cup or 60 ml of cold water called for). For flavoring, use 1 tablespoon finely grated lemon rind instead of vanilla.

Orange sponge cake: Prepare as directed, but for the liquid ingredient use 2 tablespoons of orange juice combined with 2 tablespoons of cold water (instead of the ¼ cup or 60 ml of cold water). For flavoring the cake, use 1 tablespoon finely grated orange rind in place of vanilla.

Chocolate sponge cake: Whisk ⅓ cup (20 g) of sifted cocoa into ¼ cup (60 ml) of boiling water. Cool to room temperature, then prepare the cake precisely as directed, using the cocoa-water mixture instead of plain water as the liquid ingredient.

Mocha sponge cake: Whisk ¼ cup (15 g) of sifted cocoa and 2 tablespoons of freeze-dried coffee crystals into ¼ cup (60 ml) of boiling water. Cool to room temperature, then prepare the cake as directed, using the mocha infusion as the liquid ingredient in the cake.

Mocha-hazelnut roll

SERVES 8 TO 10

Ruinously rich—the stuff of many a chocoholic's dreams. And yet this showy dessert is not difficult to make. Just make sure that the eggs you use are not the new jumbo size. (If they are, the cake will overflow its pan, making one unholy mess in the oven.) Also take pains not to overbeat the egg whites—they should be billowing, soft and moist, **not** so vigorously whisked that they form stiff peaks. As a Cornell Hotel School professor of mine used to say, "More failures are caused by overbeaten egg whites than by underbeaten ones." He was right. And that lesson holds for all egg-white-leavened mixtures: soufflés, sponge and angel food cakes, quenelles and mousses as well as for this European-style torte.

TORTE:

8 medium-size	eggs, separated	8 medium-size
1¼ cups	granulated sugar	250 g
1 teaspoon	vanilla extract	1 teaspoon
½ cup	finely ground unblanched hazelnuts or almonds (or use walnuts or pecans)	120 ml
2 tablespoons	all-purpose flour	2 tablespoons
2 tablespoons	cocoa powder (not a mix)	2 tablespoons
¼ cup	sifted confectioner's (10X) sugar	20 g
Pinch	salt	Pinch

MOCHA BUTTER CREAM:

¾ cup	granulated sugar	150 g
3 tablespoons	cocoa powder (not a mix)	3 tablespoons
2 tablespoons	freeze-dried coffee crystals	2 tablespoons
½ cup	heavy cream	120 ml
1 bar (4 oz.)	German's sweet chocolate, broken into small pieces	1 bar (113 g)
1 tablespoon	Tia Maria, Kahlúa or Crème de Cacao	1 tablespoon
1 teaspoon	vanilla extract	1 teaspoon
Pinch	salt	Pinch
¾ pound (3 sticks)	unsalted butter, well chilled and cut into ½-inch (1½ cm) pats	340 g (3 sticks)

OPTIONAL DECORATION:

2 squares (1 oz. each)	bittersweet chocolate, shaved into curls with a vegetable peeler	2 squares (28 g each)

For the torte: Beat the egg yolks, granulated sugar and vanilla at highest mixer speed about 5 minutes until mixture is pale yellow and forms flat ribbons that fall back upon themselves when the beater is withdrawn. Toss the nuts well with the flour and cocoa, making certain that all lumps of cocoa and/or flour have been broken up. Stir the nut mixture into the yolk mixture, then beat hard, using a wooden spoon, until well combined and fluffy.

Beat the egg whites with 1 tablespoon of the confectioner's sugar and the salt until frothy; sprinkle another tablespoon of confectioner's sugar over the whites and beat hard until beginning to thicken; sprinkle another tablespoon of confectioner's sugar over the whites and beat hard to incorporate; finally, add the remaining tablespoon of confectioner's sugar and beat the whites until they are soft, silvery and billowing—if you tip the bowl, the meringue mixture should just flow—**not** run. Mix about 1 cup (240 ml) of the meringue into the yolk mixture to lighten it, then gently spoon the yolk mixture on top of the remaining meringue and fold in gently but thoroughly until no streaks of white or brown remain.

Spoon the batter into a lavishly buttered and floured 15½ × 10½ × 1-inch jelly-roll pan (39 × 25 × 2½ cm), spreading well into the corners and smoothing the top. Rap the pan gently on the counter two to three times to release large trapped air bubbles that would form tunnels in the torte, then bake in a moderate oven (350°F. or 175°C.) for 35 to 40 minutes or until the torte feels springy to the touch.

Remove the torte from the oven, loosen it around the edges with a sharp serrated knife, then turn out on a clean dishtowel. (No need to sprinkle the towel with sugar; the torte will not stick to it.) Carefully trim off and discard any crusty edges (leaving them on would make the torte crack as you roll it), then roll the torte up inside the towel, jelly-roll style and cool completely.

Meanwhile, prepare the mocha butter cream: Combine the granulated sugar, cocoa and coffee in a small heavy saucepan, pressing out any lumps of cocoa or sugar; stir in the cream, then drop in the pieces of chocolate. Set over moderate heat and cook, stirring constantly, about 5 minutes or until chocolate is melted and sugar completely dissolved. (Taste the mixture—no sugar grains should be discernible.) Off heat, stir in the Tia Maria, vanilla and salt and cool to room temperature.

Cream the chilled butter until fairly fluffy, then drizzle the chocolate mixture in slowly, beating hard all the while. (NOTE: *I like to do this in a food processor fitted with the metal chopping blade—4 to 5 one-minute churnings of the motor should fluff the butter up nicely. You need then only to drizzle the chocolate down the feed tube with the motor running. You can, of course, cream the butter in an electric mixer set at highest speed, then drizzle in the chocolate with the mixer running. If the butter cream seems too soft to spread easily, chill about 20 minutes, then beat hard again to fluff it.*

To assemble the torte: Unroll the cooled torte on a piece of wax paper large enough to accommodate it; spread thickly with about two-thirds of the butter cream and reroll—not too snugly or the filling will ooze out. Ease the roll onto a small oval or rectangular platter, then frost the outside lavishly with the remaining butter cream, swirling it into soft ridges and troughs running the length of the roll. Decorate, if you like, with scatterings of chocolate curls. Chill the roll several hours, then slice—slightly on the diagonal—using a sharp serrated knife. Make the slices fairly thin because the torte is rich. Also let the slices stand at room temperature 10 to 15 minutes before serving if the filling seems cold and stiff.

NOTE: *This roll freezes well. Chill long enough in the refrigerator or freezer to harden the butter cream "frosting," then wrap snugly in aluminum foil or plastic food wrap. Unwrap before thawing; otherwise the filling will soften too much for the roll to be handled neatly. Also, slice the roll while still fairly firm, then bring almost to room temperature before serving.*

Old-fashioned angel food cake

MAKES A 10-INCH (25 CM) TUBE CAKE

The secret of a tender, high-rising angel food cake is beating the whites just until they peak softly—no more, no less. They should be billowing and moist, never dry or stiff, or they will collapse when you fold in the other ingredients. To help stabilize the egg whites and to whiten them, I sprinkle a little cream of tartar over them when they are at the frothy stage. I also add a little sugar—gradually—as I continue beating the whites, which also increases their stability. I call for the whites here by the cup measure instead of by the egg because eggs vary so in size and because precision is critical to the cake's success. It is the air beaten into the egg whites together with the steam formed from the moisture in the whites that leaven the cake. (Moisture expands 1600 times as it turns to steam, so you can imagine its leavening power.)

1½ cups	egg whites (you will need 8 to 9 large eggs), at room temperature	350 ml
¼ teaspoon	salt	¼ teaspoon
¾ teaspoon	cream of tartar	¾ teaspoon
1¼ cups	sifted sugar	250 g
1 teaspoon	vanilla extract	1 teaspoon
1 teaspoon	lemon juice	1 teaspoon
½ teaspoon	almond extract	½ teaspoon
1 cup	sifted cake flour	80 g

In a very large mixing bowl and using a rotary beater or balloon whip, beat the egg whites until frothy. Sprinkle in the salt and cream of tartar and beat until the bubbles are smaller and the whites are beginning to turn silver. Sprinkle in 1 tablespoon of the sugar and beat a little longer until whites are beginning to thicken. Sprinkle in another tablespoon of the sugar, add the vanilla, lemon juice and almond extract and beat until the whites are foamy-white but not stiff. Now sift the remaining sugar with the cake flour onto a piece of wax paper. Continue beating the whites until they form soft peaks when the beater is withdrawn.

Sift a little (not more than ¼ cup or 60 ml) of the sugar-flour mixture over the whites and fold in gently, using a large rubber spatula, just until no dry flecks or streaks show. Do not overmix. Continue adding and folding in the sugar-flour mixture the same way, using about eight separate additions in all and handling the batter gently at all times so that you don't break down the beaten whites.

Pour the batter into an **ungreased** 10-inch (25 cm) tube pan and smooth the top as evenly as possible with a rubber spatula. Place the cake on the middle rack of a slow oven (300°F. or 150°C.) and bake for 1 hour and 10 to 15 minutes until the cake has pulled from the sides of the pan and is pale tan and springy to the touch. NOTE: *This is a lower than usual oven temperature, but it produces an angel food cake of supreme tenderness and uncommon fragility. It goes without saying that you should step lightly about the house while the cake bakes and encourage the children to do their roughhousing outside.*

As soon as the cake is done, remove it from the oven, invert it at once and cool upside down in the pan until it has reached room temperature. Carefully loosen the cake around the outside and around the central tube, using a thin-blade spatula, then turn out on a cake plate. When cutting the cake, use a sharp serrated knife and a gentle sawing motion so that you don't compact the cake and destroy its light, spongy texture.

Fresh blackberry cobbler with whole-wheat shortbread topping

SERVES 6

Because I've always liked whole wheat bread, I decided to see if my favorite cobbler could be made with about 50 percent whole wheat flour instead of all white flour. It can. Deliciously, I'm pleased to report. If you like, substitute an equal quantity of fresh blueberries, dewberries, loganberries or pitted, dark sweet red cherries for the blackberries. I'm sure that fresh peaches would be superb prepared this way, too, provided the juice of a lemon is added to keep the peaches moist and bright.

½ cup	sugar	100 g
3 tablespoons	cornstarch	3 tablespoons
2 teaspoons	finely grated lemon rind	2 teaspoons
1 quart	fresh blackberries, washed and stemmed	1 L
1 tablespoon	unsalted butter, cut into bits	1 tablespoon
	WHOLE WHEAT SHORTBREAD:	
1 cup	sifted all-purpose flour	100 g
1 cup	unsifted whole wheat flour	130 g
⅓ cup	sugar	65 g
1 tablespoon	baking powder	1 tablespoon
¼ teaspoon	salt	¼ teaspoon

⅓ cup	firmly packed vegetable shortening	60 g
5 tablespoons (⅔ stick)	unsalted butter, cut into pats	5 tablespoons (⅔ stick)
½ cup	milk	120 ml

Combine the sugar, cornstarch and lemon rind in a large mixing bowl, pressing out any lumps of sugar or cornstarch. Dump in the berries and toss well to mix. Set aside for the moment.

For the shortbread: Combine the all-purpose and whole wheat flours, the sugar, baking powder and salt in a large mixing bowl. Add the shortening and butter and cut in, using a pastry blender, until uniformly crumbly. Drizzle in the milk, tossing briskly all the while with a fork just until the dough holds together.

Stir the berry mixture well, dump into an unbuttered 2-quart (2 L) baking dish and dot evenly with 1 tablespoon butter. Spoon the shortbread dough on top in clumps, then spread evenly until the berries are completely covered. Bake, uncovered, in a hot oven (400°F. or 205°C.) for 10 minutes; lower the oven heat to moderate (350°F. or 175°C.) and bake 25 to 30 minutes longer or until the berries are bubbling and the shortbread touched with brown.

Remove the cobbler from the oven and cool 30 minutes before serving. NOTE: *I like to drizzle a little light cream over each portion, but the cobbler can certainly stand alone on its own merits.*

Orange cake-and-custard pie

MAKES A 9-INCH (23 CM) OPEN-FACE PIE

The reason I call this a "cake-and-custard" pie is that during baking the filling separates into two distinct layers: custard on the bottom and sponge cake on top. How come? It's simply that the egg white, beaten to stiff peaks and folded in at the last minute, separates from the heavier yolk mixture and floats to the top.

1 cup	sugar	200 g
¼ cup	sifted cake flour	20 g
¼ cup	orange juice	60 ml
1 tablespoon	finely grated orange rind	1 tablespoon
¼ teaspoon	almond extract	¼ teaspoon
1 large	egg, separated	1 large
2 tablespoons	melted unsalted butter	2 tablespoons
½ cup	half-and-half cream	120 ml
½ cup	milk	120 ml
A 9-inch	unbaked pie shell	A 23 cm

Spoon 1 teaspoon of sugar from the cup onto a piece of wax paper and set aside. Combine the remaining sugar and the flour in a mixing bowl, pressing out any lumps. Stir in the orange juice and rind and almond extract. Beat in the egg yolk, then mix in first the melted butter, then the half-and-half, then the milk. Beat the egg white and reserved teaspoon of sugar to stiff, glossy peaks and fold into the orange mixture until no streaks of white or orange remain. Pour into the pie shell and bake in a moderate oven (350°F. or 175°C.) for 35 to 40 minutes until puffy and lightly browned. Remove the pie from the oven and cool 20 to 25 minutes before cutting. The filling will fall slightly, but that is as it should be. Cut into wedges and serve.

VARIATIONS

Lemon cake-and-custard pie: Prepare exactly as directed, but substitute freshly squeezed (not bottled) lemon juice and rind for the orange and omit the almond extract.

Lime cake-and-custard pie: Prepare as directed, but substitute 3 tablespoons of freshly squeezed (not bottled) lime juice and 1½ teaspoons freshly grated lime rind for the orange juice and rind; omit the almond extract.

Open-face Dutch almond-apple pie

MAKES A 9-INCH (23 CM) PIE

This is a good recipe. And such an easy one, too, particularly if you have a processor with which to buzz up the almond cream filling. The best apples to use are super-tart ones because of the richness of the almond cream.

4 pounds	tart green apples	2 kg (scant)
2 tablespoons	lemon juice	2 tablespoons
2 ounces	marzipan, cut into small pieces	60 g
2 tablespoons	unsalted butter	2 tablespoons
½ cup	firmly packed light brown sugar	105 g
2 tablespoons	flour	2 tablespoons
1 large	egg, lightly beaten	1 large
1 cup	half-and-half cream	240 ml
A 9-inch	unbaked pie shell with a high fluted edge	A 23 cm

Peel and core the apples, then slice thin directly into a large bowl. Sprinkle with lemon juice, toss well and set aside for the moment. Cream the marzipan, butter, sugar and flour until creamy-smooth. (In a food processor fitted with the metal chopping blade, this will mean three to four 5-second churnings, with the work bowl being scraped down between each.) Blend in the egg and cream (a couple of fast zaps of the food processor motor).

Now dump about three-fourths of the apple slices into the pie shell, leveling the surface. Arrange the remaining apple slices in a sunburst pattern on top. Now slowly pour all but ¼ cup (60 ml) of the almond mixture evenly over the apples; reserve the final ¼ cup (60 ml) to use as a glaze.

Bake the pie, uncovered, in a hot oven (400°F. or 205°C.) for 15 minutes; reduce the heat to moderate (350°F. or 175°C.) and bake 20 minutes. Remove the pie from the oven and carefully spoon the reserved almond mixture on top, making sure that all apple slices are evenly glazed. Return the pie to the oven and bake 15 minutes longer until lightly browned. Cool the pie 30 minutes before cutting.

Caramel-glazed upside-down fresh peach tart

MAKES A 10-INCH (25 CM) TART

This tart is very much like the classic Tarte Tatin (a caramel-glazed, open-face, French apple tart), in fact, if you substitute apples for peaches, you will have a Tarte Tatin—well, almost. The authentic Tarte Tatin has a puff pastry (*feuilletage*) base, whereas this one is made with the rich short pastry known as *pâte brisée*. I like it just as well; besides, it's infinitely easier to prepare. (I make it a day ahead of time and keep it in the refrigerator until I'm ready to use it.) NOTES: *I find firm-ripe peaches best for this recipe because they will hold their shape when sliced thin, also because they darken less quickly than dead-ripe peaches. For arranging the sliced peaches in the bubbling-hot caramel syrup, I use chopsticks or small tongs so there's no danger of burning my fingers. For making and baking the tart, the best pan to use is a heavy iron or cast aluminum skillet that measures 10 inches (25 cm) across and has a heatproof handle.*

1 recipe	Pâte Brisée (see Index)	1 recipe
1 cup + 3 tablespoons	sugar	240 g
¼ pound (1 stick)	unsalted butter, cut into pats	115 g (1 stick)
5 large (about 2¼ pounds)	firm-ripe peaches	5 large (about 1 kg)
1 large	lemon, juiced	1 large
¼ teaspoon	freshly grated nutmeg	¼ teaspoon

Prepare the *pâte brisée* as directed, wrap snugly in plastic food wrap or wax paper and store in the refrigerator; do this several hours ahead of time.

Place the sugar and butter in a heavy 10-inch (25 cm) ovenproof skillet and set over low heat. Meanwhile, peel the peaches and slice uniformly thin, letting the slices drop into a large shallow bowl; sprinkle each layer of peaches lightly with lemon juice to keep them from darkening. TIP: *I find it easiest to slice the peaches whole, peeled but not pitted. With a very sharp paring knife, cut straight down to the pit, then make a second cut parallel to the first and about ⅛ inch (½ cm) from it. To loosen the slice, twist the knife slightly in the second cut; the slice will pop right out. Continue in this manner until each peach is sliced.* Keep an eye on the skillet as you slice the peaches; as soon as the butter has melted, stir it and the sugar well to combine. Continue to heat the butter and sugar over low heat, without stirring, until the two begin to caramelize—turn a pale amber color.

Now starting in the center of the skillet and working very carefully, arrange the peach slices in concentric circles, each slice (and each circle) overlapping the previous one slightly so that you have a sunburst design. Once you have completed the design, it doesn't much matter how you add the remaining peaches because they won't show; do make certain, however, that the final layer of peaches is fairly level. When all of the peaches are in the skillet, turn the heat to its lowest point and cook the peaches in the caramel syrup for 20 minutes; do not cover the skillet and do not disturb the peaches. At this point, remove the *pâte brisée* from the refrigerator and set on the counter to soften slightly, but do not unwrap it.

Transfer the skillet to a hot oven (400°F. or 205°C.) and bake the peaches, uncovered, for 5 minutes. Remove the skillet from the oven and sprinkle the peaches evenly with the nutmeg. Allow to cool on a wire rack while you roll out the pastry. Also raise the oven heat to very hot (450°F. or 230°C.).

Unwrap the *pâte brisée*, shape into a ball, then flatten with your hands on a lightly floured pastry cloth. Even up any ragged edges with your hands, then roll the pastry gently, using quick short strokes and working from the center outward until you have a circle that measures 10 inches (25 cm) in diameter and about ½ inch (1½ cm) thick. Lay the rolling pin across the center of the pastry circle, gently lop half of the pastry over the rolling pin, then lift it and ease into the skillet flat on top of the peaches. Even up any ragged edges and patch any holes by pinching the pastry together. With a sharp-pronged fork, prick the pastry lightly all over to allow steam to escape and keep the pastry from buckling or breaking.

Set the tart in the very hot oven and bake, uncovered, for 20 minutes or until the pastry is lightly browned. Remove the tart from the oven, set on a trivet and cool for 10 minutes so that the syrup has a chance to thicken somewhat. Now place a large (about 12-inch or 30 cm in diameter) heatproof plate on top of the skillet and, protecting both hands with potholders, quickly invert the skillet so that the tart slides out onto the plate. Lift off the skillet and if any peaches have stuck to it or been dislodged from the sunburst design—inevitable, I'm afraid—simply pick them up and replace them in the design. No one will be the wiser. Let the tart cool 20 to 30 minutes, then cut into slim wedges and serve. Pass a bowl of softly whipped cream, if you like; it makes a nice—though far from necessary—topping.

VARIATION:

Tarte Tatin: Prepare precisely as directed for the peach tart, but substitute 5 large peeled, cored and thinly sliced apples for the peaches.

Basic & multipurpose recipes

Collected here are some fundamentals and recipes referred to elsewhere in this book—including pastries and stocks, a trio of delicious starches (risotto, wild rice and *Spaetzle*), sauces basic and elaborated and flavored butters.

Basic piecrust

MAKES ENOUGH FOR A SINGLE-CRUST 9- OR 10-INCH (23 OR 25 CM) PIE

This recipe has served me well for many years. I sometimes make it using half shortening and half lard or butter (I favor lard for meat pies; butter for apple, peach or pear pies). But whatever fat I use, I make certain that it's good and cold, for the secret of flaky pastry is distributing tiny flecks of chilled fat evenly throughout the pastry, which will melt during baking, forming crisp leaves. Overmanipulating the pastry will break the particles of fat down too much; using water that is too warm will melt them. In either case, you will toughen the pastry. NOTE: *For a double-crust pie, I prefer to make two batches of this recipe rather than to double the ingredients, because I've never been particularly lucky working with large quantities of pastry (I tend to overmix at the water-adding stage unless I use an unusually broad and shallow bowl). You'll notice that the Suet Pastry that follows is essentially a double recipe. It is also a shorter pastry (one containing more shortening, in this case shortening plus suet), so it stays light and crisp.*

1¼ cups	sifted all-purpose flour	125 g
½ teaspoon	salt	½ teaspoon

⅓ cup (firmly packed)	vegetable shortening	60 g
4–5 tablespoons	ice water	4–5 tablespoons

Sift the flour and salt together into a medium-size mixing bowl. Using a pastry blender or two knives, cut the shortening into the dry ingredients until crumbly—about the texture of uncooked oatmeal. Drizzle the ice water evenly over the surface of the fat-flour mixture, tossing briskly all the while with a fork. The second the pastry clings together, take it from the bowl and shape loosely into a ball on a lightly floured pastry cloth. The pastry is now ready to roll and fill as specific recipes instruct.

Suet pastry

MAKES ENOUGH FOR A DOUBLE-CRUST 9- OR 10-INCH
(23 OR 25 CM) PIE

Before the development of creamy vegetable shortenings, natural animal fats—principally butter, lard and suet—were what cooks used to shorten their breads and pastries. Butter and lard are still widely used, but not suet. Too bad, I think, because suet—the snowy, brittle fat encasing the kidneys of beef—adds crispness and flavor perfectly suited to savory pies. Suet, however, should not be substituted measure for measure for lard or vegetable shortening because it lacks the shortening power necessary for flaky-tender pastries. I find one part suet to two parts lard or vegetable shortening an ideal ratio.

2½ cups	sifted all-purpose flour	250 g
1 teaspoon	salt	1 teaspoon
½ cup (firmly packed)	vegetable shortening	95 g
¼ cup	finely minced suet	20 g
½ cup (about)	ice water	120 ml (about)

Sift the flour and salt together into a large shallow bowl. Cut the shortening into the dry ingredients, using a pastry blender or two knives, until the texture of coarse meal; add the suet and toss gently but thoroughly to mix. Now scatter the ice water, about 2 tablespoons at a time, over the surface of the fat-flour mixture, tossing briskly with a fork. As soon as the mixture holds together, stop adding water. NOTE: *The amount of water needed to make a pastry hold together will vary somewhat according to the composition of the flour (this may differ slightly from season to season and from one part of the country to another), how carefully you sifted and measured the flour, even according to how humid the weather is.* Lightly shape the pastry into a ball. It is now ready to roll and fill as individual recipes direct.

Pâte brisée
(RICH SHORT PASTRY)

MAKES ENOUGH FOR A 9- OR 10-INCH (23 OR 25 CM) SINGLE-CRUST PIE

This is the classic French pastry chefs use for a multitude of pies and tarts. It is exceedingly tender and must be kept well chilled, otherwise it will be too soft and sticky to roll. NOTE: *Because this pastry absorbs atmospheric moisture, do not make it in rainy or humid weather.*

1½ cups	sifted all-purpose flour	150 g
1 tablespoon	sugar	1 tablespoon
½ teaspoon	salt	½ teaspoon
¼ pound (1 stick)	unsalted butter, well chilled and cut into small cubes	115 g (1 stick)
1 medium-size	egg, lightly beaten with 1 tablespoon milk or light cream	1 medium-size

Combine the flour, sugar and salt in a medium-size mixing bowl, or place all three ingredients in the work bowl of a food processor fitted with the metal chopping blade and combine by churning briefly 2 to 3 times. Add the butter, distributing it evenly over the surface of the dry ingredients and cut in with a pastry blender until uniformly crumbly. If you are using the processor, switch the machine on and off quickly 5 times. Scrape the work bowl sides down with a rubber spatula; also gently stir the mixture up from the bottom of the bowl. Give the motor another 5 on-offs, again scrape the work bowl down and give another 5 on-offs. At this point inspect the mixture. It should be a little rougher in texture than oatmeal. If still too coarse, scrape the work bowl down once again and process with 5 more quick bursts of speed. Now drizzle the egg mixture evenly over the pastry "crumbs." If mixing by hand, toss briskly with a fork just until the mixture holds together. If using the processor, incorporate the egg mixture with 6 to 8 on-offs of the motor. If you overmix at this point, you will have a tough pastry.

Wrap the pastry snugly in wax paper or plastic food wrap and chill for about an hour before rolling. Use a lightly floured pastry cloth and stockinette-covered rolling pin, both of which facilitate rolling rich, tender pastries. Add only enough flour to keep pastry from sticking and roll as individual recipes instruct.

Pralin
(GROUND ALMOND BRITTLE)

MAKES ABOUT 1½ CUPS (350 ML)

Confectioners and bakers rely upon *pralin* to impart color, flavor and texture to a variety of pastries and tortes. It is also sometimes stirred into cream fillings or soufflé "batters" or sprinkled on top of freshly frosted cakes. I use it in making Dacquoise, that butter-cream-filled, crisp meringue torte (see Index). If stored in an airtight jar, *pralin* will keep well in the freezer for about six months. You need only dip into the jar and use a little bit at a time. I even like *pralin* sprinkled over vanilla or chocolate ice cream.

¾ cup	blanched almonds	130 ml
½ cup	superfine sugar	100 g
¼ cup	cold water	60 ml

Spread the almonds out on a pie tin, place uncovered in a slow oven (300°F. or 150°C.) and toast, stirring often, 20 to 30 minutes until pale golden. Remove from the oven and let cool. Meanwhile, combine the sugar and water in a very small but heavy pan (I use a butter warmer) and bring to a simmer over moderate heat. Cover briefly (this is to dissolve any sugar crystals that may have collected on the sides of the pan), then lower the heat slightly and cook the syrup until it thickens and turns the color of straw—if you keep the heat low enough, this will take 30 to 40 minutes. Do not stir the syrup as it cooks, because it will become granular. As soon as the syrup is pale amber, stir in the nuts and turn out at once onto a buttered pie tin. When the brittle has cooled to room temperature, break it into chunks, then grind very fine in a food processor equipped with the metal chopping blade or in an electric blender at high speed (three to four 20-second churnings should do the job). If you have neither processor nor blender, bundle the *pralin* into a dishtowel and pulverize by pounding with a mallet or the side of a meat clever.

Veal stock

MAKES 1½ QUARTS (1½ L)

Whenever you're preparing breast of veal, ask the butcher for the bony rib ends, which can be simmered into an all-purpose stock, then used as the foundation of soups, stews and sauces. This recipe makes a particularly fragrant stock. It freezes well, too.

4½–5 pounds	veal rib ends	2–2¼ kg
8 quarts, in all	water	8 L, in all
3 medium-size	yellow onions, peeled and each stuck with a clove	3 medium-size
1 medium-size	carrot, peeled and sliced thin	1 medium-size
1 medium-size	celery rib, sliced thin	1 medium-size
2 sprigs	fresh thyme or ¼ teaspoon crumbled leaf thyme	2 sprigs
2 sprigs	fresh parsley	2 sprigs

Place rib ends and 4 quarts of water in a large kettle. Set over moderate heat, bring to a simmer, then let bubble gently for 10 minutes. Drain the rib ends, rinse well to remove scum; then wash and rinse the kettle. Return rib ends to kettle, add another 4 quarts of water and all remaining ingredients and simmer, uncovered, about 8 hours. Strain the broth, discarding bones and other solids, cool to room temperature, then cover and refrigerate overnight.

Next day, lift off and discard layer of fat on top of the stock (the stock will be jellied). Return stock to moderate heat and simmer, uncovered, for about 2 hours or until reduced to about 1½ quarts (1½ L). Line a colander with several thicknesses of cheesecloth and set over a heatproof bowl. Pour in the stock and let it drip through.

If you intend to use the stock within the week, simply cover and refrigerate. Otherwise, pour into 1-pint (½ L) freezer containers, filling each to within ½ inch (1½ cm) of the top. Snap on lids, label, date and quick-freeze. NOTE: *This stock will keep well at 0°F. (− 18°C.) for about six months.*

Brown meat glaze

MAKES ¼ CUP (60 ML)

Nothing more than dramatically reduced beef broth, this glaze is a wonderfully handy flavor enhancer. Stored tightly covered in the refrigerator, it will keep well for several weeks. Use to enrich soups, gravies, sauces—particularly those pan sauces integral to so many veal *scallopine* dishes.

To make: Boil 2 cups (500 ml) rich beef broth (preferably homemade, but you may use a top-quality canned broth) in a small heavy saucepan, uncovered, over moderate heat for about 30 minutes, or until reduced to ¼ cup (60 ml). Cool to room temperature, strain through several thicknesses of cheesecloth, pour into a small glass jar, cover and store in the refrigerator.

Court bouillon

MAKES ABOUT 2½ QUARTS (2½ L)

This is a good all-round medium to use when poaching fish or shellfish. The Rich Court Bouillon below is a better choice to use as the foundation of fish soups, sauces and soufflés because of its more aromatic flavor.

1 pound	trimmings and bones from white fish such as cod, flounder or haddock	½ kg
1 medium-size	yellow onion, peeled and quartered	1 medium-size
1 large	celery rib, trimmed and sliced thin	1 large
4 large	parsley sprigs	4 large
10 large	peppercorns	10 large

2 quarts	cold water	2 L
1 pint	dry white wine	½ L
To taste	salt	To taste

Place all ingredients in a large stainless steel or enameled kettle, bring to a simmer over moderate heat and adjust the burner heat so that the kettle liquid stays at a tremble and does not boil actively. Set the lid on the kettle askew and simmer for 1 hour. Set a fine-mesh sieve over a large heatproof bowl, line it with several thicknesses of cheesecloth, pour in the court bouillon and let it drip through unattended (if you force the liquid out, you will "muddy" the court bouillon). Discard the strained-out solids, add salt to the court bouillon and use as individual recipes direct.

VARIATION:

Rich court bouillon: Prepare as directed, but to the kettle add a peeled and thinly sliced carrot, a peeled and slivered garlic clove, a nice sprig each of fresh thyme and dill (or ½ teaspoon crumbled leaf thyme and ¼ teaspoon dill weed) and, if you like, ½ small bay leaf (do not crumble).

Risotto

SERVES 4

There are several requisites for making risotto properly: You must use the short-grain Italian (Arborio) rice, a heavy saucepan, a moderately low heat and finally, you must have plenty of patience. You must be prepared to stand over a hot stove, stirring the pot, for about forty minutes. So choose carefully the day on which you intend to prepare a risotto. The trick is to add the liquid (in this case a mixture of chicken broth and water) to the rice slowly and in stages so that each grain absorbs the moisture, swells and cooks through evenly. The rice should be *al dente*, held together with a creamy, buttery mixture, not gummy, starchy or crumbly. Making perfect risotto requires practice, so don't be discouraged if it isn't precisely right the first time around. You must develop a practiced eye (not to mention a magic touch)—knowing exactly how much liquid to add, how vigorously to stir, how much heat to apply. (I find that I have best results if I keep the burner heat moderately low.)

1 large	shallot, peeled and minced	1 large
2 tablespoons	unsalted butter	2 tablespoons
1 tablespoon	olive oil (top quality) or vegetable oil	1 tablespoon
1 cup	Arborio rice (obtainable in specialty shops)	240 ml
1¾ cups	simmering chicken broth	415 ml
1¼ cups	simmering water	300 ml
To taste	salt and freshly ground black pepper	To taste

Stir-fry the shallot in the butter and olive oil in a medium-size heavy saucepan over moderate heat 2 to 3 minutes until limp; add the rice and stir-fry 2 minutes until every grain is golden and translucent; now reduce the heat to moderately low. Combine the chicken broth and water and adjust burner under this mixture so that it stays at a slow simmer. Pour ⅓ cup (80 ml) of the broth mixture into the rice and heat, stirring all the while, until all of the liquid has been absorbed by the rice. This should take 3 to 4 minutes. Continue in this manner, adding the broth mixture ⅓ cup (80 ml) at a time and cooking the rice until it has absorbed each batch of broth before you add the next one. You will need to add the liquid in eleven to twelve installments and to cook the rice 3 to 4 minutes after each addition. Do not try to hurry the process by raising the burner heat because you may scorch the rice; or the rice may become gummy on the outside but remain hard and chalky inside. When you have added about half the broth mixture, you will notice that the rice grains have doubled in size and are becoming gelatinous on the outside. At this point you must stir more slowly; otherwise you may bruise, break or mash the rice.

When you have only two or three more additions of liquid left to stir into the rice, take up a grain and taste it. When done, the rice will be tender-firm all the way through; there will be no crumbly center and no taste of raw starch. Take the risotto from the heat the minute it passes these tests of doneness, season to taste with salt and pepper, and serve in place of potatoes with veal, pork or chicken.

VARIATION:

Cheese risotto: Prepare precisely as directed above, but along with the final addition of liquid stir in 5 tablespoons of freshly grated Parmesan cheese and 1 tablespoon of unsalted butter. Stir just until the butter and cheese melt, then serve.

Boiled wild rice

SERVES 4

My method of cooking wild rice may be a bit unorthodox, but I like it because the rice has plenty of crunch and will not, when used to stuff chicken, turkey or game birds, become gummy or gluey.

1 cup	wild rice, washed well	240 ml
2 cups	cold water	½ L
2 tablespoons	unsalted butter or bacon drippings	2 tablespoons
To taste	salt and freshly ground black pepper	To taste

Place the rice and water in a heavy medium-size saucepan and bring to a boil, uncovered, over moderately high heat. Adjust the burner so that the water bubbles gently, then boil the rice uncovered for about 20 minutes or until the level of the water has dropped well below that of the rice. NOTE: *When you tilt the pan, there should be very little water visible.* Cover the pan, reduce the heat to low and cook the rice about 10 minutes longer or until it has puffed up a bit and all water has evaporated. If at this point a bit of water remains, simply turn the burner heat up again and boil the rice uncovered a minute or two longer until the rice is dry. Fork in the butter or bacon drippings, then season to taste with salt and pepper.

VARIATION:

Wild rice with carrot and onion: Cook the rice as directed, using a half-and-half mixture of beef or chicken broth and water. Stir-fry 1 medium-size peeled and chopped onion and 1 medium-size peeled and chopped carrot in 3 tablespoons unsalted butter, or in bacon drippings, about 5 minutes over moderate heat until limp and golden. Crumble in a pinch each of leaf rosemary and thyme, and mellow over the heat about 1 minute. Stir the onion mixture into the cooked wild rice, season to taste with salt and pepper and serve. NICE ADDITIONS: *About ½ cup (120 ml) crisp crumbled bacon and/or coarsely chopped pecans or walnuts and/or ¼ pound (115 g) thinly sliced mushrooms that have been lightly browned in a little butter.*

Homemade egg Spaetzle

SERVES 4

Serve these German noodles in place of potatoes with roasts or ragouts. The simplest way to shape them is by pushing the batter through a metal *spaetzle* press (it resembles a potato ricer and can be bought at specialty kitchen shops) or through a fine colander.

1 cup + 2 tablespoons	sifted all-purpose flour	115 g
⅛ teaspoon	freshly grated nutmeg	⅛ teaspoon
½ teaspoon	salt	½ teaspoon
1 large	egg	1 large
6 tablespoons	milk	6 tablespoons
3–4 gallons	boiled salted water (for cooking spaetzle)	12–16 L
¼ cup	melted unsalted butter	60 ml

To mix in a food processor: Place flour, nutmeg and salt in a work bowl fitted with the metal chopping blade and whirl briskly to mix. Add egg and milk and beat hard (about 3 to 4 one-minute churnings of the motor) until batter is elastic and shows bubbles on the surface.

To hand-mix: Mix dry ingredients in a bowl; combine egg and milk and add all at once; beat hard until batter is bubbly and elastic.

Push the batter through a *spaetzle* press (or colander) into kettle of rapidly boiling salted water. Cook the *spaetzle* uncovered for 8 minutes, stirring occasionally. With a slotted spoon, lift the *spaetzle* to a large bowl of ice water and let stand until nearly ready to serve—but no longer than an hour or two.

Drain the *spaetzle* well in a colander, then warm 4 to 5 minutes in the melted butter in a large sauté pan over moderately low heat, stirring now and then. Serve at once.

Basic white (or cream) sauces

EACH MAKES 1 CUP (240 ML)

The standard White Sauce (sometimes called Cream Sauce because it is the color and consistency of cream) performs all manner of culinary magic from thickening cream soups to propping up soufflés to binding croquettes together. Indeed, how the sauce will be used determines whether it should be thick or thin. Traditionally, the thickener used is flour and the liquid is milk. But the fat may vary. Usually it is butter (or margarine), but if you are making gravy, you will want to use the fat skimmed from the pan drippings.

SOME TIPS: Always mellow the flour in the butter 1 to 2 minutes to take off the raw starchy edge. . . . Always have the milk at room temperature before you add it to the fat-flour mixture (roux), because if it is refrigerator-cold, the butter will lump the instant the milk touches it and you will find it more difficult to make a silky-smooth sauce. . . . Stir the sauce constantly as it thickens to prevent lumping (I generally move a wooden spoon over the bottom of the pan in large figure-eights, then move out to encircle the pan after every fourth or fifth figure-eight to get up any roux that may have lodged around the edge). . . . Once the sauce has thickened, lower the heat and mellow it 3 to 5 minutes, stirring often, so that the flour is thoroughly cooked. If, despite all precautions, your white sauce lumps, fret not. Simply press it through a fine sieve, or, if the sauce is a thin or medium one, buzz the lumps out in a food processor fitted with the metal chopping blade by churning for about one minute nonstop.

NOTE: *If a recipe calls for cooling a white sauce, as soufflés usually do, a "skin" will form on the surface of the sauce unless you take some preventive measure. You can: (1) Stir the sauce frequently as it cools; (2) cover the sauce with a thin layer of melted butter (this must be poured off before you use the sauce); or (3) partially cool the sauce, stirring all the while, then place a piece of plastic food wrap flat on the* surface of the sauce. (The reason for partially cooling the sauce is to allow all steam to escape; if you seal it under plastic, it will condense into large droplets of water, which will fall into and thin the sauce—often to the point that it can no longer be used for its original purpose.)

Very thin white sauce (used primarily to thicken cream soups made with potatoes or other starchy vegetables):

1 to 2 tablespoons	unsalted butter, margarine or fat drippings	1 to 2 tablespoons
1½ teaspoons	flour	1½ teaspoons
1 cup	milk, at room temperature	240 ml
To taste	salt and white pepper	To taste

Thin white sauce (used to thicken cream soups made of nonstarchy vegetables and bisques):

1 to 2 tablespoons	unsalted butter, margarine or fat drippings	1 to 2 tablespoons
1 tablespoon	flour	1 tablespoon
1 cup	milk, at room temperature	240 ml
To taste	salt and white pepper	To taste

Medium white sauce (used in creaming or scalloping meats, fish, fowl and vegetables, also for thickening standard gravies and sauces):

2 tablespoons	unsalted butter, margarine or fat drippings	2 tablespoons
2 tablespoons	flour	2 tablespoons
1 cup	milk, at room temperature	240 ml
To taste	salt and white pepper	To taste

Thick white sauce (used as the base of soufflés made with starchy, heavy or thick purées):

3 tablespoons	unsalted butter, margarine or fat drippings	3 tablespoons
3 tablespoons	flour	3 tablespoons
1 cup	milk, at room temperature	240 ml
To taste	salt and white pepper	To taste

Very thick white sauce (used as the foundation of soufflés made with non-starchy or thin purées, also as a binder for croquettes):

4 tablespoons (¼ cup)	unsalted butter, margarine or fat drippings	4 tablespoons (60 ml)
4 tablespoons (¼ cup)	flour	4 tablespoons (60 ml)
1 cup	milk, at room temperature	240 ml
To taste	salt and white pepper	To taste

Standard preparation (for all white sauces): Melt the butter in a small heavy saucepan over moderate to moderately low heat, but do not allow it to brown. Blend in the flour to make a smooth paste, mellow for a minute or two, then set the pan off the heat. Add the milk and beat vigorously until incorporated with the roux (fat-flour mixture), return to moderate heat and cook and stir until thickened and smooth—about 3 minutes. Turn the heat to its lowest point and allow the sauce to mellow about 5 minutes, stirring occasionally, until there are no traces of a raw flour taste.

SOME EASY VARIATIONS ON MEDIUM WHITE SAUCE:

Mustard sauce: Blend 3 tablespoons of mild French mustard and 1 to 2 tablespoons white or red wine vinegar into 1 cup of finished White Sauce. Serve with ham, or over boiled green beans or broccoli. A *good addition:* ¼ cup (60 ml) finely minced chutney.

Mild cheese sauce: Mix ½ cup (120 ml) of grated mild Cheddar or American cheese into 1 cup (240 ml) of finished White Sauce along with a good pinch of ground nutmeg; heat and stir until the cheese melts.

Nippy cheese sauce: Mix ¼ cup (60 ml) grated sharp Cheddar cheese and 2 to 3 tablespoons freshly grated Parmesan or Romano cheese into 1 cup (240 ml) of finished White Sauce along with ⅛ teaspoon cayenne pepper; heat and stir until uniformly smooth. Now add, if you like, a couple of tablespoons of good strong beer or ale, dry white wine or medium-dry sherry.

Gruyère sauce: Mix ½ cup (120 ml) grated Gruyère cheese into 1 cup (240 ml) of finished White Sauce along with a good pinch of ground nutmeg or mace; heat and stir until the cheese melts, then blend in 1 to 2 tablespoons of dry white wine and, if you like, a pinch of cayenne. Wonderful over toasted English muffins.

Roquefort, gorgonzola or blue cheese sauce: Mix ¼ to ⅓ cup (60 to 80 ml) of crumbled Roquefort, Gorgonzola or blue cheese into 1 cup (240 ml) of finished White Sauce along with 1 tablespoon medium-dry sherry or Port. Heat and stir until the cheese is melted. This sauce is marvelous over baked potatoes.

Mushroom sauce: Mix ⅓ cup (80 ml) of Duxelles (see recipe in this section) into 1 cup (240 ml) of finished White Sauce. Delicious over baked potatoes, boiled green beans or spinach.

Herb sauce: Minced fresh basil, mint, flat-leaf or curly parsley, chives, tarragon, chervil, fresh coriander (also known as *cilantro* or Chinese parsley) all make aromatic sauces for poultry, fish, shellfish, potatoes and other vegetables such as carrots, beets, broccoli, Brussels sprouts, green peas and beans. Usually 3 to 4 tablespoons of freshly minced herb per 1 cup (240 ml) of finished White Sauce will be sufficient (keep tasting as you add an herb). Let the herb mellow in the sauce about 5 minutes before serving. With the basil, chives, parsley and coriander, 2 to 3 tablespoons freshly ground Parmesan and a pinch of freshly grated nutmeg will enhance the flavor. And I often slip in a tablespoon or two of dry white wine.

Béchamel sauce

MAKES 2 CUPS (½ L)

Béchamel is nothing more than the French version of White Sauce (see preceding recipes). It is made with butter (not drippings) and usually contains some heavy cream. The principle liquid may be milk or a light veal or chicken stock. Velouté (see the variation below) is similar, but contains no cream or milk. Its foundation is chicken, veal or fish stock, which varies according to the food to be sauced.

4 tablespoons	unsalted butter (no substitute)	4 tablespoons
4 tablespoons	flour	4 tablespoons
1⅔ cups	veal or chicken stock or milk, at room temperature	395 ml
⅓ cup	heavy cream, at room temperature	80 ml
To taste	salt and white pepper	To taste

Melt the butter in a medium-size heavy saucepan over moderately low heat and blend in the flour to make a smooth paste; mellow 2 to 3 minutes, then remove from the heat. Combine the stock and cream, pour into the flour paste, return to moderately low heat and cook and stir until thickened and smooth—3 to 5 minutes. Season with salt and pepper, then turn heat to its lowest point and allow the sauce to mellow, stirring often, about 5 minutes.

VARIATIONS:

Velouté sauce: Prepare precisely as directed for Béchamel, but use 2 cups (½ L) of veal, chicken or fish stock in place of the stock and cream mixture.

Caper sauce: Prepare the Velouté as directed, then swirl in 4 tablespoons of unsalted butter, a tablespoon at a time, stirring well after each addition. Mix in ¼ cup (60 ml) of drained fine capers and serve over broiled or poached salmon, tuna or swordfish.

Parsley sauce

MAKES 2 CUPS (½ L)

Here's a versatile sauce that can be used for "creaming" carrots, turnips, potatoes, turkey, chicken, ham, even hard-cooked eggs. It also makes an excellent sauce for carrots, green beans, limas, green peas, boiled whole new potatoes and Carrot Pancakes (see Index).

4 tablespoons	unsalted butter	4 tablespoons
4 tablespoons	flour	4 tablespoons
2 cups	milk at room temperature	½ L
½ teaspoon	salt	½ teaspoon
Pinch	white pepper	Pinch
Pinch	freshly grated nutmeg or mace (optional)	Pinch
3 tablespoons	minced parsley	3 tablespoons

Melt the butter in a small heavy saucepan over moderate heat, then blend in the flour. Add the milk all at once. Heat, stirring constantly, until thickened and smooth. Blend in the salt, pepper, nutmeg (if you like) and parsley. Turn the heat to its lowest point and allow the sauce to mellow about 10 minutes, stirring often to prevent a skin from forming on the surface.

VARIATIONS:

Fresh dill sauce: Prepare as directed but substitute ¼ cup (60 ml) snipped fresh dill for the 3 tablespoons of minced parsley. Serve over boiled new potatoes, butter-browned mushroom caps or broiled, steamed or poached lean white fish.

Fresh mint sauce: Prepare as directed but substitute 3 tablespoons of minced fresh mint for the parsley. Use for "creaming" diced carrots, green beans or peas or as a sauce for boiled new potatoes.

Cheese sauce: Prepare as directed but omit the parsley and add 1 cup (240 ml) coarsely grated Cheddar cheese along with 2 tablespoons of grated Parmesan and, if you like, 1 teaspoon of Dijon mustard and/or Worcestershire sauce. Use as a sauce for baked potatoes, steamed green beans, broccoli, cauliflower or cabbage.

Sauce Espagnole

MAKES ABOUT 1½ CUPS (350 ML)

This is my shortcut version of the long-winded classic. I think you'll find it surprisingly good, and I doubt that any but the most discriminating palate will know the difference.

1 medium-size	yellow onion, peeled and finely minced	1 medium-size
1 small	carrot, peeled and minced	1 small
1 tablespoon	minced parsley	1 tablespoon
¼ teaspoon	crumbled leaf thyme	¼ teaspoon
½ small	bay leaf, crumbled	½ small
4 tablespoons	unsalted butter	4 tablespoons
4 tablespoons	flour	4 tablespoons
½ cup	dry white wine	120 ml
2 cups	strong beef broth	½ L
1 tablespoon	tomato paste	1 tablespoon
To taste	salt and freshly ground black pepper	To taste

Stir-fry the onion, carrot, parsley, thyme and bay leaf in the butter in a small heavy saucepan over moderate heat 12 to 15 minutes until nicely browned. Blend in the flour and mellow about 10 minutes over moderate heat, stirring often, until the mixture turns a rich amber color. Combine the wine, broth and tomato paste, pour in all at once and heat, stirring constantly, until thickened and smooth—3 to 5 minutes. Turn heat to its lowest point and let the sauce bubble gently, stirring now and then, about half an hour or until glistening brown and richly flavored. Strain through a fine sieve, then season to taste with salt (it's unlikely that you'll need any salt if the broth is well salted) and pepper. Use in making Bordelaise Sauce, which follows, or the Sauce Madère below.

VARIATION:

Sauce madère (Madeira Sauce): Prepare the Sauce Espagnole as directed, then mix in ¼ cup (60 ml) of medium-dry (Verdelho) or medium-sweet (Boal) Madeira wine just before serving. This sauce is superlative served over baked ham, grilled beef, broiled or roast chicken.

Bordelaise sauce

MAKES ABOUT 1½ CUPS (350 ML)

The classic topper for grilled chops and steaks, Bordelaise descends from the glistening brown French sauce known as Espagnole.

1 large	shallot, peeled and minced	1 large
2 tablespoons	unsalted butter	2 tablespoons
⅔ cup	dry red wine	160 ml
Pinch	crumbled leaf thyme	Pinch
1 cup	Sauce Espagnole (see above)	240 ml
¼ cup	finely diced bone marrow, blanched 2 minutes in boiling water and drained very dry	60 ml
½ cup	strong beef broth	120 ml
1 teaspoon	finely minced parsley	1 teaspoon
Light sprinkling	freshly ground black pepper	Light sprinkling

Stir-fry the shallot in the butter in a small heavy saucepan over low heat about 10 minutes until limp and golden. Add the wine and thyme and boil uncovered until reduced to about ¼ cup (60 ml)—about 15 minutes. Stir in the Sauce Espagnole and simmer slowly, stirring often, about 5 minutes. Add the marrow, beef broth, parsley and pepper, simmer 2 to 3 minutes longer, then serve.

Processor hollandaise sauce

MAKES 1½ CUPS (350 ML)

The food processor, I think, is worth its price if for no other reason than that it makes faultless Hollandaise in about two minutes flat. This recipe, together with the variations below and the Béarnaise, which follows, are all recipes I developed for *Jean Anderson's Processor Cooking*, published in 1979 by William Morrow and Company. I offer them here again because they are the easiest (no more worries about curdling)—and the best. NOTE: *You can also make each of these sauces in an electric blender set at high speed.*

2 tablespoons	lemon juice	2 tablespoons
1 jumbo	egg	1 jumbo
Pinch	salt	Pinch
Pinch	white pepper	Pinch
½ cup (1 stick)	melted unsalted butter	120 ml (1 stick)
½ cup	corn oil or peanut oil	120 ml

Place the lemon juice, egg, salt and pepper in the work bowl of a food processor fitted with the metal chopping blade or in the container of an electric blender and whir once or twice to blend. Now with the motor running, drizzle in the butter, then the oil, in a very fine stream. Let the motor run nonstop for about 20 seconds after all of the butter and oil have been incorporated.

VARIATIONS:

Mousseline sauce: Prepare the Hollandaise as directed, then fold in ½ cup (120 ml) of heavy cream that has been whipped to stiff peaks. This sauce is superb ladled over delicate broiled or poached white fish. It's also good with any green vegetables that are compatible with Hollandaise—green beans, broccoli and asparagus, to name three.

Figaro sauce: Prepare the Hollandaise as directed, then blend in 2 tablespoons of tomato purée and 1 tablespoon of minced fresh parsley. Delicious with grilled salmon or swordfish.

Mustard hollandaise: Prepare the Hollandaise as directed, then blend in 2 tablespoons of Dijon mustard. Serve over seafood or green vegetables.

Processor béarnaise sauce

MAKES ABOUT 1½ CUPS (350 ML)

2 tablespoons	fresh tarragon leaves (or ¾ teaspoon crumbled leaf tarragon)	2 tablespoons
2 tablespoons	fresh chervil leaves (or ¾ teaspoon crumbled leaf chervil)	2 tablespoons
1 medium-size	shallot, peeled and finely minced	1 medium-size
¼ cup	tarragon vinegar	60 ml
2 tablespoons	dry white wine or vermouth	2 tablespoons
1 jumbo	egg	1 jumbo
¼ teaspoon	salt	¼ teaspoon
Pinch	freshly ground black pepper	Pinch
½ cup (1 stick)	melted unsalted butter	120 ml (1 stick)
½ cup	corn oil or peanut oil	120 ml

In a small, covered saucepan, boil the tarragon, chervil, shallot, vinegar and wine about 3 minutes or until the herbs are wilted; uncover and boil until the liquid reduces to 2 tablespoons. Empty into a food processor fitted with the metal chopping blade or into the container of an electric blender and cool 5 minutes. Break the egg into the work bowl or blender, add the salt and pepper, cover and whir briefly once or twice to blend. Now, with the motor running, drizzle the butter in a very fine stream, then the corn oil. Beat the Béarnaise for another 20 seconds nonstop after all of the butter and oil have been incorporated. Serve over broiled steaks, chops or fish.

Beurre blanc
(WHITE BUTTER SAUCE)

MAKES ½ CUP (120 ML)

My version of the exquisite French sauce used to dress seafood, asparagus, broccoli and artichokes.

1 large	shallot, peeled and finely minced	1 large
⅓ cup	dry white wine	80 ml
1 tablespoon	white wine vinegar	1 tablespoon
2 tablespoons	crème fraîche or heavy cream	2 tablespoons
6 tablespoons	unsalted butter, cut into bits	6 tablespoons

In a small, heavy, uncovered saucepan, boil the shallot, wine and vinegar 3 to 5 minutes until reduced by three-fourths. Strain, return the liquid to the pan, add the *crème fraîche* and let it bubble just once. Turn the heat down low and whisk the butter in, bit by bit, beating hard all the while. Pour into a heated sauceboat and serve.

Flavored butters

EACH MAKES ABOUT ½ CUP OR 120 ML

These are a snap to make (particularly if you have a food processor) and can be shaped into logs, foil-wrapped, frozen, then sliced into pats and used to season grilled steaks, chops, fish and fowl. I also find them an easy way to bestow elegance upon simply steamed or boiled vegetables. The process for making the different flavored butters is more or less the same: the butter is creamed until fluffy (but not so much that it begins to liquefy), then the flavoring is beaten in. The flavored butter should next be chilled until firm enough to shape into a log or stick, wrapped and stored in the refrigerator or freezer. MAXIMUM STORAGE TIMES: About ten days in the refrigerator, four months in the freezer.

Anchovy butter: Cream ¼ pound or 115 g (1 stick) of unsalted butter until fluffy-light, then beat in 2 teaspoons of anchovy paste, 1 tablespoon of lemon juice and a pinch of freshly ground black pepper. Chill, shape and wrap as directed above. Particularly good with broiled salmon, swordfish, tuna, scrod or flounder. Also good on broiled steaks, chops or chicken.

Chives butter: Cream ¼ pound or 115 g (1 stick) of unsalted butter until light, then beat in 2 tablespoons of finely snipped fresh chives. Chill, shape and wrap as directed above. Delicious in baked potatoes, as a seasoner for green beans or summer squash; also good over broiled steaks, chops, chicken, salmon, swordfish or tuna.

Dill butter: Cream ¼ pound or 115 g (1 stick) of unsalted butter until light, then beat in 3 tablespoons of finely snipped fresh dill and 1 teaspoon of lemon juice. Chill, shape and wrap as directed. Superb with broiled, poached or sautéed fish, also as a seasoner for fresh asparagus, green beans, broccoli, beets, carrots and summer squash.

Garlic butter: Cream ¼ pound or 115 g (1 stick) of unsalted butter until light, then beat in a large, peeled, minced and crushed garlic clove. NOTE: *I sometimes also mix in a tablespoon or two of freshly grated Parmesan cheese and a pinch of crumbled leaf marjoram.* Chill, shape and wrap as directed. Use in making garlic bread or as a topper for grilled steaks, chops or chicken.

Lemon butter: Cream ¼ pound or 115 g (1 stick) of unsalted butter until light, then beat in 2 tablespoons of lemon juice and ½ teaspoon of finely grated lemon rind. Chill, shape and wrap as directed. Delicious with all fish and shellfish, also as a seasoner for asparagus, beans, broccoli, carrots and summer squash.

Maître d'hôtel butter: Cream ¼ pound or 115 g (1 stick) of unsalted butter until fluffy-light, then beat in 2 tablespoons of finely minced parsley, 2 tablespoons of lemon juice, ¼ teaspoon of salt and ⅛ teaspoon of white pepper. Chill, shape and wrap as directed. Delicious with all fish, grilled steaks and chops.

Marchands de vin butter: Sauté a large peeled and minced shallot in 1 tablespoon of butter in a small heavy saucepan over moderate heat 2 to 3 minutes until limp and golden; add ½ cup (120 ml) dry red wine and boil hard until reduced to a thick glaze on the bottom of the pan—about 3 minutes; remove from the heat and cool. Meanwhile, cream ¼ pound or 115 g (1 stick) of unsalted butter until fluffy-light; beat in the shallot mixture along with 1 tablespoon of lemon juice, 1 tablespoon of finely minced parsley, ½ teaspoon of bottled meat extract and a hefty grinding of black pepper. Chill, shape and wrap as directed. Magnificent over grilled steaks and chops.

Mustard butter: Cream ¼ pound or 115 g (1 stick) of unsalted butter until light, then beat in 2 tablespoons of Dijon mustard and 1 tablespoon of lemon juice. Chill, shape and wrap as directed. Serve over grilled steaks, chops, chicken, swordfish or salmon. Or use to season green beans, broccoli or asparagus.

Orange butter: Cream ¼ pound or 115 g (1 stick) of unsalted butter until light, then beat in 2 tablespoons of lemon juice and 1 teaspoon of finely grated orange rind. Chill, shape and wrap as directed. Serve over grilled chicken, swordfish, salmon, pompano or red snapper. Or use to season green peas.

Parsley butter: Cream ¼ pound or 115 g (1 stick) of unsalted butter until light, then beat in 2 tablespoons of finely minced parsley and 1 teaspoon of lemon juice. Chill, shape and wrap as directed. Delicious over grilled steaks, chops, chicken or fish. Or use to season whole boiled potatoes.

Tarragon butter: Cream ¼ pound or 115 g (1 stick) of unsalted butter until light, then beat in 3 tablespoons of finely minced fresh tarragon and 1 tablespoon of lemon juice or tarragon vinegar. NOTE: *I also sometimes beat in 1 tablespoon of Dijon mustard.* Chill, shape and wrap as directed. Superb over most fish, also over lobster, shrimp and crab. I also like Tarragon Butter over grilled tomatoes, steaks, chops and chicken (particularly if I have added the mustard).

Duxelles
(MUSHROOM PASTE)

MAKES 1½ CUPS (350 ML)

I always keep a little jar of *Duxelles* on hand to use in seasoning soups, sauces, stuffings and all manner of casseroles. The mushrooms are highly concentrated, so a few tablespoons will have considerable impact. Tightly covered in a glass jar, the *Duxelles* will keep well in the refrigerator for ten days to two weeks; frozen, it will keep safe for several months. Simply uncap the jar and dip out as much *Duxelles* as you need, then recap and return the balance to the refrigerator or freezer.

3 medium-size	shallots, peeled and minced	3 medium-size
3 tablespoons	unsalted butter	3 tablespoons
1 pound	mushrooms, wiped clean and minced	½ kg
Pinch	freshly grated nutmeg	Pinch
2 tablespoons	dry white wine	2 tablespoons
¼ teaspoon	salt	¼ teaspoon
Light sprinkling	freshly ground black pepper	Light sprinkling

Stir-fry the shallots in the butter in a large heavy skillet over low heat about 10 minutes until very soft (do not brown). Meanwhile, bundle the mushrooms in a large clean dishtowel, twist the loose ends into a gooseneck, then twist tighter and tighter, forcing as much liquid from the mushrooms as possible. (Save the liquid for a soup or stock.) When mushrooms are quite dry, dump them into the skillet and add the nutmeg; sauté over moderate heat, stirring often, 10 to 12 minutes. Sprinkle the wine evenly over the surface and cook another 5 minutes or so until the mixture is thick and pastelike. Stir in the salt and pepper, spoon into a storage jar and set in the refrigerator or freezer.

Pesto sauce

MAKES ABOUT 1½ CUPS (350 ML)

 I am so fond of *pesto* that whenever fresh basil is in season (May through July), I make multiple batches of it, then freeze it in half-pint containers so that I can enjoy it throughout the winter. The food processor, by the way, has revolutionized the making of *pesto* and put it within the realm of every cook who can lay her hands on a hefty supply of basil. For each pound of pasta, you'll need ½ to ¾ cup (120 to 180 ml) of *pesto*, so the quantity this recipe makes will dress two to three pounds (1 to 1½ kg) altogether—enough for six to eight servings. The pasta I prefer for *pesto* is thin spaghetti (No. 9), cooked *al dente*.

2 cups (firmly packed)	*fresh basil leaves, well washed and patted very dry on paper toweling*	*½ L (firmly packed)*
2 medium-size	*garlic cloves, peeled*	*2 medium-size*
2 tablespoons	*lightly toasted* pignoli *(pine nuts)*	*2 tablespoons*
½ cup	*olive oil (top quality)*	*120 ml*
½ teaspoon	*salt*	*½ teaspoon*
⅛ teaspoon	*freshly ground black pepper*	*⅛ teaspoon*

Place all ingredients in the work bowl of a food processor fitted with the metal chopping blade; buzz 30 seconds nonstop. Scrape the sides of the work bowl down with a rubber spatula, then buzz 30 seconds longer. If the mixture is not uniformly smooth, buzz another 30 to 60 seconds. Spoon into a 1-pint (½ L) preserving jar, cover tight and store in the refrigerator; the *pesto* will keep well for about two weeks. Take out amounts as needed to dress pasta, and let it stand at room temperature about half an hour before using. TIP: *The easiest way I've found to dress pasta with* pesto *is to drain the pasta well, return it to the kettle in which I cooked it, add 2 tablespoons of olive oil or softened butter, then to toss the pasta in the oil or butter until evenly coated. I then add the* pesto *and toss well again. Freshly grated Parmesan should be passed separately.*

NOTE: *See Index for directions for toasting* pignoli.

Swedish dill and mustard sauce

MAKES 1½ CUPS (350 ML)

Normally this sauce is stationed on a *smörgåsbord* table near the pickled herring so that guests can spoon hefty dollops of it over the herring. I think it's marvelous with cold poached salmon or sea bass, with cold poached scallops, lobster, shrimp or lump crab meat. NOTE: *It's important to let* *the sauce mellow several hours in the refrigerator before you serve it so that the flavors have a chance to mingle with and temper one another. If you have a blender or food processor, so much the better. You'll be able to make the sauce in about 2 minutes flat. If not, mince the dill very fine and beat the sauce well with a whisk.*

1 cup	feathery dill clusters (measure moderately loosely packed)	240 ml
1 tablespoon	sugar	1 tablespoon
¼ cup	Dijon mustard	60 ml
1 tablespoon	prepared mild yellow mustard	1 tablespoon
1 cup	heavy cream	240 ml

Place all ingredients in the container of an electric blender or in a food processor equipped with the metal chopping blade. Buzz 30 seconds, scrape the blender cup or work bowl sides down with a rubber spatula, then buzz another 30 seconds. Have a look at the sauce—it should be slightly thinner than sour cream, thin enough to pour. If it is not thick enough, buzz for another 20 to 30 seconds, just until the cream begins to thicken. Spoon into a bowl, cover and chill 3 to 4 hours before serving.

PART TWO

Recipe Collection:

Particular Favorites

Appetizers
& hors
d'oeuvre

Fresh basil sorbet

SERVES 6 TO 8

This is not a dessert but a between-the-courses, palate-clearing ice. It's very tart and best when served after the fish and before the meat course.

3 medium-size bunches	fresh basil (you will need about 4 cups or 1 L lightly packed leaves)	3 medium-size bunches
5 cups	boiling water	1¼ L
½ cup (about)	sugar	120 ml (about)
1 envelope	plain gelatin	1 envelope
2 medium-size	lemons, juiced	2 medium-size

Carefully separate the basil leaves from the stems; discard the stems and any seriously blemished leaves. Wash the reserved basil leaves carefully in cool water, then pile them in a medium-size heatproof bowl. Pour the boiling water over the basil, then let cool to room temperature.

In a medium-size heavy saucepan, combine the sugar and gelatin. Add 4 cups (1 L) of the basil infusion, set over moderate heat and heat, stirring frequently, about 5 minutes or until sugar and gelatin both dissolve. Set aside.

In a food processor fitted with the metal chopping blade (or in an electric blender), purée the basil leaves in the 1 cup (240 ml) remaining infusion. NOTE: *The leaves should be as uniformly fine as possible, so you may need to give the processor or blender four to five 15-second churnings.* Combine the basil purée with the gelatin mixture, then stir in the lemon juice. Taste and if too tart to suit you, add another tablespoon or two of sugar.

Pour the mixture into two refrigerator trays or into one large shallow aluminum pan and freeze until firm. Break into small chunks and beat very hard, a few at a time, until fluffy in an electric mixer set at high speed or in a food processor equipped with the metal chopping blade. Pack the sorbet into freezer containers and store in the freezer.

VARIATION:

Fresh mint sorbet: This is gorgeously refreshing and an appropriate first-course introduction to roast leg of lamb. Simply follow the recipe above, substituting an equal quantity of mint for basil. Reduce the quantity of sugar slightly—to 2 to 3 tablespoons or to suit your own taste.

Eggplant caviar

SERVES 6 TO 8

Integral to every *meze*, that staggering procession of Turkish hors d'oeuvre, is this "poor man's" caviar made with eggplant. It's splendid as a cocktail hors d'oeuvre because it can be made a day or two ahead, because it's more exotic than the usual "dunk" and because it can be neatly dipped up on triangles of toast or pita bread. Mounded on shredded romaine, it also makes a superlative salad.

3 tablespoons	sesame oil	3 tablespoons
3 tablespoons	olive oil	3 tablespoons
2 large	eggplants, halved lengthwise (do not peel)	2 large
2 tablespoons	lemon juice	2 tablespoons
1/4 cup	minced parsley	60 ml
2 medium-size	garlic cloves, peeled and crushed	2 medium-size
1/4 teaspoon	ground cinnamon	1/4 teaspoon
1 1/2 teaspoons	salt	1 1/2 teaspoons
1/8 teaspoon	freshly ground black pepper	1/8 teaspoon

Combine sesame and olive oils; brush cut surface of each eggplant half with 1 tablespoon of the oil mixture. Stand eggplant halves, cut sides up, on a baking sheet and bake, uncovered, in a very hot oven (425°F. or 220°C.) for about 45 minutes or until richly browned and very soft. Cool until easy to handle, then scrape eggplant flesh into a large bowl; discard the skins. Mash eggplant well, then add the balance of oil mixture along with all remaining ingredients. Mix well, cover and chill at least 24 hours before serving. Let eggplant caviar stand at room temperature 30 minutes, mound into a pretty serving dish and garnish, if you like, with lemon and/or tomato wedges. Accompany with small triangles of toast or pita bread.

Smoked sablefish pâté

SERVES 4 TO 6

 At the Boschendal Wine Estate near Paarl, South Africa, this pâté, featured at the luncheon buffet, is made with smoked angelfish. Since angelfish is not widely available here, I've worked out a couple of variations using the varieties of smoked fish known to Americans. (They can be bought in most specialty food shops and kosher delicatessens.)

½ pound	smoked raw sablefish (black cod), boned and sliced, OR smoked cooked sturgeon, pike, whitefish, carp or halibut, boned and sliced	225 g
5 tablespoons	slightly chilled unsalted butter	5 tablespoons
⅛ teaspoon	freshly grated nutmeg	⅛ teaspoon
⅛ teaspoon	freshly ground black pepper	⅛ teaspoon

Buzz all ingredients until creamy in a food processor fitted with the metal chopping blade (three 15-second churnings should do it) or beat until fluffy in an electric mixer set at high speed. Serve with canapé-size slices of whole-grain bread as an accompaniment to cocktails or, better yet, dry white wine.

VARIATION:

To make with finnan haddie: If you should be unable to buy any of the varieties of smoked fish named above, you can make a fair approximation of the smoked angelfish pâté using smoked haddock (finnan haddie). But you must first poach it in milk to leach out some of the saltiness. Place ½ pound (225 g) finnan haddie in a medium-size saucepan, add 1½ cups (350 ml) cold milk and bring slowly to a simmer; simmer, uncovered, 10 minutes. Drain haddock well and cool to room temperature. Then buzz with butter, nutmeg and pepper as directed in the recipe above.

Sill à la Tula Brettman
(SWEDISH APPETIZER OF HERRING, EGGS, LEEKS AND DILL)

SERVES 4 TO 6

 A popular *smörgåsbord* component, this recipe comes from a friend's Stockholm cousin, who often serves the dish at the start of a meal accompanied by baby new potatoes that have been boiled and rolled in melted butter and snipped dill. It's unusually easy to make and can, in fact, be assembled well ahead of time and refrigerated until you are ready to serve it.

1 jar (9 oz.)	herring tidbits in wine, drained well	1 jar (225 g)
2 medium-size	leeks, trimmed, washed and sliced thin	2 medium-size
¼ cup	chopped parsley	60 ml
¼ cup	freshly snipped dill	60 ml
2 large	hard-cooked eggs, peeled and finely chopped	2 large
2 tablespoons	fine dry bread crumbs	2 tablespoons
3 tablespoons	melted unsalted butter	3 tablespoons

Into a buttered 9-inch (23 cm) pie pan layer the ingredients this way (sprinkling each successive layer over the preceding one as evenly as possible): the herring, the leeks (separate them into rings as you scatter them over the herring), the parsley, the dill, the chopped eggs, and finally, the bread crumbs. Drizzle the melted butter evenly over all, then bake, uncovered, in a moderate oven (350°F. or 175°C.) for 15 minutes. Spoon onto small plates and serve.

Soups

Cod and haddock chowder

SERVES 8

Two of New England's favorite "chowder fish" combined in a single recipe. The trick is just to warm the fish through, never to let them boil in the milk mixture, because they will toughen and the milk will curdle.

2 ounces	salt pork, cut into small cubes	60 g
1 large	Spanish or Bermuda onion, peeled and coarsely chopped	1 large
Pinch	freshly grated nutmeg or mace	Pinch
4 medium-size	Maine or Eastern potatoes, peeled and cut into small cubes	4 medium-size
2 teaspoons (about)	salt	2 teaspoons (about)
2½ cups	water	600 ml
1 pound	boned and skinned fresh cod	½ kg
1 pound	fresh haddock fillets	½ kg
3 cups	milk, at room temperature	¾ L
1 cup	heavy cream, at room temperature	240 ml
3 tablespoons	minced parsley	3 tablespoons
2 tablespoons	unsalted butter	2 tablespoons
⅛ teaspoon	white pepper	⅛ teaspoon

In a large heavy kettle set over moderate heat, render the cubes of salt pork about 10 minutes until all of the fat has cooked out, leaving crisp browned bits. Lift these with a slotted spoon to paper toweling to drain; reserve. Dump the onion into the kettle drippings and stir-fry over moderate heat 10 to 12 minutes until touched with brown. Add the nutmeg, potatoes and the salt and stir-fry 3 to 4 minutes until golden. Pour in the water, bring it to a simmer, adjust the burner heat so that the water stays at a slow simmer, then cover and cook about 10 minutes or until the potatoes are firm-tender. Add the cod and haddock, again bring the water to a simmer, then cover and cook about 10 minutes, just until the fish will flake at the touch of a fork; break the fish into bite-size chunks with the fork. Pour in the milk and cream and bring slowly to serving temperature—**do not allow to boil.** Add the parsley, butter and white pepper and as soon as the butter melts, sprinkle in the reserved browned salt pork. Taste the chowder for salt and add more, if needed. Ladle into large soup bowls and put out a big basket of oyster crackers and/or pilot biscuits.

Funchal fish chowder

SERVES 6 TO 8

 Madeira cooks make this suprisingly delicate chowder with whatever the nets have fetched up, a variety of fish unavailable here. The best American combination, I find, is a half-and-half mixture of lean and oily fish. For mellower flavor, make this chowder the day before you plan to serve it. Cool slightly, cover and refrigerate without delay. Serve within 24 hours.

4 medium-size	yellow onions, peeled and sliced thin	4 medium-size
2 large	garlic cloves, peeled and crushed	2 large
3 tablespoons	unsalted butter	3 tablespoons
3 tablespoons	olive oil	3 tablespoons
2 large	bay leaves	2 large
¼ cup	dry Madeira wine (Sercial)	60 ml
3 medium-size	juicily ripe tomatoes, peeled, cored, seeded and chopped fine	3 medium-size
3 medium-size	all-purpose potatoes, peeled and cut into ¼-inch (¾ cm) cubes	3 medium-size
2 tablespoons	minced parsley	2 tablespoons
4	whole cloves	4
¼ teaspoon	white pepper	¼ teaspoon
2 quarts	water	2 L
1 pound	boned, skinned halibut, haddock or cod	½ kg
1 pound	boned, skinned swordfish or mackerel	½ kg
1 tablespoon (about)	salt	1 tablespoon (about)

	GARNISHES:	
12 slices (about ½ inch thick)	French or Italian bread (use slim baguettes)	12 slices (about ½ cm thick)
4 tablespoons	unsalted butter	4 tablespoons
½ cup	freshly grated Parmesan cheese	120 ml
3 tablespoons	minced parsley	3 tablespoons

Stir-fry onions and garlic in butter and oil in a large heavy kettle over moderate heat about 15 minutes until limp and lightly browned. Add bay leaves, wine, tomatoes, potatoes, parsley, cloves, pepper and water, cover and simmer slowly 1 hour. Uncover and simmer 2 hours longer at least—until liquid has cooked down and flavors are concentrated but well blended. Add fish, breaking up clumps; simmer 5 minutes only. Cool, cover and refrigerate until about 20 minutes before serving.

Bring chowder slowly to serving temperature; remove bay leaves and add salt to taste. Meanwhile, prepare garnishes: Lightly brown bread on both sides in butter in a large heavy skillet over moderately high heat; drain on paper toweling.

To serve, ladle chowder into soup plates, float two slices of bread on each, scatter a tablespoon of Parmesan into each portion and sprinkle with parsley. Pass additional Parmesan.

Badische schneckensuppe
(BLACK FOREST SNAIL SOUP)

 SERVES 4 TO 6

The finest meal I ate during a recent week's tour of Germany's Black Forest was at Ritter-Durbach, a cozily beamed and paneled turn-of-the-century inn run by the Brunner family. Originally the grandmother and mother did the cooking; today it's the son, Wilhelm, whose mix of regional, classical and *nouvelle cuisine* dishes lures gourmands from France and the Benelux countries (and impressed Michelin critics enough to award Ritter-Durbach two stars). My own luncheon began with this exquisite soup.

5 tablespoons	unsalted butter, at room temperature	5 tablespoons
2 tablespoons	finely minced shallots	2 tablespoons
1 tablespoon	finely minced garlic	1 tablespoon
½ pound	mushrooms, wiped clean and minced fine	225 g
1 cup	Riesling wine	240 ml
1 cup	beef broth	240 ml
1 cup	chicken broth	240 ml

1 cup	crème fraîche *or* Devon *or* heavy cream	240 ml
¼ teaspoon	pulverized anise seed	¼ teaspoon
1 can (7½ oz.)	escargots, drained (reserve liquid) and minced fine	1 can (212 g)
1 tablespoon	minced fresh chives	1 tablespoon
1 tablespoon	minced parsley	1 tablespoon
1 tablespoon	flour	1 tablespoon
2 large	egg yolks, lightly beaten	2 large
2 teaspoons	Pernod	2 teaspoons

In a large heavy saucepan set over low heat, melt 4 tablespoons of the butter. Add shallots and sauté 5 minutes; add garlic and sauté 1 minute more (do not allow to brown). Add mushrooms and stir-fry 15 minutes over lowest heat. Mix in wine, beef and chicken broth and cream and simmer, uncovered, 20 minutes. Add anise, escargots (and their liquid), chives and parsley. Knead remaining tablespoon of butter with flour to form a *beurre manié*, then pinch off bits of it and whisk into the simmering soup, one at a time, so that mixture thickens slowly and evenly. Beat about a tablespoon of the hot soup into the egg yolks, then add 3 additional tablespoons, one at a time, whisking vigorously; stir back into soup. Mix in Pernod and let soup mellow a minute or two over low heat. (Do not allow to boil or the soup will curdle.) Ladle into soup bowls and serve as a first course.

Lamb and lentil soup with mint

SERVES 6

It was in Lebanon that I first tasted this soup—or rather one very much like it, for this is my interpretation of the soup I enjoyed immensely at a little restaurant high above the Mediterranean's eastern shore.

1½ cups	dried lentils, washed and sorted	350 ml
5 cups (1 quart + 1 cup)	cold water	1 L + 240 ml
5 tablespoons	unsalted butter	5 tablespoons
2 medium-size	yellow onions, peeled and chopped	2 medium-size
1 large	garlic clove, peeled and minced	1 large
1 medium-size	sweet green pepper, cored, seeded and coarsely chopped	1 medium-size
2 medium-size	carrots, peeled and coarsely chopped	2 medium-size
½ teaspoon	crumbled leaf basil	½ teaspoon

½ teaspoon	crumbled leaf marjoram	½ teaspoon
¼ teaspoon	crumbled leaf thyme	¼ teaspoon
1 can (1 lb.)	tomatoes (do not drain)	1 can (454 g)
½ pound	lean ground lamb shoulder	225 g
2 tablespoons	flour	2 tablespoons
1 can (13¾ oz.)	beef broth	1 can (407 ml)
2 tablespoons	lemon juice or cider vinegar	2 tablespoons
½ teaspoon	salt (or to taste)	½ teaspoon
⅛ teaspoon (about)	freshly ground black pepper	⅛ teaspoon (about)
2 tablespoons	freshly chopped mint	2 tablespoons

Boil the lentils in the water in a large, uncovered, heavy saucepan over moderate heat until tender, about 45 minutes. Meanwhile, melt 3 tablespoons of the butter in a very heavy skillet over moderate heat, add the onions and garlic and stir-fry 8 to 10 minutes until limp and lightly browned. Add the green pepper and carrots, the basil, marjoram and thyme and sauté 10 minutes longer. Add the tomatoes, then the lamb, breaking up large lumps, and cook about 10 minutes or until no redness remains in the lamb. Melt the remaining 2 tablespoons of butter in a small saucepan; blend in the flour, then add the broth and cook, stirring constantly, until thickened and smooth—about 3 minutes. Stir the lemon juice into the broth and add to the lentils along with the lamb mixture. Cover and simmer over lowest heat 1½ to 2 hours longer or until flavors are well blended. Season to taste with salt and pepper, stir in the mint, then ladle into large soup plates and serve with triangles of toasted pita bread.

Kuttelsuppe mit morcheln
(TRIPE SOUP WITH MORELS)

SERVES 8

 A beautiful soup, delicately balanced as to flavor, that is the creation of Peter Wehlauer, chef-owner of Burg Windeck near Baden-Baden, Germany, one of the Black Forest's outstanding restaurants. Located in a medieval castle atop a high hill, Burg Windeck overlooks miles of vineyards and orchards that twill the Rhine slopes and plain.

1 ounce	dried morels (available in specialty food shops)	30 g
1½ cups	cold water	350 ml
1 pound	fresh honeycomb tripe (or frozen, thawed), washed well and cut into fine julienne	½ kg

3 quarts	slightly salted boiling water	3 L
1 small	yellow onion, peeled and stuck with 4 cloves	1 small
2 cups	chicken broth	½ L
2 cups	beef broth	½ L
3 tablespoons	unsalted butter	3 tablespoons
¼ cup	fine carrot julienne	60 ml
¼ cup	fine celery julienne	60 ml
¼ cup	fine leek julienne	60 ml
¾ cup	Riesling wine	180 ml
1 cup	heavy cream	240 ml
Pinch	ground nutmeg	Pinch
½ teaspoon (about)	salt	½ teaspoon (about)
⅛ teaspoon (about)	white pepper	⅛ teaspoon (about)

Soak morels in the 1½ cups cold water 2 to 3 hours until soft; drain, reserving liquid. Pour soaking liquid through a cheesecloth-lined sieve (this is to remove grit) and reserve. Cut morels into fine julienne, soak about 1 hour in enough cold water to cover; drain, discard this second soaking water, and rinse the morels again well.

Blanch the tripe 2 to 3 minutes in the boiling salted water; drain and rinse well. Place tripe in a large heavy saucepan, add onion, chicken and beef broths and simmer, tightly covered, for 3 hours or until tripe is tender. Drain tripe and reserve; strain and reserve the broth.

In a large sauté pan melt the butter over moderate heat; add carrot and sauté 4 minutes; add celery and sauté 3 minutes; add leek and sauté 1 minute. Add tripe and toss lightly in butter to coat. Add reserved broth, Riesling, cream, reserved morel liquid and morels. Simmer, uncovered, 10 minutes. Season to taste with nutmeg, salt and white pepper and serve as a first course or as an entrée accompanied by a crisp green salad and crusty chunks of bread.

Maultaschen
(SWABIAN BROTH WITH SPINACH-AND-MEAT-STUFFED "RAVIOLI")

SERVES 6 TO 8

Originally a Lenten specialty of the Baden-Württemberg area of Germany, these spinach-filled pasta pillows are now often fortified with ground veal, pork, bacon and salami. The trick is to roll the pasta dough as thin as possible, incorporating minimal flour. (Too much flour will toughen the dough, as overworking it will also.) This particular recipe comes from the Kurhotel Mitteltal, one of the fine family spas lazing in the folds of the Black Forest near Baden-Baden. NOTE: *The processor makes short shrift of both the pasta dough and the filling.*

PASTA DOUGH:

2 small	eggs	2 small
2 tablespoons	cooking oil	2 tablespoons
2 tablespoons	cold water	2 tablespoons
2 cups minus 2 tablespoons	sifted all-purpose flour	188 g
¼ teaspoon	salt	¼ teaspoon

FILLING:

2 ounces	slab bacon, but in ½-inch (1½ cm) cubes	60 g
1 medium-size	yellow onion, peeled and minced	1 medium-size
1 tablespoon	unsalted butter	1 tablespoon
¼ pound	finely ground veal shoulder	115 g
¼ pound	finely ground lean pork shoulder	115 g
2 ounces	salami, finely ground	60 g
1 package (10 oz.)	frozen chopped spinach, thawed and squeezed as dry as possible	1 package (283 g)
2 tablespoons	fine soft bread crumbs	2 tablespoons
5 tablespoons	heavy cream	5 tablespoons
1 large	egg yolk	1 large
¾ teaspoon	crumbled leaf thyme	¾ teaspoon
½ teaspoon	salt	½ teaspoon
¼ teaspoon	ground allspice	¼ teaspoon
¼ teaspoon	freshly ground black pepper	¼ teaspoon
⅛ teaspoon	ground nutmeg	⅛ teaspoon

BROTH:

2 quarts	nicely seasoned beef broth or brown veal stock	2 L

Prepare the dough first: In a processor work bowl fitted with the metal chopping blade, whirl the eggs, oil and water 2 to 3 seconds to combine. Add half the flour and mix lightly, using 3 to 4 on-offs of the motor. Add remaining flour and salt and mix, using 3 to 4 on-offs of the motor. Do not overmix or the dough will be rubbery. Divide dough in half, wrap each snugly in plastic food wrap and let stand at room temperature 1 hour.

Meanwhile, prepare the filling: Sauté the bacon in a small skillet over low heat 4 to 5 minutes; drain on paper toweling. Pour off drippings in skillet, add the butter and stir-fry onion over low heat 3 to 4 minutes until translucent; cool. In processor work bowl fitted with the metal chopping blade, grind to very fine the bacon and onion with all remaining filling ingredients, using short bursts of speed and scraping down sides of work bowl as needed; mixture will be quite thick and pastelike.

To shape Maultaschen: The easiest way is to use a ravioli maker (available at specialty kitchen shops and not at all expensive). Divide each dough half in half again; roll one out on a very lightly floured pastry cloth with a lightly floured stockinette-covered rolling pin until as thin as tissue paper and slightly larger than the dimensions of the ravioli maker. Fold dough over rolling pin and ease on top of ravioli maker; unfold dough and fit into depressions. Spoon 1 teaspoon filling into each depression. Roll second piece of dough as before and ease on top of ravioli maker; unfold. Remove stockinette from rolling pin and roll hard over the "ravioli" so that you cut and seal them in one operation. Flip ravioli maker upside down to remove *Maultaschen* and arrange in one layer on a large tray; cover snugly with plastic food wrap to prevent drying. Roll, fill and cut the remaining *Maultaschen* the same way. Add to tray and re-cover. NOTE: *These may be made as much as a day ahead and kept refrigerated until about 1 hour before serving. Just make certain that the* Maultaschen *are kept tightly sealed in plastic wrap so that they do not dry out or absorb refrigerator odors.*

To cook: Let tightly covered *Maultaschen* stand at room temperature 45 minutes. Pour the broth into a large shallow kettle, set over medium heat and bring to a simmer. Adjust heat so that surface of broth just trembles, add 6 to 8 *Maultaschen* (as many as possible but without crowding) and cook, uncovered, 8 minutes; turn them all over, cover and cook 8 minutes longer. Remove to a heated platter with a slotted spoon; cover with a bowl turned upside down and keep warm. Cook the remaining *Maultaschen* the same way.

To serve: Place 4 to 5 *Maultaschen* in each of 6 to 8 large soup plates, ladle in enough broth to cover and serve as a main course. The perfect accompaniment: green beans or asparagus vinaigrette. NOTE: *Another way to serve* Maultaschen *is not in broth but tossed in melted butter (preferably butter in which you have sautéed a little minced onion or shallots).*

Sopa de legumes à Minho
(VEGETABLE SOUP FROM THE MINHO PROVINCE)

SERVES 8 TO 10

On a recent swing through Portugal, I was served variations of this robust soup at five different *pousadas* (government inns), but the best of all was that at the Pousada de São Teotónio on the Minho River, the northern boundary separating Portugal and Spain. For best results, do as Portuguese cooks do: Let the soup bubble lazily on the stove for the better part of the day, refrigerate it overnight, then reheat and serve the next day. NOTE: *This soup freezes well.*

2 large	garlic cloves, peeled and minced	2 large
4 large	yellow onions, peeled and coarsely chopped	4 large
4 large	leeks (or 8 large scallions), washed, trimmed and sliced thin	4 large
¼ cup	olive oil	60 ml
2 cups	finely shredded cabbage	½ L
1 pound	turnips, peeled and coarsely chopped	½ kg
1 large	carrot, peeled and coarsely chopped	1 large
2 pounds	Maine or Eastern potatoes, peeled and sliced thin	1 kg
2 large	bay leaves (do not crumble)	2 large
½ teaspoon	crumbled leaf marjoram	½ teaspoon
¼ teaspoon	crumbled leaf thyme	¼ teaspoon
¼ teaspoon	crumbled leaf rosemary	¼ teaspoon
Pinch	ground nutmeg	Pinch
⅛ teaspoon	freshly ground black pepper	⅛ teaspoon
1 quart	rich chicken stock or broth	1 L
6 cups	water	1½ L
1 medium-size	carrot, peeled and cut in matchstick strips	1 medium-size
3 cups	very finely sliced cabbage	¾ L
2 cups	very finely sliced fresh young spinach	½ L
¼ cup	minced parsley	60 ml
2½ teaspoons	salt	2½ teaspoons

Stir-fry garlic, onions and leeks in oil in a large heavy kettle over moderate heat 15 minutes until golden; add shredded cabbage, turnips, chopped carrot, potatoes, herbs, nutmeg and pepper and sauté, stirring now and then, 20 minutes. Add chicken stock and water, bring to a simmer, adjust heat so mixture bubbles gently, cover and cook 5 to 6 hours, stirring occasionally. With a potato masher, mash potatoes and other vegetables to a rough purée.

Add carrot matchsticks, re-cover and simmer 2 hours. Add sliced cabbage and simmer, **uncovered,** 45 minutes. Add spinach and parsley and simmer, uncovered, 10 minutes. Stir in salt, adjusting amount, if needed, to taste. Cool soup to room temperature, cover and refrigerate overnight.

Next day, bring soup slowly to serving temperature. Ladle into large soup plates and serve with crusty chunks of *Pão* (see Index).

Polish mushroom soup
with homemade egg noodles

SERVES 4 TO 6

There's a terrific little Polish restaurant called the Baltyk on New York's unfashionable Lower East Side where everything is "home-cooked"—daily—using the freshest possible ingredients. One of the house specialties is a spectacular mushroom soup. I order it every time I dine at the Baltyk and have devised this version, which comes quite close to the original.

¼ pound (6 slices)	lean sliced bacon, cut crosswise into julienne strips	115 g (6 slices)
2 medium-size	yellow onions, peeled and chopped	2 medium-size
4 large	shallots, peeled and minced (or use scallions)	4 large
1 medium-size	carrot, peeled and chopped	1 medium-size
1 pound	mushrooms, wiped clean	½ kg
2 tablespoons	snipped fresh dill (or ½ teaspoon dill weed)	2 tablespoons
½ teaspoon	ground mace	½ teaspoon
¼ teaspoon	ground allspice	¼ teaspoon
¼ teaspoon	crumbled leaf rosemary	¼ teaspoon
¼ teaspoon	crumbled leaf thyme	¼ teaspoon
½ cup	dry white wine	120 ml
2 cans (13¾ oz. each)	beef broth	2 cans (407 ml each)
1 cup	water	240 ml
4 tablespoons	unsalted butter	4 tablespoons
2 tablespoons	minced parsley	2 tablespoons
	EGG NOODLES:	
1 cup (about)	sifted all-purpose flour	100 g (240 ml)
½ teaspoon	salt	½ teaspoon
⅛ teaspoon	freshly grated nutmeg	⅛ teaspoon
2 medium-size	eggs	2 medium-size

Fry bacon in a large heavy saucepan over moderate heat until crisp and brown, about 10 minutes; lift bacon crumbles to several thicknesses of paper toweling to drain and set aside. In the drippings stir-fry the onions and shallots about 5 minutes over moderate heat until limp and golden; add carrot and sauté about 5 minutes. Mince about one-third of the mushrooms, add to saucepan and stir-fry 5 minutes. Meanwhile, slice the remaining mushrooms about ½ inch (1½ cm) thick and set aside. To the saucepan mixture add 1 tablespoon of the minced dill (or all of the dill weed), the mace, allspice, rosemary and thyme. Warm 1 to 2 minutes; add wine, broth and water, cover and simmer 1½ hours. Meanwhile, stir-fry the sliced mushrooms in 3 tablespoons of the butter in a large heavy skillet over low heat about 10 minutes. (Mushroom slices should be uniformly, glisteningly brown but still somewhat firm.) Reserve.

Now prepare the egg noodles: In a processor fitted with the metal chopping blade, combine flour, salt and nutmeg with a few short bursts of speed. Add eggs and mix with 3 to 4 five-second churnings or until dough rides up on the central spindle. If it seems soft, beat in a tablespoon or two more of flour. The noodle dough should be about the consistency of piecrust dough. (If making by hand, knead the eggs into the combined dry ingredients until springy.) Shape dough into a ball, place on well-floured wax paper, then fold paper over, enclosing dough; let stand at room temperature about ¾ hour. Meanwhile, begin heating a very big kettle of lightly salted water. (I use my large spaghetti kettle.)

When noodle dough has rested sufficiently, roll tissue-thin on a well-floured pastry cloth with a well-floured, stockinette-covered rolling pin. Lightly flour surface of dough and roll up loosely, jelly-roll style; slice about ¼-inch (¾ cm) thick. Again, allow noodles to rest.

To finish the soup: Strain the saucepan mixture, reserving both solids and liquid. Return liquid to saucepan and set, uncovered, over low heat. Purée solids along with about half the reserved crumbled bacon in a food processor fitted with the metal chopping blade, using 3 to 4 five-second churnings and scraping the sides of the work bowl down between each. Or, if you prefer, press the solids through a fine sieve or put through a food mill. Stir the purée into the soup liquid along with the sautéed mushrooms, the remaining tablespoon of butter, minced dill (if used) and the parsley. Let mellow, uncovered, over low heat.

Cook the noodles in rapidly boiling salted water about 5 minutes, until no raw floury taste remains. (Noodles should still be a bit firm.) Drain well and stir noodles into soup along with the remaining bacon crumbles. Warm 3 to 5 minutes, stirring gently, ladle into large soup plates and serve as a main course.

Callaloo

SERVES 10 TO 12

Callaloo is a Caribbean plant with leaves as big as elephant's ears. It is also the jade-green soup made from those leaves, and nowhere is it more delicious than at Ross Point Inn on the island of Grenada. Audrey Hopkin, the owner's wife, is by all accounts the best cook around. The soup is very good, too, at La Belle Creole restaurant near that sugary stretch of Grenadian beach known as Grand Anse. That restaurant, a part of the Blue Horizons Cottage Hotel, is owned by Audrey Hopkin's son, Arnold, who admits that "Mama has had a hand in the kitchen here, too." Mostly it's her recipes that are used, plus the know-how that Arnold picked up from her. Real Callaloo is impossible to make here because callaloo leaves are unavailable and fresh coconuts are a rarity in most parts of the country. But I've worked out a very good approximation of the original by using a mixture of Swiss chard and spinach and a "coconut milk" extracted from canned flaked coconut. Try to use fresh vegetables in making Callaloo because you may safely freeze any leftovers—not so if you use frozen vegetables.

2 large	yellow onions, peeled and chopped	2 large
1 large	garlic clove, peeled and minced	1 large
1 medium-size	green pepper, cored, seeded and chopped	1 medium-size
4 tablespoons	bacon or ham drippings	4 tablespoons
2 cups	boiling water	½ L
1 can (3½ oz.)	flaked coconut	1 can (99 g)
¾ pound	Swiss chard, stalks separated from the leaves, each washed and chopped, or 1 package (10 oz. or 283 g) frozen chopped spinach	⅓ kg
¾ pound	spinach, stemmed, washed and chopped, or 1 package (10 oz. or 283 g) of frozen chopped spinach	⅓ kg
¾ pound	tender young okra, washed, stemmed and sliced or 1 package (10 oz. or 283 g) frozen cut okra	⅓ kg
1 pound	Maine or Eastern potatoes, peeled and cut into small dice	½ kg
1 pound	sweet potatoes or yams, peeled and cut into small dice	½ kg
3½ cups (about)	beef broth, homemade or canned	830 ml (about)
2 tablespoons	freshly snipped chives	2 tablespoons
¼ teaspoon	crumbled leaf thyme	¼ teaspoon
¼ teaspoon	freshly grated nutmeg	¼ teaspoon
¼ pound	dried beef, chopped fine	115 g
¼ teaspoon	cayenne pepper	¼ teaspoon
½ teaspoon (about)	salt	½ teaspoon (about)
Light sprinkling	freshly ground black pepper	Light sprinkling

Stir-fry the onions, garlic and green pepper in the bacon drippings in a large heavy kettle set over moderate heat 10 to 15 minutes until limp and lightly browned. Meanwhile, pour the boiling water over the coconut and steep 10 minutes; buzz in a food processor fitted with the metal chopping blade about 2 minutes nonstop (or whirl in an electric blender at high speed). Dump the coconut mixture into a fine sieve set over a heatproof bowl, then using a wooden spoon, press as much liquid from the coconut as possible. When all liquid is extracted, discard the coconut. Set the liquid aside.

Now add to the onion mixture in the kettle the Swiss chard, spinach and okra and stir-fry about 5 minutes. Pour in the reserved coconut "milk," add the potatoes (both the Maine and the sweet), the broth, chives, thyme and nutmeg. Adjust the burner heat so that the mixture simmers gently, cover and cook 3 hours. Now purée about three-fourths of the Callaloo, doing it in three to four batches, in a food processor fitted with the metal chopping blade (or in an electric blender at high speed, or by forcing through a food mill). Return the puréed Callaloo to the soup left in the kettle, add the dried beef, cayenne, salt and black pepper, cover and simmer slowly for 30 minutes. Taste for salt and add more, if needed; also thin the soup with a little additional beef broth if it seems very thick. Serve as a first course or main dish, accompanied by crisp crackers.

Sweet red and green pepper soup

SERVES 4 TO 6

 **T**his recipe evolved out of an attempt to use up some red and green peppers that were nearing the point of no return, and it's perfectly delicious if I do say so, myself (P.S., friends agree). NOTE: *In order to achieve a mellow "browned butter" flavor, you must work the roux (flour and butter paste) very slowly, letting it turn gradually from blond to amber to russet. Hurrying the process will give the soup a bitter taste.* Accompany this soup with open-face grilled cheese sandwiches cut in triangles and a crisp green salad and you have a light but nutritious lunch or supper.

6 tablespoons	unsalted butter	6 tablespoons
4 tablespoons	flour	4 tablespoons
4 small	scallions, washed, trimmed and sliced	4 small
2 medium-size	sweet red peppers, washed, cored, seeded and cut into matchstick strips	2 medium-size
1 medium-size	sweet green pepper, washed, cored, seeded and cut into matchstick strips	1 medium-size
⅛ teaspoon	crumbled leaf thyme	⅛ teaspoon
⅛ teaspoon	crumbled leaf basil	⅛ teaspoon
⅛ teaspoon	freshly grated nutmeg	⅛ teaspoon
1 quart	rich beef broth	1 L
2 tablespoons	tomato paste	2 tablespoons
To taste	salt and freshly ground black pepper	To taste

In a medium-size heavy saucepan set over moderately low heat, blend 4 tablespoons of the butter with the flour; continue to work the mixture with a wooden spoon for about 30 mimutes or until it turns a rich red-brown. Meanwhile, stir-fry the scallions and red and green peppers in the remaining 2 tablespoons butter in a large heavy skillet over moderate heat 3 to 5 minutes just until lightly glazed but still quite crisp; mix in the thyme, basil and nutmeg, mellow a minute more over moderate heat, then remove from the heat and reserve. When the roux has reached the proper russet hue, remove from the heat and whisk in the broth, 1 cup at a time, beating vigorously after each addition until smooth. Set over moderate heat and cook, stirring constantly, until thickened and smooth and no starch taste remains—3 to 5 minutes. Blend in the tomato paste, then stir in reserved skillet mixture and salt and pepper to taste. Let peppers warm about 5 minutes in the thickened broth, then ladle into soup bowls and serve.

Meats

Espetada
(GRILLED SKEWERS OF BEEF WITH GARLIC AND BAY LEAVES)

SERVES 6

In the mountain villages of Madeira (to my mind earth's most beautiful island), *espetada* (pronounced ESH-peh-TAH-da) are skewered on green bay laurel sticks and grilled outdoors over glowing coals. I include directions here for broiling them indoors or out.

3 pounds	beef tenderloin, cut into 1-inch (2½ cm) cubes	1½ kg
4 large	garlic cloves, peeled and finely slivered	4 large
4 large	bay leaves, crumbled	4 large
⅓ cup (⅔ stick)	melted unsalted butter	80 ml (⅔ stick)
½ teaspoon	freshly ground black pepper	½ teaspoon
½ teaspoon	salt	½ teaspoon

Place all ingredients in a shallow baking dish and toss well. Let stand at room temperature 2 hours, tossing mixture occasionally. Or, if you prefer, marinate 24 hours in the refrigerator, then let stand 2 hours at room temperature; the flavor will be richer. Thread beef on 6 long metal skewers, dividing total amount evenly; heat marinade 2 to 3 minutes, brush lightly over *espetada*, then broil as follows:

In the broiler: Lay skewers on broiler pan, place 5 to 6 inches (13 to 15 cm) from the heat, then broil about 6 minutes, turning frequently, for very rare, 8 minutes for rare and 10 for medium rare. Brush frequently with remaining marinade. Serve with crusty bread chunks for sopping up drippings and any remaining marinade (heat it before serving).

Over charcoal: Pour remaining marinade in a small heavy saucepan and set at edge of a grill, adjusted so that it is about 5 inches (13 cm) above white-hot coals. Lay skewered beef on grill and broil 5 minutes, turning often, for very rare, 7 minutes for rare and 9 for medium rare. Ladle a little hot marinade over each portion, then pass the balance along with chunks of French or Italian bread.

Lis Brewer's skipperlabskovs
(DANISH SAILOR'S STEW)

SERVES 6

Lis Brewer, an old and dear friend who is an executive with Hilton International, is also one of the best cooks I know, partly because she has visited so many exotic dots on the map, paying particular attention to the local cuisines, and also because she was born and brought up in a Danish household in Argentina. This particular recipe comes from her Danish collection. "It's what Danish cooks make whenever they're feeling financially strapped," she says. With good reason, for this husky soup stretches less than a pound (only a third of a kilo) of ground beef over six copious servings.

¾ pound	lean ground beef chuck	340 g
2 large	yellow onions, peeled and coarsely chopped	2 large
3 tablespoons	unsalted butter	3 tablespoons
1 quart	boiling water or beef or veal stock	1 L
6	peppercorns	6
1 small	bay leaf	1 small
⅛ teaspoon	freshly grated nutmeg	⅛ teaspoon
Pinch	crumbled leaf thyme	Pinch
2 teaspoons (about)	salt	2 teaspoons (about)
4 large	Maine or Eastern potatoes, peeled and cubed	4 large
2 tablespoons	minced fresh parsley	2 tablespoons
2 tablespoons	minced fresh dill	2 tablespoons

Stir-fry the beef and onions in the butter in a large heavy kettle over moderate heat 8 to 10 minutes—breaking up large clumps of meat—just until the onions are limp and golden and the meat no longer red. (Do not brown the meat.) Turn the heat down low, add the water, peppercorns, bay leaf, nutmeg, thyme and salt, cover and cook slowly for ½ hour. Add the potatoes, re-cover and simmer over lowest heat about 3 hours or until potatoes have disintegrated and flavors are well blended. Remove the bay leaf, mix in the parsley and dill and mellow 3 to 5 minutes. Taste for salt and add more, if needed. Ladle into large soup plates and serve, scattering a little extra minced parsley over each portion, if you like.

Beef and mushroom ragout with paprika–sour cream gravy

SERVES 6 TO 8

Like most stews, this one is even better the second day. Serve with noodles, *spaetzle* (see Index) or potatoes.

3 pounds	boned lean beef chuck, cut in 1-inch (2½ cm) cubes	1½ kg
2 tablespoons	unsalted butter	2 tablespoons
2 tablespoons, in all	peanut or vegetable oil	2 tablespoons, in all
3 large	yellow onions, peeled and coarsely chopped	3 large
2 large	garlic cloves, peeled and minced	2 large
1 pound	mushrooms, wiped clean and sliced thin	½ kg
3 tablespoons	paprika (preferably Hungarian sweet rose paprika)	3 tablespoons
1 large	bay leaf, crumbled	1 large
¼ teaspoon	crumbled leaf thyme	¼ teaspoon
2 cups	dry white wine	½ L
¾ cup	water	180 ml
1 teaspoon (about)	salt	1 teaspoon (about)
⅛ teaspoon (about)	freshly ground black pepper	⅛ teaspoon (about)
1 pint	sour cream, at room temperature	½ L

Brown the beef, about one-third of the total amount at a time, in a mixture of the butter and 1 tablespoon of the oil in a large heavy kettle over moderately high heat; as the beef browns, transfer it to a large bowl. Add the remaining tablespoon of oil to the kettle, dump in the onions, garlic and mushrooms and stir-fry 8 to 10 minutes until nicely browned. Sprinkle in the paprika, bay leaf and thyme and stir-fry 1 to 2 minutes. Return the beef to the kettle, add the wine, water, salt and pepper, cover and simmer slowly, stirring now and then, 1½ to 2 hours or until the meat is fork-tender. Blend in the sour cream, taste for salt and pepper and add more, if needed, then ladle into a large tureen and serve at table.

Forfar bridies
(SCOTTISH BEEF, SUET AND ONION PIES)

SERVES 8

The Scots, I think, have received unduly bad press about their culinary incompetence and meat-and-potatoes mentality. There are, to be sure, perfectly wretched Scottish cooks (as indeed there are clumsy French, Italian or Chinese cooks). But the Scottish women in my family were skilled in the kitchen, and it is to them that I owe my interest in and love of good food. *Forfar Bridies*, the Scottish equivalent of Cornish Pasties, demonstrate how delicious frugal Scottish fare can be. This particular version is one I've jazzed up ever so slightly by adding a pinch of leaf thyme and a tablespoon of freshly minced parsley (for a truly authentic recipe, you've only to omit these two ingredients). The best meat to use is beef chuck. It should be trimmed of all excess fat, membranes and sinew, then moderately finely chopped—**not ground,** which would give the meat an altogether different texture. NOTE: *You can processor-chop the beef provided you trim it meticulously, cut it into 1-inch (2½ cm) cubes and partially freeze these. Equip the processor with the metal chopping blade, snap the motor on, then drop the partially frozen cubes down the feed tube—no more than five or six of them per batch or you may "gum up the works" and stall the motor.* Do not attempt to chop the suet in the processor. The machine's speed and power will reduce it to paste. What you want are small granules or crumbles that can be tossed with the meat and onion.

1½ pounds	lean boneless beef chuck, trimmed of fat and sinew and chopped moderately fine	675 g
½ cup	moderately finely chopped suet	40 g
1 large	yellow onion, peeled and minced	1 large
2 tablespoons	all-purpose flour	2 tablespoons
1 tablespoon	minced fresh parsley	1 tablespoon
Pinch	crumbled leaf thyme	Pinch
½ teaspoon	salt	½ teaspoon
⅛ teaspoon	freshly ground black pepper	⅛ teaspoon
1 recipe	Suet Pastry (see Index)	1 recipe

Toss all ingredients (except pastry) well until uniformly mixed; set aside. Prepare the suet pastry as directed and shape lightly into a ball. Divide into three equal portions, then roll, one at a time, on a lightly floured pastry cloth with a stockinette-covered rolling pin until as thin as piecrust (about ⅛ inch or ½ cm). Using a saucer as a pattern, cut into circles about 6 inches (15 cm) across. With a pastry brush, moisten edge of each circle all around with cold water. Place about

½ cup (120 ml) of the meat mixture in the center of each circle, fold over to form half-moons, then crimp the edges with the tines of a fork to seal. Ease the filled pies onto a baking sheet and prick the tops decoratively to allow steam to escape during baking. (I usually use a table fork and make a sunburst pattern, radiating from the center out toward the curved edge.)

Bake the pies, uncovered, in the middle shelf of a hot oven (400°F. or 205°C.) for 10 minutes; reduce heat to moderately slow (325°F. or 165°C.) and bake 40 to 45 minutes longer or until nicely browned and bubbly. Serve hot or cold.

NOTE: *Forfar Bridies freeze well. Cool to room temperature, then place baking sheet of unbaked pies in the freezer. When they are finally firm—after an hour or two— wrap each individually and snugly in several layers of plastic food wrap. These will keep well for about a month at 0°F. (− 18°C.). To bake, place unwrapped but still solidly frozen pies on a baking sheet; bake as directed for 10 minutes but in a very hot oven (425°F. or 220°C.), then lower heat to moderately slow as above and bake until bubbly and brown—about 45 minutes.*

Rolled breast of veal stuffed with spinach, sultanas and pine nuts

SERVES 6 TO 8

 Beloved by French and Italian cooks, veal breast is not a cut of which Americans are particularly fond. A pity, because it's one of the cheapest cuts of veal available today (a third the price of chops, a fourth of *scaloppine*), and when properly cooked—long and slow in either a little or a lot of liquid—it is remarkably succulent. This is the cut to bone and roll around a variety of savory stuffings. The spinach stuffing below is an old favorite—authoritative enough to add interest to the delicate veal, but not so strong as to overwhelm it. Browning the onions in butter is essential to the flavor of the stuffing, but go at it slowly, letting the onions and garlic caramelize gently. If you brown them too fast, they will develop an acrid aftertaste.

	BREAST OF VEAL:	
5–6 pounds	breast of veal, boned and trimmed of excess fat (use bones for making Veal Stock; see Index)	2–2¾ kg
1 teaspoon	salt	1 teaspoon
⅛ teaspoon	freshly ground black pepper	⅛ teaspoon
½ teaspoon	rubbed sage	½ teaspoon
¼ teaspoon	crumbled leaf rosemary	¼ teaspoon

STUFFING:

1 medium-size	yellow onion, peeled and chopped fine	1 medium-size
1 large	garlic clove, peeled and minced	1 large
4 tablespoons	unsalted butter	4 tablespoons
½ pound	mushrooms, wiped clean and chopped fine	225 g
¼ cup	coarsely chopped pine nuts (pignoli)	60 ml
½ teaspoon	rubbed sage	½ teaspoon
¼ teaspoon	crumbled leaf thyme	¼ teaspoon
¼ teaspoon	crumbled leaf rosemary	¼ teaspoon
1 package (10 oz).	frozen chopped spinach, partially thawed in a sieve and broken into chunks	1 package (283 g)
1 cup	soft whole wheat bread crumbs	240 ml
⅓ cup	golden seedless raisins (sultanas), coarsely chopped	80 ml
2 tablespoons	dry sherry, Port or Madeira	2 tablespoons
½ teaspoon	salt	½ teaspoon
⅛ teaspoon	freshly ground black pepper	⅛ teaspoon

POACHING MEDIUM:

1 can (13¾ oz.)	chicken broth	1 can (407 ml)
6 cups (1½ quarts)	water	1½ L
1 cup	dry white wine	240 ml
1 medium-size	carrot, peeled and sliced thin	1 medium-size
4 medium-size	scallions, washed, trimmed and sliced thin	4 medium-size
3 large	sprigs fresh parsley	3 large
2 medium-size	sprigs fresh thyme (or ½ teaspoon crumbled leaf thyme)	2 medium-size
1 small	sprig fresh rosemary (or ¼ teaspoon crumbled leaf rosemary)	1 small
¼ teaspoon (about)	salt	¼ teaspoon (about)
Light sprinkling	freshly ground black pepper	Light sprinkling

To prepare the breast of veal: Pound veal firmly on both sides with the blunt edge of a meat cleaver or edge of a heavy plate; combine salt, pepper, sage and rosemary and rub on both sides of meat. Lay meat, inner side up (the side from which the bones were removed), on a tray and set aside.

For the stuffing: Stir-fry onion and garlic in butter in a large heavy skillet over moderately low heat about 10 minutes until golden brown; mix in mushrooms, pine nuts, sage, thyme and rosemary, turn heat to low and sauté about 5 minutes to mellow the flavors. Stir in spinach and cook, stirring now and then, about 10 minutes until spinach is completely thawed and its juices evaporated. Mix in remaining stuffing ingredients, adjusting salt and pepper to taste, and sauté 2 to 3 minutes more—just to blend flavors.

To stuff the veal: Spoon stuffing down center of meat and shape into a fat "sausage"; just make sure that you leave margins of about 1½ inches (4 cm) at each end. Now pull sides of veal up and over stuffing, overlapping one edge over the other. Sew shut, using soft white string and a heavy needle. The best stitch to use is a simple overcast stitch. Do make certain that you don't sew too close to the edge of the meat or the seam will burst open during cooking as the stuffing swells. TIP: *I find it handy to use a thimble to push the needle into the meat and a pair of small pliers to pull it through.* When seam is sewn, tuck in ends as neatly as possible to enclose filling, then sew both ends of roll shut, using the overcast stitch.

To poach the veal: Place stuffed breast of veal in a large heavy kettle (a 5-quart or 5 L size is perfect); add all poaching medium ingredients and bring to a simmer over moderate heat. Adjust burner heat so that kettle liquid barely ripples, cover and poach veal 2 to 2½ hours or until you can pierce meat easily with a sharp-pronged fork.

To make pan sauce: Carefully lift meat from kettle to a heated plate, cover loosely with foil and keep warm. Boil kettle mixture hard for 20 minutes until reduced by about half. Purée mixture in a food processor, blender or food mill; return to kettle and boil uncovered 15 to 20 minutes or until the consistency of a thin white sauce.

To serve: Carefully remove strings from veal, taking care not to tear meat. Slice the roll about ½ inch (1½ cm) thick and arrange overlapping on a heated platter. Spoon some of the sauce down the center of the meat and pass the remainder. Garnish with ruffs of greenery (a few young spinach leaves, if you have them) and wedges of lemon or orange.

Bacon-basted breast of veal with bulgur-raisin-walnut stuffing

SERVES 6

With the simple addition of curry powder, you can dramatically change the character of this recipe (see Variation below).

	BREAST OF VEAL:	
5–6 pounds	bone-in breast of veal (have butcher make a pocket for the stuffing)	2–2¾ kg
½ teaspoon	crumbled leaf rosemary	½ teaspoon
⅛ teaspoon	freshly ground black pepper	⅛ teaspoon
1 pound	sliced lean bacon	½ kg

STUFFING:

1 cup	*bulgur wheat*	240 ml
2 cups	*cold water*	½ L
½ cup	*golden seedless raisins (sultanas)*	120 ml
½ cup	*dry Madeira (Sercial), Port or sherry*	120 ml
2 medium-size	*yellow onions, peeled and chopped*	2 medium-size
1 large	*shallot, peeled and minced (or 1 scallion)*	1 large
2 tablespoons	*unsalted butter*	2 tablespoons
¼ teaspoon	*crumbled leaf thyme*	¼ teaspoon
⅛ teaspoon	*crumbled leaf rosemary*	⅛ teaspoon
1 cup	*moderately finely chopped walnuts*	240 ml
1 large	*egg, lightly beaten*	1 large
1 tablespoon	*walnut, hazelnut or olive oil*	1 tablespoon
½ teaspoon	*salt*	½ teaspoon
Pinch	*freshly ground black pepper*	Pinch

Rub the veal well with a mixture of the rosemary and pepper; refrigerate for the time being.

For the stuffing: Soak the bulgur wheat in the water and the sultanas in the Madeira for about 2 hours. The bulgur will swell and soften, eliminating the need to parboil it; drain off excess water. Drain the raisins well, reserving 2 tablespoons of the soaking wine. Stir-fry the onions and shallot in the butter in a medium-size heavy skillet over moderate heat about 5 minutes until limp and golden (do not brown); add the thyme and rosemary and mellow 1 to 2 minutes over moderate heat. Add the onion mixture to the drained bulgur along with the drained raisins, 2 tablespoons reserved soaking wine, walnuts, egg, walnut oil, salt and pepper; toss lightly but thoroughly to mix.

Upend the veal so that you can spoon the stuffing directly into the pocket. Pack the stuffing in lightly at the beginning, pushing it into the bottom corners, then spoon in enough additional stuffing to come to within one inch (2½ cm) of the top. NOTE: *Spoon leftover stuffing into a buttered 1-quart (1 L) casserole, cover and refrigerate; you will bake it just before serving.* Using 6 to 8 poultry pins, skewer the opening shut, then lace tightly with twine, crisscrossing it from pin to pin just as if you were lacing your shoes. Stand the veal on its rib ends in a large shallow roasting pan and drape with the bacon, overlapping the slices so that the veal is entirely hidden.

Set the veal, uncovered, in a very hot oven (450°F. or 230°C.) and brown 30 minutes. Lower heat to moderately slow (325°F. or 165°C.) and bake 2 hours longer or until a fork will pierce the meat easily.

Remove the veal from the oven and let stand at room temperature 25 to 30 minutes. At the same time, put the covered casserole of leftover stuffing into the moderately slow oven—it will be done at about the time the veal is ready to slice. NOTE: *The purpose of letting the veal rest is to make carving easier; during this period the juices will settle and the meat will firm up.* Remove the poultry pins and twine from the veal, then transfer it to a large heated platter. To carve, simply slice down between the ribs. Pass the extra stuffing as "seconds."

VARIATION:

Curried breast of veal with curried bulgur stuffing: This is so easy: Mix 1 teaspoon of curry powder with the ½ teaspoon crumbled leaf rosemary and ⅛ teaspoon pepper and rub over the veal breast as directed. Also, prepare the stuffing exactly as directed, but blend 2 teaspoons of curry powder into the stir-fried onions along with the thyme and rosemary. From this point, proceed as directed. That's all there is to it!

Veal chops with sweet red and green peppers

SERVES 4

Perfectly delicious and as colorful as the Italian flag. Serve with boiled rice, Risotto (see Index) or buttered egg noodles and a green vegetable or salad.

4 (1-inch-thick)	veal loin or rib chops, each about ⅓–½ pound (160–225 g)	4 (2½ cm thick)
2–3 tablespoons	olive oil	2–3 tablespoons
½ teaspoon	salt	½ teaspoon
⅛ teaspoon	freshly ground black pepper	⅛ teaspoon
1 medium-size	Bermuda or Spanish onion, peeled, halved and sliced thin	1 medium-size
1 small	sweet red pepper, washed, cored, seeded and cut in thin slivers	1 small
1 small	sweet green pepper, washed, cored, seeded and cut in thin slivers	1 small
1 cup	dry white wine	240 ml
2 tablespoons	Brown Meat Glaze (see Index) or 1 teaspoon beef extract	2 tablespoons
2 large	bay leaves	2 large
¼ teaspoon	crumbled leaf rosemary	¼ teaspoon

Trim the chops of all excess fat. Heat 2 tablespoons of the oil in a large heavy skillet over moderately high heat and brown the chops about 3 to 4 minutes on a side. (Reduce heat if they begin to sputter badly.) Lift chops to a plate, sprinkle with salt and pepper and set aside. If skillet drippings seem skimpy, add an additional tablespoon of oil. Dump in the onion and peppers and stir-fry 1 to 2 minutes—just until lightly glazed but still quite crisp; remove to a plate and reserve. Add the wine and meat glaze to the skillet and boil about 5 minutes, scraping up browned bits, until reduced to a nice thick glaze on the bottom of the skillet. Return chops to skillet, add bay leaves, sprinkle in the rosemary, turn heat to low, cover and simmer 15 minutes. Transfer veal chops to a heated platter and keep warm. Remove and discard bay leaves. Raise heat under skillet to high and boil hard once again to reduce pan drippings to a rich brown glaze—1 to 2 minutes. Dump the reserved peppers into the skillet, toss lightly in the glaze just long enough to heat them through, then pour all on top of the veal chops and serve.

Veal scallops breaded with ground hazelnuts

SERVES 2

This is a recipe I worked out when I had some finely ground hazelnuts left over after making a chocolate-nut torte. You can substitute finely ground unblanched almonds, if you like, in which case a combination of peanut oil and butter would be preferable for browning the *scaloppine*. The nuts must be finely ground—almost floury—otherwise they will not stick to the meat.

½ pound	veal scaloppine, *pounded very thin*	225 g
¼ teaspoon	salt	¼ teaspoon
⅛ teaspoon	freshly ground black pepper	⅛ teaspoon
¼ cup	very finely ground unblanched raw hazelnuts or almonds	60 ml
2 tablespoons	hazelnut or peanut oil	2 tablespoons
2 tablespoons	unsalted butter	2 tablespoons
2 tablespoons	Brown Meat Glaze (see Index)	2 tablespoons
¼ cup	water	60 ml

Halve large *scaloppine*, salt and pepper each lightly on both sides and let stand at room temperature 15 minutes. Press each piece of veal firmly into ground nuts—first one side, then the other—to coat lightly but evenly. Heat oil and 1 tablespoon of the butter in a heavy 12-inch (30 cm) skillet over moderately high heat until a bread cube will sizzle in it. Quickly brown the *scaloppine*—about 3 minutes per side. Remove to a small heated platter, cover loosely with foil and keep warm. Add remaining tablespoon of butter to the skillet, also the meat glaze and water, and heat, stirring constantly, about 2 minutes, until pan sauce cooks down by about one-third. Pour over *scaloppine* and serve at once.

Saltimbocca alla Romana
(VEAL SCALOPPINE WITH PROSCIUTTO AND SAGE)

SERVES 4

Because the *scaloppine* for this recipe will be folded and wrapped in prosciutto, you'll need four to five large pieces (about 7 × 4 inches or 18 × 10 cm each **after** pounding). The prosciutto, by the way, is so salty that you will need to add very little—if any—salt to the veal (taste the prosciutto before salting the *scaloppine*). I like to serve *saltimbocca* on a bed of buttered chopped spinach, but this certainly isn't necessary.

1 pound	veal scaloppine, *pounded very thin*	½ kg
Light sprinkling	salt and freshly ground black pepper	Light sprinkling
¼ pound	thinly sliced prosciutto	115 g
2 tablespoons	finely minced fresh sage (or 1 teaspoon rubbed sage)	2 tablespoons
4 tablespoons	unsalted butter	4 tablespoons
⅔ cup	dry white wine	160 ml
2 packages (10 oz. each)	frozen chopped spinach, cooked by package directions, drained and seasoned to taste with salt, pepper and butter	2 packages (283 g each)

Lightly sprinkle *scaloppine* on both sides with salt (optional) and with pepper. Lay slices of prosciutto on veal (about 2 per scallop), overlapping and piecing as needed to cover veal. Fold in half so that the prosciutto is on the outside, making almost square "envelopes," then just before sealing, sprinkle a little sage inside each; fasten with wooden picks. Sauté quickly in butter in a heavy 10-inch (25 cm) skillet over moderately high heat 2 to 3 minutes per side. Transfer to heated plate, remove wooden picks, cover loosely with foil and keep warm. Pour wine into skillet and boil, stirring constantly, about 2 minutes, until browned bits dissolve and sauce thickens slightly. Spoon spinach onto a small heated platter, arrange a row of *saltimbocca*, one piece overlapping the next, down the center and top with pan sauce. Garnish with lemon wedges or twists and serve at once.

Émincé de veau

SERVES 4

I'm particularly fond of this Swiss dish. It isn't difficult to make, but there are a few points to bear in mind: First, have all implements and ingredients at hand and ready to use because there should be no stopping once you begin the recipe; second, make certain that the butter in the skillet is sizzling hot before you add the veal; and finally, do not brown the veal, merely cook it until it turns milky-white—a matter of a minute or two. *Scaloppine* is a tender cut of veal, and no amount of cooking will make it any more tender than it is in the raw state. So your purpose in making *Éminté de Veau* is to preserve as much of that original tenderness as possible. The best accompaniment? Shredded fried potatoes, noodles or rice.

1 pound	veal scaloppine, *sliced ⅜ inch (1 cm) thick and cut into strips about 2½ × ⅜ inch (6½ × 1 cm)*	½ kg
4 tablespoons, in all	unsalted butter	4 tablespoons, in all
2 medium-size	shallots, peeled and minced	2 medium-size
⅛ teaspoon	crumbled leaf thyme	⅛ teaspoon
⅛ teaspoon	freshly grated nutmeg	⅛ teaspoon
½ pound	mushrooms, wiped clean and sliced thin	225 g
⅓ cup	dry white wine	80 ml
1½ cups	heavy cream, at room temperature	350 ml
½ teaspoon	salt	½ teaspoon
Light sprinkling	freshly ground black pepper	Light sprinkling

Stir-fry half the veal in 1½ tablespoons sizzling hot butter in a large heavy skillet over high heat just until milky-white—1 to 2 minutes; lift veal to a large bowl with a slotted spoon and reserve. Add another 1½ tablespoons of the butter to the skillet, let it foam up and subside, then stir-fry the remaining veal the same way and transfer to bowl. Add the remaining tablespoon of butter to the skillet and, when it melts, add the shallots; turn heat to moderately low and stir-fry shallots about 2 minutes until limp and golden. Mix in the thyme and nutmeg, and let mellow a minute or two. Add the mushrooms and stir-fry about a minute; turn the heat down low, clap the lid on the skillet and let the mushrooms cook 10 minutes or until they have given up most of their juices. Pour in the wine, turn heat up high and boil, uncovered, 3 to 5 minutes until juices cook down, leaving a fairly thick glaze. Smooth in the cream, then let it boil 3 to 5 minutes until reduced by nearly half and about the consistency of sour cream. NOTE: *An interesting point about cream—the richer it is (the higher the butterfat content), the less danger there is of its curdling. Milk, when boiled, is very likely to curdle, half-and-half cream less likely to, although it must be treated gently. Heavy cream, on the other hand, will bubble away over surprisingly high heat without curdling—sweet cream, that is. Sour cream, because of its acid content, curdles the instant it boils.*

Return the veal to the skillet along with any juices that may have accumulated in the bottom of the bowl, turn burner heat down low and warm the veal in the mushroom-cream sauce 3 to 5 minutes. Mix in the salt and freshly ground black pepper and serve.

Königsberger Klopse
(GERMAN MEATBALLS WITH ANCHOVIES AND CAPERS)

SERVES 4 TO 6

If you've ever wondered why some meatballs are light and others leaden, you may be interested to know that the liquid ingredient can make all the difference. Meatballs made with milk, for example, tend to be denser and drier than those made with water or broth because milk protein curds (coagulates) during cooking. For truly light and fluffy meatballs, use club soda (as does this recipe) because it has almost a leavening effect. NOTE: *You'll need very little salt for these meatballs because of the brininess of the anchovies and capers.*

	MEATBALLS:	
1 pound	ground veal shoulder	½ kg
½ pound	ground pork shoulder	225 g
2 cups	moderately fine soft bread crumbs	½ L
2 tablespoons	minced parsley	2 tablespoons
1 tablespoon	drained minced capers	1 tablespoon
1 tablespoon	finely grated lemon rind	1 tablespoon
1 large	egg, lightly beaten	1 large
2 teaspoons	anchovy paste	2 teaspoons
¼ teaspoon	salt	¼ teaspoon
⅛ teaspoon	white pepper	⅛ teaspoon
¾ cup	club soda	180 ml
	POACHING LIQUID:	
1 can (13¾ oz.)	beef broth	1 can (407 ml)
1 quart	water	1 L
	SAUCE:	
3 tablespoons	unsalted butter	3 tablespoons
2 medium-size	shallots, peeled and minced (or use scallions)	2 medium-size
3 tablespoons	flour	3 tablespoons
2 cups	reduced Poaching liquid (above)	½ L
¼ cup	drained small capers	60 ml
½ cup	sour cream, at room temperature	120 ml

For the meatballs: Mix all meatball ingredients together, using your hands. NOTE: *Do not taste this mixture because it contains raw pork; also be sure to wash your hands well in hot soapy water when you have finished working with the meat mixture.* Cover mixture and chill 2 to 3 hours until firm enough to shape easily. Roll into balls about the size of golf balls, arrange in one layer on a large tray, cover and chill 1 to 2 hours.

To poach: Bring beef broth and water to a simmer in a large heavy saucepan over moderate heat. Drop half the meatballs into the liquid, and when it returns to a slow simmer, adjust burner heat as needed so that it ripples steadily but gently. Poach the meatballs uncovered for 20 minutes; remove to a heatproof bowl, using a slotted spoon, cover loosely with foil and keep warm. Poach the balance of the meatballs the same way and transfer to the bowl with a slotted spoon. Re-cover with foil and keep warm.

For the sauce: Boil poaching liquid hard until it has reduced to 2 cups—about 20 minutes. Meanwhile, melt the butter in a small heavy saucepan over moderately low heat; add shallots and stir-fry about 5 minutes until limp and golden but not brown. Blend in flour and mellow 2 to 3 minutes over low heat. When poaching liquid has reduced sufficiently, whisk about half of it into the flour paste, stir this mixture back into pan of poaching liquid and cook, stirring constantly, until thickened and smooth—about 3 minutes. Stir in the capers, then return all meatballs to pan and warm them very slowly in the sauce for 10 to 15 minutes with the kettle lid set on askew. NOTE: *If you turn burner heat to lowest point, you can hold the meatballs at this point for nearly an hour; just make certain that the sauce does not boil. (Use a flame-tamer underneath the saucepan.) And if the sauce should thicken too much, thin with a little water.*

When ready to serve, smooth the sour cream into the sauce and warm, stirring ever so gently so as not to damage the fragile meatballs, for about 5 minutes longer. Serve with boiled new potatoes and an assertive green vegetable such as Brussels sprouts or broccoli.

Viennese veal and bacon dumplings with mushroom-wine sauce

SERVES 6

Sheer velvet! But a difficult recipe, alas, unless you have a food processor to grind the veal and pork to a paste and to mince the bacon, shallots and mushrooms. Accompany by tiny new potatoes, boiled in their skins, and freshly cooked buttered asparagus lightly seasoned with lemon and dill.

DUMPLINGS:

1 cup	water	240 ml
¼ pound (1 stick)	unsalted butter	115 g (1 stick)
1¼ teaspoons	salt	1¼ teaspoons
1 cup	sifted all-purpose flour	100 g
7 large	eggs	7 large
¼ pound (about 5 slices)	lean bacon, cooked until crisp and crumbled	115 g (about 5 slices)

2 large	shallots, peeled (or use scallions)	2 large
1 pound	finely ground veal shoulder	½ kg
½ pound	finely ground pork shoulder	225 g
¼ teaspoon	white pepper	¼ teaspoon
¼ teaspoon	freshly grated nutmeg	¼ teaspoon
	POACHING LIQUID:	
4 quarts	water	4 L
1 tablespoon	salt	1 tablespoon
1 medium-size	yellow onion, peeled and stuck with 4 cloves	1 medium-size
2 large	bay leaves	2 large
	SAUCE:	
1 small	yellow onion, peeled and minced	1 small
4 tablespoons	unsalted butter	4 tablespoons
6 medium-size	mushrooms, wiped clean and minced	6 medium-size
⅛ teaspoon	freshly grated nutmeg	⅛ teaspoon
3 tablespoons	flour	3 tablespoons
1 cup	dry white wine	240 ml
1 cup	Poaching liquid (above)	240 ml
1 cup	heavy cream	240 ml
1 large	egg yolk, lightly beaten	1 large
2 tablespoons	minced parsley	2 tablespoons
To taste	salt and freshly ground black pepper	To taste

Prepare the dumplings first: Bring water, butter and salt to a boil in a small heavy saucepan over high heat. Off heat, dump in all of the flour and beat hard with a wooden spoon until mixture comes together in a ball. (It's the same technique that you use in making *choux* paste—in fact, this **will be** a *choux* paste, the "glue" that will hold these ultra-delicate dumplings together.) Now break an egg into the flour paste and beat hard until mixture comes together again. (It will look badly clotted at first.) Add a second egg, then a third, beating hard after each addition until mixture is again thick and smooth. Cover loosely and set aside to cool.

Place bacon and shallots in a food processor fitted with the metal chopping blade and mince very fine, using 2 to 3 ten-second churnings of the motor and scraping the work bowl down with a rubber spatula between each churning. Add the veal and pork and 3 of the remaining eggs and beat hard until uniformly smooth (about 2 half-minute churnings). Empty about half this mixture into a large bowl and reserve. To the meat mixture remaining in the food processor, add the final egg, the cooled *choux* paste, the white pepper and nutmeg. Combine, using 4 to 5 short bursts of speed. Add this mixture to the reserved meat mixture and combine by beating hard with a wooden spoon. The mixture should be absolutely homogenous. Cover with plastic food wrap and chill 1 to 2 hours until a good shaping consistency (about that of mashed potatoes).

To shape and poach the dumplings: Place water, salt, clove-studded onion and bay leaves in a very large kettle set over moderate heat and bring to a boil: adjust burner heat as needed so that surface of liquid barely ripples. If it bubbles too vigorously, the fragile dumplings will disintegrate as they cook. Your aim is to poach them slowly, **gently,** just until they are done clear through—necessary because they contain raw pork. Using a tablespoon dipped in cold water, scoop up a heaping spoonful of the veal mixture, then with a second tablespoon dipped in cold water, sculpt into a smooth, egg-shaped dumpling. I find it easiest to use the back of the second tablespoon for shaping in the beginning (that is, the convex side), then to apply the final, smoothing touches with the concave side. You'll have to dip the spoons constantly in cold water (so have a small bowl of it handy) as you shape the dumplings to prevent them from sticking to the spoons. Ease each dumpling into the simmering poaching liquid as you shape it, and when a dozen or so are in the kettle (about half the veal mixture), set the lid on askew and cook gently for 25 minutes. With a slotted spoon, transfer the dumplings to a large shallow aluminum pan that has been rinsed out in hot water, arranging them in one layer. Cover loosely with foil and keep warm. Now shape and poach the remaining dumplings the same way. When they are done, add to the pan, cover snugly with foil and keep hot by setting in a very slow oven (250°F. or 120°C.). NOTE: *If the oven heat is low enough, you can hold the dumplings successfully at this point for about half an hour.*

For the sauce: It's a good idea to begin the sauce while the second batch of dumplings is cooking so that both are done at about the same time. Stir-fry the onion in the butter in a small heavy saucepan over moderately low heat about 5 minutes until limp and golden (do not brown). Add the mushrooms and nutmeg and stir-fry another 5 minutes, until juices ooze out of mushrooms. Blend in the flour and let mellow 2 to 3 minutes over low heat. Combine the wine and poaching liquid called for and whisk into the skillet mixture; cook, stirring constantly, until thickened and no raw floury taste remains—about 3 minutes. Now simmer the sauce, uncovered, for 15 minutes to reduce slightly. Smooth in the heavy cream and simmer, uncovered, 15 to 20 minutes. Blend a little of the hot sauce into the egg yolk, then stir back into pan and turn burner heat to lowest point. Stir in parsley, salt and pepper to taste, and heat, stirring gently, 2 to 3 minutes longer. (Do not allow to boil or sauce may curdle.)

To serve, mound the dumplings on a deep, heated platter, then drizzle with about half the sauce. Pass the remaining sauce separately so that guests can help themselves to more.

Tomato bredie
(SPICY CAPE MALAY LAMB AND TOMATO STEW)

SERVES 6 TO 8

Cape cooks (from South Africa's Cape Province) make *bredies* out of a dozen different vegetables—potatoes, cauliflower, cabbage, spinach, green beans, endive and so on. But to my taste, the tomato *bredie* is the best, perhaps because the acid of the tomatoes renders the chunks of lamb meltingly tender. Like all *bredies*, this one should be ladled atop fluffy boiled rice.

3 tablespoons	butter or margarine	3 tablespoons
2 pounds	boned lean lamb shoulder, cut in 1-inch (2½ cm) cubes	1 kg
3 medium-size	yellow onions, peeled and sliced thin	3 medium-size
4 large	leeks, trimmed, washed and sliced thin	4 large
4 large	scallions, trimmed, washed and sliced thin (include some green tops)	4 large
2 large	garlic cloves, peeled and minced	2 large
1 (1-inch) cube	fresh ginger root, peeled and minced	1 (2½ cm) cube
1–2	jalapeño peppers (fresh or canned), cored, seeded and minced (depending on how "hot" you like things)	1–2
½ teaspoon	crumbled leaf thyme	½ teaspoon
½ teaspoon	crumbled leaf marjoram	½ teaspoon
¼ teaspoon	crushed coriander seeds	¼ teaspoon
⅛ teaspoon	crushed fennel seeds	⅛ teaspoon
⅛ teaspoon	crushed cumin seeds	⅛ teaspoon
2 large	cardamom pods (brown seeds only, crushed)	2 large
6	black peppercorns, crushed	6
2 cans (1 lb. each)	tomatoes (do not drain)	2 cans (454 g each)
1 cup	dry white wine	240 ml
2 tablespoons	tomato paste	2 tablespoons
2 tablespoons	finely chopped chutney	2 tablespoons
½ teaspoon (about)	salt	½ teaspoon (about)

Melt 2 tablespoons of the butter in a large heavy kettle over moderately high heat; brown the lamb a little at a time and drain on paper toweling. Add remaining 1 tablespoon butter and stir-fry onions, leeks, scallions, garlic, ginger and jalapeño peppers 8 to 10 minutes until limp and touched with brown. Mix in thyme, marjoram, crushed coriander, fennel, cumin, cardamom seeds and peppercorns; stir-fry 2 to 3 minutes to release flavors. Return lamb to kettle; add tomatoes, breaking up large clumps, the wine and tomato paste. Adjust heat so mixture bubbles gently, cover and simmer 2 to 2½ hours until lamb is fork-tender. Blend in chutney, season to taste with salt, then simmer, uncovered, 20 to 30 minutes longer until *bredie* is nice and thick—about the consistency of pasta sauce. Serve on mounds of fluffy boiled rice.

Schweinemedaillons
(PORK MEDALLIONS WITH MUSHROOMS IN COGNAC-CREAM SAUCE)

SERVES 4 TO 6

I feasted upon this elegant German dish at Baden-Baden's Badischer Hof, a 450-year-old monastery turned hotel. The mushrooms used were fresh Black Forest mushrooms *(Steinpilze)*, rarely available here, alas, except in dried form (shops specializing in German foods carry them). You can, of course, substitute our familiar white mushrooms with good results. Serve with boiled new potatoes or, better yet, with homemade *Spaetzle* (see Index).

1–1¼ pounds	fresh pork tenderloin, sliced ½ inch (1½ cm) thick	½ kg
5 tablespoons	unsalted butter	5 tablespoons
¼ cup	Cognac	60 ml
¼ cup	dry white wine	60 ml
½ cup	beef broth or consommé	120 ml
1 pound	mushrooms, wiped clean and sliced thin	½ kg
¼ cup	finely minced shallots	60 ml
1 tablespoon	dried minced Black Forest mushrooms (optional)	1 tablespoon
1 pint	half-and-half cream	½ L
To taste	salt and freshly ground black pepper	To taste

Brown the pork in 2 tablespoons of the butter in a large heavy skillet over moderately high heat; remove to a shallow baking dish, cover with foil and keep warm. Deglaze the skillet with Cognac and wine, add broth and reduce by two-thirds; pour over the pork, re-cover and set in a warm oven (250°F. or 120°C.).

Add the remaining 3 tablespoons butter to the skillet and sauté mushrooms and shallots 3 to 5 minutes over moderate heat until juices ooze out; add dried mushrooms, if you like, and sauté about 5 minutes longer or until mushrooms are limp and juices have evaporated. Stir pork medallions (and all their liquid) back into skillet, add half-and-half and simmer over medium-low heat 10 to 15 minutes until cream reduces by half and is the consistency of a thin white sauce. Season to taste with salt and pepper.

Pork chops braised with finocchio and tomatoes

SERVES 4

Here's an imaginative recipe that you can partially prepare a day ahead of time, then finish in less than an hour. Just make sure, if you do make the recipe in two installments, that you let the refrigerated pork chops come to room temperature before baking them. Serve with boiled rice or pasta shells dressed with garlic and oil.

1 large	yellow onion, peeled and chopped	1 large
1 small (¼-pound)	finocchio (fennel) bulb, washed, trimmed, halved and sliced thin	1 small (115 g)
1 large	garlic clove, peeled and minced	1 large
3 tablespoons	olive oil	3 tablespoons
½ teaspoon	crumbled leaf basil	½ teaspoon
¼ teaspoon	crumbled leaf oregano	¼ teaspoon
⅛ teaspoon	crumbled leaf thyme	⅛ teaspoon
1 can (1 lb.)	tomatoes (do not drain)	1 can (454 g)
1 tablespoon	dry vermouth	1 tablespoon
1 tablespoon	salt	¼ teaspoon (about)
Pinch (about)	freshly ground black pepper	Pinch (about)
4 (1-inch-thick)	pork loin or rib chops, each about ⅓–½ pound (160–225 g)	4 (2½ cm thick)

Stir-fry the onion, finocchio and garlic in 2 tablespoons of the oil in a medium-size heavy skillet over moderate heat about 5 minutes until limp and golden; add basil, oregano and thyme and mellow 1 to 2 minutes over moderate heat. Add tomatoes and their juice, breaking up large clumps, and the vermouth, cover and cook over moderate heat 15 minutes. Then uncover and cook over moderately high heat about 10 minutes longer until quite thick and dry; season to taste with salt and pepper. Set aside.

In a large heavy skillet set over moderately high heat, brown the pork chops lightly on both sides in the remaining tablespoon of oil; transfer to a large shallow casserole or baking dish large enough to accommodate all chops in a single layer. Pour finocchio-tomato mixture evenly on top. NOTE: *You may prepare the recipe up to this point as much as 24 hours ahead of time. Cool to room temperature, then cover and refrigerate. Before proceeding, let covered casserole stand at room temperature 1 hour.*

Bake for 40 minutes in a moderate oven (350°F. or 175°C.), then uncover and bake 15 to 20 minutes longer. Transfer the chops to a heated platter, smother with the finocchio-tomato sauce and garnish, if you like, with a few feathery green finocchio tops.

Glazed pork and sweet potato pudding ring

SERVES 8

This gossamer meat pudding is elegant enough for a party, particularly if you mound the center with buttered artichoke hearts, asparagus tips, broccoli flowerets or zucchini rounds.

6 slices	firm-textured white bread, crumbled	6 slices
1 cup	milk	240 ml
½ pound	boned lean pork shoulder, ground twice	225 g
½ pound	boneless smoked ham, ground twice	225 g
1 small	yellow onion, peeled and finely grated	1 small
4 large	eggs, separated	4 large
2 medium-size	sweet potatoes, boiled, peeled and mashed	2 medium-size
1 tablespoon	minced parsley	1 tablespoon
1 teaspoon	dry mustard	1 teaspoon
½ teaspoon	crumbled leaf thyme	½ teaspoon
½ teaspoon	crumbled leaf marjoram	½ teaspoon
¼ teaspoon	ground cloves	¼ teaspoon
¼ teaspoon	ground cinnamon	¼ teaspoon
¼ teaspoon	ground allspice	¼ teaspoon
⅛ teaspoon	ground nutmeg or mace	⅛ teaspoon
1 teaspoon	salt	1 teaspoon
⅛ teaspoon	freshly ground black pepper	⅛ teaspoon
	GLAZE:	
¼ cup	firmly packed light brown sugar	60 ml
2 tablespoons	water	2 tablespoons

Soak the bread in the milk in your largest mixer bowl 10 minutes, then beat hard until fluffy. NOTE: *If you have a food processor, soak the bread in the work bowl fitted with the metal chopping blade, then cream, using two 5-second churnings.* Add the pork, ham and onion and beat hard until smooth (three 10-second churnings with the processor). Beat in the egg yolks and all remaining ingredients except the glaze. Whip the egg whites to soft peaks and fold thoroughly but gently into ham mixture. Pack into a lavishly greased 6-cup (1½ L) ring mold; set the mold in a large shallow baking pan and pour enough hot water into the pan to come halfway up the mold. Bake, uncovered, in a slow oven (300°F. or 150°C.) for 2 hours or until the pudding is set like custard and begins to pull from the edges of the mold.

Remove the pudding from the oven and from the hot water bath; cool 20 minutes. Using a thin-blade spatula, loosen the pudding carefully around the edges and center tube of the mold. Invert onto a flameproof platter; set aside for the moment.

For the glaze: Combine the sugar and water in a very small heavy saucepan and boil 2 to 3 minutes until syrupy. Drizzle evenly over the pudding ring, then set 5 to 6 inches (13 to 15 cm) from the broiler unit and brown quickly—1 to 2 minutes.

Fill the center of the mold with a perfectly cooked green vegetable (see those suggested in the headnote) and serve.

Soy-and-ginger-glazed spareribs

SERVES 4

Forget about etiquette, pick the bones up and gnaw them! Serve with boiled rice and a salad of tropical fruits: mangoes, papayas, kiwi, grapefruit, oranges—any combination you fancy.

4 pounds	spareribs	1¾ kg
4 cups (1 quart)	boiling water	1 L
	GLAZE	
1 cup	dark soy sauce	240 ml
1 cup	apple juice or cider	240 ml
⅓ cup	Calvados or brandy	80 ml
½ cup	firmly packed light brown sugar	120 ml
3 large	garlic cloves, peeled and finely chopped	3 large
2 tablespoons	finely minced fresh ginger root	2 tablespoons

Spread the ribs out in a very large roasting pan, pour in the water, cover snugly with aluminum foil and set in a moderate oven (350°F. or 175°C.) for 1 hour (this amounts to a parboiling or steaming). Meanwhile, combine all glaze ingredients and place in a very large bowl. When the ribs have cooked 1 hour, take them from the oven, cool until easy to handle and drain off all pan drippings. Cut the ribs into serving-size pieces—usually chunks two to three ribs wide. Place the ribs in the glaze, turning so that all pieces are coated, cover and marinate for 24 hours in the refrigerator. Turn the ribs in the marinade several times.

When ready to proceed, arrange the ribs in a large shallow roasting pan, pour the marinade over all and bake, uncovered, in a moderate oven (350°F. or 175°C.) for 1 to 1½ hours until the meat all but falls from the bones. Turn the ribs every 30 minutes or so in the marinade so that they will be evenly glazed. NOTE: *If the marinade becomes skimpy or threatens to boil away, stir in a little hot water.*

Roast juniper-scented saddle of venison with spiced vegetable gravy

SERVES 6

Venison is a great specialty of the Black Forest of Germany, and luckily for those of us who like it, it is becoming more available in American meat markets. Because it is so lean, venison must be cooked carefully, usually with additional fat. Naturally tender cuts such as the rack (ribs) and the saddle (loin and leg) can never be made more tender than they are in the raw state. The idea, then, is to preserve as much of the natural tenderness as possible. This recipe from the resort hotel Dollenberg in Germany's Black Forest does precisely that: The venison is draped with bacon, then roasted quickly in a hot oven so that none of the natural juices are lost. It is also accompanied by a superlative vegetable gravy. NOTE: *You can use this same recipe—with great success—for a saddle of baby lamb of approximately the same weight.*

1 saddle (about 5 pounds)	venison, trimmed of sinew and larded well (have butcher grind trimmings for you)	1 saddle (2–2½ kg)
8 large	juniper berries, minced very fine	8 large
12 large	black peppercorns, pulverized	12 large
1 tablespoon	kosher (or coarse) salt	1 tablespoon
½ pound	thinly sliced bacon	225 g
	GRAVY:	
1 medium-size	yellow onion, peeled and chopped	1 medium-size
1 medium-size	carrot, peeled and chopped	1 medium-size
¼ cup	minced celery root	60 ml
4 tablespoons, in all	unsalted butter	4 tablespoons, in all
¼ pound	ground venison trimmings (from butcher)	115 g
¼ teaspoon	crumbled leaf thyme	¼ teaspoon
¼ teaspoon	crumbled leaf rosemary	¼ teaspoon
⅛ teaspoon	ground cloves	⅛ teaspoon

⅛ teaspoon	*freshly ground black pepper*	⅛ teaspoon
1 cup	*drained canned tomatoes*	240 ml
1 can (13¾ oz.)	*beef broth*	1 can (407 ml)
½ cup	*dry red wine*	120 ml
1 cup	*heavy cream*	240 ml
To taste	*salt*	To taste

Rub saddle of venison all over with mixture of juniper berries, peppercorns and salt. Let stand at room temperature 1 hour.

For the gravy: Stir-fry the onion, carrot and celery root in 2 tablespoons of the butter in a heavy skillet over moderate heat about 10 minutes until lightly browned; transfer to a medium-size heavy saucepan. Brown the venison trimmings in the remaining butter—2 to 3 minutes—over high heat. Add thyme, rosemary, cloves and pepper and allow to mellow 1 to 2 minutes over moderate heat; transfer to saucepan. Add the tomatoes, broth and wine to the saucepan and simmer, uncovered, 1½ hours. Purée the mixture, half the total amount at a time, in a food processor with the metal chopping blade or in an electric blender. Return to pan, add the cream and salt to taste and simmer slowly, uncovered, about 30 minutes or until slightly thickened. (Do not allow mixture to boil or it may curdle.)

To roast the venison: Stand the venison on its rib ends on a rack in a shallow roasting pan; drape the bacon slices on top, overlapping slightly, so that venison is completely covered. Roast in a very hot oven (450°F. or 230°C.) 40 to 45 minutes. The venison will be rare, but that is as it should be (overcooking will toughen it). Remove from oven and let stand 15 minutes to allow juices to settle.

To serve: Carve into thick slices by cutting down between the ribs. Pass the gravy separately so that guests may help themselves.

Ragout of venison with chestnuts and mushrooms

SERVES 8

Shoulder of venison, like shoulder of beef, lamb or pork, is a well-exercised and therefore fairly tough cut. The way to tenderize it is through slow, moist cooking, which converts the sinew to gelatin. This unusual recipe is my interpretation of a stew I tasted recently in a little country inn near Baden-Baden in Germany's Black Forest. NOTES: *You may substitute lean beef chuck, if you like, for the venison, or pork or lamb shoulder. The dried mushrooms and frozen chestnuts nowadays are available in most specialty food shops.*

3 pounds	boned venison shoulder, cut in 1-inch (2½ cm) cubes	1½ kg
⅜ pound (1½ sticks)	unsalted butter (approximately)	170 g (1½ sticks)
1 tablespoon	minced shallots or scallions	1 tablespoon
3 medium-size	yellow onions, peeled and coarsely chopped	3 medium-size
1 pound	medium-size mushrooms, wiped clean and sliced thin	½ kg
½ teaspoon	crumbled leaf thyme	½ teaspoon
¼ teaspoon	crumbled leaf rosemary	¼ teaspoon
⅛ teaspoon	ground nutmeg	⅛ teaspoon
½ pound	slab bacon, cut in ½-inch (1½ cm) cubes, blanched 15 minutes in water to cover and drained well	225 g
1 can (13¾ oz.)	beef broth	1 can (407 ml)
2 cups	dry red wine	½ L
1 package (¼ oz.)	dried minced chanterelle mushrooms	1 package (7 g)
1 package (¼ oz.)	dried minced Black Forest mushrooms	1 package (7 g)
½ pound	frozen, shelled and peeled Italian chestnuts	225 g
1 cup	whole-cranberry sauce	240 ml
1 cup	heavy cream	240 ml
To taste	salt and freshly ground black pepper	To taste

Brown one-fourth of the venison cubes in 2 tablespoons of the butter in a large heavy kettle over high heat; transfer to a bowl. Brown remaining venison in three batches, adding more butter as needed; transfer to bowl. Stir-fry the shallots and onions in 2 tablespoons of the butter 8 to 10 minutes over moderately high heat until lightly browned; add to bowl. Stir-fry the fresh mushrooms in 2 to 3 tablespoons butter about 10 minutes until limp and lightly browned. Return the venison, shallots and onions to kettle; add thyme, rosemary and nutmeg and mellow 3 to 4 minutes over low heat. Add bacon, broth, wine and dried mushrooms (both kinds), cover and simmer slowly 2 to 3 hours. Add chestnuts and cranberry sauce, re-cover and simmer 1 to 2 hours longer until venison is fork-tender. NOTE: *Cooking time will vary considerably depending upon the age of the animal and how well exercised it was (the older, more active animal will be tougher than the young one).* Stir in the cream, salt and pepper and simmer, uncovered, about ½ hour.

Serve accompanied by boiled new potatoes, egg noodles or *Spaetzle* (see Index) and a salad of crisp greens.

Poultry

Poulet au citron
(CHICKEN WITH LEMON)

SERVES 4

Lemons serve two purposes in this recipe: They flavor the sauce and help thicken it—almost like magic—to astonishing silkiness. The recipe comes from Chef Dominick Ferrière of Château du Domaine Saint-Martin in Vence, an idyllic hill-top hostelry overlooking a grand sweep of the Riviera. He teaches the finer points of *la cuisine de Provence* to hotel guests during the spring and fall. For this particular recipe, Chef Ferrière would use the plump, mild Mediterranean lemons. And plenty of them. American lemons, alas, are too tart to use so lavishly, so I've reduced the original quantity by half.

2 young (2½–3 pounds each)	broiler-fryers, split in half	2 young (1¼–1½ kg each)
Light sprinklings	salt and freshly black pepper	Light sprinklings
3–4 tablespoons	flour	3–4 tablespoons
6 tablespoons	unsalted butter	6 tablespoons
6 large	scallions, trimmed and finely chopped (include some green tops)	6 large
1 quart	dry white wine	1 L
2 large	lemons, juiced (save the rind)	2 large
3 cups	half-and-half cream	¾ L
1 cup	heavy cream	240 ml
—	the zest of the 2 lemons above, cut into fine julienne, blanched and drained	—

Sprinkle the chickens with salt and pepper, then dust lightly with flour. Melt 3 tablespoons of the butter in a very large heavy kettle over moderately low heat; sauté the chickens in the butter 7 to 8 minutes per side without browning them; transfer them to a large shallow baking pan and set, uncovered, in a moderately slow oven (325°F. or 165°C.).

Stir-fry the scallions in the kettle 5 minutes until limp. Return the chickens to the kettle, add the wine, set the kettle lid on askew and simmer 30 minutes. Remove the chickens, cover loosely with foil and keep warm. Boil the wine mixture hard for about ¾ hour or until reduced to 2 cups (½ L). At the same time, in a separate large heavy saucepan, boil the lemon juice down until it resembles glaze and barely covers the pan bottom. Pour in the half-and-half and heavy cream and boil, whisking occasionally to prevent boil-ups, until reduced to 2 cups (½ L). This will also take about ¾ hour.

Purée the reduced kettle mixture in a blender or food processor fitted with the metal chopping blade and return to the kettle. Also buzz the cream mixture in the processor or blender 30 seconds nonstop and mix into the kettle. Return the chickens to the kettle and heat to serving temperature, basting frequently with the cream sauce—about 5 minutes.

Arrange the chickens on a large heated platter and keep them warm. Whisk the remaining 3 tablespoons of butter into the sauce, then stir in the blanched lemon rind. Top the chickens with half the sauce. Garnish with twists of lemon and sprigs of fresh rosemary, rose geranium, lemon verbena or watercress. Serve with boiled rice or pilaf. Pass the remaining sauce separately.

Creamed white meat of chicken, broccoli and red peppers with fettuccine

SERVES 4

 This is not a difficult recipe, but it does require a modicum of last-minute dexterity because the chicken, broccoli, sweet red peppers and fettuccine are cooked separately, then tossed into a colorful mélange. To accompany, you need only a lightly dressed salad of delicate crisp greens.

1 large (1 pound)	whole chicken breast, halved, boned, skinned and cut into strips about as long as your little finger and ½ inch (1½ cm) wide	1 large (½ kg)
5 tablespoons	unsalted butter, at room temperature	5 tablespoons
2 large	shallots, peeled and minced	2 large
¼ teaspoon	crumbled leaf thyme	¼ teaspoon
⅛ teaspoon	crumbled leaf rosemary	⅛ teaspoon
½ cup	dry white wine	120 ml

1 cup	strong chicken broth	240 ml
1 cup	heavy cream, at room temperature	240 ml
¼ teaspoon	salt	¼ teaspoon
Light sprinkling	freshly ground black pepper	Light sprinkling
1 large	sweet red pepper, washed, cored, seeded and cut lengthwise into strips about ⅜ inch (1 cm) wide	1 large
1 medium-size	head of broccoli, trimmed, washed and divided into small flowerets	1 medium-size
1 quart	boiling water with 1 teaspoon salt added (for cooking the broccoli)	1 L
12 ounces	fettuccine	340 g
3 gallons	boiling water with 1 tablespoon salt and a few drops olive oil added (for cooking the fettuccine)	12 L
½ cup	freshly grated Parmesan cheese	120 ml

Stir-fry the chicken strips in 2 tablespoons of the butter in a medium-size heavy skillet over moderately high heat 2 to 3 minutes—just until they turn white; do not brown. With a slotted spoon, transfer the chicken to a bowl and keep warm. Add the shallots to the skillet and stir-fry in the drippings 2 to 3 minutes over moderate heat until limp and golden; do not brown. Mix in the thyme and rosemary and stir-fry a minute or so—just long enough to release their flavors. Pour in the wine, raise the heat to high and boil hard until the wine reduces, leaving only a shiny glaze on the bottom of the skillet—5 to 10 minutes. Add the chicken broth and reduce this, too, for about 20 minutes. Pour in the heavy cream, add the salt and pepper and reduce 10 to 15 minutes or until cooked down by about half. Turn the heat very low, return the chicken to the skillet and let mellow while you proceed with the recipe.

Stir-fry the red pepper strips in 1 tablespoon of the butter in a small heavy skillet over moderate heat 1 to 2 minutes—you only want to take the crisp raw edge off the peppers; remove from heat and reserve. Now parboil the broccoli in the 1 quart (1 L) of lightly salted water for 3 minutes; drain well and keep warm. Finally, boil the fettuccine in the lightly salted and oiled water about 4 minutes—just until no raw starch flavor remains; the pasta should still offer a bit of resistance to the teeth.

Drain the fettuccine well, return it to the kettle in which you cooked it, add the remaining 2 tablespoons of butter and toss well. Now dump in the cream sauce mixture, the broccoli and red pepper and toss lightly but thoroughly, using two pasta forks. NOTE: *You will not be able to distribute the broccoli and peppers evenly throughout the fettuccine, but don't worry. You can even things up as you serve.* Serve at once and pass the freshly grated Parmesan.

Murgha tikka muslam
(MILDLY CURRIED CHUNKS OF CHICKEN WITH
CREAM AND ALMONDS)

SERVES 6

I've always thought it odd that the hotter the climate, the
hotter the cuisine. But there **is** a reason for this. In many equatorial countries,
refrigeration is either faulty or unknown, so other ways of keeping food from
spoiling must be substituted. One way is through a lavish use of spices. Indeed,
many of the components of curry powder—cinnamon, cloves and chilies, to
name three—are mild preservatives. This particular curry from the Himalayan
foothills of northern India is not particularly incendiary. But you can certainly
intensify its fire by doubling the quantity of chili peppers.

3 large	whole chicken breasts, split, skinned, boned and cut into 1-inch (2½ cm) cubes	3 large
3 tablespoons	ghee (melted butter from which the milk solids have been skimmed)	3 tablespoons
2 large	yellow onions, peeled and chopped	2 large
2 large	garlic cloves, peeled and minced	2 large
A 1-inch cube	fresh ginger, peeled and minced	A 2½ cm cube
¼ teaspoon	coriander seeds	¼ teaspoon
¼ teaspoon	cumin seeds	¼ teaspoon
¼ teaspoon	peppercorns	¼ teaspoon
¼ teaspoon	crushed hot red chili peppers	¼ teaspoon
4 large	whole cloves	4 large
4 large	cardamom pods, split (use inner dark seeds only)	4 large
½ teaspoon	ground turmeric	½ teaspoon
¼ teaspoon	ground cinnamon	¼ teaspoon
1 large	lemon, juiced	1 large
¼ cup	cream of coconut (obtainable at Latin or Oriental groceries)	60 ml
¼ cup	chicken broth or water	60 ml
2 tablespoons	tomato paste	2 tablespoons
½ teaspoon (about)	salt	½ teaspoon (about)
⅓ cup	shaved blanched almonds	80 ml
¼ cup	plain yogurt, at room temperature	60 ml
¼ cup	heavy cream, at room temperature	60 ml

Brown about one-third of the chicken in 2 tablespoons of the *ghee* in a heavy, medium-size kettle over high heat; with a slotted spoon, lift the chicken as it browns to a bowl. Brown the remaining chicken the same way in the drippings and transfer to the bowl. Add the remaining tablespoon of *ghee* to the kettle, dump in the onions, garlic and ginger, turn the heat to moderate and stir-fry 8 to 10 minutes until limp and lightly browned.

Meanwhile, pulverize the coriander, cumin, peppercorns, chilies, cloves and cardamom in a mortar and pestle (or an electric blender or one of the small electric coffee grinders), then combine with the ground turmeric and cinnamon. Add the spices to the onions in the kettle and stir-fry about 2 minutes to mellow and release the flavors. Blend in the lemon juice, cream of coconut, chicken broth, tomato paste and salt. Return the chicken (and any juices that may have accumulated in the bottom of the bowl) to the kettle, bring all to a slow simmer, then adjust the heat so that the kettle liquids barely simmer. Cover and cook 1 hour in all. Uncover after 45 minutes, and if there seems to be considerable liquid, cook uncovered for the remaining 15 minutes so that the juices reduce somewhat. If the liquid seems well reduced after 45 minutes but in no danger of scorching, simply re-cover and cook 15 minutes longer.

While the chicken simmers, lightly toast the almonds. All you need do is spread them out on a pie pan, then set, uncovered, in a slow oven (300°F. or 150°C.) for about 10 minutes. Cool and reserve.

When the chicken has cooked 1 hour, combine the yogurt and cream and smooth into the kettle juices. Let mellow over lowest heat about 5 minutes. Taste for salt and add more, if needed. Stir in the almonds and serve over fluffy boiled rice.

Chicken quenelles in duxelles sauce

SERVES 6

Before food processors, no one but the most skilled chefs bothered with this exquisite but fussy recipe. But the processor makes it all a breeze. The perfect accompaniment, I think, would be fresh asparagus, crisp-tender and lightly buttered.

1½ pounds	chicken breasts (about 3 large half breasts), boned and skinned	675 g
1 teaspoon	salt	1 teaspoon
½ teaspoon	rubbed sage	½ teaspoon
¼ teaspoon	crumbled leaf thyme	¼ teaspoon
⅛ teaspoon	freshly grated nutmeg	⅛ teaspoon
⅛ teaspoon	white pepper	⅛ teaspoon
1½ cups	heavy cream	350 ml
1 very large	egg	1 very large

DUXELLES SAUCE:

2 large	shallots, peeled and minced fine	2 large
½ pound	mushrooms, wiped clean and minced very fine	225 g
2 tablespoons	unsalted butter	2 tablespoons
⅛ teaspoon	crumbled leaf thyme	⅛ teaspoon
⅛ teaspoon	freshly grated nutmeg	⅛ teaspoon
¼ cup	dry white wine	60 ml
1 cup	chicken broth	240 ml
½ cup	heavy cream	120 ml
1 very large	egg, lightly beaten	1 very large
½ teaspoon	salt	½ teaspoon

FOR POACHING THE QUENELLES:

3 quarts	chicken stock or water	3 L

Cut the chicken meat into small chunks and drop into the work bowl of a food processor fitted with the metal chopping blade. Add the salt, sage, thyme, nutmeg and pepper. Snap the motor on and buzz 30 seconds nonstop. Scrape the work bowl down well with a rubber scraper; buzz another 15 to 20 minutes nonstop or until uniformly smooth. (The mixture will be **very** thick.) Now with the motor running, drizzle the cream slowly down the feed tube; buzz 10 seconds nonstop; scrape the work bowl down and buzz another 10 seconds. Break the egg into the work bowl and incorporate with a few short bursts of speed. Scrape this mixture into a bowl, cover and chill several hours, until firm enough to shape.

Next, prepare the duxelles sauce: Stir-fry the shallots and mushrooms in a medium-size heavy skillet in the butter over moderate heat about 5 minutes or until the mushrooms have given up their juices and these have evaporated. Mix in the thyme and nutmeg and stir-fry a minute or two to heighten their flavors. Pour in the wine, turn heat up high and boil 3 to 5 minutes or until all liquids have boiled away. Transfer the mushroom mixture to a medium-size heavy saucepan, add the broth and cream and bring to a simmer over moderate heat. Quickly whisk a little of the hot sauce into the beaten egg, then stir egg mixture into the pan. Add the salt, reduce burner heat slightly and cook, stirring constantly, 2 to 3 minutes until slightly thickened—do not boil. Remove from the heat and set at the back of the stove to keep warm.

To shape and cook the quenelles: Heat the 3 quarts of stock or water in a large heavy saucepan over moderate heat until ripples appear on the surface; adjust burner heat so that the liquid stays at a gentle simmer. Now set a tall glass of ice water on the counter beside the poaching liquid and equip yourself with two tablespoons. Take up a well-rounded spoonful of the chilled chicken mixture on a tablespoon that has first been dipped into the ice water; with a second dipped tablespoon sculpt a smooth egg shape, then ease the quenelle into the poaching liquid. Continue shaping quenelles in the same manner, dipping both spoons frequently in the ice water, until you have used up about half of the chicken mixture. Poach the quenelles 4 to 5 minutes on a side—just until quivery-firm. Using a slotted spoon, lift the quenelles to a plate rinsed out in hot water, cover loosely with foil and keep warm. Shape and poach the remaining quenelles the same way.

To finish the dish: Pour the duxelles sauce into a large heavy skillet, add the quenelles and heat slowly 2 to 3 minutes; do not allow to boil or the sauce may curdle. Transfer the quenelles to a deep platter, pour the sauce evenly on top and serve. NOTE: *The quenelles are also good cold, as I discovered when I had a few left over. I refrigerated them in the leftover duxelle sauce, then took them from the refrigerator about 20 minutes before serving—just long enough to take the chill off of them.*

Colonial chicken pie with rose water, currants, prunes and raisins

 SERVES 6 TO 8

Rose water may seem an unlikely flavoring for chicken, but when combined with wine, prunes, raisins and currants, it is mellowing rather than flowery. What also enriches the flavor is the fact that the meat used comes from a roasted chicken instead of a stewed one. And where does one buy rose water? At almost any specialty food shop or Middle Eastern grocery.

¼ pound (1 stick)	unsalted butter	115 g (1 stick)
A 4-pound (about)	roasting chicken, trussed and ready to roast (reserve the heart and liver)	A 2 kg (about)
1 teaspoon	salt	1 teaspoon
¼ teaspoon	freshly ground black pepper	¼ teaspoon
3 tablespoons	dried currants	3 tablespoons
3 tablespoons	golden seedless raisins (sultanas)	3 tablespoons
6 large	prunes, pitted and coarsely chopped	6 large
A ½-inch piece	stick cinnamon	A 1½ cm piece
1 large	blade of mace	1 large
2 tablespoons, in all	light brown sugar	2 tablespoons, in all
1¼ cups, in all	dry white wine	300 ml, in all
1 tablespoon	cider vinegar	1 tablespoon
2 tablespoons	rose water	2 tablespoons
1½ cups (about)	light cream or half-and-half	350 ml (about)
3 large	egg yolks, lightly beaten	3 large

	PASTRY:	
1¼ cups	*sifted all-purpose flour*	125 g
½ teaspoon	*salt*	½ teaspoon
5 tablespoons	*lard (not vegetable shortening)*	5 tablespoons
¼ cup (about)	*cold water*	60 ml (about)

Tuck half of the butter into the body cavity of the chicken. Place the liver and heart in a small bowl, cover loosely and refrigerate until time to prepare the sauce. NOTE: *The neck and gizzard may be saved for making a soup or stock.* Rub the chicken all over with the salt and pepper. Place the chicken in a shallow roasting pan and scatter the currants, raisins and chopped prunes into the pan around the chicken; add the cinnamon stick and blade of mace. Dot the remaining butter over the chicken and fruits; sprinkle 1 tablespoon of the sugar over the chicken and pour ¾ cup (180 ml) of the wine into the pan. Roast the chicken, uncovered, in a moderate oven (350°F. or 175°C.), basting frequently with pan drippings, for about 2 hours or until it is very brown and the leg moves easily in the hip socket. Remove the chicken from the oven and cool until easy to handle. Discard the cinnamon stick and blade of mace.

While the chicken cools, prepare the sauce: Skim 2 tablespoons of the fat from the pan drippings and heat until bubbly in a medium-size saucepan. Mince the reserved chicken liver and heart, add to the saucepan and stir-fry 2 to 3 minutes until lightly browned. Add the remaining tablespoon of sugar, the remaining ½ cup (120 ml) of wine, the vinegar and rose water. Simmer, uncovered, about 10 minutes or until the wine is reduced in volume by about half. Meanwhile, lift the chicken from the roasting pan to a wire rack to finish cooling. With a slotted spoon, scoop the currants, raisins and prunes from the pan drippings and reserve. Pour the drippings into a 1-quart (1 L) measure, then add light cream until the drippings and cream total 2½ cups (600 ml); blend in the beaten egg yolks. Pour a little of the hot saucepan mixture into the cream mixture, stirring briskly, then mix all back into the saucepan and heat and stir over lowest heat 1 minute. Remove the sauce from the heat, stir in the reserved currants, raisins and prunes and season lightly with salt and pepper. Let the sauce cool while you cut the meat from the chicken.

With a sharp knife, cut the meat from the chicken, slicing the breast into nice thick slices. Layer the chicken meat into a shallow 6-cup (1½ L) casserole, pour the sauce over all and toss lightly to mix. Let stand while preparing the pastry.

To make the pastry: Place the flour and salt in a small mixing bowl, cut in the lard with a pastry blender until the texture of coarse meal, then add the water, a little at a time, tossing the mixture briskly with a fork just until the pastry clings together. Roll out on a lightly floured pastry cloth to a circle about 1½ inches (4 cm) larger in diameter than the casserole you are using. Moisten the rim of the dish, fold the pastry over the rolling pin, then ease into place on top of the casserole. Roll the pastry edges under so that they are even with the rim of the casserole, then crimp to seal, making a high fluted edge. Cut decorative steam vents over the surface of the pastry.

Bake the chicken pie in a moderate oven (350°F. or 175°C.) for 45 to 50 minutes or until the filling is bubbly and the pastry golden brown. To serve, cut pie-shaped wedges of pastry, place one on each dinner plate and top with a hefty portion of the chicken filling.

Ajiaco
(COLOMBIAN CHICKEN, POTATO AND CORN STEW WITH AVOCADO AND CAPERS)

SERVES 8 TO 10

A properly made *ajiaco* (pronounced ah-YAH-co) contains at least six different kinds of potatoes and preferably more—mealy potatoes that cook down to mush and thicken the stew, waxy potatoes that hold their shape and texture, nut-flavored "news," mellow russets. The variety of potatoes grown in the Boyaca Highlands near Bogotá is simply staggering, and Colombian cooks would use maybe a dozen different ones for *ajiaco*. This version of the Colombian "national dish" uses four popular American potatoes and approximates—it can't duplicate—the original.

A 5½–6-pound	capon or hen, disjointed and stripped of excess fat	A 2½–2¾ kg
2 quarts	rich chicken stock	2 L
2 cups	water	½ L
3 large	yellow onions, peeled and coarsely chopped	3 large
8 medium-size	scallions, trimmed and sliced thin (include some green tops)	8 medium-size
1 large	bay leaf	1 large
½ teaspoon	crumbled leaf thyme	½ teaspoon
4 tablespoons, in all	minced fresh coriander (or 4 tablespoons minced Italian parsley + ½ teaspoon ground coriander)	4 tablespoons, in all
6	peppercorns	6
3 small	baking potatoes, peeled and cubed	3 small
2 medium-size	Maine or Eastern potatoes, peeled and cubed	2 medium-size
6 medium-size	California long white potatoes, peeled and cubed	6 medium-size
8 small	new potatoes, peeled and quartered	8 small

3 medium-size ears	sweet corn, shucked and cut in 1½-inch (4 cm) chunks (or use the frozen chunks of corn, about 12 in all)	3 medium-size ears
3 teaspoons	salt (or to taste)	3 teaspoons
Generous sprinkling	freshly ground black pepper	Generous sprinkling
⅔ cup, in all	small capers, well drained	160 ml, in all
1 cup, in all	half-and-half cream, at room temperature	240 ml, in all
2 large	ripe avocados, peeled, pitted and cubed (sprinkle with lemon juice to prevent darkening)	2 large

Place chicken in a large heavy kettle, add stock, water, onions, scallions, bay leaf, thyme, 2 tablespoons of the minced coriander and the peppercorns; cover and simmer 1½ hours or until chicken is fork-tender. Remove chicken from broth and cool; cut meat from bones in bite-size pieces and reserve. Chill broth and skim off fat.

Return broth to kettle, add all potatoes, cover and simmer about 1 hour or until new potatoes are tender; add chicken and corn, cover and simmer ½ hour until corn is tender. Season to taste with salt and pepper; stir in 3 tablespoons of the capers and ¼ cup (60 ml) of the cream. Mix in remaining coriander.

To serve, place remaining capers, cream and the avocado cubes in separate serving bowls; transfer stew to a large tureen. Ladle *ajiaco* into soup plates, then top each portion with a scattering of capers and a spoonful or two of cream and avocado cubes. Pass these accompaniments so that guests can help themselves to more of each. NOTE: *You may also pass, if you like, a small bowl of minced fresh coriander or parsley—Colombians often do.*

Wine-and-butter-basted Cornish game hens with egg and olive stuffing

SERVES 4

This way of stuffing and roasting fowl is one I learned from the Portuguese, who dote upon both chickens and eggs. I decided to try their method with small game hens, which need help if they are not to dry out as they roast. My dinner guests thought this recipe a huge success and nibbled every last morsel of meat from the bones. NOTE: *Should you want to use the egg and olive stuffing for chicken, you'll find that the recipe below makes enough to stuff a 4- to 5-pound (2 to 2¼ kg) roaster.*

4 small (about 1 pound each)	Cornish game hens, preferably fresh, although thawed frozen birds will do	4 small (about ½ kg each)

EGG AND OLIVE STUFFING:

1 medium-size	yellow onion, peeled and chopped	1 medium-size
1 small	garlic clove, peeled and minced	1 small
1 small	celery rib, diced	1 small
2 tablespoons	olive oil	2 tablespoons
1 teaspoon	rubbed sage	1 teaspoon
¼ teaspoon	crumbled leaf marjoram	¼ teaspoon
¼ teaspoon	crumbled leaf thyme	¼ teaspoon
—	the game hen hearts and livers	—
2 cups	moderately coarse soft bread crumbs	½ L
2 large	hard-cooked eggs, peeled and chopped	2 large
¼ cup	minced parsley (preferably the flat-leaf Italian parsley)	60 ml
2 tablespoons	minced, pitted green olives	2 tablespoons
½ teaspoon	salt	½ teaspoon
¼ teaspoon	freshly ground black pepper	¼ teaspoon
2 tablespoons	melted unsalted butter	2 tablespoons
2 tablespoons	dry white wine	2 tablespoons

FOR BASTING THE GAME HENS:

¼ cup	melted unsalted butter	60 ml
1 tablespoon	olive oil	1 tablespoon
2 tablespoons	dry white wine	2 tablespoons

Take the giblets from the body cavity of each game hen, then mince and reserve the hearts and livers; you will use these in the stuffing. As for the remaining giblets, I wrap them in plastic food wrap and freeze to use later in making chicken broth. Now wipe the birds inside and out with a damp cloth and set aside while you prepare the stuffing.

For the egg and olive stuffing: Stir-fry the onion, garlic and celery in the olive oil in a small heavy skillet over moderate heat about 5 minutes until limp and golden. Stir in the sage, marjoram, thyme, minced hearts and livers and sauté, stirring occasionally, 2 to 3 minutes until the giblets are no longer pink. Dump the skillet mixture into a large mixing bowl, add all remaining stuffing ingredients and toss well to mix.

Now stuff each of the hens, filling the neck cavity first (you will be able to get only a teaspoon or so of stuffing into each). Spoon the stuffing in lightly—don't pack it, because it will swell as the birds roast. Fold the neck skin against the back, sealing the stuffing in, then secure with a toothpick. Now stuff the body cavity of each bird, again spooning the stuffing in lightly. TIP: *I find it easiest to upend the birds and drop the stuffing directly down into the body.* As each bird is stuffed, fold the wings against the back, then close the body cavity by tying the tail and drumsticks together. NOTE: *Wrap any remaining stuffing snugly in foil—the foil package can be baked alongside the birds.* Place the birds, breast side up, in a shallow roasting pan large enough to accommodate them all without crowding but not so large as to leave large gaps between them. Whisk together all basting ingredients, then brush each bird liberally with the mixture.

Roast the birds, uncovered, in a moderately hot oven (375°F. or 190°C.) for 1 to 1¼ hours, brushing every 15 minutes with more of the basting mixture. As soon as the birds are richly browned and you can move a drumstick easily, they are done. Remove from the oven, remove all toothpicks and string, let the birds rest for 10 minutes, then serve. Pour the pan drippings into a heated gravy boat to pass to guests, and also pass the extra stuffing in a small bowl.

Spinach, mozzarella and prosciutto-stuffed turkey breasts

SERVES 6

My friend Angela Phelan, who once owned and operated a superb restaurant in Westchester County, New York, makes marvelous stuffed chicken breasts, and this recipe, I must confess, is a variation of hers. I've substituted frozen chopped spinach for the fresh, which Angela prefers, added sautéed shallots, nutmeg, prosciutto (at Angela's suggestion) and Parmesan. If you prefer to stuff chicken instead of turkey breasts, by all means do. Just make sure that they are big—about one full pound (half a kilo) per whole breast.

3 small (1 pound each)	whole turkey breasts, boned (ask butcher to leave skin intact)	3 small (½ kg each)
¼ teaspoon	salt	¼ teaspoon
Light sprinkling	freshly ground black pepper	Light sprinkling
	STUFFING:	
2 large	shallots, peeled and minced	2 large
2 tablespoons	unsalted butter	2 tablespoons
⅛ teaspoon	crumbled leaf rosemary	⅛ teaspoon
⅛ teaspoon	freshly grated nutmeg	⅛ teaspoon
⅛ teaspoon	freshly ground black pepper	⅛ teaspoon
1 package (10 oz.)	frozen chopped spinach, thawed and drained very dry	1 package (283 g)
¼ pound	prosciutto ham, trimmed of fat and minced very fine	115 g
¼ pound	mozzarella cheese, cut into ¼-inch (¾ cm) cubes	115 g

1 cup	ricotta or pot cheese, well drained	240 ml
2 tablespoons	freshly grated Parmesan cheese	2 tablespoons
	BASTING SAUCE:	
2 tablespoons	melted unsalted butter	2 tablespoons
1 tablespoon	dry vermouth	1 tablespoon

With a very sharp knife, carefully split the turkey breasts in half by cutting straight down the center; work carefully, taking great pains not to tear or stretch the skin, because the stuffing is to go underneath it. Now, starting at the top (neck end) of a breast, work the skin free of the meat along the center so that you have a large pocket. Try not to loosen the skin at the bottom or sides. Make pockets in the two remaining breasts the same way. Sprinkle all with salt and pepper and set aside while you prepare the stuffing.

For the stuffing: Stir-fry the shallots in the butter in a medium-size heavy skillet over moderate heat about 5 minutes until limp and golden; add the rosemary, nutmeg and pepper and stir-fry 1 to 2 minutes to release their flavors. Mix in the spinach and stir-fry about 5 minutes until all juices have evaporated. Remove from the heat and cool. Meanwhile, in a large bowl, combine the prosciutto, mozzarella, ricotta and Parmesan; as soon as the spinach mixture is cool, mix it in too.

To stuff the turkey breasts: Using a tablespoon, take up a mound of the stuffing and spoon it into the pocket of a breast, pushing it all the way to the other end. Continue spooning the stuffing in, distributing it as evenly as possible, until the pocket is full. Stuff the remaining breasts the same way.

Place the stuffed breasts, skin side up, in a shallow baking pan just large enough to accommodate them in a single layer without crowding. Combine the basting sauce ingredients—the melted butter and vermouth—and brush generously and evenly over each breast. Set, uncovered, in a moderate oven (350°F. or 175°C.) and bake for 1 hour, basting with pan drippings every 10 to 15 minutes, until turkey is fork-tender. NOTE: *If you have used chicken breasts, reduce the overall cooking time by about 10 minutes.*

Serve at once, topping each portion with some of the pan drippings. Or chill the stuffed breasts and serve them cold.

Squab, green bean and red lettuce salad with warm gravy dressing

SERVES 4 TO 6

A couple of years ago when I was touring Germany's Black Forest, I ate a memorable warm quail salad at Burg Windeck, a mountaintop restaurant built inside the ruins of a medieval castle near Baden-Baden. My version of the salad, which substitutes more readily available squab for quail, is otherwise quite like the original. Serve as a first course preceding the entrée of a party dinner.

A ¾–1-pound	squab, dressed and trussed	A 340–455 g
½ pound	young green beans, cut into matchstick strips, parboiled 5 minutes and drained	225 g
2 medium-size	leeks, washed, trimmed, cut into matchstick strips, parboiled 2 minutes and drained	2 medium-size
¼ pound	celeriac, peeled, cut into matchstick strips, parboiled 3 minutes and drained	115 g
1 medium-size head	red lettuce, trimmed, washed and cut into slim shreds	1 medium-size head
	GRAVY DRESSING:	
⅓ cup	squab pan drippings (add olive oil, if necessary, to round out the measure)	80 ml
2 tablespoons	finely minced shallots or scallions	2 tablespoons
2–3 tablespoons	reduced squab stock (see recipe)	2–3 tablespoons
¼ cup	olive oil	60 ml
1 teaspoon	Dijon mustard	1 teaspoon
1 tablespoon	snipped fresh chives	1 tablespoon
1 tablespoon	minced parsley	1 tablespoon
½ teaspoon	crumbled leaf tarragon	½ teaspoon
⅛ teaspoon	crumbled leaf chervil	⅛ teaspoon
3 tablespoons	tarragon vinegar	3 tablespoons
½ teaspoon	salt	½ teaspoon
Light sprinkling	freshly ground black pepper	Light sprinkling

Roast the squab 35 to 40 minutes in a moderately hot oven (375°F. or 190°C.) until nicely browned. Remove from oven and cool until easy to handle. Pour drippings into a small heavy saucepan and set aside. Remove the squab meat from the carcass and cut into matchstick strips; also cut the crisp skin into thin strips; set both aside. Place the carcass in a small heavy saucepan, add enough cold water to cover and simmer, uncovered, for 1 hour. Strain the stock (discard carcass), then boil hard, uncovered, until reduced to 2 to 3 tablespoons (only a thin glaze will coat the bottom of the pan); reserve.

For the gravy dressing: Sauté the shallots 2 to 3 minutes in the reserved squab drippings over moderate heat until golden; off heat, add reduced squab stock and all remaining ingredients. Set over lowest heat and keep hot.

To assemble the salad: Place the squab and all other salad ingredients in a large bowl, pour the hot dressing over all, toss well and serve at once.

Fish &
shellfish

Codfish hash

SERVES 4 TO 6

Shortly before America's Bicentennial when I was researching early American recipes, I came across this exquisitely simple fish hash. The temptation, of course, is to jazz up the seasonings. But I urge you not to because the combined subtle flavors of the cod, cream and potatoes are finely—perfectly—tuned.

1 pound	boned and skinned fresh cod	½ kg
4 medium-size	Maine or Eastern potatoes, boiled until tender and cooled	4 medium-size
¾ cup	half-and-half cream	180 ml
4 tablespoons	unsalted butter	4 tablespoons
1 teaspoon	salt	1 teaspoon
⅛ teaspoon	white pepper	⅛ teaspoon

Mince the cod fine and set aside. Peel the potatoes and cut into small dice. In a large heavy skillet (not iron) set over moderate heat, heat the cream and butter until the butter melts. Add the cod and cook 2 to 3 minutes, just until it is no longer translucent. Add the potatoes, salt and pepper and simmer gently—do not boil at any time—3 to 4 minutes, just until piping hot. Serve at once for breakfast, lunch or supper.

Broiled red snapper stuffed with finocchio

SERVES 6

Fish and finocchio (fennel) may sound like an odd coupling, but they are most compatible, as this Sicilian recipe deliciously proves.

2 large	garlic cloves, peeled and minced	2 large
½ cup	olive oil (top quality)	120 ml
1½ teaspoons	fennel seeds	1½ teaspoons
1½ teaspoons	salt	1½ teaspoons
¼ teaspoon	freshly ground black pepper	¼ teaspoon
6 small (1¼ pounds each)	red snappers, cleaned (have backbones removed but heads and tails left on)	6 small (about ½ kg each)
12 medium-size	scallions, washed, trimmed and sliced thin	12 medium-size
3 medium-size	finocchio bulbs, washed, trimmed and sliced thin	3 medium-size
⅓ cup	minced parsley	80 ml

Steep garlic in oil 1 hour at room temperature. Pulverize fennel seeds with a mortar and pestle and combine with salt and pepper; reserve ½ teaspoon of this seasoning for the stuffing—the balance you will rub into the fish. Remove garlic from oil and discard; spoon 3 tablespoons oil into a large heavy skillet and set aside. Rub each fish well inside and out with the remaining oil, then with the fennel seasoning. Set skillet over moderate heat, add scallions and finocchio and stir-fry 3 to 5 minutes—just until golden but still crisp. Off heat, mix in parsley and reserved ½ teaspoon fennel seasoning.

Stuff the fish, using about half the finocchio mixture; skewer cavities shut with poultry pins. Bundle remaining finocchio mixture in foil; refrigerate it and the stuffed fish (also protected with foil) 3 to 4 hours. Let both stand at room temperature ½ hour before cooking.

Arrange fish on oiled broiler pan and broil 5 to 6 inches (13 to 15 cm) from the heat for 5 minutes; turn, top with remaining finocchio mixture and broil 5 minutes longer. Remove poultry pins and serve.

Red snapper à Madeirense

SERVES 6

Madeira's colorful morning market in the island capital of Funchal is piled high with fresh-caught *salmonete* (red mullet), which local cooks like to prepare this way. You'll find the fish more flavorful if you partially prepare it a day ahead of time so that the flavors have a chance to mellow in the refrigerator.

	SAUCE:	
2 large	yellow onions, peeled and coarsely chopped	2 large
2 large	garlic cloves, peeled and minced	2 large
3 tablespoons	olive oil	3 tablespoons
2 tablespoons	unsalted butter	2 tablespoons
5 large	vine-ripe tomatoes, peeled, cored, seeded and chopped fine	5 large
2 large	bay leaves	2 large
½ cup	dry white wine or dry vermouth	120 ml
2 tablespoons	minced parsley	2 tablespoons
¼ teaspoon	freshly ground black pepper	¼ teaspoon
½ teaspoon	salt	½ teaspoon
	FISH:	
6 small (1½ pounds each)	red snapper or trout, cleaned but with head and tail left on	6 small (675 g each)
⅔ cup	unsifted flour (for dredging)	160 ml
4 tablespoons	olive oil	4 tablespoons
	GARNISHES:	
2 tins (2 oz. each)	flat anchovy fillets, drained	2 tins (56.7 g each)
18	unpitted black olives	18
1 large	lime or lemon, sliced thin	1 large
4–5	watercress or parsley sprigs	4–5

For the sauce: Stir-fry onions and garlic in oil and butter in a large heavy skillet over moderate heat about 15 minutes until soft and lightly browned. Add remaining sauce ingredients, cover and simmer 1 hour; uncover and simmer 1 to 1½ hours longer or until sauce is about as thick as pasta sauce and the flavors are well blended. Remove bay leaves and discard.

For the fish: Dredge each fish well in flour, shaking off excess. In a heavy skillet, brown the fish gently in oil—about 2 minutes per side. Remove to a large ovenproof platter. Ladle some sauce artfully over each fish (do not cover completely). Let cool, then cover platter with foil and refrigerate until about 1 hour before serving. Reserve and refrigerate remaining sauce.

Next day—about an hour before serving—set the platter of fish on the counter; let stand 45 minutes. Empty remaining sauce into a small saucepan and warm over lowest heat, stirring as often as needed to keep it from sticking. Set fish, still covered with foil, in a moderately hot oven (375°F. or 190°C.) and heat 15 minutes.

To serve, spoon some of the reheated sauce on top of fish (leave heads and tails exposed). Decorate with crisscrosses of anchovy fillets, clusters of black olives, slices of lime or lemon and sprigs of watercress or parsley.

Individual baked mousses of flounder and cucumber with shrimp-wine sauce

SERVES 6

These quivery, exquisitely moist little mousses are a breeze to make with a food processor, but admittedly hell to make without one, because the fish must be beaten or pounded to a paste. My advice is to wait until you have a processor before attempting the recipe unless you have plenty of time and energy to spare. NOTE: *The easiest way to seed a cucumber is to quarter it lengthwise, then to slice off the seedy portions at the point of each quarter.* Allow two mousses per serving (they are really quite small), and sauce each portion lightly. NOTE: *These also can be served as a first course or fish course, in which case you can allow only one mousse per serving. There will be enough for twelve portions.*

4 large	shallots, peeled and minced	4 large
4 tablespoons	unsalted butter	4 tablespoons
1/3 cup	dry white wine or dry vermouth	80 ml
2 tablespoons	lemon juice	2 tablespoons
1 medium-size	cucumber, peeled, seeded and diced	1 medium-size
1 cup	half-and-half cream	240 ml
1 cup	heavy cream	240 ml
3 tablespoons	freshly snipped dill or 1 teaspoon dill weed	3 tablespoons
2 tablespoons	minced parsley	2 tablespoons
1 pound	flounder fillets, cut into 1½-inch (4 cm) chunks	½ kg
2 tablespoons	flour	2 tablespoons
¾ teaspoon	salt	¾ teaspoon
¼ teaspoon	white pepper	¼ teaspoon
2 large	eggs, well beaten	2 large

	SHRIMP-WINE SAUCE:	
2 tablespoons	unsalted butter	2 tablespoons
2 tablespoons	flour	2 tablespoons
½ teaspoon	salt	½ teaspoon
⅛ teaspoon	freshly grated nutmeg	⅛ teaspoon
Pinch	white pepper	Pinch
⅔ cup	milk, at room temperature	160 ml
⅓ cup	heavy cream, at room temperature	80 ml

⅓ cup	minced cooked shrimp (or use lump crab or lobster meat should you have any available)	80 ml
2 tablespoons	dry white wine	2 tablespoons

Stir-fry the shallots in the butter in a medium-size heavy skillet over moderate heat about 5 minutes until limp and golden. Pour in the wine and lemon juice and simmer slowly about 10 minutes until all liquid has cooked down to a rich golden glaze; set off the heat and cool. Meanwhile, purée the cucumber with the half-and-half in a food processor equipped with the metal chopping blade, using three to four 30-second churnings and scraping the work bowl between each; transfer the cucumber mixture to a large bowl, stir in the heavy cream, dill and parsley and set aside. NOTE: *If you have no processor, you can purée the cucumbers with the half-and-half in an electric blender at high speed, or you can blanch the pieces of cucumber in boiling water until quite limp—3 to 4 minutes—then force through a food mill.*

Now place about one-fourth of the flounder into the processor work bowl, still fitted with the metal chopping blade (no need to have rinsed the bowl or the blade), sprinkle in about 1½ teaspoons of the flour and buzz 60 seconds until very thick and pastelike; scrape the work bowl sides down, add a little of the cucumber mixture (just enough to moisten things) and buzz 60 seconds longer. Inspect the fish; if it is not velvety, purée for another 60 seconds; empty into a bowl. Purée the remaining flounder the same way in three batches, using up the remaining flour and puréeing the cooled shallot skillet mixture with the last batch. Combine the flounder and cucumber mixtures, add the salt, pepper and eggs and stir until uniformly smooth.

Ladle the mousse mixture into 12 well-buttered ¾-cup (180 ml) ramekins and set in a large shallow baking pan. Set on the middle shelf of a moderate oven (350°F. or 175°C.), then pour enough hot water into the pan (don't splash into the ramekins) to measure about 1½ inches (4 cm) deep. Bake, uncovered, for 1 hour. Remove the ramekins from the oven and from the water bath and cool 20 minutes.

Meanwhile, prepare the shrimp-wine sauce: Melt the butter in a small heavy saucepan over moderate heat, then blend in the flour to make a smooth paste. Add the salt, nutmeg and white pepper and mellow a minute or two; combine the milk and cream and pour in. Heat and stir until thickened and smooth—3 to 5 minutes—then turn the heat to its lowest point, mix in the shrimp and wine and allow the sauce to "season" while the mousses finish cooling. Stir from time to time to prevent a skin from forming on the surface of the sauce.

To serve the mousses: Loosen each around the edge with a small spatula or thin-blade knife and invert onto a heated platter or individual heated plates. Spoon sauce over each portion and pass any remaining sauce separately.

Badische Hechtklössle à la Ritter-Durbach
(PIKE DUMPLINGS IN RIESLING SAUCE)

SERVES 4 TO 6

These are the equivalent of quenelles as prepared at the two-Michelin-star Ritter-Durbach restaurant in Durbach, Germany—or, rather, my own approximation designed to be made in a food processor. NOTES: *The metric equivalents given here are precise—for the dumplings, at least—because exact proportions are essential to the recipe's success. If you intend to serve the Badische Hechtklössle as the first—or fish—course of a festive dinner, you can count on eight ample portions from the quantities given below.*

DUMPLINGS:

1 pound	fillets of pike or other lean white fish	455 g
1½ teaspoons	salt	1½ teaspoons
¼ teaspoon	white pepper	¼ teaspoon
1 large	egg	1 large
1 cup + 1 tablespoon	heavy cream	250 ml

POACHING BROTH:

3 tablespoons	unsalted butter	3 tablespoons
1 small	leek, trimmed, washed and chopped	1 small
2 tablespoons	finely minced shallots	2 tablespoons
¼ cup	coarsely chopped celery root	60 ml
1 medium-size bunch	parsley (use stems only; reserve tops for other uses)	1 medium-size bunch
1 medium-size bunch	fresh dill (use stems only; reserve tops for other uses)	1 medium-size bunch
½ cup	Riesling wine	120 ml
3 bottles (8 oz. each)	clam juice	3 bottles (237 ml each)
5 cups	water	1¼ L
⅛ teaspoon	crushed black peppercorns	⅛ teaspoon

RIESLING SAUCE:

3 cups	reduced Poaching Broth (above)	700 ml
1 cup	Riesling wine	240 ml
1 tablespoon	lemon juice	1 tablespoon
⅓ cup	crème fraîche or heavy cream	80 ml
2 large	egg yolks, lightly beaten	2 large

| ⅓ cup | heavy cream, softly whipped | 80 ml |
| 2 tablespoons | unsalted butter, at room temperature | 2 tablespoons |

For the dumplings: In a food processor fitted with the metal chopping blade, buzz fish, salt and pepper 30 seconds; scrape work bowl down, add egg and flick motor on and off several times to incorporate. Carefully remove chopping blade, scrape fish mixture clinging to it back into work bowl, cover and chill 2 hours. Reinsert chopping blade (now clean) and, with machine running, drizzle heavy cream down the feed tube. Again remove blade, scraping mixture back into work bowl, re-cover and chill 1 hour or until the consistency of mashed potatoes.

Meanwhile, prepare poaching broth: Melt butter in a large straight-sided sauté pan over low heat, add leek and shallots and sauté 5 minutes (do not brown). Add celery root and parsley and dill stems and sauté 15 minutes over low heat. Add wine, clam juice and water and simmer, uncovered, 20 minutes; add peppercorns and simmer 10 minutes longer. Strain broth, discarding solids, return to pan and heat until bubbles show on bottom (liquid should just tremble).

To shape and poach dumplings: Using a tablespoon dipped in ice water, scoop up a rounded spoonful of fish mixture and, with a second wet tablespoon, smooth into an egg-shaped dumpling. (You'll have to dip the spoons in cold water often to keep the mixture from sticking.) Shape half the fish mixture this way and ease dumplings into barely simmering broth. Poach them for 5 minutes, turn and poach 5 minutes longer or until just set but still light and quivery (about the consistency of a mousse). With a slotted spoon, lift dumplings to a large plate; cover loosely with foil. Shape and poach remaining dumplings the same way; lift to plate, cover loosely and keep warm.

For the Riesling sauce: Strain the poaching broth, return it to sauté pan and boil hard until reduced to 3 cups (700 ml). Add the Riesling and reduce this mixture by half. Turn heat to low and when mixture stops bubbling, add lemon juice. Whisk in *crème fraîche*, half of the total amount at a time. Beat 3 to 4 tablespoons of this hot sauce into the egg yolks, one spoonful at a time, then stir yolk mixture into the sauce. Whisk half the whipped cream into the sauce, then the remaining half. Finish the sauce off by adding the butter, a tablespoon at a time, and beating lightly to incorporate. (Do not allow the sauce to boil at any time or it will curdle.) Gently add the dumplings and warm 1 to 2 minutes. Serve with plenty of sauce on each portion.

Cold trout in champagne dressing à la Kurhotel Mitteltal

SERVES 4 TO 6

The creation of Chef Paul Mertschuweit of the Kurhotel Mitteltal at Baiersbronn-Mitteltal in Germany, this exquisite dish can be served as an appetizer, a salad or a main dish. I had it as an appetizer on a recent tour of the Black Forest, then came home and worked out a variation of the original that can be served as a main dish. Chef Mertschuweit serves one small trout per person, with the head and tail left on. But since mini trout are rarely available in markets here, I have taken the liberty of substituting larger trout, about a pound each, filleted and chunked. The presentation is not as perfect, but the flavor is superb. If you intend to serve this dish as an appetizer or a salad, you can count on its serving six. As a main dish, it will feed four amply.

2 (about 1 pound each)	trout, cleaned, dressed and boned at the fish market	2 (about ½ kg each)
2 quarts	cold water	2 L
1 small	yellow onion, peeled and stuck with 4 cloves	1 small
1 tablespoon	red wine vinegar	1 tablespoon
1 teaspoon	salt	1 teaspoon

CHAMPAGNE DRESSING:

¼ cup	heavy cream, whipped	60 ml
2 tablespoons	sour cream	2 tablespoons
1 tablespoon	mayonnaise	1 tablespoon
1 tablespoon	ketchup	1 tablespoon
½ large	lemon, juiced	½ large
3 tablespoons	orange juice	3 tablespoons
2 teaspoons	prepared horseradish	2 teaspoons
⅓ cup	finely snipped fresh dill	80 ml
⅓ cup	dry champagne	80 ml
3 tablespoons	Cognac or brandy	3 tablespoons
¼ teaspoon	paprika	¼ teaspoon
¼ teaspoon (about)	salt	¼ teaspoon (about)
Light sprinkling	white pepper	Light sprinkling

GARNISHES:

1 medium-size head	Boston lettuce, trimmed, washed and patted dry on paper toweling	1 medium-size head
12–18 small	dill fronds	12–18 small
12–18 small	ripe cherry tomatoes (optional)	12–18 small

Place the trout side by side on a poaching rack—either the rack of a fish poacher or one that will accommodate the fish and fit into a large shallow kettle. Bring the water, onion, vinegar and salt to a simmer over moderate heat in the poacher or kettle. Lower rack and fish into the liquid and, as soon as it returns to a gentle simmer, adjust burner heat to keep it merely trembling and poach the fish 7 to 8 minutes—just until it will flake at the touch of a fork. Lift the fish from the kettle, plunge into ice water and leave for 3 to 4 minutes to quick-chill. Then remove from the water, drain well and set aside.

For the champagne dressing: Whisk all ingredients together briskly. Taste for salt and add more, if needed.

Cut the trout into chunks about 1 inch (2½ cm) thick and divide them evenly among small plates on which you have already arranged perfect leaves of lettuce. Spoon the champagne dressing evenly over the trout and sprig each portion with a few feathery fronds of dill. For color, add 2 or 3 cherry tomatoes to each portion. Serve with champagne and crisp buttered toast points.

Pompano baked in tomato-olive-caper sauce

SERVES 6

6 small (about 1¼ pounds each)	pompano, whole, cleaned and dressed (heads and tails removed)	6 small (about 570 g each)
	SAUCE:	
1 medium-size	Spanish onion, peeled and chopped	1 medium-size
1 large	garlic clove, peeled and minced	1 large
3 tablespoons	olive oil	3 tablespoons
1 teaspoon	crumbled leaf marjoram	1 teaspoon
½ teaspoon	crumbled leaf basil	½ teaspoon
¼ teaspoon	crumbled leaf thyme	¼ teaspoon
2 large	bay leaves, crumbled	2 large
2 cans (1 lb. each)	tomatoes (do not drain)	2 cans (454 g each)
¼ cup	dry white wine or vermouth	60 ml
⅓ cup	small capers, well drained	80 ml
¾ cup	chopped pitted green olives	180 ml
1 tablespoon	sugar (if needed to mellow sauce)	1 tablespoon
½ teaspoon (about)	salt	½ teaspoon (about)
Light sprinkling	freshly ground black pepper	Light sprinkling

Arrange pompano in a shallow baking pan large enough to accommodate all six fish in one layer; cover and refrigerate. Stir-fry onion and garlic in oil over moderate heat in a large heavy skillet 8 to 10 minutes until limp and golden. Blend in marjoram, basil, thyme and bay leaves; mellow 2 to 3 minutes. Add tomatoes and wine, cover and simmer 1 hour. Break up any large tomato clumps, mix in capers, olives, sugar, if needed, and salt and pepper to taste. Cool to room temperature, pour sauce over fish and marinate 2 to 3 hours in the refrigerator.

Half an hour before cooking the fish, remove them from the refrigerator to warm slightly. Bake, uncovered, in a moderately hot oven (375°F. or 190°C.) 35 to 40 minutes or until sauce is bubbly and fish flakes at the touch of a fork.

Sicilian swordfish, sultana and pine nut croquettes alla marinara

SERVES 6

This unlikely combination is simply superb, an early Saracen (Arab) contribution to Sicily's table. The sultana raisins mellow rather than sweeten the croquettes and at the same time help keep them light and moist.

	CROQUETTES:	
1½ pounds	boned and skinned fresh swordfish, finely ground	675 g
1¾ cups	soft moderately fine bread crumbs	415 ml
1 large	egg	1 large
3 tablespoons	minced parsley	3 tablespoons
2 tablespoons	finely minced golden seedless raisins (sultanas)	2 tablespoons
¼ cup	finely minced pine nuts (pignoli)	60 ml
2 tablespoons	freshly grated Parmesan or pecorino cheese	2 tablespoons
½ teaspoon	salt	½ teaspoon
⅛ teaspoon	freshly ground black pepper	⅛ teaspoon
⅓ cup	unsifted all-purpose flour (for dredging)	80 ml
⅓ cup	olive oil (for browning croquettes)	80 ml
2 large	garlic cloves, peeled and quartered	2 large
4 large	bay leaves	4 large
	SAUCE:	
2–3 tablespoons	olive oil (use the oil in which croquettes browned)	2–3 tablespoons
1 large	yellow onion, peeled and chopped	1 large
¾ teaspoon	crumbled leaf basil	¾ teaspoon
½ teaspoon	crumbled leaf marjoram	½ teaspoon
¼ teaspoon	crumbled leaf rosemary	¼ teaspoon

¼ teaspoon	crumbled leaf thyme	¼ teaspoon
2 tablespoons	minced parsley	2 tablespoons
3 tablespoons	dry white wine or vermouth	3 tablespoons
2 cans (1 lb. each)	tomatoes (do not drain)	2 cans (454 g each)
½–1 teaspoon	salt	½–1 teaspoon
Light sprinkling	freshly ground black pepper	Light sprinkling

For the croquettes: Combine all but last 4 croquette ingredients and shape the mixture into patties about ¾ inch (2 cm) thick and 2 inches (5 cm) across. Dredge well in flour. Heat oil, garlic and bay leaves in a large heavy skillet over low heat 10 minutes; do not allow garlic to brown. Discard garlic and bay leaves. Raise heat to moderately high and brown croquettes 1 to 2 minutes per side; drain on paper toweling. Arrange them in lightly greased 9 × 9 × 2-inch baking dish (23 × 23 × 5 cm), overlapping slightly, and refrigerate.

For the sauce: In oil left from browning the croquettes, stir-fry onion over moderate heat 8 to 10 minutes until golden. Add basil, marjoram, rosemary, thyme and parsley and mellow 2 to 3 minutes. Add wine and tomatoes and simmer, uncovered, stirring occasionally, about 1 hour or until sauce is smooth and thick. Season to taste with salt and pepper, and pour evenly over croquettes. Bake, uncovered, in a moderately hot oven (375°F. or 190°C.) 35 to 40 minutes until bubbling.

Cape country curried fish, potatoes and onions

SERVES 4 TO 6

While I was in South Africa's Cape Province researching an article on the area's award-winning table wines, I encountered this spicy dish more than once and enjoyed it each time. It's fast and it's frugal and as imaginative a way to stretch one pound of fish over six portions as you're likely to find.

1 small	Spanish or Bermuda onion, peeled and sliced thin	1 small
4 tablespoons (about)	unsalted butter	4 tablespoons (about)
1 teaspoon	curry powder	1 teaspoon
½ teaspoon	chili powder	½ teaspoon
Pinch	ground cinnamon	Pinch
Pinch	ground nutmeg	Pinch
2 medium-size	Maine or Eastern potatoes, boiled, cooled, peeled and sliced	2 medium-size
1 pound	flounder fillets	½ kg

Light sprinklings	salt and freshly ground black pepper	Light sprinklings
Light sprinklings	salt and freshly ground black pepper	Light sprinklings
½ cup	unsifted all-purpose flour	120 ml
2 tablespoons	lemon juice	2 tablespoons

Stir-fry the onion, separating the slices into rings, in 2 tablespoons of the butter in a large heavy skillet over moderate heat about 5 minutes until limp and golden; blend in the curry and chili powders, the cinnamon and nutmeg and mellow a minute or two. Add the potatoes and stir-fry 3 to 5 minutes until golden. Scoop all into a large bowl and reserve. Sprinkle the flounder fillets lightly on both sides with salt and pepper, then dredge evenly in the flour. Melt the remaining 2 tablespoons of butter in the skillet, and brown the flounder fillets, about half of them at a time, allowing 2 to 3 minutes per side. When the first batch is done, lift it to a heated plate. Add a little more butter, if needed, for the second batch of fillets. When they are done, return the first batch to the skillet. Add the lemon juice and the reserved onion mixture, distributing it evenly over the fish. Cook 2 to 3 minutes longer, shaking the skillet lightly so that the onions and potatoes settle in around the fish. Serve hot with a tartly dressed green salad.

Baked stuffed fresh sardines

SERVES 6

Fresh sardines are available in many metropolitan markets. If you've never tasted them, you're in for a pleasant surprise. They are delicate, totally unlike their canned counterpart. This recipe, a Palermo specialty, brings out the best in them.

	STUFFING:	
3 cups	soft, moderately fine bread crumbs	700 ml
3 tablespoons	olive oil	3 tablespoons
⅓ cup	finely chopped pine nuts (pignoli)	80 ml
¼ cup	finely minced golden seedless raisins (sultanas)	60 ml
6	anchovy fillets, rinsed, dried and minced	6
¼ cup	minced parsley	60 ml
	FISH:	
2 pounds	fresh sardines, each about 6 inches (15 cm) long, cleaned, boned and beheaded	1 kg
16	bay leaves	16
2 tablespoons	olive oil	2 tablespoons
¼ cup	lemon juice (about 1 large lemon)	60 ml
2 tablespoons	sugar	2 tablespoons

For the stuffing: Lightly brown crumbs in oil in a large heavy skillet over moderate heat. Dump two-thirds of the crumbs into a mixing bowl and combine with remaining stuffing ingredients. Save the balance of the crumbs to use as topping.

Spoon 1 to 2 tablespoons stuffing inside each sardine and fold fish over, enclosing stuffing. Arrange sardines in one layer in an ungreased 13 × 9 × 2-inch baking dish (33 × 23 × 5 cm), tucking the bay leaves between rows of sardines, and drizzle with oil. Combine lemon juice and sugar and sprinkle evenly over fish. Top with reserved crumbs and any extra stuffing. Cover loosely and refrigerate 2 to 3 hours. Let stand 30 minutes at room temperature, then bake, uncovered, in a moderately hot oven (375°F. or 190°C.) 35 to 40 minutes or until nicely browned.

Baked salt cod with potatoes, onions and fennel

SERVES 6

1 pound	boneless salt cod	½ kg
1 pound	new potatoes, washed	½ kg
2 medium-size	Spanish onions, peeled and sliced thin	2 medium-size
1 medium-size	garlic clove, peeled and minced	1 medium-size
6 tablespoons, in all	olive oil	6 tablespoons, in all
¼ teaspoon	crumbled leaf rosemary	¼ teaspoon
⅛ teaspoon	crumbled leaf thyme	⅛ teaspoon
⅛ teaspoon	ground mace	⅛ teaspoon
¼ cup	minced parsley	60 ml
1 teaspoon	crushed fennel seeds	1 teaspoon
Generous sprinklings	freshly ground black pepper	Generous sprinklings
¼ cup	lemon juice (about 1 large lemon)	60 ml
¼ cup	water	60 ml
1 cup	soft, moderately fine bread crumbs	240 ml

Soak cod 8 hours in several changes of cold water to leach out as much salt as possible. Drain, chunk and simmer in water to cover 10 minutes or until cod flakes easily; drain and flake coarsely. Boil potatoes in their skins 20 to 30 minutes until tender; peel and slice thin. Sauté onions and garlic in 3 tablespoons of the oil in a large heavy skillet 8 to 10 minutes over moderate heat until golden. Stir in rosemary, thyme and mace.

Layer ingredients into a lightly greased 9 × 9 × 2-inch baking pan (23 × 23 × 5 cm) this way: one-third of the onions, half the cod and half the potatoes, 1 tablespoon oil drizzled evenly over all, then half of the parsley and fennel seeds topped by a generous sprinkling of pepper. Repeat each layer, then add remaining third of the onions and more pepper. Combine lemon juice and water and pour over all. Toss crumbs lightly with remaining tablespoon of oil and scatter evenly on top. Bake, uncovered, in a moderate oven (350°F. or 175°C.) about 45 minutes or until bubbling and browned.

Bacalhau à gomes de sá
(PORTUGUESE SALT COD, POTATOES AND ONION EN CASSEROLE)

SERVES 6

A couple of hours north of Lisbon by car lies the perfect walled town of Óbidos, and at its pinnacle, inside the old castle ramparts, is the Pousada do Castelo, one of the Portuguese government's splendid inns. The dining room here is the old banqueting hall, all leaded windows and beamed ceilings plus a fireplace of ox-roasting dimension. The food on the five or six times I've visited has been superb. I always order Bacalhau à Gomes de Sá here because I think the *pousada* chef prepares it better than anyone else.

1 pound	boned salt cod	½ kg
2 quarts	cold water	2 L
6 cups	boiling water	1½ L
1 tablespoon	unsalted butter	1 tablespoon
3 tablespoons, in all	olive oil (top quality)	3 tablespoons, in all
1 large	Spanish onion, peeled and sliced thin	1 large
2 pounds	California long white or new potatoes, boiled until tender, peeled and sliced thin	1 kg
⅓ cup	minced parsley	80 ml
¼ teaspoon	freshly ground black pepper	¼ teaspoon
	GARNISH:	
1 large	hard-cooked egg, peeled and cut into thin wedges	1 large
12 medium-size	unpitted black Greek olives	12 medium-size

Place the salt cod in a large bowl, pour in the cold water, cover and soak overnight in the refrigerator. Next day, drain the cod well, then rinse in several changes of cold water to leach out as much salt as possible. Now place the cod in a large heavy saucepan, pour in the boiling water, set over moderate heat, cover and simmer 10 to 12 minutes—just until the cod flakes at the touch of a fork. Drain and rinse well, then flake the cod, removing any bits of skin or bone.

In a large heavy skillet set over moderate heat, warm the butter and 1 tablespoon of the oil for about 1 minute. Add the onion, separating the slices into rings, and stir-fry 8 to 10 minutes until limp and golden; do not brown. Remove the onions from the skillet and set aside. Add the remaining 2 tablespoons of oil to the skillet, dump in the potatoes and stir-fry about 5 minutes until golden. Layer half the potatoes into a well-buttered 2-quart (2 L) shallow casserole or *au gratin* pan and sprinkle with a little of the minced parsley and pepper. Add one-third of the onion, half the cod and another scattering of parsley and pepper. Repeat the layering, ending up with onion rings on top. Sprinkle with the remaining pepper and all but a tablespoon or so of the parsley (save this to use as a garnish).

Bake the casserole, uncovered, in a moderate oven (350°F. or 175°C.) for 35 to 40 minutes until sizzling hot and touched with brown. Garnish with wedges of hard-cooked eggs and the olives, placed artfully on top of the casserole, plus a final light scattering of minced parsley.

Herring salad with apples, dill pickles and horseradish

SERVES 4 TO 6

The best herring to use for this recipe is the red-fleshed young Matjes, which can be bought in most good delicatessens and specialty food shops. This particular herring salad is a popular first course in Scandinavia and Germany.

8 large	Matjes herring fillets	8 large
1 cup	buttermilk	240 ml
1 cup	sour cream	240 ml
⅓ cup	plain yogurt	80 ml
1 medium-size	yellow onion, peeled and minced	1 medium-size
2 medium-size	tart apples, peeled, cored and chopped	2 medium-size
2 medium-size	dill pickles, minced	2 medium-size
1 tablespoon	prepared horseradish	1 tablespoon
1 tablespoon (about)	lemon juice	1 tablespoon (about)
1 tablespoon (about)	sugar	1 tablespoon (about)
To taste	salt and freshly ground black pepper	To taste

Lay the herring fillets in a shallow baking dish, add the buttermilk and marinate in the refrigerator overnight. Next day, drain and rinse the herring fillets well, then cut in bite-size pieces. Place the herring in a shallow glass or porcelain baking dish. Combine sour cream, yogurt, onion, apples, pickles, horseradish, lemon juice and sugar. Taste for lemon juice and sugar and add a little more of each, if needed—there should be a light lemon flavor and just enough sugar to mellow the tartness. Season the sauce to taste with salt and pepper, spoon over the herring and marinate several hours before serving. Toss lightly before serving.

Curried crab and papaya salad

SERVES 4

This is one of those recipes that just happen. On my way home from work several summers ago, I saw plump, golden papayas piled up at my neighborhood fruit stand. The makings of dessert, I thought, and bought a couple. Then just two doors farther along, I saw small tubs of lump crab meat nestling in drifts of crushed ice in the window of my local fish store. So I bought a pound, thinking I could stretch it over a couple of days. But "the best-laid plans . . ." A friend called and wanted to come over, bringing two more friends. So I scurried around, concocting a salad out of the crab and papayas. It was the hit of the evening. I never wrote down the makings of that original salad, but have since re-created it and recorded the ingredients of the reconstruction. NOTE: *I save the papaya shells and mound the salad into them when I'm "putting on the dog."*

2 medium-size	ripe papayas	2 medium-size
1 pound	lump crab meat, carefully picked over for bits of shell and cartilage	½ kg
2 tablespoons	minced parsley	2 tablespoons
1 tablespoon	freshly snipped dill (or ½ teaspoon dill weed)	1 tablespoon
3 tablespoons	well-drained small capers	3 tablespoons
	CURRY DRESSING:	
1 small	yellow onion, peeled and minced	1 small
2 tablespoons	unsalted butter	2 tablespoons
2 teaspoons	curry powder	2 teaspoons
Pinch	crumbled leaf thyme	Pinch
½ cup	mayonnaise	120 ml
⅓ cup	sour cream	80 ml
1 teaspoon	Dijon mustard	1 teaspoon
¼ teaspoon (about)	salt	¼ teaspoon (about)
Pinch	freshly ground black pepper	Pinch

Halve the papayas lengthwise, scoop out and discard the seeds, then, using a teaspoon, scoop out the papaya flesh, leaving shells about ¼ inch (¾ cm) thick. Drain the shells, upside down, on several thicknesses of paper toweling and reserve. Dice the papaya meat, then spread out on paper toweling to drain. NOTE: *It's important that you drain the papaya very dry; otherwise it will water down the salad.* Place the papaya in a large mixing bowl, add the crab, parsley, dill and capers—do not toss yet, but **do** refrigerate while you prepare the dressing.

For the curry dressing: Brown the onion in the butter in a small heavy skillet over moderate heat—8 to 10 minutes should do it. Blend in the curry powder and thyme, turn the heat to its lowest point and allow the curry to mellow with the onion about 5 minutes until it no longer tastes raw. Dump into a food processor fitted with the metal chopping blade (or into an electric blender), add all remaining dressing ingredients and buzz about 60 seconds to blend. Taste for salt and add a bit more, if needed.

Pour the dressing over the crab and papaya, toss lightly to mix, then cover and chill several hours until the flavors are well blended. Toss lightly again, mound into the reserved papaya shells and serve.

Lobster and asparagus salad with wheat-germ oil dressing

SERVES 4 TO 6

 It is imperative that the wheat-germ oil used in the dressing be absolutely fresh and sweet; otherwise it may spoil the salad. Taste it before using, and if it seems unusually strong, use less of it and more of the hazelnut oil.

1 large (½-pound)	frozen rock lobster tail	1 large (225 g)
1 pound	young asparagus, washed, trimmed and peeled	½ kg
1 medium-size head	Boston lettuce, washed, trimmed and cut into slim shreds	1 medium-size head
	DRESSING:	
2 large	hard-cooked eggs, shelled	2 large
2 teaspoons	finely minced shallots	2 teaspoons
1 tablespoon	finely minced fresh tarragon	1 tablespoon
2 teaspoons	finely snipped fresh chives	2 teaspoons
2 teaspoons	finely minced parsley	2 teaspoons
¼ teaspoon	salt	¼ teaspoon
Pinch	freshly ground black pepper	Pinch

¼ teaspoon	Worcestershire sauce	¼ teaspoon
1–2 tablespoons	tarragon vinegar	1–2 tablespoons
1–2 teaspoons	wheat germ oil	1–2 teaspoons
2–3 tablespoons	hazelnut, peanut or walnut oil	2–3 tablespoons

Cook the lobster tail in boiling water to cover 15 minutes; drain, plunge into ice water and shell. Halve the tail meat lengthwise, then slice each half thin. Boil the asparagus in lightly sugared and salted water 4 to 5 minutes until crisp-tender; drain and plunge into ice water. When asparagus is well chilled, drain and cut in 1-inch (2½ cm) lengths. Place lobster and asparagus in a medium-size bowl, cover and refrigerate.

For the dressing: Coarsely chop 1 hard-cooked egg and reserve. Mince the second egg and combine with all remaining dressing ingredients except the wheat germ and hazelnut oils. In a food processor fitted with the metal chopping blade, buzz this mixture about 60 seconds nonstop. Then whisk or beat the oils in slowly until dressing is thick and creamy; fold in the reserved chopped egg. If dressing seems too thick, thin with a little extra oil and/or vinegar.

To serve, make beds of lettuce on salad plates. Toss the lobster and asparagus lightly and mound on the lettuce. Top with 1 to 2 spoonfuls of dressing.

Wine-braised scampi with fresh rosemary

SERVES 6

Rosemary grows hedge-high along much of the Mediterranean shore, and its fragrance seems to hover everywhere. It imparts a lovely lemony flavor, and for that reason it is superb with fish and shellfish. The success of this particular recipe depends upon **fresh** rosemary, so if none is available, wait until it is—don't substitute dried rosemary.

3 pounds	jumbo shrimp in the shell	1½ kg
6 tablespoons, in all	olive oil (top quality)	6 tablespoons, in all
3 large	garlic cloves, peeled and quartered	3 large
8	bay leaves	8
6	tender young rosemary sprigs	6
¼ cup	dry white wine or vermouth	60 ml
Light sprinkling	freshly ground black pepper	Light sprinkling

Drizzle shrimp with 3 tablespoons of the oil, add garlic, bay leaves and rosemary and marinate 4 hours in the refrigerator. Let stand 30 minutes at room temperature before cooking. Heat remaining 3 tablespoons oil in a large, heavy sauté pan over moderately high heat 1 minute, dump in shrimp (herbs, garlic and all) and stir-fry 8 to 10 minutes until bright pink and just cooked through. Remove shrimp to a hot platter and keep warm. Add wine and pepper to pan, reduce about 1 minute over high heat, pour over shrimp and serve. Put out a big bowl for shrimp shells, also plenty of napkins. NOTE: *If you prefer to shell and devein the shrimp, do so at the outset, then marinate and stir-fry as directed, but reduce cooking time to about 5 minutes.*

Shrimp moqueca

SERVES 4 TO 6

As prepared in Bahia, this Afro-Brazilian dish would call for a thick orange palm oil known as *dendê*, which both flavors and colors the dish, and for pulpy green coconut for creaming and thickening the sauce. You can find *dendê* oil in a few big-city Latin American groceries, but it so quickly goes rancid that I prefer to substitute olive oil and a dab of paprika, which impart the proper color and approximate the flavor. I know of no place in America where green coconuts are available (Florida, perhaps? Or Southern California?), so I've resorted to steeping canned flaked coconut in boiling water, then thickening the infusion with a bit of flour. I don't pretend that this *moqueca* is authentic, but I do think it's good and a different way to prepare shrimp. Serve over fluffy boiled rice. NOTE: *Bahian women cook rice in coconut liquid; I suggest mixing in a little of the flaked coconut reserved from making the coconut infusion.*

2 cups	boiling water	½ L
1 can (3½ oz.)	flaked coconut	1 can (99 g)
1 medium-size	yellow onion, peeled and chopped	1 medium-size
1 large	garlic clove, peeled and minced	1 large
3 tablespoons, in all	olive oil	3 tablespoons, in all
½ teaspoon	paprika	½ teaspoon
¼ teaspoon	cayenne pepper	¼ teaspoon
1 pound	shelled and deveined raw shrimp (if very large, cut into chunks)	½ kg
3 tablespoons	lemon juice	3 tablespoons
2 tablespoons	minced fresh coriander (cilantro or Chinese parsley) or parsley	2 tablespoons
1 tablespoon	tomato paste	1 tablespoon
2 tablespoons	heavy cream	2 tablespoons
2 tablespoons	flour	2 tablespoons
To taste	salt and freshly ground black pepper	To taste
1½ cups	uncooked converted rice, prepared and seasoned by package directions	350 ml
½ cup	flaked coconut (reserved from steeping the coconut, above)	120 ml

Combine the boiling water and coconut in a medium-size heavy saucepan set over moderate heat and boil, uncovered, for 10 minutes; set off the heat and cool to room temperature. Then put through a fine sieve, pressing out as much of the coconut liquid as possible. Reserve ½ cup of the sieved coconut to mix into the rice later on; discard the rest. Pour out and reserve ½ cup of the coconut infusion; return the balance to the saucepan and boil, uncovered, about 10 minutes until reduced by about one-third.

In a large heavy skillet set over moderate heat, stir-fry the onion and garlic in 2 tablespoons of the olive oil 8 to 10 minutes until limp and golden. Blend in the paprika and cayenne pepper and mellow a minute or two. Add the remaining tablespoon of oil, blending in thoroughly, then dump in the shrimp and stir-fry about 2 minutes—just until the shrimp begin to turn pink. Add the lemon juice and coriander and stir-fry about a minute, then pour in the reduced coconut infusion. Blend in the tomato paste, turn heat down low and cook, stirring constantly, about 5 minutes—just until shrimp are cooked through. Stir in the heavy cream. Blend the flour with the ½ cup of reserved coconut infusion until smooth, pour into the skillet and heat, stirring constantly, until thickened and smooth—3 to 5 minutes. Season to taste with salt and pepper, turn heat to its lowest point and let the *moqueca* mellow, uncovered, about 5 minutes—just until there is no raw starch taste and the flavors are mingled.

Quickly toss the cooked rice with the ½ cup of reserved flaked coconut and bed on a deep heated platter. Pour the *moqueca* evenly over all and serve.

Low country shrimp pie

SERVES 4 TO 6

The Low Country is that swatch of coastal swampland draped with Spanish moss that stretches roughly from Charleston, South Carolina, to Savannah, Georgia. For this breakfast favorite, Low Country cooks would most likely use the tiny, sweet "crick" shrimp that inhabit their waters. But you can substitute any fresh shrimp. I like Shrimp Pie for Sunday breakfast, but I also like it as the main course of a light luncheon or supper. Fresh buttered asparagus is the perfect accompaniment.

2 large	scallions, trimmed and sliced thin (include some green tops)	2 large
2 tablespoons	unsalted butter	2 tablespoons
¼ teaspoon	freshly grated nutmeg	¼ teaspoon
⅛ teaspoon	cayenne pepper	⅛ teaspoon
5 slices	firm-textured white bread	5 slices
1 cup	milk	240 ml

¾ cup	heavy cream	180 ml
2 large	eggs, well beaten	2 large
3 tablespoons	dry Madeira or sherry	3 tablespoons
2 tablespoons	minced parsley	2 tablespoons
1 pound	shelled and deveined shrimp, cooked 2 minutes in boiling water to cover, drained and coarsely chopped	½ kg
¼ teaspoon	salt	¼ teaspoon
⅛ teaspoon	freshly ground black pepper	⅛ teaspoon

Stir-fry the scallions in the butter in a small heavy skillet over moderate heat about 5 minutes until limp and golden; smooth in the nutmeg and cayenne and mellow for a minute. Set off the heat to cool. Meanwhile, break the bread into small pieces, letting them drop directly into a large mixing bowl. Combine the milk and cream, pour over the bread and soak 15 minutes. Beat the bread-milk-cream mixture hard with a wooden spoon until it is a smooth paste. Blend in the cooled scallion mixture, the eggs, Madeira, parsley, shrimp, salt and pepper. Spoon into a well-buttered 6-cup (1½ L) casserole and bake, uncovered, in a moderate oven (350°F. or 175°C.) for 40 to 45 minutes until slightly puffed and lightly browned. Serve oven-hot.

Yankee clam and potato pie with suet pastry

SERVES 6 TO 8

You will not need to add any salt to this old-fashioned Yankee recipe—the clams and bacon are both salty—so much so, in fact, that the butter you use should be unsalted.

4 slices	bacon, snipped crosswise into julienne strips	4 slices
1 medium-size	yellow onion, peeled and chopped	1 medium-size
1 large	Maine or Eastern potato, boiled until tender, peeled and cubed	1 large
2 tablespoons	minced parsley	2 tablespoons
2 quarts	shucked littleneck or cherrystone clams (reserve liquor)	2 L
4 tablespoons	unsalted butter	4 tablespoons
4 tablespoons	flour	4 tablespoons
⅛ teaspoon	freshly grated nutmeg	⅛ teaspoon

⅛ teaspoon	ground cloves	⅛ teaspoon
⅛ teaspoon	freshly ground black pepper	⅛ teaspoon
1½ cups	liquor drained from the clams (if necessary, round the measure out with bottled clam juice)	350 ml
½ cup	half-and-half cream, at room temperature	120 ml
2 tablespoons	dry white wine	2 tablespoons
1 recipe	Suet Pastry (see Index)	1 recipe

In a large heavy skillet set over moderately low heat, fry the bacon until crisp and brown—about 10 minutes. With a slotted spoon, lift the bacon to paper toweling to drain and reserve. Pour off all drippings, then spoon 2 tablespoons of them back into the skillet. Add the onion and stir-fry over moderately low heat about 10 minutes until limp and golden. Add the potatoes and brown lightly; stir in the parsley and set the skillet off the heat.

Dump the clams and their liquor into a medium-size heavy saucepan; set over moderately low heat for about 5 minutes—just until the clams begin to ruffle about the edges. With a slotted spoon, lift the clams to a bowl and reserve. Strain the clam liquor through a fine sieve into a large measuring cup and, if necessary, add bottled clam juice until you have 1½ cups (350 ml). Set aside also.

In the saucepan in which you cooked the clams, melt the butter over moderately low heat. Blend in the flour, nutmeg, cloves and pepper and mellow a minute or two. Combine the reserved clam liquor and the cream and pour into the roux (flour-butter paste). Heat, stirring constantly, until thickened and smooth—about 3 minutes. Turn the heat to its lowest point, stir in the wine and allow the clam sauce to mellow while you prepare the pastry.

Prepare the Suet Pastry as the recipe directs, then divide in half. Roll one half into a 12-inch (30 cm) circle on a lightly floured pastry cloth and ease into a 9-inch (23 cm) pie pan. Now combine the reserved onion-and-potato mixture, the bacon crumbles, the clams and the clam sauce, stirring lightly to mix. Pour into the prepared pie shell. Roll the remaining pastry into a circle of the same size, lay a rolling pin across its center, lop half of it over the rolling pin and carefully ease on top of the pie. Now trim the pastry overhangs, top and bottom, until about 1 inch (2½ cm) larger all around than the pie pan. Roll up the edges of the top and bottom crusts together on top of the pan rim, sealing in the clam mixture, then crimp, making a high fluted edge. Make several decorative slits in the top crust to allow steam to escape as the pie bakes and to help prevent boil-over.

Set the pie on a baking sheet (to catch any drips) and bake in a hot oven (400°F. or 205°C.) for about 30 minutes or until bubbling and browned. Remove the pie from the oven and let stand at room temperature 20 minutes before cutting into wedges and serving.

Mussels à la Ingrid Olrog

SERVES 4 TO 6

 Ingrid Olrog is the Swedish cousin of my friend Margaret Perry, a travel writer who often goes to Stockholm. It was two Christmases ago that Peg watched Ingrid put together this unusual appetizer for a holiday *smörgåsbord*. "Put together," by the way, is the proper verb, for the ingredients are simply layered into a small casserole, one upon the other, then baked briefly.

1 cup	cooked, shelled mussels (or canned mussels, if you must)	240 ml
1 tin (2 oz.)	anchovy fillets, drained and rinsed well	1 tin (56.7 g)
1 cup	heavy cream, softly whipped	240 ml
2 large	hard-cooked eggs, peeled and sliced thin	2 large
1 cup	fine dry bread crumbs	240 ml
2 tablespoons	freshly grated Parmesan cheese	2 tablespoons
1 tablespoon	melted unsalted butter	1 tablespoon

Butter a 9-inch (23 cm) pie tin, then layer the ingredients into it this way: the mussels, the anchovy fillets, the heavy cream, then the egg slices. Toss the bread crumbs with the Parmesan, then drizzle in the butter and toss until well mixed. Scatter the crumbs evenly over the egg slices. Bake, uncovered, in a moderate oven (350°F. or 175°C.) for 20 minutes. Serve as a first course with small boiled potatoes.

Baked oysters and shallots on the half-shell

SERVES 4

A lovely way to introduce an elegant small dinner party.

2 large	shallots, peeled and minced	2 large
2 tablespoons	unsalted butter	2 tablespoons
2 tablespoons	dry white wine or dry vermouth	2 tablespoons
2 tablespoons	minced parsley	2 tablespoons
2 tablespoons	minced tarragon (or 1 teaspoon crumbled leaf tarragon)	2 tablespoons
24 large	oysters on the half-shell	24 large
Light sprinklings	salt and freshly ground black pepper	Light sprinklings
½ cup	moderately fine soft bread crumbs	120 ml
1 tablespoon	freshly grated Parmesan cheese	1 tablespoon
2 teaspoons	melted unsalted butter	2 teaspoons

Stir-fry the shallots in the butter in a small heavy skillet over moderate heat 3 to 5 minutes until limp and golden. Add the wine and boil a minute or two until it evaporates. Stir in the parsley and tarragon and set aside for the moment. Arrange the oysters on a baking sheet; sprinkle lightly with salt and pepper, then with the shallot mixture. Toss the crumbs with the Parmesan, drizzle in the melted butter and toss well again. Scatter the crumb mixture on top of the oysters, dividing the total amount as evenly as possible. Bake uncovered in a very hot oven (425°F. or 220°C.) for 5 to 8 minutes until bubbly and lightly browned. Serve sizzling hot.

Soufflé of sea scallops with crab sauce

SERVES 6

The problem with using scallops in a dish of this sort is that they ooze considerable liquid, which can deflate a soufflé. But there is a simple way to overcome this: Cook the scallops before you grind them and mix them into the soufflé. Also reduce the scallops liquid until it is a highly concentrated essence that will heighten the flavor of the soufflé without undermining it. NOTE: *Sea scallops give out less liquid than the smaller bay scallops, which is why I use them for this recipe. But there's another reason, too: they are cheaper. And since the scallops will be ground to paste (a processor makes short shrift of this job), their size and texture are immaterial.*

2 large	shallots, peeled and minced	2 large
6 tablespoons	unsalted butter	6 tablespoons
½ pound	sea scallops, rinsed in cool water, patted dry and sliced thin	225 g
½ cup	dry white wine or dry vermouth	120 ml
2 tablespoons	minced parsley	2 tablespoons
1 tablespoon	freshly snipped dill (or ½ teaspoon dill weed)	1 tablespoon
4 tablespoons	flour	4 tablespoons
Pinch	freshly grated nutmeg or mace	Pinch
½ teaspoon	salt	½ teaspoon
⅛ teaspoon	white pepper	⅛ teaspoon
1 cup	milk, at room temperature	240 ml
4 large	egg yolks, lightly beaten	4 large
6 large	egg whites	6 large
Pinch	cream of tartar	Pinch

FOR PREPARING THE SOUFFLÉ DISH:

	FOR PREPARING THE SOUFFLÉ DISH:	
1 teaspoon	unsalted butter	1 teaspoon
2 tablespoons	fine dry bread crumbs	2 tablespoons
	CRAB SAUCE:	
2 tablespoons	unsalted butter	2 tablespoons
2 tablespoons	flour	2 tablespoons
½ teaspoon	salt	½ teaspoon
Pinch	freshly grated nutmeg or mace	Pinch
Pinch	white pepper	Pinch
1 cup	half-and-half cream, at room temperature	240 ml
½ cup	cooked lump crab meat, picked over for bits of shell and cartilage	120 ml
1 tablespoon	medium-dry sherry, Port or Madeira	1 tablespoon

Stir-fry the shallots in 2 tablespoons of the butter in a medium-size heavy skillet over moderate heat 3 to 5 minutes until limp and golden; add the scallops and stir-fry 2 to 3 minutes, just until they have released their juices and turned opaque. With a slotted spoon, lift the scallops to a plate and reserve. Add the wine to the skillet, also any juices that may have accumulated on the plate of scallops, and boil hard until reduced to an amber glaze—about 3 minutes. Return the scallops to the skillet, add the parsley and dill and set off the heat.

In a small heavy saucepan, melt the remaining 4 tablespoons of butter over moderately low heat; blend in the flour, nutmeg, ¼ teaspoon of the salt and the pepper and mellow 1 to 2 minutes, stirring often. Pour in the milk and heat, stirring constantly, until thickened and smooth—about 3 minutes. Turn the heat to its lowest point and allow the sauce to mellow 5 minutes. Now whisk a little of the hot sauce into the egg yolks; stir back into the pan and cook and stir over lowest heat about 1 minute. Set the sauce off the heat and reserve; stir it frequently to prevent a skin from forming on the surface.

Now purée the skillet mixture in a food processor fitted with the metal chopping blade (or in an electric blender at high speed or by putting—twice—through a meat grinder fitted with the fine blade). NOTE: *The mixture should be smooth and velvety. It will take three to four 30-second churnings in the food processor or blender; be sure to scrape the sides of the work bowl or blender container down between each with a rubber scraper.* Combine the scallop paste with the cooled sauce in a large mixing bowl and set aside while you prepare the soufflé dish.

To prepare the soufflé dish: Butter well the bottom and sides of a 6-cup (1½ L) soufflé dish, paying particular attention to the juncture where sides meet bottom. Add the bread crumbs and coat the bottom and sides evenly by tilting the dish first one way, then another. Tap out excess crumbs and set the dish aside.

Sprinkle the remaining ¼ teaspoon of salt over the egg whites along with the cream of tartar. Using a whisk or rotary beater, whip the whites to soft peaks. Blend about one-fourth of the beaten whites into the scallop mixture to lighten it; dump the remaining whites on top and fold in gently but thoroughly until no streaks of white or yellow remain. Pour the soufflé batter into the prepared dish and bake, uncovered, for about 35 minutes in a moderately hot oven (375°F. or 190°C.) or until puffed, touched with brown, and the soufflé quivers gently when you nudge it.

While the soufflé bakes, prepare the crab sauce: Melt the butter in a small heavy saucepan over moderately low heat, blend in the flour, salt, nutmeg and pepper and mellow a minute or two. Pour in the cream and cook, stirring constantly, until thickened and smooth—about 3 minutes. Turn the heat to its lowest point and allow the sauce to mellow about 5 minutes until no raw starch taste lingers. Stir in the crab meat and sherry and allow the sauce to mellow over lowest heat another 5 to 10 minutes—just until the soufflé is ready—then pour the sauce into a heated sauceboat.

When the soufflé tests done, rush it to the table and serve, ladling some of the sauce over each portion and passing the balance so that dinner guests may help themselves to more if they wish.

Cold marinated bay scallops with juniper, dill and wine

SERVES 4 AS AN ENTRÉE, 6 AS AN APPETIZER

I once made the mistake of trying to rush this recipe—that is, of not giving it sufficient time in the refrigerator—and as a result the scallops were disappointingly bland. So be sure that you marinate them a full 24 hours. This is a superlative summer dish on two counts: It requires almost no cooking and the finished dish is cool and refreshing.

1 large bunch	fresh dill (there should be about 24 to 30 stalks)	1 large bunch
1½ cups	dry white wine	350 ml
1 cup	cold water	240 ml
1 tablespoon	juniper berries, crushed	1 tablespoon
1 teaspoon	dill seeds	1 teaspoon
1½ pounds	bay scallops, washed and drained	675 g
1 large	lemon, sliced thin	1 large
2 medium-size	yellow onions, peeled and sliced thin	2 medium-size

12 large	peppercorns, cracked	12 large
½ teaspoon	salt	½ teaspoon
¼ cup	white wine vinegar	60 ml

Carefully sort and wash the dill, discarding the stems and saving the feathery fronds. Place one-third of the fronds and all the wine and water in a medium-size heavy saucepan. Tie the juniper berries and dill seeds in several thicknesses of cheesecloth and drop into the pan. Bring slowly to the boil over moderately low heat. Add the scallops and cook them 10 minutes exactly—begin timing from the moment the scallops go into the pan.

Meanwhile, layer another one-third of the dill fronds in the bottom of a 2-quart (2 L), flat-bottomed, heatproof glass or china dish, place half the lemon and onion slices on top and sprinkle with half the peppercorns. When the scallops have cooked 10 minutes, transfer them with a slotted spoon to the casserole, layering them evenly on top of the onion slices; reserve the cooking liquid and keep hot. Sprinkle the scallops with salt, then cover with the remaining dill fronds, onion and lemon slices and peppercorns. Strain the cooking liquid (discard the spice bag). Stir the wine vinegar into the strained liquid, then pour into the bowl. Cover and marinate at least 24 hours in the refrigerator.

To serve, carefully remove and discard the top layer of onion and lemon slices, then with a slotted spoon, lift out the scallops, discarding any peppercorns or bits of dill that cling to them. If you intend to serve the scallops as an appetizer, mound them in stemmed goblets and garnish each portion with a small sprig of dill. For an entrée, heap the scallops on four salad plates, tuck about five small romaine leaves underneath each mound of scallops so that the tips show, then garnish with twists of lemon and sprigs of dill.

Cold curried bay scallops, shrimp and wild rice

SERVES 8 TO 10

A simply splendid entrée for a summer party buffet which can be made a day ahead.

1½ cups	wild rice, washed	350 ml
3 cups	water	¾ L
1 pound	medium-size mushrooms, wiped clean and sliced thin	½ kg
¼ cup, in all	olive oil (top quality)	60 ml, in all
¾ pound	bay scallops, rinsed and drained	340 g
¾ pound	shelled and deveined raw shrimp	340 g

1/3 cup	dry vermouth	80 ml
3 large	hard-cooked eggs, peeled and chopped	3 large
1 teaspoon (about)	salt	1 teaspoon (about)
1/8 teaspoon	freshly ground black pepper	1/8 teaspoon
3 tablespoons	minced parsley	3 tablespoons
	CURRY SAUCE:	
1 large	garlic clove, peeled and minced	1 large
1 teaspoon	finely grated fresh ginger root	1 teaspoon
12 medium-size	scallions, trimmed and coarsely chopped (include some green tops)	12 medium-size
1 tablespoon	olive oil (top quality)	1 tablespoon
1 tablespoon	curry powder	1 tablespoon
1/2 teaspoon	crumbled leaf marjoram	1/2 teaspoon
1/4 teaspoon	crumbled leaf thyme	1/4 teaspoon
1/4 teaspoon	dill weed	1/4 teaspoon
1 pint	sour cream	1/2 L
1 1/2 cups	mayonnaise	350 ml
1/4 cup	lemon juice	60 ml
1/2 teaspoon	salt	1/2 teaspoon
1/8 teaspoon	freshly ground black pepper	1/8 teaspoon

Place the wild rice and water in a heavy medium-size saucepan and set over high heat; bring to a boil, adjust burner heat so that water bubbles gently, then cook, uncovered, about 20 minutes or until most of the water has cooked away. Cover the saucepan, turn burner heat to low and cook 10 to 15 minutes longer or until all water has evaporated and rice is crunchy-tender. Cool.

Stir-fry the mushrooms in 3 tablespoons of the olive oil in a large heavy skillet over moderately high heat about 3 to 5 minutes until limp and lightly browned; with a slotted spoon, lift to a large bowl and reserve. Stir-fry the scallops and shrimp in the skillet in the remaining tablespoon of oil about 5 minutes until scallops have released their juices; with a slotted spoon, lift to a separate large bowl. Pour in the vermouth and boil down quickly with the shellfish juices until only a thickish glaze remains on the bottom of the skillet—3 to 5 minutes should be sufficient. Drain any shellfish juices that may have accumulated in the bowl of scallops and shrimp into the skillet and boil down also. Return the scallops and shrimp to the skillet and toss until lightly glazed. Empty into the bowl with the mushrooms. Add the wild rice, chopped eggs, salt, pepper and 2 tablespoons of the minced parsley. Set aside.

For the curry sauce: Stir-fry the garlic, ginger and scallions in the olive oil in a small heavy skillet over moderate heat about 3 minutes—just until the scallions and ginger are no longer bitingly raw. Smooth in the curry powder, marjoram, thyme and dill weed and let mellow over low heat about 2 minutes until no raw curry taste remains. Scrape the curry mixture into an electric blender cup or a food processor work bowl fitted with the metal chopping blade. Add the sour cream and buzz until creamy-smooth; about three 10-second bursts of speed should do it. Now add the remaining sauce ingredients and buzz another 10 to 20 seconds to incorporate.

Pour half the sauce over the wild rice mixture and toss well. Cover snugly and refrigerate until about 30 minutes before you are ready to serve. Also cover and refrigerate the remaining sauce.

To serve, toss the wild rice mixture very well, taste for salt and pepper and add more, if needed. Let the mixture stand at room temperature for 30 to 40 minutes (no longer, however) so that flavors are released and blended, then arrange in your prettiest salad bowl, lined, if you like, with crisp young romaine leaves. Scatter the remaining tablespoon of parsley on top. Pour the remaining sauce into a bowl, set it on the buffet beside the main dish and encourage guests to ladle a spoonful or two over their portions.

Vegetables & salads

Asparagus and potato purée with freshly grated parmesan

SERVES 6

If you have a food processor, use it to purée the asparagus. But **not** the potatoes! The processor will turn them to glue; to obtain the proper fluffiness, you must hand-mash them. NOTE: *I find this avocado-green purée, mounded onto slices of tomato or into butter-browned mushroom caps or artichoke bottoms, an easy way to dress up a dinner plate or platter. If I can lay my hands on fresh dill, I finely snip about two tablespoons of it and mix into the purée along with the grated Parmesan because its delicate lemony flavor enhances that of the asparagus.*

2 large (about ¾ pound)	Maine or Eastern potatoes, peeled and cut into small dice	2 large (about 340 g)
2 cups	boiling beef broth or water	½ L
2 pounds	asparagus, trimmed of coarse stalks and peeled	1 kg
3 cups	boiling water mixed with 2 teaspoons salt	¾ L
3 tablespoons	unsalted butter, at room temperature	3 tablespoons
⅛ teaspoon	freshly grated nutmeg	⅛ teaspoon
¼ cup	freshly grated Parmesan cheese	60 ml
2 tablespoons	freshly snipped dill (optional)	2 tablespoons
To taste	salt and freshly ground black pepper	To taste

Boil the potatoes in the broth in a heavy saucepan, covered, over moderate heat until very soft—20 to 25 minutes. Meanwhile, lay the asparagus stalks flat in a large heavy skillet, pour in the boiling salted water, cover, set over moderate heat and boil 10 to 12 minutes until very soft. NOTE: *For a properly smooth purée, you must overcook the asparagus, so this would be the time to use less than perfect stalks.* Drain very dry, return the asparagus to the skillet and shake briefly over moderate heat to drive off excess moisture. Now purée the asparagus in a food processor fitted with the metal chopping blade along with 1 tablespoon of the butter. Two to three 20-second churnings of the motor should do it, but do scrape the work bowl sides down between each. (If you have no food processor, purée the asparagus, about one-third of the total amount at a time, with 1 teaspoon of the butter in an electric blender at high speed. Or failing that, force the asparagus through a food mill, then add 1 tablespoon of the butter.)

Dump the hot asparagus purée into a large mixing bowl and stir in the grated nutmeg at once. (The heat of the purée will take the raw edge off the nutmeg, at the same time intensifying its flavor.) As soon as the potatoes are very soft, drain them well. (If you have used beef broth for cooking them, save it to use in a soup or sauce.) Now mash the potatoes well, adding the remaining 2 tablespoons of butter as you go. Keep mashing and beating the potatoes with a wooden spoon until they are silky-smooth, then combine them with the asparagus purée. Mix in the grated Parmesan and, if available, the dill. Season to taste with salt and pepper and serve.

Purée of green beans and scallions with fresh dill

SERVES 2 TO 4

 The French are fond of puréeing vegetables, the Scandinavians of seasoning them with freshly snipped dill and with cream. So I put the two penchants together and came up with this lovely purée. It's a snap to make in a food processor and is a marvelous accompaniment to broiled chicken or fish, particularly salmon or swordfish. It's very good, too, with roast lamb or lamb chops.

4 medium-size	scallions, trimmed and sliced (white part only)	4 medium-size
2 tablespoons	unsalted butter	2 tablespoons
1 pound	tender young green beans, tipped and snapped in half	½ kg
½ cup	beef broth	120 ml
¼ teaspoon (about)	salt	¼ teaspoon (about)
Pinch	freshly ground black pepper	Pinch
2 tablespoons (about)	heavy cream	2 tablespoons (about)
3 tablespoons	freshly snipped dill	3 tablespoons

Stir-fry the scallions in the butter in a large heavy saucepan over moderate heat 3 to 4 minutes until limp and golden. Add the beans and stir-fry about 5 minutes until bright green. Pour in the broth, adjust burner heat so that it bubbles gently, cover the beans and simmer about 15 minutes until very soft. Check the pot occasionally and stir the beans so that they do not scorch. If the pot threatens to boil dry (it shouldn't if you keep the heat low enough and cover the pot with a close-fitting lid), add a bit more broth or a little water. When the beans are very tender, uncover the pot and if there is still broth in the pan, boil rapidly, tossing the beans all the while, until it has reduced to glaze.

If you have a food processor, equip it with the metal chopping blade, dump in the beans, then add the salt and pepper and 1 tablespoon of the cream. Buzz about 30 seconds nonstop, open the work bowl and scrape its sides down with a rubber spatula, add the second tablespoon of cream and buzz nonstop for about 60 seconds. Uncover the work bowl, again scrape the sides down and if the purée seems too thick (it should be moist and just stiff enough to mound softly), add a bit more cream; buzz for 60 seconds more whether or not you added extra cream. Sprinkle in the dill and again buzz 60 seconds. NOTE: *If you do not have a food processor, put the beans through a food mill, then push through a fine sieve. Season with the salt and pepper, then beat in just enough cream to give the purée the consistency of softly whipped potatoes. Mix in the dill.*

Empty the purée into a small heavy saucepan and bring gently to serving temperature, stirring constantly. Taste for salt and add more, if needed.

Fasolakia lathera
(GREEK-STYLE GREEN BEANS IN TOMATO SAUCE)

SERVES 4

Every country *taverna* (and many a big-city one) has its version of Fasolakia Lathera, and I must have tasted dozens of them during my travels in Greece. This particular recipe is my own adaptation, a good bit less greasy than this bean dish often is and decidedly more colorful because I do not stew the beans in the tomato sauce as Greek women do. I add it shortly before serving so that the acid of the tomatoes does not have a chance to turn the beans brown.

1 medium-size	yellow onion, peeled and cut into very slim wedges	1 medium-size
2 large	garlic cloves, peeled and slivered	2 large
3 tablespoons	olive oil (top quality)	3 tablespoons
1 pound	tender young green beans, tipped and snapped in half	½ kg

2 tablespoons	finely chopped fresh mint (or 2 teaspoons mint flakes)	2 tablespoons
½ teaspoon	crumbled leaf basil	½ teaspoon
¼ teaspoon	crumbled leaf oregano	¼ teaspoon
¼ teaspoon	crumbled leaf thyme	¼ teaspoon
¼ teaspoon	crushed fennel seeds	¼ teaspoon
Light sprinkling	freshly ground black pepper	Light sprinkling
¾ cup	beef broth	180 ml
⅓ cup	dry white wine or dry vermouth	80 ml
1 can (8 oz.)	tomato sauce	1 can (226 g)
2 tablespoons	minced parsley	2 tablespoons

In a large heavy skillet set over moderate heat, stir-fry the onion and garlic in the oil about 5 minutes until limp and golden; dump in the beans, mint, basil, oregano, thyme, fennel and pepper and stir-fry 5 to 8 minutes until the beans are an intense green. NOTE: *You will have to keep the beans moving constantly as they fry; otherwise they may burn.* Pour in the broth, turn the heat down so that it simmers gently, then cover the skillet and cook the beans 12 to 15 minutes. Meanwhile, combine the wine and the tomato sauce in a small heavy saucepan set over moderately low heat and let bubble gently, stirring now and then, until reduced by about one-third—12 to 15 minutes. As soon as the beans are crisp-tender, uncover them and raise the burner heat so that the skillet liquid reduces quickly to a rich amber glaze. Stir the beans often as the liquid reduces so that they do not scorch. Add the tomato sauce and parsley to the beans, toss well to mix, mellow 2 to 3 minutes over low heat, taste for salt and pepper (none may be needed) and serve.

Cold shredded beets and apples with fresh dill and sour cream

SERVES 4 TO 6

I've always liked this cool Swedish salad, which figures prominently in most *smörgåsbords*. It's particularly good as a light lunch with pickled herring and sliced cucumbers on a sweltering summer day.

1½ pounds	beets, scrubbed, boiled until tender, peeled and shredded	675 g
2 large	tart green apples, peeled, cored and shredded	2 large

DRESSING:

2 tablespoons	finely minced yellow onion	2 tablespoons
2 tablespoons	Dijon mustard	2 tablespoons
1 tablespoon	prepared horseradish	1 tablespoon
2 teaspoons	sugar	2 teaspoons
¼ teaspoon	salt	¼ teaspoon
Pinch	freshly ground black pepper	Pinch
1 cup	sour cream	240 ml
¼ cup	freshly snipped dill	60 ml

Place the beets and apples in a medium-size mixing bowl and toss well. Now combine all dressing ingredients by buzzing in a food processor fitted with the metal chopping blade for about 60 seconds nonstop; scrape the sides of the work bowl down and buzz 60 seconds longer. (If you do not have a processor, buzz in an electric blender at high speed until creamy-smooth, or simply whisk all ingredients together.) Pour over the beets and apples and toss well. Cover and marinate several hours in the refrigerator. Toss well again and serve.

Lemon-glazed cabbage rolls stuffed with chicken and rice

SERVES 6

 Cabbage rolls are easier to make than they sound. And if you have a processor to grind the chicken and chop the onion and cabbage, you'll find that it all goes quickly. You will need a big cabbage for this recipe, but it must also be firm (i.e., fresh). NOTE: *The easiest way I know to limber and loosen the individual leaves is just to boil the entire head of cabbage about 15 minutes in enough water to cover. Sever each leaf where it joins the base, then hold the cabbage upside down under a stream of cool water so that the pressure of the water separates the leaves. The idea is to loosen the leaves as gently as possible without ripping or puncturing them.*

A 4-pound	firm cabbage, trimmed of coarse or blemished outer leaves	A 1¾ kg
4 quarts	boiling water	4 L

STUFFING:

1 medium-size	yellow onion, peeled and chopped	1 medium-size
2 large	shallots, peeled and minced	2 large
4 tablespoons	unsalted butter	4 tablespoons

1 teaspoon	crumbled leaf marjoram	1 teaspoon
½ teaspoon	crumbled leaf thyme	½ teaspoon
½ teaspoon	finely grated lemon rind	½ teaspoon
¼ teaspoon	crumbled leaf rosemary	¼ teaspoon
⅛ teaspoon	freshly grated nutmeg	⅛ teaspoon
2½ cups	coarsely chopped cabbage (use the trimmings)	600 ml
⅓ cup	uncooked converted rice	80 ml
¼ cup	minced parsley	60 ml
1½ teaspoons	salt	1½ teaspoons
⅛ teaspoon	freshly ground black pepper	⅛ teaspoon
½ pound	boned and skinned chicken breast (1 large whole breast)	225 g
7 tablespoons	club soda	7 tablespoons

FOR COOKING THE CABBAGE ROLLS:

1 can (13¾ oz.)	beef broth	1 can (407 ml)
1 can (13¾ oz.)	chicken broth	1 can (407 ml)

LEMON GLAZE:

2 tablespoons	cornstarch	2 tablespoons
¼ cup	cold water	60 ml
1½ cups	broth (reserved from cooking the cabbage rolls)	350 ml
1 tablespoon	unsalted butter	1 tablespoon
½ teaspoon	finely grated lemon rind	½ teaspoon
Pinch	freshly grated nutmeg	Pinch
To taste	salt and freshly ground black pepper	To taste

Place the cabbage in a large kettle, add the boiling water, cover, set over moderate heat and boil 15 minutes. Drain the cabbage, then submerge in cold water until cool enough to handle. Turn the cabbage upside down and sever each leaf stem from the base. Hold the cabbage under cool running water and let the pressure of the water loosen first one leaf, then another. Carefully lift the leaves from the cabbage as the water separates them and drain on several thicknesses of paper toweling. Continue in this manner until you reach the heart of the cabbage where the leaves are too small to stuff. Reserve these leaves. Also cut out and reserve the coarse central rib in each leaf, then chop enough of the reserved leaves and ribs to total 2½ cups (600 ml); you will use these in the stuffing.

NOTE: *If some of the inner leaves still seem too stiff to roll, simmer them 5 to 10 minutes in enough water to cover until they are pliable.* Let the cabbage leaves drain on paper toweling while you prepare the stuffing.

For the stuffing: Stir-fry the onion and shallots in the butter in a large heavy skillet over moderate heat 10 to 12 minutes until limp and nicely browned. NOTE: *This browning of the onion and shallots is essential for proper flavor because a slight caramelization (sweetening) takes place.* Add the marjoram, thyme, lemon rind, rosemary and nutmeg and stir-fry 1 to 2 minutes to release and intensify the flavors. Dump in the chopped cabbage and stir-fry about 5 minutes over moderate heat until limp and golden. Now mix in the rice, parsley, salt and pepper, remove from the heat and let cool while you prepare the chicken.

Cut the chicken into small chunks, then grind to paste in a food processor fitted with the metal chopping blade, adding the club soda a tablespoon at a time, until light and fluffy. Stop the machine occasionally and scrape down the sides of the work bowl. I find that about three to four 15- to 20-second churnings of the motor do the job nicely. NOTE: *If you do not have a food processor, you can purée the chicken, a little bit at a time, with a tablespoon or two of the club soda in an electric blender at high speed. Failing that, grind the chicken several times in a meat grinder fitted with the fine blade, then beat hard with the club soda until light and fluffy.* Mix the chicken into the cooled skillet mixture.

To stuff the cabbage: Place a cabbage leaf on the counter with the stem end facing you. If the bottom of the leaf still seems too coarse or stiff to roll, simply trim it off. And if the leaf seems giant-size, cut in half right down the central rib. Place a heaping teaspoon of the stuffing about an inch (2½ cm) in from the base of the leaf, fold the right and left sides over the stuffing, then fold the base of the leaf over the stuffing and roll up snuggly toward the leaf tip. Place the cabbage roll, seam side down, on a rack in a large heavy kettle. I use a round cake rack in an enameled cast-iron kettle that measures 9½ inches (24½ cm) across. Now stuff and roll the remaining cabbage leaves the same way and arrange, seam side down, on the rack. NOTE: *There will be more rolls than you can accommodate in a single layer. No matter, simply place the extra rolls on top.*

To cook the cabbage rolls: Pour the beef and chicken broth into the kettle and weight the cabbage rolls down with a heavy plate. Set the kettle over moderate heat and bring the broth to a simmer. Adjust the burner heat so that the broth just trembles, then cover the kettle and cook the cabbage rolls 1 hour. Drain the cabbage rolls, reserving 1½ cups (350 ml) of the broth for the glaze. (Save any remaining broth to use in a soup or sauce.) Keep the cabbage rolls warm while you prepare the glaze.

For the glaze: Combine the cornstarch with the cold water to make a smooth paste. Pour the reserved 1½ cups (350 ml) of broth into a small saucepan, blend in the cornstarch and cook and stir over moderate heat about 3 minutes—just until the mixture bubbles up, clears and no longer tastes of raw starch. Swirl in butter; add lemon rind, nutmeg and salt and pepper to taste.

To serve, mound the cabbage rolls on a heated platter, pour some of the glaze on top, then pass the remainder separately so that guests may help themselves to more.

Carrot pancakes with parsley sauce

SERVES 4 TO 6

These pancakes are particularly good topped with a light parsley sauce. Carrots and parsley, by the way, are related. Both belong to a large botanical family that also includes Queen Anne's lace and caraway. How do you serve carrot pancakes? As a main course accompanied by buttered broccoli or asparagus, green beans, peas or zucchini. NOTE: *This pancake batter can be made a day ahead of time and refrigerated until you are ready to use it.*

	PANCAKE BATTER:	
¼ pound	carrots, peeled and finely shredded	115 g
1 medium-size	yellow onion, peeled and finely minced	1 medium-size
4 tablespoons	melted unsalted butter	4 tablespoons
½ teaspoon	crumbled leaf marjoram	½ teaspoon
¼ teaspoon	crumbled leaf thyme	¼ teaspoon
Pinch	crumbled leaf rosemary	Pinch
Pinch	freshly grated nutmeg	Pinch
1 cup	sifted all-purpose flour	100 g
1 teaspoon	salt	1 teaspoon
⅛ teaspoon	freshly ground black pepper	⅛ teaspoon
2 large	eggs, lightly beaten	2 large
1 cup	milk	240 ml
	SAUCE:	
1 recipe	Parsley Sauce (see Index)	1 recipe

Stir-fry the carrots and onion in 3 tablespoons of the butter in a large heavy skillet over moderate heat 5 minutes. Add the marjoram, thyme, rosemary and nutmeg and stir-fry 2 to 3 minutes longer, just enough to mellow and release the flavors. Set off the heat to cool.

Place the flour in a mixing bowl, add the salt and black pepper and stir to combine. Make a well in the center of the dry ingredients. Combine the eggs, milk, remaining tablespoon of melted butter, and cooled carrot mixture. Add all at once to the flour and stir just enough to mix. NOTE: *If you do not intend to make the pancakes right away, pour the batter into a 1-quart (1 L) jar or plastic container, cover tight and set in the refrigerator.*

When you are ready to cook the pancakes, heat a lightly oiled griddle or large skillet over moderately high heat until a drop of water will dance about the surface. Using 2 to 3 tablespoons of batter for each pancake, ladle onto the hot griddle and brown about 2 minutes or until small holes appear on the surface of the pancakes. With a pancake turner, turn the pancakes over and brown the flip side about a minute. Lift the browned pancakes to a hot plate and keep warm while you cook the balance. To serve, allow about four pancakes per portion and top each with a ladling of parsley sauce.

Spicy East Indian braised cauliflower

SERVES 6

What impressed me most, I think, on my first trip to India was how good the curried vegetables were—this skillet cauliflower, for example, which I ordered every chance I got. I was also fascinated by the fact that Indian cooks used clarified butter (*ghee*) both for frying and for flavoring meats and vegetables. *Ghee* does not blacken as does unclarified butter because it is the milk solids that burn, and these, of course, are skimmed off in the making of *ghee*. The flavor of *ghee* is mellower than that of unclarified butter, almost golden (if a flavor may be described as "golden"). Cauliflower prepared this way is best with lamb, ham, pork or chicken.

A 2½-pound	*cauliflower, trimmed, divided into flowerets and washed*	A 1¼ kg
1 quart (4 cups)	*boiling water mixed with 2 teaspoons salt*	1 L
1 large	*yellow onion, peeled and chopped*	1 large
1 tablespoon	*finely minced fresh ginger*	1 tablespoon
5 tablespoons, in all	*ghee (melted unsalted butter from which the milk solids have been skimmed)*	5 tablespoons, in all
1 teaspoon	*curry powder*	1 teaspoon
1 teaspoon	*chili powder*	1 teaspoon
½ teaspoon	*ground coriander*	½ teaspoon
¼ teaspoon	*ground turmeric*	¼ teaspoon
Pinch	*ground cinnamon*	Pinch
1 teaspoon	*salt*	1 teaspoon
Pinch	*freshly ground black pepper*	Pinch

Parboil the cauliflowerets in the boiling salted water in a heavy covered saucepan over moderate heat about 15 minutes until crisp-tender; drain well and reserve. In a very large heavy skillet set over moderate heat, stir-fry the onion and ginger in 3 tablespoons of the *ghee* 8 to 10 minutes until limp and lightly browned. Turn heat to low, blend in the curry and chili powders, the coriander, turmeric and cinnamon and stir-fry 2 to 3 minutes to mellow the flavors. Add the remaining *ghee* and the drained cauliflower and stir-fry 3 to 5 minutes, just until evenly coated with the curry mixture. Reduce heat to its lowest point, sprinkle the salt and pepper over the cauliflower, toss once again, cover and simmer 15 minutes—this is really more to mellow and mingle the flavors than to cook the cauliflower. Uncover, toss well again and serve.

Baked whole cauliflower crumbled with hazelnuts

SERVES 6

If hazelnuts are unavailable, substitute finely ground unblanched almonds, or pecans or walnuts and, if necessary, use walnut or peanut oil in place of the hazelnut oil. It's important that you brown the butter when you begin the sauce so that the lovely browned-butter flavor carries through. And it is imperative that you do not overcook the cauliflower or it will fall apart.

A 1¾–2-pound	firm, snowy cauliflower, trimmed of green leaves and the coarse stem end	A ⅘–1 kg
1 quart	boiling water mixed with 2 teaspoons salt	1 L
	SAUCE:	
2 tablespoons	unsalted butter	2 tablespoons
1 tablespoon	hazelnut oil	1 tablespoon
3 tablespoons	flour	3 tablespoons
1 cup (about)	milk	240 ml (about)
½ cup	half-and-half cream	120 ml
1 large	egg yolk, lightly beaten	1 large
⅓ cup	freshly grated Parmesan cheese	80 ml
½ teaspoon	salt	½ teaspoon
⅛ teaspoon	freshly grated nutmeg or mace	⅛ teaspoon
Light sprinkling	freshly ground black pepper	Light sprinkling
	TOPPING:	
1 cup	fine soft bread crumbs	240 ml
⅓ cup	finely ground unblanched hazelnuts	80 ml
2 tablespoons	freshly grated Parmesan cheese	2 tablespoons
1 tablespoon	hazelnut oil	1 tablespoon
2 teaspoons	melted unsalted butter	2 teaspoons

Boil the whole cauliflower in the salted water in a covered, heavy saucepan over moderate heat about 20 minutes—just until you can pierce it relatively easily with a sharp-pronged fork; the cauliflower should still be quite firm. Drain well, place in a 9-inch (23 cm) pie pan and cool to room temperature.

Meanwhile, prepare the sauce: Brown the butter in a small heavy saucepan over moderately low heat 3 to 5 minutes until a rich topaz color. (If you hurry the browning, the butter will blacken and taste bitter.) Add the hazelnut oil, then blend in the flour to make a smooth paste. Combine ¾ cup (180 ml) of the milk with the half-and-half, pour into the saucepan and heat, stirring constantly, until thickened and smooth—about 3 minutes. Turn the heat down low and allow the sauce to mellow several minutes until no raw floury taste remains. Whisk a little of the hot sauce into the beaten egg, then stir the egg mixture into the pan and cook, stirring constantly, about 2 minutes; do not boil or the sauce may curdle. Mix in the Parmesan, salt, nutmeg and pepper, remove from the heat, and cool the sauce about 15 minutes, stirring often to prevent a skin from forming on the surface.

While the sauce cools, prepare the topping: Toss the bread crumbs, hazelnuts and grated Parmesan together to combine, drizzle in the hazelnut oil and melted butter and toss well again.

Using a rubber spatula, spread about half the cooled sauce evenly and thickly over the cauliflower; reserve the remaining sauce. Let air-dry about 5 minutes, then pat the crumb mixture evenly and thickly over all, starting at the top of the cauliflower and working your way down to the base. Scoop up any crumbs that fall into the pie pan as you work, and pat them firmly into place.

Bake the cauliflower, uncovered, in a moderately hot oven (375°F. or 190°C.) for 15 to 20 minutes or until the crumb coating is a rich golden brown. While the cauliflower bakes, pour the reserved sauce into a small heavy saucepan, then blend in enough of the remaining ¼ cup (60 ml) of milk until about the consistency of a medium white sauce. Bring slowly to serving temperature, stirring often to prevent sticking or scorching.

To serve, ease the cauliflower onto a heated plate, then cut into wedges just as you would a molded mousse or plum pudding. Pass the sauce separately.

Fresh sweet corn soufflé with shallots and rosemary

SERVES 4

Soufflés terrify inexperienced cooks. Needlessly, I think, because they are less likely to collapse than is commonly believed. The secret of their success lies in the beating of the egg whites. Our tendency is to beat the daylights (and the air) out of the whites, at which point they **will** collapse when folded into the heavier soufflé base. Properly beaten, the egg whites should peak softly, **not** stiffly, and they should flow, **not** run from the bowl. TIP: *You can help stabilize the egg whites if you beat them with a little salt (or in the case of a dessert soufflé, with a little sugar). The salt (or sugar), dissolving into the liquid of the whites, makes for greater volume as well as for greater stability.*

FOR PREPARING THE SOUFFLÉ DISH:

1 teaspoon	unsalted butter (at room temperature)	1 teaspoon
2 tablespoons	fine dry bread crumbs	2 tablespoons

FOR THE SOUFFLÉ:

3 tablespoons	unsalted butter	3 tablespoons
2 large	shallots, peeled and minced	2 large
¼ teaspoon	crumbled leaf rosemary	¼ teaspoon
Pinch	crumbled leaf marjoram	Pinch
Pinch	freshly grated nutmeg	Pinch
3 tablespoons	flour	3 tablespoons
1 cup	milk, at room temperature	240 ml
1 teaspoon, in all	salt	1 teaspoon, in all
⅛ teaspoon	freshly ground black pepper	⅛ teaspoon
4 large	eggs, separated	4 large
1½ cups	fresh cream-style corn (you'll need about 3 medium-size ears; see page 232)	350 ml

Prepare the soufflé dish first so that it will be ready to receive the soufflé mixture the instant you have finished folding in the beaten whites. (Soufflés wait for no cook once the whites have been beaten.) Butter the bottom and sides of a 5-cup (1¼ L) soufflé dish, then add the bread crumbs and coat the bottom and sides evenly by tilting the dish first to one side and then to the other. Tap out excess crumbs and set the dish aside while you prepare the soufflé.

For the soufflé: Melt the butter in a medium-size heavy saucepan over moderate heat, add the shallots, rosemary, marjoram and nutmeg and stir-fry 3 to 5 minutes until limp and golden. Blend in the flour to make a smooth paste, then add the milk, ½ teaspoon of the salt and the pepper, and cook, stirring constantly, until thickened and smooth—about 3 minutes. Whisk the egg yolks lightly in a small bowl, mix a little of the hot sauce into the yolks, beating all the while, then stir back into the saucepan. Reduce the burner heat to low and cook, stirring constantly, about 2 minutes—do not boil the sauce or it may curdle. Remove from the heat, stir in the corn, transfer all to a large bowl, then cool to room temperature, whisking now and then so that a skin does not form on the surface of the sauce.

Sprinkle the remaining ½ teaspoon of salt evenly over the egg whites, then beat to soft peaks. Mix about one-fourth of the beaten whites into the corn mixture; this is to lighten it so that it will be easier to fold in the balance of the egg whites. Dump the remaining whites on top of the corn mixture and, using a rubber spatula, fold in gently but thoroughly until no streaks of white or yellow remain.

Pour the soufflé mixture into the prepared dish and bake, uncovered, in a moderate oven (350°F. or 175°C.) for 45 to 50 minutes until puffy and touched with brown. Rush the soufflé to the table and serve.

Baked mousse of eggplant and tahini

SERVES 6

I've been partial to *baba ghannouj*, the Middle Eastern eggplant and sesame dip, ever since I tasted it in Beirut ten years ago, so I began to experiment to see if I could make it into a more substantial dish that could accompany an entrée. My original intention was to make a *baba ghannouj* soufflé, but I had forgotten one cardinal principle of egg cookery: oil instantly collapses beaten egg whites. We all know, of course, that a speck of yolk in a bowl of whites will keep them from mounting to stiff peaks. It's the same principle. *Tahini* (sesame seed paste, which can be bought at any Middle Eastern or specialty grocery) is very oily. So of course no soufflé based upon *tahini* would rise properly. I then began thinking in terms of a baked mousse and worked out this recipe. It's a superb accompaniment to roast leg of lamb, and the variation that follows makes an excellent though offbeat stuffing for a breast or cushion shoulder of lamb.

2 medium-size (about 1 pound each)	plump, firm eggplants, trimmed of stems and halved lengthwise	2 medium-size (about ½ kg each)
1 tablespoon	toasted sesame seed oil	1 tablespoon
1 tablespoon	olive oil	1 tablespoon
5 large	eggs, separated	5 large
1 small	garlic clove, peeled and crushed	1 small
¼ cup	tahini (sesame seed paste)	60 ml
2 tablespoons	lemon juice	2 tablespoons
½ cup	fine dry bread crumbs	120 ml
2 tablespoons	freshly grated Parmesan cheese	2 tablespoons
⅛ teaspoon	freshly ground black pepper	⅛ teaspoon
½ teaspoon	salt	½ teaspoon
	FOR PREPARING THE CASSEROLE:	
1 tablespoon	olive oil	1 tablespoon
¼ cup	fine dry bread crumbs	60 ml

Brush the cut surface of each eggplant half with the combined sesame and olive oils. Place in the broiler 6 inches (15 cm) from the heat and broil 10 minutes until dark brown. Transfer to a moderate oven (350°F. or 175°C.) and roast, uncovered, for 10 to 15 minutes or until quite soft. Place the egg yolks and garlic in the work bowl of a food processor fitted with the metal chopping blade, or in an electric blender cup, and combine, using two to three short bursts of speed. Using a large spoon, scoop the eggplant flesh from the skins; discard as many seeds as possible. Then with the processor or blender motor running, drop the eggplant, scoop by scoop, into the beaten eggs; continue beating until smooth. Add the *tahini* and lemon juice and buzz 10 seconds or so until smooth. NOTE: *If you have neither processor nor blender, beat the eggs lightly in a large bowl and stir in the garlic. Force the eggplant through a food mill and combine with the eggs. Blend in the* tahini *and lemon juice, beating hard until smooth.*

If you have used the processor or blender, transfer the eggplant mixture to a large bowl. Stir in the bread crumbs, Parmesan and pepper and set aside.

To prepare the casserole: Brush a 2-quart (2 L) casserole generously with oil, then dump in the crumbs and coat the bottom and sides evenly by tilting it this way and that; tap out excess crumbs.

Beat the egg whites with the salt to soft peaks, then fold about one-third of them into the eggplant mixture to lighten the eggplant mixture and facilitate folding in the balance of the beaten whites. Dump the remaining whites on top of the eggplant mixture and fold in gently but thoroughly. Pour into the prepared casserole, then bake, uncovered, in a moderately hot oven (375°F. or 190°C.) for 30 minutes. Rush to the table and serve.

VARIATION:

Eggplant and tahini stuffing: Prepare as directed, but increase the quantity of fine dry bread crumbs to ¾ cup (180 ml). If you like a stronger garlic flavor, use 2 garlic cloves instead of one. Use to stuff a breast or cushion shoulder of lamb (see recipe in the lamb section of the Meat chapter). Bake any remaining stuffing separately in a small buttered and crumbed baking dish; just set it, uncovered, in the oven for the last 30 minutes of roasting.

Lauchkuchen
(GERMAN LEEK CAKE)

SERVES 6 TO 8

 First cousin to quiche, this Kirsch-spiked leek tart (for it is more tart than cake) is baked in a multileaved phyllo crust. It's the specialty of Burg Windeck, a medieval mountaintop castle a few miles south of Baden-Baden, Germany, which in the loving hands of Peter Wehlauer and his wife, Marianne, has emerged as one of the Black Forest's most talked-about restaurants.

	CRUST:	
½ cup (1 stick)	unsalted butter, melted	120 ml (1 stick)
½ (1-lb.) package	phyllo leaves (fresh or thawed, if frozen)	225 g
	FILLING:	
3 large	leeks, trimmed, washed and sliced thin	3 large
2 tablespoons	unsalted butter	2 tablespoons
½ pound	Emmenthaler cheese, coarsely grated	225 g
3 very large	eggs, lightly beaten	3 very large
1¼ cups	milk	300 ml
1¼ cups	half-and-half cream	300 ml
1 tablespoon	Kirsch	1 tablespoon
½ teaspoon	salt	½ teaspoon
⅛ teaspoon	ground nutmeg	⅛ teaspoon
⅛ teaspoon	ground white pepper	⅛ teaspoon

For the crust: Brush the bottom and sides of a 9 × 9 × 2-inch flameproof dish (23 × 23 × 5 cm) with melted butter. Unfold phyllo leaves according to package directions. Brush top leaf with melted butter, fold in half horizontally and fit into baking dish, letting excess overhang evenly to left and right. Brush a second leaf with melted butter, fold and fit into dish at right angles to the first leaf so that there is overhang both top and bottom. Continue building up layers of phyllo the same way until you have used eight full leaves. Make certain that each successive leaf is placed in the dish at right angles to the preceding one and also that the overhang is liberally brushed with melted butter to prevent drying. When last leaf is in place, carefully roll overhang under on top of the dish rim. Let "crust" air-dry while you prepare filling.

For the filling: Sauté leeks in the butter in a small skillet over medium-high heat 5 minutes until golden; do not brown. Scatter leeks over the crust; top with grated cheese. Combine remaining ingredients and pour into crust. Bake, uncovered, in a slow oven (300°F. or 150°C.) for 45 to 50 minutes until set like custard. Remove *Lauchkuchen* from oven and cool 30 minutes. Cut into large squares and serve as a first course or a light luncheon entrée.

Minted green peas
cooked in cream with rivvels

SERVES 4

***R**ivvels* are Pennsylvania Dutch egg dumplings used to stretch a modicum of food over many portions. They are chewy rather than fluffy, an interesting textural contrast to green peas. Unless mixed with a light touch, however, *rivvels* will be tough. The proper method of mixing to use is the Muffin Method, that is combine all dry ingredients in a bowl, make a well in the center, pour the combined liquids in all at once, then stir lightly just until mixed—no longer. TIP: *If you add a pea pod or two to the peas as they cook, they will have a just-picked flavor.* This dish is very filling and can be served as the main course of a light luncheon or supper, accompanied by one or more colorful vegetables.

2 cups	half-and-half cream	½ L
1½ cups	freshly shelled green peas (you'll need about 1½ pounds or ⅔ kg of peas in the pod)	350 ml
2 tablespoons	minced fresh mint (or 1 tablespoon mint flakes)	2 tablespoons
1 teaspoon	sugar	1 teaspoon
Pinch	freshly grated nutmeg	Pinch
1 tablespoon	unsalted butter	1 tablespoon
To taste	salt and freshly ground black pepper	To taste
	RIVVELS:	
¾ cup	sifted all-purpose flour	75 g
¼ teaspoon	salt	¼ teaspoon
⅛ teaspoon	freshly grated nutmeg	⅛ teaspoon
1 small	egg, lightly beaten	1 small
3 tablespoons	half-and-half cream	3 tablespoons

Bring the 2 cups half-and-half to a simmer in a large heavy saucepan over moderate heat, add the peas (and, if you like, a couple of pea pods), the mint, sugar and nutmeg, adjust the burner heat so that the cream barely simmers (if it boils, it may curdle), cover and cook about 10 to 15 minutes until the peas are tender and no longer raw-tasting.

Meanwhile, prepare the rivvels: Combine the flour, salt and nutmeg in a medium-size mixing bowl; also combine the egg and 3 tablespoons half-and-half. Make a well in the center of the dry ingredients, pour the egg mixture in and stir briskly with a fork just until all dry ingredients are moistened and hold together. If you beat the *rivvel* batter any longer, it will toughen.

As soon as the peas are tender, discard any pea pods you may have added to the pot and begin adding the *rivvels*: They are shaped simply by dropping the batter into the peas by spoonfuls; use the quarter-teaspoon of a measuring spoon set and distribute them as evenly as possible among the peas. Cover and simmer 5 to 8 minutes, just until the *rivvels* cook through and are no longer doughy. Season the peas with the butter, then salt and pepper them to taste. Ladle into soup bowls and serve.

Snow peas in lemon and shallot sauce

SERVES 4 TO 6

I've always been fond of the Cantonese specialty Lemon Chicken, and wondered if there might not be a similar way of seasoning fresh snow peas. This recipe is the result. Serve with broiled baby lamb chops or chicken.

1 pound	young and tender snow peas, washed	½ kg
2 quarts	water mixed with 1 tablespoon salt	2 L
	SAUCE:	
2 tablespoons	unsalted butter	2 tablespoons
2 large	shallots, peeled and minced	2 large
1 teaspoon	finely minced fresh ginger	1 teaspoon
1 teaspoon	finely grated lemon rind	1 teaspoon
1 teaspoon	sugar	1 teaspoon
4 teaspoons	cornstarch	4 teaspoons
1¼ cups	chicken or beef broth	300 ml
1 tablespoon	soy sauce	1 tablespoon
¼ teaspoon	salt	¼ teaspoon
Light sprinkling	freshly ground black pepper	Light sprinkling

Tip the snow peas and remove all strings; place in a large heavy saucepan and set aside. Pour the salted water into a large saucepan, set over low heat and slowly bring to a boil.

Meanwhile, prepare the sauce: Melt the butter in a small heavy saucepan over moderately low heat, add the shallots, ginger, lemon rind and sugar and sauté slowly, stirring often, 8 to 10 minutes until lightly browned. Mix the cornstarch with the broth until smooth, pour into the saucepan, raise the heat to moderate and cook, stirring constantly, until the mixture bubbles up, thickens and turns clear—about 3 minutes. Mix in soy sauce, salt and pepper, turn heat to its lowest point and keep the sauce warm while you cook the snow peas.

As soon as the salted water comes to a full rolling boil, pour it over the peas. Cover the saucepan, set over high heat and boil the peas 1 minute exactly. Drain the peas in a colander, return them to the saucepan, then shake lightly over moderate heat about 1 minute to drive off excess moisture. Pour the sauce over the peas, toss lightly to mix and serve.

Roasted red and green peppers marinated with fresh basil

SERVES 2 TO 4

It's essential to use a top-quality, aromatic olive oil for this recipe, one that is assertive enough to temper the pungency of the peppers and basil. I use one of the rich, thick, green French olive oils now available in specialty food shops. They are expensive, it's true, but because of their pronounced flavor, you'll find that you will use less of them than you would of a cheaper oil. Serve these peppers as part of an antipasto, as a salad on a bed of shredded romaine or as a cold vegetable.

2 large	sweet red peppers	2 large
2 large	sweet green peppers	2 large
1 tablespoon	olive oil (top quality)	1 tablespoon
2 tablespoons	finely minced fresh basil	2 tablespoons
1/4 teaspoon (about)	salt	1/4 teaspoon (about)
Light sprinkling	freshly ground black pepper	Light sprinkling
2 tablespoons	lemon juice	2 tablespoons

Place the peppers in a pie pan, set 2 inches (5 cm) from the broiler flame and broil, turning every 5 minutes or so, until the skins are uniformly blackened. Quick-chill the peppers by setting under cool running water, then remove the blackened skins; they will slake right off if you hold the peppers under running water and rub them gently. Halve each pepper, remove core and seeds, then pat very dry between several thicknesses of paper toweling. Quarter each pepper lengthwise, then slice each quarter crosswise about 3/4 inch (2 cm) thick and slightly on the bias. Place the peppers in a small bowl, add the olive oil, basil, salt and pepper and toss well. Let stand at room temperature 1 to 2 hours. Taste for salt and add more, if needed, then drizzle with lemon juice.

Finnish creamed new potatoes and onions with fresh dill

SERVES 6

One of the loveliest "comfort foods" I know and, alas, glutted with calories. You can reduce the calorie content significantly by using half-and-half in place of the heavy cream, but the dish won't be as soul-satisfying. TIP: *To peel the onions easily—tearlessly—blanch them for 2 minutes in boiling water, then plunge immediately into ice water. The skins will slip off as easily as peach skins.*

2 pounds	uniformly small new potatoes (about 18–20), scrubbed well but not peeled	1 kg
1 can (13¾ oz.)	chicken broth	1 can (407 ml)
1 pound	uniformly small silverskin onions (about 10–12), peeled	½ kg
Pinch	ground mace	Pinch
1 cup	heavy cream or half-and-half	240 ml
1 tablespoon	unsalted butter	1 tablespoon
1 tablespoon	freshly minced dill (or ¼ teaspoon dill weed)	1 tablespoon
½ teaspoon	salt	½ teaspoon
Light sprinkling	freshly ground black pepper	Light sprinkling

Simmer the potatoes slowly in the broth in a large heavy, covered saucepan over moderately low heat 15 minutes. Add the onions and mace, re-cover and simmer 30 to 40 minutes longer or until potatoes and onions can be pierced easily by a fork. NOTE: *This may seem a very long time to cook potatoes, but you are simmering— not boiling—them.* Using a slotted spoon, lift the potatoes and onions to a bowl and keep warm. Raise heat under saucepan to high and quickly reduce the broth by half by boiling hard for 3 to 5 minutes. Add the cream and boil hard another 2 to 3 minutes or until reduced by about one-third. Add the butter and dill, turn heat to low and as soon as the butter melts, return the potatoes and onions to the pan. Warm about 5 minutes in the cream, turning the potatoes and onions often. Season with salt and pepper, ladle into soup bowls and serve, accompanying each portion with plenty of the cream.

Roesti
(SWISS POTATO PANCAKE)

SERVES 4

Ever since I first tasted *Roesti* in Zurich some twenty-five years ago, I've been experimenting with the different varieties of American potatoes, trying to come up with the perfect *Roesti*. I first tried baking potatoes because their flavor is so nutlike, but the *Roesti* did not have the proper texture. I next tried the super-waxy California Long Whites, but the *Roesti* turned an unappetizing gray. I finally settled upon plain old-fashioned all-purpose Maine or Eastern potatoes. The *Roesti* they make becomes exquisitely crunchy outside but softens to creaminess inside. More important, all-purpose potatoes are waxy enough to hold the *Roesti* together. NOTE: *It is important to use a well-tempered frying pan for Roesti. I use a round-bottomed skillet that measures 8 inches (20 cm) across and have found it the perfect size for this recipe.* Serve *Roesti* with roast beef or pork or braised veal.

5 medium-size (1¼ pounds)	Maine or Eastern potatoes, scrubbed	5 medium-size (½ kg)
¾ teaspoon	salt	¾ teaspoon
⅛ teaspoon	freshly ground black pepper	⅛ teaspoon
2 tablespoons	melted unsalted butter	2 tablespoons
1 tablespoon	peanut or corn oil	1 tablespoon

Peel the potatoes one by one and shred moderately coarsely, using the second-coarsest side of a four-sided grater. If you are lucky enough to have a food processor, equip it with the shredding disk and machine-shred the potatoes. When all the potatoes are shredded, add the salt and pepper and toss well to mix.

Heat the butter and oil in a medium-size heavy skillet over moderate heat, tilting the skillet first to one side, then to the other, so that the skillet sides are well greased as well as the bottom. When the fat is good and hot, dump in the potatoes and press down firmly with a pancake turner. Cook, uncovered, for 15 minutes, keeping the heat between moderate and moderately low—there should be a gentle sizzling sound throughout, not an angry spitting or hissing. Carefully loosen the pancake around the edges with a spatula, then invert on a large plate. NOTE: *If some shreds of potato stick to the skillet despite all precautions, simply pick them up, set in place on the browned side of the pancake and press gently. Also scrape up and discard any dark brown bits in the skillet.* Now ease the *Roesti* back into the skillet, uncooked side down, and again press down firmly with the pancake turner. Cook, uncovered, 15 minutes longer. Invert the *Roesti* onto a heated dinner plate, cut into quarters and serve.

Peloponnesian potato salad

SERVES 6

I've always thought it odd that the small experiences of travel manage to separate themselves from the big ones and hang themselves up forever in your memory. This potato salad—and the luncheon where I enjoyed it—is just such an experience. I had spent the morning climbing the Acrocorinth, the mountain that rears directly behind the Doric ruins of Corinth on the Peloponnesus of Greece, then collapsed into a dining chair at the local *Xenia* (government inn). I didn't expect much in the way of food and was really too tired to eat anyway. But then came this glorious potato salad, studded with salty chunks of feta cheese, black olives and coarsely chopped fresh mint. I was revived within minutes and, to my dismay, wolfed down a second helping. I make this potato salad often today, and each bite spins me straight back to that lovely luncheon on an open terrace high above the Gulf of Corinth. NOTE: *The feta and olives are so salty that you will probably not need to salt the salad.* Accompany, if you like, with cold roast lamb or chicken or baked ham, but the salad is really hearty enough to serve as the main course. Snappily dressed sliced ripe tomatoes or asparagus or artichoke hearts vinaigrette will nicely round out the meal.

2 pounds	medium-size waxy potatoes (California long whites are good), boiled until tender, peeled and cubed	1 kg
1 medium-size	yellow onion, peeled and minced	1 medium-size
6 large	black Greek olives, pitted and diced	6 large
1 small	garlic clove, peeled and finely minced	1 small
¼ pound	feta cheese, cut into small cubes	115 g
2 tablespoons	minced fresh mint	2 tablespoons
2 tablespoons	minced fresh parsley	2 tablespoons
1 teaspoon	minced fresh marjoram (or ¼ teaspoon crumbled leaf marjoram)	1 teaspoon
⅛ teaspoon	freshly ground black pepper	⅛ teaspoon
6 tablespoons (about)	olive oil (top quality)	6 tablespoons (about)
2 tablespoons	lemon juice	2 tablespoons

Place the potatoes, onion, olives, garlic, feta, mint, parsley, marjoram and pepper in a large mixing bowl and toss lightly. Drizzle with 4 tablespoons of the olive oil and toss lightly again; pour the lemon juice evenly on top, then drizzle with the remaining 2 tablespoons of oil and toss once again. Cover and marinate in the refrigerator several hours.

Before you serve the salad, let it stand at room temperature for at least 30 minutes (but no longer than 1 hour) so that the flavors will intensify. If the salad seems dry—and it may because the potatoes will absorb both the oil and the lemon juice—moisten with a little additional olive oil or, if you prefer, with a little chicken broth (a good way to keep the calories from getting out of hand). Also taste the salad for salt and add a little, if needed (it isn't likely that it will). Toss the salad well once again and serve on crisp beds of romaine. (Romaine is also known as cos lettuce and comes originally from the Greek island of Cos.)

Baked spinach balls with tomato-wine sauce

SERVES 4 TO 6

My all-time favorite spinach recipe is this one, which was given to me by Mrs. Charles A. Volpi of Napa County, California, whom I interviewed several years ago for a series I was writing for *Family Circle* magazine called "America's Great Grass Roots Cooks." NOTE: *The Tomato-Wine Sauce is equally delicious served over freshly cooked pasta.*

SPINACH BALLS:

1 medium-size	yellow onion, peeled and finely minced	1 medium-size
2 medium-size	garlic cloves, peeled and minced	2 medium-size
2 tablespoons	unsalted butter	2 tablespoons
2 cups	finely chopped cooked spinach, pressed dry in a fine sieve (you'll need four 10-oz. or 283 g packages frozen spinach or 1½ pounds or ⅔ kg fresh)	½ L
½ teaspoon	salt	½ teaspoon
⅛ teaspoon	freshly ground black pepper	⅛ teaspoon
¼ cup	moderately fine dry bread crumbs	60 ml
⅓ cup	freshly grated Parmesan cheese	80 ml
1 large	egg	1 large

TOMATO-WINE SAUCE:

1 medium-size	yellow onion, peeled and minced	1 medium-size
1 large	garlic clove, peeled and minced	1 large
2 tablespoons	olive oil (top quality)	2 tablespoons
2 teaspoons	minced fresh sage (or 1 teaspoon crumbled leaf sage)	2 teaspoons
1 quart	tomato sauce (use your favorite)	1 L
½ cup	dry white wine	120 ml
To taste	salt and freshly ground black pepper	To taste

For the spinach balls: In a large heavy skillet set over moderately low heat, sauté the onion and garlic in the butter about 15 minutes, stirring occasionally, until very limp and golden but not brown. Mix in the spinach, salt and pepper, cover, turn heat to lowest point and steam 15 minutes. Off heat, blend in the bread crumbs, Parmesan and egg. Chill the mixture for several hours or until firm enough to shape. NOTE: *You can quick-chill it by setting in the freezer.*

Meanwhile, prepare the sauce: Sauté the onion and garlic in the oil in a large heavy skillet over moderately low heat about 15 minutes, stirring occasionally, until limp; do not allow to brown. Add the sage and stir-fry 5 minutes. Blend in the tomato sauce and wine and simmer, uncovered, about 10 minutes; cover and simmer 1 to 1½ hours or until the flavors are well blended. Season to taste with salt and pepper.

When the spinach mixture is firm enough to shape, roll into 1-inch (2½ cm) balls. Arrange in one layer in a buttered 9 × 9 × 2-inch (23 × 23 × 5 cm) flameproof baking dish and bake, uncovered, in a moderate oven (350°F. or 175°C.) for 30 minutes. Spoon into a vegetable dish or onto individual plates and top with a generous ladling of sauce. Pass extra sauce so that guests may help themselves to as much as they wish. NOTE: *Save any leftover sauce and use later to dress spaghetti. Stored in an airtight jar in the refrigerator, it will keep well for several days.*

Les spaghettis de courgettes à la ciboulette
(ZUCCHINI SPAGHETTI WITH CHIVES SAUCE)

SERVES 4

Slimmest strands of zucchini cooked just until *al dente*, then dressed with a creamy chives sauce. This is the creation of Guy Tricon and Jean André, the brilliant young chef-owners of the Restaurant La Mourrachonne at Mouans-Sartoux in the hills above Cannes. They serve this dish as a first course—a little mound of zucchini "pasta" bracketed by the chives sauce and a fresh tomato-basil *coulis* (you can substitute your own favorite fresh tomato sauce). It is simply glorious. The recipe that follows is my interpretation of the original.

3 pounds	tender young zucchini, peeled and cut lengthwise into thin pastalike strands about 4 inches (10 cm) long	1½ kg
2–3 teaspoons	salt	2–3 teaspoons
2 tablespoons	unsalted butter	2 tablespoons
Light sprinkling	freshly ground black pepper	Light sprinkling
	CHIVES SAUCE:	
2 medium-size	leeks, washed, trimmed and chopped fine	2 medium-size
6 medium-size	shallots, peeled and chopped fine	6 medium-size
1 small	celery rib, trimmed and chopped fine	1 small
1 very small	carrot, peeled and chopped fine	1 very small
2 tablespoons	unsalted butter	2 tablespoons
¼ teaspoon	crumbled leaf thyme	¼ teaspoon
1 small	bay leaf	1 small
½ cup	dry white wine	120 ml
1 pint	half-and-half cream	½ L
To taste	salt and white pepper	To taste
½ medium-size	lemon, juiced	½ medium-size
¼ cup	snipped fresh chives	60 ml

Spread the zucchini out in one layer on several thicknesses of paper toweling; sprinkle liberally with salt, top with more toweling, weight down and let stand 2 to 3 hours. This is to draw the bitter juices out of the zucchini and to firm it up so that it will be less apt to cook down to mush.

Meanwhile, prepare the chives sauce: Stir-fry the leeks, shallots, celery and carrot in the butter in a heavy saucepan over moderately low heat 10 minutes—do not brown. Add the thyme, bay leaf and wine and boil hard until only 2 tablespoons of the wine remain. Add the cream and boil until reduced by half. Remove the bay leaf. Purée the mixture in an electric blender or in a food processor equipped with the metal chopping blade; return the sauce to the pan, season to taste with salt and pepper and keep warm. Just before you are ready to serve, stir in the lemon juice and chives and let mellow a minute or two.

To cook the "pasta," stir-fry the zucchini in the 2 tablespoons butter in a very large skillet over moderate heat about 2 minutes—just until *al dente*. Season to taste with salt and pepper. To serve, twirl the cooked zucchini on a fork and place a mound in the center of each plate. Wreathe with the hot chives sauce or, if you prefer, spoon chives sauce on one side and your favorite light tomato sauce to the other.

Zucchini stuffed with sweet Italian sausages, shallots and Parmesan

SERVES 4

This is one of those accommodating recipes that can be prepared one day and baked the next. NOTE: *Because of the saltiness of the sausages and Parmesan, you will not need to add salt to the stuffing.*

4 medium-size	tender young zucchini, washed and halved lengthwise	4 medium-size
2 cups	boiling water	½ L
1 tablespoon	olive oil	1 tablespoon
	STUFFING:	
2 medium-size	sweet Italian sausages	2 medium-size
2 large	shallots, peeled and minced	2 large
¼ teaspoon	crumbled leaf basil	¼ teaspoon
¼ teaspoon	crumbled leaf marjoram	¼ teaspoon
⅛ teaspoon	crumbled leaf thyme	⅛ teaspoon
Light sprinkling	freshly ground black pepper	Light sprinkling
1¼ cups	fine soft bread crumbs	300 ml
3 tablespoons, in all	freshly grated Parmesan cheese	3 tablespoons, in all

Lay the zucchini halves, cut sides up, on a large round rack and set in a large heavy skillet. Pour in the water, cover the skillet, set over moderate heat and steam the zucchini for 10 to 15 minutes—just until firm-tender. Remove the zucchini from the heat and cool until easy to handle. Using a teaspoon, scrape out the seedy central portion of each zucchini, leaving shells about ¼ inch (¾ cm) thick. Chop the seedy portions, drain in a fine sieve and reserve. Also drain the zucchini halves by placing them upside down on several thicknesses of paper toweling. Let stand while you prepare the stuffing.

For the stuffing: Slit the casing of each sausage and push the meat into a large heavy skillet. Break up the clumps of meat as much as possible with a wooden spoon, set the skillet over moderately low heat and stir-fry the sausage, continuing to break up the meat until it is uniformly fine and crumbly, 5 to 10 minutes. Do not brown the sausage; merely cook it through. Add the minced shallots to the skillet along with the basil, marjoram, thyme and pepper and stir-fry 2 to 3 minutes until limp. Stir in the reserved chopped zucchini, remove the skillet from the heat and cool 10 minutes. Mix in the bread crumbs and 2 tablespoons of the Parmesan cheese.

To stuff the zucchini: Turn the zucchini right side up and brush each with olive oil. Now spoon the stuffing into each hollow, mounding it up lightly. Sprinkle each with grated Parmesan, dividing the remaining tablespoon of cheese evenly.

Place the stuffed zucchini in one layer in a large shallow baking pan. NOTE: *If you do not intend to bake the zucchini straightaway, cover the pan with foil and refrigerate until about 1 hour before you are ready to serve them. Bring the zucchini from the refrigerator, uncover and let stand at room temperature 30 minutes, just long enough to take the chill off.* Bake, uncovered, in a moderate oven (350°F. or 175°C.) for about 30 minutes or until lightly browned.

Pasta, rice, eggs & cheese

Whole wheat pasta dressed with bay scallops and fresh basil

SERVES 4

This is one of the loveliest ways I know to prepare scallops. Be sure not to overcook them.

2 large	shallots, peeled and minced	2 large
1 medium-size	garlic clove, peeled and minced	1 medium-size
3 tablespoons	unsalted butter	3 tablespoons
1 pound	bay scallops, washed in cool water and drained well (halve any scallops that seem large)	½ kg
⅓ cup	dry white wine or dry vermouth	80 ml
2 tablespoons	lemon juice	2 tablespoons
1 cup	heavy cream	240 ml
½ cup	half-and-half cream	120 ml
½ cup	minced fresh basil	120 ml
3 tablespoons	minced parsley	3 tablespoons
Light sprinklings	salt and freshly ground black pepper	Light sprinklings
2 cups	whole wheat macaroni, cooked by package directions until al dente and drained well	½ L
2 tablespoons	melted unsalted butter	2 tablespoons

Stir-fry the shallots and garlic in the butter in a large heavy skillet over moderate heat 2 to 3 minutes until limp; add the scallops and stir-fry about 2 minutes, just until they release all of their juices. With a slotted spoon, lift the scallops to a large plate and reserve. Add the wine and lemon juice to the skillet and quickly boil down the liquid until reduced to a rich pale amber glaze; drain any liquid that may have collected on the plate of scallops into the skillet and reduce also. Smooth in the heavy cream and half-and-half and simmer, uncovered, 8 to 10 minutes until reduced by about one-third. Return the scallops to the skillet and simmer slowly, 2 to 3 minutes. Sprinkle in the basil, parsley, salt and pepper. Turn heat to its lowest point and let the sauce mellow while you attend to the pasta. As soon as you have drained the macaroni, return it to the kettle in which you cooked it, add the melted butter and toss well to mix. Mound the pasta on a deep platter, smother with the scallops sauce and serve.

Fettuccine verde with shrimp and ground walnut sauce

SERVES 4

Sinfully rich but oh, so good.

2 large	shallots, peeled and minced	2 large
1 medium-size	garlic clove, peeled and minced	1 medium-size
4 tablespoons, in all	unsalted butter	4 tablespoons, in all
1 tablespoon	olive oil	1 tablespoon
1 pound	small raw shrimp, shelled and deveined	½ kg
½ cup	walnut meats	120 ml
Pinch	crumbled leaf rosemary	Pinch
Pinch	crumbled leaf thyme	Pinch
Pinch	freshly grated nutmeg	Pinch
⅓ cup	dry vermouth	80 ml
1 cup	half-and-half cream, at room temperature	240 ml
½ cup	heavy cream, at room temperature	120 ml
¼ cup	freshly grated Parmesan cheese	60 ml
1 tablespoon	minced parsley	1 tablespoon
To taste	salt and freshly ground black pepper	To taste
1 pound	green fettuccine, cooked by package directions until al dente and drained	½ kg

Stir-fry the shallots and garlic in 2 tablespoons of the butter and the tablespoon of olive oil in a large heavy skillet over moderate heat 3 minutes. Dump in the shrimp and stir-fry 3 to 4 minutes until they turn pink. With a slotted spoon, lift the shrimp to a large plate and reserve. Add the walnuts, rosemary, thyme and nutmeg to the skillet and stir-fry 3 to 4 minutes; now add the vermouth and any liquid that may have accumulated on the plate of shrimp and boil hard until reduced to an amber glaze—about 3 minutes. Dump the skillet mixture into a food processor fitted with the metal chopping blade (or into the container of an electric blender), pour in the half-and-half and purée—three to four 30-second churnings should do the job.

Pour the purée into a medium-size heavy saucepan, add the heavy cream and simmer uncovered, stirring often, 8 to 10 minutes until slightly reduced. Add the reserved shrimp, the Parmesan, parsley, salt and pepper, turn the heat to its lowest point and allow the sauce to mellow while you deal with the pasta.

As soon as the fettuccine has been drained, return it to the pan in which you cooked it, add the remaining 2 tablespoons of butter and toss well to mix. Mound the fettuccine on a heated deep platter and ladle the shrimp sauce on top. To accompany: the tartest, crispest and coolest of salads—nothing more other than a well-chilled, dry white wine.

Fettuccine verde with creamed shallots

SERVES 2

The elegance of this recipe belies the ease with which it can be made. It requires about fifteen minutes—start to finish. Accompany with a sharply dressed salad of arugula and romaine.

2 very large	shallots, peeled and chopped	2 very large
3 tablespoons, in all	unsalted butter, at room temperature	3 tablespoons, in all
⅛ teaspoon	crumbled leaf rosemary	⅛ teaspoon
⅛ teaspoon	crumbled leaf marjoram	⅛ teaspoon
¼ cup	dry vermouth	60 ml
1 cup	heavy cream, at room temperature	240 ml
½ teaspoon	salt	½ teaspoon
Light sprinkling	freshly ground black pepper	Light sprinkling
½ pound	green fettuccine, cooked by package directions until al dente and drained	225 g
1 tablespoon	minced parsley	1 tablespoon

Stir-fry the shallots in 1 tablespoon of the butter in a medium-size heavy skillet over moderate heat 2 to 3 minutes—just until limp and golden; do not brown. Stir in the rosemary and marjoram and stir-fry 1 to 2 minutes to release the herbs' flavors. Add the vermouth, raise the heat under the skillet and boil hard about 5 minutes until only a thin glaze remains on the bottom of the skillet. Off heat, pour in the cream; return to high heat and boil about 5 minutes to thicken slightly. Season with salt and pepper.

As soon as you have drained the fettuccine, return it to the kettle in which you cooked it, add the remaining 2 tablespoons of butter and toss well until the butter melts. Add the parsley to the shallots mixture, quickly pour over the fettuccine, toss well again and serve. NOTE: *Resist the temptation to serve grated Parmesan with this recipe. The strength and saltiness of the cheese will overpower the delicacy of the sauce.*

Pasta and broccoli salad with sweet red pepper, pignoli and feta

SERVES 6

A dazzling red, white and green salad that is hearty enough for a main course. It should be served at room temperature.

1 medium-size	sweet red pepper, washed, cored, seeded and diced	1 medium-size
4 large	scallions, washed, trimmed and sliced thin (include some tops)	4 large
A 2-pound head	broccoli, trimmed of leaves and stems and divided into small florets	A 1 kg head
2 tablespoons	olive oil	2 tablespoons
1 tablespoon	toasted sesame seed oil	1 tablespoon
1/3 cup	pine nuts (pignoli)	80 ml
3 cups	small shell macaroni, cooked by package directions until al dente and drained well	3/4 L
1/4 pound	feta cheese, cut into small dice	115 g
1/2 teaspoon	salt	1/2 teaspoon
Light sprinkling	freshly ground black pepper	Light sprinkling
	LEMON AND SESAME DRESSING:	
1 large	garlic clove, peeled and minced	1 large
1 tablespoon	minced fresh ginger root	1 tablespoon
1 teaspoon	sugar	1 teaspoon
1/2 teaspoon	crumbled leaf marjoram	1/2 teaspoon
1/2 teaspoon	crumbled leaf basil	1/2 teaspoon
1/4 teaspoon	crumbled leaf thyme	1/4 teaspoon

2 tablespoons	toasted sesame seed oil (available in Oriental groceries)	2 tablespoons
4–6 tablespoons	olive oil	4–6 tablespoons
1 large	lemon, juiced	1 large

Place the pepper and scallions in a large mixing bowl. Stir-fry the broccoli in the olive and sesame oils in a large heavy skillet over high heat 4 to 5 minutes until crisp-tender and bright green. Dump on top of the peppers and scallions. Spread the pine nuts out on a pie pan and toast 12 to 14 minutes in a slow oven (300°F. or 150°C.) until a nice honey brown. Dump on top of the broccoli—do not mix—and set aside for the time being.

At this point, prepare the dressing: Place all dressing ingredients (use 4 tablespoons of the olive oil) in the container of an electric blender or in the work bowl of a food processor fitted with the metal chopping blade and buzz about 30 seconds until blended. Set aside.

Dump the cooked and drained macaroni into the mixing bowl, add about two-thirds of the dressing and toss lightly. Cover loosely and let stand at room temperature about 1 hour so that the flavors have a chance to mingle. Add the feta cheese, salt, pepper and remaining dressing. Toss again lightly, cover loosely and let stand at room temperature ½ hour longer. If the salad seems dry, add 1 to 2 tablespoons of the remaining olive oil and toss lightly again. Serve as a main course with perfectly ripe sliced tomatoes and a hot bread.

Rice, egg, tuna and tomato salad

SERVES 6

An unusual combination, it's true, but an unusually good one that's perfect for a light luncheon.

1 can (14 oz.)	solid white tuna, drained and flaked	1 can (370 g)
4 cups (1 quart)	cooked unseasoned rice, cooled	1 L
2 large	hard-cooked eggs, peeled and minced	2 large
1 large	firm-ripe tomato, cored, seeded and moderately finely chopped (do not peel)	1 large
½ cup	chopped pitted black olives (preferably Greek)	120 ml
1 medium-size	yellow onion, peeled and minced	1 medium-size
¼ cup	minced parsley	60 ml
1¼ cups	mayonnaise (preferably homemade)	300 ml
1 large	lemon, juiced	1 large
¼ cup (about)	milk	60 ml (about)
To taste	salt and freshly ground pepper	To taste

Mix all ingredients together well, cover and marinate in the refrigerator for at least 4 hours. Toss well again, moisten, if needed, with a little additional milk, and add more salt and pepper, if necessary. Serve as is, or in hollowed-out tomatoes or avocado halves or on crisp leaf lettuce.

Chicken and rice salad al pesto

SERVES 6 TO 8

I like this warm-weather salad because it can be made a day or so ahead and kept in the refrigerator. Also because it can be so easily dressed up by serving in hollowed-out sweet red peppers, tomatoes or avocado halves. It is best served at room temperature.

1½ pounds	chicken breasts (about 3 large half breasts)	675 g
1 quart	cold water	1 L
¼ cup	dry vermouth	60 ml
1 small	bay leaf	1 small
1 small	thyme sprig (optional)	1 small
3 cups	chicken stock (from cooking the breasts)	¾ L
1½ teaspoons (about)	salt	1½ teaspoons (about)
1½ cups	converted rice	350 ml
½ cup	lightly toasted pine nuts (pignoli)	120 ml
½ recipe	Pesto Sauce (see Index)	½ recipe
5–6 tablespoons	lemon juice	5–6 tablespoons
⅛ teaspoon	freshly ground black pepper	⅛ teaspoon
—	olive oil (if needed)	—

Bring the chicken breasts to a simmer in a mixture of the water and vermouth in a large heavy saucepan over moderate heat; add the bay leaf and, if available, the thyme; reduce heat so that the water barely bubbles, cover and simmer gently 45 minutes. Remove the chicken breasts from the stock and cool until easy to handle. Strain the stock; pour 3 cups (¾ L) of the stock into a medium-size heavy saucepan and mix in 1 teaspoon of the salt. Bring to a boil over high heat, stir in the rice, reduce heat so that the stock just ripples and cook, uncovered, 10 to 12 minutes or until the stock drops well below the level of the rice. Cover the rice and cook 10 minutes; uncover and cook 5 minutes more until all stock has cooked away and rice is *al dente*.

While the rice cooks, remove the chicken meat from the bones and cut into small cubes. Place in a large mixing bowl, add the pine nuts, the cooked rice and the Pesto Sauce and toss well. Scatter 5 tablespoons of the lemon juice and the pepper over all; toss well again. Taste for salt and lemon juice and add more of each, if needed. Also, if the mixture seems a little dry, add a tablespoon or so of olive oil and toss again. Let stand at room temperature about 20 minutes before serving. Or cover and refrigerate until about 45 minutes before serving. Let salad stand on the counter—still covered—for about half an hour. Toss well, and if mixture seems dry, add a little olive oil. Serve as a main course accompanied by sliced tomatoes; or serve in hollowed-out tomatoes and accompany by green beans or asparagus vinaigrette.

NOTE: *To toast pine nuts* (**pignoli**)*, spread the nuts out in a pie pan, then set, uncovered, in a very slow oven (300°F. or 150°C.) for 10 to 12 minutes, stirring now and then. The nuts should be a pale amber color. Take them out immediately, then dump onto several thicknesses of paper toweling to drain (the nuts are quite oily).*

Sweets

Prinzregententorte Café Luitpold

MAKES A 9-INCH (23 CM), 6-LAYER TORTE

The *Prinzregententorte* (Prince Regent Cake) is Bavaria's unofficial "chocolate sweet"—six thin vanilla sponge layers sandwiched together with the richest chocolate butter cream imaginable. This particular recipe comes from Munich's famous Café Luitpold, which opened on January 1, 1888, in a Renaissance palace in the historic heart of the Bavarian capital and soon became a favorite among such writers, musicians and artists as Henrik Ibsen, Johann Strauss (the younger) and Paul Klee. Twenty years ago the old coffee house was bought by master pastry chef Paul Buchner and restored to its original glory. And today, as in Ibsen's day, *Prinzregententorte* reigns supreme among chocolate lovers. It is not the easiest cake to make, but I've simplified the method by baking three layers in springform pans (which can be halved when cool) instead of baking each of the six layers individually on baking sheets as Luitpold chefs do. The cake is unusually porous and spongy, so it doesn't break as you split the layers. NOTE: *It's best to bake and assemble the* Prinzregententorte *one day and to serve it the next—the flavors get together better.*

	SPONGE CAKE:	
6 large	egg yolks	6 large
1 cup	sugar	200 g
Pinch	salt	Pinch
1 teaspoon	vanilla extract	1 teaspoon
¼ pound (1 stick)	unsalted butter, melted and cooled to room temperature	115 g (1 stick)
7 large	egg whites	7 large
1⅓ cups	sifted cake flour	105 g

482

CHOCOLATE BUTTER CREAM FILLING:

1 cup	sugar	200 g
½ cup	water	120 ml
5 large	egg yolks	5 large
7 squares (1 oz. each)	semisweet chocolate, melted over simmering water	7 squares (28 g each)
1½ pounds (6 sticks)	unsalted butter, cut into ½-inch (1½ cm) pats	680 g (6 sticks)

APRICOT GLAZE:

⅓ cup	sieved apricot jam, warmed just enough to spread easily	80 ml

CHOCOLATE COATING:

6 squares (1 oz. each)	semisweet chocolate, melted over simmering water	6 squares (28 g each)
½ cup	boiling water	120 ml

For the cake: Beat the yolks with ⅓ cup (65 g) of the sugar, the salt and vanilla until pale yellow and fluffy; drizzle in the melted butter, beating hard until mayonnaiselike. Beat the egg whites until frothy, then gradually add the remaining ⅔ cup (135 g) sugar, beating hard to stiff, glossy peaks. Pour the yolk mixture on top of the whites and fold in gently. Add the flour in about eight additions, sifting each one over the batter and folding in with a light touch. Divide the batter evenly among three lavishly greased and floured 9-inch (23 cm) springform pans or layer cake pans (about 1⅓ cups or 315 ml of batter per pan). Rap the bottom of each pan smartly on the counter three times to release large trapped air bubbles and to level the batter in the pan.

Bake the layers in a moderate oven (350°F. or 175°C.) for 12 to 15 minutes or until pale tan and cakes feel springy. Do not overbake them or they will be rubbery. Remove the layers from the oven and cool upright in their pans on wire racks for 5 minutes; loosen and remove the springform sides and bottoms. NOTE: *If using layer cake pans, loosen the cakes carefully and invert on wire racks.* Cool to room temperature.

For the chocolate butter cream filling: Combine the sugar and water in a small heavy saucepan set over moderate heat and bring to the soft ball stage (236°F. or 114°C.) without stirring. Meanwhile, beat the egg yolks until thick and pale; drizzle the hot syrup into the yolks, beating hard all the while. Beat in the melted chocolate and continue beating until the mixture cools to room temperature. Now beat in the butter, pat by pat, until the filling is fluffy-light.

To assemble the torte: With a sharp serrated knife, split the layers in half horizontally, using a gentle sawing motion. Place the bottom layer on a cut-to-fit cardboard circle on a cake rack set on a paper-covered counter. Spread with the chocolate butter cream, making the layer of filling as thick as the layer of cake. Repeat until all layers are in place. Frost the sides of the torte as smoothly as possible with the chocolate butter ceam, but leave the top plain. Quick-chill the torte until the butter cream is firm—abuut 30 minutes. Remove the torte from the refrigerator and spread the top evenly with apricot glaze; refrigerate torte about 45 minutes or until glaze is no longer sticky.

Meanwhile, prepare the chocolate coating: Whisk the melted chocolate until creamy, then beat in the boiling water—the mixture should be absolutely smooth. Cool almost to room temperature or until the chocolate is a good spreading consistency. Pour about two-thirds of the chocolate over the torte so that it oozes evenly across the top and eases down the sides; direct and smooth the chocolate with a spatula. Apply the remaining chocolate smoothly around the sides of the torte, filling in any skimpy spots—your aim is for as even a chocolate coating as possible, rather as if the entire torte had been dipped in chocolate. Once again, quick-chill the torte to set the chocolate.

Store the torte in the refrigerator about 12 hours before serving, then let it stand at room temperature about 1 hour. Cut the pieces small—the *Prinz-regententorte* is unconscionably rich!

Ginger cake

MAKES A 10-INCH (25 CM) TUBE CAKE

This spicy cake has a compact texture akin to that of pound cake. It's a great specialty at Reid's Hotel, a posh Victorian establishment on the island of Madeira, where it is baked in long institutional loaves, then gussied up with frosting for the pastry cart. I prefer the cake unadorned because it's quite rich enough without the added frosting calories.

4 cups	sifted all-purpose flour	400 g
1 teaspoon	baking soda	1 teaspoon
1 teaspoon	baking powder	1 teaspoon
1 teaspoon	ground cinnamon	1 teaspoon
1 teaspoon	ground ginger	1 teaspoon
½ teaspoon	ground cloves	½ teaspoon
½ teaspoon	ground nutmeg	½ teaspoon
¼ pound (1 stick) + 3 tablespoons	unsalted butter, at room temperature	160 g (1 stick + 3 tablespoons)
⅔ cup (firmly packed)	vegetable shortening	120 g
1⅔ cups	sugar	335 g
⅓ cup	light molasses or dark corn syrup	80 ml

5 large	eggs, separated	5 large
1/3 cup	sweet Madeira wine (Boal or Malmsey)	80 ml
1 cup	milk	240 ml

Sift the flour with the baking soda, baking powder and spices onto a piece of wax paper and set aside. Cream the butter, shortening and sugar until fluffy-light. Add the molasses and cream well; beat the egg yolks in, one at a time. Combine the Madeira and the milk. Add the sifted dry ingredients to the creamed mixture alternately with the combined liquids, beginning and ending with the dry ingredients. Beat the egg whites to soft peaks and fold in gently but completely.

Pour the batter into a well-greased and floured 10-inch (25 cm) tube pan and bake in a moderately slow oven (325°F. or 165°C.) for about 1 hour and 15 minutes or until the cake begins to pull from the sides of the pan and feels springy to the touch. Cool the cake upright in its pan on a wire rack 10 minutes; loosen with a spatula, then turn the cake out on the rack and cool to room temperature before cutting. Serve plain or frost, if you like, with your favorite butter cream frosting to which you have added about 1 tablespoon of Madeira wine and 2 to 3 tablespoons of chopped preserved ginger.

Mohntorte
(AUSTRIAN POPPY-SEED CAKE)

MAKES A TWO-LAYER 2-INCH (13 CM) CAKE

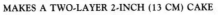 **A** most unusual cake, wholly unlike the poppy-seed cakes of America that contain only light scatterings of the seeds. This cake is simply filled with fluffy **ground** poppy seeds and owes its density, darkness and unusual biting flavor to them. NOTE: *Ground fresh poppy seeds can be bought in specialty food shops, also in many health food stores. Make certain that they are fresh; poppy seeds quickly go rancid. Do not attempt to substitute whole poppy seeds for the ground because they have an entirely different texture and will cause the cake to fail.*

4 tablespoons	unsalted butter	4 tablespoons
3/4 cup	sugar	150 g
1 tablespoon	Vanilla Sugar (to make Vanilla Sugar, see Index)	1 tablespoon
1 large	egg, lightly beaten	1 large
2 3/4 cups	finely ground fresh poppy seeds	650 ml
1 cup	milk	240 ml
2 cups	sifted all-purpose flour	200 g
1 tablespoon	baking powder	1 tablespoon

VANILLA BUTTER CREAM ICING:

4 tablespoons	unsalted butter	4 tablespoons
2 cups	unsifted confectioner's (10X) sugar	200 g
2 tablespoons	Vanilla Sugar	2 tablespoons
2–3 tablespoons	light or heavy cream	2–3 tablespoons

Cream the butter, sugar and 1 tablespoon vanilla sugar until smooth, then beat in the egg. Stir in the poppy seeds and ⅓ cup (80 ml) of the milk. Sift the flour with the baking powder, then add alternately to the poppy-seed mixture with the remaining milk, beginning and ending with the dry ingredients and stirring only enough to mix after each addition. NOTE: *I usually work the flour in in four additions.* Spoon the batter—it will be very thick—into a well-greased and floured 9-inch (23 cm) springform pan, smoothing the surface as evenly as possible.

Bake in a moderately slow oven (325°F. or 165°C.) for 40 minutes or until the cake begins to pull from the sides of the pan and feels springy to the touch. Remove the cake from the oven as soon as it tests done and cool upright in the pan on a wire rack for 10 minutes. Loosen around the edge of the cake with a thin-blade spatula, then unclamp and remove the springform pan sides. Invert the cake on a large flat plate, remove the pan bottom, then invert once again so that the cake is right side up; cool completely.

With a serrated knife, very carefully split the cake in two horizontally and set the two layers aside while you prepare the icing. NOTE: *I keep both layers on cut-to-fit cardboard disks, which simplifies handling them.*

For the vanilla butter cream icing: Cream the butter, confectioner's sugar and vanilla sugar until uniformly crumbly, then beat in just enough cream to give the icing a good spreading consistency.

To assemble the cake: Center the bottom layer (still on its cardboard disk) on a large flat cake plate, then spread smoothly with about half of the icing. Ease the top layer into place, cut side down, of course, and spread the top of the cake with the remaining icing, swirling it around any way you fancy for a decorative touch. Leave the sides of the cake plain. When serving, cut the slices small; this is an excruciatingly rich cake.

Torta de limão
(LEMON TORTE)

SERVES 6

Another of Portugal's devastating, completely flourless "egg sweets," this one from the Pousada do Castelo, a lovely government-run inn built inside the walls of the medieval royal castle at Óbidos some two hours north of Lisbon.

1⅔ cups	sugar	335 g
5 extra large	eggs	5 extra large
¼ cup	lemon juice	60 ml
1 tablespoon	finely grated lemon rind	1 tablespoon

Beat 1 cup (200 g) of the sugar with the eggs at high mixer speed about 5 minutes or until the color and consistency of mayonnaise; fold in lemon juice and rind. Spread mixture evenly in a lavishly greased and floured jelly-roll pan (15½ × 10½ × 1 inch or 39 cm × 25 cm × 2½ cm). Be sure that pan corners and sides are generously greased and floured, too—otherwise the torte will not unmold easily.

Bake in a very hot oven (425°F. or 220°C.) 12 to 15 minutes—just until torte billows and browns. The surface will be startlingly uneven, but this is as it should be. While torte bakes, spread wax paper on kitchen counter and cover with a clean dish towel. Sprinkle the remaining sugar heavily over the towel, covering an area slightly larger than that of the pan. The instant the torte is done, loosen quickly around edges with a knife and invert on sugared towel. Lifting one end of the towel, encourage torte to roll up on itself, jelly-roll fashion. Let towel-wrapped, rolled-up torte stand at room temperature 3 to 4 hours (it will magically make its own custardy filling).

To serve, cut torte slightly on the diagonal into slices about ½ inch (1½ cm) thick; allow two slices per person.

Dacquoise
(LAYERED HAZELNUT-MERINGUE TORTE WITH MOCHA-PRALINE FILLING)

MAKES A THREE-LAYER 9-INCH (23 CM) TORTE

I first tasted this ambrosial dessert not in France but at the Coach House in Greenwich Village, to my mind one of New York City's most consistently good restaurants, thanks to the talents of chef-owner Leon Lianides. This is not the Coach House recipe but one I have worked out myself. It is not the classic Dacquoise—I add rather more toasted hazelnuts than usual, also cocoa, coffee and coffee liqueur. NOTE: *Do not attempt to make this recipe in rainy or humid weather because the meringue will absorb atmospheric moisture—even in the oven—and never crisp properly. If I intend to make the Dacquoise well ahead of time—a good idea because of the complexity of the recipe—I store it in the freezer snugly wrapped in plastic food wrap once the filling has firmed up.*

MERINGUE:

1 cup	shelled hazelnuts or filberts	240 ml
8 large	egg whites	8 large
¼ teaspoon	cream of tartar	¼ teaspoon

¼ teaspoon	salt	¼ teaspoon
1½ cups	superfine sugar	300 g
1 teaspoon	vanilla extract	1 teaspoon
¼ teaspoon	almond extract	¼ teaspoon
½ cup	sifted confectioner's (10X) sugar	45 g

MOCHA-PRALINE FILLING:

⅔ cup	sugar	135 g
1 tablespoon	cocoa powder (not a mix)	1 tablespoon
5 large	egg yolks	5 large
½ cup	scalding-hot mix	120 ml
2 teaspoons	freeze-dried coffee crystals	2 teaspoons
1 teaspoon	vanilla extract	1 teaspoon
¾ pound (3 sticks, about)	ice-cold unsalted butter, cut into slim pats	340 g (3 sticks, about)
1 tablespoon	coffee or mocha liqueur	1 tablespoon
⅓ cup	Pralin (see Index)	80 ml

First, toast the hazelnuts: Spread the nuts out in a pie tin, set, uncovered, in a slow oven (300°F., or 150°C.) and toast for 35 to 45 minutes, just until the skins begin to buckle and the nuts are pale amber. Remove the nuts from the oven and remove the skins this way: Bundle about one-third of the nuts in a small terry towel and rub them briskly. Most of the dark skins will come off; don't worry about any recalcitrant bits—they will not affect the recipe other than adding nice color to the meringue. Repeat the towel rub until all nuts have been skinned. Let the nuts cool to room temperature, then grind very fine in a food processor equipped with the metal chopping blade (three to four 15-second churnings of the motor should be about right). If you have no processor, you'll have to hand-mince the nuts; I've never found a blender efficient at grinding nuts because they seem to clump about the blade at the bottom of the cup and churn into an oily mass. Your object should be ground nuts about as fine as cornmeal, so keep chopping until they are just the right mixture. NOTE: *The fineness of the grind is critical to the meringue's success; if the nut "meal" is too large, it will sink to the bottom of the fragile meringue layers instead of being distributed evenly.*

Now begin the meringue: Beat the egg whites until barely frothy, then sprinkle in the cream of tartar and salt. Beat just enough to incorporate, then begin adding the superfine sugar gradually, beating hard all the while. When about half of the sugar has been added, beat in the vanilla and almond extracts. Continue adding the sugar gradually and beating hard until all the sugar has been incorporated and the meringue is as thick and glossy as "seven-minute icing." (In an electric mixer, this can be done in 1 to 2 minutes at highest speed after all of the sugar has been added.) Add the confectioner's sugar to the ground hazelnuts and toss well to dredge. NOTE: *Hazelnuts are very oily and the confectioner's sugar coats them nicely so that this oil does not come into contact with—and deflate—the carefully beaten meringue.* Now turn three 9-inch (23 cm) layer cake tins upside down; lavishly butter and flour the bottoms. Using about three separate additions, gently but thoroughly fold the hazelnut–confectioner's sugar mixture into the meringue. Spread the hazelnut meringue thickly and smoothly on the pan bottoms, dividing the total amount evenly. Bake the meringues for 2½ to 3 hours in a keep-warm oven (250°F. or 120°C.) or until they feel firm and dry, then turn the heat off and leave the meringues in the oven to crisp somewhat. NOTE: *Hazelnut meringues take longer to bake than plain meringues because of the added moisture of the nuts.*

While the meringues bake, prepare the filling: Combine the sugar and cocoa powder, pressing out all lumps. Beat the egg yolks in and continue beating hard until thick. Drizzle in the scalded milk, beating hard all the while. Pour the mixture into a small heavy saucepan set over moderately low heat and cook, stirring constantly, 2 to 3 minutes until thick and custardlike. Pour into a bowl (or a food processor work bowl fitted with the metal chopping blade) and mix in the coffee crystals and vanilla. Now beat the butter in, one pat at a time. Beat the mixture hard after each addition (if you are using the processor, simply let it run nonstop and drop the butter pats down the feed tube); do not add successive butter pats until the previous one has been completely assimilated. This is a tedious job, so you must have patience. If you add the butter too fast, it will melt and thin the mixture; it must be thoroughly incorporated each time, so that by the time you have added all the butter, the filling will be cool and the consistency of a fluffy butter cream. If it still seems thin, beat in another ½ to 1 stick of well-chilled butter, pat by pat. As soon as all the butter has been incorporated, stir in the coffee liqueur. Cover and refrigerate the filling until you are ready for it. Keep the *pralin* at room temperature.

To assemble the dacquoise: Remove the meringues from the oven, very carefully loosen each with a large spatula and transfer to wire racks to cool. Center one meringue on a cake plate only slightly larger than it in diameter. Remove the filling from the refrigerator and beat hard until fluffy-light. Spread about one-third of the filling on the meringue and sprinkle with one-third of the *pralin*. Add a second meringue, pressing over so lightly into the filling below, spread with another one-third of the filling and sprinkle with another one-third of the *pralin*. Top with the final meringue, pressing gently into the layers underneath, spread with the remaining filling and sprinkle the last of the *pralin* evenly on top.

Set the Dacquoise in the freezer for about half an hour—just long enough to firm up the filling, then wrap carefully in plastic food wrap and store in the freezer. To serve, remove the Dacquoise from the freezer about 45 minutes before you intend to cut it, unwrap immediately and let stand on the counter. This will give the filling a chance to soften. To serve, cut into wedges with a serrated knife. NOTE: *Any leftover Dacquoise should be stored in the refrigerator.*

Vacherin aux framboises
(RASPBERRY-MERINGUE TORTE)

SERVES 8

~~~~~~ **T**his celestial dessert is the creation of Chef Dominick Ferrière of the Château du Domaine Saint-Martin, a historic, antique-filled country estate turned luxurious inn in Provence. With its gull's-eye view over the Côte d'Azur, it is my idea of heaven on earth. Despite its theatricality, my adaptation of Chef Ferrière's dessert is simple to make—three poufs of meringue sandwiched together with raspberry ice. NOTE: *Do not attempt this recipe in rainy or humid weather because the meringue will go soggy.*

	MERINGUE:	
8 large	egg whites	8 large
2 cups	superfine sugar	400 g

	RASPBERRY ICE:	
1 cup	sugar	200 g
2 cups	water	475 ml
2 packages (10 oz. each)	frozen raspberries, thawed, puréed and sieved	2 packages (283 g each)
½ large	lemon, juiced	½ large

Prepare the meringue first: Beat the egg whites until frothy. Add the sugar gradually, beating hard, and continue beating until the meringue is as thick and glossy as "seven-minute icing." (In an electric mixer, this can be done in 1 to 2 minutes at highest speed after all the sugar is incorporated.) Turn three 8-inch (20 cm) layer cake tins upside down; lavishly butter and flour the bottoms. Spread the meringue thickly and smoothly on the pan bottoms, dividing the total amount evenly. Bake for 2 hours in a very slow oven (250°F. or 120°C.), then turn the heat off and leave the meringues in the oven to crisp and dry.

For the raspberry ice: Boil the sugar and water 15 to 20 minutes until the mixture reduces to 1¾ cups (415 ml); cool to room temperature. Combine with the raspberries and lemon juice. Freeze until mushy; beat hard; freeze until almost firm; beat hard, then again freeze until almost firm.

To assemble: Place one meringue on a large dessert plate. TIP: *To remove the meringue easily from the pan bottom, twist it ever so slightly and it will pop right off.* Quickly spread the meringue with half the raspberry ice; add a second meringue, spread as before with raspberry ice, then top with the remaining meringue, pressing down gently. Freeze several hours before serving.

To serve, let the dessert stand at room temperature about 5 minutes, then cut into wedges just as you would a cake, using a very sharp knife dipped into boiling water.

Chocolate chiffon pie

SERVES 8

This cool, shimmery pie is adapted from a recipe served aboard that *grande dame* of the sea, the RMS *Queen Elizabeth 2*. I've simply pared the proportions down to family size and substituted a crumb crust for the one of crushed rusks the QE 2 chef uses (the right rusks not being readily available here). You can use any crumb crust—graham cracker, vanilla wafer or chocolate wafer—following these basic proportions: 1½ cups (350 ml) fine crumbs, ¼ cup (60 ml) melted butter and 2 to 3 tablespoons of sugar—just enough to sweeten. Simply mix all together and pat firmly over the bottom and up the sides of a 9-inch (23 cm) pie pan. The crust is then ready to fill.

2 tablespoons	cornstarch	2 tablespoons
⅓ cup	sugar	65 g
1 envelope	plain gelatin	1 envelope
1 cup	milk	240 ml
3 large	eggs, separated	3 large
3 squares (1 oz. each)	semisweet chocolate, melted over simmering water	3 squares (28 g each)
Pinch	salt	Pinch
½ cup	heavy cream, whipped	120 ml
1 teaspoon	vanilla extract	1 teaspoon
A 9-inch	crumb crust	A 23 cm
	OPTIONAL GARNISHES:	
½ cup	heavy cream, whipped	120 ml
1 square (1 oz.)	semisweet chocolate, shaved into curls with a vegetable peeler	1 square (28 g)

Blend the cornstarch, sugar and gelatin in a small heavy saucepan, whisk in the milk, set over moderate heat and cook and stir about 5 minutes until thickened and smooth and no raw cornstarch flavor remains. Lightly beat the egg yolks, blend in a little of the hot mixture, then stir the yolk mixture into pan. Remove from the heat and mix in the melted chocolate. Whip the egg whites to soft peaks with the salt. Mix about one-fourth of the beaten whites into the chocolate mixture, then pour chocolate mixture over whites. Dump the whipped cream on top and fold the two into the chocolate mixture together—gently but thoroughly—until no streaks of white or brown remain. Stir in the vanilla and pour into the crumb crust. Chill several hours until firm. Decorate before serving, if you like, with fluffs of whipped cream and a scattering of chocolate curls.

Fresh peach soufflé

SERVES 4 TO 6

The foundation for this dessert soufflé is one cup of puréed fresh peaches thickened with both cornstarch and egg yolks. It contains no fat or flour as do savory soufflé bases, and thus the end result is lighter, moister and more fragile. I find that the soufflé puffs more dramatically if I chill the dish in which I intend to bake it, then set the dish on a heavy baking sheet (one that won't buckle as it heats) on the middle rack of the oven. I also bake this soufflé in a moderately hot oven (moderate or moderately low heats are more conventional temperatures for soufflés), so that it will both rise and "set" more quickly. NOTE: *Perfectly cooked, a soufflé will be soft and moist inside—it should just quiver when you nudge the dish in the oven.* This soufflé profits by a sauce. Make a purée of fresh peaches spiked with lemon and sugar or, if you prefer, Vanilla Sauce (see Index) served at room temperature. NOTE: *The basic proportions for this soufflé may be used for almost any fruit soufflé; see those suggested in the variations at the end of this recipe.*

FOR PREPARING THE SOUFFLÉ DISH:

2 teaspoons	unsalted butter, at room temperature	2 teaspoons
2 tablespoons	sugar	2 tablespoons

SOUFFLÉ:

1 cup	puréed dead-ripe peaches (about 3 medium-size peaches)	240 ml
2 tablespoons	lemon juice	2 tablespoons
½ cup	sugar	100 g
3 tablespoons	cornstarch	3 tablespoons
4 large	egg yolks	4 large
¼ cup	heavy cream	60 ml
1 tablespoon	rum	1 tablespoon
6 large	egg whites, at room temperature	6 large
Pinch	salt	Pinch

GLAZE:

2 teaspoons	sifted confectioner's (10X) sugar	2 teaspoons

Prepare the soufflé dish first so that you will waste no time getting the soufflé into the oven once it's mixed: Butter a 2-quart (2 L) soufflé dish well, then spoon in the sugar and coat the bottom and sides of the dish evenly by tilting the dish first to one side and then to another. Tap out excess sugar. Set the dish in the refrigerator while you prepare the soufflé.

For the soufflé: Combine the peach purée and lemon juice in a medium-size heavy saucepan. Combine ⅓ cup (65 g) of the sugar with the cornstarch in a small bowl, pressing out all lumps; dump into the peach mixture and stir well to blend. Set over moderate heat and heat, stirring constantly, 2 to 3 minutes—just until the mixture thickens and turns clear. Set off the heat. Lightly beat the egg yolks with the cream, whisk in a little of the hot peach mixture, then stir yolk mixture into pan. Set over moderately low heat and cook, stirring constantly, about 2 minutes, just until heated through; do not allow to boil or the sauce may curdle. Pour the hot sauce at once into a large heatproof bowl and stir in the rum. Cool to room temperature, stirring often to prevent a skin from forming on the surface of the sauce, then place a piece of wax paper or plastic food wrap flat on the surface of the sauce and quick-chill by setting in the freezer for about 30 minutes. (This chilling is to thicken the sauce so that it forms a stronger foundation for the soufflé.)

Place the egg whites in a large bowl and sprinkle the salt on top. Using a balloon whip or rotary beater, beat until frothy. Sprinkle in about 1 tablespoon of the remaining sugar and beat until the whites begin to turn silvery. Sprinkle in another tablespoon of the remaining sugar and beat to soft peaks. Now sprinkle in all remaining sugar and continue beating until the egg whites almost, **but not quite,** form stiff peaks. They should be billowing and moist, not dry.

Mix about one-third of the beaten whites into the chilled peach mixture to lighten it, then pour the remaining beaten whites on top and fold in gently but thoroughly until no streaks of white or orange remain. Pour the soufflé batter into the prepared soufflé dish, set on a sturdy baking sheet and place on the middle rack of a moderately hot oven (375°F. or 190°C.). Bake the soufflé for 20 minutes. Very carefully open the oven and sift the confectioner's sugar glaze evenly on top. Gently close the oven and bake the soufflé 10 to 15 minutes longer until puffed and browned but still soft inside—nudge the dish gently; if the soufflé quivers lightly, it is done.

Rush the soufflé to the table and serve as is or with a sauce if you prefer.

VARIATIONS:

Fresh nectarine or plum soufflé: Prepare exactly as directed, but substitute 1 cup (240 ml) of puréed ripe nectarines or plums for the peaches. Also, use 1 tablespoon each lemon and orange juice instead of 2 tablespoons lemon juice.

Fresh papaya soufflé: Prepare exactly as directed, but substitute 1 cup (240 ml) of puréed ripe papayas for the peaches and 2 tablespoons of freshly squeezed lime juice for the lemon juice.

Fresh raspberry soufflé: Prepare as directed, but substitute 1 cup (240 ml) of puréed **and sieved** black or red raspberries for the peaches; flavor with 1 tablespoon of *framboise* (raspberry *eau de vie*) instead of rum.

Fresh strawberry soufflé: Prepare as directed, but substitute 1 cup (240 ml) of puréed **and sieved** ripe strawberries for the peaches; flavor with 1 tablespoon of Cointreau instead of rum.

Fresh pear soufflé: Prepare as directed, but substitute 1 cup (240 ml) of puréed dead-ripe pears for the peaches; flavor with 1 tablespoon of Poire William (pear *eau de vie*) instead of rum.

Chocolate rum soufflé

SERVES 6

Lovely and light and easy to make. It's best to prepare the chocolate base several hours ahead of time. Then all you have left to do is beat the whites and fold them in before baking. The soufflé dish should be prepared ahead of time, too. Butter it well, then coat with a generous sprinkling of granulated sugar. This, by the way, is the French way of preparing a soufflé dish, and I prefer it to the way I was taught—which was no preparation at all. The theory was: Don't grease a soufflé dish because the egg whites will not be able to cling to the sides of the dish and climb to stratospheric heights. But the sugar coating, of course, provides plenty of purchase, so the soufflé rises straight up. An additional bonus: The butter and sugar coating bakes into a wonderfully crisp crust, providing a welcome contrast to the soufflé itself. Finally, it simplifies cleanup because the soufflé scarcely sticks to the dish at all.

¾ cup	sugar	150 g
2 cups	milk	475 ml
4 tablespoons	unsalted butter	4 tablespoons
5 tablespoons	all-purpose flour	5 tablespoons
5 tablespoons	cocoa powder (not a mix)	5 tablespoons
4 large	eggs, separated	4 large
1 tablespoon	rum	1 tablespoon
1 teaspoon	vanilla extract	1 teaspoon
Pinch	salt	Pinch

Heat ½ cup (100 g or 120 ml) of the sugar with the milk in a small heavy saucepan over moderate heat just to the scalding point (when bubbles appear around the edge of the pan and steam rises from the surface but the milk itself does not bubble). Meanwhile, melt the butter in a medium-size heavy saucepan over moderate heat and blend in the flour and cocoa to make a thick paste. Off heat, whisk in the milk mixture; return to moderate heat and whisk and stir until thick and smooth, about 3 minutes. Lightly whisk the egg yolks, then blend a little of this chocolate mixture into the yolks; stir the yolk mixture into pan and cook and stir over low heat 2 to 3 minutes. Remove from heat, mix in rum and vanilla and cool to room temperature, whisking often to prevent a skin from forming on the surface of the sauce. NOTE: *You may prepare the recipe up to this* point several hours ahead of time; simply cover and refrigerate the chocolate base. About two hours before you intend to serve, set the sauce on the counter and whisk hard. Let stand for about an hour. Timing is now of the essence. The soufflé will take about 40 to 45 minutes to bake, so gauge the serving of dinner accordingly.

Beat the egg whites with the salt and 1 tablespoon of the remaining sugar until frothy. Scatter another tablespoon of sugar over the whites and beat until they begin to turn silvery. Scatter another tablespoon of sugar over the whites and beat hard to incorporate. Scatter the final tablespoon of sugar over the whites and beat just until they are moist and billowing and peak softly. Mix about 1 cup (240 ml) of the beaten whites into the chocolate base to lighten it so that folding in the remaining whites can be done more efficiently. Now gently pour the chocolate mixture on top of the beaten whites and fold in gently but thoroughly until no streaks of white or brown remain. Pour into prepared soufflé dish and bake in a moderate oven (350°F. or 175°C.) until puffy and lightly browned; the soufflé should just quiver when you nudge the dish. NOTE: If you want a "top-hat" soufflé (raised center portion), simply draw a ring in the unbaked soufflé with a thin-blade spatula about 2 inches (5 cm) in from the edge of the dish and concentric to it, then bake as directed.

The instant the soufflé is done, rush it to the table and serve.

Pine honey parfait with raspberry sauce

SERVES 6 TO 8

Pine honey, unique to Germany's Black Forest, is dark and heavy with the slightest hint of evergreen. It's unavailable here, but I have approximated its woodsy flavor by teaming an infusion of juniper berries with dark wildflower honey for my version of a dessert I tasted one spring evening at the Kurhotel Mitteltal near Baden-Baden.

5 large	juniper berries, lightly crushed	5 large
¾ cup	water	180 ml
10 large	egg yolks	10 large
1½ cups	**unsifted** confectioner's (10X) sugar	350 ml
3 tablespoons	very dark honey	3 tablespoons
1 pint (2 cups)	heavy cream, whipped	½ L
	RASPBERRY SAUCE:	
1 package (10 oz.)	frozen raspberries, thawed (do not drain)	1 package (283 g)
2 tablespoons	eau de vie de framboise	2 tablespoons
	OPTIONAL GARNISH:	
¼ cup	finely chopped blanched pistachios	60 ml

Boil the juniper berries in the water until water reduces to ½ cup (120 ml); strain (discard juniper), return liquid to lowest heat and keep warm. Beat the egg yolks with the confectioner's sugar (at highest speed if you use a mixer) until creamy-thick and the color of mayonnaise. Bring the juniper infusion quickly to the boil, then trickle into the egg mixture, beating vigorously. Mix in the honey, fold in the whipped cream and freeze until soft-firm. Beat the mixture once at the mushy stage.

For the raspberry sauce: Purée the raspberries in a food processor equipped with the metal chopping blade (or in an electric blender or by forcing through a food mill). Sieve to remove seeds. Combine raspberry purée with the *framboise*, pour into a pint (½ L) jar, cover and refrigerate until ready to use.

To serve: Layer the parfait and thin drizzlings of the sauce into stemmed parfait glasses. Top each portion, if you like, with a sprinkling of finely chopped blanched pistachio nuts.

Badische cream

SERVES 8 TO 10

The irony of this sublime dessert is that it comes from the elegant Brenner's Park-Hotel in Baden-Baden, which is famous for its firming-up, slimming-down regimes. It's showy—reds and pinks and creams layered into a crystal bowl. I use a footed three-quart (3 L) bowl about 7 inches (18 cm) across that resembles an outsize brandy snifter.

	VANILLA CREAM:	
½ cup	sugar	120 ml
1 envelope	plain gelatin	1 envelope
1 pint	milk	½ L
½ large	vanilla bean, slit lengthwise	½ large
4 large	egg yolks, lightly beaten	4 large
1 pint	heavy cream, whipped	½ L
	RASPBERRY CREAM:	
¼ cup	sugar	60 ml
1 envelope	plain gelatin	1 envelope
½ cup	milk	120 ml
1 large	egg yolk, lightly beaten	1 large
1 package (10 oz.)	frozen raspberries, thawed, puréed and sieved to remove seeds	1 package (283 g)
1 pint (2 cups)	heavy cream, whipped	½ L

VANILLA SAUCE:

1 pint	milk	½ L
½ cup	sugar	120 ml
½ large	vanilla bean, slit lengthwise	½ large
4 large	egg yolks, lightly beaten	4 large

RASPBERRY SAUCE:

| 1 package (10 oz.) | frozen raspberries, thawed, puréed and sieved to remove seeds | 1 package (283 g) |
| 1¼ cups | **unsifted** confectioner's (10X) sugar | 300 ml |

OPTIONAL GARNISHES:

| 5–6 large | perfect fresh raspberries | 5–6 large |
| 3–4 sprigs | rose geranium, lemon verbena or mint | 3–4 sprigs |

For the vanilla cream: Combine the sugar and gelatin in a small heavy saucepan; blend in the milk, add vanilla bean, set over moderately low heat and cook, stirring constantly, about 10 minutes until gelatin and sugar dissolve. Discard vanilla bean. Whisk a little of the hot mixture into the egg yolks, stir the yolk mixture into pan and cook, stirring constantly over low heat, 3 to 4 minutes until slightly thickened. (Do not allow to boil or mixture will curdle.) Quick-chill by setting pan in a bowl of crushed ice and beating hard. When thick and syrupy, fold in whipped cream. Set aside for the time being.

For the raspberry cream: Combine the sugar and gelatin in a small heavy saucepan, blend in the milk, set over low heat and cook, stirring constantly, 8 to 10 minutes until sugar and gelatin dissolve. Whisk a little of the hot mixture into the egg yolk, stir the yolk mixture into pan and cook and stir 1 to 2 minutes. Off heat, blend in the raspberry purée. Quick-chill by setting pan in a bowl of crushed ice and beating hard. When partially set, fold in the whipped cream; set aside.

For the vanilla sauce: Combine the milk and sugar in a small heavy saucepan, drop in the vanilla bean and bring just to a simmer. Remove from heat; discard vanilla bean. Whisk a little of the hot mixture into the egg yolks, stir the yolk mixture into pan, set over low heat and cook and stir 2 to 3 minutes until thickened like custard (do not boil). Cool, beating frequently to prevent a skin from forming on the top of the sauce.

For the raspberry sauce: Combine raspberry purée and confectioner's sugar.

To assemble the Badische cream: Spoon about one-third of the raspberry sauce into a tall 3-quart crystal bowl (3 L). Carefully spoon half the raspberry cream on top; spoon another third of the raspberry sauce around the edges so that it trickles down into the pink layer. Quick-chill in the freezer about 10 minutes to firm up slightly. Top with half the vanilla cream; quick-chill 10 minutes. Add the remaining raspberry cream and raspberry sauce, again spooning it around the edge so that it oozes down into the preceding layers. Quick-chill as before. Top with the remaining vanilla cream, quick-chill, then pour the vanilla sauce evenly on top. Cover and refrigerate 5 to 6 hours before serving. Garnish, if you like, with a small cluster of fresh raspberries and sprigs of rose geranium, lemon verbena or mint.

Madeira wine jelly

SERVES 4 TO 6

A jellied wine rather than a true jelly, this English dessert can be made equally well with a ruby (sweet) Port or with Marsala. It remains a great favorite in the American South, a holdover of plantation days when wealthy landowners imported wines by the barrel and bottled them under family labels.

2 envelopes	plain gelatin	2 envelopes
¾ cup	sugar	180 ml
2 cups	water	475 ml
1 strip (about 2 inches by ½ inch)	lemon rind (yellow part only)	1 strip (about 5 by 1½ cm)
1 small	cinnamon stick, broken in half	1 small
2½ cups	sweet Madeira wine (Malmsey or Boal) or ruby Port or Marsala	590 ml
1 cup	light cream (optional topping)	240 ml

Combine gelatin and sugar in a small heavy saucepan, pressing out any lumps. Add water, lemon rind and cinnamon; heat and stir over moderate heat about 5 minutes until sugar and gelatin dissolve. Cool to room temperature. Remove lemon rind and cinnamon. Carefully mix in wine. Chill 24 hours or until set. To serve, spoon into crystal goblets, alternating spoonfuls, if you like, with drizzlings of cream.

Delicias de laranja
(DELICIOUS ORANGE DESSERT)

SERVES 6

This cool, cloud-light orange mousse is the specialty of Chef Henrique of Reid's Hotel on the Portuguese resort island of Madeira. Winston Churchill used to come here to paint and few Old World hotels can match Reid's for location or luxury. Like so many other Portuguese desserts, this one is eggy and rich and ravishingly good.

2 envelopes	plain gelatin	2 envelopes
2 medium-size	oranges, juiced	2 medium-size
2 tablespoons	finely grated orange rind	2 tablespoons
1 cup	sugar	240 ml
1 quart	milk, scalded	1 L
12 large	eggs, separated	12 large
6 tablespoons	confectioner's (10X) sugar	6 tablespoons

Soften gelatin in orange juice 5 minutes. Add rind, sugar and softened gelatin mixture to hot milk; stir until dissolved. Beat yolks lightly, mix in a little hot milk, then stir yolk mixture into pan. Set over low heat and cook, stirring constantly, 15 to 20 minutes until slightly thickened—about like thin custard sauce. Do not boil or mixture will curdle. Remove from heat.

Beat egg whites to soft peaks, gradually adding confectioner's sugar. Gently but thoroughly fold beaten whites into orange mixture. Pour into a large bowl and chill 24 hours. Serve in stemmed goblets.

Sopa dourada
(SOUP OF GOLD)

SERVES 4 TO 6

 This rich-as-sin dessert, one of Portugal's infamously caloric "egg sweets," appears daily on the pastry cart at the palatial Pousada da Rainha Santa Isabel in Estremoz, one of the government's superb regional inns. Like many savory soups, *Sopa Dourada* should be made a day ahead of time so that its flavors mellow.

3 slices	stale firm-textured white bread, cut into ¼-inch (¾ cm) cubes	3 slices
4 tablespoons, in all	unsalted butter	4 tablespoons, in all
2 tablespoons, in all	vegetable oil	2 tablespoons, in all
1¼ cups	sugar	300 ml
1 cup	water	240 ml
5 large	egg yolks	5 large
1 large	egg	1 large
⅛ teaspoon	ground cinnamon	⅛ teaspoon
⅛ teaspoon	ground nutmeg	⅛ teaspoon
Pinch	salt	Pinch
2 tablespoons	almond paste (it must be softly malleable)	2 tablespoons
Light sprinklings	ground cinnamon	Light sprinklings

Sauté half the bread cubes in 1 tablespoon each butter and oil in a large heavy skillet over moderate heat. When crisply golden, drain on paper toweling. Wipe skillet clean with paper toweling and brown remaining bread cubes the same way in 1 tablespoon each butter and oil; drain on toweling as before and reserve.

Combine sugar and water in a small heavy saucepan; insert candy thermometer and bring to 230°F. (110°C.) without stirring. Meanwhile, beat egg yolks, egg, ⅛ teaspoon cinnamon, nutmeg and salt in a double boiler top until frothy; set aside. Cream remaining 2 tablespoons butter with almond paste until smooth; reserve. When syrup reaches proper temperature, drizzle slowly into egg mixture, beating hard with a whisk or a hand electric mixer set at medium speed. Place over simmering water and beat 10 minutes, until the consistency of hollandaise. Remove from heat. Whisk a little hot sauce into creamed almond paste, stir almond paste mixture into double boiler top and beat until smooth. Add bread cubes, stir lightly and cool to room temperature.

Spoon into 4 to 6 small crystal goblets, cover and refrigerate at least 24 hours. About 30 minutes before serving, remove goblets from refrigerator, sprinkle each portion lightly with cinnamon and let stand at room temperature.

Rote Grütze
(GERMAN RED BERRY DESSERT)

SERVES 6 TO 8

 My Bavarian friend Hedy Wuerz introduced me to this tartly refreshing "sweet." *Rote*, of course, means *red*. And *Grütze?* "It really is a kind of grain," explains Hedy. "I don't know why this word is part of the title unless maybe women once made the dessert with grain." Whatever its origin, *Rote Grütze* is simply splendid. "It's mostly a summer dessert in Germany," Hedy continues. "We would use all the red berries of summer for making it. Red currants and cherries, too." In America, Hedy has learned to make *Rote Grütze* with frozen berries. "It is almost as good," she says, "and, of course, frozen berries are available the year round." NOTE: Rote Grütze *will have better flavor if made one day and served the next. It also "sets up" more quickly and prettily in individual dishes than in a single large bowl. Hedy uses large stemmed goblets and spoons sweetened cream on top just before serving.*

2 packages (10 oz. each)	frozen raspberries, thawed (drain and reserve juice)	2 packages (283 g each)
1 package (16 oz.)	frozen strawberries, thawed and put through a food mill	1 package (454 g)
1 pound	dark, sweet red cherries, stemmed, pitted and quartered, or 1 can (1 lb. or 454 g) dark, sweet, pitted cherries (drain and reserve juice)	½ kg

1 quart (about)	natural red grape juice or cranberry juice	1 L (about)
¾ cup	sugar	180 ml
1 tablespoon	finely grated lemon rind	1 tablespoon
1 large	lemon, juiced	1 large
⅔ cup	unsifted cornstarch	160 ml
1 cup	dry red wine	240 ml
	TOPPING:	
1 cup	heavy cream	240 ml
1 tablespoon	Vanilla Sugar (see below)	1 tablespoon

Combine the raspberry juice, puréed strawberries and, if using canned cherries, the cherry juice in a 1-quart (1 L) measure. Pour in enough red grape or cranberry juice to total 1 quart (1 L); pour this mixture into a large heavy saucepan (not aluminum) and add 2 additional cups (½ L) of the grape or cranberry juice. Stir in the sugar, lemon rind and lemon juice and bring to a boil over moderate heat, stirring often. Meanwhile, combine the cornstarch with the red wine to make a thin smooth paste. As soon as the saucepan mixture comes to a boil, pour in the cornstarch mixture, whisking vigorously. Reduce heat at once to low and cook and stir 3 minutes—just until the saucepan mixture bubbles up once again, is thickened and clear and no raw starch flavor remains. Stir in the reserved raspberries and the cherries, heat about 1 minute longer, then cool to room temperature. Spoon into individual serving dishes and refrigerate at least 8 hours.

Shortly before serving, prepare the topping: Beat the cream with the vanilla sugar briefly, just until slightly thickened and still thin enough to pour. Top each portion with a generous ladling of the cream and serve.

To make vanilla sugar: Fill a 1-pint (½ L) jar with confectioner's (10X) sugar, then insert 1 to 2 vanilla beans, pushing them well down into the sugar. Cover tight and let "season" several weeks before using. NOTE: *This is a handy sugar to have on hand for flavoring all manner of desserts and dessert sauces. Leave the vanilla beans in the sugar and keep replenishing it as you use it. Kept tightly covered in a cool spot, vanilla sugar will last almost indefinitely.*

Grapefruit granita

SERVES 6

I can't think of a more cooling hot-weather dessert (it's relatively low in calories, too—less than 200 per serving). The corn syrup used in the recipe serves a dual purpose: It helps sweeten the *granita* and also keeps it from becoming gritty or grainy. The *granita* is delicious as is or topped by fresh sliced strawberries or Quick Cardinal Sauce (see Index).

½ cup	sugar	120 ml
1 envelope	plain gelatin	1 envelope
1 tablespoon	finely grated grapefruit rind	1 tablespoon
1 cup	water	240 ml
3 cups	pink grapefruit juice (you'll need about 3 medium-size grapefruit)	700 ml
½ cup	light corn syrup	120 ml

Combine sugar, gelatin, grapefruit rind and water in a small heavy saucepan; set over moderate heat and stir until sugar and gelatin dissolve, about 5 minutes. Remove from heat and combine with grapefruit juice and corn syrup. Freeze until mushy-firm, then beat at high mixer speed or churn in a food processor (about half of the total amount at a time) fitted with the metal chopping blade until light and fluffy. Return to freezer, again freeze until mushy-firm, then beat as before until light and fluffy. Spoon into two 1-quart (1 L) freezer containers, cover and store in freezer. Let the *granita* stand at room temperature 15 to 20 minutes before spooning into dessert dishes.

Raspberry-strawberry semifreddo

SERVES 6 TO 8

 Semifreddo is the Italian equivalent of our soft ice cream, though in truth it often contains no cream at all. This one, for example, contains only puréed berries, lemon, sugar and, to keep it nice and velvety, gelatin and corn syrup. This recipe is a good basic one with which to improvise: Substitute any berries or combination of berries for the raspberries and strawberries and increase the sugar and/or corn syrup as needed to temper their tartness.

½ cup	sugar	120 ml
1 envelope	plain gelatin	1 envelope
1 cup	water	240 ml
1 cup	light corn syrup	240 ml
¼ cup	lemon juice	60 ml
1 teaspoon	finely grated lemon or orange rind	1 teaspoon
2 packages (10 oz. each)	frozen raspberries, thawed slightly	2 packages (283 g each)
1 package (10 oz.)	frozen strawberries, thawed slightly	1 package (283 g)

Combine the sugar and gelatin in a small heavy saucepan, pressing out any lumps. Blend in the water and corn syrup, set over moderate heat and cook, stirring frequently, 3 to 5 minutes or until sugar and gelatin both dissolve. Off heat, mix in the lemon juice and rind; cool. Meanwhile, purée the raspberries in an electric blender at high speed or in a food processor equipped with the metal chopping blade; dump into a large fine sieve set over a large bowl. Purée the strawberries the same way and dump into the sieve. With a wooden spoon, stir the purée until all has passed through the sieve, leaving the seeds behind.

Stir the reserved gelatin mixture into the purée, then pour into a large shallow bowl or pan—I find the 13 × 9 × 2-inch size (33 × 23 × 5 cm) perfect—and freeze until mushy. Quickly beat the mush until fluffy in an electric mixer set at high speed, or in a food processor fitted with the metal chopping blade. NOTE: *In the processor, you'll be able to beat only about half the total amount at a time.* Again freeze until mushy, beat as before, then freeze until mushy-firm. Spoon into crystal goblets and serve as is, or drizzled with a little cream or Vanilla Sauce (see Index).

Fresh papaya sherbet

SERVES 6 TO 8

Although food faddists attribute magical fountain-of-youth powers to papaya, no scientist, alas, has ever proved that claim. It is true, however, that papain, the enzyme in papaya, is an effective meat tenderizer. (Indeed, many commercial tenderizers are nothing more than concentrated, crystallized papain.) It is also true that papaya is high in vitamins A and C and low in calories. It's one of the most refreshing fruits I know, particularly when buzzed into sherbet.

¾ cup	sugar	180 ml
1 envelope	plain gelatin	1 envelope
⅓ cup	light corn syrup	80 ml
1½ cups	milk or half-and-half cream	350 ml
2–3 large (4½–5 pounds, total)	fully ripe papayas	2–3 large (2–2¼ kg, total)
¼ cup	fresh lime juice	60 ml

Combine the sugar and gelatin in a small heavy saucepan, pressing out any sugar lumps. Blend in the corn syrup and milk, then cook and stir over moderate heat about 5 minutes or until both the sugar and the gelatin dissolve. Halve the papayas, discard seeds, then scoop the flesh directly into a food processor fitted with the metal chopping blade; add lime juice and purée, using two to three 60-second churnings of the motor. Combine papaya purée and gelatin mixture in a large shallow bowl, then freeze about 3 hours or until mushy. Beat the semifrozen mixture until fluffy in an electric mixer at high speed, or in the food processor fitted with the metal chopping blade. NOTE: *If you use the processor, you'll have to beat the sherbet in several batches.* Return the mixture to the bowl, again freeze until mushy, then beat once more until fluffy. Pack into freezer containers and store in the freezer. Let the sherbet soften slightly before serving.

NOTE: *For an even velvetier sherbet, freeze in a hand-cranked or electric freezer or in one of the new ice cream machines. Follow the manufacturer's directions precisely, using the proportion of rock salt to ice that is recommended.*

VARIATIONS:

Fresh melon sherbet: The basic recipe above can also be used for making a lovely, fragrant melon sherbet. Any melon will do—as long as it is perfectly ripe: honeydew, Crenshaw, cantaloupe, Persian melon, even watermelon. Simply substitute an equal weight of melon for papaya and, if you like, use ¼ cup (60 ml) lemon juice instead of the lime juice called for. Mix and freeze as directed.

Fresh mango sherbet: Simply substitute 4½ to 5 pounds (about 2 kg) fresh whole mangoes for the papayas, then proceed as recipe directs.

Grenadian fresh nutmeg ice cream

SERVES 8 TO 10

Indonesian nutmeg trees were transplanted to the West Indies in the mid-nineteenth century and flourished so on Grenada that this southernmost of the Windwards is now called "The Isle of Spice." On a recent visit there, I toured a nutmeg plantation and was surprised to see that the nutmeg tree looks very much like the peach tree, and that the nutmeg, the seed, is enclosed in a peachlike fruit. The nutmeg is so beautiful when gathered—jet black underneath a scarlet webbing of mace—that native women make jewelry of it. They also use nutmeg in dozens of island recipes, both savory and sweet, including this exquisite ice cream, which is a specialty of the Spice Island Inn. For truly fragrant flavor, use freshly grated nutmeg because it's much sweeter and less astringent than the commercially ground. For the silkiest of ice creams, freeze in a hand-cranked or electric freezer. (Refrigerator ice cream, despite many beatings, will be more crystalline.)

1 quart	milk	1 L
1 pint	half-and-half cream	½ L
8 large	eggs	8 large
1½ cups	sugar	350 ml
1 can (14 oz.)	sweetened condensed milk	1 can (396 g)
4 medium-size	whole nutmegs, freshly grated	4 medium-size
3 cups	heavy cream	700 ml

Combine milk and half-and-half in a large heavy saucepan, set over moderately low heat and bring just to the point where steam rises from the liquid (do not boil). Meanwhile, blend eggs with sugar, whisk a little hot milk into egg mixture, stir egg mixture into pan and cook, stirring constantly, over low heat, 5 to 8 minutes until the consistency of custard; do not boil or custard will curdle. Remove from heat, mix in condensed milk and nutmeg and cool to room temperature.

For refrigerator ice cream: Pour ice cream mixture into a 13 × 9 × 2-inch (33 × 23 × 5 cm) aluminum pan and freeze until mushy-firm. Whip cream to soft peaks and set aside. Beat ice cream in largest mixer bowl at high speed until fluffy; fold in whipped cream, return to pan and again freeze until mushy-firm. Beat again until fluffy, return to pan and freeze until soft-firm.

For freezer ice cream: Stir unwhipped heavy cream into cooled ice cream mixture; chill 2 hours. If you have a 1-gallon (4 L) freezer, you'll be able to freeze all of the ice cream at once; if not, you'll have to do two to three batches, depending upon the capacity of your freezer. (Never fill freezer canister more than two-thirds full with ice cream mix because it will expand dramatically as it freezes.) Assemble freezer according to manufacturer's directions and freeze the ice cream, using 1 part rock salt to 8 parts crushed ice. When ice cream is "done," an electric freezer will automatically shut off and a hand-cranked freezer will be impossible to turn. Remove canister from freezer bucket. Open, being careful not to get salt into ice cream, remove dasher, plug hole in canister lid and re-cover canister. Return canister to freezer bucket, pack in crushed ice, adding about 1 part rock salt to every 4 parts ice. Cover with heavy paper or towels and let ice cream season 30 minutes before serving.

Quick crimson sauce

MAKES ABOUT 2½ CUPS (600 ML)

An easy, elegant dessert sauce that will dress up puddings, ices, sherbets, ice creams and a broad range of fruit desserts. Try serving it over fresh sliced peaches, oranges or strawberries or over whole blueberries, raspberries or blackberries.

1 package (10 oz).	frozen raspberries, thawed	1 package (283 g)
1 package (10 oz.)	frozen sliced strawberries, thawed	1 package (283 g)
2 tablespoons	lemon juice	2 tablespoons
2 tablespoons	Cointreau or Kirsch	2 tablespoons

Purée, then sieve berries. Mix in lemon juice and Cointreau, pour into a 1-quart (1 L) jar, cover tight and store in the refrigerator. The sauce will keep well for about a week.

Appendix

The basic metric units: When it comes to buying and preparing food, the metric units that will concern us most are those used to measure **weight (grams), volume (liters)** and **length (meters),** all of which are neatly computed in increments or multiples of ten. Here, adapted from a U.S. Department of Commerce, National Bureau of Standards chart, is a simple chart of metric multiples and prefixes, which apply to grams, liters and meters (as indeed they do to all other metric measures with the exception of temperature). The Base Units are those from which all portions and multiples evolve. Set in **boldface** type are the specific measures that you will use most often when shopping and cooking; these are also the ones used in recipes throughout this book. INCIDENTAL INTELLIGENCE: All metric prefixes for quantities larger than the Base Unit are from the Greek (*kilo,* for example), and all of those denoting quantities smaller than the Base Unit are Latin (*centi* and *milli* to name two of the most commonly used).

Multiples and prefixes

KILO = 1,000 × the Base Unit **(kilogram,** for example, equals 1,000 **grams)**

HECTO = 100 × the Base Unit (this is not used in cooking)

DEKA = 10 × the Base Unit (not used in cooking)

BASE UNITS: **Gram . . . Liter . . . Meter.** These three you must learn in order to cook and shop wisely.

DECI = 0.1 or 1/10 of the Base Unit (European cooks often use deciliters when measuring liquids—one deciliter equals about 1/2 cup—but we Americans are not expected to).

CENTI = 0.01 or 1/100 of the Base Unit **(centimeter** is the linear measurement I use in this book to denote pan sizes, pastry thicknesses and the like).

MILLI = 0.001 or 1/1000 of the Base Unit **(milliliter** is the increment into which the new metrically calibrated measuring cups are subdivided and the one I use throughout this book for volume measures of less than one liter whenever precise measures are critical to a recipe's success. For less meticulous measuring, I resort to the European habit of calling for 1/2 and 3/4 liter and so on).

About terminology and abbreviations: So that there will be no confusion, here are the metric measures I used throughout this book together with their abbreviations:

FOR ALL LINEAR MEASURES:

centimeter **(cm)**

FOR WEIGHTS:

gram **(g)** for weights of less than one kilogram (1,000 grams)

kilogram **(kg)** for weights of 1,000 grams or more

FOR VOLUME:

milliliters **(ml)** for quantities of less than one liter (1,000 milliliters)

liter **(L)** for quantities of 1,000 milliliters or more

TEMPERATURE:

Celsius **(C)**

ABOUT CONVERSIONS AND THE AMERICAN/METRIC EQUIVALENTS IN THE CHARTS THAT FOLLOW:

The **ml, L, g, kg** and **cm** equivalents in the center columns of the charts, headed **Approximate,** are the ones used throughout this book. The **Precise** equivalents in the right-hand columns show you the extent of error—usually minute—in the approximate columns.

Next, I may be telling you more than you really care to know, but the equivalent conversion charts in this Appendix reflect the current state of the art, which is referred to in the lingo of the technicians as "soft conversion." In its simplest form, this means that you start with the American measures and convert them to their metric equivalents arithmetically, by formula. This gives you an accurate but awkward, odd-numbered equivalent, which mercifully can easily be rounded off to a reasonable figure without sabotaging recipes. If you look, however, at the charts for common can and frozen-food package sizes, precise metric equivalents are given because this is consumer information each manufacturer must state exactly. I imagine that these weird-looking digits have helped to give metrics a bad name. Who, for example, really wants to know that an 8-oz. bottle of clam juice contains 237 ml?

The liquor industry, on the other hand, has provided us with an example of "hard conversion." Its products are now sold in bottles designed to hold metric quantities—multiples or simple subdivisions of the liter—and that's the end of it; no strange calculations harking back to ounces and quarts appear on their labels. When hard conversion takes over in the food industry, a bottle of clam juice might hold a sensible 250 ml and all other products will be sold in metric amounts meaningful to the consumer.

At that point, for cookbook writers, anyway, conversion charts will have no further function except one—to update their recipes to all-metric and unload the old American measures once and for all.

American/metric volume equivalents
(usually used for measuring liquids)

AMERICAN MEASURE FLUID OUNCES, CUPS	METRIC MEASURE (MILLILITERS, LITERS)	
	APPROXIMATE	PRECISE*
1 teaspoon	5 ml	5 ml
1 tablespoon (.5 fl. oz.)	15 ml	15 ml
⅛ cup (2 Tbsp., 1 fl. oz.)	30 ml	29.57 ml
¼ cup (4 Tbsp., 2 fl. oz.)	60 ml	59 ml
⅓ cup	80 ml	79 ml
½ cup (8 Tbsp., 4 fl. oz.)	120 ml	118 ml
⅔ cup	160 ml	157 ml
¾ cup (12 Tbsp., 6 fl. oz.)	180 ml	178 ml
⅞ cup	210 ml	207 ml
1 cup (16 Tbsp., 8 fl. oz.)	240 ml (.25 or ¼ L)	237 ml
1¼ cups	300 ml	296 ml
1⅓ cups	315 ml	316 ml
1½ cups (24 Tbsp., 12 fl. oz.)	350 ml (.33 or ⅓ L)	355 ml
1⅔ cups	395 ml	394 ml
1¾ cups	415 ml	414 ml
2 cups (1 pint, 16 fl. oz.)	475 ml or 500 ml (.5 or ½ L)	473 ml
2¼ cups	535 ml	532 ml

*Decimals in the calculations have been rounded off to the nearest whole number.

Conversion formulas:

TO CONVERT FLUID OUNCES TO MILLILITERS (ML):
Multiply **ounces** by 30 (approximate conversion) or 29.57 (precise conversion).

TO CONVERT MILLILITERS (ML) TO FLUID OUNCES:
Multiply **milliliters** by .03 (approximate conversion) or .034 (precise conversion).

TO CONVERT QUARTS TO LITERS (L):
Multiply **quarts** by 1 (approximate conversion) or .95 (precise conversion).

TO CONVERT LITERS (L) TO QUARTS:
Multiply **liters** by 1 (approximate conversion) or by 1.057 (precise conversion).

AMERICAN MEASURE FLUID OUNCES, CUPS	METRIC MEASURE (MILLILITERS, LITERS)	
	APPROXIMATE	PRECISE*
2⅓ cups	550 ml	553 ml
2½ cups	590 ml or 600 ml	592 ml
2⅔ cups	630 ml	631 ml
2¾ cups	650 ml (.66 or ⅔ L)	652 ml
3 cups (1½ pints, 24 fl. oz.)	700 ml	710 ml
3¼ cups	770 ml (.75 or ¾ L)	769 ml
3⅓ cups	790 ml	789 ml
3½ cups	830 ml	828 ml
3⅔ cups	860 ml	858 ml
3¾ cups	890 ml	887 ml
4 cups (1 quart, 32 fl. oz.)	950 ml or 1 L	946 ml
1 quart + 3 tablespoons	1 L	1 L (1000 ml)
5 cups	1.25 L or 1¼ L	1183 ml
6 cups (1½ quarts)	1.5 L or 1½ L	1420 ml
2 quarts (½ gallon)	2 L	1892 ml
3 quarts	3 L	2838 ml
4 quarts (1 gallon)	4 L	3784 ml (3.75 L)

American/metric equivalents for weights

AMERICAN MEASURE (OUNCES AND POUNDS)	GRAM WEIGHT	
	APPROXIMATE	PRECISE*
0.035 ounce	—	1 g
¼ ounce	7 g	7 g
½ ounce	15 g	14 g
¾ ounce	20 g	21 g
1 ounce	30 g	28.35 g
2 ounces	60 g	57 g
3 ounces	85 g	85 g
4 ounces (¼ pound)	115 g	113 g
5 ounces	140 g	142 g
5¼ ounces (⅓ pound)	160 g	154 g
6 ounces	170 g	170 g
7 ounces	200 g	198 g
8 ounces (½ pound)	225 g (.25 or ¼ kg)	226 g
9 ounces	250 g	255 g
10 ounces	285 g	284 g
10½ ounces (⅔ pound)	300 g	298 g
12 ounces (¾ pound)	340 g (.33 or ⅓ kg)	341 g
16 ounces (1 pound)	455 g (.5 or ½ kg)	454 g
17½ ounces	—	500 g (.5 or ½ kg)
20 ounces (1¼ pounds)	570 g (.5 or ½ kg)	567 g
24 ounces (1½ pounds)	675 g (.66 or ⅔ kg)	680 g

*Decimals in the calculations up to 2000 g have been rounded off to the nearest whole number.

Conversion formulas:

TO CONVERT OUNCES TO GRAMS (G):
Multiply the number of **ounces** by 28.35.

TO CONVERT GRAMS (G) TO OUNCES:
Multiply the number of **grams** by .035.

TO CONVERT POUNDS TO KILOGRAMS (KG):
Multiply the number of **pounds** by .45.

TO CONVERT KILOGRAMS (KG) TO POUNDS:
Multiply the number of **kilograms** by 2.2.

AMERICAN MEASURE (OUNCES AND POUNDS)	GRAM WEIGHT	
	APPROXIMATE	PRECISE*
26 ounces (1⅝ pounds)	750 g (.75 or ¾ kg)	737 g
28 ounces (1¾ pounds)	800 g (.8 or ⅘ kg)	794 g
32 ounces (2 pounds)	1 kg	907 g
35 ounces (2.2 pounds)	—	1000 g (1 kg)
2½ pounds	1.25 or 1¼ kg	1134 g
3 pounds	1.33 or 1⅓–1.5 or 1½ kg	1361 g
3½ pounds	1.5 or 1½ kg	1588 g
4 pounds	1.75 or 1¾–1.8 or 1⅘ kg	1814 g
4.4 pounds	—	2000 g (2 kg)
4½ pounds	2 kg	2 kg
5 pounds	2.25 or 2¼ kg	2.25 kg
5½ pounds	2.5 or 2½ kg	2.5 kg
6 pounds	2.75 or 2¾ kg	2.7 kg
6½ pounds	3 kg	2.9 kg
7 pounds	3.25 or 3¼ kg	3.15 kg
7½ pounds	3.33 or 3⅓ kg	3.4 kg
8 pounds	3.5 or 3½ kg	3.6 kg
8½ pounds	3.8 or 3⅘ kg	3.8 kg
9 pounds	4 kg	4 kg
9½ pounds	4.25 or 4¼ kg	4.3 kg
10 pounds	4.50 or 4½ kg	4.5 kg

American/metric equivalents for linear measures

AMERICAN MEASURE (INCHES, FEET)	METRIC MEASURES (CENTIMETERS, METERS)	
	APPROXIMATE	PRECISE
¹⁄₁₆ inch	¼ cm	0.2 cm
⅛ inch	½ cm	0.4 cm
¼ inch	¾ cm	0.6 cm
⅜ inch	1 cm	0.95 cm
½ inch	1½ cm	1.3 cm
⅝ inch	1½ cm	1.6 cm
¾ inch	2 cm	1.9 cm
1 inch	2½ cm	2.54 cm
1½ inches	4 cm	3.8 cm
2 inches	5 cm	5 cm
2½ inches	6½ cm	6.4 cm
3 inches	8 cm	7.6 cm
3½ inches	9 cm	8.9 cm
4 inches	10 cm	10.2 cm
4½ inches	11 cm	11.4 cm
5 inches	13 cm	12.7 cm
5½ inches	14 cm	13.9 cm
6 inches	15 cm	15.2 cm
7 inches	18 cm	17.8 cm
8 inches	20 cm	20.3 cm

Conversion formulas:

TO CONVERT INCHES TO CENTIMETERS (CM):
Multiply the number of **inches** by 2.54.

TO CONVERT CENTIMETERS (CM) TO INCHES:
Multiply the number of **centimeters** by .394.

AMERICAN MEASURE (INCHES, FEET)	METRIC MEASURES (CENTIMETERS, METERS)	
	APPROXIMATE	PRECISE
9 inches	23 cm	22.9 cm
10 inches	25 cm	25.4 cm
11 inches	28 cm	27.9 cm
12 inches (1 foot)	30 cm	30.48 cm
13 inches	33 cm	33 cm
14 inches	35 cm	35.5 cm
15 inches	38 cm	38 cm
16 inches	40 cm	40.6 cm
17 inches	43 cm	43 cm
18 inches (1½ feet)	45 cm	45.6 cm
19 inches	48 cm	48.2 cm
20 inches	50 cm	50.8 cm
21 inches	53 cm	53.3 cm
22 inches	55 cm	55.8 cm
23 inches	58 cm	58.4 cm
24 inches (2 feet)	60 cm	60.9 cm
30 inches (2½ feet)	76 cm	76.2 cm
36 inches (3 feet, 1 yard)	91 cm	91.44 cm
39 inches	1 meter	1 meter

Some Fahrenheit/Celsius temperature equivalents

FAHRENHEIT		CELSIUS
0°	Recommended Freezer Temperature	−18°
32°	Water Freezes	0°
98.6°	Normal Body Temperature	37°
115°		46°
120°		49°
125°		52°
130°		54°
135°		57°
140°		60°
160°		71°
165°		74°
170°		77°
175°		79°

FAHRENHEIT	DEGREE OF DONENESS	CELSIUS

Meat roasting (internal meat temperatures)

FAHRENHEIT	DEGREE OF DONENESS	CELSIUS
125°	Rare Roast Beef	52°
125° to 130°	Rare Roast Lamb	52° to 54°
135° to 140°	Medium Rare Roast Beef and Lamb	57° to 60°
140°	Well-Done for Precooked Hams	60°
150° to 155°	Medium Roast Beef	65° to 68°
160° to 165°	Medium Roast Lamb, Medium-Well Beef, Well-Done Hams	71° to 74°
170°	Well-Done Roast Veal and Pork	77°
175° to 180°	Well-Done Roast Lamb	79° to 82°
180° to 185°	Well-Done Roast Turkey	82° to 85°

Deep-fat frying

FAHRENHEIT		CELSIUS
325° to 350°		165° to 175°
350° to 365°		175° to 185°
365° to 375°		185° to 190°
375° to 400°		190° to 205°

Conversion formulas:

TO CONVERT FAHRENHEIT TO CELSIUS: Subtract 32 and divide by 1.8.

TO CONVERT CELSIUS TO FAHRENHEIT: Multiply by 1.8 and add 32.

FAHRENHEIT		CELSIUS
180°	Water Simmers (at sea level)	82°
212°	Water Boils (at sea level)	100°
225°		107°
250°	Keep-Warm Oven	120°
275°	Very Slow Oven	135°
300°	Slow Oven	150°
325°	Moderately Slow Oven	165°
350°	Moderate Oven	175°
375°	Moderately Hot Oven	190°
400°	Hot Oven	205°
425°	Very Hot Oven	220°
450°	Very Hot Oven	230°
500°	Extremely Hot Oven	260°

FAHRENHEIT		CELSIUS

Jellymaking and candymaking

218° to 220°	Jelly Sheets	103° to 104°
230° to 234°	Candy Syrup Spins a Thread	110° to 112°
234° to 240°	Soft Ball (Candy)	112° to 116°
244° to 248°	Firm Ball (Candy)	118° to 120°
250° to 266°	Hard Ball (Candy)	120° to 130°
270° to 290°	Soft Crack (Candy)	132° to 143°
300° to 310°	Hard Crack (Candy)	150° to 154°

Refrigerator temperature (for maximum safekeeping of food)
33° to 45°   0.5° to 1.8°

Recommended temperature for wine storage:
55°   13°

Recommended water temperature for dissolving yeast:
105° to 115°   41° to 46°

Recommended canning temperatures:

185°	Hot water bath	85°
212°	Boiling water bath	100°

American/metric equivalents for commonly used staples

You may need to check precise metric measures for baking, where the proportion of ingredients, one to the other, is critical to the recipe's success. NOTE: *To avoid awkward decimals, all precise measures have been rounded off to the nearest whole number, i.e. 99.68 = 100 and 100.23 = 100.*

All-purpose flour

Sifted (then lightly spooned into a dry-cup measure and leveled off with the edge of a spatula)

AMERICAN MEASURE	APPROXIMATE GRAM WEIGHT	PRECISE GRAM WEIGHT
¼ cup	25 g	25 g
⅓ cup	35 g	33 g
½ cup	50 g	50 g
⅔ cup	65 g	66 g
¾ cup	75 g	75 g
1 cup	100 g	100 g

Unsifted (spooned directly from bag or canister into a dry-cup measure and leveled off with the edge of a spatula)

AMERICAN MEASURE	APPROXIMATE GRAM WEIGHT	PRECISE GRAM WEIGHT
¼ cup	30 g	28 g
⅓ cup	40 g	37 g
½ cup	60 g	57 g
⅔ cup	75 g	75 g
¾ cup	85 g	85 g
1 cup	115 g	113 g

Cake flour

Sifted (then lightly spooned into a dry-cup measure and leveled off with the edge of a spatula)

AMERICAN MEASURE	APPROXIMATE GRAM WEIGHT	PRECISE GRAM WEIGHT
¼ cup	20 g	20 g
⅓ cup	25 g	26 g
½ cup	40 g	40 g
⅔ cup	55 g	53 g
¾ cup	60 g	60 g
1 cup	80 g	80 g

Unsifted (spooned directly from bag or canister into a dry-cup measure and leveled off with the edge of a spatula)

AMERICAN MEASURE	APPROXIMATE GRAM WEIGHT	PRECISE GRAM WEIGHT
¼ cup	30 g	27 g
⅓ cup	35 g	35 g
½ cup	55 g	54 g
⅔ cup	70 g	70 g
¾ cup	80 g	80 g
1 cup	110 g	106 g

Whole wheat flour, unsifted (spooned directly from bag or canister into a dry-cup measure and leveled off with the edge of a spatula). NOTE: *Whole wheat flour is not sifted because the sifter separates out most of the husk and bran.*

AMERICAN MEASURE	APPROXIMATE GRAM WEIGHT	PRECISE GRAM WEIGHT
¼ cup	35 g	32 g
⅓ cup	45 g	42 g
½ cup	65 g	64 g
⅔ cup	85 g	84 g
¾ cup	100 g	96 g
1 cup	130 g	128 g

Rye flour, unsifted (spooned directly from bag or canister into a dry-cup measure and leveled off with the edge of a spatula). NOTE: *Like whole wheat flour, rye flour is not sifted because the sifter will remove most of the husk and bran that give it character.*

AMERICAN MEASURE	APPROXIMATE GRAM WEIGHT	PRECISE GRAM WEIGHT
¼ cup	25 g	23 g
⅓ cup	30 g	31 g
½ cup	45 g	46 g
⅔ cup	60 g	61 g
¾ cup	70 g	69 g
1 cup	95 g	92 g

Cornmeal (granular), unsifted (spooned directly from bag or canister into a dry-cup measure and leveled off with the edge of a spatula)

AMERICAN MEASURE	APPROXIMATE GRAM WEIGHT	PRECISE GRAM WEIGHT
¼ cup	40 g	38 g
⅓ cup	50 g	50 g
½ cup	75 g	76 g
⅔ cup	100 g	100 g
¾ cup	115 g	113 g
1 cup	150 g	151 g

Granulated sugar (spooned directly from bag or canister into a dry-cup measure and leveled off with the edge of a spatula)

AMERICAN MEASURE	APPROXIMATE GRAM WEIGHT	PRECISE GRAM WEIGHT
¼ cup	50 g	50 g
⅓ cup	65 g	66 g
½ cup	100 g	100 g
⅔ cup	135 g	132 g
¾ cup	150 g	150 g
1 cup	200 g	200 g

Light and dark brown sugar (firmly packed into a dry-cup measure with the top flush with the rim)

AMERICAN MEASURE	APPROXIMATE GRAM WEIGHT	PRECISE GRAM WEIGHT
¼ cup	55 g	54 g
⅓ cup	70 g	71 g
½ cup	105 g	106 g
⅔ cup	140 g	141 g
¾ cup	160 g	160 g
1 cup	215 g	213 g

Confectioner's (10X) sugar

Sifted (then spooned lightly into a dry-cup measure and leveled off with the edge of a spatula)

AMERICAN MEASURE	APPROXIMATE GRAM WEIGHT	PRECISE GRAM WEIGHT
¼ cup	20 g	21 g
⅓ cup	30 g	28 g
½ cup	45 g	43 g

AMERICAN MEASURE	APPROXIMATE GRAM WEIGHT	PRECISE GRAM WEIGHT
⅔ cup	55 g	56 g
¾ cup	65 g	64 g
1 cup	85 g	85 g

Unsifted (spooned directly from bag or canister into a dry-cup measure and leveled off with the edge of a spatula)

AMERICAN MEASURE	APPROXIMATE GRAM WEIGHT	PRECISE GRAM WEIGHT
¼ cup	25 g	25 g
⅓ cup	35 g	33 g
½ cup	50 g	50 g
⅔ cup	65 g	65 g
¾ cup	75 g	74 g
1 cup	100 g	99 g

Cornstarch

Sifted (then spooned lightly into a dry-cup measure and leveled off with the edge of a spatula)

AMERICAN MEASURE	APPROXIMATE GRAM WEIGHT	PRECISE GRAM WEIGHT
¼ cup	30 g	28 g
⅓ cup	40 g	38 g
½ cup	60 g	57 g
⅔ cup	75 g	76 g
¾ cup	85 g	85 g
1 cup	115 g	113 g

Unsifted (spooned directly from bag or canister into a dry-cup measure and leveled off with the edge of a spatula)

AMERICAN MEASURE	APPROXIMATE GRAM WEIGHT	PRECISE GRAM WEIGHT
¼ cup	35 g	32 g
⅓ cup	45 g	42 g
½ cup	65 g	64 g
⅔ cup	85 g	84 g
¾ cup	100 g	98 g
1 cup	130 g	128 g

Cocoa powder (not a mix)

Sifted (then spooned lightly into a dry-cup measure and leveled off with the edge of a spatula)

AMERICAN MEASURE	APPROXIMATE GRAM WEIGHT	PRECISE GRAM WEIGHT
¼ cup	15 g	16 g
⅓ cup	20 g	21 g
½ cup	35 g	33 g
⅔ cup	45 g	43 g
¾ cup	50 g	49 g
1 cup	65 g	64 g

Unsifted (spooned directly from bag or canister into a dry-cup measure and leveled off with the edge of a spatula)

AMERICAN MEASURE	APPROXIMATE GRAM WEIGHT	PRECISE GRAM WEIGHT
¼ cup	20 g	20 g
⅓ cup	25 g	26 g
½ cup	40 g	39 g
⅔ cup	55 g	52 g
¾ cup	60 g	59 g
1 cup	80 g	78 g

Butter and margarine (firmly packed into a dry-cup measure and leveled off with the edge of a knife)

AMERICAN MEASURE	APPROXIMATE GRAM WEIGHT	PRECISE GRAM WEIGHT
¼ cup (½ stick, 2 oz.)	60 g	57 g
⅓ cup (⅔ stick)	75 g	75 g
½ cup (1 stick, 4 oz.)	115 g	114 g
⅔ cup (1 stick + 2 Tbsp. and 2 tsp.)	150 g	150 g
¾ cup (1½ sticks, 6 oz.)	170 g	170 g
1 cup (2 sticks, ½ lb.)	225 g	227 g
1½ cups (3 sticks, ¾ lb.)	340 g	341 g
2 cups (4 sticks, 1 lb.)	455 g	454 g

Vegetable shortening (firmly packed into a dry-cup measure and leveled off with the edge of a knife)

AMERICAN MEASURE	APPROXIMATE GRAM WEIGHT	PRECISE GRAM WEIGHT
¼ cup	45 g	46 g
⅓ cup	60 g	61 g
½ cup	95 g	93 g
⅔ cup	120 g	121 g
¾ cup	140 g	138 g
1 cup	185 g	184 g

American/metric equivalents for some common can, jar and bottle sizes

AMERICAN MEASURE (FLUID OUNCES, CUPS)	CAN NUMBER	CONTENTS	METRIC MEASURE (GRAMS, MILLILITERS)
2 ounces	—	Anchovy Fillets	56.7 g
3½ ounces	—	Flaked Coconut	99 g
4 ounces (½ cup)	—	Slivered Almonds	113 g
5⅓ fluid ounces (⅔ cup)	—	Evaporated Milk	158 ml
6 ounces (¾ cup)	—	Tomato Paste, Shelled Pecans	170 g
7 ounces	—	Tuna Fish, Green Chili Peppers	198 g
8 ounces (1 cup)	—	Tomato Sauce, Fruits, Vegetables, Shelled Walnuts	226 g
8 fluid ounces (1 cup)	—	Clam Juice	237 ml
10 fluid ounces	—	Coconut Milk	296 ml
10½ ounces	—	Corned Beef, Stews, Fruits	298 g
11 ounces	—	Fruits	312 g
12 ounces (1½ cups)	—	Vegetables, Tomato Paste	340 g
12 fluid ounces (1½ cups)	—	Vegetable Juices	355 ml
13 fluid ounces (1⅔ cups)	—	Evaporated Milk	384 ml
13¾ fluid ounces (1¾ cups)	—	Beef, Chicken Broth	407 ml

American/metric equivalents for some common frozen food package sizes

AMERICAN MEASURE (OUNCES, FLUID OUNCES)	CONTENTS	METRIC MEASURE (GRAMS, MILLILITERS)
6 ounces	Chinese Pea Pods	170 g
6 fluid ounces	Frozen Juice Concentrates	177 ml
9 ounces	Some Vegetables	255 g
10 ounces	Most Fruits and Vegetables	283 g

AMERICAN MEASURE (FLUID OUNCES, CUPS)	CAN NUMBER	METRIC CONTENTS	MEASURE (GRAMS, MILLILITERS)
14 ounces (1¾ cups)	300	Baked Beans, Cranberry Sauce, Sweetened Condensed Milk, Tuna Fish	396 g
14½ ounces	—	Tomatoes	411 g
15 ounces	—	Kidney Beans, Tomato Sauce	425 g
15½ ounces	—	Pineapple Chunks, Spaghetti Sauce	439 g
16 ounces (2 cups)	303	Tomatoes, Vegetables, Fruits	454 g
17 ounces (1 lb. 1 oz.)	—	Fruit Cocktail, Vegetables	482 g
20 ounces (1 lb. 4 oz.)	2	Chick Peas, Crushed Pineapple, Soups	567 g
28 ounces (1 lb. 12 oz.)	2½	Tomatoes, Tomato Purée, Baked Beans, Sliced Peaches	794 g
32 ounces (2 lbs.)	—	Spaghetti Sauce	907 g
46 ounces (2 lbs. 14 oz.)	5	Family-Size Fruits, Vegetables (10 to 12 servings)	1304 g
46 fluid ounces (5¾ cups)	5	Tomato Juice, Vegetable Juice, Apple Juice	1360 ml

AMERICAN MEASURE (OUNCES, FLUID OUNCES)	CONTENTS	METRIC MEASURE (GRAMS, MILLILITERS)
12 ounces	Some Fruits	340 g
12 fluid ounces	Fruit Juice Concentrates	355 ml
16 ounces	Some Fruits and Vegetables	454 g

American/metric equivalents for can and bottle sizes for soft drinks, mixers, beers, wines and spirits

AMERICAN MEASURE (FLUID OUNCES, CUPS)	CONTENTS	METRIC MEASURE (MILLILITERS, LITERS, TO NEAREST WHOLE NUMBER)

Soft drinks and mixers

AMERICAN MEASURE (FLUID OUNCES, CUPS)	CONTENTS	METRIC MEASURE
10 fluid ounces (1¼ cups)	Club Soda, Ginger Ale, Colas, Tonic Water, Bitter Lemon	296 ml
12 fluid ounces (1½ cups)	Colas, Diet Colas, Ginger Ale, Root Beer, etc., in Cans	355 ml
28 fluid ounces (3½ cups)	Colas, Ginger Ale, Seltzer, Club Soda	828 ml
33.8 fluid ounces (1 qt. + 3 Tbsp.)	Club Soda, Ginger Ale, Colas, Diet Colas, Root Beer, Tonic Water	1 L (1000 ml)
67.6 fluid ounces (2 qts. + ⅓ cup)	Colas, Diet Colas, Root Beer	2 L (2000 ml)

Beers and ales

AMERICAN MEASURE	CONTENTS	METRIC MEASURE
12 fluid ounces (1½ cups)	Domestic and Imported Ales and Beers	355 ml
16 fluid ounces (2 cups)	Domestic and Some Imported Beers	473 ml
33.8 fluid ounces (1 qt. + 3 Tbsp.)	Domestic Beers	1 L (1000 ml)

Wines and champagnes

(NOTE: *Although all wines and champagnes are now sold by the liter—or fractions or multiples thereof—you may still encounter some old stock, and for that reason, I also include metric equivalents for fifths and quarts.*)

AMERICAN MEASURE (FLUID OUNCES, CUPS)	CONTENTS	METRIC MEASURE (MILLILITERS, LITERS, TO NEAREST WHOLE NUMBER)
6 fluid ounces (the "split"—¾ cup)	Domestic and Imported Wines and Champagne	177 ml
25.4 fluid ounces (3 cups)	Domestic and Imported Wines	750 ml (.75 L)

*The bottle sizes most commonly used today for wines, champagnes and liquors.

AMERICAN MEASURE (FLUID OUNCES, CUPS)	CONTENTS	METRIC MEASURE (MILLILITERS, LITERS, TO NEAREST WHOLE NUMBER)
25.6 fluid ounces (⅘ quart or a "fifth")	Domestic and Imported Wines	757 ml
32 fluid ounces (4 cups or 1 quart)	Domestic Wines	946 ml
*33.8 fluid ounces (1 quart + 3 Tbsp.)	Domestic and Imported Wines and Champagnes	1 L (1000 ml)
*50.7 fluid ounces (1½ quarts—a magnum)	Domestic and Imported Wines and Champagnes	1.5 L (1500 ml)
64 fluid ounces (½ gallon)	Domestic Jug Wines	1.9 L (1892 ml)
*135 fluid ounces (4¼ quarts)	Domestic Jug Wines	4 L (4000 ml)

Liquors

(NOTE: *Like wines, hard liquors are now sold altogether by metric volumes, but because you may encounter old stock marked in the familiar American pints, fifths, quarts, etc., I include the metric equivalents for these.*)

AMERICAN MEASURE (FLUID OUNCES, CUPS)	METRIC MEASURE (MILLILITERS, LITERS, TO NEAREST WHOLE NUMBER)
*1.5 fluid ounces ("the mini")	44 ml
*6.8 fluid ounces (about ¾ cup)	200 ml
13 fluid ounces (⅘ pint)	384 ml
16 fluid ounces (1 pint)	473 ml
*16.9 fluid ounces	500 ml
*25.4 fluid ounces (almost ⅘ quart)	750 ml
25.6 fluid ounces (⅘ quart or a "fifth")	757 ml
32 fluid ounces (1 quart)	946 ml
*33.8 fluid ounces (1 quart + 3 Tbsp.)	1 L (1000 ml)
*59 fluid ounces (almost ½ gallon)	1.75 L (1750 ml)
64 fluid ounces (½ gallon)	1.9 L (1892 ml)

American/Metric Equivalents for commonly used pots, pans and casseroles

AMERICAN MEASURE	METRIC EQUIVALENT
Saucepans	
1 pint (2 cups)	½ L
1 quart (4 cups)	1 L
1½ quarts (6 cups)	1½ L
2 quarts (8 cups)	2 L
3 quarts (12 cups)	3 L
4 quarts (16 cups, 1 gallon)	4 L
Soufflé dishes, casseroles	
1 quart	1 L
1½ quarts	1½ L
2 quarts	2 L
2½ quarts	2½ L
3 quarts	3 L
Dutch ovens	
3 quarts	3 L
4 quarts (one gallon)	4 L
6 quarts (1½ gallons)	6 L
8 quarts (2 gallons)	8 L

AMERICAN MEASURE	METRIC EQUIVALENT
Skillets	
5-inch	13 cm
8-inch	20 cm
10-inch	25 cm
12-inch	30 cm
Baking pans	
8-inch round cake or pie tin	20 cm (diameter)
9-inch round cake or pie tin	23 cm
10-inch round springform pan or pie tin	25 cm
8 × 8 × 2-inch pan	20 × 20 × 5 cm
9 × 9 × 2-inch pan	23 × 23 × 5 cm
9 × 5 × 3-inch loaf pan	23 × 13 × 8 cm
13 × 9 × 2-inch pan	33 × 23 × 5 cm
15½ × 10½ × 1-inch jelly-roll pan	39 × 25 × 2½ cm

Index

Crab(s) *(cont.)*
types of, 164
Cranberries, jugged beef with mushrooms and, 47–49
Cranberry beans, 204
Cream gravy
for chicken, 124
Dijon-, 33
for roast beef, 33
tarragon-Dijon-, 33
Cream sauce, 350–51
Brussels sprouts with chestnuts or grapes in, 213
cognac-, pork medallions with mushrooms in, 400–401
-mustard, chicken scallops in, 127–28
-shallot, braised loin of veal with, 55–56
variations on, 351–53
Crimson sauce, 505
Crofter's scones, 315–16
Croquettes
potato, veal-stuffed, 72–74
swordfish, sultana and pine nut, alla marinara, 430–31
Crustaceans, 153
See also names of crustaceans
Cucumber(s), 235–37
amount per serving, 235
cooking methods, 235
à la dijonnaise, 236–37
general data on, 235
minted crescents with yogurt, 236
mousse of flounder and, with shrimp-wine sauce, 424–25
preparation of, 235
quality of, 235
Scandinavian style, 235
season for, 235
to seed, 235, 424
shrimp stir-fried with water chestnuts, ginger and, 173
storage of, 235
types of, 235
Currants, chicken pie colonial style, with rose water, prunes, raisins and, 413–15
Curry(ied)
bay scallops, shrimp and wild rice, cold, 447–49
carrots and onion, braised, 222–23

chicken chunks with cream and almonds, 410–11
crab and papaya salad, 436–37
fish, potatoes and onions, 431–32
lamb, 92–93
kurma, 96–97
Rock Cornish game hens with raisin, rice and pine nut stuffing, 130–31
veal
breast with curried bulgur stuffing, 391
and vegetable loaf with sour cream gravy, 70–71
Custard-and-cake pie
lemon, 338
lime, 338
orange, 337–38

Dacquoise, 487–89
Danish style
bacon, 113
meatballs, 109–10
sailor's stew, 384–85
Dannenbaum, Julie, 265
Date muffins, 318
Delicias de laranja, 498–99
DeMartino, Mike, 154, 170
Desserts, *see* Sweets (desserts)
Deviled crab, 166–67
Deviled lamb shanks, crusty crumbed, 93–94
Dijon-cream gravy, 33
Dijon-cream-tarragon gravy, 33
Dijonnaise, cucumbers à la, 236–37
Dill
appetizer of herring, egg, leeks and, 367–68
bay scallops sautéed, with vermouth and, 184–85
beets and apples with sour cream and, 453–54
beets with sour cream and, 208–9
butter, 359
cold marinated bay scallops with juniper, wine and, 446–47
haddock baked with wine, cream and, 161
and mustard sauce, 361–62
navy bean salad with lemon and, 206–7
potatoes and onions creamed with, 467–68